ACCA

PAPER P1

GOVERNANCE, RISK AND ETHICS

PRACTICE & REVISION KIT

BPP Learning Media is the **sole ACCA Platinum Approved Learning Partner – content** for the ACCA qualification. In this, **the only Paper P1 Practice and Revision Kit to be reviewed by the examiner**:

- We discuss the **best strategies** for revising and taking your ACCA exams

- We show you how to be well **prepared** for your exam

- We give you **lots of great guidance** on tackling questions

- We show you how you can **build your own exams**

- We provide you with **three** mock exams including the **December 2011 exam**

- We provide the **ACCA examiner's answers** as well as our own to the June and December 2010 exams as an additional revision aid

FOR EXAMS IN 2012

BPP
LEARNING MEDIA

First edition 2007
Sixth edition January 2012

ISBN 9781 4453 8000 1
(previous ISBN 9780 7517 9408 3)

E-ISBN 9781 4453 2425 8

British Library Cataloguing-in-Publication Data
A catalogue record for this book
is available from the British Library

Published by

BPP Learning Media Ltd
BPP House, Aldine Place
London W12 8AA

www.bpp.com/learningmedia

Printed in the United Kingdom

We are grateful to the Association of Chartered Certified Accountants for permission to reproduce past examination questions. The suggested solutions in the exam answer bank have been prepared by BPP Learning Media Ltd, except where otherwise stated.

Your learning materials, published by BPP Learning Media Ltd, are printed on paper sourced from sustainable, managed forests.

Contents

Question index

The headings in this checklist/index indicate the main topics of questions, but questions are expected to cover several different topics.

BPP
LEARNING MEDIA

39 Crawley Gossop	25	45	32	175
40 Environmental and social issues	25	45	32	177
41 Edted	25	45	33	180
42 Code of conduct	25	45	33	182
43 Drofdarb	25	45	34	185
44 David Hunter	25	45	35	188
45 Penrice	25	45	36	190
46 JH Graphics (Examiner question)	25	45	36	192
47 Professor Cheung's views (Pilot paper)	25	45	37	195
48 Football club (12/07)	25	45	37	197
49 Anne Hayes (6/08)	25	45	38	201
50 Hogg Products (12/08)	25	45	39	204
51 Policy speech (6/09)	25	45	39	207
52 John Wang (12/09)	25	45	40	210
53 Happy and healthy (6/10)	25	45	41	213
54 JGP (12/10)	25	45	42	216
55 Ann Koo (6/11)	25	45	43	219

Section A questions

56 VCF	50	90	44	221
57 Wilberforce Humphries	50	90	45	227
58 Partner	50	90	47	232
59 Integrated Broadcasting Organisation	50	90	48	237
60 ChemCo (Pilot paper)	50	90	50	242
61 Worldwide Minerals (12/07)	50	90	51	247
62 Rowlands and Medeleev (6/08)	50	90	52	253
63 Swan Hill (12/08)	50	90	54	259
64 Global-bank (6/09)	50	90	55	265
65 Mary Jane (12/09)	50	90	57	270
66 Hesket Nuclear (6/10)	50	90	59	275
67 ZPT (12/10)	50	90	61	280
68 Bobo (6/11)	50	90	63	287

Mock exam 1

Questions 69 to 72

Mock exam 2

Questions 73 to 76

Mock exam 3 (December 2011)

Questions 77 to 80

Planning your question practice

Our guidance from page xxxix shows you how to organise your question practice, either by attempting questions from each syllabus area or **by building your own exams** – tackling questions as a series of practice exams.

Using your BPP Learning Media products

This Kit gives you the question practice and guidance you need in the exam. Our other products can also help you pass:

- **Learning to Learn Accountancy** gives further valuable advice on revision

- **Passcards** provide you with clear topic summaries and exam tips

- **Success CDs** help you revise on the move

- **i-Pass CDs** offer tests of knowledge against the clock

You can purchase these products by visiting www.bpp.com/mybpp.

BPP
LEARNING MEDIA

Topic index

Listed below are the key Paper P1 syllabus topics and the numbers of the questions in this Kit covering those topics.

If you need to concentrate your practice and revision on certain topics or if you want to attempt all available questions that refer to a particular subject, you will find this index useful.

Syllabus topic	Question numbers
Accountancy as a profession	17(c)
Agency	3, 7(a), 10(a), 64(c), 66(c)
ALARP	21(b), Mock 3 Q1(c)
American Accounting Association model	44(a), 65(a)
Audit committee	2(a), 16(c), 33, 36(c), 42, Mock 1 Q4(b), Mock 2 Q3(a)
Board of directors	3, 5, 6(c), 9, 13(b), 22, 59(a), 60, 65(d), Mock 1 Q4
Chairman	9, 12, 13(c), Mock 3 Q2(b)
Charities	16
Chief executive	9, 64(e), 68(d), Mock 3 Q2(b), Mock 3 Q3(a)
Conflicts of interest	8, 15(a), 41(c), 58(d)
Confidentiality	63, 65(a)
Control environment	17, 56, Mock 2 Q1(a)
Control procedures	17, 20, 56, Mock 2 Q2(c)
Corporate citizen	41, 57(d)
Corporate ethical codes	42, 46, 50, 59(d), Mock 3 Q1(a)
Corporate governance	1-14, 15(c) 22, 33, 56, 59(b), 60, 61, 67, Mock 1 Q1, Mock 1 Q2, Mock 1 Q4, Mock 2 Q1, Mock 2 Q2, Mock 3 Q2
Corporate governance codes	7, 9(c), Mock 2 Q2(a)
Corporate governance concepts	56(c)
Deontological approach	47(c), 50(c), 59(c)
Directors' performance assessment	2
Directors' remuneration	1-3, 8, 12(c), 14, 23(a), 27(c), 57(b), Mock 1 Q1(d), Mock 1 Q2(d), Mock 3 Q3(a)
Directors' vacation of office	12(a)
Employee responsibilities	49
Entrepreneurial risk	29(c)
Environmental auditing	45(b), 54(b)
Environmental issues	39-41, 45, 54, 60(e), 61, 62(d), 66(d), Mock 1 Q1, Mock 3 Q1
Environmental management systems	39, 41
Environmental reporting	39, 40, 45(a), 60(e), Mock 1 Q1(c), Mock 3 Q1(b)
Ethics	14(c),17, 39-55, 60, 63(c), 65(a), 67(b), 68, Mock 1 Q1, Mock 2 Q1, Mock 2 Q3, Mock 3 Q1, Mock 3 Q4
Ethical theories	41, 46, 47, 49(c), 50(c), 56, 57(e), 59(c), 68

Syllabus topic	Question numbers
Risk manager	29(a)
Risk monitoring	20, Mock 1 Q4
Risk perception	21(c), Mock 3 Q1(c)
Rules-based approaches	11(a), 38(a), Mock 3 Q2(a)
Sarbanes-Oxley	6(a), 11(a), 58(d)
Shareholders	56
Social issues	40, 66(d)
Social responsibility	30(d), 40, 57(d), 58(a), Mock 1 Q1, Mock 3 Q4
Stakeholders	4, 40(c), 46, 48, 58(a), 62(a), 64(d), 66(a), Mock 1 Q1(a)
Strategic risks	54(c), 57(a), 59(a), 63(b), 67(c), Mock 1 Q3(c), Mock 2 Q1(c)
Sustainability	54(a),62(d), Mock 1 Q1(c)
Teleological approach	47(c), 50(c)
Trade unions	66(b)
Transaction cost theory	45(c)
Transparency	16(b), 56(c), 61(a), 63(c)
Tucker's 5 question model	44(b), 63(a)
Utilitarianism	57(e), 59(c)

Helping you with your revision – the ONLY P1 Practice and Revision Kit to be reviewed by the examiner!

BPP Learning Media – the sole Platinum Approved Learning Partner - content

As ACCA's **sole Platinum Approved Learning Partner – content**, BPP Learning Media gives you the **unique opportunity** to use **examiner-reviewed** revision materials for the 2012 exams. By incorporating the examiner's comments and suggestions regarding syllabus coverage, the BPP Learning Media Practice and Revision Kit provides excellent, **ACCA-approved** support for your revision.

Tackling revision and the exam

Using feedback obtained from ACCA examiners as part of their review:

- We look at the dos and don'ts of revising for, and taking, ACCA exams

- We focus on Paper P1; we discuss revising the syllabus, what to do (and what not to do) in the exam, how to approach different types of question and ways of obtaining easy marks

Selecting questions

We provide signposts to help you plan your revision.

- A full **question index**

- A **topic index** listing all the questions that cover key topics, so that you can locate the questions that provide practice on these topics, and see the different ways in which they might be examined

- **BPP's question plan** highlighting the most important questions and explaining why you should attempt them

- **Build your own exams**, showing how you can practise questions in a series of exams

Making the most of question practice

At BPP Learning Media we realise that you need more than just questions and model answers to get the most from your question practice.

- Our **Top tips** included for certain questions provide essential advice on tackling questions, presenting answers and the key points that answers need to include

- We show you how you can pick up **Easy marks** on some questions, as we know that picking up all readily available marks often can make the difference between passing and failing

- We include **marking guides** to show you what the examiner rewards

- We include **examiners' comments** to show you where students struggled or performed well in the actual exam

- We refer to the **2011 BPP Study Text** (for exams in 2012) for detailed coverage of the topics covered in questions

- In a bank at the end of this Kit we include the **examiner's answers** to the June and December 2011 papers. Used in conjunction with our answers they provide an indication of all possible points that could be made, issues that could be covered and approaches to adopt.

Attempting mock exams

There are three mock exams that provide practice at coping with the pressures of the exam day. We strongly recommend that you attempt them under exam conditions. **Mock exams 1 and 2** reflect the question styles and syllabus coverage of the exam; **Mock exam 3** is the December 2011 paper.

Revising P1

Topics to revise

Firstly we must emphasise that you will need a good knowledge of the **whole syllabus**. Any part of the syllabus could be tested within compulsory Question 1. Having to choose two out of three optional questions does not really represent much choice if there are areas of the syllabus you are keen to avoid. Although (like all syllabuses) this syllabus may have seemed a lot when you were studying, we actually believe that it is not as large as some of the syllabuses you have previously studied.

That said, there are certain topics that are stressed in the syllabus and by the examiner, and therefore are core:

- Concepts underpinning corporate governance, in particular integrity, accountability and transparency
- Stakeholders in organisations and in decisions
- The agency problem
- Features of, and arguments for and against, principles vs rules based approaches
- Sarbanes-Oxley
- Corporate governance best practice in relation to the board, board committees, remuneration and reporting
- Elements of control environment
- The main control procedures
- Risk assessment framework
- The main strategies for dealing with risks
- The key ethical positions
- Kohlberg's framework
- Methods of ethical decision-making
- Gray, Owen, Adams seven positions on corporate social responsibility
- Meaning of sustainability

Your knowledge of other topic areas needs to demonstrate breadth. You need to have a good idea of:

- The different types of risks (not just financial) that it can face
- The elements of control and risk management systems
- The impact of culture
- The main elements of corporate and professional codes
- The main areas discussed in corporate social responsibility debates

Reading articles

The examiner has stressed the importance of reading the technical articles published in *Student Accountant* that relate to P1. We've reproduced in this kit the articles the examiner has written about the syllabus and his approach to the paper, also the article about the verbs used in question requirements. Other articles relating to P1 are available on ACCA's website. Some of the articles are written by the examiner and all are reviewed by him.

It's also useful to keep reading the business pages during your revision period and not just narrowly focus on the syllabus. Remember that the examiner has stressed that this paper is about how organisations respond to real-world issues, so the more you read, the more practical examples you will have of how organisations have tackled real-life situations.

Question practice

You should use the Passcards and any brief notes you have to revise these topics, but you mustn't spend all your revision time passively reading. **Question practice is vital**; doing as many questions as you can in full will help develop your ability to analyse scenarios and produce relevant discussion and recommendations. The question plan on page xliii tells you what questions cover so that you can choose questions covering a variety of organisations and risk situations.

You should make sure you leave yourself enough time during your revision to practise 50 mark Section A questions as you cannot avoid them, and the scenarios and requirements of Section A questions are more complex. You should also leave yourself enough time to do the three mock exams.

Passing the P1 exam

Displaying the right qualities

The examiner will expect you to display the following qualities.

Qualities required	
Fulfilling the higher level question requirements	This means that when you are asked to show higher level skills such as **assessment or evaluation**, you will only score well if you demonstrate them. Merely describing something when you are asked to evaluate it will not earn you the marks you need.
Identifying the most important features of the organisation and its environment	You must use your **technical knowledge and business awareness** to identify the key features of the scenario.
Sorting the information in the scenario	You will get a lot of information, particularly in the Section A scenario, and will be expected to **evaluate how useful** it is and **use it** to support answers such as comparisons and discussions. Over 50% of marks in most questions are likely to be available for direct application of knowledge to the scenario.
Selecting relevant real-life examples	You may gain credit for using **good examples**, providing you use the examples to illustrate your understanding of the points in the scenario.
Using the governance and ethical frameworks	Remember that the examiner has emphasised the importance of accountants showing awareness of their responsibilities. You may be expected to **apply the frameworks** to determine what the problem is (for example which stakeholders should be considered) and to identify appropriate solutions.
Criticising the approaches you use	You may be expected not only to **apply** guidance such as **corporate governance codes** or **principles-based ethical guidance**, but also criticise the approaches you use.
Arguing well	You may be expected to discuss both sides of a case, or present an argument in favour or against something. You will gain marks for the **quality** and **logical flow of your arguments**.
Making reasonable recommendations	The measures you recommend must be **appropriate** for the organisation; you may need to discuss their strengths and weaknesses, as there may be costs of adopting them. The recommendations should clearly state what has to be done.

Avoiding weaknesses

The examiner has highlighted weaknesses in many answers which you must try to avoid:

- **Failing to provide what the question verbs require** (discussion, evaluation, recommendation) or to write about the topics specified in the question requirements

- **Failing to apply your answers to the scenario**

You will also enhance your chances significantly if you ensure you avoid these mistakes as well:

- **Repeating the same material** in different parts of answers

- **Quoting chunks of detail** from the question that don't add any value

- **Forcing irrelevancies into answers**, for example irrelevant definitions or theories, or examples that don't relate to the scenario

- **Giving long lists or writing down all that's known** about a broad subject area, and not caring whether it's relevant or not

- **Focusing too narrowly on one area** – for example only covering financial risks when other risks are also important

- **Letting your personal views prevent you from answering the question** – the question may require you to construct an argument with which you personally don't agree

- **Unrealistic or impractical recommendations**

- **Vague recommendations** - instead of just saying improve risk management procedures, you should discuss precisely **how** you would improve them

- **Failing to answer sufficient questions** because of poor time management

- **Not answering all parts of optional questions**

The examiner has also commented that the way some students lay out their answers is unhelpful. They do not clearly label the part of the question they are attempting or answer all parts at the same time.

Using the reading time

We recommend that you spend the first part of the 15 minutes reading time choosing the Section B questions you will do, on the basis of your knowledge of the syllabus areas being tested and whether you can fulfil all (preferably), or most (at least), of the question requirements. Remember that Section B questions will normally be in three or more parts and can cover different parts of the syllabus, and you should be happy with all the areas that the questions you choose cover. We suggest that you should note on the paper any initial ideas that come to you about these questions, but don't go through them in detail.

However don't spend all the reading time going through and analysing the Section B question requirements in detail; leave that until the three hours writing time. Instead you should be looking to spend as much of the reading time as possible looking at the Section A scenario, as this will be longer and more complex than the Section B scenarios and cover more of the syllabus. You should highlight and annotate the key points of the scenario on the question paper.

Choosing which questions to answer first

Spending most of your reading time on the Section A scenario will mean that you can get underway with planning and writing your answer to the Section A question as soon as the three hours start. It will give you more actual writing time during the one and a half hours you should allocate to it and it's writing time that you'll need. Comments from examiners of other syllabuses that have similar exam formats suggest that students appear less time-pressured if they do the big compulsory question first.

During the second half of the exam, you can put Section A aside and concentrate on the two Section B questions you've chosen.

However our recommendations are not inflexible. If you really think the Section A question looks a lot harder than the Section B questions you've chosen, then do one of those first, but **DON'T run over time on it.** You must have an hour and a half to tackle the Section A question and you will feel under much more pressure on it if you leave it till last. If you do one of the Section B questions first, and then tackle the Section A question having had initial thoughts on it during the reading time, you should be able to generate more ideas and find the Section A question is not as bad as it looks.

Remember also that small overruns of time during the first half of the exam can add up to your being very short of time towards the end.

Tackling questions

Scenario questions

You'll improve your chances by following a step-by-step approach to scenarios along the following lines.

Step 1   Read start of scenario

The opening sentence or paragraph should give you important details that set the scenario in its business context. Don't however read all of the scenario straightaway.

Step 2   Read the requirement

You need to identify the knowledge areas being tested and what information will therefore be significant.

Step 3   Identify the action verbs

These convey the level of skill you need to exhibit and also the structure your answer should have. A lower level verb such as define will require a more descriptive answer; a higher level verb such as evaluate will require a more applied, critical answer.

The examiner has stressed that **higher level requirements and verbs** will be most significant in this paper, for example critically evaluating a statement and arguing for or against a given idea or position.

Action verbs that are likely to be frequently used in this exam are listed below, together with their intellectual levels and guidance on their meaning.

Intellectual level		
1	Define	Give the meaning of
1	Explain	Make clear
1	Identify	Recognise or select
1	Describe	Give the key features
2	Distinguish	Define two different terms, viewpoints or concepts on the basis of the differences between them
2	Compare and contrast	Explain the similarities and differences between two different terms, viewpoints or concepts
2	Contrast	Explain the differences between two different terms, viewpoints or concepts
2	Analyse	Give reasons for the current situation or what has happened
3	Assess	Determine the strengths/weaknesses/ importance/ significance/ability to contribute
3	Examine	Critically review in detail
3	Discuss	Examine by using arguments for and against
3	Explore	Examine or discuss in a wide-ranging manner
3	Criticise	Present the weaknesses of/problems with the actions taken or viewpoint expressed, supported by evidence
3	Evaluate/critically evaluate	Determine the value of in the light of the arguments for and against (critically evaluate means weighting the answer towards criticisms/arguments against).
3	Construct the case	Present the arguments in favour or against, supported by evidence
3	Recommend	Advise the appropriate actions to pursue in terms the recipient will understand

Also make sure you identify all the action verbs; some question parts may have more than one.

Step 4   Identify what each part of the question requires

Think about what frameworks or theories you could choose if the question doesn't specify which one to use.

When planning, you will need to make sure that you aren't reproducing the same material in more than one part of the question.

Also you're likely to come across part questions with two requirements that may be at different levels; a part question may for example ask you to explain X and discuss Y. You must ensure that you **fulfill both requirements** and that your discussion of Y shows greater depth than your explanation of X (for example by identifying problems with Y or putting the case for and against Y).

Step 5   Check the mark allocation to each part

This shows you the depth anticipated and helps allocate time.

Step 6   Read the whole scenario through, highlighting key data

In the front pages of the text we discussed what the key data would be for questions covering different areas of the syllabus:

Corporate governance	• Weaknesses in arrangements described
	• Relating arrangements described to governance best practice
	• Relating arrangements to underlying principles
Control systems	• Adequacy of control systems (what's missing)
	• Appropriateness of control systems (do they address key risks/problems)
	• Overall control environment/culture and influence on effectiveness of control processes
Risks	• Most significant risks (strategic/relate to key changes)
	• Most significant uncertainties
	• Consequences of risks materialising
	• Evidence of risk awareness in organisation
	• Factors determining risk response (risk appetite, size of organisation)
Ethics	• Ethical issues at stake
	• Ethical position of organisation
	• Ethical position of individuals
	• Factors that determine ethical positions
	• Importance of stakeholders

Put points under headings related to requirements (eg by noting in the margin to what part of the question the scenario detail relates).

Step 7   Consider the consequences of the points you've identified

Remember that in the answer you will often have to provide recommendations based on the information you've been given. Consider also that you may have to criticise the code, framework or model that you've been told to use. The examiner sees expression of views as very important. You may have to bring in wider issues or viewpoints, for example the views of different stakeholders.

Step 8   Write a plan

You may be able to do this on the question paper as often there will be at least one blank page in the question booklet. However any plan you make should be reproduced in the answer booklet when writing time begins.

Consider carefully when planning your answer to Section A the sorts of issues that will earn you professional marks. How should you present your answer? Do the arguments you use have a logical flow and are they supported by material from the scenario?

Make sure that you have identified **all** the question requirements, all the points you intend to make are **relevant** and your answer will be **applied to the scenario** when required.

Step 9   Write the answer

Make every effort to present your answer clearly. The pilot paper and other questions suggest that the examiner will be looking for you to make a number of clear points. The best way to demonstrate what you're doing is to put points into separate, succinct, paragraphs with clear headers.

Remember that **depth of discussion** will be important. Discussions will often consist of paragraphs containing 2-3 sentences. Each paragraph should:

- **Make a point**

- **Explain the point** (you must demonstrate why the point is important)

- **Illustrate the point** (with material or analysis from the scenario, perhaps an example from real-life)

In this exam a number of requirement verbs will expect you to express a viewpoint or opinion, for example construct an argument, criticise, evaluate. When expressing an opinion, you need to provide:

- **What the question wants**; for example if you are asked to criticise something, don't spend time discussing its advantages. In addition if a scenario provides a lot of information about a situation, and you are (say) asked to assess that situation in the light of good practice, your assessment is unlikely to be favourable.

- **Evidence** from theory or the scenario – again we stress that the majority of marks in most questions will be given for applying your knowledge to the scenario

Gaining the easy marks

Knowledge of the core topics that we list under topics to revise should present you with some easy marks. The pilot paper suggests that there will be some marks available on certain part questions for definitions, explanations or descriptions that don't have to be related to the scenario. However don't assume that you can ignore all the scenarios and still pass!

As P1 is a Professional level paper, 4 or 5 **professional level marks** will be awarded in the compulsory question. Some of these should be easy to obtain. The examiner has stated that some marks may be available for presenting your answer in the form of formal business letters, briefing notes, memos, presentations, press releases, narratives in an annual report and so on. You may also be able to obtain marks for the format, layout, logical flow and persuasiveness of your answer.

What you write should always sound professional, and you will be awarded marks for good introductions and conclusions. You must use the format the question requires. You must also lay your answer out so that somebody could actually read it and use it. A good way to end all documents is to invite further communication.

How you make the document persuasive will depend on who you are and who the recipients are. If you are writing to shareholders you should consider how much information you need to provide. If you are trying to convince the reader that a decision is right, you should focus on the benefits. If you are apologising for something that has gone wrong, you need to reassure the reader and ensure they are happy with the information you provide.

Reports

A report should have the following formal elements at the top:

- Title
- Report writer
- Report recipient
- Date

It should include:

- An introduction summarising its scope, terms of reference and the information used
- Findings/points made, in sections with headings. The points should be specific and factual
- Recommendations/conclusions at the end

It should be written in the first person. (I)

Memorandum

A memorandum should have the same formal elements at the top as a report. Its recipient should be referred to as you. A memo should finish with a conclusion or recommendation – you should not end it with yours faithfully.

Letter

A letter should include:

- The address of the sender
- The date it is written
- If to a single recipient, the recipient's name and address at the top.

It should have:

- An introductory paragraph, setting out the reasons why the letter is written

- A clear and logical flow of content

- A personal element, using the first person (I, our company) and referring to the recipients and their interests

- A concluding paragraph, re-emphasising the purpose of the letter and, if appropriate, inviting further action by the recipient(s) (eg please get in touch if you would like further information)

If it is a business letter, addressed formally (Dear Sir), it should be signed Yours faithfully. If the addressee is named, it should be signed yours sincerely.

Speech or statement at meeting

A speech should:

- Be easy to read out. If you answer any questions requiring speeches **during your revision** you should read your answer to yourself to see whether you say it easily (Do **NOT** however, read your answer aloud in the actual exam!)

- Begin with a formal introduction, for example Welcome Ladies and Gentlemen

- Provide an overview of what will be covered

- Connect each section with narrative designed to make the speech sound convincing, logical and persuasive

- **Not** contain bullet points (how would you deliver them)

- End with an invitation to respond: 'Thank you for listening. I now open the floor to questions'.

Briefing notes

These may be required for use at a board meeting or to inform external stakeholders such as institutional shareholders. They should:

- Start with the key points, with background information later on or in appendices
- Be written in the third person, referring to the directors or the company'

Press or website statement

The statement should have:

- A first paragraph that emphasises the key points
- Background information later in the statement or in appendices
- A third person narrator

Management narratives in annual report

The narrative should have:

- A first paragraph that clearly introduces the purpose of the statement
- A narrative that clearly supports this purpose
- A clear structure, with separate points being distinguished
- A third person narrator

Article in newspaper or magazine

The article should be clearly focussed on the issues to be discussed and designed to attract the reader's attention by the use of paragraph 'headlines'. The article must be tailored to the readership of the publication, explaining (or maybe better not using) terms they are unlikely to know. Generally articles should have short sentences and avoid the use of the passive. The article may not necessarily be unbiased. The question requirements may ask you to use the article to promote an argument or viewpoint, and the article would then have to be slanted in that direction.

Exam information

Format of the exam

		Number of marks
Section A:	1 compulsory case study	50
Section B:	Choice of 2 from 3 questions (25 marks each)	50
		100

Time: 3 hours plus 15 minutes reading time

Section A will be a compulsory case study question with typically four or five sub-requirements relating to the same scenario information. The question will usually assess and link a range of subject areas across the syllabus. It will require students to demonstrate high-level capabilities to understand the complexities of the case and evaluate, relate and apply the information in the case study to the requirements.

The examiner has stressed the importance of reading the case in detail, taking notes as appropriate and getting a feel for what the issues are. Scenarios may be drawn from any situation involving aspects of governance; this is likely to be, but need not be, in an organisational setting.

Professional marks will be available in Section A for presentation, logical flow of argument and quality of argument.

Section B questions are more likely to assess a range of discrete subject areas from the main syllabus section headings; they may require evaluation and synthesis of information contained within short scenarios and application of this information to the question requirements.

Although one subject area is likely to be emphasised in each Section B question, students should not assume that questions will be solely about content from that area. Each question will be based on a shorter case scenario to contextualise the question.

The paper will have a global focus.

Additional information

The Study Guide provides more detailed guidance on the syllabus.

December 2011

Section A

1 Ethical codes; voluntary and mandatory disclosure; internal controls; risk assessment and management

Section B

2 Principles or rules; chairman and chief executive; comply or explain

3 Chief executive remuneration; market risk; proxy voting

4 Corporate social responsibility

The December 2011 exam is Mock exam 3 in this kit.

June 2011

Examiner's comments. As in previous exam reports, I would remind candidates preparing for P1 exams not only to ensure they have studied the entire P1 study guide (and not 'question spotted'), but also to make themselves familiar with the content of technical articles on P1. These are published in Student Accountant magazine and are also posted on the ACCA website.

December 2010

Examiner's comments. First, there is still evidence that candidates are not correctly or fully reading the questions. I will discuss the specifics below but in, for example, Q1(c)(i) and also Q3(c), many candidates seemed not to realise what the question was actually asking. Perhaps some candidates answered the question they wish had been asked rather than the actual question set.

Second, it was frustrating to see that many candidates were unable to bring the content of one of my technical articles into their answers when it was appropriate to do so. The content on environmental auditing for Q2 (b) was covered in a technical article in Student Accountant. Perhaps the fact that the article was published some time ago made some candidates think the content would not be covered.. Technical articles should be studied carefully by all P1 candidates including those written by the examiner and by other authors.

Third, there is ample scope for improvement in the development of level 3 intellectual outcomes like 'construct' and 'criticise' (such as in Q1(c) (ii), Q2 (a) and Q4 (d)). Being able to operate at 'level 3' is important at the professional level in ACCA exams (and in professional life) and there was evidence that some candidates lacked an insight into what these verbs meant.

June 2010

Examiner's comments. Firstly, I sadly must repeat comments made in previous examiner's reports about the four professional marks in Q1. Many candidates did not gain many professional marks in writing the statement required in Q1(d). Secondly, the ethical reasoning questions, Q2c and Q4c, were both done poorly overall. This suggests that candidates are less well prepared for these tasks than they might be.

December 2009

Examiner's comments. As in previous diets, Question 1 was a multi-part requirement covering a wide range of outcomes from the study guide. The Section B questions tended to be located within one area of the study guide but, as in previous papers, also contained supporting requirements from other areas. All questions were based on case scenarios and marks were often awarded for application to the case material.

June 2009

Examiner's comments. There was evidence of 'question spotting' or 'question guessing' by over-relying on exam tips. This meant that some candidates concentrated on a few areas that they thought and hoped would come up on the paper. Importantly, however, this revision may have been at the expense of content they thought would not come up. The danger of this strategy was realised in some of the responses to Q1(a) on Kohlberg. Because Kohlberg was on a previous paper (December 2007), some candidates evidently thought that it wouldn't come up again so soon – and it did. It was disappointing that marks went unawarded to candidates who made the wrong question-spotting guess.

The other potential question-spotting error was on the content of recent technical articles. When an examiner writes a technical article in Student Accountant, it does not necessarily signal that the content of that article will be in the next exam paper, or indeed in any future exam paper. It might be that an examiner wants to clarify or re-emphasise an important area or it may be to update material in the light of recent events.

This, then, is a general warning against question-spotting and question-guessing. All candidates should learn and revise all of the content of the P1 study guide. They should also practice using all past papers and study the model answers for each one.

The level of analysis, where required, was often poor. This applied to questions specifically asking for answers using the context of the case such as Q3 (b). In question 3(c) most candidates could not use the deep green ethical position to assess Ivor Nahum's remarks and this was not necessarily because they didn't understand what the deep green position is. It was because they were unable to tie their book learning to the case. This lack of analytical and evaluative ability was why many candidates failed to pass the exam.

December 2008

Examiner's comments. It is very important that all candidates study carefully all previous papers along with the answers. Examiner's reports enable candidates and tutors to see the areas that were done well and not so well by candidates.

I would like to make two overall points. First there is still ample evidence that some candidates are yet to learn the importance of the verb used in the question. Second, some candidates underachieved in the exam because of a failure to read the questions carefully enough. In some cases, candidates answered the question they wished had been set rather than the one that was actually set.

June 2008

Examiner's comments. 'Candidates who performed well in the paper were those who, in addition to having a good understanding of the P1 subject matter, were able to bring two other important intellectual skills to bear on the examination.

1. It was important to correctly interpret the verb in the question and use that as the basis for their answers. This meant that if the question asked candidates to 'explain' or 'describe' and the answer just contained (say) a list of points, few marks were awarded. Similarly, where a question asked candidates for a higher level skill such as 'evaluate', 'assess',' construct' or 'criticise', answers that did not address the content at the level required were poorly rewarded. Candidates must not 'explain' when they are meant to 'construct' or 'criticise', and they must not 'identify' when they are meant to 'describe'.

2. It was important to correctly analyse the case materials given in the exam paper, especially when specifically instructed to do so in the question. The exam questions contained numerous instructions to work with information from the case. For example:

   Q1 (a)(i) ... and identify from the case...
   Q1 (c) ... using information from the case...
   Q2 (a) ... and describe three threats to auditor independence in the case
   (Other types of wording are used to mean the same thing).

   The important thing to realise is that if the question specifically asks for answers to be based on the case then marks will not be awarded for non case-based answers. This was a frequent cause of poor performance in the exam.'

December 2007

Examiner's comments. 'Candidates that performed well in the exam were those who, in addition to having studied and revised the syllabus in depth, were able to answer at the levels of the verbs used in the questions. Because P1 is a professional level paper, many verbs were at cognitive level 3 – verbs like assess, evaluate, critically evaluate and construct. Candidates that achieved good marks in the paper were those able to demonstrate these skill levels when required in the exam. Candidates that were expecting to be able to answer the questions of the exam using 'book work' or 'rote learning' knowledge generally failed to address the level 2 and level 3 skill requirements and thereby failed the exam.'

Pilot paper

Supplementary questions

Analysis of past papers

The table below provides details of when each element of the syllabus has been examined and the question number and section in which each element appeared.

Covered in Text chapter		Dec 2011	Jun 2011	Dec 2010	Jun 2010	Dec 2009	Jun 2009	Dec 2008	Jun 2008	Dec 2007	Pilot paper
	GOVERNANCE AND RESPONSIBILITY										
1	Scope of governance		3a,b	1a,c	1a,b		1d	1c	1a	1a,4a,c	1a,3b
1	Agency				1c		1c		3a		
3	Board of directors	2b	1d,4c	3a,b		1c,2a,b,c	1e,3a,d	2c	3c	1c,3a,b	1a,c,d,2c
3,5	Board committees		3c					2c,3c	3b		
3	Directors' remuneration	3a			2a,b		3c			2c	2a,b
2	Different approaches to governance	2a			4a				4a	3c	
2,11	Corporate social responsibility			4d					1d		1e
3	Reporting and disclosure	1b, 2c, 3c	1c	3c			3b	1d			
	INTERNAL CONTROL AND REVIEW										
4,7,8	Management control systems				3a,b			3a		1d	4a
4,7,8,10	Internal control, audit and compliance	1c	1a		3c	1b	1b	3a,b	1e,2a		
8	Internal control and reporting			1c					4b,c		
8	Management information					1d					
	IDENTIFYING AND ASSESSING RISK										
5	Risk and the risk management process		2a				4a,c				
6	Risk categories	1c, 3b		2c,4a				1b,3c	1c		1b,4b
5,6,7,8	Risk identification, measurement and assessment	1c	2c		1d				1b		
	CONTROLLING RISK										
5,8	Risk targeting and monitoring					4c		2a			
5,7,8	Risk reduction and control		2d	4b,c		4a, b	4b	2b		2b	
5,7	Risk, avoidance, retention and modelling		2b					2b		2a	
	PROFESSIONAL VALUES AND ETHICS										
9	Ethical theories		1b	1b			1a	1a,4c		1b	3c
9,11	Different approaches to ethics and social responsibility	4a, b,c	1d			1a	2c			4b	
10	Professions and the public interest		4b				2a		2b		4c
10	Professional practice and codes of ethics	1a		2a,b,c		3a		4a,b			3a
10	Conflicts of interest and consequences of unethical behaviour		4a		2c,4c	3c	2b		2a		
9,10	Ethical characteristics of professionalism					4b	3b		2c		
11	Social and environmental issues				1d				1d		1e

IMPORTANT!

The table above gives a broad idea of how frequently major topics in the syllabus are examined. It should not be used to question spot and predict for example that Topic X will not be examined because it came up two sittings ago. The examiner's reports indicate that the examiner is well aware some students try to question spot. You can assume that he will therefore take care to ensure that the exams avoid falling into a predictable pattern, and may examine the same topic two sittings in a row for example.

Useful websites

The websites below provide additional sources of information of relevance to your studies for *Advanced Financial Management.*

- www.accaglobal.com

  ACCA's website. The students' section of the website is invaluable for detailed information about the qualification, past issues of Student Accountant (including technical articles) and interviews with examiners.

- www.bpp.com

  Our website provides information about BPP products and services, with a link to the ACCA website.

- www.ft.com

  This website provides information about current international business. You can search for information and articles on specific industry groups as well as individual companies.

- www.economist.com

  Here you can search for business information on a week-by-week basis, search articles by business subject and use the resources of the Economist Intelligence Unit to research sectors, companies or countries.

- www.invweek.co.uk

  This site carries business news and articles on markets from Investment Week and International Investment.

- www.pwcglobal.com/uk

  The PricewaterhouseCoopers website includes UK Economic Outlook.

- www.cfo.com

  Good website for financial officers.

- www.bankofengland.co.uk

  This website is useful for sourcing Bank of England publications.

Key articles

EXAMINER'S APPROACH TO PAPER P1, PROFESSIONAL ACCOUNTANT

by **David Campbell**
22 Feb 2007

Paper P1, *Professional Accountant* is a new compulsory paper in the Essentials module at the Professional level of the ACCA Qualification. It is an exciting, challenging, and innovative paper that aims to enrich students' understanding of a number of important issues as they prepare to take their place as members of the professional accounting community.

Following in-depth consultation on the development of the new ACCA Qualification and guidance on ethics and governance teaching from IFAC and others, it was decided to create a new paper – Professional Accountant – to examine a number of areas relevant to the broad themes of professionalism, responsibility, accountability, and ethics. In terms of syllabus content, these themes are handled in the context of corporate governance, internal control, risk, and professional and business ethics. These areas form the basis of the new Paper P1 syllabus.

Content from a number of other parts of the new ACCA Qualification is relevant to the Paper P1 syllabus (refer to the 'linked papers' diagram in the *Syllabus*). Most obviously, it forms a prominent part of the qualification's emphasis on ethics. Professionalism and ethics are both at the heart of the new ACCA Qualification. They are covered in 11 of the 16 exam papers – including all papers at Professional level – and three of the Essentials performance objectives as part of the practical experience requirement. Underpinning the syllabus and the practical experience is the Professional Ethics module. The aim of the Professional Ethics module is to give students exposure to a range of ethical perspectives and can be completed once eligible to take Paper P1. Ideally, the Professional Ethics module should be taken at the same time as – or soon after – completing Paper P1. In addition, the Paper P1 syllabus builds on and develops content studied previously in Paper F1, *Accountant in Business* and Paper F8, *Audit and Assurance*.

It is important to study an ACCA-approved textbook for Paper P1. They are written especially for the syllabus, and are reviewed by the examiner, making them invaluable in terms of coverage and insight into what is examinable. The syllabus for Paper P1, possibly more than any of the other papers, is eclectic in nature and draws on material from a number of different disciplines. Students are strongly encouraged to read around the subject area, especially those students new to the content of the syllabus. A number of recommended books are listed at the end of the *Study Guide*.

Syllabus and relational diagram

Although the syllabus contains five areas (refer to the 'relational diagram' in the *Syllabus*), it is important to understand that all of these, taken together, comprise a logical 'whole'. All areas are interconnected and, in total, the syllabus represents a set of issues essential to the understanding of how accounting – especially in a business context – contributes to, and is underpinned by, governance and ethics. Although these have always been important to the accountancy profession, a number of well-publicised recent corporate failures and scandals have highlighted the need for sound governance and ethical behaviour. Society invests a great deal of trust in its professions and it is crucial that accounting professionals repay that trust and maintain the level of respect and regard in which they have been traditionally held. Accordingly, accountants need to be aware of their responsibilities to investors, to society, and to the highest standards of

professional probity and competence. The content of the Paper P1 syllabus will help students explore and develop these themes.

Part A of the syllabus focuses of corporate governance, responsibility, and accountability. This means exploring aspects of, for example, the agency relationship between directors and shareholders, the meaning of governance, the role and types of directors, issues of responsibility, and the meaning and limits of accountability. It aims to introduce these important themes while also encouraging students to think about the ethical assumptions made by accountants collectively as a profession.

The next three parts of the syllabus – B, C and D – focus specifically on issues that have, in recent corporate failures, been the most problematic. These include internal control, the identification and assessment of risk, and controlling and mitigating risk. The Paper P1 syllabus singles these out for separate consideration because, although they are integral to corporate governance as a whole, they play a crucial part in an accountant's responsibility to act in the public interest and in the interests of shareholders.

Sound systems of internal analysis, control, and audit underpin all effective corporate governance systems. Effective management at the strategic level rests on the assumption that internal activities can be controlled, verified, and reported on internally. If management loses control of internal systems and procedures, any claim of sound governance is lost – as was the case at Baring's Bank, when a single uncontrolled trader lost large amounts of money on derivatives markets. The same is true of risk. Being aware of all possible risks, understanding their potential impact, as well as the probability of occurrence, are important safeguards for investors and other stakeholders.

All of these preceding sections are underpinned by Paper P1's important consideration of both professional and business ethics – Part E of the syllabus. Ethical assumptions underpin and 'surround' any profession and system of governance. The accountancy profession, just as in medicine or law, is governed by certain ethical frameworks that inform practice and guide practitioners. This part of the Paper P1 syllabus explores some of these assumptions, while also looking at some of the ethical theories that help to explain them. This part of the syllabus will always be assessed to some degree in the compulsory section of the exam but not necessarily exclusively in that section.

Study Guide and intellectual levels

The *Study Guide*, which breaks the syllabus down into separate sections, is on the ACCA website. The superscript numbers at the end of each objective in the *Study Guide* indicate the level at which students should understand a particular subject or topic area. These levels of understanding, known as cognitive levels, are important as they indicate the depth to which each part of the syllabus may be examined.

Because Paper P1 is at the Professional level, the higher cognitive challenges – represented by the number 3 – are prominent. This means that this paper is more likely to use higher levels of questioning; whereas level 1 tasks might concern knowledge and comprehension (such as 'list', 'define', 'identify', 'calculate'), levels 2 and 3 are more challenging. Level 2 tasks concern application and analysis ('contrast', 'explain', 'discuss', and so on), and level 3 tasks concern synthesis and evaluation. Level 3 requirements might therefore include 'construct', 'evaluate', 'assess', 'formulate', or 'advise'.

It is likely that each Paper P1 exam will contain several questions at levels 2 and 3, and the *Study Guide* reflects this emphasis on higher cognitive levels. It is important to realise that if *Study Guide* sections require learning at levels 2 or 3, then it is possible that the exam will test that area at that cognitive level. The marking scheme will reflect this, and answers that do not attempt to answer at the higher cognitive level will be rewarded accordingly. If, therefore, a question asks a candidate to 'assess' or 'evaluate' an argument or a statement, answers that merely 'describe' will not be well rewarded.

Ethical and governance codes

Paper P1 covers two areas that, in some countries, are underpinned by 'codes' or 'guidelines' that attempt to regulate practice. In the light of recent corporate governance failures, governments and professional bodies have introduced these codes so as to reduce the 'freedom of movement' for managers, and to make their duties and responsibilities unambiguous in certain circumstances. The UK was among the first to introduce such initiatives, with the Cadbury Code back in 1992, but the intervening years have seen many other codes springing up in different parts of the world. Some apply to single jurisdictions, such as in Singapore, the UK, and the US, while other codes are intended to apply internationally. IFAC's and ACCA's Codes of Ethics are examples of ethical codes, while the Organisation for Economic Co-operation and Development (OECD) and International Corporate Governance Network (ICGN) both have international codes of corporate governance.

In the Paper P1 *Study Guide*, I have highlighted the fact that whereas a general knowledge of codes is important, line-by-line detail is not required. While the UK codes (such as the Combined Code, first published in 2003) provide a good summary of provisions in corporate governance, other countries and agencies have also produced equivalent guidelines. Students may be required to demonstrate familiarity with a code when answering a question, but it will be acceptable to refer to a local code if more appropriate, or to one of the international codes. ACCA's Code of Ethics applies broadly, and IFAC's Code of Ethics applies to all professional accountants whose professional bodies are members of IFAC (such as ACCA). If students live in a jurisdiction with its own code of ethics (such as the ICPAS code in Singapore), it will be acceptable to refer to that code where appropriate.

Explicit reference is made in the *Study Guide* to Sarbanes–Oxley, which is the legal underpinning of corporate governance in the US. Sarbanes–Oxley is the most influential corporate governance instrument of recent times and has changed practice globally, mainly because of the international dominance of US business.

Exam format

The exam will contain two sections. Section A will contain Question 1, which will be worth a total of 50 marks and which will be compulsory. It will be based on a case study scenario of several hundred words. The requirements will include several distinct tasks (listed as (a), (b), (c), etc) and will sample the syllabus quite broadly. Question 1 might contain elements of governance, risk, internal control, and will include some aspect of ethics.

One of the features of the Professional level exam papers is the awarding of 'professional marks'. These are marks allocated not for the content of an answer, but for the degree of professionalism with which certain parts of the answer are presented. They will usually be awarded in Section A (the compulsory part of the exam paper) and will total 4 to 6 marks.

It may be, for example, that one requirement asks you to present your answer in the form of, say, a letter, a presentation, a memo, a report, briefing notes, or similar. Some marks may be awarded for the form of the answer in addition to the content of the answer. This might be for the structure, content, style and layout, or the logical flow of arguments in your answer. You should assume that if the question asks for a specific format of answer that some marks may be awarded for an effective presentation of that format.

Section B will contain three questions (Questions 2, 3 and 4) and students will be invited to attempt two from the three questions set. Each question in Section B will, accordingly, be worth a total of 25 marks. In contrast to Question 1, it is likely that the questions in Section B will explore one part of the syllabus in a little more depth. Students should not assume, however, that each question in Section 2 will examine only one part of the syllabus. It is more likely that each will contain an emphasis on one part of the syllabus, while including content from other parts as well. All of the three questions in Section B will be based on a short scenario.

The *Pilot Paper*, which is on the ACCA website, is an illustration of the way the future papers will look and feel. In addition to the *Pilot Paper* – which students will want to study in some depth and eventually attempt – additional pilot questions will also be published.

David Campbell is examiner for Paper P1

Gareth Owen explains how the design of the new ACCA Qualification can help students learn more effectively.

testing, testing, one, two, three

☑ **For the new ACCA Qualification, all** *Study Guides* **refer to three intellectual levels. These represent the three bands of intellectual or cognitive ability required to study a particular subject or topic area.**

It is recommended best practice in accounting education to give students as much guidance as possible on how much study is required in order to achieve syllabus aims and objectives. Students therefore need to be aware of the depth at which they will be assessed in any given area. This article explains how the system of intellectual levels should be used in relation to the ACCA syllabus, and looks in detail at the *Study Guides*.

WHAT ARE INTELLECTUAL LEVELS?
In the 1950s, educational psychologist Benjamin Bloom identified six main cognitive domains relating to study:
☐ knowledge
☐ comprehension
☐ application
☐ analysis
☐ synthesis
☐ evaluation.

According to Bloom, the level of cognitive difficulty increases from the recall of knowledge to the evaluation of complex ideas and situations resulting in appropriate decisions or recommendations.

Best practice suggests that professional accounting syllabuses should use three (rather than six) broad bands of cognitive difficulty to help students and their teachers gauge how much preparation is needed, and the level of difficulty they may encounter, in meeting various educational capabilities.

ACCA had adopted three ascending levels of cognitive difficulty, where 1 represents knowledge and comprehension, 2 is application and analysis, and 3 is synthesis and evaluation. These cognitive bands consolidate Bloom's six-level taxonomy.

WHAT KINDS OF CAPABILITIES ARE RELATED TO THESE LEVELS?
Level 1
Knowledge and comprehension require demonstration of the following capabilities:
☐ retention and recall of knowledge
☐ understanding of major accounting and business ideas, techniques, and theories
☐ use of knowledge and techniques in new but familiar situations
☐ recognition of fundamental cause and effect in accounting.

Level 2
Application and analysis require demonstration of the following capabilities:
☐ analysis of unfamiliar situations to prepare reports and solve problems using relevant concepts and theories

☐ recognition of subtle or hidden information patterns and trends within financial and other information, and the ability to interpret these
☐ the ability to infer from given information and draw conclusions.

Level 3
Synthesis and evaluation require demonstration of the following capabilities:
☐ creation of new ideas from, or new insights into, existing knowledge
☐ generalisation, comparison, and discrimination using complex and unstructured information
☐ assessment and evaluation of complex information
☐ use of reasoned argument to infer and make judgements
☐ presentation and justification of valid recommendations.

Do the modules of the syllabus correspond to the intellectual levels?
The new ACCA Qualification syllabus is divided into two main levels, each containing two modules: the Fundamentals level contains the Knowledge and Skills modules, and the Professional level contains the Essentials and Options modules. While both modules in the Professional level are broadly assessed at the same cognitive level, the Skills module papers are set at a higher

intellectual level than the Knowledge module papers. This is also reflected in the time allowed for the respective exams within these modules.

While there are three broad levels within the syllabus, these do not always match the cognitive levels described above. Therefore, it is not the case that every capability in the Knowledge module is assessed at Level 1, and that all Professional level capabilities are assessed at Level 3.

How does learning develop throughout the qualification?
As students progress through the qualification, they both broaden and deepen their capabilities at all stages.

The Knowledge module is predominantly about the breadth and comprehension of knowledge, although there may also be some application or simple analysis. Students would therefore expect to see most capabilities set at Level 1, although in some subject areas there may be a few Level 2 requirements, particularly if the area is not developed further in subsequent papers.

In the Skills module, students should expect to see mostly Level 2 capabilities being assessed, but also to find a number of Level 1 capabilities which will be built on. In some exceptional cases, some Level 3 capabilities will be identified, particularly in areas which are not being taken further at the Professional level.

This shows that even within the higher level modules there is still a need to acquire and comprehend new knowledge before more difficult capabilities relating to this new knowledge can be assessed.

At the Professional level, students should still expect to find a few Level 1 capabilities, as new knowledge is introduced, and before this knowledge can be applied, analysed, synthesised, and evaluated.

Figure 1 shows, in broad terms, the proportion of capabilities assessed at each intellectual level within each discrete module or modules.

FIGURE 1: APPROXIMATE DISTRIBUTION OF LEVEL 1, 2 AND 3 CAPABILITIES IN THE NEW ACCA QUALIFICATION SYLLABUS

Knowledge module	Skills module	Professional level

☒ Level 1
☒ Level 2
☐ Level 3

Which verbs are associated with which levels?

Bloom and other academics have suggested the types of verbs associated with each cognitive level, and these are listed in **Table 1** below. Some of the verbs Bloom lists are not relevant to a profession accountancy qualification, so only relevant verbs are included.

Please note that certain verbs (such as describe, explain, calculate) and other verbs found within the *Study Guides*, may be designated at different levels. This recognises that these verbs need to reflect the varying intellectual demands these requirements may make on students in different situations. For example, under one subject area, a sub-objective might be '*Explain* the structure of a T account[1]'. Another could be: '*Explain* how a warrant works as a derivative financial

instrument[2]'. Not all the verbs listed in **Table 1** will necessarily be used by examiners in their question requirements, nor is this an exhaustive list. The verbs given are merely indicative of the capabilities examiners want students to acquire from the *Study Guide*, in order to meet a range of exam requirements.

The *Study Guide* will often contain more verbs than an examiner would ever use in an exam. This, however, does not mean that students shouldn't develop these capabilities. An example is given below.

In Paper F1, *Accountant in Business* learning outcome A1(b) asks students to describe various organisational structures as follows: 'Describe the different ways in which organisations may be structured: entrepreneurial, functional, matrix, divisional, departmental, by geographical area, and by product.'

However, an objective test question might be written as follows: 'Which of the following forms of organisational structure always requires staff to report to both functional and product managers?
a   Divisional
b   Departmental
c   Matrix (correct answer)
d   Entrepreneurial'

To answer the question correctly, the student must understand the nature, scope, and definition of each type of organisational structure. This would have been taught and learned through reading, and possibly writing, an explanation of each. Therefore, although this capability would not need explicit demonstration in the examination, the examiner will assume the successful student has this capability.

Should I refer to the *Study Guide* and to the intellectual levels when using examinable documents?

It is important that students should refer closely to both the *Study Guide* and the designated intellectual level of each capability when looking at examinable documents. This helps in two ways:
☐   If a document such as an accounting standard or a statute is listed, then students can refer to the area in the *Study Guide* relating to the content of that document, to identify the specific areas to be covered.
☐   By noting the intellectual levels and the verbs used, better guidance is given about the breadth and depth of knowledge required for each aspect.

Should I be worried about the inclusion of intellectual levels?

No one should worry about the inclusion of references to intellectual levels within the *Study Guides*. This new feature is intended to help students and tuition providers tailor their learning and determine the depth required to study various aspects of the syllabus.

The inclusion of intellectual levels is not intended to be prescriptive, and examiners have the freedom to assess the syllabus as they decide. However, they will need to refer to the *Study Guide* when setting their exams.

It is hoped that the inclusion of intellectual levels within the *Study Guides* will help examiners and students match each other's expectations more closely when setting and taking ACCA examinations. ▣

Gareth Owen is qualifications development manager at ACCA

TABLE 1: TYPICAL VERBS ASSOCIATED WITH INTELLECTUAL LEVELS

Level 1	List, define, describe, explain, select, calculate, identify, compare
Level 2	Apply, compare, analyse, compute, derive, reconcile, prepare, interpret, value, contrast, relate, classify, solve, implement
Level 3	Formulate, modify, rearrange, create, compose, design, develop, highlight, summarise, assess, evaluate, justify, decide, infer, advise, recommend, discuss, report

Planning your question practice

We have already stressed that question practice should be right at the centre of your revision. Whilst you will spend some time looking at your notes and Paper P1 Passcards, you should spend the majority of your revision time practising questions.

We recommend two ways in which you can practise questions.

- Use **BPP's Learning Media question plan** to work systematically through the syllabus and attempt key and other questions on a section-by-section basis

- **Build your own exams** – attempt questions as a series of practice exams

These ways are suggestions and simply following them is no guarantee of success. You or your college may prefer an alternative but equally valid approach.

BPP's Learning Media's question plan

The BPP Learning Media plan below requires you to devote a **minimum of 45 hours** to revision of Paper P1. Any time you can spend over and above this should only increase your chances of success.

Step 1   **Review your notes** and the chapter summaries in the Paper P1 **Passcards** for each section of the syllabus.

Step 2   **Answer the key questions** for that section. These questions have boxes round the question number in the table below and you should answer them in full. Even if you are short of time you must attempt these questions if you want to pass the exam. You should complete your answers without referring to our solutions.

Step 3   **Attempt the other questions** in that section. For some questions we have suggested that you prepare **answer plans or do the calculations** rather than full solutions. Planning an answer means that you should spend about 40% of the time allowance for the questions brainstorming the question and drawing up a list of points to be included in the answer.

Step 4   Attempt **Mock exams 1, 2 and 3** under strict exam conditions.

Syllabus section	2011 Passcards chapters	Questions in this Kit	Comments	Done ☑
Governance and responsibility	1 - 3	3	Answer in full. This is a good example of a what's wrong with these corporate governance arrangements and how can they be improved question.	☐
		7	Answer in full. This question was an extra example question published by the examiner, and is a very good example of the style of question that he asks, particularly the links between the question requirement and the scenario.	☐
		8	Answer in full. This pilot paper question covers well the issues of directors' independence and remuneration.	☐
		9	Answer in full. This December 2007 question is a good test of a number of different areas of corporate governance.	☐
		10	Answer in full. This question from June 2008 is an example of a common exam scenario – a company with various corporate governance weaknesses which the question requirements pick up.	☐
		11	Answer in full. From June 2008 a scenario that the examiner seems to like – a conference where opposing views on a key syllabus area are aired.	☐
		12	Answer in full. A good test from a recent exam of various issues relating to the key figures of chairman and chief executive.	☐
		13	Answer in full. This December 2009 question covers quite a number of issues relating to board operation.	☐
		14	Answer in full. This question from June 2010 covers the very topical area of director's remuneration.	☐
		15	Answer in full. This question from December 2010 provides good coverage of the appointment of non-executive directors and reporting on governance issues.	☐
		16	Answer in full. This June 2011 question is quite broad for a 25 mark question, bringing in a number of important areas. It's also about charities, and is a useful reminder that not all questions you see will be about companies.	☐

Syllabus section	2011 Passcards chapters	Questions in this Kit	Comments	Done ☑
Internal control and environment	4 - 5	17	Answer in full. This pilot paper question demonstrates how the examiner expects students to analyse internal control; it also shows that even 25 mark questions will cover areas across the syllabus, as it also covers reputation risk and ethical responsibilities.	☐
Risk assessment, response and monitoring	6-8	18	Answer in full. This question is a good test of your ability to recommend realistic risk management policies for an organisation.	☐
		20	Prepare an answer plan for this question.	☐
		22	Prepare an answer plan for this question.	☐
		25	Answer in full. This question gives you practice in analysing what numerical data tells you about risk levels	☐
		26	Answer in full. This question provides calculation practice and also covers financial risk, an important area of the syllabus.	☐
		27	Answer in full. This December 2007 question tests your knowledge of the strategies used to manage risk, and covers the important area of risk culture within an organisation which the examiner regards as very significant.	☐
		28	Answer in full. From December 2008, a good test of the major risk management strategies and the role and personnel of the risk management committee.	☐
		29	Answer in full. This June 2009 question requires you to discuss very different views of how risks should be managed.	☐
		30	Answer in full. This December 2010 question covers embedding risk awareness, which is a particular interest in the examiner, and also the application of corporate social responsibility in a practical situation.	☐
		31	Answer in full. This question from June 2011 is the first time that a number of topics that have recently been introduced to the syllabus have been examined.	☐
		34	Jot down the main issues you would discuss in this question.	☐
		35	Answer in full. This question covers a number of important issues connected with internal audit.	☐

Syllabus section	2011 Passcards chapters	Questions in this Kit	Comments	Done ☑
		36	Answer in full.	☐
			This December 2008 question examines your ability to apply your knowledge of internal control and internal audit, by testing it in the context of a company that has many shortcomings in these areas.	
		37	Answer in full.	☐
			This question from December 2009 looks at the role of risk culture and external audit's role in ensuring it is enforced.	
		38	Answer in full.	☐
			This question looks at monitoring, an important component of internal control systems.	
Professional values and ethics	9 – 11	40	Prepare an answer plan for this question.	☐
		41	Prepare an answer plan for this question.	☐
		44	Answer in full.	☐
			This question provides important practice in applying the AAA model and Tucker's 5 questions.	
		46	Answer in full.	☐
			A supplementary question issued by the examiner, testing various significant aspects of ethics.	
		47	Answer in full.	☐
			This pilot paper question shows how the examiner tests ethical theories.	
		48	Answer in full.	☐
			This December 2007 question brings together responsibilities with a discussion of Gray, Owen and Adams' CSR positions.	
		49	Answer in full.	☐
			This June 2008 question is a good example of the sort of ethical dilemma that you may have to consider.	
		50	Answer in full.	☐
			This December 2008 question combines how organisations enforce ethics and promote themselves by being ethical, with application of different ethical stances to a scenario, which is a key skill in the P1 exam.	
		51	Answer in full.	☐
			A good wide-ranging question from June 2009, bringing together various issues in this part of the syllabus.	
		52	Answer in full.	☐

Syllabus section	2011 Passcards chapters	Questions in this Kit	Comments	Done ☑
		53	Answer in full. These two recent questions are examples of a problem that may arise in practice, of an accountant getting too close to a client.	☐
		54	Answer in full. This question from December 2010 covers in detail the important areas of environmental risks and auditing.	☐
		55	Answer in full. This June 2011 question covers the topical area of bribery and other types of illegal and unethical conduct.	☐
Case studies		60-68	Answer in full. Answer these wide-ranging case study questions to give yourself practice in tackling lengthy questions.	☐

Build your own exams

Having revised your notes and the BPP Passcards, you can attempt the questions in the Kit as a series of practice exams. You can organise the questions in the following ways.

- Either you can attempt complete past exam papers; recent papers are listed below:

	Pilot	Dec 07	Jun 08	Dec 08	Jun 09	Dec 09	Jun 10	Dec 10	Jun 11
Section A									
1	60	61	62	63	64	65	66	67	68
Section B									
2	8	27	49	28	51	13	14	54	31
3	47	9	10	36	12	52	38	15	16
4	17	48	11	50	29	37	53	30	55

- Or you can make up practice exams, either yourself or using the suggestions we have listed below.

	Practice exams								
	1	2	3	4	5	6	7	8	9
Section A									
1	67	56	57	68	63	60	61	62	64
Section B									
2	9	33	8	7	17	47	31	43	29
3	35	27	28	30	16	3	6	10	11
4	54	46	55	51	50	36	48	15	49

Whichever practice exams you use, you must attempt **Mock exams 1, 2 and 3** at the end of your revision.

Questions

GOVERNANCE AND RESPONSIBILITY

Questions 1 to 16 cover governance and responsibility, the subject of Part A of the BPP Study Text for Paper P1.

1 Remuneration   45 mins

X Group is a company that has been listed on the local Stock Exchange for the last five years. The most recent accounts and associated documents published by X Group include the following information.

Corporate governance disclosures in the accounts

These include:

'The (two) non-executive directors constitute the remuneration committee.'

'No member of the committee has a personal financial interest, other than as a shareholder, in the matters to be decided. There are no conflicts of interest arising from cross directorships....'

'The Chairman has a service contract with a notice period of three years. This was originally drawn up in 20X2 and was considered at that time to afford protection for the Group against the loss of the services of a key executive. ....the Board does not intend to seek to vary the terms.'

Chief Executive's remuneration

The remuneration package was as follows:

	£
Salary	516,000
Bonus	50,000
Employee profit-sharing scheme	8,000
Benefits	21,000

He has a contract that is subject to renewal every three years. The Group contribution to his pension scheme was £85,000.

The bonus is determined by the remuneration committee, and is non-pensionable. It is based on the committee's assessment of the annual performance of the company and the individual's contribution thereto. The bonus may not exceed 25% of salary. Participation in the employee profit-sharing scheme is limited to £8,000. The benefits relate to the use of a company car and accommodation.

In addition to the above, the contract provides that the Chief Executive can receive, as part of his remuneration package, the following.

(i) A conditional allocation of ordinary shares, which may be approved annually by the Remuneration Committee, based on a percentage of salary not exceeding 50%.

Shares are held by trustees during the measurement period of three years.

Vesting (formal ownership and possession) of the shares is subject to a performance test at the end of the period. The test involves ranking the total shareholder return (TSR) against those of other top 100 companies (FT-SE 100).

(1) An upper quartile ranking will produce 100% vesting, a lower quartile zero.

(2) The calculation of intermediate points is linear.

The shares required are purchased in the market. Conditional allocations are expected to be at 50% of salary (the maximum).

(ii) Share options may be granted, at the market price at the date of grant. The maximum share options granted in a three-year period cannot exceed four times annual salary. These cannot be exercised for three years, and can be exercised only if the percentage growth of the TSR of the company equals or exceeds that of the average of the FT-SE 100 companies.

Required

(a) Assess the corporate governance arrangements that have been quoted from the accounts, and advise the board on improvements that should be made.

(10 marks)

(b) Assess the extent to which each element of the remuneration package is likely to motivate the Chief Executive, and the acceptability of each element to shareholders.

(15 marks)

(Total = 25 marks)

2 Nerium Engineering

45 mins

Ken Masters is Managing Director of a medium-sized engineering company. His company has carried out a couple of projects over the last year for Nerium Engineering, a recently listed company. The board of Nerium Engineering has subsequently contacted Ken about becoming a non-executive director of the company.

Nerium's board has told Ken that his responsibilities as a director would include being a member of Nerium's audit and remuneration committees. The audit committee has only just been established and its terms of reference have yet to be finally agreed. Ken is unsure what such a role might involve and, as an engineer without a finance qualification, he is also unsure as to whether he is the right person for such a committee.

The remuneration committee has by contrast been established for just over two years. Ken understands the main role of the remuneration committee but is worried about the responsibilities that he will be taking on. In particular he is concerned about widespread condemnation of 'fat cat' salaries and rewards, and criticisms of situations where senior executives have been forced to resign when their company has performed very badly but have taken a large pay-off when they leave. He is worried that in some cases, non-executive directors on remuneration committees have been accused of failing to do their job properly by allowing excessive remuneration packages. He has been pondering the following quote from the UK Corporate Governance Code:

'Levels of remuneration should be sufficient to attract, retain and motivate directors of the quality required to run the company successfully, but a company should avoid paying more than is necessary for this purpose. A significant proportion of executive directors' remuneration should be structured so as to link rewards to corporate and individual performance.'

Historically Nerium Engineering has rewarded its directors largely on the basis of the earnings the company has achieved. The directors have received quite a small basic salary, but a large profit-related bonus.

Required

(a) Explain the possible role and responsibilities of the audit committee and the main qualities that a member of such a committee should possess.

(12 marks)

(b) Describe the basic principles that should be applied to test the acceptability of a performance measure.

(5 marks)

(c) Critically evaluate the bases that might be used for measuring the performance of senior executives, with a view to establishing a remuneration system that rewards individuals for achievement.

(8 marks)

(Total = 25 marks)

3 Mega Mart

45 mins

MegaMart plc is a medium sized retailer of fashion goods with some 200 outlets spread throughout the UK. A publicly quoted company on the London Stock Market, it has pursued a growth strategy based on the aggressive acquisition of a number of smaller retail groups. This growth has gone down well with shareholders, but a significant slowdown in retail sales has resulted in falling profits, dividends and, as a consequence, its share price. MegaMart had been the creation of one man, Rex Lord, a high profile entrepreneur, convinced that his unique experience of the retail business gained through a lifetime working in the sector was sufficient to guide the company through its current misfortunes. His dominance of the company was secured through his role as both Chairman and Chief Executive of the company. His control of his board of directors was almost total and his style of management such that his decisions were rarely challenged at board level. He felt no need for any non-executive directors drawn from outside the company to be on the board. Shareholders were already asking questions on his exuberant lifestyle and lavish entertainment, at company expense, which regularly made the headlines in the popular press. Rex's high profile personal life also was regularly exposed to public scrutiny and media attention.

As a result of the downturn in the company's fortunes some of his acquisitions have been looked at more closely and there are, as yet, unsubstantiated claims that MegaMart's share price had been maintained through premature disclosure of proposed acquisitions and evidence of insider trading. Rex had amassed a personal fortune through the acquisitions, share options and above average performance related bonuses, which had on occasion been questioned at the Shareholders' Annual General Meeting. His idiosyncratic and arrogant style of management had been associated with a reluctance to accept criticism from any quarter and to pay little attention to communicating with shareholders.

Recently, there has been concern expressed in the financial press that the auditors appointed by MegaMart, some twenty years ago, were also providing consultancy services on his acquisition strategy and on methods used to finance the deals.

Required

(a) Explain the nature of the agency problem that exists in MegaMart. **(3 marks)**

(b) Assess the extent to which MegaMart's corporate governance arrangements and situation fail to constitute governance best practice. **(12 marks)**

(c) Rex Lord has consistently resisted the appointment of independent, non-executive directors to the board of MegaMart plc. Construct a case for MegaMart appointing independent non-executive directors. **(10 marks)**

(Total = 25 marks)

4 Stakeholders   45 mins

Lynne Howard is about to begin a business studies course at university. She has obtained a guest ticket at a major conference through one of the organisers. In a keynote speech at the conference, a junior government minister referred to the impact stakeholder theory has had and the importance of businesses showing responsibility towards all their stakeholders.

Lynne is confused as she thought that businesses were basically responsible to their owners/shareholders and therefore would seek to maximise profits. She wonders how, if there are interested parties other than shareholders whom the business must respect, what the consequences will be and how a business decides whose interests are most important.

Required

(a) Distinguish between stakeholders on the basis of their level of involvement in the business, how much the business's activities affect them, how much power and influence they have and how much they participate in the business, and explain the significance of the classifications. **(10 marks)**

(b) Describe how Mendelow's system provides a means for showing the significance of different stakeholders. **(5 marks)**

(c) Assess the views expressed by the government minister on how businesses should respond to stakeholder concerns. **(10 marks)**

(Total = 25 marks)

5 SPV

45 mins

SPV is listed on the stock exchange of a central European country. The company manufactures a wide range of pharmaceutical products including modern drugs used in preventing and treating cancer, AIDS and similar diseases. SPV has three factories where drugs are produced and one research and development facility.

The board of directors comprises the chairman/CEO, three executive and two non-executive directors (NEDs). Separate audit and remuneration committees are maintained, although the chairman has a seat on both of those committees. The NEDs are appointed for two and usually three 4-year terms of office before being required to resign. The internal auditor currently reports to the board (rather than the financial accountant) on a monthly basis, with internal audit reports normally being actioned by the board.

There have recently been problems with the development of a new research and development facility. On a number of occasions the project has fallen behind schedule and the costs have been much greater than expected. Because of developments that have taken place elsewhere in the pharmaceuticals industry while the project was being completed, concern has been expressed that the facility cannot now represent value for money. A couple of large institutional investors has raised concerns about this, and have indicated their intention to raise the issue at the annual general meeting and possibly vote against the accounts.

Throughout the project one of the non-executive directors criticised the way the project had been approved and monitored. She claimed that the board had been led by the senior managers in the Research and Development department and had acted as no more than a rubber stamp for what they wanted to do. She is threatening to resign at the annual general meeting on the grounds that the board is failing to function effectively and she does not wish to be held responsible for decisions on which she has had no effective input. As a result, the other non-executive director has also raised questions about the way the board is functioning.

Required

(a)   Explain the main responsibilities of the board and assess the ways in which SPV's board appears to have failed to fulfil its responsibilities.   **(12 marks)**

(b)   Assess the structures for corporate governance within SPV in the light of corporate governance best practice and recommend any improvements you consider necessary to those structures.   **(13 marks)**

(Total = 25 marks)

6 LL

45 mins

LL is a listed company based in the country of Tyne. The corporate governance code in Tyne, enforced by Tyne's stock exchange, is based on the OECD principles of corporate governance.
Robert Ferris, the Chairman of LL, has recently returned from a meeting with Thelma Chambers, who is the representative of Elm Lodge International bank, the institutional investor with the largest shareholding in LL. He discussed the results of the meeting with Terrance Collier, LL's chief executive.

Robert told Terrance that he had mentioned to Thelma that LL may try to expand its operations into America and he wondered whether LL should therefore seek a stock market listing in America. Thelma said that, in her opinion, this would be a very good idea, as it would force LL to comply with the Sarbanes-Oxley legislation and meet higher standards of corporate governance than the regime in Tyne, which she considered too lax. Terrance however commented that this was another example of the 'dreaded Thelma's interference'. From what he could tell Sarbanes-Oxley took a 'one size fits all' approach and would involve lots of useless bureaucracy.

Robert also said that Thelma had raised the possibility of LL including a business review in the next set of accounts. He said Thelma was enthusiastic about this idea, saying it would provide Elm Lodge with greater information and assurance about how the company was being run. Terrance commented that the business review was just another irrelevant document and the accounts were far too long anyway.

Robert also discussed with Terrance the adverse comments Thelma had on the quality of the reports by the board committee (audit, remuneration, nomination and risk) chairmen. Thelma felt these reports were brief and uninformative, and gave little idea of the work the committees had done. Terrance commented that he'd never seen why the board's functioning needed to be complicated by a lot of committees, but that the committee chairmen were clearly doing their jobs properly if those were Thelma's feelings.

Required

(a)   Evaluate Thelma's suggestion that it would be better if LL had to comply with the Sarbanes-Oxley legislation.
(8 marks)

(b)   Explain how publication of a business review by LL could enhance the assurance given to investors.
(10 marks)

(c)   Explain the principles that should determine the content of the reports by board committees in the annual financial statements and prepare a brief example of a disclosure that a nomination committee would make about the recruitment of a new chief executive. **(7 marks)**

(Total = 25 marks)

7 Sentosa House (Examiner question)   45 mins

Sonia Tan, a fund manager at institutional investor Sentosa House, was reviewing the annual report of one of the major companies in her portfolio. The company, Eastern Products, had recently undergone a number of board changes as a result of a lack of confidence in its management from its major institutional investors of which Sentosa House was one. The problems started two years ago when a new chairman at Eastern Products (Thomas Hoo) started to pursue what the institutional investors regarded as very risky strategies whilst at the same time failing to comply with a stock market requirement on the number of non-executive directors on the board.

Sonia rang Eastern's investor relations department to ask why it still was not in compliance with the requirements relating to non-executive directors. She was told that because Eastern was listed in a principles-based jurisdiction, the requirement was not compulsory. It was simply that Eastern chose not to comply with that particular requirement. When Sonia asked how its board committees could be made up with an insufficient number of non-executive directors, the investor relations manager said he didn't know and that Sonia should contact the chairman directly. She was also told that there was no longer a risk committee because the chairman saw no need for one.

Sonia telephoned Thomas Hoo, the chairman of Eastern Products. She began by reminding him that Sentosa House was one of Eastern's main shareholders and currently owned 13% of the company. She went on to explain that she had concerns over the governance of Eastern Products and that she would like Thomas to explain his non-compliance with some of the stock market's requirements and also why he was pursuing strategies viewed by many investors as very risky. Thomas reminded Sonia that Eastern had outperformed its sector in terms of earnings per share in both years since he had become chairman and that rather than question him, she should trust him to run the company as he saw fit. He thanked Sentosa House for its support and hung up the phone.

Required

(a)   Explain what an 'agency cost' is and discuss the problems that might increase agency costs for Sentosa House in the case of Eastern Products. **(7 marks)**

(b)   Describe, with reference to the case, the conditions under which it might be appropriate for an institutional investor to intervene in a company whose shares it holds. **(10 marks)**

(c)   Evaluate the contribution that a risk committee made up of non-executive directors could make to Sonia's confidence in the management of Eastern Products. **(4 marks)**

(d)   Assess the opinion given to Sonia that because Eastern Products was listed in a principles-based jurisdiction, compliance with the stock market's rules was 'not compulsory'. **(4 marks)**

(Total = 25 marks)

8 Frank Finn (Pilot paper)

45 mins

In a recent case, it emerged that Frank Finn, a sales director at ABC Co, had been awarded a substantial over-inflation annual basic pay award with no apparent link to performance. When a major institutional shareholder, Swanland Investments, looked into the issue, it emerged that Mr Finn had a cross directorship with Joe Ng, an executive director of DEF Co. Mr Ng was a non-executive director of ABC and chairman of its remuneration committee. Swanland Investments argued at the annual general meeting that there was 'a problem with the independence' of Mr Ng and further, that Mr Finn's remuneration package as a sales director was considered to be poorly aligned to Swanland's interests because it was too much weighted by basic pay and contained inadequate levels of incentive.

Swanland Investments proposed that the composition of Mr Finn's remuneration package be reconsidered by the remuneration committee and that Mr Ng should not be present during the discussion. Another of the larger institutional shareholders, Hanoi House, objected to this, proposing instead that Mr Ng and Mr Finn both resign from their respective non-executive directorships as there was 'clear evidence of malpractice'. Swanland considered this too radical a step, as Mr Ng's input was, in its opinion, valuable on ABC's board.

Required

(a) Explain FOUR roles of a remuneration committee and how the cross directorship undermines these roles at ABC Co. **(12 marks)**

(b) Swanland Investments believed Mr Finn's remuneration package to be 'poorly aligned' to its interests. With reference to the different components of a director's remuneration package, explain how Mr Finn's remuneration might be more aligned to shareholders' interests at ABC Co. **(8 marks)**

(c) Evaluate the proposal from Hanoi House that both Mr Ng and Mr Finn be required to resign from their respective non-executive positions. **(5 marks)**

(Total = 25 marks)

9 Seamus O'Brien (12/07)

45 mins

At a recent international meeting of business leaders, Seamus O'Brien said that multi-jurisdictional attempts to regulate corporate governance were futile because of differences in national culture. He drew particular attention to the Organisation for Economic Co-operation and Development (OECD) and International Corporate Governance Network (ICGN) codes, saying that they were, 'silly attempts to harmonise practice'. He said that in some countries, for example, there were 'family reasons' for making the chairman and chief executive the same person. In other countries, he said, the separation of these roles seemed to work. Another delegate, Alliya Yongvanich, said that the roles of chief executive and chairman should always be separated because of what she called 'accountability to shareholders'.

One delegate, Vincent Viola, said that the right approach was to allow each country to set up its own corporate governance provisions. He said that it was suitable for some countries to produce and abide by their own 'very structured' corporate governance provisions, but in some other parts of the world, the local culture was to allow what he called, 'local interpretation of the rules'. He said that some cultures valued highly structured governance systems while others do not care as much.

Required

(a) Explain the roles of the chairman in corporate governance. **(5 marks)**

(b) Assess the benefits of the separation of the roles of chief executive and chairman that Alliya Yongvanich argued for and explain her belief that 'accountability to shareholders' is increased by the separation of these roles. **(12 marks)**

(c) Critically evaluate Vincent Viola's view that corporate governance provisions should vary by country. **(8 marks)**

(Total = 25 marks)

10 Rosh (6/08)

Mary Hobbes joined the board of Rosh and Company, a large retailer, as finance director earlier this year. Whilst she was glad to have finally been given the chance to become finance director after several years as a financial accountant, she also quickly realised that the new appointment would offer her a lot of challenges. In the first board meeting, she realised that not only was she the only woman but she was also the youngest by many years.

Rosh was established almost 100 years ago. Members of the Rosh family have occupied senior board positions since the outset and even after the company's flotation 20 years ago a member of the Rosh family has either been executive chairman or chief executive. The current longstanding chairman, Timothy Rosh, has already prepared his slightly younger brother, Geoffrey (also a longstanding member of the board) to succeed him in two years' time when he plans to retire. The Rosh family, who still own 40% of the shares, consider it their right to occupy the most senior positions in the company so have never been very active in external recruitment. They only appointed Mary because they felt they needed a qualified accountant on the board to deal with changes in international financial reporting standards.

Several former executive members have been recruited as non-executives immediately after they retired from full-time service. A recent death, however, has reduced the number of non-executive directors to two. These sit alongside an executive board of seven that, apart from Mary, have all been in their posts for over ten years.

Mary noted that board meetings very rarely contain any significant discussion of strategy and never involve any debate or disagreement. When she asked why this was, she was told that the directors had all known each other for so long that they knew how each other thought. All of the other directors came from similar backgrounds, she was told, and had worked for the company for so long that they all knew what was 'best' for the company in any given situation.

Mary observed that notes on strategy were not presented at board meetings and she asked Timothy Rosh whether the existing board was fully equipped to formulate strategy in the changing world of retailing. She did not receive a reply.

Required

(a)   Explain 'agency' in the context of corporate governance and criticise the governance arrangements of Rosh and Company. **(12 marks)**

(b)   Explain the roles of a nomination committee and assess the potential usefulness of a nominations committee to the board of Rosh and Company. **(8 marks)**

(c)   Define 'retirement by rotation' and explain its importance in the context of Rosh and Company.   **(5 marks)**

(Total = 25 marks)

11 West vs Leroi (6/08)

At an academic conference, a debate took place on the implementation of corporate governance practices in developing countries. Professor James West from North America argued that one of the key needs for developing countries was to implement rigorous systems of corporate governance to underpin investor confidence in businesses in those countries. If they did not, he warned, there would be no lasting economic growth as potential foreign inward investors would be discouraged from investing.

In reply, Professor Amy Leroi, herself from a developing country, reported that many developing countries are discussing these issues at governmental level. One issue, she said, was about whether to adopt a rules-based or a principles-based approach. She pointed to evidence highlighting a reduced number of small and medium sized initial public offerings in New York compared to significant growth in London. She suggested that this change could be attributed to the costs of complying with Sarbanes-Oxley in the United States and that over-regulation would be the last thing that a developing country would need. She concluded that a principles-based approach, such as in the United Kingdom, was preferable for developing countries.

Professor Leroi drew attention to an important section of the Sarbanes-Oxley Act to illustrate her point. The key requirement of that section was to externally report on – and have attested (verified) – internal controls. This was, she argued, far too ambitious for small and medium companies that tended to dominate the economies of developing countries.

Professor West countered by saying that whilst Sarbanes-Oxley may have had some problems, it remained the case that it regulated corporate governance in the 'largest and most successful economy in the world'. He said that rules will sometimes be hard to follow but that is no reason to abandon them in favour of what he referred to as 'softer' approaches.

Required

(a)   There are arguments for both rules and principles-based approaches to corporate governance.

  (i)   Describe the essential features of a rules-based approach to corporate governance.   **(3 marks)**

  (ii)   Construct the argument against Professor West's opinion, and in favour of Professor Leroi's opinion that a principles-based approach would be preferable in developing countries. Your answer should consider the particular situations of developing countries.   **(10 marks)**

The Sarbanes-Oxley Act contains provisions for the attestation (verification) and reporting to shareholders of internal controls over financial reporting.

Required

(b)   Describe the typical contents of an external report on internal controls.   **(8 marks)**

(c)   Construct the arguments in favour of Professor Leroi's remark that external reporting requirements on internal controls were 'too ambitious' for small and medium companies.   **(4 marks)**

(Total = 25 marks)

12 TQ (6/09)   45 mins

TQ Company, a listed company, recently went into administration (it had become insolvent and was being managed by a firm of insolvency practitioners). A group of shareholders expressed the belief that it was the chairman, Miss Heike Hoiku, who was primarily to blame. Although the company's management had made a number of strategic errors that brought about the company failure, the shareholders blamed the chairman for failing to hold senior management to account. In particular, they were angry that Miss Hoiku had not challenged chief executive Rupert Smith who was regarded by some as arrogant and domineering. Some said that Miss Hoiku was scared of him.

Some shareholders wrote a letter to Miss Hoiku last year demanding that she hold Mr Smith to account for a number of previous strategic errors. They also asked her to explain why she had not warned of the strategic problems in her chairman's statement in the annual report earlier in the year. In particular, they asked if she could remove Mr Smith from office for incompetence. Miss Hoiku replied saying that whilst she understood their concerns, it was difficult to remove a serving chief executive from office.

Some of the shareholders believed that Mr Smith may have performed better in his role had his reward package been better designed in the first place. There was previously a remuneration committee at TQ but when two of its four non-executive members left the company, they were not replaced and so the committee effectively collapsed. Mr Smith was then able to propose his own remuneration package and Miss Hoiku did not feel able to refuse him. He massively increased the proportion of the package that was basic salary and also awarded himself a new and much more expensive company car. Some shareholders regarded the car as 'excessively' expensive. In addition, suspecting that the company's performance might deteriorate this year, he exercised all of his share options last year and immediately sold all of his shares in TQ Company.

It was noted that Mr Smith spent long periods of time travelling away on company business whilst less experienced directors struggled with implementing strategy at the company headquarters. This meant that operational procedures were often uncoordinated and this was one of the causes of the eventual strategic failure.

Miss Hoiku stated that it was difficult to remove a serving chief executive from office.

(a) (i) Explain the ways in which a company director can leave the service of a board. **(4 marks)**

(ii) Discuss Miss Hoiku's statement that it is difficult to remove a serving chief executive from a board. **(4 marks)**

(b) Assess, in the context of the case, the importance of the chairman's statement to shareholders in TQ Company's annual report. **(5 marks)**

(c) Criticise the structure of the reward package that Mr Smith awarded himself. **(4 marks)**

(d) Criticise Miss Hoiku's performance as chairman of TQ Company. **(8 marks)**

(Total = 25 marks)

13 Sam Mesentery (12/09)   45 mins

Sam Mesentery was appointed a director of Ding Company in October this year taking on the role of financial controller. He had moved himself and his family to a new country to take up the post and was looking forward to the new challenges. When he arrived he learned that he was on the 'operating board' of Ding Company and that there was a 'corporate board' above the operating board that was senior to it. This surprised him as in the companies he had worked for in his own country, all directors in the company were equal. The corporate board at Ding was small, with five directors in total, while the operating board was larger, with ten members.

After a few days in the job he received an e-mail requiring him to report to Annette Hora, the managing director. She said that she had regretfully received two complaints from another senior colleague about Sam's behaviour. First, Sam had apparently made a highly inappropriate remark to a young female colleague and second, his office was laid out in the wrong way. Not only was his desk positioned in breach of fire regulations but also, he was told that it was normal to have the desk facing towards the door so that colleagues felt more welcomed when they went in. 'It's company policy' she said abruptly. Sam remembered the conversation with the young female colleague but was unaware of anything inappropriate in what he had said to her. He said that he positioned his desk so he could get the best view out of the window when he was working.

The following day he arrived at work to find that the corporate board was in an emergency meeting. There had been a sudden and dramatic change in the circumstances of one of Ding's major suppliers and the corporate board later said that they needed to meet to agree a way forward and a strategy to cope with the change. Annette said that because of the competitive nature of its resource markets, Ding had to act fast and preferably before its competitors. Hence the necessity of a two-tier board structure. She said there was no time for lengthy discussions which was why the operating board was excluded. Sam was told that Ding operated in a 'complex and turbulent' environment and when strategic factors in the environment changed, the company often had to respond quickly and decisively.

It was a month later that Sam first met with Arif Zaman, Ding's non-executive chairman. After Arif asked Sam how he was settling in, Sam asked Arif why he preferred a two-tier board structure and Arif replied that actually it was Annette's idea. He said that she prefers it that way and because he is a non-executive member doesn't feel able to challenge her opinion on it. Because 'it seems to work' he had no plans to discuss it with her. He went on to say that he was an old friend of Annette's and was only in post to satisfy the corporate governance requirements to have a non-executive chairman. He said that he saw his role as mainly ceremonial and saw no need to take any direct interest in the company's activities. He said that he chaired some board meetings when he was available and he sometimes wrote the chairman's statement in the annual report.

Required

(a) Explain the content of a director's induction programme and assess the advantages of such a programme for Sam. **(8 marks)**

(b) Using information from the case, critically evaluate Annette's belief that two-tier boards are preferable in complex and turbulent environments such as at Ding Company. **(8 marks)**

(c) Assess Arif Zaman's understanding of his role as non-executive chairman. **(9 marks)**

(Total = 25 marks)

14 Tomato Bank (6/10)　　　　　　　　　　　　　45 mins

Five years ago, George Woof was appointed chief executive officer (CEO) of Tomato Bank, one of the largest global banks. Mr Woof had a successful track record in senior management in America and his appointment was considered very fortunate for the company. Analysts rated him as one of the world's best bankers and the other directors of Tomato Bank looked forward to his appointment and a significant strengthening of the business.

One of the factors needed to secure Mr Woof's services was his reward package. Prior to his acceptance of the position, Tomato Bank's remuneration committee (comprised entirely of non-executives) received a letter from Mr Woof saying that because his track record was so strong, they could be assured of many years of sustained growth under his leadership. In discussions concerning his pension, however, he asked for a generous non-performance related pension settlement to be written into his contract so that it would be payable whenever he decided to leave the company (subject to a minimum term of two years) and regardless of his performance as CEO. Such was the euphoria about his appointment that his request was approved. Furthermore in the hasty manner in which Mr Woof's reward package was agreed, the split of his package between basic and performance-related components was not carefully scrutinised. Everybody on the remuneration committee was so certain that he would bring success to Tomato Bank that the individual details of his reward package were not considered important.

In addition, the remuneration committee received several letters from Tomato Bank's finance director, John Temba, saying, in direct terms, that they should offer Mr Woof 'whatever he wants' to ensure that he joins the company and that the balance of benefits was not important as long as he joined. Two of the non-executive directors on the remuneration committee were former colleagues of Mr Woof and told the finance director they would take his advice and make sure they put a package together that would ensure Mr Woof joined the company.

Once in post, Mr Woof led an excessively aggressive strategy that involved high growth in the loan and mortgage books financed from a range of sources, some of which proved unreliable. In the fifth year of his appointment, the failure of some of the sources of funds upon which the growth of the bank was based led to severe financing difficulties at Tomato Bank. Shareholders voted to replace George Woof as CEO. They said he had been reckless in exposing the company to so much risk in growing the loan book without adequately covering it with reliable sources of funds.

When he left, the press reported that despite his failure in the job, he would be leaving with what the newspapers referred to as an 'obscenely large' pension. Some shareholders were angry and said that Mr Woof was being 'rewarded for failure'. When Mr Woof was asked if he might voluntarily forego some of his pension in recognition of his failure in the job, he refused, saying that he was contractually entitled to it and so would be keeping it all.

Required

(a)　Criticise the performance of Tomato Bank's remuneration committee in agreeing Mr Woof's reward package.

(10 marks)

(b)　Describe the components of an appropriately designed executive reward package and explain why a more balanced package of benefits should have been used to reward Mr Woof.　**(10 marks)**

(c)　Construct an ethical case for Mr Woof to voluntarily accept a reduction in his pension value in recognition of his failure as chief executive of Tomato Bank.　**(5 marks)**

(Total = 25 marks)

15 KK (12/10)

45 mins

KK is a large listed company. When a non-executive directorship of KK Limited became available, John Soria was nominated to fill the vacancy. John is the brother-in-law of KK's chief executive Ken Kava. John is also the CEO of Soria Supplies Ltd, KK's largest single supplier and is, therefore, very familiar with KK and its industry. He has sold goods to KK for over 20 years and is on friendly terms with all of the senior officers in the company. In fact last year, Soria Supplies appointed KK's finance director, Susan Schwab, to a non-executive directorship on its board. The executive directors of KK all know and like John and so plan to ask the nominations committee to appoint him before the next AGM.

KK has recently undergone a period of rapid growth and has recently entered several new overseas markets, some of which, according to the finance director, are riskier than the domestic market. Ken Kava, being the dominant person on the KK board, has increased the risk exposure of the company according to some investors. They say that because most of the executive directors are less experienced, they rarely question his overseas expansion strategy. This expansion has also created a growth in employee numbers and an increase in the number of executive directors, mainly to manage the increasingly complex operations of the company. It was thought by some that the company lacked experience and knowledge of international markets as it expanded and that this increased the risk of the strategy's failure. Some shareholders believed that the aggressive strategy, led by Ken Kava, has been careless as it has exposed KK Limited to some losses on overseas direct investments made before all necessary information on the investment was obtained.

As a large listed company, the governance of KK is important to its shareholders. Fin Brun is one of KK's largest shareholders and holds a large portfolio of shares including 8% of the shares in KK. At the last AGM he complained to KK's chief executive, Ken Kava, that he needed more information on directors' performance. Fin said that he didn't know how to vote on board reappointments because he had no information on how they had performed in their jobs. Mr Kava said that the board intended to include a corporate governance section in future annual reports to address this and to provide other information that shareholders had asked for. He added, however, that he would not be able to publish information on the performance of individual executive directors as this was too complicated and actually not the concern of shareholders. It was, he said, the performance of the board as a whole that was important and he (Mr Kava) would manage the performance targets of individual directors.

Required

(a) Explain the term 'conflict of interest' in the context of non-executive directors and discuss the potential conflicts of interest relating to KK and Soria Supplies if John Soria were to become a non-executive director of KK Limited. **(8 marks)**

(b) Assess the advantages of appointing experienced and effective non-executive directors to the KK board during the period in which the company was growing rapidly. **(7 marks)**

(c) Explain the typical contents of a 'best practice' corporate governance report within an annual report and how its contents could help meet the information needs of Fin Brun. **(10 marks)**

(Total = 25 marks)

16 HHO (6/11)

In the country of Laland, aid organisations registered as charities are not subject to the same financial reporting requirements as limited companies (this is not the case in many other countries where they are treated equally in law). One person to take advantage of this is Horace Hoi who has led his vigorous campaign in favour of animal protection for the past 25 years. As a highly competent self-publicist for his charity and an engaging media performer, he has raised the public profile of his charity substantially. He can and does raise large amounts of money for his charity through his personal charm and passionate appeals on television and in large meetings of supporters. His charity is called the 'Horace Hoi Organisation' (HHO) and its stated aim is to 'stop animals suffering'. Mr Hoi has recently become the subject of criticism by the media because of allegations that he lived a lavish lifestyle and personally owned a large mansion and a number of classic cars. The HHO recently bought a private jet to support

Mr Hoi in his travels around the world for speaking engagements and for his work for the HHO charity. One journalist reported that most of the donors to HHO are well-meaning individuals, mainly of modest means, that care greatly about animal suffering and who would be 'horrified' if they knew of the luxury in which Mr Hoi lived.

Despite the fact that Mr Hoi had claimed that he personally takes only a modest salary from the organisation for his work, a journalist recently estimated Mr Hoi's personal wealth, thought to be gained from the HHO, to be around $10 million. When challenged to disclose the financial details of the HHO and Mr Hoi's own personal earnings, a HHO spokesman simply replied that this was not required under the law in Laland and that the HHO was therefore fully compliant with the law. The HHO has refused to join a group of other charities that have undertaken to make full financial disclosures despite it not being mandatory in law. The HHO says that although it does produce financial information for the charity and tax authorities, it has no intention of making this information public. The HHO also makes no disclosures about its governance structures and was once criticised as being 'intentionally opaque in order to hide bad practice'.

In yielding to the media pressure to provide some information on its financial affairs, HHO eventually published a pie chart on its website saying that its expenditure was divided between animal shelters (57%), field work helping animals (32%), administration (6%) and other causes (5%). This was the totality of its public financial disclosure.

Required

(a) Discuss the ways in which charities differ from public listed companies and explain how these differences affect their respective governance structures. **(9 marks)**

(b) Define 'transparency' and construct the case for greater transparency in the governance of the Horace Hoi Organisation. **(8 marks)**

Audit committees can have a role in reviewing internal controls and addressing areas of deficiency.

Required

(c) Explain how an audit committee might assist in addressing the apparent internal control deficiencies at HHO. **(8 marks)**

(Total = 25 marks)

INTERNAL CONTROL AND RISK

Questions 17 to 38 cover internal control and risk, the subject of Part B of the BPP Study Text for Paper P1.

17 FF Co (Pilot paper)   45 mins

As part of a review of its internal control systems, the board of FF Co, a large textiles company, has sought your advice as a senior accountant in the company.

FF's stated objective has always been to adopt the highest standards of internal control because it believes that by doing so it will not only provide shareholders with confidence in its governance but also enhance its overall reputation with all stakeholders. In recent years, however, FF's reputation for internal control has been damaged somewhat by a qualified audit statement last year (over issues of compliance with financial standards) and an unfortunate internal incident the year prior to that. This incident concerned an employee, Miss Osula, expressing concern about the compliance of one of the company's products with an international standard on fire safety. She raised the issue with her immediate manager but he said, according to Miss Osula, that it wasn't his job to report her concerns to senior management. When she failed to obtain a response herself from senior management, she decided to report the lack of compliance to the press. This significantly embarrassed the company and led to a substantial deterioration in FF's reputation.

The specifics of the above case concerned a fabric produced by FF Co, which, in order to comply with an international fire safety standard, was required to resist fire for ten minutes when in contact with a direct flame. According to Miss Osula, who was a member of the quality control staff, FF was allowing material rated at only five minutes fire resistance to be sold labelled as ten minute rated. In her statement to the press, Miss Osula said that there was a culture of carelessness in FF and that this was only one example of the way the company approached issues such as international fire safety standards.

Required

(a)   Describe how the internal control systems at FF Co differ from a 'sound' system of internal control, such as that set out in the Turnbull guidance, for example.   **(10 marks)**

(b)   Define 'reputation risk' and evaluate the potential effects of FF's poor reputation on its financial situation.
                                                                                                (8 marks)

(c)   Explain, with reference to FF as appropriate, the ethical responsibilities of a professional accountant both as an employee and as a professional.   **(7 marks)**

(Total = 25 marks)

18 LinesRUs   45 mins

The LinesRUs Company is responsible for maintaining the railway infrastructure for the rail network in a large European country. Main areas of responsibility for the company include:

- Ensuring that the railway tracks are safe
- Signalling equipment is installed correctly and works properly
- Maintenance of overhead power lines for electric trains

Income is fixed each year dependent on the number of train services being operated and is paid via a central rail authority. The company is granted a sole franchise each year to provide services on the rail network.

Work is scheduled in accordance with the amount of income, and to provide LinesRUs with an acceptable operating profit. Any additional work over and above standard maintenance (eg due to foreseen factors such as bridges being damaged by road vehicles and unforeseen factors such as car drivers falling asleep and driving their cars onto railway tracks) is negotiated separately and additional income obtained to repair the infrastructure in these situations.

A lot of maintenance work is relatively simple (eg tightening nuts and bolts holding railway tracks together) but is extremely important as an error may result in a train leaving the rails and crashing. The board of LinesRUs is aware of many of these risks and attempts to include them in a risk management policy.

However, recently a train was derailed causing the death of 27 passengers. Initial investigations show that faulty maintenance was the cause of the derailment. One of the unforeseen consequences of the crash has been a fall in the numbers of people using trains with a subsequent fall in income for train operators. LinesRUs are being sued by the train operators for loss of income, and the national press are suggesting LinesRUs must be incompetent and are calling for a re-evaluation of the method of providing maintenance on the rail network.

Required

(a)   Advise the directors of LinesRUs of the main stages of a structured risk analysis approach that will be appropriate to the company's needs.   **(15 marks)**

(b)   Using the TARA framework, construct four possible strategies for managing the risk that rail crashes could occur. Your answer should describe each strategy and explain how each might be applied in the case.

(10 marks)

(Total = 25 marks)

19 Doctors' practice   45 mins

A doctors' practice, with six doctors and two practice nurses, has decided to increase its income by providing day surgery facilities. The existing building would be extended to provide room for the surgical unit and storage facilities for equipment and drugs. The aim is to offer patients the opportunity to have minor surgical procedures conducted by a doctor at their local practice, thus avoiding any unfamiliarity and possible delays to treatment that might result from referral to a hospital. Blood and samples taken during the surgery will be sent away to the local hospital for testing but the patient will get the results from their doctor at the practice. It is anticipated that the introduction of the day surgery facility will increase practice income by approximately 20 per cent.

Required

(a)   (i)   Describe the additional risks that the doctors' practice may expect to face as a consequence of the introduction of the new facility.   **(9 marks)**

        (ii)   Explain how a risk management model might be used to understand and control such risks.
(5 marks)

(b)   Explain the meaning of the term 'risk appetite' and discuss who should take responsibility for defining that appetite in the context of the scenario outlined above.   **(5 marks)**

(c)   Analyse how an internal audit of the practice may contribute to an assessment of its risk management procedures.   **(6 marks)**

(Total = 25 marks)

20 IDAN   45 mins

Company overview

IDAN is a large banking and financial services group that is listed on both the London Stock Exchange and the New York Stock Exchange. The group has over 20 million customers throughout the world and operates in 35 countries on four continents. The IDAN Group is composed of a mix of retail and commercial businesses that include corporate and investment banking, private banking and commercial banking.

Trends within the Financial Services Sector

Although IDAN has not received any UK or US government help during the recent financial downturn, the directors believe that the bank may be affected by changes in government and central bank policy and volatility in worldwide markets. At present the governments and central banks of both countries are under pressure to revive their economies by stimulating demand.

The Board of Directors of IDAN is aware that a number of trends within the sector will also require the bank to review its business strategy and substantially re-design a number of its operating and information systems. Current issues that are having an impact on the financial services sector include:

- The elimination within the UK of the use of personal signatures as the authorisation for credit and debit card transactions and their replacement with personal identification (PIN) numbers.
- The increasing use, by personal customers, of both telephone and internet banking services. Over 40% of bill payments, standing order amendments and balance transfers by such customers were processed in this way during the last 12 months compared with 28% the previous year.
- A growth in the number of cases being sent to the financial ombudsman or the financial industry regulator relating to claims of mis-selling or incorrect advice on the part of financial services companies in the supply of a range of savings and investment products.
- As a result of threats of terrorist activity, money laundering legislation has been introduced or tightened in all of the countries in which IDAN has banking operations.

The board is currently reviewing future investment policy and the future opportunities and threats facing each business, with a view to deciding priorities across the group for use of the surpluses available to invest.

Required

(a)   Using information from the case, explain the main categories of risk that are faced by a bank such as IDAN.

(8 marks)

(b)   Construct a case for risk categorisation being an essential part of a risk management system.   **(5 marks)**

(c)   For every one of the four issues identified in the question, recommend the controls that might be introduced to minimise IDAN's exposure to such risks.   **(12 marks)**

(Total = 25 marks)

21 Ceedee   45 mins

Ceedee is a listed company that manufactures, markets and distributes a large range of components throughout Europe and the United States of America, supplying products to over 0·5 million customers in 20 countries. Ceedee holds stocks of about 100,000 different electronic components.

Two years ago Ceedee established a specialist components department ('SCD') to undertake the manufacture of customised components, such as a microprocessor that has been programmed with a specific set of instructions supplied by the customer. SCD can also make complex parts and assemblies. SCD does not generate a large proportion of Ceedee's revenue, but it has been very profitable since it began 3 years ago because SCD can charge high profit margins. SCD employs 17 highly skilled technicians who work in a sophisticated electronics workshop.

Almost all of the work undertaken by SCD is 'jobbing work' ie for very small quantities, sometimes only a single unit. This is because SCD's customers often build prototypes of products that they plan to test before committing themselves to full-scale production. If the prototype is successful and the customer then requires larger quantities of the component SCD directs them to another division of Ceedee.

SCD has been approached by ZZ, a specialist manufacturer of extremely expensive high performance cars. ZZ is in the process of developing a new car that will be one of the fastest in the world. The car will be designed to be driven on public roads, but the owners of such cars often take them to private race tracks where they can be driven at very high speeds.

ZZ has designed an electronics system to enable an average driver to drive the car safely at high speed. The system will monitor the engine, brakes and steering and will compensate for errors that could cause a crash. The system will, for example, sense that the car is about to skid and will compensate for that. The electronics system will be based on a circuit board that ZZ wishes to have built by SCD.

Building ZZ's circuit board will pose a number of challenges for SCD. The circuit board will be subject to a great deal of vibration when the car is driven at speed. The cars are expected to last for a very long time and so there could be problems if the circuit boards deteriorate with age. The circuit board will be installed in an inaccessible part of the car where it will be difficult to inspect or maintain.

Many of the components on the board will be manufactured by SCD, but some crucial components will be supplied by a third party that has already been selected by ZZ.

ZZ is prepared to order a large number of circuit boards but only if they are hand built by SCD. That is partly because the cars will not be built in sufficient volume to make it possible for another division of Ceedee to mass-produce the boards and partly because ZZ wishes to be able to update and modify the design of the circuit boards in response to feedback from owners. SCD's Production Manager believes that the ZZ contract will create sufficient work to keep 7 technicians almost fully occupied. SCD will have to recruit and train additional staff in order to service this contract.

When notifying the board of this significant opportunity, Ceedee's chief executive emphasised the importance of thorough risk assessment, and reducing the risks associated with the high-profile project to levels that were as low as reasonably practicable. However a newly appointed non-executive director pointed out that it would be difficult to measure many of the risks, and wondered if Ceedee should focus on managing risks that could be measured precisely.

Required

(a)   Assess FOUR significant risks associated with accepting the order from ZZ.   **(9 marks)**

(b)   Explain the ALARP principle and advise the board on the steps it can take to reduce the risks identified in (a) to levels that are as low as reasonably practicable.   **(9 marks)**

(c)   Explain the difference between subjective and objective risk perception, and criticise the non-executive director's view that the board should focus on managing risks that can be measured precisely.   **(7 marks)**

(Total = 25 marks)

22 Cerberus   **45 mins**

During the past three years, Cerberus, a large defence contractor in the UK and USA, has been adversely affected by a series of internal control failures. These incidents resulted in major losses being incurred and brought the company to the brink of collapse. Although the threat of company failure now appears to have receded, the shareholders, who have seen their investment in the company decrease dramatically, recently replaced the board of directors. The new board is determined to ensure that the company avoids any such problem in the future and believes that this has to be done by the board demonstrating greater concern about the operation of internal controls and fulfilling relevant corporate governance requirements.

One particular problem Cerberus has had over the last couple of years is a total failure of its information systems. The new directors realise that if they are to review controls fairly, better information systems will be required. They have also noted the previous directors apparently heard nothing about employee concerns with the systems through the company's informal grapevine. The previous directors were only notified and took action after the control failures had occurred, which was too late.

The new directors also want to be particularly sure of UK and US reporting requirements in relation to internal controls, since at present Cerberus is required to report under both jurisdictions.

Required

(a)   Advise the new board of the key responsibilities of board members in relation to ensuring the effectiveness of internal controls.   **(7 marks)**

(b)   Explain the methods used to assess the effectiveness of controls and advise the board on the information required to support a fair assessment.   **(12 marks)**

(c)   Describe the best practice requirements that govern reporting of the results of internal control reviews to stock markets such as those in the UK and US.   **(6 marks)**

(Total = 25 marks)

23 B Bank

45 mins

The B Bank is a large international bank. It employs 6,000 staff in 250 branches and has approximately 500,000 borrowers and over 1,500,000 savers. The bank, which was founded in 1856, has an excellent reputation for good customer service. The bank's share price has increased, on average, by 12% in each of the last 10 years.

There has been much adverse media coverage in many countries, including B Bank's home country, about the alleged excessive bonuses received by the directors of banks. A meeting of central bank governors from many nations failed to reach agreement on how to limit the size of directors' bonuses. The governor of the central bank in B Bank's home country is particularly concerned about this issue, and consequently put forward the following proposal:

'Directors of banks will be asked to pay a fee to the bank for the privilege of being a director. This fee will be set by the remuneration committee of each bank. Directors will be paid a bonus based solely on appropriate profit and growth indicators. The more the bank succeeds, the higher will be the bonus. This proposal directly links performance of the bank to directors' pay. I see this as a more realistic option than simply limiting salaries or bonuses by statute as proposed at the recent central bank governors' conference.'

The constitution of the board of B Bank is in accordance with the internationally agreed code of corporate governance.

Overall board strategy has been to set targets based on previous (profitable) experience, with increased emphasis on those areas where higher potential profits can be made such as mortgage lending (this is discussed below). The bank's executive information systems are able to compute relative product profitability, which supports this strategy. This strategy generated substantial profits in recent years. The last major strategy review took place four years ago. Non-executive directors do not normally query the decisions of the executive directors.

In recent years, the profile of the major shareholders of the bank has moved. Traditionally the major shareholders were pension funds and other longer term investors but now these are overshadowed by hedge funds seeking to improve their short-term financial returns.

One of the major sources of revenue for the bank is interest obtained on lending money against securities such as houses (termed a "mortgage" in many countries) with repayments being due over periods varying between 15 and 25 years. Partly as a result of intense competition in the mortgage market, the values of the mortgages advanced by B Bank regularly exceed the value of the properties, for example B Bank has made advances of up to 125% of a property's value. Internal reports to the board estimate that property prices will reverse recent trends and will rise by 7% per annum for at least the next 10 years, with general and wage inflation at 2%. B Bank intends to continue to obtain finance to support new mortgages with loans from the short-term money-markets.

Required

(a)   Evaluate the proposal made by the governor of the central bank.   **(10 marks)**

(b)   Assess the risk management strategy in B Bank (except for consideration of directors' remuneration). Your assessment should include recommendations for changes that will lower the bank's exposure to risk.

(15 marks)

(Total = 25 marks)

24 JDM

45 mins

JDM Construction is a construction company. The company completed the building of 30 apartments in December 20X3 and immediately sold 15 of them for $125,000 each. However, no apartments have been sold since that date. It is now 30 June 20X4.

The total cost of building the apartments was $75,000 each. It is thought that the only additional cash flows that will arise will be for marketing and selling the remaining 15 apartments.

The Marketing Director of JDM has forecast the following changes in property prices during the next five years:

Market Forecast

20X4	10% decrease
20X5	2% decrease
20X6	5% increase
20X7	8% increase
20X8	5% increase

In response to the declining market, the Marketing Director has proposed and financially evaluated the two possible alternative marketing strategies shown below.

Marketing strategy 1

Sell the properties at a discounted price of $115,000 each. This would require a marketing campaign that involves spending $210,000. Market research suggests that there is a 70% chance that all of the apartments would be sold within six months but a 30% chance that none will be sold. Under this strategy all money will be paid and received by 31 December 20X4.

Marketing strategy 2

This strategy requires spending $75,000 on advertising. The Marketing Director expects that all the remaining 15 apartments will be sold under this strategy. Marketing Strategy 2 involves offering potential buyers the choice of three different deals, as detailed below:

Deal 1

Customers can buy an apartment at a reduced price of $95,000, if they agree to a rapid transfer of ownership. A 10% deposit is payable immediately, and the remaining balance is payable in eight weeks' time.

The Marketing Director expects that eight apartments will be sold under this arrangement.

Deal 2

Purchasers will be given the opportunity to purchase an apartment for $110,000, with a guarantee that if they wish to sell at any time during the next five years, JDM will purchase the property back at this initial price. Under this deal all sales receipts will be received within the next three months.

The marketing director expects to sell five apartments under this arrangement and that they will all be repurchased by 20X7.

Deal 3

Customers will be given the opportunity to purchase an apartment for $105,000, payable in three months' time, plus a further payment of $25,000 payable after 10 years, or when the customer sells the apartment, whichever occurs first.

The Marketing Director expects that two apartments will be sold under this arrangement.

Financial evaluation of Strategies 1 and 2

	Expected NPV $000
Strategy 1	950
Strategy 2	
Immediate advertising	(75)
Deal 1	750
Deal 2	103
Deal 3	240
Total for Strategy 2	1,018

Required

(a) Discuss the impact on the decision of which strategy to choose of the board's risk appetite. **(4 marks)**

(b) Analyse the other factors that will influence the decision. **(9 marks)**

JDM is a relatively new company, which until now has operated in a buoyant market. In view of the recent economic downturn, the Board has realised that JDM needs a more formal system for considering risk.

Required

(c) Construct an appropriate risk management process for the company. **(12 marks)**

(Total = 25 marks)

25 Product choice   45 mins

Vinnick is a USA based global consumer electronics company. Vinnick's board is currently reviewing the system for costing and project appraisal of all new product proposals.

All costs and revenues are based on information provided by the electronic engineers and marketing staff responsible for each individual project. It is assumed that all development is fully completed prior to initial marketing, and so no redesign costs are allowed once a product is launched. The rapid rate of technology change within the industry has led the company to assume a maximum product life of seven years.

The tables below give details of the company-wide incremental cash flows for two new consumer products. All cash flows are assumed to occur at the year end. Regulatory constraints mean that the company cannot invest in both developments. The company-wide hurdle rate for capital investments is 7.5% per year but the Finance Director is considering introducing risk-adjusted rates, which would give a discount rate of 8.5% per year for Product 1 and 10% per year for Product 2. The net present values generated by each of the products, using both the standard hurdle rate and the risk-adjusted hurdle rates, are also given in the tables.

Product 1 would be manufactured and assembled in China and transferred to company-owned retail outlets in the USA. Product 2 would be assembled in the Czech Republic from components shipped in from Taiwan and then sold to third party distributors across Western Europe.

Product 1	Year(s)	Annual sales revenue $ Million (based on ex factory prices)	Design and development costs $ Million	Annual manufacturing and distribution costs $ Million
	1	Nil	200	Nil
	2	Nil	400	Nil
	3	280		120
	4-7	420		180
NPV at 7.5% pa	$244 million			
NPV at 8.5% pa	$217 million			

Product 2	Year(s)	Annual sales revenue $ Million (based on ex factory prices)	Design and development costs $ Million	Annual manufacturing and distribution costs $ Million
	1	Nil	6,400	Nil
	2	1,250	Nil	600
	3	2,000	Nil	750
	4-6	3,500	nil	1,200
NPV at 7.5% pa	$430 million			
NPV at 10% pa	($45 million)			

The non-executive chairman of Vinnick wishes to see a financial analysis of the two products, as he believes that this is the only objective way of judging between them. The chief executive believes however that other risks will be important in deciding whether to go ahead.

(a) Discuss the extent to which the board can rely on the financial information given above and analyse the financial indications that the information provides. **(11 marks)**

(b) Assess the other significant business risks that may influence the investment decision. **(9 marks)**

(c) Explain how the investment decision may be influenced by the profile of, and risks relating to, Vinnick's existing products. **(5 marks)**

(Total = 25 marks)

26 X   45 mins

X is a small company based in England. The company had the choice of launching a major new product range in either England or France but lack of funding meant that it could not do both. The company bases its decisions on Expected Net Present Value (ENPV) and current exchange rates. As a result of this methodology, and the details shown below, it was decided to launch in England (with an ENPV of £2,839,000) and not France (with an ENPV of £2,556,000).

England		France	
£000	*Probability*		*Probability*
Launch costs		**Launch costs**	
14,500	0.1	19,000	1.0
12,000	0.9		
Annual cash flows		**Annual cash flows**	
6,500	0.4	9,000	0.5
4,200	0.4	7,000	0.2
2,400	0.2	3,000	0.3

The annual cash flows are based on contribution margins of 10% for England and 20% for France where it is expected that sales volumes will be lower. It is thought that the product will sell for four years only.

The monetary values are expressed in the local currency, £, and have been converted (where necessary) at the current exchange rate.

The company has discounted the cash flows using a cost of capital of 10% per year.

Launch costs will be financed by a long-term loan. The Finance Director of X is concerned about interest rate risk however, and is unsure about whether to opt for a fixed or floating rate loan.

LXN currently has £2,000 million of assets and the following long-term debt in its statement of financial position.

£15 million [(6% fixed rate) redeemable 20X9]
£18 million [(Sterling LIBOR plus 3%) redeemable 20X7]

All rates are quoted as an annual rate.

It has now been forecast that the Euro is likely to strengthen against sterling by 5% in each of the next four years.

Required

(a) Calculate and briefly assess the revised Expected Net Present Value if the product is launched in France. **(5 marks)**

(b) Identify the different risks associated with each launch option and discuss how these may be managed by the company. **(8 marks)**

(c) Discuss the factors that should be taken into account by the Treasurer of X when deciding whether to raise fixed rate or floating rate debt for the expansion project and whether to hedge the resulting interest rate exposure. **(12 marks)**

(Total = 25 marks)

27 Southern Continents (12/07 amended)

45 mins

The risk committee at Southern Continents Company (SCC) met to discuss a report by its risk manager, Stephanie Field. The report focused on a number of risks that applied to a chemicals factory recently acquired by SCC in another country, Southland. She explained that the new risks related to the security of the factory in Southland in respect of burglary, to the supply of one of the key raw materials that experienced fluctuations in world supply and also an environmental risk. The environmental risk, Stephanie explained, was to do with the possibility of poisonous emissions from the Southland factory.

The SCC chief executive, Choo Wang, who chaired the risk committee, said that the Southland factory was important to him for two reasons. First, he said it was strategically important to the company. Second, it was important because his own bonuses depended upon it. He said that because he had personally negotiated the purchase of the Southland factory, the remunerations committee had included a performance bonus on his salary based on the success of the Southland investment. He told Stephanie that a performance-related bonus was payable when and if the factory achieved a certain level of output that Choo considered to be ambitious. 'I don't get any bonus at all until we reach a high level of output from the factory,' he said. 'So I don't care what the risks are, we will have to manage them.'

Stephanie explained that one of her main concerns arose because the employees at the factory in Southland were not aware of the importance of risk management to SCC. She said that the former owner of the factory paid less attention to risk issues and so the staff were not as aware of risk as Stephanie would like them to be. 'I would like to get risk awareness embedded in the culture at the Southland factory,' she said.

Choo Wang said that he knew from Stephanie's report what the risks were, but that he wanted somebody to explain to him what strategies SCC could use to manage the risks. He was wary of excessive costs and therefore wanted Southern Continents to employ practical strategies to reduce risk as much as was reasonable.

Required

(a) Describe four strategies that can be used to manage risk and identify, with reasons, an appropriate strategy for each of the three risks mentioned in the case. **(12 marks)**

(b) Explain the meaning of Stephanie's comment: 'I would like to get risk awareness embedded in the culture at the Southland factory.' **(5 marks)**

(c) Explain the benefits of performance-related pay in rewarding directors and critically evaluate the implications of the package offered to Choo Wang. **(8 marks)**

(Total = 25 marks)

28 Chen Products (12/08)

45 mins

Chen Products produces four manufactured products: Products 1, 2, 3 and 4. The company's risk committee recently met to discuss how the company might respond to a number of problems that have arisen with Product 2. After a number of incidents in which Product 2 had failed whilst being used by customers, Chen Products had been presented with compensation claims from customers injured and inconvenienced by the product failure. It was decided that the risk committee should meet to discuss the options.

When the discussion of Product 2 began, committee chairman Anne Ricardo reminded her colleagues that, apart from the compensation claims, Product 2 was a highly profitable product.

Chen's risk management committee comprised four non-executive directors who each had different backgrounds and areas of expertise. None of them had direct experience of Chen's industry or products. It was noted that it was common for them to disagree among themselves as to how risks should be managed and that in some situations, each member proposed a quite different strategy to manage a given risk. This was the case when they discussed which risk management strategy to adopt with regard to Product 2.

Required

(a) Describe the typical roles of a risk management committee. **(6 marks)**

(b) Using the TARA framework, construct four possible strategies for managing the risk presented by Product 2.

Your answer should describe each strategy and explain how each might be applied in the case. **(10 marks)**

Risk committee members can be either executive or non-executive.

Required

(c)   (i)   Distinguish between executive and non-executive directors. **(2 marks)**

(ii)   Evaluate the relative advantages and disadvantages of Chen's risk management committee being non-executive rather than executive in nature. **(7 marks)**

(Total = 25 marks)

29 H and Z (6/09)   45 mins

John Pentanol was appointed as risk manager at H&Z Company a year ago and he decided that his first task was to examine the risks that faced the company. He concluded that the company faced three major risks, which he assessed by examining the impact that would occur if the risk were to materialise. He assessed Risk 1 as being of low potential impact as even if it materialised it would have little effect on the company's strategy. Risk 2 was assessed as being of medium potential impact whilst a third risk, Risk 3, was assessed as being of very high potential impact.

When John realised the potential impact of Risk 3 materialising, he issued urgent advice to the board to withdraw from the activity that gave rise to Risk 3 being incurred. In the advice he said that the impact of Risk 3 was potentially enormous and it would be irresponsible for H&Z to continue to bear that risk.

The company commercial director, Jane Xylene, said that John Pentanol and his job at H&Z were unnecessary and that risk management was 'very expensive for the benefits achieved'. She said that all risk managers do is to tell people what can't be done and that they are pessimists by nature. She said she wanted to see entrepreneurial risk takers in H&Z and not risk managers who, she believed, tended to discourage enterprise.

John replied that it was his job to eliminate all of the highest risks at H&Z Company. He said that all risk was bad and needed to be eliminated if possible. If it couldn't be eliminated, he said that it should be minimised.

The risk manager has an important role to play in an organisation's risk management.

Required

(a)   (i)   Describe the roles of a risk manager. **(4 marks)**

(ii)   Assess John Pentanol's understanding of his role. **(4 marks)**

(b)   With reference to a risk assessment framework as appropriate, criticise John's advice that H&Z should withdraw from the activity that incurs Risk 3. **(6 marks)**

Jane Xylene expressed a particular view about the value of risk management in H&Z Company. She also said that she wanted to see 'entrepreneurial risk takers'.

Required

(c)   (i)   Define 'entrepreneurial risk' and explain why it is important to accept entrepreneurial risk in business organisations. **(4 marks)**

(ii)   Critically evaluate Jane Xylene's view of risk management. **(7 marks)**

(Total = 25 marks)

30 UU (12/10)

During the global economic recession that began in mid 2008, many companies found it difficult to gain enough credit in the form of short-term loans from their banks and other lenders. In some cases, this caused working capital problems as short-term cash flow deficits could not be funded.

Ultra-Uber Limited (UU), a large manufacturer based in an economically depressed region, had traditionally operated a voluntary supplier payment policy in which it was announced that all trade payables would be paid at or before 20 days and there would be no late payment. This was operated despite the normal payment terms being 30 days. The company gave the reason for this as 'a desire to publicly demonstrate our social responsibility and support our valued suppliers, most of whom, like UU, also provide employment in this region'. In the 20 years the policy had been in place, the UU website proudly boasted that it had never been broken. Brian Mills, the chief executive often mentioned this as the basis of the company's social responsibility. 'Rather than trying to delay our payments to suppliers,' he often said, 'we support them and their cash flow. It's the right thing to do.' Most of the other directors, however, especially the finance director, think that the voluntary supplier payment policy is a mistake. Some say that it is a means of Brian Mills exercising his own ethical beliefs in a way that is not supported by others at UU Limited.

When UU itself came under severe cash flow pressure in the summer of 2009 as a result of its bank's failure to extend credit, the finance director told Brian Mills that UU's liquidity problems would be greatly relieved if they took an average of 30 rather than the 20 days to pay suppliers.

In addition, the manufacturing director said that he could offer another reason why the short-term liquidity at UU was a problem. He said that the credit control department was poor, taking approximately 50 days to receive payment from each customer. He also said that his own inventory control could be improved and he said he would look into that. It was pointed out to the manufacturing director that cost of goods sold was 65% of turnover and this proportion was continuously rising, driving down gross and profit margins. Due to poor inventory controls, excessively high levels of inventory were held in store at all stages of production. The long-serving sales manager wanted to keep high levels of finished goods so that customers could buy from existing inventory and the manufacturing director wanted to keep high levels of raw materials and work-in-progress to give him minimum response times when a new order came in.

One of the non-executive directors (NEDs) of UU Limited, Bob Ndumo, said that he could not work out why UU was in such a situation as no other company in which he was a NED was having liquidity problems. Bob Ndumo held a number of other NED positions but these were mainly in service-based companies.

Required

(a)   Define 'liquidity risk' and explain why it might be a significant risk to UU Limited.   **(5 marks)**

(b)   Define 'risk embeddedness' and explain the methods by which risk awareness and management can be embedded in organisations.   **(7 marks)**

(c)   Examine the obstacles to embedding liquidity risk management at UU Limited.   **(8 marks)**

(d)   Criticise the voluntary supplier payment policy as a means of demonstrating UU's social responsibility.   **(5 marks)**

(Total = 25 marks)

31 YGT (6/11)

The board of YGT discussed its need for timely risk information. The consensus of the meeting was that risk consultants should be engaged to review the risks facing the company. One director, Raz Dutta, said that she felt that this would be a waste of money as the company needed to concentrate its resources on improving organisational efficiency rather than on gathering risk information. She said that many risks 'didn't change much' and 'hardly ever materialised' and so can mostly be ignored. The rest of the board, however, believed that a number of risks had recently emerged whilst others had become less important and so the board wanted a current assessment as it believed previous assessments might now be outdated.

The team of risk consultants completed the risk audit. They identified and assessed six potential risks (A, B, C, D, E and F) and the following information was discussed when the findings were presented to the YGT board:

Risk A was assessed as unlikely and low impact whilst Risk B was assessed as highly likely to occur and with a high impact. The activities giving rise to both A and B, however, are seen as marginal in that whilst the activities do have value and are capable of making good returns, neither is strategically vital.

Risk C was assessed as low probability but with a high potential impact and also arises from an activity that must not be discontinued although alternative arrangements for bearing the risks are possible. The activity giving rise to Risk C was recently introduced by YGT as a result of a new product launch.

Risk D was assessed as highly likely but with a low potential impact, and arose as a result of a recent change in legislation. It cannot be insured against nor can it be outsourced. It is strategically important that the company continues to engage in the activity that gives rise to Risk D although not necessarily at the same level as is currently the case.

In addition, Risks E and F were identified. Risk E was an environmental risk and Risk F was classed as a reputation risk. The risk consultants said that risks E and F could be related risks. In the formal feedback to the board of YGT, the consultants said that the company had to develop a culture of risk awareness and that this should permeate all levels of the company.

Required

(a)   Criticise Raz Dutta's beliefs about the need for risk assessment. Explain why risks are dynamic and therefore need to be assessed regularly. **(8 marks)**

(b)   Using the TARA framework, select and explain the appropriate strategy for managing each risk (A, B, C and D). Justify your selection in each case. **(6 marks)**

(c)   Explain what 'related risks' are and describe how Risks E and F might be positively correlated. **(5 marks)**

The risk consultants reported that YGT needed to cultivate a culture of risk awareness and that this should permeate all levels of the company.

Required

(d)   Explain and assess this advice. **(6 marks)**

(Total = 25 marks)

32 Internal audit effectiveness
45 mins

Meg Richardson is the newly-appointed finance director of Crucero, a quoted company. Meg has just been asked by the chairman to advise him on the effectiveness of the existing internal audit department.

The chairman explained that internal audit has been established in the company for many years. The chief internal auditor, who has held this post for many years, has reported direct to the chairman. He has always had a right of access to the Board, and, since the establishment of an Audit Committee, has worked closely with that committee.

However, there had been increasing friction in recent years between the chief internal auditor and Meg's predecessor as finance director. Internal audit was regarded by Meg's predecessor as expensive, slow, cumbersome, and ineffective.

The chief internal auditor has seen the internal audit department's main objective as being supporting the work of external audit by reviewing compliance with internal accounting procedures relating to accounting for sales, purchases, payroll and non-current assets. Meg's predecessor would have preferred internal audit to spend far more time assessing business value for money; he was particularly concerned with investor demands for growth in profits and would have liked internal audit recommendations to contribute to this growth.

Required

(a)   Advise the chairman whether Meg should carry out the assessment of internal audit, or, if not, who should do so. **(8 marks)**

(b)   Recommend specific objectives for the internal audit department related to the aims of the department, explaining how performance of the internal audit department against each of its objectives could be evaluated, and providing for each objective an example of a performance measure that could assist in this.
(17 marks)

(Total = 25 marks)

33 Audit committees   45 mins

KPN is a major hotel group that will shortly be seeking a flotation on the stock market. At present the company does not have any non-executive directors or an audit committee. One of KPN's most significant local competitors, NN has recently collapsed; certain of the competitor's shareholders have raised issues about the ineffectiveness of the non-executive directors and in particular the failure of the audit committee to deal with major accounting problems.

As this news story is topical, the directors of KPN want to understand why NN's non-executive directors might have failed to exercise sufficient supervision, and how the audit committee that KPN will be required to establish can function effectively.

NN was also criticised for failing to respond adequately to customer complaints. The directors of KPN are therefore considering the introduction of formal arrangements for hearing and dealing with complaints.

Required

(a)   Assess the factors that might limit the contribution of non-executive directors to improving corporate governance. **(10 marks)**

(b)   Recommend how the effectiveness of audit committees can be enhanced. **(7 marks)**

(c)   Explain what improvements will be needed in control systems if the formal arrangements for dealing with customers were introduced, and explain their impact on the role of the audit committee. **(8 marks)**

(Total = 25 marks)

34 PNY   45 mins

PNY is a book publisher. Each year, it publishes over 10,000 new book titles that range from popular fiction through to specialist guides on 120 different towns worldwide. Over 50,000 titles are stocked in its warehouse awaiting sale to book wholesalers, and recently individual consumers via its Internet site.

Over the last few years, significant amounts of new technology in the form of on-line trading with suppliers and use of the Internet as a selling medium have been implemented into PNY by outside contractors. However, no independent audit of the Internet trading site has been carried out and the site is left to run more as a marketing tool than selling media. There have been relatively few sales from the site since it started operating. No specific reasons have been put forward for lack of sales. A perpetual inventory system has also been in use for the last two years, providing real time information on inventory balances with the aim of reduction of inventory losses due to theft.

Four staff are employed in the internal audit department. The staff have worked in the company for 10 years. Important family and social commitments have meant they do not want to move location and they have little ambition for promotion. The chief internal auditor reports to the Finance Director, who also sets the remuneration levels of internal audit department staff. Training within internal audit is limited to one day's update on audit procedures each year, the lack of staff mobility being given as a reason not to provide detailed training schemes. The company has not established an audit committee.

Internal audit testing methods focus on substantive testing of transactions, tracing those transactions through the accounting system as far as possible. Where there is a break in the audit trail, where possible, the transaction is located again after the break and testing continues. Testing of inventory takes place at the year end when a full inventory count is carried out in association with the external auditors.

Risk management policies in PNY are under the control of the Finance Director. The policy is written by the Head of Accounts and then agreed by the board.

PNY has recently received a number of complaints about one of its biggest-selling ranges. The range manager responsible for this range has recently retired. A review has found numerous errors in the books in this range including spelling mistakes, factual errors and errors in putting the books together such as pages not following in sequence and contents pages not agreeing with the rest of the book. Over the last few years the experienced staff who used to look after the range have departed. Their replacements have been younger employees who have lacked experience of publishing. The range manager did not fulfil company policies in regard to the training he should have given them, and these employees were mostly given a number of titles each to look after, and left to work on those titles by themselves.

Required

(a) Explain how risk management and control systems can be used to prevent and detect poor quality such as has been recently found in PNY's major range. **(8 marks)**

(b) Critically assess the current staffing, role and reporting responsibilities of the internal audit department.
(11 marks)

(c) Recommend how the problems affecting the internal audit department can be overcome. **(6 marks)**

(Total = 25 marks)

35 Franks & Fisher (Examiner question)   45 mins

The board of Franks & Fisher, a large manufacturing company, decided to set up an internal control and audit function. The proposal was to appoint an internal auditor at mid-management level and also to establish a board level internal audit committee made up mainly of non-executive directors.

The initiative to do so was driven by a recent period of rapid growth. The company had taken on many more activities as a result of growth in its product range. The board decided that the increased size and complexity of its operations created the need for greater control over internal activities and that an internal audit function was a good way forward. The need was highlighted by a recent event where internal quality standards were not enforced, resulting in the stoppage of a production line for several hours. The production director angrily described the stoppage as 'entirely avoidable' and the finance director, Jason Kumas, said that the stoppage had been very costly.

Mr Kumas said that there were problems with internal control in a number of areas of the company's operations and that there was a great need for internal audit. He said that as the head of the company's accounting and finance function, the new internal auditor should report to him. The reasons for this, he said, were because as an accountant, he was already familiar with auditing procedure and the fact that he already had information on budgets and other 'control' information that the internal auditor would need.

It was decided that the new internal auditor needed to be a person of some experience and with enough personality not to be intimidated nor diverted by other department heads who might find the internal audits an inconvenience. One debate the board had was whether it would be better to recruit to the position from inside or outside the company. A second argument was over the limits of authority that the internal auditor might be given. It was pointed out that while the board considered the role of internal audit to be very important, it didn't want it to interfere with the activities of other departments to the point where their operational effectiveness was reduced.

Required

(a) Explain, with reference to the case, the factors that are typically considered when deciding to establish internal audit in an organisation. **(10 marks)**

(b) Construct the argument in favour of appointing the new internal auditor from outside the company rather than promoting internally. **(6 marks)**

(c) Critically evaluate Mr Kumas's belief that the internal auditor should report to him as finance director.
(4 marks)

(d) Define 'objectivity' and describe characteristics that might demonstrate an internal auditor's professional objectivity. **(5 marks)**

(Total = 25 marks)

36 Gluck and Goodman (12/08)   45 mins

Susan Paullaos was recently appointed as a non-executive member of the internal audit committee of Gluck and Goodman, a public listed company producing complex engineering products. Barney Chester, the executive finance director who chairs the committee, has always viewed the purpose of internal audit as primarily financial in nature and as long as financial controls are seen to be fully in place, he is less concerned with other aspects of internal control. When Susan asked about operational controls in the production facility Barney said that these were not the concern of the internal audit committee. This, he said, was because as long as the accounting systems and financial controls were fully functional, all other systems may be assumed to be working correctly.

Susan, however, was concerned with the operational and quality controls in the production facility. She spoke to production director Aaron Hardanger, and asked if he would be prepared to produce regular reports for the internal audit committee on levels of specification compliance and other control issues. Mr Hardanger said that the internal audit committee had always trusted him because his reputation as a manager was very good. He said that he had never been asked to provide compliance evidence to the internal audit committee and saw no reason as to why he should start doing so now.

At board level, the non-executive chairman, George Allejandra, said that he only instituted the internal audit committee in the first place in order to be seen to be in compliance with the stock market's requirement that Gluck and Goodman should have one. He believed that internal audit committees didn't add materially to the company. They were, he believed, one of those 'outrageous demands' that regulatory authorities made without considering the consequences in smaller companies nor the individual needs of different companies. He also complained about the need to have an internal auditor. He said that Gluck and Goodman used to have a full time internal auditor but when he left a year ago, he wasn't replaced. The audit committee didn't feel it needed an internal auditor because Barney Chester believed that only financial control information was important and he could get that information from his management accountant.

Susan asked Mr Allejandra if he recognised that the company was exposing itself to increased market risks by failing to have an effective audit committee. Mr Allejandra said he didn't know what a market risk was.

Required

Internal control and audit are considered to be important parts of sound corporate governance.

(a) (i) Describe FIVE general objectives of internal control. **(5 marks)**

    (ii) Explain the organisational factors that determine the need for internal audit in public listed companies. **(5 marks)**

(b) Criticise the internal control and internal audit arrangements at Gluck and Goodman as described in the case scenario. **(10 marks)**

(c) Define 'market risk' for Mr Allejandra and explain why Gluck and Goodman's market risk exposure is increased by failing to have an effective audit committee. **(5 marks)**

(Total = 25 marks)

37 Saltoc (12/09)

After a major fire had destroyed an office block belonging to Saltoc Company, the fire assessment reported that the most likely cause was an electrical problem. It emerged that the electrical system had suffered from a lack of maintenance in recent years due to cost pressures. Meanwhile in the same week, it was reported that a laptop computer containing confidential details of all of Saltoc's customers was stolen from the front seat of a car belonging to one of the company's information technology (IT) mid-managers. This caused outrage and distress to many of the affected customers as the information on the laptop included their bank details and credit card numbers. Some customers wrote to the company to say that they would be withdrawing their business from Saltoc as a result.

When the board met to review and consider the two incidents, it was agreed that the company had been lax in its risk management in the past and that systems should be tightened. However, the financial director, Peter Osbida, said that he knew perfectly well where systems should be tightened. He said that the fire was due to the incompetence of Harry Ho the operations manager and that the stolen laptop was because of a lack of security in the IT department led by Laura Hertz. Peter said that both colleagues were 'useless' and should be sacked. Neither Harry nor Laura liked or trusted Peter and they felt that in disputes, chief executive Ken Tonno usually took Peter's side.

Both Harry and Laura said that their departments had come under severe pressure because of the tight cost budgets imposed by Peter. Ken Tonno said that the last few years had been 'terrible' for Saltoc Company and that it was difficult enough keeping cash flows high enough to pay the wage bill without having to worry about 'even more' administration on risks and controls. Peter said that Harry and Laura both suffered in their roles by not having the respect of their subordinates and pointed to the high staff turnover in both of their departments as evidence of this.

Mr Tonno asked whether having a complete risk audit (or risk review) might be a good idea. He shared some of Peter's concerns about the management skills of both Harry and Laura, and so proposed that perhaps an external person should perform the risk audit and that would be preferable to one conducted by a colleague from within the company.

Required

(a)   Describe what 'embedding' risk means with reference to Saltoc Company.   **(6 marks)**

(b)   Assess the ability of Saltoc's management culture to implement embedded risk systems.   **(8 marks)**

(c)   Explain what external risk auditing contains and construct the case for an external risk audit at Saltoc Company.   **(11 marks)**

(Total = 25 marks)

38 COSO (6/10)

The Committee of Sponsoring Organisations (COSO) of the Treadway Commission is an American voluntary, private sector organisation and is unconnected to government or any other regulatory authority. It was established in 1985 to help companies identify the causes of fraudulent reporting and to create internal control environments able to support full and accurate reporting. It is named after its first chairman, James Treadway, and has issued several guidance reports over the years including important reports in 1987, 1992 and 2006.

In 2009, COSO issued new 'Guidance on monitoring internal control systems' to help companies tighten internal controls and thereby enjoy greater internal productivity and produce higher quality reporting. The report, written principally by a leading global professional services firm but adopted by all of the COSO members, noted that 'unmonitored controls tend to deteriorate over time' and encouraged organisations to adopt wide ranging internal controls. It went on to say that, the 'assessment of internal controls [can] ... involve a significant amount of ... internal audit testing.'

After its publication, the business journalist, Mark Rogalski, said that the latest report contained 'yet more guidance from COSO on how to make your company less productive by burdening it even more with non-productive things to do' referring to the internal control guidance the 2009 report contains. He said that there was no industry sector-specific advice and that a 'one-size-fits-all' approach to internal control was 'ridiculous'. He further argued that there was no link between internal controls and external reporting, and that internal controls are unnecessary for effective external reporting.

Another commentator, Claire Mahmood, wrote a reply to Rogalski's column pointing to the views expressed in the 2009 COSO report that, 'over time effective monitoring can lead to organisational efficiencies and reduced costs associated with public reporting on internal control because problems are identified and addressed in a proactive, rather than reactive, manner.' She said that these benefits were not industry sector specific and that Rogalski was incorrect in his dismissal of the report's value. She also said that although primarily concerned with governance in the USA, the best practice guidance from COSO could be applied by companies anywhere in the world. She said that although the USA, where COSO is based, is concerned with the 'rigid rules' of compliance, the advice ought to be followed by companies in countries with principles-based approaches to corporate governance because it was best practice.

Required

(a)   Distinguish between rules-based and principles-based approaches to internal control system compliance as described by Claire Mahmood and discuss the benefits to an organisation of a principles-based approach.

(7 marks)

Mr Rogalski is sceptical over the value of internal control and believes that controls must be industry-specific to be effective.

Required

(b)   Describe the advantages of internal control that apply regardless of industry sector and briefly explain the statement, 'unmonitored controls tend to deteriorate over time'. Your answer should refer to the case scenario as appropriate. **(10 marks)**

The COSO report explains that 'assessment of internal controls [can] ... involve a significant amount of ... internal audit testing.'

Required

(c)   Define 'internal audit testing' and explain the roles of internal audit in helping ensure the effectiveness of internal control systems. **(8 marks)**

(Total = 25 marks)

PROFESSIONAL VALUES AND ETHICS

Questions 39 to 55 cover professional values and ethics, the subject of Part C of the BPP Study Text for Paper P1.

39 Crawley Gossop

45 mins

Crawley Gossop plc is a manufacturer of household cleaning materials. Thanks to a technological development in its manufacturing process some years ago, the company was able to gain and sustain for some time a significant competitive advantage over its rivals. As a result Crawley Gossop has greatly expanded over the last few years and obtained a listing on its local stock exchange three years ago.

However Crawley Gossop's success has had some unpopular consequences. Greatly increased activity at the company's biggest factory has angered the local community because of the disruption caused by increased traffic and site expansion. Crawley Gossop has also recently been fined for exceeding local statutory emission limits over a period of time. As a result environmental groups are threatening to encourage boycotts of Crawley Gossop's goods. Its board has discussed the shortcomings that have led to the fines and have concluded the company's environmental management systems and policies need to be strengthened. One of the board has looked into the European Union's Eco-Management and Audit Scheme (EMAS) and the directors intend to discuss at the next board meeting whether Crawley Gossop should adopt the scheme. One of the non-executive directors has already circulated the board with the view that the EMAS regime is too inflexible and Crawley Gossop's annual report should include a detailed voluntary environmental report, tailored to its own circumstances.

Crawley Gossop's auditors, Broadfield Bewbush, have also faced criticisms from environmental groups. The spokeswoman of one group has stated that 'If Broadfield Bewbush had any professional ethics, they would resign as auditors. By continuing as auditors, they are helping to prop up a company that has an appalling record of acting against the public interest. Crawley Gossop's accounts give no indication of how much damage it is doing to the local environment.'

Required

(a)   Construct the case for implementation of EMAS by Crawley Glossop.   **(10 marks)**

(b)   Describe the main influences upon the content of an environmental report.   **(5 marks)**

(c)   Critically evaluate the view that accountants should not act for clients who are perceived to be acting against the public interest.   **(10 marks)**

(Total = 25 marks)

40 Environmental and social issues

45 mins

Z plc is a publicly quoted company. Its products are based on raw materials grown in tropical countries and processed either in these countries or in the eventual sales markets. Processing is undertaken partly by Z plc and partly by sub-contractors. The products are branded and sold worldwide, but mainly in the United Kingdom and North America. They are sold to consumers through a very large number of outlets.

The non-executive directors have for some time expressed concern that the company has not developed any systems of environmental or social reporting to shareholders, although many comparable companies already publish such information as part of their Annual Report. A government minister has now stated that legislation will be considered if all companies do not make progress on reporting on social and environmental policies.

The chief executive has always regarded reporting as ideally never exceeding legal requirements.

Required

(a)   Construct a case for including a report on environmental and social issues in the annual report.   **(6 marks)**

(b)   Identify the main issues that could be covered in the environmental and social report.   **(8 marks)**

(c)   Analyse the impact of business partners and other stakeholders on the content of the environmental and social report.   **(5 marks)**

(d)   Identify the information that the board requires to review the company's progress on environmental and social issues.   **(6 marks)**

(Total = 25 marks)

41 Edted   45 mins

The directors of Edted have raised a number of concerns connected with corporate social responsibility. Extracts from the discussion on social responsibility at the last board meeting are as follows.

Extracts from board meeting minutes

The chairman commented that he had read that companies were benefiting in terms of image and more sales from 'ethical' consumers if they were perceived as good corporate citizens. He was unclear of the exact meaning of the term corporate citizenship.

The sales director commented that a key element of good corporate citizenship was managing the company's relationship with the natural environment. He therefore regarded it as top priority for the company to introduce an effective environmental management system.

The finance director was more sceptical of the concept of corporate citizenship, claiming that staff co-operation would be necessary if the company was to act as, and be perceived as, a good corporate citizen. She suspected that this would depend on the factors in their background that determined their ethical approaches: 'We ourselves can't teach our employees to be good citizens'.

Required

(a)   Explain the concept of corporate citizenship and describe the issues that influence an organisation's position on corporate citizenship.   **(5 marks)**

(b)   Describe the main issues that Edted will face if it adheres to the European Union's Eco-Management and Audit Scheme (EMAS) and explain how requirements would differ if it adopted the ISO 14000 standards.

(9 marks)

(c)   Evaluate the finance director's viewpoint that Edted cannot overcome the influences in individuals' backgrounds that determine their approach to ethics.   **(11 marks)**

(Total = 25 marks)

42 Code of conduct   45 mins

The Managing Director of a company which makes and sells defence equipment worldwide has had a most unhappy meeting with his Chairman.

They have both just read a newspaper report of a statement made by a disgruntled ex-employee, after a court case for compensation for his dismissal.

In the statement, the ex-employee stated that the company had been selling equipment in breach of a United Nations embargo, and that such sales have been made on a number of occasions.

The Chairman is concerned because:

(i)   He did not anticipate such unfortunate public criticism of the company

(ii)   He was not aware of such irregular sales

(iii) He thought all possible had been done, by establishing an audit committee in line with the UK Corporate Governance Code recommendations, to ensure that such problems would never arise

(iv)   He thought the internal audit department should have detected *all* actions contrary to the Company code of conduct and reported them to him immediately.

Required

(a)   Describe the membership of, and evaluate the case for, establishing an audit committee in a company.

(8 marks)

(b)   Explain how an audit committee may contribute to the solution of problems such as those outlined above.

(6 marks)

(c)   Assess the extent to which the internal audit department can be involved in ensuring compliance with the Company code of conduct.   **(4 marks)**

(d)   Recommend other steps that may be required to ensure that decisions taken within a company are ethical.

(7 marks)

(Total = 25 marks)

43 Drofdarb   **45 mins**

Drofdarb plc is a British publicly owned company, which competes mainly on the UK market for sporting goods: replica kits, training equipment, leisurewear and sporting accessories such as balls and pads. It has a Board of Directors that comprises the following:

Chairman	Mr S McNamara
Chief Executive	Mr I Harris
Finance Director	Mr C McKenna
Executive Director (Clothing)	Mr D Solomona
Executive Director (Equipment)	Mr J Langley
Non-Executive Director	Mr S Hape
Non-Executive Director	Mr A Lynch

The Chairman, Mr McNamara, is concerned that Drofdarb's previously good reputation as a good 'corporate citizen' may have become tarnished after the following:

*   The introduction of a new computer system combining manufacturing, ordering and accounting procedures in the last 12 months

*   Press reports suggesting widespread non-compliance with the corporate governance regulations among FTSE 350 companies, especially in relation to non-executive directors

*   Rumours of poor controls within the finance function at Drofdarb leading to allegations of financial irregularities.

The finance function is staffed mostly by ACCA members and students – any claims regarding the quality and integrity of his staff are hotly refuted by the FD Mr McKenna, who feels that the company already does enough to meet the requirements for good internal controls.

Mr McNamara has been assessed as independent in his role as Chairman, leaving a need for a third non-executive director (NED) to make the balance of independent to non-independent board members 50:50. A vacancy is to be advertised in the next month.

Mr McKenna has suggested that instead of repeating the lengthy and expensive recruitment process that preceded the appointment of both Mr Hape and Mr Lynch, the company should consider the appointment of Mr B McDermott. His credentials are as follows:

*   Current executive director of Sdeel plc – a competitor of Drofdarb's

*   Previously the external auditor of Drofdarb – he resigned his position as senior partner two years ago in favour of a more commercial role

*   Mr McDermott was appointed by Sdeel because of his knowledge of the industry and his family's connections with Sdeel's historical owners, who had sold up and bought into Drofdarb some 20 years before – he currently owns a 2% shareholding in Drofdarb as well as 'a few shares to balance his portfolio' in Sdeel plc.

Mr McNamara is keen for the board to be seen to be following good corporate governance practices. He is also mindful of the requirements of the Turnbull Committee in ensuring internal controls are sufficient and that no problems exist with trusting staff.

Required

(a)   Describe the fundamental ethical principles that should be present in all finance staff, and recommend what needs to be done in the business to encourage staff to act ethically.   **(9 marks)**

(b)   Explain the main elements of a risk-based approach by the board to internal controls, and discuss the limitations of a risk-based approach.   **(6 marks)**

(c)   (i)   Describe the roles of a non-executive director.   **(4 marks)**

         (ii)   Evaluate the suitability of Mr B McDermott to be an independent non-executive director of Drofdarb.
            (6 marks)

(Total = 25 marks)

44 David Hunter   45 mins

David Hunter is currently serving as a non-executive director on the board of a nationalised concern, The Electricity Provision Corporation (EPC), in a country in Asia. EPC operates a number of coal-fired power stations and transmits energy through a national grid which it controls. The electricity generated is then sold to the general public by private sector electricity distribution companies.

David Hunter is concerned about the ethical implications of a couple of issues that were discussed at EPC's most recent board meeting which was held yesterday. As a non-executive director, he believes he has a particular responsibility to consider ethical issues carefully.

(a)   A general election campaign has recently begun in this country. The governing party has indicated that it intends to maintain EPC as a nationalised industry if it wins the general election, although it will be seeking efficiency improvements. The opposition party has indicated that it intends to privatise all industries that are currently nationalised. Early yesterday morning before the board meeting, EPC's Managing Director was suddenly asked by senior civil servants in the Ministry of Energy to provide a major commitment to cost cutting in the next ten days. The Managing Director is aware that the Minister of Energy will be making a major election speech in a fortnight's time.

(b)   A recent United Nations report ranked EPC's home country in the Top 10 of its worst polluters, as measured by CO_2 emissions per head of population. This report has been seized upon by environmental groups who have called for a month of action during the general election campaign. They wish to highlight the environmental damage being caused by the government's environmental policies and to highlight the need to switch to alternative technologies such as wind power generation.

         In the last few days small groups of protestors have broken through perimeter fences at two of EPC's power stations and managed to delay deliveries of coal by chaining themselves across railway tracks. There have been some reports in the press of heavy handed treatment being meted out by the security firm hired by EPC to deal with the protests. EPC's Managing Director has dismissed these reports, saying the protestors' solutions are impractical, they have no rights of access, and that EPC is entitled to take whatever action is required against the protestors to protect its property and maintain electricity supplies.

Required

(a)   Using the American Accounting Association model to support your answer, recommend to David Hunter the course of action the board should take in responding to the civil servants' request for information.
            (15 marks)

(b)   Using Tucker's model for decision-making, assess the factors that EPC's board should consider when dealing with the current protests by environmental groups.   **(10 marks)**

(Total = 25 marks)

45 Penrice

45 mins

A new government has recently been elected in the country of Munrofaure. Political commentators believe that a major reason for the change of government has been recent excesses in the country's corporate and financial sectors, with the new government being elected on a platform of dealing with these. The new government's Minister for Business has already criticised many of the companies operating in the country for being too inwardly directed and lacking transparency and accountability. He has called on companies to demonstrate their commitment to building a relationship of trust with the wider community in which they operate.

Pravina Tank is the newly appointed Chief Executive Officer of Penrice, one of the major manufacturing companies in Munrofaure. Penrice has faced particular criticism from campaigners for fuller corporate disclosure because of the lack of information provided in Penrice's accounts. Pravina is considering how to demonstrate Penrice's commitment to fuller disclosure, particularly of the company's impact on the environment, and how to achieve verification of the other steps Penrice is taking to limit its impact on the environment.

Pravina also believes that Penrice has become too inwardly focused over the years, partly because its significant acquisitions have resulted in considerable vertical integration, with the result that all stages of the supply chain of many goods it produces are now located in-house. Pravina feels that many of Penrice's managers have concentrated their efforts on low-risk activities that are guaranteed to result in adequate performance, but have limited growth prospects. Penrice's biggest institutional shareholder has recently indicated that it would like the company to deliver higher growth in profitability.

Required

(a)   Identify the costs that could be incorporated into Penrice's accounts using full cost accounting, and evaluate the case for Penrice publishing information using full cost accounting. **(9 marks)**

(b)   Explain the main elements of an environmental audit and construct the case for an external environmental audit of Penrice. **(8 marks)**

(c)   Assess the behaviour of managers at Penrice from the perspective of transaction cost theory and recommend ways in which managers can be directed towards taking steps to improve Penrice's profitability. **(8 marks)**

(Total = 25 marks)

46 JH Graphics (Examiner question)

45 mins

The board of JH Graphics, a design and artwork company, was debating an agenda item on the possible adoption of a corporate code of ethics. Jenny Harris, the chief executive and majority shareholder, was a leading supporter of the idea. She said that many of the large companies in the industry had adopted codes of ethics and that she thought it would signal the importance that JH Graphics placed on ethics. She also said that she was personally driven by high ethical values and that she wanted to express these through her work and through the company's activities and policies.

Alan Leroy, the creative director, explained that he would support the adoption of the code of ethics as long as it helped to support the company's long-term strategic objectives. He said that he could see no other reason as the company was 'not a charity' and had to maximise shareholder value above all other objectives. In particular, he was keen, as a shareholder himself, to know what the code would cost to draw up and how much it would cost to comply with it over and above existing costs.

Jenny argued that having a code would help to resolve some ethical issues, one of which, she suggested, was a problem the company was having over a particular image it had recently produced for a newspaper advertisement. The image was produced for an advertising client and although the client was pleased, it had offended a particular religious group because of its content and design.

When it was discovered who had produced the 'offending' image, some religious leaders criticised JH Graphics for being insensitive and offensive to their religion. For a brief time, the events were a major news story. As politicians, journalists and others debated the issues in the media, the board of JH Graphics was involved in intense discussions and faced with a dilemma as to whether or not to issue a public apology for the offence caused by the image and to ask the client to withdraw it.

Alan argued that having a code of ethics would not have helped in that situation, as the issue was so complicated. His view was that the company should not apologise for the image and that he didn't care very much that the image offended people. He said it was bringing the company free publicity and that was good for the business. Jenny said that she had sympathy for the viewpoint of the offended religious leaders. Although she disagreed with them, she understood the importance to some people of firmly-held beliefs. The board agreed that as there seemed to be arguments both ways, the decision on how the company should deal with the image should be Jenny's as chief executive.

Required

(a) Analyse Jenny's and Alan's motivations for adopting the code of ethics using the normative-instrumental forms of stakeholder theory. **(8 marks)**

(b) Assess Jenny's decision on the possible apology for the 'offending' image from conventional and pre-conventional moral development perspectives. **(4 marks)**

(c) Explain and assess the factors that the board of JH Graphics might consider in deciding how to respond to the controversy over the offending image. **(10 marks)**

(d) Comment on the legitimacy of the religious group's claims on JH Graphics's activities. **(3 marks)**

(Total = 25 marks)

47 Professor Cheung's views (Pilot paper) 45 mins

At a recent conference on corporate social responsibility, one speaker (Professor Cheung) argued that professional codes of ethics for accountants were not as useful as some have claimed because:

'they assume professional accountants to be rules-driven, when in fact most professionals are more driven by principles that guide and underpin all aspects of professional behaviour, including professional ethics.'

When quizzed from the audience about his views on the usefulness of professional codes of ethics, Professor Cheung suggested that the costs of writing, implementing, disseminating and monitoring ethical codes outweighed their usefulness. He said that as long as professional accountants personally observe the highest values of probity and integrity then there is no need for detailed codes of ethics.

Required

(a) Critically evaluate Professor Cheung's views on codes of professional ethics. Use examples of ethical codes, where appropriate, to illustrate your answer. **(12 marks)**

(b) With reference to Professor Cheung's comments, explain what is meant by 'integrity' and assess its importance as an underlying principle in corporate governance. **(7 marks)**

(c) Explain and contrast a deontological with a consequentialist based approach to business ethics. **(6 marks)**

(Total = 25 marks)

48 Football club (12/07) 45 mins

When a prominent football club, whose shares were listed, announced that it was to build a new stadium on land near to its old stadium, opinion was divided. Many of the club's fans thought it a good idea because it would be more comfortable for them when watching games. A number of problems arose, however, when it was pointed out that the construction of the new stadium and its car parking would have a number of local implications. The local government authority said that building the stadium would involve diverting roads and changing local traffic flow, but that it would grant permission to build the stadium if those issues could be successfully addressed. A number of nearby residents complained that the new stadium would be too near their homes and that it would destroy the view from their gardens. Helen Yusri, who spoke on behalf of the local residents, said that the residents would fight the planning application through legal means if necessary. A nearby local inner-city wildlife reservation centre said that the stadium's construction might impact on local water levels and therefore upset the delicate balance of animals and plants in the wildlife centre. A local school, whose pupils often visited the wildlife centre, joined in the opposition, saying that whilst the school supported the building of a new stadium in principle, it had concerns about disruption to the wildlife centre.

The football club's board was alarmed by the opposition to its planned new stadium as it had assumed that it would be welcomed because the club had always considered itself a part of the local community. The club chairman said that he wanted to maintain good relations with all local people if possible, but at the same time he owed it to the fans and the club's investors to proceed with the building of the new stadium despite local concerns.

Required

(a)   Define 'stakeholder' and explain the importance of identifying all the stakeholders in the stadium project.

(10 marks)

(b)   Compare and contrast Gray, Owen and Adams's 'pristine capitalist' position with the 'social contractarian' position. Explain how these positions would affect responses to stakeholder concerns in the new stadium project.

(8 marks)

(c)   Explain what 'fiduciary responsibility' means and construct the case for broadening the football club board's fiduciary responsibility in this case.

(7 marks)

(Total = 25 marks)

49 Anne Hayes (6/08)   45 mins

It was the final day of a two-week-long audit of Van Buren Company, a longstanding client of Fillmore Pierce Auditors. In the afternoon, Anne Hayes, a recently qualified accountant and member of the audit team, was following an audit trail on some cash payments when she discovered what she described to the audit partner, Zachary Lincoln, as an 'irregularity'. A large and material cash payment had been recorded with no recipient named. The corresponding invoice was handwritten on a scrap of paper and the signature was illegible.

Zachary, the audit partner, was under pressure to finish the audit that afternoon. He advised Anne to seek an explanation from Frank Monroe, the client's finance director. Zachary told her that Van Buren was a longstanding client of Fillmore Pierce and he would be surprised if there was anything unethical or illegal about the payment. He said that he had personally been involved in the Van Buren audit for the last eight years and that it had always been without incident. He also said that Frank Monroe was an old friend of his from university days and that he was certain that he wouldn't approve anything unethical or illegal. Zachary said that Fillmore Pierce had also done some consultancy for Van Buren so it was a very important client that he didn't want Anne to upset with unwelcome and uncomfortable questioning.

When Anne sought an explanation from Mr Monroe, she was told that nobody could remember what the payment was for but that she had to recognise that 'real' audits were sometimes a bit messy and that not all audit trails would end as she might like them to. He also reminded her that it was the final day and both he and the audit firm were under time pressure to conclude business and get the audit signed off.

When Anne told Zachary what Frank had said, Zachary agreed not to get the audit signed off without Anne's support, but warned her that she should be very certain that the irregularity was worth delaying the signoff for. It was therefore now Anne's decision whether to extend the audit or have it signed off by the end of Friday afternoon.

Required

(a)   Explain why 'auditor independence' is necessary in auditor-client relationships and describe THREE threats to auditor independence in the case.

(9 marks)

Anne is experiencing some tension due to the conflict between her duties and responsibilities as an employee of Fillmore Pierce and as a qualified professional accountant.

Required

(b)   (i)   Compare and contrast her duties and responsibilities in the two roles of employee and professional accountant.

(6 marks)

       (ii)   Explain the ethical tensions between these roles that Anne is now experiencing.

(4 marks)

(c)   Explain how absolutist (dogmatic) and relativist (pragmatic) ethical assumptions would affect the outcome of Anne's decision.

(6 marks)

(Total = 25 marks)

50 Hogg Products (12/08)

45 mins

Hogg Products Company (HPC), based in a developing country, was recently wholly acquired by American Overseas Investments (AOI), a North American holding company. The new owners took the opportunity to completely review HPC's management, culture and systems. One of the first things that AOI questioned was HPC's longstanding corporate code of ethics.

The board of AOI said that it had a general code of ethics that HPC, as an AOI subsidiary, should adopt. Simon Hogg, the chief executive of HPC, disagreed however, and explained why HPC should retain its existing code. He said that HPC had adopted its code of ethics in its home country which was often criticised for its unethical business behaviour. Some other companies in the country were criticised for their 'sweat shop' conditions. HPC's adoption of its code of ethics, however, meant that it could always obtain orders from European customers on the guarantee that products were made ethically and in compliance with its own highly regarded code of ethics. Mr Hogg explained that HPC had an outstanding ethical reputation both locally and internationally and that reputation could be threatened if it was forced to replace its existing code of ethics with AOI's more general code.

When Ed Tanner, a senior director from AOI's head office, visited Mr Hogg after the acquisition, he was shown HPC's operation in action. Mr Hogg pointed out that unlike some other employers in the industry, HPC didn't employ child labour. Mr Hogg explained that although it was allowed by law in the country, it was forbidden by HPC's code of ethics. Mr Hogg also explained that in his view, employing child labour was always ethically wrong. Mr Tanner asked whether the money that children earned by working in the relatively safe conditions at HPC was an important source of income for their families. Mr Hogg said that the money was important to them but even so, it was still wrong to employ children, as it was exploitative and interfered with their education. He also said that it would alienate the European customers who bought from HPC partly on the basis of the terms of its code of ethics.

Required

(a)   Describe the purposes and typical contents of a corporate code of ethics.   **(9 marks)**

'Strategic positioning' is about the way that a company as a whole is placed in its environment and concerns its 'fit' with the factors in its environment.

(b)   With reference to the case as appropriate, explain how a code of ethics can be used as part of a company's overall strategic positioning.   **(7 marks)**

(c)   Assess Mr Hogg's belief that employing child labour is 'always ethically wrong' from deontological and teleological (consequentialist) ethical perspectives.   **(9 marks)**

(Total = 25 marks)

51 Policy speech (6/09)

45 mins

In a major policy speech, Government finance minister Mrs Wei Yttria said that the audit and assurance industry's work should always be judged by the effect it has on public confidence in business. She said that it was crucial that professional services such as audit and assurance should always be performed in the public interest and that there should be no material threats to the assurer's independence. Enron and other corporate failures happened, she said, because some accountants didn't understand what it was to act in the public interest. She stressed that it was important that firms should not provide more than one service to individual clients. If a firm audited a client then, she said, it shouldn't provide any other services to that client.

Mr Oggon Mordue, a financial journalist who had worked in audit and assurance for many years, was in the audience. He suggested that the normal advice on threats to independence was wrong. On the contrary in fact, the more services that a professional services firm can provide to a client the better, as it enables the firm to better understand the client and its commercial and accounting needs. Mrs Yttria disagreed, saying that his views were a good example of professional services firms not acting in the public interest.

Mr Mordue said that when he was a partner at a major professional services firm, he got to know his clients very well through the multiple links that his firm had with them. He said that he knew all about their finances from providing audit and assurance services, all about their tax affairs through tax consulting and was always in a good position to provide any other advice as he had acted as a consultant on other matters for many years including advising on mergers, acquisitions, compliance and legal issues. He became very good friends with the directors of client companies, he said. The clients, he explained, also found the relationship very helpful and the accounting firms did well financially out of it.

Another reporter in the audience argued with Mr Mordue. Ivor Nahum said that Mr Mordue represented the 'very worst' of the accounting profession. He said that accounting was a 'biased and value laden' profession that served minority interests, was complicit in environmental degradation and could not serve the public interest as long as it primarily served the interests of unfettered capitalism. He said that the public interest was badly served by accounting, as it did not address poverty, animal rights or other social injustices.

Required

(a) Explain, using accounting as an example, what 'the public interest' means as used by Mrs Yttria in her speech. **(5 marks)**

This requirement concerns ethical threats. It is very important for professional accountants to be aware of ethical threats and to avoid these where possible.

Required

(b) (i) With reference to the case as appropriate, describe five types of ethical threat. **(5 marks)**
     (ii) Assess the ethical threats implied by Mr Mordue's beliefs. **(8 marks)**

(c) Assess Ivor Nahum's remarks about the accounting profession in the light of Gray, Owen & Adams' deep green (or deep ecologist) position on social responsibility. **(7 marks)**

(Total = 25 marks)

52 John Wang (12/09)   45 mins

John Wang is a junior partner and training manager at Miller Dundas, a medium sized firm of auditors. He oversees the progress of the firm's student accountants. One of those under John's supervision, Lisa Xu, recently wrote in her progress and achievement log about a situation in an audit that had disturbed her.

On the recent audit of Mbabo Company, a medium sized, family-run business and longstanding client of Miller Dundas, Lisa was checking non-current asset purchases when she noticed what she thought might be an irregularity. There was an entry of $100,000 for a security system for an address in a well-known holiday resort with no obvious link to the company. On questioning this with Ellen Tan, the financial controller, Lisa was told that the system was for Mr Martin Mbabo's holiday cottage (Martin Mbabo is managing director and a minority shareholder in the Mbabo Company). She was told that Martin Mbabo often took confidential company documents with him to his holiday home and so needed the security system on the property to protect them. It was because of this, Ellen said, that it was reasonable to charge the security system to the company.

Ellen Tan expressed surprise at Lisa's concerns and said that auditors had not previously been concerned about the company being charged for non-current assets and operational expenses for Mr Mbabo's personal properties.

Lisa told the engagement partner, Potto Sinter, what she had found and Potto simply said that the charge could probably be ignored. He did agree, however, to ask for a formal explanation from Martin Mbabo before he signed off the audit. Lisa wasn't at the final clearance meeting but later read the following in the notes from the clearance meeting: 'discussed other matter with client, happy with explanation'. When Lisa discussed the matter with Potto afterwards she was told that the matter was now closed and that she should concentrate on her next audit and her important accounting studies.

When John Wang read about Lisa's concerns and spoke to her directly, he realised he was in an ethical dilemma. Not only should there be a disclosure requirement of Mr Mbabo's transaction, but the situation was made more complicated by the fact that Potto Sinter was senior to John Wang in Miller Dundas and also by the fact that the two men were good friends.

Required

(a) Explain the meaning of 'integrity' and its importance in professional relationships such as those described in the case. **(5 marks)**

(b) Criticise Potto Sinter's ethical and professional behaviour in the case. **(10 marks)**

(c) Critically evaluate the alternatives that John Wang has in his ethical dilemma. **(10 marks)**

(Total = 25 marks)

53 Happy and healthy (6/10)

45 mins

'Happy and healthy' is a traditional independent health food business that has been run as a family company for 40 years by Ken and Steffi Potter. As a couple they have always been passionate campaigners for healthy foods and are more concerned about the quality of the foods they sell than the financial detail of their business. Since the company started in 1970, it has been audited by Watson Shreeves, a local audit firm. Mr Shreeves has overseen the Potters' audit for all of the 40 year history (rotating the engagement partner) and has always taken the opportunity to meet with Ken and Steffi informally at the end of each audit to sign off the financial statements and to offer a briefing and some free financial advice in his role as what he calls, 'auditor and friend'. In these briefings, Mr Shreeves, who has become a close family friend of the Potters over the years, always points out that the business is profitable (which the Potters already knew without knowing the actual figures) and how they might increase their margins. But the Potters have never been too concerned about financial performance as long as they can provide a good service to their customers, make enough to keep the business going and provide continued employment for themselves and their son, Ivan. Whilst Ken and Steffi still retain a majority shareholding in 'Happy and healthy' they have gradually increased Ivan's proportion over the years. They currently own 60% to Ivan's 40%. Ivan was appointed a director, alongside Ken and Steffi, in 2008.

Ivan grew up in the business and has helped his parents out since he was a young boy. As he grew up, Ken and Steffi gave him more and more responsibility in the hope that he would one day take the business over. By the end of 2009, Ken made sure that Ivan drew more salary than Ken and Steffi combined as they sought to ensure that Ivan was happy to continue in the business after they retired.

During the audit for the year ended 31 March 2010, a member of Watson Shreeves was performing the audit as usual when he noticed a dramatic drop in the profitability of the business as a whole. He noticed that whilst food sales continued to be profitable, a large amount of inventory had been sold below cost to Barong Company with no further explanation and it was this that had caused the reduction in the company's operating margin. Each transaction with Barong Company had, the invoices showed, been authorised by Ivan.

Mr Shreeves was certain Ken and Steffi would not know anything about this and he prepared to tell them about it as a part of his annual end of audit meeting. Before the meeting, however, he carried out some checks on Barong Company and found that it was a separate business owned by Ivan and his wife. Mr Shreeves's conclusion was that Ivan was effectively stealing from 'Happy and healthy' to provide inventory for Barong Company at a highly discounted cost price. Although Mr Shreeves now had to recommend certain disclosures to the financial statements in this meeting, his main fear was that Ken and Steffi would be devastated if they found out that Ivan was stealing and that it would have long-term implications for their family relationships and the future of 'Happy and healthy'.

Required

(a) Explain how a family (or insider-dominated) business differs from a public listed company and, using evidence from the case, explore the governance issues of a family or insider-dominated business.

(10 marks)

(b) Mr Shreeves is a professional accountant and auditor. Explain why he is considered a professional by society and describe the fundamental principles (or responsibilities) of professionalism that society expects from him and all other accountants.   **(7 marks)**

(c) Discuss the professional and ethical dilemma facing Mr Shreeves in deciding whether or not to tell Ken and Steffi about Ivan's activity. Advise Mr Shreeves of the most appropriate course of action.   **(8 marks)**

(Total = 25 marks)

54 JGP (12/10)

45 mins

At a board meeting of JGP Chemicals Limited, the directors were discussing some recent negative publicity arising from the accidental emission of a chemical pollutant into the local river. As well as it resulting in a large fine from the courts, the leak had created a great deal of controversy in the local community that relied on the polluted river for its normal use (including drinking). A prominent community leader spoke for those affected when she said that a leak of this type must never happen again or JGP would suffer the loss of support from the community. She also reminded JGP that it attracts 65% of its labour from the local community.

As a response to the problems that arose after the leak, the JGP board decided to consult an expert on whether the publication of a full annual environmental report might help to mitigate future environmental risks. The expert, Professor Appo (a prominent academic), said that the company would need to establish an annual environmental audit before they could issue a report. He said that the environmental audit should include, in addition to a review and evaluation of JGP's safety controls, a full audit of the environmental impact of JGP's supply chain. He said that these components would be very important in addressing the concerns of a growing group of investors who are worried about such things. Professor Appo said that all chemical companies had a structural environmental risk and JGP was no exception to this. As major consumers of natural chemical resources and producers of potentially hazardous outputs, Professor Appo said that chemical companies should be aware of the wide range of ways in which they can affect the environment. CEO Keith Miasma agreed with Professor Appo and added that because JGP was in chemicals, any environmental issue had the potential to affect JGP's overall reputation among a wide range of stakeholders.

When the board was discussing the issue of sustainability in connection with the environmental audit, the finance director said that sustainability reporting would not be necessary as the company was already sustainable because it had no 'going concern' issues. He said that JGP had been in business for over 50 years, should be able to continue for many years to come and was therefore sustainable. As far as he was concerned, this was all that was meant by sustainability.

In the discussion that followed, the board noted that in order to signal its seriousness to the local community and to investors, the environmental audit should be as thorough as possible and that as much information should be made available to the public 'in the interests of transparency'. It was agreed that contents of the audit (the agreed metrics) should be robust and with little room left for interpretation – they wanted to be able to demonstrate that they had complied with their agreed metrics for the environmental audit.

Required

(a) Explain 'sustainability' in the context of environmental auditing and criticise the finance director's understanding of sustainability. **(6 marks)**

(b) Explain the three stages in an environmental audit and explore, using information from the case, the issues that JGP will have in developing these stages. **(9 marks)**

(c) Define 'environmental risk'. Distinguish between strategic and operational risks and explain why the environmental risks at JGP are strategic. **(10 marks)**

(Total = 25 marks)

55 Ann Koo (6/11)

The IFAC code of professional ethics (2009), adopted as being relevant to ACCA members and students, contains the following advice.

'A professional accountant in business or an immediate or close family member may be offered an inducement. Inducements may take various forms, including gifts, hospitality, preferential treatment, and inappropriate appeals to friendship or loyalty. Offers of inducements may create threats to compliance with the fundamental principles [of professionalism].'

Executive director and qualified accountant Ann Koo was in charge of awarding large outsourcing contracts for a large public listed company. When her family fell into debt, she looked for a way to make some additional income. When her company was seeking to place a contract for a large outsourced service, without inviting other tenders from which to select, she accepted a bid from one supplier who said it would pay her $50,000 as a 'thank you' once the contract was awarded. She justified her behaviour by reminding herself that she obtained her job partly because she was an accountant and that she had worked extremely hard to obtain her accounting qualification. She believed she was entitled to make a 'higher personal return' on her investment of time and effort in her accountancy training and through successful qualification as a professional accountant.

Required

(a) Briefly describe the five types of ethical threats in the IFAC code of professional ethics (2009) and discuss how accepting excessive 'gifts' or 'hospitality' can give rise to some of these threats within this case.

(9 marks)

(b) Criticise Ann Koo's beliefs and behaviour, and explain why accepting the $50,000 conflicts with her duty to uphold the public interest. **(10 marks)**

The IFAC code also highlights the need for:

'up-to-date education [for directors] on ethical issues and the legal restrictions and other regulations around potential insider trading.'

Required

(c) Explain what 'insider dealing/trading is and why it is an unethical and often illegal practice. **(6 marks)**

(Total = 25 marks)

56 VCF

90 mins

VCF is a small listed company that designs and installs high technology computer numerical control capital equipment used by multinational manufacturing companies. VCF is located in one Pacific country, but almost 90% of its sales are exported. VCF has sales offices in Europe, Asia, the Pacific, Africa, and North and South America and employs about 300 staff around the world.

VCF has annual sales of $200 million but the sales value of each piece of equipment sold is about $3 million so that sales volume is relatively low. Sales are always invoiced in the currency of the country where the equipment is being installed. The time between the order being taken and the final installation is usually several months. However a deposit is taken when the order is placed and progress payments are made by the customer before shipment and upon delivery, with the final payment being made after installation of the equipment.

The company has international patents covering its technology and invests heavily in research and development (R&D about 15% of sale) and marketing costs to develop export markets (about 25% of sales). VCF's manufacturing operations are completely outsourced in its home country and the cost of sales is about 20%. The balance of costs is for installation, servicing and administration, amounting to about 15% of sales. Within each of the cost classifications the major expenses (other than direct costs) are salaries for staff, all of whom are paid well above the industry average, rental of premises in each location and travel costs. Area managers are located in each sales office and have responsibility for achieving sales, installing equipment and maintaining high levels of after-sales service and customer satisfaction.

Although the head office is very small, most of the R&D staff are located in the home country along with purchasing and logistics staff responsible for liaising with the outsource suppliers and a small accounting team that is primarily concerned with monthly management accounts and end of year financial statements.

VCF has a 40% shareholding held by Jack Viktor, an entrepreneur who admits to taking high risks, both personally and in business. The Board of four is effectively controlled by Viktor who is both Chairman and Chief Executive. The three other directors were appointed by Viktor. They are his wife, who has a marketing role in the business, and two non-executive directors, one an occasional consultant to VCF and the other a long-term family friend. Board meetings are held quarterly and are informal affairs, largely led by Viktor's verbal review of sales activity.

Viktor is a dominating individual who exercises a high degree of personal control often by-passing his area managers. Because the company is controlled by him Viktor is not especially concerned with short-term profits but with the long-term. He emphasises two objectives: sales growth to generate increased market share and cash flow; and investment in R&D to ensure the long-term survival of VCF by maintaining patent protection and a technological lead over its competitors.

Viktor is in daily contact with all his offices by telephone. He travels extensively around the world and has an excellent knowledge of VCF's competitors and customers. He uses a limited number of non-financial performance measures, primarily concerned with sales, market share, quality and customer satisfaction. Through his personal contact and his twin objectives, Viktor encourages a culture committed to growth, continual innovation, and high levels of customer satisfaction. This is reinforced by high salary levels, but Viktor readily dismisses those staff not committed to this objectives.

The company has experienced rapid growth over the last 10 years and is very profitable although cash flow is often tight. A high margin is achieved because VCF is able to charge its customers premium prices. The equipment sold by VCF enables faster production and better quality than its competitors can offer.

Viktor has little time for traditional accounting. Product costing is not seen as valuable because the cost of sales is relatively low and most costs incurred by VCF, particularly R&D and export marketing costs, are incurred a long time in advance of sales being made. R&D costs are not capitalised in VCF's balance sheet.

Although budgets are used for expense control and monthly management accounts are produced, they have little relevance to Viktor who recognises the fluctuations in profit caused by the timing of sales of low volume but high value capital equipment. Viktor sees little value in comparing monthly profit figures against budgets because sales are erratic. However Viktor depends heavily on a spreadsheet to manage VCF's cash flow by using sensitivity analysis against his sales and cash flow projects. Cash flow is a major business driver and is controlled tightly using the spreadsheet model.

The major risks facing VCF have been identified by Viktor as:

- Competitor infringement of patents, which VCF always meets by instituting legal actions
- Adverse movements in the exchange rate between the home country and VCF's export markets, which VCF treats as an acceptable risk given that historically, gains and losses have balanced each other out.
- The reduction in demand for the equipment due to economic reasons
- A failure of continued R&D investment to maintain technological leadership; and
- A failure to control costs.

Viktor considers that the last three of these risks are addressed by his policy of outsourcing manufacture and continuous personal contact with staff, customers and competitors.

When VCF became listed, the board appointed an external non-executive director, a senior partner from a local firm of lawyers. However she only served as a non-executive director for a few months before resigning, as she had reservations about the way the board ran the company and the role of Viktor. In particular she objected to Viktor's references to corporate governance codes as 'irrelevant to real-world business'.

Required

(a) Identify and assess the existing controls within VCF (including those applied by Viktor). **(13 marks)**

(b) Write a report to the Board of VCF recommending improvements to the company's:

  (i) Corporate governance **(6 marks)**

  (ii) Risk management strategy **(6 marks)**

  (iii) Internal controls **(6 marks)**

  Professional marks for structure, clarity, logical flow and layout of the statement. **(4 marks)**

(c) (i) Evaluate the importance of the following underlying principles in the context of the corporate governance of VCF:

    (1) Fairness
    (2) Accountability
    (3) Transparency
    (4) Independence **(12 marks)**

  (ii) Identify the ethical viewpoint that treats implementation of corporate governance recommendations as the best means of maximising the value of VCF. **(3 marks)**

  (Total = 50 marks)

57 Wilberforce Humphries   90 mins

Wilberforce Humphries is a construction company based and listed in a European country that is not an EU member state. The Wilberforce Humphries group structure comprises three divisions operating in different construction business segments and all operating both in the group's home country and other countries in Europe. The three divisions are:

- House building
- Offices construction
- Major construction projects

Wilberforce Humphries has established itself as a builder of high quality housing and apartments. The Wilberforce Humphries group has been able to command premium prices, because of its good designs and quality specifications. However Wilberforce Humphries has seen the type of house building change in the last decade, with a higher percentage of lower priced houses and apartments being built. Wilberforce Humphries has also seen a change in the timing of when customers purchase their houses or apartments; they are making their decisions later in the construction process rather paying a deposit prior to any construction work commencing on the housing unit.

Most of the construction work undertaken by the office building division is specifically commissioned. Its international office building construction work is very small compared to many other international companies. However, it has a substantial market share in the office construction market in its home country, although the volume of new office construction in its home country has fallen in the last five years. With the demands of international competition and the innovative features that Wilberforce Humphries now incorporates into its office buildings as standard, far exceeding legal requirements, margins have decreased from the levels achieved a decade ago.

Work undertaken by the major construction projects has recently included motorways, bridges and a sports stadium. Over the last three years the division has been awarded more contracts than it had undertaken in the previous years. As a result the company has recruited a significant number of new employees into this division and also used sub-contractors to provide more flexibility.

However although Wilberforce Humphries has repeatedly used the same sub-contracting companies, the make-up of the teams used on projects that undertake the work have changed far too often. Despite supervision by the sub-contractors' management, there are large numbers of unskilled workers who are not capable of completing certain stages of construction to the required standard, which causes delays while the faulty work is rectified. Additionally, as sub-contactors are paid a fixed fee for various stages of construction, they want to complete the job in the least possible time. This leads to jobs being rushed and not professionally completed.

Wilberforce Humphries has also had two major accidents over the last year involving the deaths of several construction workers. One accident involved Wilberforce Humphries's own employees, the other subcontractors. The company's response has been to focus training on safety awareness and accident prevention procedures.

Wilberforce Humphries has twelve directors, of whom six are independent non-executive directors. Recruitment of new directors and remuneration of executive directors is decided by the chief executive and chairman; the remuneration of the chief executive is decided by the chairman. The company has an audit committee staffed by the independent non-executive directors, but does not have a separate internal audit function, instead the external auditors are employed to carry out internal audit work on the main areas of concern in the accounts.

Recently as a result of an approach from one of the company's main competitors, the chairman decided that the chief executive and two of the other executive directors should be offered improved basic salary and benefit packages and contracts with two-year notice periods.

Over the last couple of years, the company's personnel director has been pushing the development of a corporate responsibility framework, including enhancing the company's reporting of responsibility issues. The main issues in the most recent report were as follows.

- Organisational framework – establishment of an advisory social responsibility committee that meets quarterly and reports to the main board.

- Health and safety issues – 100% of staff and 90% of contractors inducted in health and safety issues.

- Environment – trained 90% of site management and 60% of subcontractors in environmental issues.

- Employees – results of third employee survey published and action plan to address issues drawn up. Introduced new HR strategy concerning working hours and performance related pay. Increase of 20% in training hours per employee.

For the last few years the government of Wilberforce Humphries's home country has been planning to sell for development a large amount of land in a largely undeveloped area of the country, about 70 kilometres east of the capital city. Media speculation feared that it would become another tourist area and this would not help local companies and local people with their housing needs. The government has launched an initiative to move people out of currently over-crowded cities to better housing elsewhere. The government also wants to attract companies in the IT industries to the area. All office buildings are to be built with the latest high tech equipment.

The government has recently finalised the sale of the land to Wilberforce Humphries. The government has given outline planning permission for Wilberforce Humphries's plans for the entire area, but formal government approval will still be required prior to the start of any specific construction work.

There has been a growing amount of adverse publicity concerning this development. Most of the area's few inhabitants do not like the idea of their isolation being destroyed by new development. Environmental lobbyists are concerned that the area currently has a few endangered species of small wildlife animals, which are dependent on the existing habitat. While every effort has been made to preserve as many trees as possible, to enhance the appeal of the completed development, there will be a need to clear a large area of forest where some of the housing and the commercial office buildings area would be constructed.

Required

(a)   Identify the main strategic and operational risks that Wilberforce Humphries faces in the context of its building operations and advise the board on how a risk management framework can be used to address these risks. **(16 marks)**

(b)   Briefly evaluate the decision to award the directors enhanced employment rewards and advise the board on improvements that should be made to the decision-making process affecting directors' remuneration.
(8 marks)

(including 2 professional marks)

(c)   Evaluate whether an internal audit function staffed by Wilberforce Humphries' own staff would provide more effective assurance than internal audit work carried out by the company's external auditors. **(8 marks)**

(d)   Write a memo to the board recommending how the company's existing corporate responsibility framework can be made more effective. **(10 marks)**

(including 2 professional marks)

(e)   Explain why the company's decision to undertake the new investment can be justified from a utilitarian perspective and discuss the criticisms of adopting this approach. **(8 marks)**

(Total = 50 marks)

58 Partner

90 mins

Jaitinder Sharma is a partner of a large, expanding international firm of accountants. Her firm has recently marketed itself as having specialisms in advising on corporate governance, corporate social responsibility and risk management. Jaitinder has just returned from holiday to find the following correspondence concerning her clients.

A new client of Jaitinder's firm, Stuart Brand, which is a large manufacturer, has recently come bottom of a survey of a number of companies measuring responsiveness to the concerns of stakeholders and society as a whole. The company's share price has fallen as a result and the managing director is therefore very concerned. He wants to know how the company can respond better to stakeholder pressures, and be seen as a more responsible corporate citizen.

Pierre Renoir is a tax client of Jaitinder's firm. He was a member of parliament but lost his seat in the last general election. One of the opportunities he has been offered since is to become an independent non-executive director of Loire Boucher, a company in his former constituency that is about to seek a stock market listing. Although Pierre Renoir has got on well with Loire Boucher's managing director, he has reservations about how well controlled the company is. In response to his concerns the managing director has forwarded him documentation about the control systems being operated. Pierre Renoir would like to know how to judge this information.

The audit of one of Jaitinder's clients, Garmeant 4 You, is imminent. The only audit senior available has had limited experience of the clothing industry in which Garmeant for You operates. Jaitinder wishes to discuss the following issues with the senior in relation to this client:

- In recent years Garmeant 4 You has suffered a number of setbacks and has also seen many of its competitors suffer losses and cease trading. Garmeant 4 You has been able to stay profitable only because of its particular customer base and because it sold high quality clothes that commanded a premium price. However, Garmeant 4 You has seen its margins on many product lines reduced greatly and also it has lost many of its smaller customers, who choose to import, at much lower prices, clothing produced in Asia, particularly China. Many European companies have spent millions of Euros establishing manufacturing bases in countries which have much lower operating costs.

- Over the last few years Garmeant 4 You has increased its loans and its overdraft to finance operations with the result that its gearing is somewhat above the industry average. Two years ago it refinanced with a ten year loan, which was to purchase some new machinery. and to invest in a design centre.

- Three major retailers account for 60% of Garmeant 4 You's sales revenue between them. Most contracts with retailers are renewed at the start of each fashion season. Garmeant 4 You is currently in negotiations with its second most important customer, accounting currently for 18% of sales revenue, which is threatening not to renew its contract next time.

- Garmeant 4 You has had a skilled, very dedicated workforce who have always adapted to new machinery and procedures and have been instrumental in suggesting ways in which quality could be improved. The machinery that is used to sew garments is very sophisticated but it is always the skills of the machine operatives which can make the difference to a finished garment. Additionally, Garmeant 4 You has always completed certain finishing touches by hand and this quality is appreciated by its customers.

- Many of Garmeant 4 You's customers have needed to speed up the process of supplying clothing to their shops for competitive reasons. Garmeant 4 You has aimed to achieve shorter lead times from design to delivery of finished products. The company has recently opened a new design centre, using computer aided design techniques, which has helped its customers to appreciate the finished appearance of new designs. It has also contributed to speeding up the process from design board to finished article. Garmeant 4 You has also benefited from working closer with its customers and this has resulted in additional orders.

Jaitinder has also been contacted by Marie Arcidiacono, the chair of Quintus Inc's audit committee. Marie is concerned that the company's managing director is seeking to have the company delisted in the United States and listed on a European stock exchange that operates a similar code to the UK Corporate Governance Code. Marie is concerned of what the implications might be for Quintus Inc. In writing to Jaitinder Marie knows she is going against the views of Quintus's Managing Director and Marie is therefore also concerned that Jaitinder may be facing a conflict of interest in advising her.

Required

(a) Assess the extent to which stakeholder concerns may impact upon the business strategy of Stuart Brand, and construct a case for enhanced reporting of corporate social responsibility issues by the company.

(9 marks)

(b) Prepare a memo for Jaitinder to send to Pierre Renoir advising him on the criteria he can use to assess the adequacy of Loire Boucher's control systems. **(16 marks)**

(including 4 professional marks)

(c) Provide an analysis for the audit senior or the main business risks faced by Garmeant 4 You. **(12 marks)**

(d) Discuss whether Jaitinder is facing a conflict of interest in advising Marie Arcidiacono and advise Marie Arcidiacono of the implications of changing from the Sarbanes-Oxley regime to the European regime.

(13 marks)

(Total = 50 marks)

59 Integrated Broadcasting Organisation   90 mins

Ben Jackson has recently been appointed as Managing Director of the Integrated Broadcasting Organisation (IBO), the biggest broadcaster in a large European country, Tara. Ben Jackson has previously worked for this company in a senior management role, and was then headhunted to be Chief Executive of one of IBO's main rivals. He has recently been recruited back to IBO, and he will be responsible for dealing with a number of recent controversies that culminated in the early retirement of the previous Managing Director.

IBO runs national television and radio channels, and also broadcasts worldwide through satellite. Its drama and comedy productions enjoy a high international reputation and IBO gains significant income from sales of these productions on DVD and to foreign broadcasters. Its other major sources of income include a levy on sales of radios and televisions, programme sponsorship, donations to benefit specific programming strands such as education and subscription channels dedicated to its old shows and national sporting events. IBO has competitors in Tara in both radio and television broadcasting, that are funded by advertising, digital subscription and other commercial activities. These include the Network Group, which owns a commercial television group as well as

Tara's biggest selling newspaper, the Daily Network. All the major broadcasters are currently investing heavily in new media technologies to command higher subscription uptake. Technology is also developing so that laptops and mobile phones are increasingly being used as TV devices.

IBO is governed by a Management Board consisting of the Managing Director, seven other executive directors and eight trustees.

The eight trustees come from a variety of backgrounds. Liz Shaw is a member of the Council of the Advertising Authority which enforces advertising standards in Tara. Peri Brown is managing director of a large independent production company in IBO's home country that supplies programmes to IBO. Jamie McCrimmon is a member of the Upper House of Tara's legislature who represents the governing party. Ian Chesterton is chair of Tara's Arts Council. Harry Sullivan is a non-executive director of the Network Group. Steven Taylor is on the board of Tara's Integrated Transport Authority. Victoria Waterfield is on the executive committee of the Civic Values Trust, which sponsors a number of IBO's education programmes. Zoe Herriot is a well-known economist and Vice-Chair of Tara's Arts authority.

The board's remuneration committee is staffed solely by trustees. The other board committees (Appointments, Audit, Finance, Strategy and Editorial Standards) are staffed 50:50 by trustees and Executive Directors

Ben Jackson has reservations about these arrangements and wishes to introduce a model of corporate governance that is based on internationally accepted guidance such as the UK Corporate Governance Code.

IBO is currently planning a major drama production, an adaptation of the classic romantic novel *Life and Love in Landra*. IBO is expecting large home country audiences, and heavy sales on DVD and to other international broadcasters. The Landran government has offered IBO very generous terms to film in the country, believing that the production will generate employment opportunities and indirect benefits through increased tourism. The production's authenticity will also be aided by being filmed in Landra, since there are a number of very detailed descriptions of the country in the novel and these are relevant to its plot.

However plans to film in Landra have caused concern in IBO's own country. International observers have reported that there was mass vote rigging in the most recent presidential elections. The country's former leader of the opposition is currently in jail on corruption charges that are widely believed to be without foundation, whereas strong evidence has been produced about corrupt activities of the ruling party and indeed the president himself. International pressure groups and politicians in IBO's home country who are sympathetic to the opposition party have been calling for an international boycott of Landra. Recently a major European bank closed all its operations in the country and withdrew its staff.

IBO has recently also suffered heavy criticism in connection with its popular reality television show *The Toughest Trek*. The show puts members of the public, supposedly selected through a rigorous but fair audition process, through a series of demanding tests and apparently films them reacting spontaneously. However leaks to the press from the production office's files have revealed that some applicants have been rejected without audition because they are 'too old or too ugly'. Instead some of the participants in the programme have been actors and actresses, chosen for their good looks. In addition some of the dialogue in the programme has been scripted in order to increase viewer tension.

An internal inquiry into the programme has revealed that the production team did not breach such specific guidelines to programme-makers that are in place. However the main emphasis in IBO has been always been on complying with the organisation's ethical code based on the principles in the organisation's founding charter, the 'three Is' of Integrity, Intelligence and Independence. Media critics have however suggested that the three Is that apply to the IBO are Inanity, Illusion and Immorality.

Required

(a) Analyse the strategic risks faced by IBO and explain the role that the Management Board should take in managing those risks. **(15 marks)**

(b) Prepare a memo advising Ben Jackson of shortcomings in the current governance arrangements and recommending improvements. **(13 marks)**

(including 4 professional marks)

(c)   (i)   Assess the decision on whether to go ahead with filming the production in Landra from Kohlberg's conventional and post-conventional perspectives. **(5 marks)**

    (ii)   Construct a case for going ahead from the utilitarian perspective of ethics and criticise a decision to go ahead from the deontological perspective. **(8 marks)**

(d)   Criticise the approach to ethics currently taken by IBO's ethical code and recommend improvements that should be made to the ethical guidance that IBO provides. **(9 marks)**

(Total = 50 marks)

60 Chemco (Pilot paper)   90 mins

Chemco is a well-established listed European chemical company involved in research into, and the production of, a range of chemicals used in industries such as agrochemicals, oil and gas, paint, plastics and building materials. A strategic priority recognised by the Chemco board some time ago was to increase its international presence as a means of gaining international market share and servicing its increasingly geographically dispersed customer base. The Chemco board, which operated as a unitary structure, identified JPX as a possible acquisition target because of its good product 'fit' with Chemco and the fact that its geographical coverage would significantly strengthen Chemco's internationalisation strategy. Based outside Europe in a region of growth in the chemical industry, JPX was seen by analysts as a good opportunity for Chemco, especially as JPX's recent flotation had provided potential access to a controlling shareholding through the regional stock market where JPX operated.

When the board of Chemco met to discuss the proposed acquisition of JPX, a number of issues were tabled for discussion. Bill White, Chemco's chief executive, had overseen the research process that had identified JPX as a potential acquisition target. He was driving the process and wanted the Chemco board of directors to approve the next move, which was to begin the valuation process with a view to making an offer to JPX's shareholders. Bill said that the strategic benefits of this acquisition was in increasing overseas market share and gaining economies of scale.

While Chemco was a public company, JPX had been family owned and operated for most of its thirty-five year history. Seventy-five percent of the share capital was floated on its own country's stock exchange two years ago, but Leena Sharif, Chemco's company secretary, suggested that the corporate governance requirements in JPX's country were not as rigorous as in many parts of the world. She also suggested that the family business culture was still present in JPX and pointed out that it operated a two-tier board with members of the family on the upper tier. At the last annual general meeting, observers noticed that the JPX board, mainly consisting of family members, had 'dominated discussions' and had discouraged the expression of views from the company's external shareholders. JPX had no non-executive directors and none of the board committee structure that many listed companies like Chemco had in place. Bill reported that although JPX's department heads were all directors, they were not invited to attend board meetings when strategy and management monitoring issues were being discussed. They were, he said, treated more like middle management by the upper tier of the JPX board and that important views may not be being heard when devising strategy. Leena suggested that these features made the JPX board's upper tier less externally accountable and less likely to take advice when making decisions. She said that board accountability was fundamental to public trust and that JPX's board might do well to recognise this, especially if the acquisition were to go ahead.

Chemco's finance director, Susan Brown, advised caution over the whole acquisition proposal. She saw the proposal as being very risky. In addition to the uncertainties over exposure to foreign markets, she believed that Chemco would also have difficulties with integrating JPX into the Chemco culture and structure. While Chemco was fully compliant with corporate governance best practice, the country in which JPX was based had few corporate governance requirements. Manprit Randhawa, Chemco's operations director, asked Bill if he knew anything about JPX's risk exposure. Manprit suggested that the acquisition of JPX might expose Chemco to a number of risks that could not only affect the success of the proposed acquisition but also, potentially, Chemco itself. Bill replied that he would look at the risks in more detail if the Chemco board agreed to take the proposal forward to its next stage.

Finance director Susan Brown had obtained the most recent annual report for JPX and highlighted what she considered to be an interesting, but unexplained, comment about 'negative local environmental impact' in its accounts. She asked chief executive Bill White if he could find out what the comment meant and whether JPX had any plans to make provision for any environmental impact. Bill White was able to report, based on his previous dealings with JPX, that it did not produce any voluntary environmental reporting. The Chemco board broadly supported the idea of environmental reporting although company secretary Leena Sharif recently told Bill White that she was unaware of the meaning of the terms 'environmental footprint' and 'environmental reporting' and so couldn't say whether she was supportive or not. It was agreed, however, that relevant information on JPX's environmental performance and risk would be necessary if the acquisition went ahead.

Required

(a) Evaluate JPX's current corporate governance arrangements and explain why they are likely to be considered inadequate by the Chemco board. **(10 marks)**

(b) Manprit suggested that the acquisition of JPX might expose Chemco to a number of risks. Illustrating from the case as required, identify the risks that Chemco might incur in acquiring JPX and explain how risk can be assessed. **(15 marks)**

(c) Construct the case for JPX adopting a unitary board structure after the proposed acquisition. Your answer should include an explanation of the advantages of unitary boards and a convincing case FOR the JPX board changing to a unitary structure. **(10 marks)**
(including 2 professional marks)

(d) Explain FOUR roles of non-executive directors (NEDs) and assess the specific contributions that NEDs could make to improve the governance of the JPX board. **(7 marks)**

(e) Write a memo to Leena Sharif defining 'environmental footprint' and briefly explaining the importance of environmental reporting for JPX. **(8 marks)**
(including 2 professional marks)

(Total = 50 marks)

61 Worldwide Minerals (12/07) 90 mins

The board of Worldwide Minerals (WM) was meeting for the last monthly meeting before the publication of the year-end results. There were two points of discussion on the agenda. First was the discussion of the year-end results; second was the crucial latest minerals reserves report.

WM is a large listed multinational company that deals with natural minerals that are extracted from the ground, processed and sold to a wide range of industrial and construction companies. In order to maintain a consistent supply of minerals into its principal markets, an essential part of WM's business strategy is the seeking out of new sources and the measurement of known reserves. Investment analysts have often pointed out that WM's value rests principally upon the accuracy of its reserve reports, as these are the best indicators of future cash flows and earnings. In order to support this key part of its strategy, WM has a large and well-funded geological survey department which, according to the company website, contains 'some of the world's best geologists and minerals scientists'. In its investor relations literature, the company claims that:

'our experts search the earth for mineral reserves and once located, they are carefully measured so that the company can always report on known reserves. This knowledge underpins market confidence and keeps our customers supplied with the inventory they need. You can trust our reserve reports – our reputation depends on it!'

At the board meeting, the head of the geological survey department, Ranjana Tyler, reported that there was a problem with the latest report because one of the major reserve figures had recently been found to be wrong. The mineral in question, mallerite, was WM's largest mineral in volume terms and Ranjana explained that the mallerite reserves in a deep mine in a certain part of the world had been significantly overestimated. She explained that, based on the interim minerals report, the stock market analysts were expecting WM to announce known mallerite reserves of 4·8 billion tonnes. The actual figure was closer to 2·4 billion tonnes. It was agreed that this difference was sufficient to affect WM's market value, despite the otherwise good results for the past year. Vanda Monroe, the finance director, said that the share price reflects market confidence in future earnings. She said that an announcement of an incorrect estimation like that for mallerite would cause a reduction in share value. More importantly for WM itself, however, it could undermine confidence in the geological survey department. All agreed that as this was strategically important for the company, it was a top priority to deal with this problem.

Ranjana explained how the situation had arisen. The major mallerite mine was in a country new to WM's operations. The WM engineer at the mine said it was difficult to deal with some local people because, according to the engineer, 'they didn't like to give us bad news'. The engineer explained that when the mine was found to be smaller than originally thought, he was not told until it was too late to reduce the price paid for the mine. This was embarrassing and it was agreed that it would affect market confidence in WM if it were made public.

The board discussed the options open to it. The chairman, who was also a qualified accountant, was Tim Blake. He began by expressing serious concern about the overestimation and then invited the board to express views freely. Gary Howells, the operations director, said that because disclosing the error to the market would be so damaging, it might be best to keep it a secret and hope that new reserves can be found in the near future that will make up for the shortfall. He said that it was unlikely that this concealment would be found out as shareholders trusted WM and they had many years of good investor relations to draw on. Vanda Monroe, the finance director, reminded the board that the company was bound to certain standards of truthfulness and transparency by its stock market listing. She pointed out that they were constrained by codes of governance and ethics by the stock market and that colleagues should be aware that WM would be in technical breach of these if the incorrect estimation was concealed from investors. Finally, Martin Chan, the human resources director, said that the error should be disclosed to the investors because he would not want to be deceived if he were an outside investor in the company. He argued that whatever the governance codes said and whatever the cost in terms of reputation and market value, WM should admit its error and cope with whatever consequences arose. The WM board contains three non-executive directors and their views were also invited.

At the preliminary results presentation some time later, one analyst, Christina Gonzales, who had become aware of the mallerite problem, asked about internal audit and control systems, and whether they were adequate in such a reserve-sensitive industry. WM's chairman, Tim Blake, said that he intended to write a letter to all investors and analysts in the light of the mallerite problem which he hoped would address some of the issues that Miss Gonzales had raised.

Required

(a) Define 'transparency' and evaluate its importance as an underlying principle in corporate governance and in relevant and reliable financial reporting. Your answer should refer to the case as appropriate.   **(10 marks)**

(b) Explain Kohlberg's three levels of moral development and identify the levels of moral development demonstrated by the contributions of Gary Howells, Vanda Monroe and Martin Chan.   **(12 marks)**

(c) Critically discuss FOUR principal roles of non-executive directors and explain the potential tensions between these roles that WM's non-executive directors may experience in advising on the disclosure of the overestimation of the mallerite reserve.   **(12 marks)**

(d) Draft a letter for Tim Blake to send to WM's investors to include the following:

   (i)   why you believe robust internal controls to be important; and
   (ii) proposals on how internal systems might be improved in the light of the overestimation of mallerite at WM.

Note: four professional marks are available within the marks allocated to requirement (d) for the structure, content, style and layout of the letter.   **(16 marks)**

(Total = 50 marks)

62 Rowlands and Medeleev (6/08)   90 mins

Rowlands & Medeleev (R&M), a major listed European civil engineering company, was successful in its bid to become principal (lead) contractor to build the Giant Dam Project in an East Asian country. The board of R&M prided itself in observing the highest standards of corporate governance. R&M's client, the government of the East Asian country, had taken into account several factors in appointing the principal contractor including each bidder's track record in large civil engineering projects, the value of the bid and a statement, required from each bidder, on how it would deal with the 'sensitive issues' and publicity that might arise as a result of the project.

The Giant Dam Project was seen as vital to the East Asian country's economic development as it would provide a large amount of hydroelectric power. This was seen as a 'clean energy' driver of future economic growth. The government was keen to point out that because hydroelectric power did not involve the burning of fossil fuels, the power would be environmentally clean and would contribute to the East Asian country's ability to meet its internationally agreed carbon emission targets. This, in turn, would contribute to the reduction of greenhouse gases in the environment. Critics, such as the environmental pressure group 'Stop-the-dam', however, argued that the project was far too large and the cost to the local environment would be unacceptable. Stop-the-dam was highly organised and, according to press reports in Europe, was capable of disrupting progress on the dam by measures such as creating 'human barriers' to the site and hiding people in tunnels who would have to be physically removed before proceeding. A spokesman for Stop-the-dam said it would definitely be attempting to resist the Giant Dam Project when construction started.

The project was intended to dam one of the region's largest rivers, thus creating a massive lake behind it. The lake would, the critics claimed, not only displace an estimated 100,000 people from their homes, but would also flood productive farmland and destroy several rare plant and animal habitats. A number of important archaeological sites would also be lost. The largest community to be relocated was the indigenous First Nation people who had lived on and farmed the land for an estimated thousand years. A spokesman for the First Nation community said that the 'true price' of hydroelectric power was 'misery and cruelty'. A press report said that whilst the First Nation would be unlikely to disrupt the building of the dam, it was highly likely that they would protest and also attempt to mobilise opinion in other parts of the world against the Giant Dam Project.

The board of R&M was fully aware of the controversy when it submitted its tender to build the dam. The finance director, Sally Grignard, had insisted on putting an amount into the tender for the management of 'local risks'. Sally was also responsible for the financing of the project for R&M. Although the client was expected to release money in several 'interim payments' as the various parts of the project were completed to strict time deadlines, she anticipated a number of working capital challenges for R&M, especially near the beginning where a number of early stage costs would need to be incurred. There would, she explained, also be financing issues in managing the cash flows to R&M's many subcontractors. Although the major banks financed the client through a lending syndicate, R&M's usual bank said it was wary of lending directly to R&M for the Giant Dam Project because of the potential negative publicity that might result. Another bank said it would provide R&M with its early stage working capital needs on the understanding that its involvement in financing R&M to undertake the Giant Dam Project was not disclosed. A press statement from Stop-the-dam said that it would do all it could to discover R&M's financial lenders and publicly expose them. Sally told the R&M board that some debt financing would be essential until the first interim payments from the client became available.

When it was announced that R&M had won the contract to build the Giant Dam Project, some of its institutional shareholders contacted Richard Markovnikoff, the chairman. They wanted reassurance that the company had fully taken the environmental issues and other risks into account. One fund manager asked if Mr Markovnikoff could explain the sustainability implications of the project to assess whether R&M shares were still suitable for his environmentally sensitive clients. Mr Markovnikoff said, through the company's investor relations department, that he intended to give a statement at the next annual general meeting (AGM) that he hoped would address these environmental concerns. He would also, he said, make a statement on the importance of confidentiality in the financing of the early stage working capital needs.

Any large project such as the Giant Dam Project has a number of stakeholders.

Required

(a) (i) Define the terms 'stakeholder' and 'stakeholder claim', and identify from the case FOUR of R&M's external stakeholders as it carries out the Giant Dam Project; **(6 marks)**

     (ii) Describe the claim of each of the four identified stakeholders. **(4 marks)**

(b) Describe a framework to assess the risks to the progress of the Giant Dam Project. Your answer should include a diagram to represent the framework. **(6 marks)**

(c) Using information from the case, assess THREE risks to the Giant Dam Project. **(9 marks)**

(d) Prepare the statement for Mr Markovnikoff to read out at the AGM. The statement you construct should contain the following.

    (i)   A definition and brief explanation of 'sustainable development'. **(3 marks)**

    (ii)   An evaluation of the environmental and sustainability implications of the Giant Dam Project.

    (8 marks)

    (iii)   A statement on the importance of confidentiality in the financing of the early stage working capital needs and an explanation of how this conflicts with the duty of transparency in matters of corporate governance. **(6 marks)**

    Professional marks for layout, logical flow and persuasiveness of the statement. **(4 marks)**

Internal controls are very important in a complex civil engineering project such as the Giant Dam Project.

Required

(e) Describe the difficulties of maintaining sound internal controls in the Giant Dam Project created by working through sub-contractors. **(4 marks)**

(Total = 50 marks)

63 Swan Hill (12/08)   90 mins

The scientists in the research laboratories of Swan Hill Company (SHC, a public listed company) recently made a very important discovery about the process that manufactured its major product. The scientific director, Dr Sonja Rainbow, informed the board that the breakthrough was called the 'sink method'. She explained that the sink method would enable SHC to produce its major product at a lower unit cost and in much higher volumes than the current process. It would also produce lower unit environmental emissions and would substantially improve product quality compared to its current process and indeed compared to all of the other competitors in the industry.

SHC currently has 30% of the global market with its nearest competitor having 25% and the other twelve producers sharing the remainder. The company, based in the town of Swan Hill, has a paternalistic management approach and has always valued its relationship with the local community. Its website says that SHC has always sought to maximise the benefit to the workforce and community in all of its business decisions and feels a great sense of loyalty to the Swan Hill locality which is where it started in 1900 and has been based ever since.

As the board considered the implications of the discovery of the sink method, chief executive Nelson Cobar asked whether Sonja Rainbow was certain that SHC was the only company in the industry that had made the discovery and she said that she was. She also said that she was certain that the competitors were 'some years' behind SHC in their research.

It quickly became clear that the discovery of the sink method was so important and far reaching that it had the potential to give SHC an unassailable competitive advantage in its industry. Chief executive Nelson Cobar told board colleagues that they should clearly understand that the discovery had the potential to put all of SHC's competitors out of business and make SHC the single global supplier. He said that as the board considered the options, members should bear in mind the seriousness of the implications upon the rest of the industry.

Mr Cobar said there were two strategic options. Option one was to press ahead with the huge investment of new plant necessary to introduce the sink method into the factory whilst, as far as possible, keeping the nature of the sink technology secret from competitors (the 'secrecy option'). A patent disclosing the nature of the technology would not be filed so as to keep the technology secret within SHC. Option two was to file a patent and then offer the use of the discovery to competitors under a licensing arrangement where SHC would receive substantial royalties for the twenty-year legal lifetime of the patent (the 'licensing option'). This would also involve new investment but at a slower pace in line with competitors. The licence contract would, Mr Cobar explained, include an 'improvement sharing' requirement where licensees would be required to inform SHC of any improvements discovered that made the sink method more efficient or effective.

The sales director, Edwin Kiama, argued strongly in favour of the secrecy option. He said that the board owed it to SHC's shareholders to take the option that would maximise shareholder value. He argued that business strategy was all about gaining competitive advantage and this was a chance to do exactly that. Accordingly, he argued, the sink method should not be licensed to competitors and should be pursued as fast as possible. The operations director said that to gain the full benefits of the sink method with either option would require a complete refitting of the factory and the largest capital investment that SHC had ever undertaken.

The financial director, Sean Nyngan, advised the board that pressing ahead with investment under the secrecy option was not without risks. First, he said, he would have to finance the investment, probably initially through debt, and second, there were risks associated with any large investment. He also informed the board that the licensing option would, over many years, involve the inflow of 'massive' funds in royalty payments from competitors using the SHC's patented sink method. By pursuing the licensing option, Sean Nyngan said that they could retain their market leadership in the short term without incurring risk, whilst increasing their industry dominance in the future through careful investment of the royalty payments.

The non-executive chairman, Alison Manilla, said that she was looking at the issue from an ethical perspective. She asked whether SHC had the right, even if it had the ability, to put competitors out of business.

Required

(a)   Assess the secrecy option using Tucker's model for decision-making.   **(10 marks)**

(b)   Distinguish between strategic and operational risks, and explain why the secrecy option would be a source of strategic risk.   **(10 marks)**

Mr Cobar, the chief executive of SHC, has decided to draft two alternative statements to explain both possible outcomes of the secrecy/licensing decision to shareholders. Once the board has decided which one to pursue, the relevant draft will be included in a voluntary section of the next corporate annual report.

Required

(c)   (i)   Draft a statement in the event that the board chooses the secrecy option. It should make a convincing business case and put forward ethical arguments for the secrecy option. The ethical arguments should be made from the stockholder (or pristine capitalist) perspective.   **(8 marks)**

        (ii)   Draft a statement in the event that the board chooses the licensing option. It should make a convincing business case and put forward ethical arguments for the licensing option. The ethical arguments should be made from the wider stakeholder perspective.   **(8 marks)**

        (iii)   Professional marks for the persuasiveness and logical flow of arguments: two marks per statement.
                                                                                                        (4 marks)

Corporate annual reports contain both mandatory and voluntary disclosures.

Required

(d)   (i)   Distinguish, using examples, between mandatory and voluntary disclosures in the annual reports of public listed companies.   **(6 marks)**

        (ii)   Explain why the disclosure of voluntary information in annual reports can enhance the company's accountability to equity investors.   **(4 marks)**

                                                                                                 (Total = 50 marks)

64 Global-bank (6/09)   90 mins

Global-bank is a prominent European bank with branches throughout Europe and investment arms in many locations throughout the world. It is regarded as one of the world's major international banks. Through its network of investment offices throughout the world, fund managers trade in local investment markets and equities. Futures and derivative traders also operate. Its primary listing is in London although it is also listed in most of the other global stock markets including New York, Hong Kong, Frankfurt and Singapore. As with similar banks in its position, Global-bank's structure is complicated and the complexity of its operations makes the strategic management of the company a demanding and highly technical process. Up until the autumn of 20X8, investors had a high degree of confidence in the Global-bank board as it had delivered healthy profits for many years.

In the autumn of 20X8, it came to light that Jack Mineta, a Global-bank derivatives trader in the large city office in Philos, had made a very large loss dealing in derivatives over a three-month period. It emerged that the losses arose from Mr Mineta's practice of ignoring the company trading rules which placed limits on, and also restricted, the type of financial instruments and derivatives that could be traded.

The loss, estimated to be approximately US$7 billion, was described by one analyst as 'a huge amount of money and enough to threaten the survival of the whole company'. As soon as the loss was uncovered, Mr Mineta was suspended from his job and the police were called in to check for evidence of fraud. The newspapers quickly reported the story, referring to Mr Mineta as a 'rogue trader' and asking how so much money could be lost without the bank's senior management being aware of it. It turned out that Mr Mineta's line manager at the Philos office had ignored the trading rules in the past in pursuit of higher profits through more risky transactions. Mr Mineta had considerably exceeded his trading limit and this had resulted in the huge loss. It later emerged that Mr Mineta had been dealing in unauthorised products which were one of the riskiest forms of derivatives.

At a press conference after Mr Mineta's arrest, Global-bank's chief executive, Mrs Barbara Keefer, said that her first priority would be to ask the Philos office why the normal internal controls had not been effective in monitoring Mr Mineta's activities. It emerged that Mr Mineta had in the past been one of Global-bank's most profitable derivatives traders. Some journalists suggested to Mrs Keefer that the company was happy to ignore normal trading rules when Mr Mineta was making profits because it suited them to do so.

Another derivatives trader in the Philos office, Emma Hubu, spoke to the media informally. She said that Mr Mineta was brilliant and highly motivated but that he often said that he didn't care about the trading rules. Miss Hubu explained that Mr Mineta didn't believe in right and wrong and once told her that 'I'm in this job for what I can get for myself – big risks bring big returns and big bonuses for me.' She also explained that the culture of the Philos office was driven by Mr Mineta's line manager, Juan Evora. She said that Mr Evora knew that Mr Mineta was breaking trading rules but was also very profits driven and kept compliance information from head office so that the nature of Mr Mineta's trading was not uncovered. The compliance information was required by head office but several failures to return the information had not been acted upon by head office. Mr Evora's bonus was directly linked to the size of the Philos office's profits and all of the derivatives traders, including Mr Mineta, were regularly reminded about the importance of taking risks to make big returns. Miss Hubu said that trading rules were not enforced and that head office never got involved in what went on in Philos as long as the annual profits from the Philos derivative traders were at or above expectations.

It emerged that the lack of correct information from Philos and elsewhere meant that Global-bank's annual report statement of internal control effectiveness was not accurate and gave an unduly favourable impression of the company's internal controls. In addition, the company's audit committee had been recently criticised by the external auditors for a lack of thoroughness. Also, the audit committee had recently lost two non-executive members that had not been replaced.

The amount lost by Mr Mineta made it necessary to refinance the Global-bank business and when the board recommended a US$5 billion rights issue, some of the institutional investors demanded an extraordinary general meeting (EGM). Global-bank's largest single shareholder, the Shalala Pension Fund, that held 12% of the shares, was furious about the losses and wanted an explanation from Mrs Keefer on why internal controls were so ineffective. When the Shalala trustees met after the losses had been reported, it was decided to write an urgent letter to Mrs Keefer expressing the trustees' disappointment at her role in the internal control failures at Global-bank. The letter would be signed by Millau Haber, the chairman of the Shalala trustees.

At the EGM, Mrs Keefer made a statement on behalf of the Global-bank board. In it she said that Mineta had been a rogue trader who had wilfully disregarded the company's internal controls and was, in breaking the company's trading rules, criminally responsible for the theft of company assets. She denied that the main Global-bank board had any responsibility for the loss and said that it was a 'genuinely unforeseeable' situation.

Kohlberg's theory of the development of moral reasoning contains three levels, with each level containing two stages or 'planes'. It is a useful framework for understanding the ways in which people think about ethical issues.

(a) (i)   Explain the three levels of Kohlberg's theory.   **(6 marks)**

     (ii) Identify the level that Mr Mineta operated at and justify your choice using evidence from the case.
                                                                                                                 (4 marks)

     (iii) Identify, with reasons, the stage (or 'plane') of Kohlberg's moral development most appropriate for a
           professional bank employee such as Mr Mineta as he undertakes his trading duties.   **(2 marks)**

(b) Explain FIVE typical causes of internal control failure and assess the internal control performance of Global-
     bank in the case scenario.   **(10 marks)**

(c) Analyse the agency relationship that exists between the board of Global-bank and the trustees of the Shalala
     Pension Fund.   **(4 marks)**

(d) Distinguish between narrow and wide stakeholders and identify three narrow stakeholders in Global-bank
     (based on Evan & Freeman's definition) from information in the case. Assess the potential impact of the
     events described on each narrow stakeholder identified.   **(10 marks)**

(e) You have been asked to draft a letter from Millau Haber, chairman of the Shalala trustees, to Mrs Keefer as a
     result of concerns over the events described in the case. The letter should explain the roles and
     responsibilities of the chief executive in internal control, and criticise Mrs Keefer's performance in that role.
                                                                                                             (10 marks)

     Professional marks are available in part (e) for the structure, content, style and layout of the letter. **(4 marks)**

                                                                                                      (Total = 50 marks)

65 Mary Jane (12/09)   **90 mins**

The Mary Jane was a large passenger and vehicle ferry operating between the two major ports of Eastport and
Northport across a busy section of ocean known as the 'Northport route'. Prior to this, the Mary Jane had operated
for many years in the much calmer waters of the 'Southsea route' but she had been transferred to the Northport
route because her large size meant that more profit could be made by carrying more passengers and vehicles per
journey. She was capable of carrying up to 1,000 passengers, 300 cars and 100 lorries per trip. The Mary Jane
belonged to Sea Ships Company, a long established international company with a fleet of five ships operating on
routes in other parts of the world. The Mary Jane had large doors at both the front and rear. Vehicles would drive in
through the rear doors in Eastport and when she arrived in Northport, the Mary Jane would dock the other way
round so that the vehicles could drive straight out using the forward doors. There were two doors at each end,
upper and lower, and it was important that all four doors were securely closed before setting out to sea.

As with all marine operations, the safety procedures aboard the Mary Jane were subject to regulation, but her
design left one weakness which was eventually to prove a disaster. From the main control bridge of the ship, it was
not possible to see the front or rear doors, which meant that it wasn't possible to check from the main control
bridge that they were closed upon departure from a port. On the night of 7 November, the Mary Jane was leaving
Eastport in a storm for a crossing to Northport, a journey which should have taken five hours. It was dark and the
weather was very poor. When she was only a few kilometres out from the Eastport harbour, water entered the car
decks through the upper rear doors that had been left open after the Mary Jane had left port. The stormy conditions
meant that the waves were very high and on this occasion, high enough so that when a large wave hit, the water
entered through the open rear doors. Once enough water had entered her car decks, the Mary Jane began to lean to
30 degrees before completely falling over onto her side. The speed of the event, less than two minutes, meant that
escape via lifeboats wasn't possible and the Mary Jane sank with the loss of many lives.

Among the survivors was first officer Ned Prop. Mr Prop later told how a recent change to staff reporting
procedures had produced a situation in which the responsibility for checking that the rear doors were closed before
sailing had changed. He said that, under the new system, two people were responsible for safety on the car deck
but each person assumed that the other had checked that the upper rear doors had been closed. A reporting system
in which each department head (car deck, navigation, etc.) on the ship separately reported readiness for sea to the
captain at the beginning of each journey had been abandoned because it was too inconvenient to operate. Mr Prop
said that the normal procedure was that if they didn't hear anything to the contrary by the departure time, he and
Captain Mullet assumed that all was well throughout the ship and they could put to sea.

Mr Prop told how procedures on board ship often relied on 'human teamwork' rather than 'following paperwork systems'. It also emerged that, on the day of the disaster, a mistake in loading vehicles onto the wrong decks had delayed the ship's departure and created pressure to leave as soon as possible after all the vehicles were loaded. Mr Prop said that this too may have been a contributory factor to the confusion over who should have checked that the rear doors were closed. Mr Prop's superior officer, Captain Mullet, was drowned in the disaster. Sea Ships Company, the Mary Jane's owner, was one of the longest established and most respected companies listed on the stock exchange. Although best known for its ferry operations, it had diversified into other activities in recent years. It was considered by investment analysts to be a 'steady and reliable' investment and the company chief executive, Wim Bock, had often said that Sea Ships Company employed 'the highest standards of corporate ethics'. It also valued its reputation as a well-run company and believed that the company's value was primarily due to its reputation for 'outstanding customer care'. The board often claimed that Sea Ships was a socially responsible company.

When Sea Ships' board met to discuss how to proceed after the disaster, Wim Bock said that the company could expect to receive substantial claims from victims' relatives. He also reported that, because of a regrettable oversight in the company's legal department, only a proportion of that liability would be covered by the company's insurance. There would also be punitive fines from the courts, the size of which would, a legal adviser said, reflect the scale of Sea Ships' negligence in contributing to the disaster. The finance director, Jill Wha, reported that if the company met the expected uninsured liabilities in full, even if reduced on appeal, it would severely threaten future cash flows as it would most likely have to sell non-current assets (most of its ships) to settle the claims. If large punitive fines were also imposed after the legal process, Mr Bock said that the company may not survive.

The government ordered an enquiry and a senior official was appointed to investigate the disaster. In her conclusions, enquiry chairman Caroline Chan said that in addition to the human error in not ensuring that the upper rear doors had been closed, it had also emerged that the Mary Jane had been travelling above the local shipping speed limit out of Eastport harbour. The excess speed had caused increased turbulence in the water and this was made much worse by the storm on the night in question. The combination of these factors meant that water gradually entered the open upper rear doors and this eventually caused the ship to lean and then capsize. Mrs Chan said that contrary to the board's perception of itself as a well-run company, she had encountered a 'culture of carelessness' at Sea Ships and that the internal control systems were inadequate for safely operating a fleet of ships. She reserved particular criticism for the board of Sea Ships saying that it was unbalanced, lacked independent scrutiny and, because none of the existing directors had ever served on board a ship, lacked representation from technically qualified nautical officers.

After the enquiry was concluded, but before the level of claims and punitive damages had been set by the courts, a document emerged within the company confirming that certain independent advice had been received from an external consultant. The advice was received at the time of the Mary Jane's transfer from the Southsea route to the Northport route. Because the Northport route is a much rougher area of sea, the advice concerned structural changes to the Mary Jane that would make her safer in rougher seas. Had the advice been followed, the Mary Jane would have had additional doors inserted inside the car deck to act as a second internal bulkhead to prevent water flooding the whole deck. Water would still have entered through the open rear doors on the night of 7 November, but would have been kept sealed in that rear section of the car deck and the Mary Jane would not have sunk. The company had received the advice but had not acted upon it as it would have required an expensive refit for the Mary Jane. This advice was then 'lost' in the company and only emerged later on.

The independent consultant's advice was that the Mary Jane should have received structural work to make her safe for operating in the rougher seas of the Northport route. Sea Ships Company did not act on the advice.

Required

(a) Using the seven-step American Accounting Association (AAA) model for ethical decision-making, examine the company's dilemma on whether or not to disclose this information publicly. **(14 marks)**

(b) Using information from the case, identify and analyse the internal control failures at Sea Ships Company and on the Mary Jane. **(12 marks)**

(c) Assess the contribution that non-executive directors might have made in improving the corporate governance at Sea Ships Company. **(8 marks)**

(d) Draft a memo from chief executive Wim Bock to the senior officers on the other ships in the Sea Ships fleet informing them of vital internal control and risk issues following the loss of the Mary Jane. The memo should include the following, all placed in the context of the case.

(i) An assessment, based on information in the case, of the importance for the board of Sea Ships to have all the information relating to key operational internal controls and risks. **(6 marks)**

(ii) An explanation of the qualitative characteristics of information needed by the Sea Ships' board for the assessment of internal controls and risks. **(6 marks)**

Professional marks will additionally be awarded in part (d) for drafting a memo that is clear, has a logical flow, is persuasive and is appropriately structured. **(4 marks)**

(Total = 50 marks)

66 Hesket Nuclear (6/10)   90 mins

Hesket Nuclear (HN) is a nuclear power station in Ayland, a large European country. The HN plant is operated by Hesket Power Company (HPC), which in turn is wholly owned by the government of Ayland. Initially opened in the late 1950s, the power station grew in subsequent decades by the addition of several other facilities on the same site. HN now has the ability to generate 5% of Ayland's entire electricity demand and is one of the largest nuclear stations in Europe. At each stage of its development from the 1950s to the present day, development on the site was welcomed by the relevant local government authorities, by the businesses that have supported it, by the trade union that represents the majority of employees (called Forward Together or FT for short) and also by the national Ayland government. A nuclear reprocessing facility was added in the 1980s. This is a valuable source of overseas income as nuclear power producers in many other parts of the world send material by sea to HN to be reprocessed. This includes nuclear producers in several developing countries that rely on the cheaper reprocessed fuel (compared to 'virgin' fuel) that HN produces.

HPC is loss-making and receives a substantial subsidy each year from the government of Ayland. HPC has proven itself uneconomic but is deemed politically and environmentally necessary as far as the government is concerned. The government of Ayland has reluctantly accepted that large subsidies to HPC will be necessary for many years but considers nuclear power to be a vital component of its energy portfolio (along with other energy sources such as oil, gas, coal, renewables and hydroelectric) and also as a key part of its 'clean' energy strategy. Unlike energy from fossil fuels (such as coal, gas and oil), nuclear power generates a negligible amount of polluting greenhouse gas. HN also provides much needed employment in an otherwise deprived part of the country. The HN power station underpins and dominates the economy of its local area and local government authorities say that the HN plant is vital to the regional economy.

Since it opened, however, the HN power station has been controversial. Whilst being welcomed by those who benefit from it in terms of jobs, trade, reprocessing capacity and energy, a coalition has gradually built up against it comprising those sceptical about the safety and environmental impact of nuclear power. Some neighbouring countries believe themselves to be vulnerable to radioactive contamination from the HN plant. In particular, two countries, both of whom say their concerns about HN arise because of their geographical positions, are vocal opponents. They say that their geographical proximity forced them to be concerned as they are affected by the location of the HN plant which was not of their choosing.

The government of Beeland, whose capital city is 70 km across the sea from HN (which is situated on the coast), has consistently opposed HN and has frequently asked the government of Ayland to close HN down. The Beeland government claims that not only does 'low-level' emission from the site already contaminate the waters separating the two countries but it also claims that any future major nuclear 'incident' would have serious implications for the citizens of Beeland. There is some scientific support for this view although opinion is divided over whether Beeland is being irrational in its general opposition to HN.

The government of Ceeland is also a vocal opponent of HN. Ceeland is located to the north of Beeland and approximately 500 km away from Ayland. Some nuclear scientists have said that with such a large stretch of water between the HN plant and Ceeland, even a much-feared incident would be unlikely to seriously impact on Ceeland. Some commentators have gone further and said that Ceeland's concerns are unfounded and 'borne of ignorance'. FT, the trade union for HN employees, issued a statement saying that Ceeland had no reason to fear HN and that its fears were 'entirely groundless'.

HN's other vocal and persistent opponent is No Nuclear Now (NNN), a well-organised and well-funded campaigning group. Describing itself on its website as 'passionate about the environment', it describes HN's social and environmental footprint as 'very negative'. NNN has often pointed to an environmentally important colony of rare seals living near the HN plant. It says that the seals are dependent on a local natural ecosystem around the plant and are unable to move, arguing that the animals are at significant risk from low-level contamination and would have 'no chance' of survival if a more serious radioactive leak ever occurred. NNN points to such a leak that occurred in the 1970s, saying that such a leak proves that HN has a poor safety record and that a leak could easily recur.

Each time an objection to the HN power station is raised, FT, the trade union, robustly defends the HN site in the media, and argues for further investment, based on the need to protect the jobs at the site. Furthermore, the radiation leak in the 1970s led to FT uniting with the HPC board to argue against those stakeholders that wanted to use the leak as a reason to close the HN site. The combination of union and HPC management was able to counter the arguments of those asking for closure.

HN places a great deal of emphasis on its risk management and often publicises the fact that it conducts continual risk assessments and is in full compliance with all relevant regulatory frameworks. Similarly, FT recently pointed out that HN has had an 'impeccable' safety record since the incident in the 1970s and says on its website that it is 'proud' that its members are involved in ensuring that the company is continually in full compliance with all of the regulatory requirements placed upon it.

The board of HPC, led by chairman Paul Gog, is under continual pressure from the government of Ayland to minimise the amount of government subsidy. Each year, the government places challenging targets on the HPC board requiring stringent cost controls at the HN power station. In seeking to reduce maintenance costs on the expiry of a prior maintenance contract last year, the board awarded the new contract to an overseas company that brought its own workers in from abroad rather than employing local people. The previous contract company was outraged to have lost the contract and the move also triggered an angry response from the local workforce and from FT, the representative trade union.

FT said that it was deplorable that HPC had awarded the contract to an overseas company when a domestic company in Ayland could have been awarded the work. The union convenor, Kate Allujah, said that especially in the nuclear industry where safety was so important, domestic workers were 'more reliable' than foreign workers who were brought in purely on the basis of cost and in whose countries safety standards in similar industries might not be so stringent. HPC said that it had done nothing illegal as the foreign workers were allowed to work in Ayland under international legal treaties. Furthermore, it argued that pressure by FT to raise wages over recent years had created, with the government's subsidy targets, the cost pressure to re-tender the maintenance contract.

On HN's 50th anniversary last year, NNN published what it called a 'risk assessment' for the HN power station. It said it had calculated the probabilities (P) and impacts (I) of three prominent risks.

Risk of major radioactive leak over the next 10 years: P = 10%, I = 20
Risk of nuclear explosion over the next 50 years: P = 20%, I = 100
Risk of major terrorist attack over next 10 years: P = 10%, I = 80

Impacts were on an arbitrary scale of 1–100 where 100 was defined by NNN as 'total nuclear annihilation of the area and thousands of deaths'.

The governments of Beeland and Ceeland seized upon the report, saying that it proved that HN is a genuine threat to their security and should be immediately closed and decommissioned. HN's risk manager, Keith Wan, vigorously disagreed with this assessment saying that the probabilities and the impacts were 'ridiculous', massively overstated and intended to unnecessarily alarm people. HN's public relations office was also angry about it and said it would issue a rebuttal statement.

Required

(a)   Distinguish between voluntary and involuntary stakeholders, identifying both types of stakeholders in Hesket Nuclear. Assess the claims of THREE of the involuntary 'affected' stakeholders identified.   **(12 marks)**

The trade union, Forward Together, has had a long relationship with HN and represents not only the main workforce but also the employees of the maintenance company replaced by the foreign workers.

Required

(b)   Explain the roles of employee representatives such as trade unions in corporate governance and critically evaluate, from the perspective of HPC's board, the contribution of Forward Together in the governance of HPC. **(10 marks)**

(c)   Explain what an agency relationship is and examine the board of HPC's current agency relationship and objectives. Briefly explain how these would differ if HPC was a company with private shareholders. **(10 marks)**

As a part of HPC's public relations effort, it has been proposed that a response statement should be prepared for the company's website to help address two major challenges to their reputation.

Required

(d)   Draft this statement to include the following:

  (i)   Referring to the NNN report, explain why accurate risk assessment is necessary at Hesket Nuclear. **(8 marks)**

  (ii)   Explain what a social and environmental 'footprint' is and construct the argument that HN's overall social and environmental footprint is positive. **(6 marks)**

  Professional marks will additionally be awarded in part (d) for drafting a statement that is clear, has a logical flow, is persuasive and is appropriately structured. **(4 marks)**

(Total = 50 marks)

67 ZPT (12/10)   90 mins

In the 2009 results presentation to analysts, the chief executive of ZPT, a global internet communications company, announced an excellent set of results to the waiting audience. Chief executive Clive Xu announced that, compared to 2008, sales had increased by 50%, profits by 100% and total assets by 80%. The dividend was to be doubled from the previous year. He also announced that based on their outstanding performance, the executive directors would be paid large bonuses in line with their contracts. His own bonus as chief executive would be $20 million. When one of the analysts asked if the bonus was excessive, Mr Xu reminded the audience that the share price had risen 45% over the course of the year because of his efforts in skilfully guiding the company. He said that he expected the share price to rise further on the results announcement, which it duly did. Because the results exceeded market expectation, the share price rose another 25% to $52.

Three months later, Clive Xu called a press conference to announce a restatement of the 2009 results. This was necessary, he said, because of some 'regrettable accounting errors'. This followed a meeting between ZPT and the legal authorities who were investigating a possible fraud at ZPT. He disclosed that in fact the figures for 2009 were increases of 10% for sales, 20% for profits and 15% for total assets which were all significantly below market expectations. The proposed dividend would now only be a modest 10% more than last year. He said that he expected a market reaction to the restatement but hoped that it would only be a short-term effect.

The first questioner from the audience asked why the auditors had not spotted and corrected the fundamental accounting errors and the second questioner asked whether such a disparity between initial and restated results was due to fraud rather than 'accounting errors'. When a journalist asked Clive Xu if he intended to pay back the $20 million bonus that had been based on the previous results, Mr Xu said he did not. The share price fell dramatically upon the restatement announcement and, because ZPT was such a large company, it made headlines in the business pages in many countries.

Later that month, the company announced that following an internal investigation, there would be further restatements, all dramatically downwards, for the years 2006 and 2007. This caused another mass selling of ZPT shares resulting in a final share value the following day of $1. This represented a loss of shareholder value of $12 billion from the peak share price. Clive Xu resigned and the government regulator for business ordered an investigation into what had happened at ZPT. The shares were suspended by the stock exchange. A month later, having failed to gain protection from its creditors in the courts, ZPT was declared bankrupt. Nothing was paid out to shareholders whilst suppliers received a fraction of the amounts due to them. Some non-current assets were acquired by competitors but all of ZPT's 54,000 employees lost their jobs, mostly with little or no termination payment. Because the ZPT employees' pension fund was not protected from creditors, the value of that was also severely reduced to pay debts which meant that employees with many years of service would have a greatly reduced pension to rely on in old age.

The government investigation found that ZPT had been maintaining false accounting records for several years. This was done by developing an overly-complicated company structure that contained a network of international branches and a business model that was difficult to understand. Whereas ZPT had begun as a simple telecommunications company, Clive Xu had increased the complexity of the company so that he could 'hide' losses and mis-report profits. In the company's reporting, he also substantially overestimated the value of future customer supply contracts. The investigation also found a number of significant internal control deficiencies including no effective management oversight of the external reporting process and a disregard of the relevant accounting standards.

In addition to Mr Xu, several other directors were complicit in the activities although Shazia Lo, a senior qualified accountant working for the financial director, had been unhappy about the situation for some time. She had approached the finance director with her concerns but having failed to get the answers she felt she needed, had threatened to tell the press that future customer supply contract values had been intentionally and materially overstated (the change in fair value would have had a profit impact). When her threat came to the attention of the board, she was intimidated in the hope that she would keep quiet. She finally accepted a large personal bonus in exchange for her silence in late 2008.

The investigation later found that Shazia Lo had been continually instructed, against her judgement, to report figures she knew to be grossly optimistic. When she was offered the large personal bonus in exchange for her silence, she accepted it because she needed the money to meet several expenses related to her mother who was suffering a long-term illness and for whom no state health care was available. The money was used to pay for a lifesaving operation for her mother and also to rehouse her in a more healthy environment. Shazia Lo made no personal financial gain from the bonus at all (the money was all used to help her mother) but her behaviour was widely reported and criticised in the press after the collapse of the company.

The investigation found that the auditor, JJC partnership (one of the largest in the country), had had its independence compromised by a large audit fee but also through receiving consultancy income from ZPT worth several times the audit fee. Because ZPT was such an important client for JJC, it had many resources and jobs entirely committed to the ZPT account. JJC had, it was found, knowingly signed off inaccurate accounts in order to protect the management of ZPT and their own senior partners engaged with the ZPT account. After the investigation, JJC's other clients gradually changed auditor, not wanting to be seen to have any connection with JJC. Accordingly, JJC's audit business has since closed down. This caused significant disturbance and upheaval in the audit industry.

Because ZPT was regarded for many years as a high performing company in a growing market, many institutional investors had increased the number of ZPT shares in their investment portfolios. When the share price lost its value, it meant that the overall value of their funds was reduced and some individual shareholders demanded to know why the institutional investors had not intervened sooner to either find out what was really going on in ZPT or divest ZPT shares. Some were especially angry that even after the first restatement was announced, the institutional investors did not make any attempt to intervene. One small investor said he wanted to see more 'shareholder activism', especially among the large institutional investors.

Some time later, Mr Xu argued that one of the reasons for the development of the complex ZPT business model was that it was thought to be necessary to manage the many risks that ZPT faced in its complex and turbulent business environment. He said that a multiplicity of overseas offices was necessary to address exchange rate risks, a belief challenged by some observers who said it was just to enable the ZPT board to make their internal controls and risk management less transparent.

Required

Because of their large shareholdings, institutional investors are sometimes able to intervene directly in the companies they hold shares in.

(a) (i)   Explain the factors that might lead institutional investors to attempt to intervene directly in the management of a company. **(6 marks)**

     (ii) Construct the case for institutional investors attempting to intervene in ZPT after the first results restatement was announced. **(6 marks)**

(b) Distinguish between absolutist and relativist approaches to ethics and critically evaluate the behaviour of Shazia Lo (the accountant who accepted a bonus for her silence) using both of these ethical perspectives.

(10 marks)

The ZPT case came to the attention of Robert Nie, a senior national legislator in the country where ZPT had its head office. The country did not have any statutory corporate governance legislation and Mr Nie was furious at the ZPT situation because many of his voters had been badly financially affected by it. He believed that legislation was needed to ensure that a similar situation could not happen again. Mr Nie intends to make a brief speech in the national legislative assembly outlining the case for his proposed legislation and some of its proposed provisions.

Required

Draft sections of the speech to cover the following areas:

(c) (i) Explain the importance of sound corporate governance by assessing the consequences of the corporate governance failures at ZPT.   **(10 marks)**

(ii) Construct the case for the mandatory external reporting of internal financial controls and risks.

(8 marks)

(iii) Explain the broad areas that the proposed external report on internal controls should include, drawing on the case content as appropriate.   **(6 marks)**

Professional marks will be awarded in part (c) for the structure, flow, persuasiveness and tone of the answer.   **(4 marks)**

(Total = 50 marks)

68 Bobo (6/11)   90 mins

The Bobo car company decided to launch a new model of car to compete in the highly competitive 'economy' market. Although Bobo was a long-established and profitable car manufacturer with a wide range of vehicles in other markets (such as family cars, four-wheel drives, etc), it had not entered the economy market because it believed profit margins would be too low. Company research showed that this was the car market segment with the smallest unit profits. The appointment of James Tsakos as chief executive changed that, however, as he believed that Bobo should offer a model in every category of car. It was announced that the new economy car, when launched, would be called the 'Bobo Foo'. The key concepts in the new model were conveyed to the design team led by executive director and head of design, Kathy Yao: cheap to buy, economical to run, cheap to repair, easy to park, fun to drive.

At the outset, James Tsakos met to discuss the new model with Kathy Yao. Because it was to enter the economy market, the minimisation of unit costs would be absolutely paramount. Mr Tsakos had some posters printed to hang in the design offices that read: 'The Bobo Foo – keep it cheap!' They were all signed personally by Mr Tsakos to emphasise the message to the design team as they were designing the car.

As well as repeating the 'Keep it cheap' message as often as possible, Mr Tsakos also instructed Kathy Yao that rather than the usual 43 months it took to develop a new model of car 'from the drawing board to the road', he wanted the Bobo Foo ready in 25 months. This, again, was about saving on costs to increase the eventual unit profits once the Bobo Foo was on sale. The design team was placed under a lot of pressure by Mr Tsakos, and Kathy Yao became stressed with the demand to complete the project in such a short time period. She privately told colleagues that the period was too short to ensure that all design features were safety tested. (This case took place before rigid safety regulations were imposed by governments so legal issues can be ignored.)

Kathy Yao's team worked out that one way of reducing manufacturing costs would be to position the car's fuel tank slightly differently from usual. She calculated that a small amount could be saved on producing each unit of production if the fuel tank was placed behind the rear axle rather that on top of the axle as was the normal practice. Along with other cost saving measures, this was incorporated into the finished prototype. In order to shorten the time to market, the factory started to be prepared for production of the Bobo Foo (called 'tooling up') as soon as the completed design was available but before the prototype was fully tested.

When the prototype Bobo Foo went through a range of crash tests, the positioning of the fuel tank was shown to be a potential fire risk in the event of a rear collision. No action was taken in the light of this observation because, as part of the low-cost strategy for the Bobo Foo, the factory had already been tooled up and was ready to begin production. The board decided that it would have been too expensive to retool the production line to a modified design and so it went into production as it was.

The Bobo Foo quickly became a big seller and sold half a million units of the model a year, making it appear that the Bobo Foo was another successful product for the Bobo Company. Some time later, however, a lorry crashed into the back of a Bobo Foo containing three young women. Upon impact, the fuel tank was ruptured causing a fire in which all three passengers in the car were killed. The company then began to receive other claims from lawyers acting for people killed or injured by fires started by several rear-end collisions and fuel tank damage. Bobo accepted legal advice to pay compensation for each injury or loss of life caused by the fuel tank design fault.

The board then met to discuss the options for the Bobo Foo. Kathy Yao said her team had worked out that the cars could be made safe by adding some reinforcing metalwork around the tank area. Vernon Vim, the finance director, said that there were two options in the light of what Kathy had said. First was the 'universal recall' option. The company could recall, at its own expense, all Bobo Foos to make the modifications suggested by Kathy Yao and retool the production line to ensure safe positioning of the fuel tank on all future cars. The second option, the 'compensation option', was not to recall the existing cars nor to make changes to the production line but to continue to pay full compensation to victims or their families if, or when, a serious or fatal liability arose as a result of fuel tank damage from rear collisions.

Vernon Vim produced some calculations to illustrate the dilemma. They showed that, assuming that the Bobo Foo will be produced for ten years, the universal recall option would amount to $750 million over those ten years whilst the compensation option was likely to amount to approximately $200 million in total.

Vernon Vim said that even allowing for substantial errors in the calculation, there was still at least a three-fold difference in cost between the two options. Because the board's bonuses were partly based on the company's annual profits, he said that the board should simply continue to pay compensation claims and not issue the universal recall. He reminded the board that the difference between the two options was half a billion dollars over ten years.

Kathy Yao said that the company should consider the universal recall option and think about retooling the production line to ensure the safe repositioning of the fuel tank on future production. It was important, she believed, for customers to know they could trust Bobo cars for their safety and that customers associated the brand with social responsibility. She said this was an important part of the company's strategic positioning and that the company should comply with the expectations that society has of a large company like Bobo.

Chief executive James Tsakos was concerned about complying with the expectations of shareholders and with how events might affect the company's share price and longer term prospects. The company's reputation as a strong investment was very important and any long-term damage to the brand would be very unfortunate. He said that issuing a universal recall would send out a terrible signal to the financial markets and would damage confidence.

After a lengthy and heated discussion of the two options, it was decided that the 'compensation option' would be adopted. This was for financial reasons and it was decided that any discussion of the decision in public should be avoided because of the potential risk to reputation that may arise.

An unknown member of the board, outraged by the decision, informed the media about the choice the board had made and about the design process that led to the Bobo Foo (thereby acting as a 'whistleblower'). With a great deal of resulting negative publicity for Bobo on TV, radio and in the press, the institutional shareholders demanded an extraordinary general meeting to discuss the relevant issues with the board. In particular, the shareholders wanted to hear the chief executive explain why the board took the decision it did. In particular, they wanted to hold James Tsakos accountable for the decision: to establish how he understood his role as chief executive and how he arrived at the decision not to issue a universal recall on the Bobo Foo.

Required

(a) The fuel tank risk with the Bobo Foo was subsequently classified by an insurance company as a product and a safety risk.

Explore the circumstances leading to the fuel tank problem. Identify and explain internal control measures capable of mitigating the risk in future car development projects.

Note: Ignore any possible legal or regulatory issues that may arise. **(12 marks)**

(b) Explain Kohlberg's three levels of moral development and identify, with reasons, the levels of development exhibited by James Tsakos, Kathy Yao and Vernon Vim. **(12 marks)**

(c) Distinguish between annual general meetings (AGMs) and extraordinary general meetings (EGMs). Explain the purpose of each and the advantages of holding an EGM to discuss the issues raised by the whistleblower. **(8 marks)**

(d) Prepare a statement for Mr Tsakos, the chief executive, to read at the EGM to address the following areas.

(i) An explanation of the roles of the chief executive in managing the issues described in the case at Bobo Company; **(8 marks)**

(ii) A defence of the company's decisions on the Bobo Foo from a 'pristine capitalist' ethical perspective (using Gray, Owen & Adams's framework). **(6 marks)**

Professional marks will additionally be awarded in part (d) for drafting a statement that is clear, has a logical flow, is persuasive and is appropriately structured. **(4 marks)**

(Total = 50 marks)

Answers

Note

These answers have been written by BPP and are based on Study Text content that the examiner has reviewed.

1 Remuneration

(a) **The two non-executive directors constitute the remuneration committee**

Membership of remuneration committee

The recommendations fulfil the requirement in many governance reports that the **remuneration committee** should consist **wholly of non-executive directors**. The main purpose of the committee should be to recommend the remuneration of executive directors. Having the committee staffed by non-executive directors means that executive directors do **not decide their own remuneration**.

Numbers of non-executive directors

Most reports also recommend that the board should include a **significant number of non-executive directors** in order that their views should carry sufficient weight. The UK Corporate Governance Code for example recommends that at least half the board should be non-executive directors. It may be that the board of this company is small, and non-executive directors are two out of four, although for a listed company this is unlikely.

Reliance on directors

The UK Corporate Governance Code also identifies the issue of not placing **undue reliance on certain directors**. It is possible that the company will be relying too much on its non-executive directors if there are only two of them, as they will be required to attend board meetings, carry out various duties as full board members and staff various board committees. If they have limited time available because of commitments elsewhere, they may not be able to pay sufficient attention to all their duties. For this reason the **minimum number of non-executive directors** that the Cadbury report recommended was **three**.

Personal financial interests

Independence

The UK Corporate Governance Code stresses that a key role of non-executive directors is to bring an independent judgement to the board's decision-making. Hence most or all **non-executive directors should be independent** of the company; this means that apart from their shareholdings and fees as directors, they should have no financial interests. This includes **participation in the company's share option or performance-related pay scheme**, or being a member of the company's pension scheme.

The company seems to have reasonable guidelines in place to ensure independence.

Cross-directorships

The UK Corporate Governance Code also states that **non-executive directors should not have cross-directorships with executive directors**. This means that executive directors of Company A should not be non-executive directors of Company B if non-executive directors of Company A are executive directors of Company B. Cross-directorships could result in agreements to set each others' remuneration at a higher level than what is considered desirable.

Again the provisions in place should guarantee that cross-directorships are not a problem.

Chairman's service contract

Problems of lengthy service contracts

This statement highlights the potential problem a remuneration committee faces when determining the length of a service contract. A **long service contract** may help retain a key member of the management team. However a long notice period means that there are **financial disincentives to remove the director** – the compensation for loss of office is likely to be high. This may in practice mean that a **fundamental shareholder right**, to remove a director, is **undermined**.

Limiting service contracts

The UK Corporate Governance Code recommends that **service contracts** should normally be for **one year**, although a longer period may be acceptable if the director has been appointed from outside, on **initial appointment**. Exceptional circumstances may have existed when the chairman was given his original contract but would not apply long-term, and hence his service contract should now be for a shorter period.

(b) **Salary**

The basic salary of £516,000 is substantial, suggesting that the Chief Executive is a **highly-paid and highly sought-after director** able to effectively and profitably steer a large public company. Although not directly performance related, his salary can be expected to increase in line with the fortunes of the company. Its size has probably affected his decision to stay with the company.

As the chief executive's employment contract will determine his salary, shareholders are likely to have been concerned when he was first appointed with the rigour of the appointment process, did the nomination committee appoint someone who appeared to be worth that sort of money. They will also be worried about how strict the **conditions** are in the contract for a future uplift in salary, and, if an uplift is granted, the **evidence** that the conditions have been fulfilled.

Bonus

The size of bonus is more under the control of the Chief Executive since it is **related to the performance of the company** (which is, after all, his primary concern). The maximum bonus of 25% of salary is considerable (a possible £129,000 based on last year's salary). There are no specific criteria for its achievement, however. It is based on the Remuneration Committee's assessment. This may mean that the level of the bonus is **susceptible to company politics**, which **may reduce its motivational effect**.

Since it is based on annual performance, shareholders may be concerned that the bonus **encourages a short-term view**, but that will depend on how the Remuneration Committee carry out their brief.

Employee profit-sharing scheme

Although this is linked to the performance of the company, the £8,000 maximum payment means that it is **insignificant** in comparison to the rest of the package, so is unlikely to worry shareholders. If the Chief Executive performs adequately this payment is almost certain to be made.

Other benefits, including pension contribution

As with the salary, these are **substantial** (particularly the £85,000 pension contribution). It is unlikely that these are performance related and so will have **limited motivational effect**. For this reason they will concern shareholders, and shareholders will also be worried about the control exercised over the benefits given, especially if they increase significantly in the future. The £21,000 other benefits may not be a major concern at present.

Conditional allocations of shares

At an initial value of 50% of salary, these shares could represent a **significant part** of the package and thus have a **large motivational impact**. Such an incentive is **good from the shareholders' point of view** since not only is it directly related to shareholder return but the three-year time scale discourages short-term thinking.

An **area of concern for the Chief Executive** may be the **volatility of share values**. If the stock market falls, his shares' value may be diminished even if the company's relative performance is good. Alternatively, the group could perform well in its market sector but if the sector has not performed well in relation to the FT-SE 100, the bonus could be reduced (even to nothing).

Share options

These could also be very **lucrative** and so provide a **strong motivational force**. Their **value is dependent on the state of the stock market**, however, which is **out of the Chief Executive's control**. A **sliding scale** such as that used with the share allocations would **have a better motivational impact** than an 'all or nothing' target.

From the shareholder point of view, this is a **sensible form of remuneration** for the Chief Executive as the focus is on shareholder return over three years. Whether the target of above average FT-SE 100 performance is fair depends on the company. If it is an average FT-SE company the Chief Executive will consider the target reasonable. Shareholders may consider that an above average performance is needed, however.

Overall effect of the total package

The motivational effect of the package is linked to how easily the Chief Executive can control the internal and external environment of the group and therefore its fortunes. There is a relatively large fixed element to the package. Although the Chief Executive may not feel the need to increase his earnings beyond this fixed level, his personal ambitions should be considered. **People are usually motivated by success itself** as well as the financial rewards that accompany it. This may alleviate shareholder concerns about the size of the fixed element.

Both the share schemes are potentially very valuable to the Chief Executive and are **linked to long-term success**. Shareholders may consider this an appropriate financial motivator for the group to use since they are directly related to shareholder return.

2 Nerium Engineering

(a) (i) **Role and responsibilities**

Monitoring accounts

One of the main roles of the audit committee is to **monitor the integrity of the financial statements** of the company. This will mean that the audit committee should **review the significant financial reporting issues and judgements** made in connection with the preparation of the financial statements that are prepared by the company. The audit committee should also **review the clarity and completeness of disclosures** in the financial statements.

Review of control systems

The audit committee should **review the company's internal financial control system** and, unless addressed by a separate risk committee or by the board itself, **risk management systems**. The audit committee should **assess the scope and effectiveness of the systems** established by management to identify, assess, manage and monitor financial and non financial risks.

Whistleblowing arrangements

The audit committee should **review arrangements** by which staff of the company may, in confidence, raise concerns (whistleblow) about possible improprieties in matters of financial reporting, financial control or any other matters.

Monitoring internal audit

The audit committee also has responsibilities for the **internal audit** function and should monitor and **review the effectiveness of the company's internal audit function**. If there is no internal audit function, the audit committee should consider whether there is a need for one each year and make recommendations to the board.

Maintaining relations with external auditors

In general terms the audit committee is responsible for overseeing the company's **relations with the external auditor**. The audit committee has primary responsibility for making recommendations on the **appointment, reappointment and removal** of the external auditors. The audit committee should assess the **qualification, expertise, resources, effectiveness and independence** of the external auditors annually. The audit committee should approve the **terms of engagement and the remuneration** to be paid to the external auditor. The audit committee should also **recommend to the board the policy** in relation to the provision of **non-audit services** by the external auditor, to ensure that the provision of such services does not impair the external auditor's independence or objectivity.

(ii)   **Knowledge of company and its environment**

All new audit committee members should be given an **induction programme** and all members should receive **training** on an ongoing basis.

Independence

Corporate governance reports such as the UK Corporate Governance Code require all members of the audit committee to be **independent non-executive directors**. Independence means having no financial or other connection with the company other than receiving directors' fees and possibly owning shares. The UK Corporate Governance Code suggests that non-executive directors may not be independent if during the last three years they have had a material business relationship with the company, so this suggests Ken may not be considered independent

Financial experience

Ken does not need to have an accountancy qualification to serve on an audit committee. Governance reports require that at least **one** member of the audit committee should have significant, recent and relevant **financial experience**, for example as an auditor or finance director of a listed company. Ideally this person should have a relevant **professional qualification**.

Financial literacy

However given the role and responsibilities of the audit committee, governance reports suggest there is a need for some degree of **financial literacy** amongst the other members of the audit committee. This will vary according to the nature of the company. Ken's experience as Managing Director should mean he has sufficient knowledge to fulfil this requirement, although this may be more of a problem if Nerium is involved in significant specialist treasury activities.

Overview of business

Individual members of the audit committee should have an **overview of the company's business** and be able to identify the main business and financial dynamics and risks. Clearly Ken would have the requisite knowledge as Managing Director of an engineering company.

(b)   **Performance measures**

A performance measure should follow a number of basic principles.

Link with strategy

The measure should be **clearly linked** to the **strategic goals** of the company.

Individual performance

A performance measure for an individual should, as far as possible, **reflect the contribution** of that individual to achieving the performance.

Interests of shareholders

The performance measure should be **identifiable with the interests of shareholders** and the wider stakeholder community.

Flexibility

The measure should **require the minimum of adjustment** to ensure consistency in the light of any strategic and operational changes that occur.

Difficult to distort

The measure should not be able to be manipulated easily, nor should there be **incentive or opportunity** to manipulate it. Possibly manipulation is less likely if the performance measure is one of a number of different **qualitative and quantitative, financial and non-financial measures**, a sort of **balanced scorecard.**

(c) **Types of measure**

Measures for monitoring the performance of a company, and individuals, can be grouped into three categories, market-based measures, earnings-based measures and internal performance measures.

(i) **Earnings-based measures of performance**

These measures were used when Nerium was an unlisted company, but may still be appropriate now it is listed. They are based on indications of returns earned, such as EPS, growth in EPS and return on investment. These measures are linked to external shareholder interests, the key financial objective of maximising **profit and company value**. They provide a definite indicator of what has happened, and it is easy for external shareholders to view trends.

Drawbacks of measures

Although widely used in incentive packages, earnings-based measures have several weaknesses. They are **short-term measures of profit,** and ignore the longer term, ie what an individual has achieved that will affect future results rather than historical results. Accounting profit can be **prone to manipulation**, unlike share price movements and dividend payments. A further criticism is that an earnings-based measure **ignores risk:** if a company increases profits by investing in high-risk projects, profits might go up but shareholder value could fall.

(ii) **Market-based measures of performance**

These are based on the **movement in the market price of the company's shares** over a given time period. An advantage of this method of performance measure is that it is **aligned closely** to the **creation of shareholder value**, which is generally assumed to be the prime objective of a company. A widely-used market-based measure is **Total Shareholder Return** (TSR) which is a measure of the return earned by shareholders over a given period, in terms of dividends received and movements in the share price. The return is expressed as a percentage of the share price at the start of the period.

Drawbacks of measures

A drawback to market-based measures is that share price movements **fluctuate continually with supply and demand**, and the prices that are used to measure the rise or fall in the share price over a period might not be properly representative of their true market worth. A further limitation of market-based measures is that although they can measure company performance, they **cannot identify which individuals contributed** to the achievement of the return.

(iii) **Internal performance measures**

These are measures of performance derived from **internal reporting systems**, but that are of significance to shareholders. Internal measures can be both **financial and non-financial**. Financial measures include cash flow return on investment or shareholder value added. Non-financial measures can relate to any key performance objective, such as customer satisfaction (however measured) or the creation of intellectual capital. With the growth in the use of the balanced scorecard approach to setting performance targets, it seems likely that many incentive schemes will be based on internal measures.

Drawbacks of measures

The main problems with internal measures include the difficulty of **benchmarking certain performance indicators** against what is achieved in other companies. Other companies may not publish the data required, particularly as regards non-financial measures. In addition when a number of different measures is used, it can be difficult to **assess the relative importance** of each.

3 Mega Mart

(a) **Agency problem**

Rex Lord has been using MegaMart plc as a vehicle to **pursue his own ends**, thus depriving the shareholders and other stakeholders of their legitimate expectations. There appears to be a serious **agency problem** within the company with the shareholders (the principals) being unable to exercise control over Rex Lord, their agent/manager. Rex has been maximising his personal rewards, and appears also to have been pursuing his own objective of growth (and hence personal glory) rather than profit and share price maximisation.

(b) **Contraventions of corporate governance best practice**

In order to do this he has contravened several well-established **rules of corporate governance** that are incorporated in, for example, the London Stock Exchange UK Corporate Governance Code.

(i) **Directors**

Leading management roles

There are **two leading management roles:** running the Board and running the company. There should be a clear division of responsibilities so that there is a balance of power and no single person has unfettered powers of decision-making. Rex Lord's clear **exploitation of his power** illustrates why this is a good rule. The board cannot make a Chief Executive truly accountable for management if it is itself led by the Chief Executive. A further reason for splitting the job is that **the two roles of Chairman and Chief Executive** are **demanding roles**, and it is difficult for the same person to have the time or ability to do both jobs well.

Non-executive directors (NEDs)

Governance reports state that there should be a **strong and independent body of NEDs** with a recognised senior member other than the Chairman. The UK Corporate Governance Code states that at least half the board should be **independent NEDs** This is to ensure that their views carry sufficient weight and that power and information is not concentrated in the hands of one or two individuals. MegaMart does not have the non-executive presence to provide this assurance.

(ii) **Remuneration**

Remuneration committee

Governance reports acknowledge that remuneration levels should be **enough to attract directors of sufficient calibre**, but companies should not pay more than is necessary. Directors should not be involved in setting their own remuneration. A **remuneration committee**, staffed by independent NEDs, should determine specific remuneration packages. Quite clearly, MegaMart has failed to conform with these requirements as far as Rex Lord's remuneration is concerned, with the result that there appears to have been no adequate scrutiny of his complex and possibly excessive remuneration arrangements.

(iii)   **Accountability and audit**

Familiarity

There are two significant threats to the **independence of the auditors** that should be reviewed both by them and by MegaMart's audit committee (which should be made up of NEDs). The first is that having been in post for 20 years, there is a danger that the auditors have become **complacent and even acquiescent** in their relationship with Rex Lord. In any event, governance codes suggest that the partner in charge of the audit should change after a maximum of five years.

Self-interest

The second threat is associated with the **provision of services other than audit**. There is a risk that the auditors effectively act in a management role, doing things that should be reserved to the directors and managers of the company. The Sarbanes-Oxley legislation prohibits auditors providing **appraisal or valuation services**, or **management functions**.

(iv)   **Relations with shareholders**

Communication with institutional shareholders

Rex Lord appears to have failed to abide by the guidance that companies should **communicate directly with institutional shareholders** and use the AGM as a constructive means of communication with **private investors**. The Hermes Principles, for example, state that companies should seek an honest, open and ongoing dialogue with shareholders. They should clearly **communicate the plans** that they are pursuing and the likely **financial and wider consequences of those plans**.

(v)   **Compliance with the UK Corporate Governance Code**

As a quoted company, MegaMart should include in its financial statements a **narrative report of how it applied the principles** of the UK Corporate Governance Code and a statement as to whether it **complied with its specific provisions**. We are not told whether or not this was done. There is also a danger that the board may regard disclosure of non-compliance as by itself an acceptable alternative to compliance. Non-compliance is only justified if there are good reasons, and these should be disclosed in the accounts.

(c)   **Position of NEDs**

As discussed above, quoted companies such as MegaMart should have an influential and numerically significant body of NEDs. As already mentioned, these directors should form both the **audit and remuneration committees**. All members of the remuneration committee and a majority of the audit committee should be independent NEDs.

Contribution of NEDs

Strategic experience of business

NEDs should bring to their role **wide experience of business** and possibly of organisations in other spheres. This should enable them to give **good strategic advice** to the board as a whole and to individual directors, possibly in a mentoring role. They should also be prepared to **challenge the strategic decisions** of the executive directors. The recent performance of MegaMart suggests that strategy should have been more robustly discussed than it seems to have been.

Scrutiny

NEDs should **scrutinise the performance of executive management** in meeting goals and objectives. This would be particularly important for MegaMart given recent poor performance linked with the high rewards given to Rex Lord. In their role as members of the audit committee, they should also **scrutinise the performance of the auditors** and question whether there are conflicts of interest.

Risk management

Non-executive directors should satisfy themselves that **financial information** is **accurate** and that **financial controls and systems of risk management are robust**. Given MegaMart's acquisition of smaller retail groups, the group's risk management systems should have evolved to meet changing demands, and NEDs would need to monitor whether this was happening.

Ethical problems

NEDs should be alert for the emergence of problems with an **ethical dimension** or issues of **corporate social responsibility**. Independent NEDs, in particular, should be able to act as a kind of **conscience** for the board as a whole. Strong NEDs may have raised questions over issues such as **premature disclosure of information**; NEDs on the audit committee might have taken the responsibility to investigate the insider dealing allegations.

Advice on appointments

NEDs may have a valuable role to play in the **selection and appointment of new board members**. They should be alert for issues such as board succession and bringing in directors with external experience, which appear to have been neglected at MegaMart.

4 Stakeholders

Text reference. Chapter 1.

Top tips. Starting (a) with a definition of stakeholders is good technique. The primary/secondary and active/passive methods of classification link in with Mendelow's matrix in (b).

(c) starts with a statement of what appears to be the minister's view and then discusses the criticisms of it. Using clear criteria is designed to counter the problem of management not setting priorities, but this then leads to the complication of how to keep some stakeholders satisfied whilst pursuing the best interests of others. It's important also to consider the moral and ethical normative viewpoints (acting towards stakeholders in a certain way because it's morally right rather than it's in a business's best interests). Enlightened self-interest is suggested as possibly the best way of dealing with the conflicting viewpoints and complications.

Easy marks. You must be aware of the different ways of classifying stakeholders in (a), although the usefulness of these methods may have been difficult to discuss. Mendelow's matrix in (b) also represents fundamental knowledge.

(a)   **Definition of stakeholders**

A stakeholder in an organisation is any person or group with an **interest in what the organisation does**.

(i)   **Internal, connected and external stakeholders**

One commonly used way of classifying stakeholders is by their **level of involvement with the business**. **Internal stakeholders** are the insiders, the managers and employees, whose objectives are likely to have a strong and immediate influence on how the business is run. **Connected stakeholders** include **shareholders**, whose prime interest is a return on their investment, **bankers** (interested in the security of any loan they make), **customers** (products and services) and **suppliers** (payment and future business). **External stakeholders** include the **government**, **local authorities**, **pressure groups**, **the community at large**, **professional bodies**. They are likely to have quite diverse objectives and have varying abilities to ensure that the company meets them.

This method of classification is useful for analysing what the **objectives of stakeholders** are likely to be and how the stakeholders are **likely to apply pressure**.

(ii) **Narrow and wide stakeholders**

This classification groups stakeholders by how much they are affected by the **activities** of the business. **Narrow stakeholders** are those **most affected** by the organisation's strategy – shareholders, managers, employees, suppliers, dependent customers. **Wide stakeholders** are those **less affected** by the organisation's strategy – government, less dependent customers and the wider community.

This way can help businesses decide which stakeholders are likely to be **most interested** in their activities. In addition, if the stance the government minister is taking is felt to be valid, this method helps businesses decide to which stakeholders' interests it should pay most attention.

(iii) **Primary and secondary stakeholders**

This method classifies stakeholders by **how much power and influence** they could potentially exercise over the business. **Primary stakeholders** are those **without whose support** (or lack of opposition) the business will have **difficulty continuing**. These include major customers and suppliers, also the government and regulators. **Secondary stakeholders** are those **whose loss of support won't affect continuation**, such as members of the local community.

This classification is a good way of emphasising **power** over the business and whose support managers must retain.

(iv) **Active and passive stakeholders**

This method groups stakeholders by **how much they participate in a business's activities and particularly influence decision-making**. **Active stakeholders** include managers and shareholders and also others who seek to exert an influence such as regulators or pressure groups. **Passive stakeholders** are those who do not normally seek to influence strategy such as many shareholders, local communities and government.

This classification is most useful as an indicator of **how much time and effort** directors and managers will need to spend dealing with the interests of stakeholders. It is less effective as an indicator of potential shareholder power and influence. Some passive stakeholders, for example shareholders holding a significant % of shares, may intervene effectively if they feel that there is a fundamental threat to their interests.

(b) **Use of stakeholder theory**

Stakeholder theory provides a **framework** for mapping the **differing concerns of stakeholders**, focusing on **interest in activities and power held**.

Mendelow classifies stakeholders on a matrix whose axes are **power held and likelihood of showing an interest** in the organisation's activities. These factors will help define the type of relationship the organisation should seek with its stakeholders, and how it should view their concerns. Stakeholders in the bottom right of the matrix are more significant because they combine the highest power and influence.

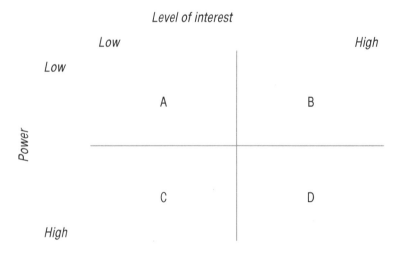

(i) **Key players are found in segment D**: the organisation's strategy must be **acceptable** to them, at least. An example would be a major customer.

(ii) **Stakeholders in segment C** must be treated **with care**. While often passive, they are capable of moving to segment D. Large institutional shareholders might fall into segment C.

(iii) **Stakeholders in segment B** do not have great ability to influence strategy, but their views can be important in **influencing more powerful stakeholders**, perhaps by lobbying. Community representatives and charities might fall into segment B.

(iv) **Stakeholders in segment A** require **minimal effort**

(c) **Fundamental stakeholder view**

The **fundamental stakeholder view**, which the government minister may be implying, asserts that a commercial organisation must aim to satisfy all its stakeholders, and that it is the job of management to **balance somehow** the interests of the different stakeholders.

Accountability to shareholders

Many would take issue with this view. Critics such as Milton Friedman have suggested that **managers are employed to serve the owners of the business**, that is shareholders. The main interest of the owners of a business is **long term increase in the value of their wealth**. Managers are accountable to shareholders for that wealth. If managers are argued to have wider social responsibilities towards stakeholders, then they have to act in some ways that are not in the interest of the owners, **their principals**. They will be spending money for purposes other than which they are authorised. They therefore are not acting properly as agents, but making decisions about **social responsibility** that are the responsibility of government.

Accountability to whom

If it is accepted that businesses have responsibilities to stakeholders other than shareholders, there is then the problem of the **limits of accountability** to each group. Ultimately it is argued that managers who are accountable to **everyone are effectively accountable to no one**. Managers have **unfettered power** to determine organisational priorities, and the balance between different stakeholders will be achieved by managerial discretion. The problem with this is that they will favour their own interests, and the organisation's system goals, over other ones. The balance might be heavily loaded in their favour.

Criteria to use to determine priorities

Managers thus need to **prioritise rationally the interest of certain stakeholders**. The classification of stakeholders described above provides a method, with managers spending most time on stakeholders whose **interest and power** over the business is greatest. However critics would claim that the narrow and wide stakeholder classification is most significant and businesses need to pay most attention to those whose who are most affected by businesses' activities – their **narrow stakeholders**.

Satisficing

There is also the issue of how much the business needs to **satisfice the concerns of certain stakeholders**, to do enough to keep them happy even if they are not primarily pursuing their interests. Some of these stakeholders' interests are clearcut and businesses will have to work within the framework of keeping them happy. Businesses will need to **fulfil regulations** to avoid the attention of legal authorities and fulfil lending terms if they are to continue to receive loan finance. Other stakeholders' positions are less clear. Even If it is acknowledged that shareholders are not the only significant stakeholders, **what levels of return** should businesses regard as a minimum to meet the interests of shareholders.

In addition what is the extent to which businesses must operate within a **framework of moral laws**. Some critics emphasise that business managers cannot **avoid their normal moral obligations**, particularly **avoiding harm to others, respecting the autonomy of others, telling the truth and honouring agreements**. Only after fulfilling these can they maximise shareholder wealth and fulfil other stakeholder interests.

Enlightened self-interest

Enlightened self-interest can be seen as the stakeholder argument in weaker form, that **economic success is most easily achieved by keeping all significant stakeholders happy. Employees, customers and suppliers** are clearly key stakeholders; without them a business could not exist at all. Keeping stakeholders such as regulatory authorities, pressure groups and the local community happy can be seen as ensuring that **management time is not diverted** into combating them, and hence managers can concentrate on achieving economic success.

5 SPV

> **Text reference**. Chapter 3.
>
> **Top tips.** There are various ways of grouping the responsibilities of the board, so your answer to (a) may not have followed the same structure, although it should have brought out much the same points. You would only have received limited credit if you failed to cover the weaknesses with what SPV's board has been doing. Note that (a) includes control system issues as well as corporate governance, since the board is responsible for ensuring control systems are adequate and identifying major weaknesses.
>
> (b) is designed to allow you to focus on the weaknesses in the corporate governance structures of SPV. The weaknesses are mainly directed around the composition of the board and its major sub-committees.
>
> **Easy marks**. If you have a good understanding of the corporate governance requirements, there is enough material in the scenario to enable you to score well on (b).

(a) **Role of board**

Each individual board of directors will take on particular tasks peculiar to their own company and these will be different from company to company. However there are three key tasks that will be addressed by all boards of directors to one degree or another.

Strategic management

The development of the strategy of the company will almost certainly be led by the board of directors. At the very least they will be responsible for **setting the context for the development of strategy**, defining the nature and focus of the operations of the business and determining the mission statement and values of the business. Strategic development will also consist of **assessing the opportunities and threats** facing the business, **considering, developing and screening the strategic proposals and selecting and implementing appropriate strategies**. Some or all of this more detailed strategic development may be carried out by the board, but also may be delegated to senior management with board supervision.

In the case of SPV the board appears to have had inadequate involvement in the development of strategy. Whilst the board may use advice from expert managers, the board should also have challenged what they provided and carried out its own analysis; possible **threats from rivals** appear to have been inadequately considered.

Control

The board of directors is ultimately responsible for the **monitoring and control** of the activities of the company. They are responsible for the financial records of the company and that the financial statements are drawn up using appropriate accounting policies and show a true and fair view. They are also responsible for the **internal checks and controls in the business** that ensure the financial information is accurate and the assets are safeguarded. The board will also be responsible for the direction of the company and ensuring that the managers and employees work towards the **strategic objectives** that have been set. This can be done by the use of plans, budgets, quality and performance indicators and benchmarking.

Again what has happened with the projects appear to indicate board failings. It seems that the board failed to spot **inadequacies in the accounting information** that managers were receiving about the new project, and did not ensure that **action was taken by managers to control** the overruns in time and the excessive costs that possibly the accounting information may have identified. The board also seems to have failed to identify inadequacies in the information that it was receiving itself.

Shareholder and market relations

The board of directors also has an important role externally to the company. The board are responsible for **raising the profile of the company and promoting the company's interests** in its own and possibly other market places. The board has an important role in managing its relationships with its shareholders. The board is responsible for **maintaining relationships and dialogue** with the shareholders, in particular the institutional shareholders. As well as the formal dialogue at the annual general meeting many boards of directors have a **variety of informal methods** of keeping shareholders informed of developments and proposals for the company. Methods include informal meetings, company websites, social reports, environmental reports etc.

The institutional shareholders' intention to vote against the accounts is normally seen as a **last resort** measure, if other methods of exercising their influence and communicating their concerns have failed. This indicates that the board has **failed to communicate effectively** with the institutional shareholders.

(b)   **Suggestions for corporate governance**

Composition of the board

Corporate governance requirements normally indicate that the board of directors should comprise **equal numbers of executive and non-executive directors**. By having only two non-executive directors, SPV may not be following requirements. SPV needs to appoint at least one more non-executive director to the board. There is also a **lack of any relevant financial experience** amongst the non-executive directors. Again, corporate governance regulations normally suggest that at least one NED has **financial experience** so they can monitor effectively the financial information that the board is reviewing. Making the new appointee an accountant would also help to fulfil this requirement.

Role of chairman/CEO

Corporate governance regulations normally require that the roles of the **chairman** (the person running the board) and the **CEO** (the person running the company) are split. The reason for this is to ensure that no one person has too much influence over the running of the company. The only exception to this rule is that the roles can be combined for a short period of time where the company faces significant difficulties and giving more power to one person will assist in overcoming those difficulties (eg Marks & Spencer in 2003). As SPV does not appear to have any significant difficulties at present, then the roles of chairman and CEO should be split at the earliest opportunity.

Appointment and nomination committees

Issues that are not clear with the current structures relate to the **composition of those committees**. Corporate governance requirements indicate **these committees** will **normally comprise independent NEDs**, including the senior NED. This is to limit the extent of power of the executive directors. SPV needs to ensure that this requirement is being followed. The chairman of the board will be allowed to sit on the audit and remuneration committees if he's an independent NED, to ensure that decisions made are in agreement with the overall objectives.

Service contracts

Service contracts for NEDs normally should last for a **maximum of 3 years**, with appointment for a **third term** being classed as **unusual**. The duration of contracts is limited to ensure **payments for early termination of contracts** are **not excessive**. The re-appointment provisions apply to ensure that new NED's are being appointed as directors on a regular basis. NEDs who have been on the board for a few years may become **too familiar with the operations** of the company and therefore not provide the necessary external independent check that they are supposed to do.

Internal audit

The internal audit department usually reports to the financial accountant as that person may have a **vested interest** in not taking any action on the reports, especially where reports are critical of the accountant. In that sense, reporting to the board is acceptable. However, the board as a whole may **not have the time** to **review internal audit reports** and again may be tempted to ignore them if they are critical of the board itself. Corporate governance regulations indicate that the internal audit department **should report to the audit committee** with reports being forwarded to the board. This ensures that the report is heard by the NEDs, who can then ensure that internal audit recommendations are implemented where appropriate, by the board.

In SPV, the internal auditor needs to report to the audit committee, for reasons already mentioned above.

6 LL

(a)   **Advantages of compliance with Sarbanes-Oxley**

Enforcement of key provisions

From Thelma's viewpoint, adherence to Sarbanes-Oxley means that LL **must comply** with certain important features of corporate governance, rather than being allowed to explain non-compliance. One example is the audit committee. Sarbanes-Oxley requires all listed companies to establish an audit committee consisting of independent directors, one of whom should be a **financial expert**.

Internal controls

Sarbanes-Oxley is stronger than most principles-based codes in requiring accounts to include an **audited assessment of financial reporting controls**. Most principles-based codes require disclosures about risk management and board review, but not assessment of effectiveness.

Accountability

Sarbanes-Oxley **enforces director accountability** by requiring the chief executive and chief finance officer to provide **certification** of the appropriateness and fair presentation of the accounts. If the accounts later have to be restated, these individuals **forfeit their bonuses**.

Ethics

Sarbanes-Oxley promotes corporate ethics by requiring companies to report on whether they have **adopted a code of ethics for senior financial officers**. This should help ensure that the right 'tone' is established at the top of the organisation.

Disadvantages of compliance with Sarbanes-Oxley

Extra bureaucracy

Terrance's observation that Sarbanes-Oxley has resulted in increased demands appears to have been borne out in practice, with the US stock markets becoming less popular as a place for initial public listings. **High compliance costs** appear to be significant factors in these decisions.

Costs of multiple compliance

As well as compliance with Sarbanes-Oxley, LL will still need to provide evidence of its compliance with its own local governance regime. This will involve the company **incurring the costs of compliance with two regimes**, without perhaps giving some investors much, if any, extra assurance.

Over-focus on compliance

The emphasis in the Sarbanes-Oxley regime has been on compliance with all aspects of the legislation. This can distract companies' attention from issues that are not closely regulated by Sarbanes-Oxley, but are important to investors like Elm Lodge bank, such as **improvement in information flows**.

Inflexibility

Sarbanes-Oxley requirements do **not allow any leeway or judgement** in a number of areas, for example forbidding auditors from carrying out specified non-audit services. A principles-based regime can emphasise the importance of auditor independence, but leave it to companies' audit committees' judgement on how this may best be achieved.

(b) **Participation of shareholders**

The first advantage from Thelma's viewpoint is that the content of the review is flexible and is not confined to areas **required by laws and regulations**. In the **UK shareholders and other interest groups** have been encouraged to help determine the content of companies' business reviews. Given Thelma's concern about the information provision in LL's accounts, this could be a useful opportunity to make matters better.

Disclosures about the nature, strategies and objectives of the business

The statement can disclose the **objectives** the business has for preserving value and the **strategies** for achieving these objectives within the business environment. This will be valuable for investors such as Elm Lodge who will be able to compare their views of how the business should develop with those of the directors. It would force Terrance as chief executive to provide clear information about what he aims to achieve, which Thelma currently appears to feel he is reluctant to do.

Development and performance

The review should also provide information about the **development and performance** of the business in the current period and in the future. This will provide **yardsticks** for investors to assess the directors' **stewardship** of the company. The descriptions in the report should reduce the information asymmetry between investors and directors, and demonstrate whether the directors are implementing, and will implement, their strategies effectively. The forward-looking nature of the information here is particularly important, as it is additional to the historical information in the accounts, and is of prime interest to investors who are concerned about future value. Here the impact of LL's future plans to expand geographically would be information that investors would want discussed.

Risks and uncertainties

The review can form an important part of the company's reporting on the **principal risks** it faces. Investors concerned about the security of their investments will be interested in the company's views and may wish to compare their **understanding of the risks** with the directors. The risks of future changes in strategies will be particularly important here. This disclosure will require input from the risk committee chairman and alleviate one of the areas that particularly concerns Thelma.

Position and resources of the business

The review can also include **disclosure of the business's resources and financial position**. If the business is involved in treasury activities, it can include details of its treasury policies, which may concern investors as an important risk area. The directors' views on future financial strategies are likely to be important with LL, as its planned expansion into America may involve seeking a **listing** there.

(c) **Compliance with legislation or best practice**

In some jurisdictions governance codes **specify the content of committee reports**. Perhaps the most important example is the remuneration report, which is required in many places to give a number of specific disclosures about how directors' remuneration is determined. More widely, governance reports can often be used to provide a general framework. The Cadbury report provides a list of the **main responsibilities of the audit committee**, and disclosures could demonstrate how the committee has fulfilled each responsibility.

Information for investors

The other main principle, as with the Operating and Financial Review, is providing information that will be of use to shareholders.

Constitution of committees

To aid investors' understanding, the committee reports ought to include details of the committee's **terms of reference** or be cross-referenced to where the terms of reference can be found. Information about the qualifications of the committee, for example the **financial qualifications and experience** of the audit committee, will also be helpful.

Operation of committees

Details about the **frequency** of **committee meetings and the attendance of members** should help investors determine whether board committees are fulfilling certain responsibilities. For example, if the risk committee only meets once a year, it is unlikely to be conducting the **regular review of risks and control systems** demanded by **governance reports**. In order to judge how effective the committee can be, investors will also need disclosures about the **information supplied** to the committee, and the committee's rights to take **independent advice**.

Changes in environment

The committee report should include details of the major changes in the company's environment that affect the **work of the committee**. The risk committee's report should give details of how they have responded to major changes in the company's risks. If LL was to change its listing and adhere to Sarbanes-Oxley, the audit committee's report should contain details of how its work had been affected.

One-off reporting

As well as details of the committee's regular workload, investors may be particularly interested in full details of **one-off investigations or assignments** by the audit or risk committees, or full details of the recruitment process for a new chief executive by the nomination committee.

Example disclosure

The nomination committee conducted a thorough search process to identify candidates for the position of Chief Executive, aided by X Co, the committee's appointed search consultants. As a result of this process Brenda Boyle was identified as a candidate with the desired experience. She met with members of the nomination committee, and her appointment was recommended to the board, who approved her appointment as Chief Executive.

7 Sentosa House

Text references. Chapters 1, 2 and 5.

Top tips. This question is likely to be a good example of the question design that the examiner will use. The company circumstances are very closely integrated into the question requirements. This is also a good illustration of how a scenario might have to be analysed from the viewpoint of a specific stakeholder.

Note the marking scheme in (a); you will get 2 marks for a clear definition in (a) but just knowing the definition won't be enough to pass that part. The key elements that incur agency costs are means of obtaining information and controls established over the agent. Most of the marks are available for relating agency costs to the scenario and discussing why they might be increased.

In (b) you need to think about threats to value and the various problems associated with a cavalier attitude towards control – including risks to your own reputation for being associated with it.

(c) sees the risk committee as having a similar monitoring remit to the audit committee, and hence needing to be composed of non-executive directors. This is not necessarily the case under many corporate governance regimes, and companies may have more flexibility in the role they give to risk committees and staffing risk committees with executive directors. However to pass this part you have to focus here on the circumstances described in the question.

(d) represents a core point in relation to principles-based regimes. It illustrates the significance of listing rules and investor reaction. Remember also that a principles based-regime implies companies comply or explain why not. Stating that the company hasn't complied because compliance isn't compulsory is **never** an adequate explanation.

Easy marks. All question parts appear to be of roughly equal difficulty. (b) though has a lower level question verb than the other parts – describe (see Gareth Owen's article in the front pages) so is less demanding in terms of application skills required.

			Marks
(a)	2 marks for definition of agency costs	2	
	1 mark for each problem identified and briefly discussed	5	
			7
(b)	1 mark for each relevant point identified and briefly described on conditions for intervention	7	
	1 mark for each relevant point made on Eastern Products	3	
			10
(c)	1 mark for each relevant point made		4
(d)	1 mark for each relevant point made		4
			25

(a) **Definition of agency costs**

Agency costs arise from the need of **principals** (here shareholders) to monitor the activities of agents (here the board, particularly the chairman). This means that principals need to **find out what the agent is doing**, which may be difficult because they may not have as much information about what is going on as the agent does. Principals also need to **introduce mechanisms to control the agent** over and above normal analysis. Both finding out and introducing mechanisms will incur costs that can be viewed in terms of money spent, resources consumed or time taken.

Problems with agency costs in Eastern Products

Attitudes to risk

The first reason for increased agency costs is that the company's attitude to risk is a major area of concern on which Sentosa requires **more information**, since the **risk appetite** appears significantly greater than what would normally be expected in this sector.

Unwillingness of chairman to be monitored

Agency costs will certainly increase because Thomas Hoo is **unwilling to supply any information about the reasons for his policies**, certainly indicating arrogance and also a **lack of willingness to accept accountability**. This means that Sentosa will have to **find out from other sources**, for example any non-executive directors who are on the board. Alternatively they may contact other investors and take steps to put more pressure on Thomas Hoo, for example by threatening to requisition an extraordinary general meeting.

Inadequacy of existing mechanisms

Agency costs will also increase because existing mechanisms for communicating concerns appear to be **inadequate**. There are **insufficient non-executive directors** on the board to exert pressure on Thomas Hoo. There is **no risk management committee** to monitor risks. The investor relations department is **insufficiently informed and unhelpful**. Thomas Hoo has abruptly dismissed the one-off phone call. Because of the seriousness of the concerns, ideally there should be **regular meetings** between Thomas Hoo and the major shareholders, **requiring preparation** from both parties and increasing agency costs.

Combining shareholder concerns

Thomas Hoo may be able to ignore shareholder concerns, because of the **shareholding patterns**. Although institutional shareholders are concerned, those who want to take action may not together hold a sufficiently large shareholding to enforce their views. Building a shareholder alliance will also increase agency costs.

(b)   **Active intervention**

Active intervention by an institutional shareholder by making an attempt, for example, to change the board is regarded as a serious step, and may result in a **significant increase in agency costs**. However there are a number of reasons why it might happen.

Threats to value of shareholding

Institutional shareholders may intervene if they perceive that management's policies could lead to a fall in the value of the company and hence the **value of their shares**. There could be concerns over strategic decisions over products, markets or investments or over **operational performance**. Although they can in theory sell their shares, in practice it may be difficult to offload a significant shareholding without its value falling. Here although Eastern Products is currently making high returns, Sentosa may judge that the **risk of a major strategy** going wrong is **too high**.

Lack of confidence in management integrity

Institutional investors may intervene because they feel management cannot be trusted. At worst they may fear **management fraud**; this could be a worry in this scenario given that Thomas Hoo has done away with a key component of the control system (the risk committee) without good reason.

Failure to control management

Institutional investors may take steps if they feel that there is **insufficient influence** being **exercised by non-executive directors** over executive management. The disappearance of the risk committee is also a symptom of this problem.

Lack of control systems

Intervention would be justified if there were **serious concerns about control systems**. Thomas Hoo's actions may indicate a fundamental flaw in control arrangements with management able to bypass whatever systems are in place.

Failure to address shareholder concerns

Even if there is no question of dishonesty, there may be intervention if institutional investors feel that management is **failing to address their legitimate viewpoints**. Institutional investors' own investors may exert pressure on them **not to invest in high-risk companies**, or **companies with a poor ethical reputation**. Thomas Hoo is solely focused on returns whilst **failing to address the issue of risk**.

Failure to comply with stock market requirements

Eastern Products' failure to comply with corporate governance concerns appear to be quite blatant. The institutional investors may be concerned that they will **suffer criticism** if they are perceived as conniving in these breaches because they have not taken action. It may also **threaten the value of their shareholding** if the stock market turns against Eastern Products.

(c)   **Importance of risk committees**

Risk committees are considered to be **good practice in most worldwide governance regimes**, particularly in situations like this where there are doubts about the attitudes of executive management. A risk committee staffed by non-executive directors can provide an **independent viewpoint** on Eastern Products' overall response to risk; a significant presence of non-executive directors, as required by governance guidelines, would be able to **challenge Thomas's attitudes**.

Determining overall exposure to risk

The first contribution the committee can make is to pressure the board to determine what constitutes **acceptable levels of risk**, bearing in mind the likelihood of the risks materialising and Eastern Products' ability to **reduce the incidence and impact** on the business.

Monitoring overall exposure to risk

Once the board has **defined acceptable risk levels**, the committee should **monitor whether Eastern Products is remaining within those levels**, and whether **earnings are sufficient** given the levels of risks that are being borne.

Reviewing reports on key risks

There should be a regular system of reports to the risk management committee covering areas known to be of **high risk**, also **one-off reports** covering conditions and events likely to arise in the near future. This should facilitate the monitoring of risk.

Monitoring the effectiveness of the risk management systems

The committee should **monitor the effectiveness of the risk management systems**, focusing particularly on **executive management attitudes towards risk** and the **overall control environment and culture**. A risk management committee can judge whether there is an emphasis on effective management or whether **insufficient attention** is being **given to risk management** due to the pursuit of high returns.

(d) **Significance of principles**

In a principles-based jurisdiction, corporate governance is underpinned by certain basic ethical concepts such as **integrity and accountability**. These should be applied willingly and clearly are not designed as an excuse for non-compliance.

Principles and requirements

In most principles-based jurisdictions, the general guidance is often combined with specific stock market requirements as here with the **number of non-executive directors**. Companies have to comply with requirements if they are to continue to enjoy a stock market listing.

Comply or explain

Other, less specific, requirements are based on what would normally be regarded as **best practice** and thus investors would expect companies to comply with them. If companies don't, they should supply good and clear reasons for non-compliance. This Eastern Products has failed to do.

Investor reaction

Even if reasons are supplied, investors can challenge them. Ultimately, if not satisfied, they **can put pressure on Eastern Products' share price** by selling their shares.

8 Frank Finn

> **Text reference.** Chapter 3.
>
> **Top tips.** Directors' remuneration is the type of subject that you are very likely to see in this exam as it is (always) topical and there's lots of corporate governance guidance covering it. In (a) 8 marks is quite a generous allocation for the role of the remuneration committee; the answer brings out what it does, the issues and complexities with which it has to engage, and the key corporate governance responsibilities of accountability (here the reporting requirements) and compliance. Your answer on cross-directorships needs to bring out the key principle (independence) and show how independence is breached. This scenario is a good illustration of why governance reports require remuneration committees to be chaired by independent non-executive directors.
>
> In (b) the description of remuneration brings out the most important issue of links with performance, but also another important issue, that of directors getting benefits on better terms than employees. Note the stress on trying to balance short and long-term priorities; the weighting of each is not easy to determine, particularly for a sales director whose short-term performance will be significant.

In (c) evaluate means you have to cover the arguments for and against. The arguments for the proposal take an absolutist view of the rules, reinforced by arguments stressing the beneficial consequences (simple solution, better for reputation).

The arguments against the proposal stress that there is doubt about malpractice and also other consequences (loss of experience unbalancing the board). Remember under most governance codes not all non-executive directors have to meet the independence criteria, but there need to be sufficient independent non-executive directors on the board to constitute a strong presence and to staff the key corporate governance committees.

Overall (c) is a good example of weighing up a strong ethical solution against a maybe weaker, but more practical, one.

Easy marks. The descriptive sections on remuneration committee and directors' remuneration certainly offer most of the marks you need to pass this question. Remember however that in your exam, the marks may be more tilted towards application. The mark allocation for explaining a level 1 verb per Gareth's Owen's article in the front pages appears to be generous.

Marking scheme

				Marks
(a)	(i)	1 mark for each valid point made for demonstrating an understanding of cross directorships	2	
	(ii)	Award up to 2 marks for each valid point made on roles of remuneration committees	8	
	(iii)	Award up to 2 marks for each valid point on undermining the roles	4	
		max		12
(b)		1 mark for each component of a director's remuneration correctly identified	4	
		1 mark for each relevant point describing how Finn's remuneration might be more aligned to shareholders' interests	5	
		max		8
(c)		Award 1 mark for each point evaluating the proposal from Hanoi House	1	
		Arguments in favour – up to 3 marks	3	
		Arguments against – up to 3 marks	3	
		max		5
				25

(a) **Complying with laws and best practice**

To ensure that executive directors do not set their own remuneration, governance codes such as the UK Corporate Governance Code suggest that the committee should be **staffed by independent non-executive directors**, who have no personal interests other than as shareholders. The committee should also ensure **compliance with any relevant legislation**, for example prohibition of loans to directors.

Establishing general remuneration policy

The remuneration committee is responsible for establishing remuneration policy, acting on behalf of shareholders, but for the **benefit of both the board and shareholders**. They should consider the **pay scales** for directors, including how much the remuneration offered by comparable companies should influence remuneration levels in its own company. It also includes considering **what relation remuneration should have to measurable performance** or enhanced shareholder value and **when** directors should receive performance-related benefits.

Determining remuneration packages for each director

The committee needs to establish packages that will **retain, attract and motivate directors** whilst taking into account the interests of shareholders as well. The committee should consider how **different aspects of the package are balanced**, also what **measures** are used to assess the performance of individual directors.

Determining disclosures

The committee should also consider what **disclosures** should be made in the remuneration committee report in the accounts, generally in the corporate governance section. The report normally includes **details of overall policies** and the **remuneration of individual directors.**

Cross-directorship

Cross-directorships are when two or more directors **sit on the boards of the same companies;** there may also be **cross-shareholdings** in both companies. The cross-directorship undermines the role of the remuneration committee because Mr Ng, its chairman, is linked with Frank Finn as fellow directors of another company. He does not have the necessary **independence** since Frank Finn, in his role as director of DEF, may be responsible for determining Mr Ng's salary. Both may therefore be tempted to act in their own interests by voting the other a high salary.

(b) **Basic salary**

Basic salary is the **salary laid down** in the director's contract of employment. The terms are determined by the contract and the original salary is not generally related to performance (although increases in it may be). Shareholder interests can be promoted by ensuring that contracts of employment are **not of excessive length**; however if remuneration packages are heavily weighted towards basic salary, as here, they may be criticised for not providing enough incentives for directors to perform well.

Performance related bonus

Directors may be paid a cash bonus for **good performance.** Performance measures need be determined carefully so that they are in **shareholders' interests**, are not **subject to manipulation of profits**, **do not focus excessively on short-term results** and **reward the individual contribution of Mr Finn.** However given that Mr Finn is a sales director, **rewards based on revenues or profits** would play an important part in rewarding performance, on an annual or more frequent basis.

Shares and share options

Share options give directors the **right to purchase shares at a specified exercise price over a specified time period in the future.** If the price of shares rises due to good company performance so that it exceeds the exercise price, the directors will be able to purchase shares at lower than their market value. Share options can be used to align Mr Finn's interests with shareholder wishes to maximise company value. They can also be used to **reward long-term performance** whereas bonuses can be used to reward short-term performance, by specifying that the options may not be exercised for some years (the UK Corporate Governance Code recommends not less than three years).

Benefits in kind

Benefits in kind could include a **car, health provisions** and **life assurance**. It may be difficult to relate these elements to directors' performance and indeed one symptom of the breakdown of the agency relationship is the directors being rewarded with excessive 'perks'. There is also the issue that these measures may be **unpopular with employees** who are not enjoying the same terms. Thus the remuneration committee should ensure that the value of these benefits is not excessive compared with other elements of the package.

Pensions

Some companies pay pension contributions for directors. As pension contributions tend to be linked to **basic salary**, they are not usually connected with performance, and again there may be a concern about directors receiving **preferential treatment,** with Mr Finn and others' pension contributions being paid at a higher rate than those of staff. The UK Corporate Governance Code stresses that the remuneration committee should consider the pension consequences and associated costs to the company of basic salary increases and changes in pensionable remuneration.

(c)   **Nature of issues**

The issues are how best to deal with a **conflict of interest** and also whether it is fair for the two directors to suffer detriment.

Arguments in favour of Hanoi's House position

Integrity

Resignation of both directors would arguably demonstrate that they are acting with **integrity** and are **putting their companies' interests before their own**. It would also demonstrate **ABC's strict adherence** to the **principles of good corporate governance**.

Removal of threat to independence

Given that corporate governance reports suggest that cross-directorships are a threat to independence, resignation is the **simplest way to remove that threat**.

Reputation risk

ABC and DEF may be vulnerable to criticisms that **'fat cat' directors** are operating on a 'you scratch my back, I'll scratch yours' basis. Resignation would **restore confidence in the remuneration committee.**

Arguments against Hanoi House's position

Evidence of malpractice

Although cross-directorships are against corporate governance best practice, it looks excessive to suggest that there is **evidence of malpractice. Frank Finn's package** may have been **poorly designed**, but this may not have been deliberate.

Loss of Mr Ng

Swanland Investment make the legitimate point that the two directors' contribution will be lost. It emphasises the complexities of corporate governance, the need to choose between the **better functioning of the board** against the **threat to independence**.

Role of other directors

Swanland's proposals emphasises that the remuneration committee does not just consist of Mr Ng; there should be **other independent non-executive directors** on it who are capable of coming to a fair decision even without Mr Ng.

9 Seamus O'Brien

Text references. Chapters 2 and 3.

Top tips. (a) is textbook material; knowledge of the UK Corporate Governance Code is particularly helpful. Your answer needs to demonstrate that the main role of the chairman is to run the board effectively. If you had just listed the chairman's ideas in a single-line bullet point list without any detailed description, you would have scored a maximum of 2 marks for this part.

In (b) you should bring out the problem of unfettered power that can result from the chairman and chief executive being the same person; this has been a significant issue in a number of corporate governance scandals. The points about the time available, separation providing two viewpoints and two sets of experience, and chairman's role as a link with the non-executive directors and shareholders are also important. The chairman will need to show detachment from executive management to provide accountability and give investors confidence, and can never do this if he is chief executive as well. The discussion on accountability needs to bring out the methods of enforcement.

As in Questions 1 and 2, the requirement to evaluate in (c) means reviewing the arguments for and against. The main arguments in favour of local codes are that governance guidance should reflect local conditions. The arguments against local variation come mainly from a globalist perspective, although also you have corporate governance practice reflecting activity elsewhere, here the international convergence in accounting guidance.

Easy marks. (a) should be five of the easiest marks on this paper.

Examiner's comments. The question highlighted which students had a basic knowledge of corporate governance, but struggled when answering questions with higher level verbs. In (a) students needed to explain (ie provide evidence of understanding of the role over and above an identification).

Good answers to (b) focused on the benefits arising from a separation of roles reducing the unfettered power of a single individual. Students appeared to be surprised by the second requirement on increased accountability to shareholders. Students need to be aware that questions ' will often ask them to think about something in the exam that they may not have read directly in the study guides or been taught in class.' (b) is a good illustration of the sort of question structure that students should expect in future exams.

Marking scheme

				Marks
(a)	1 mark for each relevant role clearly identified	max		5
(b)	'Cross mark' points made in these answers.			
	Benefits of separation of roles: Up to 2 marks for each point identified and assessed as an argument	max	10	
	Accountability and separation of roles: 1 mark for each point made explaining the comment	max	4	
		max		12
(c)	'Cross mark' points made/issues raised in the two parts of the answer			
	1 mark for each relevant point made on why corporate governance provisions should not vary by country	max	5	
	1 mark for each relevant point made on why corporate governance provisions might vary by country	max	5	
		max		8
				25

(a) **Running the board and setting its agenda**

The chairman is responsible for ensuring that the board **meets regularly** and **runs effectively** when it meets. The chairman should **encourage active participation** by all members of the board and **promote good relations between executive and non-executive directors.**

Ensuring the board receives accurate and timely information

Good information will enable the board to **take sound decisions** and **monitor the company effectively.**

Communicating with shareholders

Financial statements in many jurisdictions include a **chairman's statement** that must be compatible with other information in the financial statements. The chairman may also be **responsible for signing off the financial statements.**

Ensuring that sufficient time is allowed for discussion of controversial issues

The chairman should ensure that board meetings **focus on strategic matters**, and that the board takes account of the key issues and the concerns of all board members. The board should have enough time to **consider critical issues** and not be faced with unrealistic deadlines for decision-making.

Taking the lead in board development

The chairman is responsible for **addressing the development needs** of the board as a whole and enhancing the effectiveness of the whole team, also **meeting the development needs of individual directors**. The chairman should ensure that the induction programme for new directors is **comprehensive, formal and tailored**. The chairman should also ensure the performance of the whole board, board committees and individuals is **appraised at least once a year.**

(b)   **Benefits of splitting the roles**

Authority

There is an important difference between the authority of the chairman and the authority of the chief executive, which having the roles taken by different people will clarify. The chairman **carries the authority of the board** whereas the chief executive has the authority that is **delegated by the board.** Having the roles separate emphasises that the chairman is acting on behalf of the board, whereas the chief executive has the authority given in his **terms of appointment.** Having the same person in both roles means that **unfettered power** is concentrated into one pair of hands; the board may be ineffective in controlling the chief executive if it is led by the chief executive. The chairman provides a second **effective viewpoint** and also contributes his or her own **experience**, augmenting the board.

Time considerations

An important argument in favour of splitting the roles of chairman and chief executive is that both are very demanding functions. In large, complex organisations no one individual will have the time to do both jobs effectively. Splitting the roles means that the chairman is responsible for the functions of **leading and running the board** described in (a), the chief executive for **running the organisation and developing its strategy.**

Leadership of non-executive directors

Governance reports emphasise the importance of a strong, influential presence of **independent non-executive directors**. A **non-executive chairman** can provide effective leadership for the non-executive directors.

Information for non-executive directors

The chairman is responsible for obtaining the information that other directors require to **exercise proper oversight.** If the chairman is also chief executive, then directors may not be sure that the information they are getting is sufficient and objective enough to support their supervision. The chairman should ensure that the board is receiving sufficient information to make **informed decisions**, and should put pressure on the chief executive if the chairman believes that the chief executive is not providing adequate information.

Information for markets

Having a separate chairman means that there is a division of roles between the person **responsible for communicating business performance to markets** (the chairman), and the person **responsible for that performance** (the chief executive).

Protection of minority shareholders

A separate chairman can also ensure that executive management pays **sufficient attention to the interests of minority shareholders** and protects their interests. Seamus O'Brien's comment about family reasons highlights a situation where a separate chairman is particularly important; in companies where a founding family dominates executive management, shareholders who are not family members often feel that their interests are neglected.

Accountability

Definition

Accountability means ensuring that the chief executive is **answerable for the consequences** of his actions.

Role in appraising chief executive

A separate chairman can take responsibility for regularly appraising the chief executive's performance. The chairman may also be responsible for advising the remuneration committee on the chief executive's remuneration, having taken **account of shareholder views.**

Focal point for non-executive directors

If the non-executive directors or shareholders have **concerns about the way executive management** is running the company, a chairman not involved in executive management can offer an effective point for reporting these concerns. If however the chief executive is also the chairman, the non-executive directors may doubt his objectivity, as he is ultimately responsible for managing the company.

Ensuring accountability to shareholders

The UK Corporate Governance Code and other reports stress the role of the chairman in seeking the **views of shareholders** and ensuring **effective communication with them.** This provides a means for shareholders to raise concerns about the chief executive, and the chairman, as board representative, can **ultimately be held to account for this**.

Ensuring legal accountability

As representative of the board, the chairman can be **held responsible in law** for its activities including the supervision exercised over the chief executive.

(c)   **In favour of variation**

Varied board structures

Vincent Viola rightly highlights one key international difference, that what are felt to be appropriate corporate governance structures vary by country. In the UK for example a **single board is** responsible for all aspects of corporate governance. In other jurisdictions a **supervisory board** is **responsible for review and safeguarding stakeholder interests,** a **management board** for **executive decisions.** It is difficult for a single international code to encompass these different arrangements.

Impact of local culture

Vincent Viola also raises another issue, that to be more effective corporate governance needs to reflect **local cultural issues**. For example the King report in South Africa was designed to reflect issues that are seen as important in South Africa's development such as collectiveness, consensus and fairness. This also extends to different concepts of accountability.

Legal systems

The effectiveness of governance codes should be reinforced by legal sanctions being available against miscreant directors. Governance codes therefore need to be **compatible with differing legal regulations and systems** in different countries.

Costs

The costs of following a very structured international regime (such as one based on **Sarbanes-Oxley**) may be **very burdensome** for **companies based in less developed countries**, who are not operating worldwide.

Against variation

Concerns of global companies and investors

Companies trade across several different jurisdictions and many investors invest in different countries. Having to comply with the provisions of a number of different local codes will **increase compliance costs for companies** who are **operating in many jurisdictions**. Many European companies, for example, have expressed concern about the costs of complying with Sarbanes-Oxley, if they have interests in America, as well as their own local European codes. In addition local codes may not be able to deal with **cross-jurisdiction issues** of concern to investors, such as impediments to cross-border shareholdings.

Compatibility of financial reporting rules

A key part of debates about corporate governance has been the need to **develop robust financial reporting rules,** since investors' concerns with unreliable accounting information has meant that they have questioned corporate governance arrangements. Developments in international accounting standards are aiming to **promote greater international harmony in accounting practice**, and international convergence on governance would be consistent with this.

Investor protection

Consistent corporate governance practice worldwide can also **encourage investment**, since it should ensure investors are **treated equally in different jurisdictions**. A major concern of many international investors has been the **different levels of protection** given to domestic and foreign investors under local governance regimes.

Investor confidence

More fundamentally investors may **not have the confidence to invest in regimes** that allow local, very flexible, interpretations. They may migrate to countries where good governance is emphasised and backed by effective codes, rather than countries that 'do not care as much' and which therefore **allow bad practice**.

10 Rosh

Text references. Chapters 1 and 3.

Top tips. This is the sort of situation that will occur frequently in this exam, a board with a mix of corporate governance problems, some obvious, some not.

(a) emphasises the importance of working systematically through a scenario to ensure that you pick up all the examples that will support your answer. You need to use most of the information in the scenario. Note that criticise is a level 3 verb, so that as well as identifying problems, you also need to show why they are problems. (a) emphasises how governance should ensure board accountability; most of the problems discussed in (a) will ultimately result in less accountability.

Note that the role of the nomination committee isn't just to supervise the recruitment process whenever the main board believes the company needs a new director. Recruitment should flow naturally out of the nomination committee's ongoing review of the membership of the board. The second part of (b) is basically asking you to say that a nomination committee would benefit the board of (b) because . . . . .

(c) shows that retirement by rotation is not just a legal requirement, but a key means of ensuring accountability to shareholders. Make sure that you revise retirement by rotation if you didn't know what it was. It does not mean doing different jobs in the same organisation or succession planning.

Easy marks. The role of the nomination committee and retirement by rotation (revision from F4) should have generated easy marks.

Examiner's comments. A lot of students made the most of the many opportunities they had in (a) to criticise the current situation. Answers to (b) were more mixed, with some students confusing the work of the nomination committee with the work of the HR department. Some students appeared not to know the meaning of retirement by rotation in (c).

Marking scheme

			Marks
(a)	1 mark for each relevant point made max	4	
	1 mark for identification of each criticism max	5	
	1 mark for brief discussion of each criticism max	5	
	max		12
(b)	1 mark for each relevant role of the nominations committee max	5	
	1 mark for each relevant point on the usefulness of a nominations committee to Rosh max	4	
	max		8
(c)	1 mark for each relevant point made for definition max	2	
	1 mark for each relevant point made on importance max	3	
	1 mark for each relevant point made on applying to Rosh max	2	
	max		5
			25

(a) **Agency**

Corporate governance codes seek to provide mechanisms for **shareholders** (principals) to enforce accountability on their **agents** (the directors). Here the key shareholder-principals are the shareholders who are not family members who hold 60% of the voting shares.

Reports enforce accountability by, for example, recommending regular contact between directors and significant shareholders and emphasising the **importance of true and fair financial reporting**, so that shareholders can have the information necessary to judge directors' stewardship.

Shortcomings in governance arrangements

Recruitment of directors

The board does **not appear to recruit directors systematically**. The appointment of Mary Hobbes appears to be an attempt to correct a glaring lack of financial accounting experience on the board. However even that appointment appears flawed. It seems to be largely for reasons of ensuring accounting compliance rather considering the wider contribution a finance director should make, for example assessing the financial aspects of strategic decisions.

Diversity of directors

As a consequence of the poor recruitment procedures, the board lacks a breadth of experience. In particular the non-executive directors should, but do not, bring insights gained from **occupying senior positions in other organisations**. Some governance reports, for example the King report in South Africa, state diversity and varied demographic contribute significantly to board effectiveness; if so Rosh's board is lacking, since Mary is the only woman, and the rest of the board are all elderly.

Number of non-executive directors

Governance reports state that boards should contain a **balance of executive and non-executive directors**, so that non-executive directors are able to make a strong contribution. The UK Corporate Governance Code recommends that at **least half** the directors should be **independent non-executive directors**. Two non-executive directors out of a board of nine does not fulfil this requirement.

Lack of independence of non-executive directors

The UK Corporate Governance Code highlights service on the board of **greater than nine years** as normally indicating non-executive directors are **not independent**, and Rosh's board therefore does not have any independent non-executive directors. The fact that they have worked as **executives in Rosh** within the last five years also indicates a lack of independence. Governance reports highlight the role of independent non-executive directors in **scrutinising the board's activities** and **serving on key committees** including the audit and remuneration committees, (which Rosh does not appear to have).

Discussion of issues

Governance reports stress the importance of board meetings covering key issues for the future of the business. The Cadbury report recommends that the board should have a formal schedule of matters reserved for its decision, including **major strategic issues**. Failure to do this means that Rosh is not being directed properly. The board is unlikely to be taking proper account of changing circumstances and risks in retailing, and hence failing to set the right objectives and to manage risks effectively.

(b) **Role of nomination committee**

Review of the board

When undertaking a **regular review of the current board** as well as making new board appointments, the nomination committee needs to consider the composition and strength of the current board. This involves assessing the balance between executives and non-executives, the board's skills, knowledge and experience and the need for continuity and succession planning. The nomination committee should also consider the desirable **size** of the board and number of non-executives, and the **diversity** of backgrounds of board members.

Appointments to board

The nomination committee should **oversee the process for board appointments** and make recommendations on appointment to the main board.

Leadership arrangements

The committee should also consider the adequacy of future leadership arrangements in the company. This needs to include **succession planning** and whether the company should **recruit externally** to fill leading positions.

Role of non-executive directors

The committee should examine the **role of non-executive directors** and consider whether they are spending enough time on their duties.

Usefulness to Rosh and Company

Compliance with governance codes

An active nomination committee should ensure the board fulfils the requirements of codes such as the UK Corporate Governance Code that there should be a **formal, rigorous and transparent procedure** for the appointment of new directors. At present the board appears not to be complying.

Balance of board

A systematic review by the nomination committee should **highlight for the board** areas where the board is still lacking in terms of **skills and experience**, and also consider the **contribution and independence** of non-executive directors.

Strength of board

The nomination committee should also assess whether the board is strong enough in terms of numbers and roles undertaken to **exercise effective control** over Rosh, and to recommend to the directors whether **further executive roles need to be created**.

Succession arrangements

A nomination committee made up of independent non-executive directors should be able to **assess objectively** whether it would be best for the company if Geoffrey Rosh should become chairman, or whether another director or an outsider should succeed.

(c) **Retirement by rotation**

Retirement by rotation means that every year a certain number of directors retire from the board, and have to offer themselves for **re-election** if they wish to continue to serve. The directors retiring include directors who have been appointed during the year and then directors who have **served the longest on the board**. In most companies this means that directors serve for a **maximum of three years** before being required to retire. The chief executive may be exempt from these requirements.

Importance for Rosh

Shareholder rights

Retirement by rotation is important for Rosh because it gives shareholders who are **not members of the family** their main chance to **judge the contribution of individual directors** and deny them re-election if they have performed inadequately. It is an important mechanism to **ensure director accountability**.

Evolution of board

Compulsory retirement of directors forces directors and shareholders to consider the need for the board to **change over time**. This does not appear to have been considered at Rosh, with the result that board recruitment has stagnated. The fact that only some directors retire each year means that if board changes are felt to be necessary, they can happen gradually enough to ensure **some stability**.

Costs of contract termination

By limiting the length of service period, the **compensation paid to directors for loss of office** under their service contracts will also be limited. Contracts may well expire at the time the director is required to retire and if then the director is not re-elected, no compensation will be payable.

11 West versus Leroi

Text references. Chapters 2 and 8.

Top tips. Perhaps the most important point in (a) (i) is the lack of flexibility as this leads into (a) (ii). It's no use setting out rules that companies can't comply with because of lack of local infrastructure. Our answer also brings out the point that a principles-based approach encourages governance to develop as the companies expand, and addresses the issue raised of international investor confidence by pointing out that there are globally recognised international codes that are principles-based. Many students found the wording to (a) (ii) unclear, but the examiner was generous in rewarding students who misinterpreted the question, but produced valid arguments to support their interpretation.

In spite of the mention of Sarbanes-Oxley in the requirements to (b), your answer doesn't need to be based on what's in the Act. Basing the answer on Turnbull or other governance guidance covering external reporting would have earned you the marks you need. Note that (b) is not talking about the external auditors' letter of weakness/management letter to management.

(c) is largely framed in terms of costs-benefits, considering whether the costs will be beyond small companies, and even if small companies can afford them, whether the benefits will warrant the costs.

Note that both (a) (ii) and (c) require construction of arguments ie you only cover the points that support the view (if you had been asked to discuss, you would have had to cover fairly the points for and against). The examiner has indicated that questions asking students to construct a case will feature regularly in this exam. You should think of these types of questions as essentially asking 'Tell me why'.

Easy marks. (a) (i) and (b) should have been some of the easiest marks in this exam as they just represent textbook knowledge.

Examiner's comments. This question produced the poorest answers in this exam, although (a) (i) was well-done. (a) (ii) exposed students who were unaware of the arguments in favour of a principles-based approach, and who should not therefore have chosen this question. Similarly (b) exposed a lack of knowledge of what should be reported on internal controls. Many students misread the question and discussed external reporting or internal controls in general. In (c) a number of students failed to discuss the key issue of rigid reporting requirements bearing heavily on small companies.

Marking scheme

				Marks
(a)	(i)	1 mark for each essential feature briefly described		3
	(ii)	1 mark for each relevant point made on the advantages of principles-based max	4	
		2 marks for each relevant point on developing countries max	6	
				10
(b)	2 marks for each relevant area of content identified and briefly described			8
(c)	1 mark for each relevant valid argument put forward			4
				25

(a) (i) **Rules-based approaches**

Lack of flexibility

Rules-based approaches allow **no leeway**; the key issue is whether you have complied with the rules.

Visibility

It should be easy to **assess** whether or not a company has complied with the rules.

Aspects of governance emphasised

Rules-based approaches emphasise aspects of governance that can be verified easily, such as whether there is an **audit committee**. They place less emphasis on areas such as organisational culture that cannot be governed by clear rules.

(ii) **Overall compliance**

A principles-based approach emphasises to businesses the need to comply with the **overall spirit of governance codes**. It thus is more likely to encourage the **continuous improvement** that is particularly important in developing countries, especially in areas which are not easily covered by rules. Adopting a rules-based approach means that the focus is on conformance with a possibly limited set of rules.

Lack of local resources

A rules-based approach will only be effective if companies can draw on **sufficient local resources** to fulfil those rules. This may not be the case in developing countries. For example requiring all companies to set up an audit committee including non-executive directors with financial knowledge will be ineffective if there is an insufficient pool of individuals within the country who are willing to serve on audit committees.

Varying circumstances

Companies in developing countries are likely to develop their governance structures at different speeds as their businesses develop. Requiring all companies to meet the standards that are necessary for the **largest, most developed companies**, will not be **cost-effective**.

Local legislation

Professor Leroi highlighted the discussions going on at government level. A **rules-based approach to corporate governance** may only be effective if it is backed by government legislation; governments may not be willing to introduce this legislation because of the cost to the taxpayer and corporate sector.

International appeal

If companies in developing countries follow a recognised international principles-based code, for example the **OECD code**, this may inspire more confidence in investors than if they follow a local, rules-based, code. Investors will be judging against an internationally recognised benchmark. Also the emphasis in international codes on comply or explain encourages **transparency** by companies. This should also increase confidence because the accounts should explain clearly the company's current state of corporate governance.

(b) According to UK corporate governance guidance, the report should include the following disclosures:

Acknowledgement of board responsibility

The directors should acknowledge that they are responsible for the **company's system of internal control** and **reviewing its effectiveness**.

Management of risks

The board should disclose the **existence of a process for managing risks, how the board has reviewed the effectiveness of the process** and that the **process accords** with **guidance**.

Aims of control systems

The report should explain that the control system is **designed to manage** rather than **eliminate the risk of failure** to achieve business objectives, and can only provide **reasonable and not absolute assurance** against material misstatement or loss.

Review of control systems

The report should give a **summary of the process** that the directors (or a board committee) have used to **review the effectiveness of the system of internal control** and consider the **need for an internal audit function** if the company does not have one. The reports should also disclose the process the board has used to deal with **material internal control aspects of any significant problems** disclosed in the annual accounts.

Weaknesses in control systems

The report should give information about those **weaknesses in internal control** that have resulted in **material losses**, **contingencies or uncertainties**, which require disclosure in the financial statements or the auditors' report.

(c)   **Elaborate control systems**

The requirements of Sarbanes-Oxley and other worldwide governance guidance imply that businesses are reporting on **elaborate control systems** involving for example various board committees and varied means of assessing compliance. These systems are more complex than a small business with a few, **relatively straightforward activities**, would need.

External reporting

To be worthwhile, external reporting must be supported by a reliable assessment of how controls are operating. For smaller companies, this assessment will require **excessive time and resources** and will not be justified by the benefits it will deliver. Small companies would not have the resources to employ an internal audit department.

Audit costs

Some governance requirements, for example the Sarbanes-Oxley legislation, require auditors to attest the internal control report to give accounts users **greater assurance**. Paying for this exercise will be a significant extra cost, in addition to the audit fee, for small companies.

Shareholder assurance

A significant proportion of the shares of many small companies will be held by shareholders who are **directors or actively involved in management** and who do not need a report to inform them about the control systems.

12 TQ

Text reference. Chapter 3.

Top tips. (a) (i) illustrates the links between F4 and P1 – remember F4 material is assumed knowledge. Death, dissolution of the company and prolonged absence are other ways you could have mentioned. Knowledge of the law can help in (ii), as well as a questioning approach – how do you prove incompetence? The examiner is likely to test the assessment of poor performance by directors again in the future.

The key points in (b) are that the chairman's statement should demonstrate the accountability and the independence of the chairman.

In (c) and (d) the examiner's comments about how he uses the verb 'criticise' are very important. What he is looking for is not just, for example, a comment that the remuneration package is bad, but that it is deficient in comparison with what is regarded as best practice. The key yardstick in (c) is alignment of remuneration package against shareholders' interests, which demonstrates the package is totally unsatisfactory.

In (d) the four criteria for non-executive directors under the Higgs report – strategy, scrutiny, risk and people – are a useful framework for generating ideas. Higgs also provides a description of an effective chairman, which you can bring into your answer.

Easy marks. (a) (i) if you still remembered F4. Note though the examiner's comments about bullet points. Just providing three or four word bullets when the examiner wanted a sentence of explanation of each way would have cost you a couple of marks.

Examiner's comments. (a)(i) on the ways in which a director can leave a company was well done in most cases although as elsewhere, bullet lists were not well-rewarded. In (a) (ii), poorer answers said that it was easy to remove a serving chief executive from service. Better answers were able to draw out some of the issues surrounding the costs of removal, difficulties in proving incompetence and so on.

A common problem for (b) was failing to see that the question was asking candidates to assess the importance of the chairman's statement in the context of the case. The point was that the chairman had a particular duty to report truthfully to shareholders, and not to conceal information on executive performance that was material to shareholders. The question was not asking about the general purposes of a chairman's statement in an annual report.

(c) and (d) were both pitched at level 3 outcomes in which candidates had to show how the situations in question fell short of expectations or best practice. Overall, (c) was done better than (d). Good performance in 'criticise' questions relies on two things: a sound knowledge of the expectation or best practice against which to measure, and careful study of the case scenario.

Marking scheme

				Marks
(a)	(i)	1 mark for each way identified and explained. Half for identification only	max	4
	(ii)	1 mark for each relevant discussion point made		4
(b)		1 mark for each relevant comment made		5
(c)		1 mark for each relevant point of criticism clearly made		4
(d)		1 mark for each relevant point of criticism clearly made		8
				25

(a)　(i)　**Ways in which company directors leave a board**

Resignation

Directors can leave the board if they **resign by notice in writing.**

Disqualification

Directors may be disqualified from acting as a director if they are **disqualified by legislation or courts**, they become **bankrupt** or enter into an arrangement with creditors, or they become of **unsound mind**.

Failing to seek re-election

Directors leave a board when they are required by the **retirement by rotation** provisions in company constitutions to **seek re-election**, but they decide not to offer themselves for re-election.

Voted out

Directors also leave a board if they are nominated for re-election at an annual general meeting, but members **vote against their re-election**. Directors may be also removed from office by **ordinary resolution at a general meeting** of which **special notice** has been given to the company.

(ii)   **Service contract**

As an employee, a chief executive will have a service contract. If Mr Smith had been removed from office before the end of his contract, TQ could have faced **legal action and possible compensation for loss of office.** TQ may find it difficult to satisfy the courts that the chief executive was **incompetent.** This particularly applies to strategic decision-making where the success of decisions can only often be assessed in the longer-term, and where company failure does not provide a reliable indicator of incompetence.

Retirement by rotation

The chief executive may be required to **submit himself for re-election regularly** at annual general meetings, at which time members will have the opportunity to remove him from office. However provisions in the company's constitution may exempt the chief executive from retirement by rotation.

Special meeting of company

Some members may wish to force the chief executive's departure from office by voting him out at an extraordinary general meeting. However although some members were disgruntled, they may **not have been sufficient in number or voting powers** to be able to call a general meeting. In addition a director who is also a member may have **weighted voting rights** given to him under the constitution for such an eventuality, so that he can automatically defeat any motion to remove him as a director.

Resignation

It therefore follows that perhaps the quickest way to ensure the chief executive leaves office is to **persuade him to resign.** This could be done by the rest of the board stating that they have **lost confidence** in him. Here it seems the other directors were too cowed by Mr Smith to force the issue.

(b)   **Accountability and independence**

The chairman's statement is a separate document in the accounts that enables the chairman to demonstrate that she is acting in the **interests of shareholders.** Her commentary can also demonstrate an **independent view** of the company's affairs, drawing attention to issues that the chief executive would prefer not to be raised.

Performance of chairman

The statement can provide information about how the **chairman is exercising her role.** This information, along with analysis of the **quality and reliability of the other information in the statement,** provides the shareholders with material to enable them to judge the performance of the chairman.

Corporate governance

The chairman's statement could have provided information to shareholders about how corporate governance was operating in the company. In particular it could have explained how Mr Smith was **exercising his role**. It could also have commented on the **implications and consequences of the departure of the non-executive directors and the failure to replace them.**

Wider information provision

The chairman's statement could have included disclosures covering wider areas than those required by law or regulations. These could have given stakeholders a **better idea of the environment** within which TQ was operating and how it was responding. This should have enabled investors to carry out a more informed analysis of the **strategies** the company was pursuing, **reducing information asymmetry** between directors and shareholders. The chairman's statement could also have been focused on **future strategies and objectives**, giving readers a **different perspective to compulsory information** that tends to be **focused on historical accounting data**.

Assurance about executive management

The chairman's statement could have provided investors with further yardsticks to **judge the performance of executive management, in particular the chief executive.**

(c)   **Basic salary**

Most of Mr Smith's package is basic salary, and as such it is **unrelated to company performance and hence value to shareholders**. It therefore shields him from suffering the consequences of the poor strategic decisions he has allegedly made.

Car

The excessive amount spent on the car does **not appear to have resulted in any benefit** for TQ or its shareholders. Having such an expensive car does not appear to have been necessary for Mr Smith to perform his duties. If the car is viewed as a reward, again it is a reward that is unrelated to company performance.

Share options – long-term performance

The share options appear to have rewarded Mr Smith for TQ's performance over **too short a period of time**. They would have become worthless had he had to wait longer, and TQ had then gone into administration.

Share options – immediate exercise

In addition the benefits of share options, tying a **part of Mr Smith's remuneration package to TQ's performance**, disappeared as soon as Mr Smith exercised the options and could immediately sell the shares. Some benefit could have been retained if Mr Smith had been required to keep the shares for a period after the options were exercised, thus still maintaining his interest in ensuring TQ performed well and maintained a high share price.

(d)   **Strategy**

If the shareholders' allegations are correct, then Miss Hoiku has **failed to criticise the strategies** proposed by the chief executive, perhaps because she is frightened of him. The Higgs report suggests that the chairman and other non-executive directors should **scrutinise and challenge the strategies proposed by executives.** The chairman has responsibility for ensuring that the board spends **sufficient time discussing risk management issues.**

Scrutiny of chief executive' activities

As chairman Miss Hoiku should have **scrutinised Mr Smith's performance effectively.** She should have assessed his achievements against targets such as profit or revenues. She should also have **formally appraised his performance at least annually** and raised concerns about excessive time spent away from headquarters. **No effective appraisal** appears to have been carried out.

Agency problems

Miss Hoiku was also responsible for representing shareholder interests and ensuring that there was **goal congruence** between the **objectives of the shareholders** and the **activities of the chief executive**. Instead she has allowed a significant agency problem to develop, with the chief executive effectively voting himself a generous package that **bears little relation to what shareholders require.**

Risk management systems

The chairman should oversee the board's assessment of TQ's risk management systems. It is clear here that an **effective assessment did not take place,** since the problems with implementing strategy and **coordination of operational procedures** that derived from the absence of the chief executive were not resolved.

Failure to replace non-executive directors

The failure to replace the non-executive directors probably breaches local requirements about the proportion of non-executive directors on the board. Miss Hoiku should have ensured that the process for **recruiting new non-executive directors began** as soon as the existing directors announced they were leaving.

Committee system

The departure of the non-executive directors has resulted in a further **breach of governance best practice.** A key board committee (the remuneration committee) has not operated due to the lack of non-executive directors on the board and thus **Mr Smith's package has not been effectively scrutinised**.

Executive directors' remuneration

A remuneration committee should have been in place to **scrutinise the remuneration of the chief executive and other executive directors.** In the committee's absence Miss Hoiku was responsible for challenging executive packages rather than meekly accepting Mr Smith's proposals for his own package.

Shareholder communications

Miss Hoiku should have taken the lead in communicating with shareholders and making a considered response to shareholder concerns. Instead there appears to have been **no attempt to address shareholder concerns**, and **no explanation for this failure.** The chairman's statement appears inadequate.

13 Sam Mesentery

Text reference. Chapter 3.

Top tips. You have to adapt what you may remember about the contents of induction programmes, to pick up the strong hints in the scenario for (a). In particular ensuring the director is familiar with the company's culture is important here. If you struggled to think of any points, you should look at this area again.

In (b) the multi-tier board arrangement here appears to be similar to part of the Japanese model of governance, with the corporate board dealing with strategic issues and the operational board being made up of the main executives with a functional role. There is a case to be made for Annette's views on grounds of efficiency and clarity of purpose. However another argument in favour, that it means more control over operational directors, can be turned round to say that it also implies less control over Annette. There is also the issue of effective information provision to the main board, which of course was also a key issue in Question 1. As indicated by the mark scheme, a description of two-tier boards would have scored at maximum 2 marks. Only points that were clearly for or against the arrangement would have gained you the other marks. If you lacked the knowledge to give a good description, again you need to revise this area.

In (c) virtually everything Arif says can be challenged and the scenario therefore sets out clearly the points you need to make. Underpinning (c) are the reasons for having a separate chairman and chief executive. These include the demands of both roles, and the need for the chairman to be able to act for the shareholders in holding the chief executive to account – a vital aspect of the shareholders' enforcement of the agency relationships on the executives. This contrasts with the box-ticking of corporate governance requirements view which Arif holds. Markers would only have given marks in (c) for criticisms of Arif's conduct and views. General descriptions of the role of the chairman and non-executive directors would not have gained credit.

Easy marks. The examiner has flagged his interest in the roles of chairman and chief executive so you should have had the knowledge to demolish Arif's views in (c).

Examiner's comments. In (a) in most cases, the first task was done better than the second. The marks for 'explain the content' were mainly bookwork but it was necessary to study the problems with Sam Mesentery to gain the 'assess the advantages' marks. Candidates must be prepared to closely examine the text of case scenarios, as answers often require the placing of case evidence into a theoretical context.

(b) and (c) were less well done overall than part (a). Both required level 3 intellectual levels and a very careful analysis of the case. Candidates who did not answer at that level did not achieve a high score on these tasks. (b) was not just about the pros and cons of one type of board structure over another, but rather about their suitability in different environmental conditions, therefore this was an application question.

There was evidence of candidates not adequately reading the question in (c). It was necessary to know what the roles of a non-executive chairman are in order to compare Arif's views with those roles, but the question was not asking what the roles of a non-executive chairman are. The most common error in answering this question was listing the roles of the chairman and failing to analyse what Arif had actually said.

				Marks
(a)	1 mark for each relevant point recognised and explained. 1 mark for development of each point and assessment with regard to Sam	max		8
(b)	Evidence of understanding the meaning of unitary and two-tier boards		2	
	1 mark for each relevant point made in favour of Annette's belief	max	3	
	1 mark for each relevant point made against Annette's belief	max	3	
				8
(c)	1 mark for each relevant point of criticism recognised.			
	1 mark for development and application	max		9
				25

(a) **Build an understanding of the company**

The induction programme should ensure that the new director has a sufficient understanding of the company's **products or services, major risks** and board **operations**.

Induction will help Sam understand the **complex environment** in which Ding is operating and the nature of Ding's **resource markets**. It should also help Sam understand why the board is **constituted** as a two-tier board, and what that means for the way it operates.

Develop relations with colleagues

Induction should help new directors establish relations with their colleagues by personal meetings and by setting out how **colleagues are expected to work together**. It should prevent early clashes which could permanently damage relationships.

Here it seems that **Sam's relationship with Annette** was **not established properly** at the start and the fact that their first significant meeting was when Annette admonished Sam may impair their future relationship. Proper induction could have meant that Sam avoided the misunderstandings that have led to Annette rebuking him.

Develop relationships with external parties

Induction should give new directors the chance to start developing relations with the **key external stakeholders** with whom they will be dealing.

Here it should mean that Sam has an early opportunity to **meet Ding's auditors** and establish how they operate and the **significance of differences in auditing practices** in this country compared with the country in which Sam has previously been based. He should also be introduced to Ding's **main finance providers**.

Promote understanding of practices and culture

Induction should also allow new directors to gain an understanding of the company's practices and culture, 'our way of doing things'. This could include how directors **conduct themselves in their dealings with others** and **practical operating matters.**

Early problems have arisen as a result of Sam failing to receive **proper induction.** An induction process would have demonstrated to Sam how expectations in dealings with others differed in this country compared with his previous base, and made it less likely that he would make an **inappropriate remark.** He would also have been briefed on the **practical policies** with which he must comply, such as the positioning of his desk.

(b) **Single and two-tier boards**

Under a single board system all participants have an **equal legal responsibility** for management of the company and strategic performance. This requires the **active involvement of all board members** in the board's operation, and the participation of all directors in strategic discussions.

In the two-tier system described here, the split is between the corporate board, which has responsibilities for decision-making on **long-term strategic issues**, and the operational board which is responsible for **day-to-day matters and functional performance.**

Arguments in favour of Annette's view

Flexibility of decision-making

A small strategic board, which does not have operational demands on its time, can more **easily get together** and **respond with necessary speed** to the changes in business environment such as issues with an important supplier. Having a larger number of people involved may make it more difficult to arrange meetings. It may also mean that it takes **longer to make a decision** when meetings are held because of the need to bring everyone into discussions.

Complex nature of environment

Clearly the environment in which Ding operates requires **careful review and monitoring,** because of the **continual changes in it.** Members of the corporate board will have more time to review the environment if they do not have operational responsibilities.

Holding operational board to account

The corporate board can act as the shareholders' agent and **hold directors in charge of operations** to account.

Arguments against Annette's view

Failure to take account of all views and information

Although the corporate board is taking strategic decisions, issues such as problems with a supplier could clearly have **major operational consequences.** Members of the operational board should be advising on these as part of board discussions, but are not being given the chance to participate here. This may mean that operational board members **fail to support the decision,** which may **hinder the implementation of the strategy.**

Take over by individual

Having a smaller board in charge of the long-term direction of the company may make it easier for a **single individual to wield excessive power**. That seems to be a distinct risk here with a board of only five members and Annette's views not being challenged by Arif. A larger board consisting of all directors may mean that the **chief executive's views** are **more likely to be challenged**.

Accountability

Having two tiers of directors may lead to confusion over board **accountability**, particularly as here when strategic decisions have a major impact on operations. Who is ultimately responsible for maintaining relations with suppliers and ensuring that supply is maintained? This is particularly important if a strategic board takes an **inappropriate decision** and operational directors are forced to implement a policy with which they do not agree.

(c) **Ceremonial nature of role**

Arif's view that the role of the chairman is ceremonial seriously underestimates its importance. The chairman should be responsible for **overseeing the functioning of the board**. As such he should not simply **defer to Annette's views on board structure**. This means also that the chairman should ensure that the board **receives reliable and timely information** and that **sufficient time** is allowed for discussion of controversial issues. That does not seem to be happening here and as a result key directors are being excluded from discussions.

Compliance with corporate governance requirements

Arif's view of compliance with corporate governance guidance is also misguided. When they recommend that the **roles of chairman and chief executive** be **split,** corporate governance codes require more than the roles be held by different people. They seek a **division of responsibilities** with the chief executive running the company, but the chairman being able to **hold the chief executive to account and express the concerns of other non-executive directors and shareholders.**

Role of non-executives

Arif's inability to challenge Annette's opinions demonstrates that he is **ineffective** as a chairman and non-executive director. One of the roles of non-executive directors according to the Higgs report is to **contribute to, and challenge, the strategy** that the chief executive and other executives are promoting. As chairman Arif should be taking the lead in this.

Independence of chairman

It seems that Arif's friendship with Annette was a significant factor in his appointment and he appears to feel indebted to her. However the expectations of shareholders, whose interests the chairman represents, is that the chairman should be **objective.**

Commitment to role

Arif's view of the **level of commitment** required as chairman again demonstrates he totally misunderstands its importance. One reason why governance reports recommend splitting the roles of chairman and chief executive is that both should be demanding jobs. Arif **cannot effectively be leading the board** if he does not attend many of its meetings. His lack of direct interest in Ding does mean that he will find it **difficult to hold Annette to account.** His lack of involvement also may mean that the chairman's statement that he writes cannot provide any assurance to shareholders.

14 Tomato Bank

Text references. Chapters 1, 3 and 9.

Top tips. The problems in (a) are fairly well signposted in the scenario, emphasising the examiner's comments about the need for careful analysis of the scenario. To score high marks you need to demonstrate an understanding of the qualities and duties of non-executive directors.

The latter part of (b) brings out the agency problem which underlies the whole question. It also considers the best ways of ensuring that the remuneration package can be an effective mechanism for passing judgement on the directors' performance. Judging over a longer period provides stronger evidence, and removing entitlement on a vote of no confidence by the shareholders ensures shareholder opinions are taken into account

You could have used other frameworks as a basis for answering (c). Again concepts of agency and responsibility are important, and enhanced by the director's poor conduct.

Easy marks. Certainly the remuneration package elements in (b), although note that you had to give some description to get a mark for each. Merely listing each item would have given you half a mark at best.

Examiner's comments. (a) and (b) were done quite well overall but (c) was done poorly by most candidates.

In (a), I was pleased to see that many candidates were able to do well on this question with case analysis skills being well demonstrated by successful candidates. On questions containing verbs such as 'criticise', careful analysis of the case is usually essential in preparing good answers.

In (b), the first task, largely bookwork, was done better than the second. There were ample points in the case to pick up on and careful study of the case was rewarded with higher marks than those who merely relied on 'lists' of points.

(c) was badly done by most candidates. Although Mr Woof was legally entitled to receive the pension value, the question specifically asked candidates about the ethical case. Mr Woof could have accepted a reduction in the value of his pension in recognition of his failure as CEO. This was done poorly by a majority of candidates, thus somewhat underscoring the importance of developing ethical reasoning skills in preparation for P1 exams.

				Marks
(a)	2 marks for each criticism identified and discussed	max		10
(b)	1 mark for each component identified and described (0.5 marks for identification only)	max	5	
	1 mark for each relevant point of explanation of the benefits of a balanced package for Mr Woof	max	5	
				10
(c)	1 mark for each relevant point made	max		5
				25

(a) **Failure to consider risks**

The remuneration committee was too heavily influenced by the favourable publicity surrounding Woof. It failed to consider the **consequences** of Woof failing to deliver. Although Woof had previously been successful, this may have been by taking very risky strategies. The committee failed to consider whether Woof's package was **compatible** with the desirable risk **appetite** of the bank.

Agreeing to non-performance related element

A significant part of Woof's package was the pension element. It was not related to the bank's performance and shareholders' interests. Woof was still entitled to it despite the bank's problems, and there was **no downside risk** for him. The committee could have made the granting of the pension dependent on Woof leaving office in a satisfactory way, and not being forced out for failure.

Lack of scrutiny of elements

The committee failed to scrutinise the individual elements of the package. In particular they failed to take into account the fact that a significant part of the package was **payable after only two years**, but Woof's performance could only be judged fairly over a longer time period. The directors also should have considered whether the **balance of the different elements of the package** was appropriate.

Influenced by Woof and finance director

The committee failed to take an **objective view** of the package, but allowed itself to be **influenced by Woof's lobbying and pressure from the finance director**. Governance reports recommend that the committee is made up of non-executive directors so that they can take a **view of directors' remuneration** that is **independent** of executive directors. Instead committee members **failed to scrutinise and challenge** the proposals put forward by the finance director.

Lack of independence

Two of the non-executive directors were former colleagues of Woof's. They lacked the **independence** required by governance best practice to judge what his package should be. They should therefore have taken no part in the decisions on his remuneration.

(b) **Elements of reward package**

Basic salary

Basic salary will be in **accordance with the director's contract of employment** and is not related to the performance of the company and the director. It is determined by the **experience of the director** and the **market rate** that other companies are prepared to pay.

Short and long-term performance related bonuses

Directors may be paid a cash bonus for meeting **performance targets**. It may well be linked to the level of **accounting profits**. The bonus level may be limited to a **fixed percentage of salary or pay**.

Shares and share options

Directors may be **awarded shares** in the company with time limits on when they can be sold. They may alternatively be awarded **share options**, the right to purchase shares at a specified exercise price over a specified time period in the future. If the price of the shares exceeds the exercise price when the options can be exercised, the directors will be able to buy shares at lower than market value.

Benefits-in-kind

Benefits-in-kind can include a car, health provisions, life assurance, holidays, expenses and loans.

Pension contributions

Companies may pay directors' pension contributions. Directors may be in a **separate scheme** from employees, and have their contributions paid at a higher rate. A pre-arranged pension benefit might also be paid after a certain number of years' service.

Why more balanced package would have been appropriate

Agency costs

A package more dependent on company performance would have reduced **agency costs**. Agency costs arise out of the need for shareholders to monitor the performance of their agent (CEO) and are enhanced if the agent's interests are not aligned with theirs. A package based on results would bring the CEO's **interests more into line with shareholders**, and reduce the need for **scrutiny.**

Investors' expectations about risk

The package appears to have encouraged Woof to **pursue a high risk high growth strategy.** This will have been contrary to the **interests and expectations** of shareholders who held Tomato's shares as a **low-risk element** in a balanced portfolio. To counter this excessive risk-taking, the package could have depended on an assessment by internal audit of the **riskiness** of the sources of funding, and judgements by the remuneration committee of whether these risks were too high.

Long-term elements

It seems Woof's performance could only be judged fairly **over a number of years**, since the **demand for mortgages** is over the long-term (often 25 years). However much of the package was payable before a judgement could be made.

Past performance

In a sense the pension entitlement was awarded based on Woof's good performance at other banks. However his historic performance did **not guarantee future profit increases** for Tomato's shareholders, and his package should have been based more on what he achieved at Woof.

Manner of departure

A further way of adding balance to the package would be to have made some or all of it **conditional** on the way in which **Woof left office**. The agreement could have provided for a loss of entitlement if Woof left office as the result of a shareholders' vote.

(c)   **Accountability to shareholders**

As the agent of shareholders, Woof is accountable to them for the performance of the bank. A decision to accept a reduction indicates his **responsibility for strategic decisions**, and acknowledges that he is answerable for the consequences of his poor management.

Expectations

The case for a reduction is enhanced by Woof **knowing** that he was taken on because his reputation led the directors to believe the bank would generate much better results under his leadership. He **encouraged these expectations** by his promises of sustained growth for many years. Though the pension element was not explicitly linked to performance, Woof was given it because other directors believed that it was needed for him to agree to become CEO and deliver the growth.

Responsibility for results

The case for Woof giving up some of his pension is enhanced the **level of direct responsibility** he has for the bank's problems. Although poor economic conditions beyond Woof's control could have led to the failure of the sources of funds, Woof's excessive risk-taking has made a bad situation worse for the bank.

Flaws in granting process

A further argument for Woof returning his pension was that the procedure for granting it was **unsatisfactory.** The directors making the decision were too concerned to attract him and failed to give his package the **independent and thorough scrutiny** required.

Level of morality

Judged by Kohlberg's scale of morality, Woof appears to be operating at pre-conventional level 1, seeing the situation in terms of the rewards to which he has an **entitlement.** If he was viewing the decision at a desirable post-conventional level 3 he would take into account the views of society that he was morally not entitled to the pension or even decide independently that he should not be rewarded for failure.

15 KK

Text references. Chapter 3.

Top tips. The requirements for this question require careful reading as it's particularly easy to produce a general answer for (b) and (c) that contains much irrelevant material. In (a) the requirement to discuss suggests 2 marks will be available for each conflict of interest that you cover. Note the problem with the cross-directorship would apply even if KK did not purchase from SS.

The temptation in (b) is to base the answer around all of the Higgs report categories (strategy, scrutiny, risk and people). The answer however needs to focus on NEDs' contribution to discussions about strategy and also risk. The last point about reassurance is important in the context of the agency relationship between shareholders and executive directors. Effective NEDs can lower other agency costs.

It would be easy for an answer to (c) to be a unorganised list of disclosures. The focus needs to be on the performance and functioning of the board, as this is the main concern of Fin. Some of the headings used in the answer are similar to those in the UK Corporate Governance Code, although we also discuss communication with shareholders.

Easy marks. Identifying the conflicts of interest in (a) should have been straightforward as they are very clearly highlighted in the scenario.

Examiner's comments. (a) asked candidates to explain what a conflict of interest was and then to discuss the conflicts of interest that would arise if John Soria, the nominee for the position, became the NED of KK Company. This was done well overall, with many candidates scoring well on both tasks.

There was a difference in (b) between candidates who attempted to analyse the case and carefully consider what the question was actually asking, and those who seemed to think that questions asking about the non-executives should be answered in terms of the four general roles (people, risk, strategy, scrutiny). The question asked specifically about how NEDs would benefit the KK board during a period of growth and this required candidates to carefully consider the particular circumstances in question. Those candidates that carefully considered the case and the particular advantages that NEDs could bring during a period of rapid growth achieved the highest marks.

(c) was actually asking something quite straightforward: what would a good corporate governance section of an annual report contain. In many countries, a substantive CG section is either mandatory or prescribed under listing rules. Reports often have several pages of content called 'corporate governance' or similar. This underlines the importance of candidates being aware of a range of reporting issues. Inspecting the annual reports of most large companies would be a way of becoming familiar with corporate governance reports. One common error was to answer as if the question was asking about the contents of an annual report (chairman's statement, income statement, etc.). It was asking about the corporate governance section in an annual report and not about the annual report in its entirety.

			Marks
(a)	Explanation of conflict of interest	2	
	2 marks for each potential conflict of interest identified and explained		
	max	6	
			8
(b)	2 marks for each advantage assessed max		7
(c)	2 marks for each section explained max	8	
	Explanation of information needs of Fin Brun	2	
			10
			25

(a) **Conflicts of interest**

Non-executive directors (NEDs)' conduct and decision-making should be determined by the best interests of the company that they manage and its shareholders. A conflict of interest is an external pressure or commitment that **undermines the independence** of NEDs and could lead them to make decisions that are not in the best interests of the company or shareholders.

Conflicts of interest in KK

Personal relationships

John has very strong links with KK's board, being brother-in-law of the chief executive and friends with the rest of the board. John may not therefore wish to come into conflict with the board if it **threatens family harmony or friendships**. John may also be more inclined to take what KK board members tell him on trust because he relies on his close personal knowledge of them. Thus he may fail to query doubtful conduct or decisions when he should do so.

Relationship with supplier

John's non-executive directorship can be expected to strengthen the links between KK and Soria Supplies. (SS). A close supply chain relationship may in practice benefit both companies. However the underlying conflict of interest is that as directors of both companies, John and also Susan are expected to **promote the best interests of both**, and these may come into conflict. In particular it could ultimately be in KK's best interests to stop using SS because, for example, other suppliers offer better terms. John and Susan could not be involved in this decision because of their commitment to SS.

Cross-directorships

The cross-directorships of John and Susan (executive director of KK is NED of SS and vice-versa) are by themselves a threat to independence, even if there were no other links between KK and SS. The problem is that non-executive directors will **sit in judgement on executives** when, for example, they consider their remuneration. Having one director judge another when the other director is also judging the first director is a conflict of interest, since directors' decisions could clearly be determined by their own interests rather than their companies.

(b) **Advice on strategy**

NEDs with wide knowledge of the industry such as John has, could help advise on the **appropriateness** of **expansion strategies**. Here the right NEDs could supply what other directors are lacking, **knowledge of particular overseas markets and experience of developing a presence in these markets**.

Advice on risk

Experienced NEDs should also be able to offer an **informed opinion** about the **riskiness of rapid expansion** into new markets. Because KK is growing quickly, it is likely to face new or much increased exposure to many different risks. The NEDs may have greater knowledge of some of these risks than the less experienced executives. The NEDs should also advise on whether the increase in risk exposure has been too high, given the **returns** available and the **appetite of shareholders for new risks.**

Advice on risk management

Because the NEDs have had experience of other companies, they should also be able to **benchmark KK's risk and control management systems** against systems elsewhere, and try to ensure that they are developing along with the expansion in business. The expansion in director numbers may help, but will not be enough by itself. A **risk committee**, staffed by NEDs, could be valuable for KK.

Reassurance to investors

Experienced and effective NEDs should also offer shareholders comfort that Ken Kava does not have unrestrained powers of decision-making. Shareholders will want to believe that NEDs are **scrutinising future plans**, and **challenging strategies** that they believe to be inappropriate. For KK, experienced NEDs are particularly important for shareholders because of the **lack of experience** of many of the executive directors, which appears to mean that executives lack the confidence to challenge Ken.

(c) **Board details**

Shareholders will be interested in how the board is functioning as a **forum for decision-making** and **monitoring**. The report should contain details about the workings of the board including the frequency of, and attendance at, board meetings, and how the board's performance has been evaluated. The report should also detail changes in the composition of the board, including particularly explanations of why directors have **left the board suddenly and unexpectedly**.

Non-executive directors and board committees

Shareholders will be looking for evidence that NEDs are a strong, objective presence on the board. The report should explain whether NEDs are considered to be **independent.** NEDs will also be particularly involved in **key board committees**, the **nomination, audit, remuneration and risk committees**. The report therefore should contain details about the terms of reference and composition of these committees, as well as the frequency of meetings. Each of the main committees should provide a **report on their activities during the year.**

Accounts and audit

The report should contain certain specific disclosures for shareholders' reassurance. These include a statement of the **board's responsibility for the preparation of accounts and that the company is a going concern.** The report should contain details about any **accounting issues** that have arisen, for example the impact of changes in accounting standards or a restatement of the accounts. There should be information about **relations with auditors**, including reasons for change and steps taken to ensure auditor objectivity and independence if auditors have provided non-audit services. If the company does not have an **internal audit** function, the report should say why. The report should also include a statement about the **board's review of internal controls**.

Communication with shareholders

The report should include information about **relations with shareholders** and how communication channels have been maintained. The report can be a means of providing shareholders with the information that they have said they need. This particularly applies to the **business review,** which should give shareholders information about how the directors view **historic performance and their plans for future strategy.** This is particularly important where, as with KK, the company is developing rapidly.

Fin Brun's information needs

Fin Brun is correct in asserting that it is likely to be difficult to determine individual directors' performance from the accounts. The accounts can however provide some information to reassure Fin. The accounts should disclose why directors have been **nominated for election or re-election.** The accounts should disclose the **bonuses paid to directors,** which should have been objectively determined by a remuneration committee staffed by NEDs. These will provide an indication of how the remuneration committee has viewed performance. The report could also include **biographical details** about the directors and also details of their **main responsibilities and objectives**. This information together should help Fin determine whether directors appear to be qualified for board membership and their board roles. The accounts could also give more details about the **process for appraising individual directors**, including the frequency of assessment, the criteria used and how the results of the appraisal are actioned. These should help reassure Fin that a rigorous system is in place.

16 HHO

Text references. Chapters 1 and 3.

Top tips. Most of the differences discussed in (a) relate to issues mentioned in the scenario.

The main omission from the scenario is the role of trustees. It is important to bring out in (b) the links between transparency and accountability to different classes of stakeholder, particularly donors. It might have been helpful to think, when answering (b), about why you give money to particular charities, and what you expect to see those charities doing. Transparency here, as in other questions in this exam, is also seen as a means of reducing or halting damaging publicity about the organisation.

In (c) the answer discusses most of the major roles of the audit committee. As always, your answer needs to bring in material from the case as a justification for discussing each role. The compliance role of the audit committee is perhaps wider than it would be for a limited company, with more focus on compliance with the expectations of stakeholders and not just laws and regulations.

Easy marks. Definitions such as the definition of transparency in (b) should always be worth a couple of straightforward marks.

Examiner's comments. (a) should have been straightforward to candidates that were familiar with the relevant part of the study guide and who had studied the relevant technical article. This part was done quite well by many of those who attempted question 3.

(b) offered more of a challenge because after a relatively straightforward opening (to define transparency), a higher level verb ('construct') invited candidates to examine the case in detail and to pick out those things that were wrong at HHO and to use those issues to argue in favour of greater transparency.

ACCA examiner's answer. The ACCA examiner's answer to this question can be found at the back of this kit.

			Marks
(a)	0.5 marks for identification. 2 marks for each area of difference identified and explained max	6	
	Differences in governance structures max	3	
			9
(b)	2 marks for definition of transparency		
	2 marks for each point made for greater transparency max		8
(c)	2 marks for each relevant area of internal audit explained max		8
			25

(a) **Purpose**

The main purpose of companies is to earn a return for shareholders. Directors and staff aim to **maximise long-term cash flows**. Success is measured by **earnings per share, cash flows and share price movements.**

Charities exist to fulfil the charitable purpose for which the charity is set up. To be able to operate as a charity, this purpose will have to be a **socially beneficial or benevolent purpose as defined by the law.** Funds are donated to the charity to support its charitable purpose. The charity's governance should thus not only be concerned with maximising the income received, but also the expectations of donors about how their donations will be used.

Regulations

Companies will be subject to **companies' legislation** that applies locally, including regulations about how the company should be administered and the contents of the company's financial reports. Larger companies listed on a local stock exchange will be subject to listing rules and required to comply with the local governance codes, which include additional requirements such as the need for board committees.

Charities will be subject to a different statutory regime. They will need to fulfil the requirements of the local charitable authority to be able to operate as a charity. **Charitable status** confers certain privileges, for example exemption from taxation, that companies do not have. The **accounting information required from charities** is also likely to differ from that required for companies. In this country the information that charities have to disclose is significantly less than companies, but the same is not true in other regimes.

Stakeholders' expectations

Society expects a business to be **run profitably and efficiently** and to supply goods or services that society requires. A business is expected to **create value** for shareholders, and treat other key stakeholders, particularly employees, suppliers and customers, fairly. A business will be successful if people want to work for it, suppliers supply resources and customers buy what it offers.

A charity's main stakeholders include donors, beneficiaries and employees. All of these will be concerned about the extent to which, and the ways in which, the charity **fulfils its benevolent purposes.**

Governance arrangements

Companies are **governed by a board of directors**. Listed companies are expected to include non-executive directors as well as executive directors on their board. The shareholders can hold the board accountable through **votes at general meetings,** including votes on whether to re-elect directors and whether to approve directors' remuneration arrangements. In many countries a single board oversees the company.

Charities may have a board of executive directors to run its **operations**. However the fulfilment of the charity's purposes is **overseen** by a **board of trustees**. The trustees interpret how the charity's purposes and fiduciary duties should be applied. The trustees may include **representatives of beneficiaries**. However in many instances, as with HHO, trustees will have to look after the interests of beneficiaries who cannot represent themselves. The trustees themselves hold the executive board **accountable** for running the charity in **accordance with the charity's purposes**. This includes being sensitive to whether the executive board is acting in its own interests and not the charity's, by, for example, earning excessive salaries.

(b) **Transparency**

Transparency means **open and clear disclosure** of relevant information to stakeholders, and also not concealing information when it may affect decisions. It implies a **default position of information provision rather than concealment**.

Reassurance of donors

Donors provide the charity with the bulk of its income. They will wish to see that the charity is spending **its money in accordance with its aims and purposes**, and their monies have funded the projects promoted by Horace Hoi. In many countries multiple charities exist to promote animal welfare. The proportion of money being spent on improving animal welfare by each charity will be a major influence on donors' decisions on which charity to support. In addition donors may also be influenced by the level of detail provided by different charities, gaining greater reassurance from charities that give much more detail than HHO has provided. The lack of detail given by HHO may be counter-productive and suggest the charity has something to hide. **Reduction of criticism**

As well as being influenced by the data the charity itself provides, donor decisions will also be influenced by other information. Press criticism poses a **substantial threat to the reputation of the charity** and **could lead to a significant fall in donations and other support.** Better information would demonstrate to the media that HHO took donors' concerns seriously. It would also decrease the risk of inaccurate speculation by journalists damaging the charity.

Position of Horace Hoi

Horace Hoi's role has come under particular scrutiny and concerns have been raised about his **stewardship of the organisations' resources.** Donors and others are concerned that he is receiving excessive rewards and is spending money unnecessarily, for example on the private jet. The failure to join other charities in disclosing more information can be seen as demonstrating a poor attitude to governance. The accounts should be used to explain the business case for **potentially controversial expenditure**, for example the need for Horace Hoi to be transported rapidly around the world.

(c) ### Role of audit committee

The audit committee can help create a **culture** that emphasises discipline and control in governance. The audit committee can also contribute to improving significantly the culture of **transparency.** The committee's role will be strengthened if it consists of independent trustees or non-executive directors, at least some of whom have financial knowledge. Directors with these qualities should be able to **resist pressure** from Horace Hoi and make **informed judgements on key areas**.

Review of financial statements

The audit committee can play a particularly important role in HHO by reviewing the quality of financial information. The committee can put pressure on the other directors to **increase the level of detail of financial reporting** towards the full disclosure made by other charities. It can also review the accounting systems that provide the financial information for the public and charity and tax authorities, and press for improvements in these.

Review of internal controls

The audit committee can also look at other aspects of internal control. It should focus on the **control of the expenses** that do not relate directly to specific charitable projects, as these are a sensitive issue. It should press for **proper budgeting** of this expenditure and follow-up by executive management if actual expenditure exceeds budgets. It should also obtain evidence about the system of expenditure authorisation, focusing on **authorisation of large amounts** and **expenditure which may not be necessary** for the charity's main purpose. The audit committee also needs to assess whether adequate controls are in place to **limit the risk of fraud and non-compliance with regulations.**

Fraud

The audit committee should also consider the risk of **fraud.** Because of the sensitivities surrounding expenditure levels at HHO, the audit committee should establish a **whistleblowing channel**, enabling staff to report suspicions of fraud directly to the audit committee. The audit committee should also be able to **instigate an investigation** into fraud itself, without the approval of executive directors being required. Here there seems to be a need for the audit committee to **investigate remuneration arrangements for directors** and the **activities of Horace Hoi,** assessing whether he has misused the charity's income to fund his personal lifestyle.

Compliance and ethics

The audit committee should obtain evidence that HHO is **complying with the regulations and codes** that apply in this country to an organisation with charitable status. It should also check for compliance with voluntary codes, for example that the charity's appeals are line with the sector's best practice and do not mislead donors. More widely it could itself review **large transactions for reasonableness,** measured against the expectations of the charity's donors.

17 FF Co

Marking scheme

			Marks
(a)	Description of 'sound' control systems – up to 2 marks for each valid point	6	
	Explanation of shortcomings at FF plc – 1 mark for each valid point made	6	
	max		10
(b)	Definition of 'reputation risk' – 1 mark for each valid point made	3	
	Explanation of the financial effects of poor reputation – 1 mark for each valid point made	4	
	Recognition of the causes of FF's reputation problems – 1 mark for each valid point made	2	
	max		8
(c)	Responsibilities to employer – 1 mark for each valid point made	4	
	Responsibilities to professionalism – 1 mark for each valid point made	4	
	max		7
			25

(a) **Control systems**

The Turnbull report sees control framework as being designed to **achieve a number of objectives** and emphasises the need for the control system to be **sound;** an unsound system can undermine corporate governance. **Control systems** are often defined as being made up of two main elements – the **control environment** and **control procedures**.

Compliance with laws and regulations

Control systems should **ensure compliance with applicable laws and regulations**, also with internal policies.

FF's systems clearly have not done this; FF has **failed to follow fire safety standards** and its accounts have **failed to comply with accounting standards**. Also management have **not been able to enforce the objective** of complying with the highest standards of control.

Ensure the quality of internal and external reporting

This requires the **maintenance of proper records and processes** which generate a flow of timely and relevant information.

The qualified audit report that FF has had may be a **failure of controls**, a lack of awareness within the company of the requirements of accounting standards.

Respond to significant and changing risks

The control system should **identify what the most significant risks** are, and be capable of responding quickly to **evolving risks within the business.**

The **lack of compliance with fire reporting standards** suggests a failure within SS's systems to **identify significant risks**, not just the **direct risks of selling unsafe products** but also the **reputation risk** arising from this.

Control environment

The control environment is the **stress** placed by directors and managers, also the management style and **corporate culture and values shared by all employees.**

The Turnbull report comments that internal control systems should be **embedded in the operations of a company** and **form part of its culture.**

The scenario highlights a number of problems with the control environment within FF. Although the board have sought to promote the highest standards of internal control, the **directors failed to respond** when the issue of product safety was raised. In addition Miss Osula asserted that there was a overall **culture of carelessness** within FF.

Control procedures

Control procedures represent the specific **policies and procedures** designed to achieve objectives.

The scenario highlights a number of failings in the control procedures of FF. The **quality control** relating to the **material testing** clearly failed. The qualified audit report suggests a **failure in accounting controls**. Reporting control failings to management is a management control, part of the **system of accountabilities,** and again that failed to work as no action was taken.

(b) **Reputation risk**

Reputation risk is the risk of a **loss of reputation** of an organisation, arising from the **perceptions** others have about the implications of risks materialising. Reputation risk levels depend **not only on the levels of other risks** but **the reaction of stakeholders** to those other risks materialising – how much less of the organisation do stakeholders think, and what actions they take.

Stakeholders and financial consequences

Thus the level of reputation risk depends on the actions that stakeholders can take that can affect the organisation financially. These actions vary by stakeholder.

Shareholders

Shareholders can ultimately sell their shares, more easily if FF is **listed**, if they lack confidence in the way the company is governed. If shareholders holding a significant proportion of shares do this, FF's **share price will fall.**

Customers

If customers are concerned about the safety of FF's products, they are likely to cease buying them, causing **falls in revenues and profits**.

Law enforcement agencies

FF may face **legal action** as a result of failing to comply with standards. This could lead to **fines** and **lawyers' fees** for defending the action. FF may also be ordered to **cease manufacturing** the product that has not complied with standards, again causing **falls in revenues and profits.**

Auditors

Because of the qualified audit report, auditors are likely to scrutinise FF's records more closely in subsequent years, leading to an **increase in audit fees.**

(c) **Ethical responsibilities to employer**

Probity

Accountants should act honestly and not be swayed from fulfilling their duty to the employers by considerations of **personal interests** or **illegitimate pressures** to act other than in their employers' interests.

Professional competence

Accountants should **exercise competence and skill** in the service of the employer and maintain knowledge of best practice, legislation and techniques. Accountants should also **exercise due care** when working in the employer's interests.

Confidentiality

Accountants should respect **confidential information** that they have about their employer and should **not disclose it without proper or specific authority** or **unless there is a legal or professional right or duty to disclose.** This should apply during and after their employment.

Responsibilities towards shareholders and stakeholders

Accountants should seek to fulfil the company's objectives of trying to maximise shareholder value, also **maintaining good relationships** with **other relevant stakeholders.**

Promotion of business interests

Employees have a duty to promote their employer's **legitimate business interests** and not take actions that would be detrimental to their employer.

Responsibilities as an accountant

Public interest

Accountants have a general duty to act in the public interest; at times this may override the **duty of confidentiality**. With FF, Miss Osula's actions could be justified on the grounds that the public needed to know about potential dangers of FF's products.

Professional behaviour

Accountants should **avoid any action that discredits the profession** and **comply with laws and regulations, also ethical codes**. Again Miss Osula's **actions could be justified** on the grounds that to stay silent would have effectively been condoning a breach of regulation.

18 LinesRUs

Marking scheme

				Marks
(a)	Risk identification		4	
	Risk assessment		4	
	Risk profiling		4	
	Risk quantification		4	
	Risk consolidation		4	
	Give full credit for other similar frameworks	max		15
(b)	Risk responses. Up to 3 marks per response. To gain high marks, reference must be made to company circumstances	max		10
				25

(a) **Risk identification**

Risks cannot be managed without first realising that they exist. Managers need to maintain a **list of known or familiar risks** and the extent to which they can harm the organisation or people within it. Managers also need to be aware that unfamiliar risks may exist and maintain vigilance in case these risks occur. **Risk identification** is an **ongoing process** so that new risks and changes affecting existing risks may be identified quickly and dealt with appropriately before they result in unacceptable losses.

LinesRUs appear to have **identified some risks** in their risk management policy. However, other risks do occur and managers within LinesRUs must be able to identify and respond to those risks quickly.

Risk assessment

It may be difficult to forecast the financial affects of a risk until after a disaster has occurred. Areas such as **extra expenses, inconvenience and loss of time** can then be recognised, even if they were not thought of in initial risk analysis. In a severe situation, damage to the company's reputation could result in LinesRUs becoming bankrupt.

In this situation, there has been a loss of confidence in the company, the extent of which may not have been foreseen. This has resulted in **additional expense in terms of lost passengers** – legal advice will be needed to determine whether LinesRUs is liable and whether the company's insurance meets this liability. It is also uncertain what the **additional time and cost of repairing the track** will be and whether LinesRUs can claim additional income for this work.

Sources of information to ensure that the risk can be minimised may include **obtaining regular reports** from train operators on the state of the rail infrastructure and **monitoring news feeds** such as Reuters for early indication of potential disasters. LinesRUs should **file appropriate reports** of physical inspection of track as evidence of maintenance work carried out.

Risk profiling

This stage involves using the results of risk assessment to group risks into families. A consequence matrix is one method of doing this.

Likelihood	Consequences	
	Low	High
High	Loss of lower level staff	Loss of senior staff
Low	Loss of suppliers Major rail disaster not the company's fault	Major rail disaster affecting reputation of company. Loss of computer data on maintenance work. Loss of franchise

The analysis will be incomplete for LinesRUs because not all risks can be identified.

Risk quantification

Risks that require more detailed analysis can be quantified, and, where possible, results and probabilities calculated. The result of calculations will show average or expected result or loss, frequency of losses, chances of losses and largest predictable loss to which LinesRUs could be exposed by a particular risk.

Unfortunately, **many of the risks facing LinesRUs** are **significant**. So while quantification can be enhanced by past events such as drivers falling asleep, they appear to be one-off situations meaning that the actual event may not occur again. However, the adverse effects of the risk in terms of costs necessary to repair the rail infrastructure will be helpful enabling LinesRUs to ensure that appropriate insurance is available – effectively guarding against loss by transferring the risk.

Risk consolidation and review

Risks analysed at the divisional or subsidiary level need to be **aggregated at the corporate level**. This aggregation will be required as part of the overall review of risk that the board needs to undertake. **Systems** will be placed to **identify changes in risks as soon as they occur**, enabling management to monitor risks regularly and undertake annual reviews of the way that organisation deals with risk.

There is no information on the **organisational structure** of LinesRUs. Given the risky nature of the company's business, LinesRUs is likely to be an independent legal entity to ensure that no other companies are adversely affected should LinesRUs go out of business.

(b) **Risk responses**

Transfer

The risk is transferred to a third party. As noted above, this may not be possible if insurers are **not willing to accept the risk**. Alternative methods of risk transfer may have to be considered including asking the state for some form of insurance.

Avoidance

LinesRUs may consider whether the risk can be **avoided**. However, given that maintenance work must continue and that errors are always possible, then the risk may **crystallise**. Avoidance is not possible.

The only method of avoidance would appear to be **termination of operations**. This again may not be appropriate given this would close LinesRU's business.

Reduction

The risk can be **reduced by taking appropriate measures**. In the case of LinesRUs these will include **regular training** for maintenance staff. Management should use other methods such as newsletters to **raise awareness** of the importance of work being carried out and the potential consequences of error. There should be **maintenance and enforcement of appropriate disciplinary procedures** where breaches of work practices have been identified.

LinesRUs may also consider loss control options. These may include **hiring of lawyers** to defend LinesRUs and **release of publicity material** on the work of LinesRUs showing extent of maintenance normally carried out.

Acceptance

This is where the organisation retains the risk and if an unfavourable outcome occurs it will suffer the full loss. In the case of the rail crash, LinesRUs may have to **retain the risk** if **suitable insurance cannot be found**. Given the uncertainties regarding the costs resulting from the unfavourable outcome, insurers may be unwilling to insure for this type of event.

19 Doctors' practice

Text references. Chapter 4, 6 and 8.

Top tips. This question reinforces our comments in the front pages about thinking widely about risks. (a) requires imagination, but the way to evaluate the risks is simply to ask what could go wrong. As with any business embarking on a new venture, there may be problems with anticipating demand and obtaining finance. Note that the second part of (a) does **not** ask you to describe a risk management model in detail, rather to explain the uses of it. This question reinforces our comments in the front pages about thinking widely about risks. Elements to emphasise include assessment, profiling and action.

In (b) the risks are such that a risk manager needs to be appointed, although the practice is small enough for everyone to be involved in the decision to define risk appetite.

You need to bring into your discussion the possibility that some decisions need to be made by all the doctors, also the constraints on decision-making.

In (c) you don't need to go into detail about whether the practice should employ an internal auditor or who it should be. The question is based on the assumption that internal audit work will be performed.

Easy marks. Quite a tough question with no particularly easy parts.

(a) (i) **Additional risks**

A number of additional risks arise from the introduction of the new facility, including the following.

Operational risks

(1) **Surgical equipment failure**

The practice may face threats to its income through **failures of its surgical equipment**, meaning that it cannot provide surgical procedures whilst the equipment is unavailable.

(2) **Storage facilities failure**

Environmental failures in the storage facilities for equipment and drugs may also lead to a **loss of income** if surgical procedures cannot be provided. The practice may also face the **costs of replacing the equipment** and drugs that have been contaminated.

(3) **Security**

The additional equipment and drugs stored may make the practice **more vulnerable to theft**.

(4) **Transportation risks**

The blood and samples taken may be contaminated by storage facilities problems at the surgery, and also by deterioration during transportation. This may result in **misdiagnosis of illness** and hence the **costs of giving patients** the **wrong treatment.**

(5) **High demand**

High demand at **certain times of the year** may mean that the practice **loses income** through being **unable to meet the demand**, or **incurs increased costs** through having to pay for **extra medical and nursing care.**

You would also have scored marks if you discussed the following operational risks.

(1) **Hospital delays**

The practice may **lose income** through not being able to provide care because of **delays in testing** blood and samples at the local hospital.

(2) **Staff**

Existing staff **may not have** the **collective skills** necessary to operate the new unit. If new staff are employed, there may be a risk of **staff dissatisfaction** and hence **retention problems** with existing staff if new staff are employed on better terms.

(3) **Effect on existing care**

The resources required by the new facilities may mean **less resources are available** for existing work; hence the **areas of care** currently provided may suffer and **income** from these be **threatened.**

Legal risks

Providing more procedures may increase the risk of problems arising during treatment, and hence losses through the **costs of fighting or settling negligence claims.**

Regulatory risks

If shortcomings arise in the treatment provided, the practice's **regulatory body** may **intervene** and prevent the practice providing the surgical procedures it currently wishes to offer.

Financial risks

The new **facilities** will have to be **financed.** The practice may face problems in **meeting any finance costs** that it has to incur, particularly if the return on investment is not as good as forecast. Financing the investment may mean funds are lacking when required for other purposes, such as buying out a retiring partner.

Reputation risks

The practice may not achieve the income growth expected if the **standard of treatment** is believed to be lower than would be available in the hospital, or if because of operational difficulties **patients** were **forced to wait longer** for treatment than they would in a hospital.

(ii) **Uses of risk management model**

Iterative model

The most important feature of models is that they demonstrate how risk management is a **continual process** and experience gained from carrying out all stages can impact upon all other stages of the cycle. Review by the **risk manager** or all of the doctors of the **effectiveness of risk management** needs to be built into the process.

Organisation – wide application

Models are used to assess **organisation-wide** risks and also **specific process or unit risks.** They also are used to assess the **interaction** between risks.

Logical process

Models show that risk management is a logical process, taking the organisation through **initial risk identification,** then **identification of events** that may cause **risks to crystallise, assessment** of **how great losses** might be and in the light of these how best to **respond to risks.** This will help identify who should be responsible for which aspects of the risk management cycle.

Role of monitoring and feedback

Models emphasise the importance of **monitoring risk management procedures** and controls once they are in place. The feedback from this monitoring will **impact upon future risk assessments** and also lead to **continuous improvements in processes,** following the **principles of feedforward control.**

Decision-making

Models emphasise that the results of all stages of the risk management process should impact upon **the organisation's decision-making process** and consequently **affect strategy** and also **the appetite the organisation has for risk.** The decisions taken as a result of this will in turn feed through to the risk assessment and management processes, modifying the views taken on **key risks** and the best ways to **respond to them.**

(b) **Risk appetite**

Risk appetite is the amount of risk that the practice is prepared to **accept in exchange for returns** (the clientele effect). The new arrangements here are expected to increase income, and the risk appetite defines what risk levels will be **acceptable in exchange** for the increased income. Risk appetite also infers that the practice is willing to accept that risk has a downside as well as an upside, and the consequences of both are culturally acceptable.

Risk appetite decisions

In this situation, one of the senior partners in the practice would act as the risk manager and be responsible for analysing risk and recommending what **acceptable risk levels** might be in the **changed circumstances** for each of the major risks. However as the decision results from a major change in practices, the recommendations should certainly be approved by a majority of the doctors, and preferably be unanimous. The practice may also have to act within **constraints** imposed by government or regulator, which effectively limit the maximum amount of risk the practice can bear.

(c) **Contribution of internal audit**

Internal audit could be used to add value by operating a **risk-based approach to auditing the practice's systems.** Although the practice would not be able to employ a full-time internal auditor, it could maybe employ experienced staff from elsewhere in the health service to perform the work.

Benefits of a risk-based approach

A risk-based approach would assess whether the risk management systems are sufficient to **assess and manage risk.** A risk-based audit would question the **appropriateness of risk management systems** as a means of managing risk and would question whether the **assessment of operational systems' risk** was fair. A risk-based approach therefore combines audit of operational systems with an audit of the risk management systems.

Usefulness of systems-based auditing

Systems-based auditing would focus on the overall functioning of the practice's operational systems. Systems-based auditing concentrates on the **procedures** in place to achieve the practice's objectives and the **controls** that are in place to **manage the risks** that threaten the achievement of objectives

The systems-based audit will assess whether the **controls and procedures** in place are **appropriate** in the light of the **objectives management has decided** and the **risk management systems** that managers have adopted. It then tests whether procedures and controls are operating effectively.

20 IDAN

Text references. Chapter 6 and 7 on risks, Chapter 8 deals with the role of internal audit.

Top tips. In (a) don't worry too much if your classification of risks differed from ours. A possible alternative is credit, market, operational, reputation, compliance and business risk. It's important to link your discussion into the scenario; it's evident for example that IDAN faces a number of legal/compliance risks.

(b) is based on the usefulness of a systematic approach to risk, meaning that risk management is more effective **and** efficient. Note that the discussion of the advantages of categorisation focuses on key elements of the risk management cycle.

(c) is an interesting mix of a number of controls. You need to give specific examples and also give some consideration to the risks of introducing new systems in response to changes. Note that IT controls are a significant element. You don't need a detailed knowledge of the money laundering regulations to answer that part; a systematic approach to risk management (establishing policies, staffing, training and management review) will get you the majority of marks. You can also use your own experience of dealing with banks when discussing opening an account with a new bank or using pin numbers.

The study guide requires you to recognise and analyse the sector or industry specific nature of many business risks. If you're not involved in the banking sector the question may seem tough, but it is designed to get you to apply the main risk categories, and to use a variety of controls to deal with problem areas.

Easy marks. Categorisation of risks in (a) should have provided a gentle start to the question as most of the 'normal' major risks apply. In (c), provided you make clear by using headers which risk you're discussing, you don't have to discuss the risks in the order given in the question, and can start with those you find easiest first.

(a) **Main categories of risk**

Business risks

Business risks are the potential movements of profits caused by the **nature and type** of **operations** in which the company is involved. **Strategic risk**, the consequences of making the wrong strategic decisions, is an important element of business risk, since IDAN is faced with choosing in which areas of business to carry out further investment. IDAN also faces business risk through **failing to respond** as quickly as its competitors do to the **current changes in the business environment**.

Financial market risks

Financial market risks are the risks of losses through adverse movements in financial markets. This includes **changes in the foreign currency markets** (exchange risk), **changes in interest rates** (interest rate risk) when governments and central banks relax fiscal policy and **other changes** in securities or derivatives markets.

Legal risks

Legal risks are the risks of losses resulting from IDAN **incurring legal penalties**, or having its **operations disrupted by legal action**. IDAN faces several risks in this area, including legal penalties for failure to implement money laundering requirements effectively, and successful claims against the group for incorrect financial services advice.

Operational risks

Operational risks are the risks of losses caused by operational failures. This risk may be significant for IDAN since it is faced with having to **re-design its operational and information systems**. Problems with the design or implementation of new systems may lead to failure to provide a **proper service to customers** or **failure to supply managers** with the information they need to **supervise the business effectively**. Another significant risk is a **breakdown in the computer systems** resulting in customers being unable to use their credit or debit cards.

Fraud risks

IDAN may be vulnerable to **losses through fraud**, for example use by **unauthorised persons of PIN numbers**, or **fraudulent transactions over the telephone**.

Reputation risks

Reputation risk is the risk of adverse financial consequences such as lost business caused by failures resulting from another risk. This could arise through customers receiving a **poor service** through operational failures, **concerns over the security of systems**, and **imposition of legal penalties** because poor financial services advice was given.

(b)   **Advantages of categorisation of risks**

Event identification

Sorting risks into different categories enables the business to **identify situations or events** that will cause loss.

Risk response

Categorising risks should ensure they are dealt with in the most appropriate manner, for example developing systems to eliminate the risk of non-compliance with regulations or transfer of risk by insurance. Even when the same broad method is used for different risks, there may be variations, for example using **different insurers** to cover **operational and credit risks**.

Responsibility

Grouping risks enables the business to assess who will be responsible for dealing with them. Risks in **specialist areas** of the business may require internal or external risk management input, whereas **'mainstream' operational risks** can be dealt with by operational managers.

Monitoring

Categorisation of risks makes its easier for the directors to **fulfil their responsibilities** to ensure that the risks the business faces are managed to an acceptable level. Not only will it make risk monitoring easier, but the initial process of risk categorisation will require directors to respond to the results by ensuring appropriate systems are developed. Directors will also be able to fulfil their legal obligations to report on risk.

(c)   **Elimination of personal signatures**

Transition to new arrangements will require controls to ensure that all customers are notified of their PIN numbers. IDAN must also operate appropriate security measures to combat the **risk of fraud**:

(i)   The identification numbers supplied by IDAN to its customers should be reasonably **easy for the customer to remember**, but should **avoid combinations that can easily be guessed**.

(ii)   Customers should be instructed to **destroy IDAN's notification** of their pin number.

(iii)   IDAN should make clear to customers what they should **do if their cards are lost or stolen**. If customers **report cards** to be **missing**, those cards should be instantly cancelled.

(iv)   If customers contact IDAN **claiming to have forgotten their pin numbers**, IDAN staff should ask for **evidence of identification** such as personal details before supplying their pin numbers.

In addition, IDAN will need to ensure that its own credit and debit cards function properly when used for payment by **pre-testing** the new arrangements. Once operational, there should be alternative **back-up facilities in place**.

Increasing use of telephone and Internet banking services

Developments in new types of business carry the risk that the company's systems will not be able to cope with **increased demand**. Management therefore **need to monitor call waiting times against targets**, and **Internet response times**. Internal audit may need to carry out **detailed testing of transactions** to ensure that they have been processed accurately. **Extra training** may be required to combat problems.

Verification of identity controls will also be required to counter the risk of security breaches. This can be achieved by requiring a passcard or PIN number to be entered or quoted over the phone, along with an item of personal data such as **date of birth or mother's maiden name**. There should also be controls over the **security of the telephone system and encryption and firewall controls** to protect data transmitted by computer.

Misselling claims

Human resource controls are an important element of avoiding the **legal risk** of successful claims:

(i)   **Recruitment processes** should ensure the employment of **properly-qualified staff** and **obtaining references** on their experience.

(ii) Staff should be **trained in appropriate selling techniques and ethical behaviour**.

(iii) **Staff remuneration schemes** should be carefully reviewed to ensure that they do not encourage inappropriate selling.

(iv) **Remedial measures** should be taken against staff who have fallen below standard; they should incur **remedial training** or **dismissal** as appropriate.

IDAN should also have controls in place to ensure **staff behaviour is monitored**, for example requiring recording of all phone calls, and written records of all meetings which the customer confirms.

It should also implement a formal **complaints procedure**, which deals with **customer complaints speedily** and **actions findings**.

Money laundering

The key elements of a money laundering policy are:

(i)   **Appointing a director or senior manager as money laundering compliance officer**, backed by clear support from other directors for anti-money laundering requirements

(ii) **Establishing written policies and procedures** which cover the money laundering regulations, detail the records to be kept and periods of retention and specify when the authorities should be notified

(iii) **Verifying the identity of new customers**. This can be done for personal customers by a passport or identity card including a photograph, identifying the customer's name and permanent address. Similar confirmation of details should be obtained for companies

(iv) **Training all staff** so that they are aware of the **signs of money laundering** and know that they are **legally required** to **report their suspicions**

(v)   **Tracking large or unusual transactions**, especially those taking place over more than one country. Accounts with unusual transactions may require continual monitoring

(vi) **Regular review of policies** to ensure that they are effective and comply with any changes in regulations

21 Ceedee

Text references. Chapters 6 - 7.

Top tips. For (a) the risks are fairly clearly signposted in the unseen scenario. Note that the hints given about SCD's dependence on the new contract may equally apply to ZZ. The threat to reputation is not totally dependent on whether SCD is legally liable – SCD may suffer guilt by association, particularly if it is associated with the speed freak approach to motoring. The comment about high profitability should alert you to the need to consider other profitable uses of the scarce resource of qualified technicians.

In (b) the question is looking for sensible suggestions to reduce risks, as the only sure way of eliminating the risks is not to be involved in the project.

The main point in (c) is that the major risks arising as a result of this project have to be assessed subjectively.

Easy marks. Identifying threats and risks is generally the easiest part of a question like this, and forms the basis of the rest of your answer. Being alert for risks when you are reading through question scenarios is a key skill as we stressed in the front pages.

(a) **Liability for crashes**

If a car **manufactured by ZZ crashes**, then SCD could be held **liable** for the failure of the circuit board. If a crash happens, it may be difficult to tell whether and why a circuit board has failed and it may be difficult for SCD to prove it was not responsible. This risk is increased by the functioning of the circuit board being dependent on factors beyond SCD's control. It includes a component manufactured by ZZ, a supplier that SCD has not selected. SCD also has no control over how the circuit board is fitted in the finished car, or how conscientiously the car is maintained.

Reputation risk

Even if SCD is not held liable for problems, it may suffer a serious loss of reputation if cars manufactured by ZZ have safety problems. Toyota's problems illustrate that potential problems with car safety will be widely publicised. However responsibility for the Gulf of Mexico disaster is allocated, there is no doubt that BP and the other companies involved have all suffered **damage to their reputation.** If there are problems and SCD is blamed by ZZ or the supplier, this will damage its reputation even if the allegations are unfounded. The risk to reputation is enhanced by how the cars are being marketed. SCD could be criticised for being associated with a car with the appeal that it can supposedly be driven safely at **high speeds**, although the speeds may in fact make it more likely that its components will fail.

Problems with supplier

The component supplier may **not deliver on time** or its components may be unreliable, causing delays in the production process. If the supplier goes out of business, SCD and ZZ may have **difficulty finding a replacement supplier at short notice.** Particularly if there are only a few suppliers who can manufacture the component, a new supplier may be able to charge a much greater price, **threatening profit margins** on the contract.

Threats to profitability

The contract represents a major commitment of resources for SCD. If ZZ goes out of business or changes its supplier, SCD will be left with **surplus staff.** Commitment of technicians that are currently employed to the contract may mean that SCD is forced to **turn down more profitable opportunities** because of a lack of resources.

(b) **ALARP principle**

The ALARP principle is based on the idea that many risks cannot be avoided if, for example, a business is involved in activities that are hazardous. However the **higher the level of risk, the less is acceptable it is**. Following the ALARP principle means **reduction of risks to an acceptable level** by undertaking risk mitigation. The extent of risk mitigation is based on a trade-off between cost and the risks' remaining likelihood and impact.

Liability for crashes

SCD could build a **failsafe routine** into the circuit board. This would mean that the car could only start if the board was functioning correctly. SCD should also carry out **full and documented quality testing** on the circuit boards. It should either **test the components** it purchases from the supplier itself, or insist that the **supplier provides evidence** that it has tested the components. The agreement with ZZ should make clear that SCD is not liable for circuit board failure caused by **problems with the manufacturing process at ZZ** or **inadequate maintenance**. SCD may wish to **insure** against legal costs if the premiums are not excessive, and should hopefully be able to do so if it can satisfy the insurer that it has taken all the steps it can to ensure the circuit boards operate safely.

Reputation risk

SCD should ask ZZ to ensure drivers are fully warned about the need to drive at safe speeds and the threat to the car's safety of driving too fast. Warnings should be included in sales literature, together with the explanation that the system is designed to **make driving safer** if the car is driven at reasonable speeds. Safety warnings should also be included in the **documents** purchasers are supplied with about the car. The documentation should also include advice to keep the car **well-maintained** and have it **regularly and thoroughly serviced**. New owners could be asked to sign an agreement that the system cannot prevent all crashes.

Problems with suppliers

If SCD is able to have input into the contract with the supplier, it should insist that the contract includes requirements about the **quality and timing of supply,** and that the supplier is **liable for delays caused by its shortcomings.** The contract should also include other requirements imposed on the supplier, for example carrying out quality checks. Its contract with ZZ should make clear that SCD is **not liable for delays caused by the supplier.** The supplier contract should include a termination clause that SCD or ZZ can enforce if the supplier **fails to perform satisfactorily**. If problems begin to occur SCD and ZZ should consult with a view to finding alternative suppliers as soon as possible.

Threats to profitability

Ceedee's finance department should review ZZ's accounts and other evidence of its financial status. It should consider how **dependent ZZ's future profitability** is on the success of this new car, or whether it is very committed to any other makes. SCD should also try to **assess ZZ's plans for promoting the car**, and whether they are likely to be successful, particularly as it is an expensive car being marketed at a time of financial stringency. The contract with ZZ should include provisions for ZZ to pay **financial penalties** if it terminates the contract prematurely without good reason or fails to order a certain number of boards each year. SCD should also **plan the staffing of the contract** carefully, focusing particularly on the use of technician time, and trying to use lower grade staff for basic tasks wherever possible.

(c) **Objective and subjective risk perception**

The likelihood and impact of some risks can be measured with a high degree of certainty, and these risks can be **objectively** assessed. However it may be difficult to assign a precise value to a likelihood or impact connected with many risks, and these risks have to be **subjectively** assessed. Subjective risk assessment requires a greater degree of judgement.

Problems with non-executive's views

Seriousness of risks

One problem is that many of the most severe risks that SCD faces can **only be assessed subjectively**. Clearly the most serious risk is that someone will lose their life in an accident caused by problems with the car, but the likelihood of this happening cannot be assessed objectively.

Reputation risk

One of the most significant risks SCD faces is the consequences of a loss of reputation. The seriousness of reputation risk is dependent not only on the consequences of other risks materialising that could lead to a loss of reputation (here problems with product safety), but also how the stakeholders who deal with Ceedee will **react** to the risks **materialising**. How stakeholders will react cannot be assessed objectively, as amongst other reasons it includes the reaction of potential future customers whose current identity is unknown.

Impact of uncertainty

Even risks where the eventual outcome can be measured in precise financial terms may not be able to be assessed objectively because of the impact of **uncertainty.** The **amount of damages** that may be payable if there is an accident is **uncertain.** The **opportunity losses** of **turning down more profitable work** that could be done by the skilled technicians cannot be assessed objectively if SCD cannot be sure what the future work might be.

22 Cerberus

(a)   **Key responsibilities of board members**

Sound system of control

Corporate governance guidelines require the board to **maintain a sound system of internal control** to **safeguard shareholders' investments** and the **company's assets**. A sound system should aid operations by **responding to risks**, should **ensure the quality of reporting**, and help ensure **compliance with laws and regulations**.

Risks

In order to determine what constitutes a sound system, the board should consider the major risks that the company faces, concentrating on the identification, evaluation and management of all key risks affecting the organisation and the effectiveness of internal control (see below). The board should ensure that risk objectives with targets and indicators are **communicated to employees.** The board should also ensure that action is taken if any weaknesses are found.

Effectiveness of internal control

The board should consider the effectiveness of all internal controls, not financial controls but also operational, compliance and risk management controls. Board members need to consider the **nature and extent of the risks** which face the company and which it regards as **acceptable** for the company to bear within its particular business and the threat of such risks becoming a reality. It should assess **the company's ability to reduce the incidence and impact** on the business and to adapt to changing risks or operational deficiencies. It is possible for the board to overreact and introduce elaborate systems that will not have a significant impact and so the board therefore needs to consider the **costs and benefits** related to operating relevant controls.

Feedback

The board must not regard establishing a good control system as a one-off exercise. The **risks** that drive the development of the internal control systems will **change** as the company's **strategy** and **business environment changes.** In addition **feedback** on how the controls have been operating is an essential part of a business's control systems; the feedback the board obtains should lead to modifications and improvements.

(b) **Methods used to assess effectiveness of internal control**

Consideration of internal controls should be a regular part of the board's agenda and the board should also conduct a higher level annual review of internal control.

Regular review

The board should regularly consider the effectiveness of strategies for **identifying**, **evaluating** and **managing** the major risks, the **strength of the management and internal control environment and systems**, the **actions** being taken to **reduce the risks found**, and whether the results indicate that **internal control** should be **monitored more extensively.**

Annual review

When the board is considering annually the disclosures about internal controls in the accounts, it should conduct an **annual review** of internal control. This should be wider-ranging than the regular review; in particular it should cover the **changes** since the last **assessment** in **risks** faced, the company's **ability** to **respond** to **changes** in its business environment and whether the company's **objectives** and **risk appetite** should be **re-assessed**. The board should also reassess the **scope and quality of its monitoring** of risk and internal control.

The board should consider how well the **information systems** fulfil the board and management's **information needs**, taking into account the extent and frequency of reports to the board and communication with employees. The directors should also consider significant controls, failings and weaknesses which have or might have material impacts upon the accounts. These may have to be reported in the report on internal control. The directors should also assess whether **the public reporting** processes communicate a **balanced and understandable account** of the company's position and prospects

Information for review

To carry out effective reviews, the board needs to use a number of different sources of information. Part of the review of controls should be the quality of the reports the board is receiving.

(i) **Performance measurement and indicators**

Regular reporting of these measures should be built into the control systems. They should include not just **financial data** but also **qualitative measures** such as customer satisfaction.

(ii) **Senior management monitoring**

The board should consider reports on the **monitoring activities** undertaken by senior management below board level, such as control self-assessment and confirmation by employees of compliance with policies and codes of conduct. Management reports should highlight the impact of, and actions taken to remedy, **significant control failings and weaknesses.** Management should also report to the board risk any risk and control matters of particular importance, such as fraud, illegal acts or matters significantly affecting the company's reputation or financial position.

(iii) **Audit committee and internal audit**

The board should review regular reports from the audit committee and internal audit. The issues covered should include the committee's own activities in **reviewing control and risk management systems**, and also the **results of internal and external audit**, in particular the **control weaknesses identified.** The audit committee should also assess the **effectiveness of internal audit.**

(iv) **Staff communications**

The board should consider information communicated to them by staff on risk and control weaknesses. There should be channels of communication for staff to use to **report suspected breaches of laws, regulations or other improprieties.**

(v) **Follow-up on problems**

As part of the cycle of continual feedback, the board should review whether **changes or actions have occurred** in response to changes in risk assessment or weaknesses identified in previous reports.

(c)   **Reporting on internal control**

The reports the board provides will depend on the stock exchange rules. Two major jurisdictions with differing requirements reflecting a differing approach to corporate governance are the UK and the USA.

UK requirements

The board should disclose, as a minimum, in the accounts the existence of a **process for managing risks**, how the board has **reviewed the effectiveness** of the process and that the **process accords** with **UK guidance**. The board should also include an acknowledgement that they are responsible for the company's system of internal financial control and reviewing its effectiveness. The directors should explain that such a system is designed to **manage** rather than eliminate the risk of **failure** to **achieve business objectives**.

The board should **summarise** the process that it has **used to review the effectiveness** of the **system of internal financial control** and has considered the need for an **internal audit** function if the company does not have one. There should also be disclosure of the process the board has used to deal with **material internal control aspects of any significant problems** disclosed in the annual accounts. The accounts should contain **information** about those **weaknesses** in internal financial control that have resulted in material losses, contingencies or uncertainties that require disclosure in the financial statements or the auditor's report on the financial statements.

USA requirements

Under the Sarbanes-Oxley requirements, annual reports should contain **internal control reports** that state the responsibility of management for establishing and maintaining an **adequate internal control structure** and **procedures for financial reporting.** Annual reports should also contain an **assessment** of the **effectiveness of the internal control structure and procedures for financial reporting,** additionally disclosures of any **material weaknesses** in internal control. Auditors should report on this assessment.

If you have any further questions on these issues, please do not hesitate to get in touch.

23 B Bank

> **Text references.** Chapter 3, 6 and 7.
>
> **Top tips.** The question is on a topical area, with the scenario including some risk management weaknesses that have been identified recently in financial institutions. Some of the recommendations in the answer tie in with the 2009 UK Walker review of corporate governance in banks and other financial institutions.
>
> (a) highlights recent concerns about corporate governance weaknesses, but also involves other important syllabus issues – controllability, short-term vs long-term performance and the risk/return relationship.
>
> (b) combines corporate governance issues on strategy determination and the role of non-executives with management of lending risks. An important point is that lenders should only lend to borrowers whom they expect to meet their commitments. Security is a method of limiting the impact of borrower default, but it won't be required if all borrowers repay on time.
>
> **Easy marks.** A few fairly obvious hints in the scenario of (b).

(a)   Arguments in favour of proposal

Response to stakeholder demands

The proposal may be **popular with shareholders** and other significant **stakeholders, such as government and the media.** If the banks do not make profits, directors will be exposed to the risk of the loss of their fee.

Clear link

The **link** between bank performance and directors' remuneration appears **clear**. Directors will not be given substantial rewards if their bank fails to perform well.

Arguments against proposal

Deterrence of fee

Having to pay an initial fee may put off some potential directors who would otherwise be good candidates. This particularly applies to **non-executive directors**. They should be recruited on the basis of the **independence, financial industry capability and critical perspective** that they can bring to the board, and also the **time commitment** they can make. Because they should be assisting shareholders and other stakeholders by scrutinising executive directors' actions, it would be inappropriate for them to be charged a fee. If non-executives' remuneration is linked to performance, they will face a **conflict of interest** when advising on potentially profitable but risky strategies, and may be less willing to disagree with executive directors' proposals.

Risk and return

The scheme appears to encourage behaviour that has been criticised over the past few years, banks putting excessive resources into **speculative or uncertain activities**, and as a result making large losses. The reward system proposed would seem to appeal most to directors who are willing to take excessive risks for the chance of achieving high returns. Such individuals may regard the fee they have to pay as an acceptable charge for the chance to obtain high remuneration. A better way to ensure director commitment to long-term success may be to require them to maintain a holding of a **minimum number of shares.**

Short and long-term

Rewarding directors by bonuses based on annual profits rewards short-term performance, and does not take account of the **long-term effects** of directors' decisions. Incentives should be balanced so that a **significant proportion of remuneration** takes the form of a **long-term incentive scheme** such as **share options** with rewards only being due after a number of years has elapsed. Even shorter-term bonuses should be **paid over more than a year**, with a **limit to the proportion paid** in the first year.

Manipulation of profits

Directors may try to **manipulate profits** to maximise their bonuses in a particular year. This risk could be lessened by **clawback** provisions, where directors have to **repay bonuses based on misleading accounts.**

Controllability of profits

The reward scheme should link to the factors directors can control. However economic factors such as **interest rates and inflation** will have a significant impact on the volume of lending and borrowing and hence on a bank's results. The decisions directors make may therefore have **less impact on profits** than external influences.

(b)   **Review of strategy**

Reviews of strategy should be conducted **more regularly than once every four years.** They are fundamental to a business's success over the long-term. Decisions on mortgages can affect the bank's results for up to 25 years. Strategic decisions impact greatly on risk management, since they are influenced by the **risk appetite** of the directors and impact upon the **risks borne** and the **ways risks are managed**. Therefore board consideration of strategy and risk needs to cover regularly current and future risk appetite.

Impact of current trends

In particular the board appears to be relying too much on policies that have been successful in the past in managing predictable financial risks. It does not seem to be taking enough notice of the implication of current economic trends, where **house price inflation is greater than wage inflation.** If this trend continues, it will mean that mortgages become less affordable. A decrease in demand for mortgages will threaten bank profits. The board should consider **diversification** into other products, particularly short-term loans, as it may presently be over-committed to longer-term lending.

Role of non-executive directors

Guidance such as the Higgs and Walker reports has identified scrutiny as a key duty of non-executive directors. Ideally executive directors should formulate strategy and it should then be **rigorously discussed and challenged** if necessary by non-executive directors. The failure of non-executive directors to do this at B may lead to strategies being implemented that are not in the bank's best interests. Non-executive directors should play a much more active role in deliberations about strategy.

Relations with shareholders

B's shareholder base is changing and the board does not seem to be considering the full implications of this. The changes could lead to the **risks faced by B increasing** as the new shareholder base demands higher returns. This could result in dangerous decisions being taken as B's board tries to fulfil unrealistic expectations. **Increased communication** with shareholders should help keep expectations under control. This will be a particularly important role for senior non-executive directors.

Lending excessive amounts

B's **lending policy** seems to be primarily determined by competition. This increases its riskiness, as it seems that not enough attention is being given to the ability of **borrowers to repay**. Even if the value of loans is backed by adequate security, the best way to limit the riskiness of loans is only to lend to those who can provide **sufficient evidence of ability to repay.**

Inadequate security

B's policy of lending in excess of the properties' value increases the risk that the **security** provided by the properties will be **inadequate.** The security will only be enough if property prices continue to rise. If prices fall and lenders default, B will be left with property assets that do **not cover the value of the loan**, are **declining in value and may be difficult to sell**. Lending up to a percentage that is some way short of 100% of property value should mean that the loan can be realised even if there is some fall in prices. The commitment the mortgage payer has made of providing a certain amount of the property's value from their own resources should increase their **commitment to meet repayments** and avoid the loss of the property.

Scenario analysis

B's lending policy appears to be based on a scenario where property prices are **continuing to rise**. B does not appear to have adequately considered the possibility of **alternative scenarios** and developed plans for the possibility that prices fall.

24 JDM

> **Text references**. Chapters 4, 5 and 7.
>
> **Top tips**. In (a) we start by relating the figures to the board's risk appetite. Note the importance of patterns of cash flows as well as risk v return and the probabilities.
>
> In (b) we move onto the factors also affecting the board's perceptions of the risks, the uncertainties over the forecasts and the nature of the main (financial) risks. You also need to consider the factors affecting the risk management solutions, including whether their complexity may limit their effectiveness and whether the board can adopt its strategies depending on how the economic risks turn out.
>
> In (c) you should have scored marks for discussing the establishment of the process and the responsibilities for it, as well as the steps in the process.
>
> It's worth noting that the economic recession is a significant factor in this question It's probable that the poor economic climate will also feature in other exams over the next couple of years.
>
> **Easy marks**. You must revise Chapter 4 of the text urgently if you couldn't generate ideas for (c).

(a)   **Risk appetite**

Strategy 1 offers a **70% chance of maximising revenues** if all the apartments are sold. JDM should make a surplus of roughly $1.5 million (115,000 × 15 – 210,000). Strategy 2 has a higher **expected NPV**, although the NPV for Strategy 1 is an average figure that is very different from either of the two possibilities.

JDM's directors should take into account what they have decided **acceptable risks and risk levels** are, and their attitudes towards **risk levels versus return levels.** If the directors are risk-seeking, then arguably they will choose Strategy 1 as it offers the possibility of maximising returns. If they are risk-averse, then Strategy 2 may be chosen on the grounds that its expected net present value is higher, and its risks may not be significantly, if at all, higher. However one complexity is that **maximising revenue** in a time of recession is clearly acceptable, and Strategy 1 offers a 70% chance of doing so.

(b)   **Other factors influencing decision**

Cash flow patterns

Cash flow patterns will also complicate the board's view of risk appetite in a number of ways. Strategy 1 involves **higher initial marketing expenditure,** which may be significant if JDM is facing tight liquidity over the next few months. The **first receipts** should be **received quicker** under Strategy 2 than Strategy 1. However all the receipts will have been received under Strategy 1 by the end of this year, whereas $25,000 per apartment is due under Strategy 2 Deal 3, and Deal 2 may involve a buyback sometime over the next five years. The **greater length of time to settle payments due this year** under Strategy 1 may also make it more feasible for purchasers than the requirements to settle within weeks.

Uncertainties over figures

The market may be **sufficiently sensitive to price** that the all or nothing possibilities under Strategy 1 are the only likely ones. There may though be a possibility that some, but not all, of the apartments are sold. The figure of 70% may be debatable. The forecasts do not consider what will happen under Strategy 1 if **none of the properties are sold**.

The forecasts for Strategy 2 appear to have been based **only on the outcome forecast** by the Marketing Director. However there are various uncertainties relating to his figures that forecasts should have taken into account, particularly how the Marketing Director can be sure that the **demand for each deal** will be **as predicted**. If forecasts are wrong and prices fall more than expected or for longer than expected, there will be a loss under Strategy 2, Deal 2.

Financial risks

If the building industry is expected to come out of recession soon, this may make Strategy 1 more viable, as if JDM **cannot sell the apartments initially**, eventually it will be able to in the future at increased prices. However financing the increased working capital until the apartments are sold may be problematic under current conditions. If customers expect the **deflation in house prices to continue** for some time, they may wait until they believe that the market price has reached its lowest level before buying. Economic conditions over the next five years may make it difficult for JDM to **fund the buybacks** should buyers choose Strategy 2 Deal 2 and exercise their options. However the **protection offered to buyers** under each of the deals may make Strategy 2 much more appealing in the current climate.

Complexity of strategies

The success of the strategies in managing risk will depend on how buyers react to them. The greater **simplicity** of Strategy 1 makes it a more suitable strategy. Purchasers may struggle to decide which the best option for them is, and the numbers choosing each deal may differ from the Marketing Director's estimate.

Timeframe of strategies

For Strategy 1 if property prices eventually rise as expected, then consumers may wish to buy the apartments in future. There is also an option to delay in the decision. The board **can reconsider their strategy** if the properties don't sell.

(c)   **Risk appetite**

The board should first establish risk appetite, the **attitude to risks** and the relationship between **risk and return**. This may be determined by the risks directors feel comfortable taking or shareholder views. It will be affected by significant environmental issues such as the current recession. The board should ensure that risk appetite is directly **related to their business strategy**. It should feed into JDM's policies and procedures.

Establishment of risk management process

Formal systems for **monitoring and managing risk** need to be established. These systems require clear **board support**, and also **information and training** being provided to managers and staff to ensure that they operate effectively.

Responsibilities for risk management process

Specifying responsibilities is also a key part of establishing the risk management process. These include **responsibilities for monitoring the overall process** that the board, risk committee and the risk management function assume. It also includes establishing who is responsible for **controlling risks on a day-to-day basis**. The **risk register** should set out who is responsible for managing specific risks.

Risk identification

Risk management processes need to **identify what specific risks JDM faces.** JDM's board of the company also needs to be aware that the risks will **change over time**, so it must be on the lookout for new risks, for example those arising from more stringent building requirements or new health and safety legislation.

Risk assessment

Risk involves the use of various procedures to assess **the nature of the risk** and the **consequences** of the risk materialising. For a downside risk, the extent of any loss depends on the probability of the outcome of the loss making event, and the size of the loss in the event that the risk crystallises – that is occurs. The assessment may also cover the **expected loss**, the **probability that losses will occur** and the **largest predictable loss**.

Risk profiling

Risk profiling involves **mapping different risks** in terms of the **frequency** that they will crystallise, and the **severity** of the outcome if they do. Where the probability of the outcome is remote and the actual loss small, then no action may be taken regarding that risk. However, a high probability of the event occurring and potentially large losses will mean that serious risk management measures are required.

Risk management measures

Measures taken will vary depending on the risk:

- **Abandonment/avoidance** of risks with high likelihood of occurring and serious consequences if they do occur – for example failing to sell any properties in a development in an unpopular area.

- **Transfer**, for example by insurance, risks that have little chance of occurring, but will have serious consequences if they materialise, for example major damage to properties whilst they are being built.

- **Control** measures to reduce risks that are likely to materialise, but with limited consequences if they do, for example delays in construction.

- **Acceptance** of risks with insignificant consequences, and little possibility of materialising.

JDM's situation emphasises the importance of **changing (being able to change) risk management strategies** and policies as perceptions of risk change. One appeal of Strategy 1 is that it allows the board to reconsider its position if the strategy doesn't initially work and the properties don't sell.

Risk reporting

JDM's board needs to **establish a system of risk reporting.** Internally the frequency of reporting will depend on the significance of the risks, with key risks being monitored daily or weekly, less significant risks being monitored monthly or quarterly. There also needs to be a system for reporting to higher levels of management risks that are not being managed well. A key element of this is **residual risk reporting**, reviewing the risk exposure remaining after risk management activities have been implemented.

25 Product choice

(a)   **Verification of information**

The **realism of the net present value analysis** is very dependent on the quality of the information supplied. The figures they supply need to be verified, by staff not involved in their production or by internal auditors. They will need to review the **justification behind the assumptions** made and how much uncertainty lies behind the figures provided. They also must consider whether some **relevant costs** have been omitted from the analysis, for example costs of establishing new supplier relationships. The verifiers should also take into account how **accurate previous forecasts** have been and whether there are **weaknesses in the information gathering or forecasting processes** that have been identified by previous internal audits but not corrected.

Use of other appraisal methods

Using a higher risk-discounted factor as in the scenario takes into account the risks of the specific investment appraisal. However the **discount factor** is only one of a number of figures in the discount analysis. Vinnick needs to carry out additional **investment appraisals,** using **different assumptions** about marketing and engineering figures, also examining the impact on the figures if the **launch of products is postponed.** It also needs some idea of the probabilities of different outcomes, as this will help **calculate expected values** and the **chances of making a loss. Worst-case scenario analysis** will indicate maximum risk levels, which may also influence decisions depending on the **risk appetite** of the board.

Figures at risk-adjusted discount rate

Assuming use of the risk-adjusted discount factor fairly indicates risk would mean accepting Product 1 with a positive NPV and rejecting Product 2 because it has a negative NPV. The **risk-adjusted hurdle rate** represents a method of taking into account the risks associated with the development of a specific project and quantifying their significance based on how seriously Vinnick views them. However the variety of risks involved (discussed further below), and the difficulty of estimating their importance and ranking arguably means that the risk-adjusted rate fails to give a more reliable guide than using the company-wide hurdle rate would.

Sensitivity analysis

Simple sensitivity analysis reveals that Product 2 is much more vulnerable to making a loss if cost or revenue estimates turn out to be **over-optimistic.** Using the hurdle rate Product 1's NPV is $244 million against initial costs of $600 million, whereas Product 2's NPV is $430 million against initial costs of $6,400 million. Therefore the percentage by which Product 1's initial costs would have to increase before it made a loss is much higher than the % that Product 2's costs would have to increase.

Financial risk of Product 2

The level of **initial costs** also needs careful consideration. For Product 2 $6,400 million is a large amount of development costs so may cause **significant liquidity problems.** Having to meet the higher costs of Product 2 may also increase Vinnick's financial risk if loan finance is used and **gearing rises.**

Figures at hurdle rate

If however the hurdle rate of 7.5% is used to appraise investments, then Product 2 shows a **higher net present value**. This indicates that Vinnick may be able to make higher net revenues if it chooses Product 2 so long as it accepts the significant risk of making a loss. Whether Vinnick opts for Product 1 or Product 2 will depend on its **risk appetite**; will it prefer higher returns even though it takes greater risks to achieve them.

Product life cycle

Given the industry is changing rapidly, there is a risk that products may become **obsolete before seven years**. The estimated net present value of Product 1 is more vulnerable to a change in its life cycle, since it has the longer life cycle. Revenues from Product 2 begin to flow earlier than from Product 1, although at a fairly low level.

Use of surplus funds

As noted, Product 1 requires a much smaller early investment than Product 2. To improve the comparisons between the two products, Vinnick should consider how the spare funds (the funds that would not be needed for Product 1 but would be for Product 2) would be used. Vinnick therefore needs to consider the **rate of return** and **risk** of other investments for which the surplus funds could be used.

Postponement of Product 1

As Product 1 is a smaller-scale investment, it may be possible to **postpone** it until some years in the future, and fund it out of the eventual receipts from Product 2.

(b) **Strategic risks**

The investment decision must be **compatible with Vinnick's strategy.** The board should assess whether the products are a breakthrough into a new market sector, or whether there is **potential to expand** into other geographical markets. Whether the proposed products are **significantly differentiated** from what the competition is offering may be significant. Product 1 is being sold in Vinnick's retail outlets and the strategic impact on these outlets needs to be considered; will it require them to change their focus or will it utilise any spare capacity that they have.

Competitor risk

The board needs to consider the **different market profiles** for each product, and the risks that **competitors** will **develop their own products** ahead of Vinnick or respond more quickly on one rather than the other, accelerating the product life cycle.

Customer risk

Information is needed not only about the likely reactions of customers but the **different profiles of the customer base** for each product.

Supply and manufacturing risk

The **reliability of suppliers and manufacturing arrangements,** and the local infrastructure, needs to be considered carefully. Supply arrangements from China for some companies have been disrupted by problems within China such as electricity rationing. For Product 1 the consequences of problems in China will probably be more severe than problems in Taiwan for Product 2. If manufacturing is taking place in China, disruption there will clearly affect sales, whereas if there are problems with component suppliers in Taiwan, it may be possible to reduce the risk of lost sales by making contingency arrangements to buy components from suppliers in other countries.

Foreign exchange risk

With both products, there may be foreign exchange risks from settling in their suppliers' currencies. However **exchange risk relating to sales** will only apply to Product 2, since Product 1 sales will be in the home market.

(c) **Portfolio management**

Vinnick should view investment in both products in the light of its overall portfolio of investments. It should consider how both investments would contribute to ensuring that Vinnick had an optimum mix of **low and high risk investments.**

Correlation of risks

It should also consider the **correlation of both products** with the existing product portfolio. would investing in one ensure that risks were much better spread than investing in the other. Risks that may be positively correlated include supply risks if Vinnick already uses China or Taiwan for supplies.

International diversification

The extent of international diversification may be an issue. Product 1 will be sold in the American markets so may be **vulnerable to the American economic cycle**, whereas Product 2 will be sold all over Western Europe and hence diversified over countries with different cycles. Another point is that the risk borne by the retailer will be suffered by Vinnick's outlets for Product 1, but will be shared with third-party retailers for Product 2.

26 X

> **Text references**. Chapters 6 and 7.
>
> **Top tips**. The € **strengthening** against the £ means for UK companies that revenues and costs denominated in € will **rise**; therefore you have to multiply the sterling contribution by 1.05 each year.
>
> (b) is asking specifically for risks that differ between launching in France and England. For each risk, you would probably get 1 mark for identifying it, 1 mark for discussing how to manage it but it is not that easy to generate ideas from the limited details given.
>
> Cost, expectations/perceptions, attitudes/ appetite and mix are key elements in (c).
>
> **Easy marks**. The choice between fixed and floating rate debt is a key financing decision, so the factors in (c) are important determinants of financial risk.

(a) Expected annual cash flow $= (9{,}000{,}000 \times 0.5) + (7{,}000{,}000 \times 0.2) + (3{,}000{,}000 \times 0.3)$
$= 6{,}800{,}000$

Year (n)	0	1	2	3	4
	£000	£000	£000	£000	£
Original expected annual cash flow	(19,000)	6,800	6,800	6,800	6,800
Expected annual cash flow $\times (1.05)^n$	(19,000)	7,140	7,497	7,872	8,265
Disc factor 10%	1.000	0.909	0.826	0.751	0.683
Present value	(19,000)	6,490	6,193	5,912	5,655

Expected net present value = £5,250,000

The appreciation of the € has meant it will now be preferable to launch the product in France.

(b) **Risks associated with product launch in England**

Launch costs

The **actual net present value** will prove significantly **lower** than the expected net present value if launch costs turn out to be the less likely possibility, £14,500,000.

X should identify the factors that could cause launch costs to be £14,500,000 and take steps to **avoid these factors materialising**, for example **tight cost control**.

Risks associated with product launch in France

Exchange risks

As illustrated above, a strengthening of the € means that the product launch in France would be worthwhile. However if expectations are wrong and the **€ weakens against the £,** then the wrong decision would have been taken.

X can **reduce this risk** by **obtaining finance in France in euros** to fund the launch of the product. This would **match costs of finance against cash flows from the product**, and thus provide a **hedge against currency movements**.

Sales volume elasticity

X may find that the **availability of substitutes in France** may mean that the demand for product is more elastic than it anticipated. As a result revenues for new products are more price-sensitive and the higher margins that it is trying to obtain **result in lower annual cash flows than predicted**.

X should **reduce this risk** by being prepared to **vary the price of the product**, perhaps with a lower contribution margin in the first couple of years to get the product established. Possibly it may be able to raise margins in Years 3 and 4 once the product has become established and the demand is perhaps less elastic.

Market risks

As X is based in England, it may find it more difficult than anticipated to break into the French market if it lacks experience of it. It may not have contacts and also lack an appreciation of **different taste and cultural conditions**. X may also find it **more difficult to withdraw** from the French market once it has made the commitment to enter the market, since it may jeopardise its future chances of success abroad.

X should **reduce this risk** by **undertaking market research** and **employing French staff as agents**, to advise on the French market and to provide means of establishing sales and distribution networks.

(c)   **Factors influencing choice of fixed and floating debt**

Cost of debt

The respective **current costs** of fixed and floating rate debt, plus any **arrangement or set-up fees**, will influence the decision.

Interest rate expectations

Expectations will be a significant influence, particularly if X borrows locally in £. Taking out fixed rate debt will eliminate the risk of changes in interest rates causing changes in finance costs. Higher interest rate costs will **not only increase X's cost of finance** if the directors choose floating rate debt, but may **decrease demand**, further decreasing profit. On the other hand, expectations of lower interest rates will mean that **floating rate debt** may be a **better option**.

Mix of debt

One way in which X can **limit its exposure to interest rate movements** is by having a **mix of fixed and floating rate debt**. If the funding is raised by fixed rate debt, then because the current floating rate debt is redeemable first, after 20X7 X could have just fixed rate debt. It would hence be vulnerable to relatively expensive borrowing if rates decrease, and **termination costs** if it terminates some or all of its loans.

Factors influencing decision to hedge

Attitudes to risk

If the board is **risk-averse**, this may increase the likelihood that it chooses to hedge.

Cost of hedging

Purchasing interest rate derivatives will have a **cost**, and X will have to decide whether the cost is worth incurring in the light of the **potential magnitude and likelihood** of **losses**. The proposed expenditure and hence loan funding required is £19 million which does not seem very large in the context of £2,000 million assets. If hedging reduces the possibility of financial losses, the company may feel able to **incur more debt**, and the **cost of borrowing** may **fall** because of the decreased risk. If interest rates are expected to remain stable, the **losses from not hedging** are likely to be **small**, not justifying the cost of hedging.

27 Southern Continents

Text references. Chapters 3, 5 and 7.

Top tips. The most important feature of (a) is to link the risk management strategies to the likelihood-consequences matrix. The three risks are clearly flagged in the first paragraph. Other recommendations are possible in the second half of (a), including insurance for the burglary if the consequences are assessed as serious, but the likelihood is low. However your recommendations must follow the ALARP principle, as that is what Choo Wang clearly wants.

The key point to bring out in (b) is that risk awareness should be part of people's mentality. Elaborate systems of risk management will be ineffective unless staff see risk management as integral to their work.

The main benefit of PRP in (c) is that it solves the agency problem; don't forget though that directors need to feel motivated by it as well as shareholders benefiting. A critical evaluation implies that the majority of your review will be pointing out problems; however you do need also to discuss advantages, in particular here the package has resulted in the director being highly motivated. However his increased motivation has been at the expense of balancing risk and return. Lots of students wasted time in (c) writing all they knew about remuneration.

Easy marks. Hopefully you should have been able to define and explain the four basic risk management strategies.

Examiner's comments. (a) (i) was generally well answered, (a) (ii) rather less so. (a) (ii) should remind students that application to the case will often be an important source of marks at professional level.

(b) surprised many students. The question was about establishing risk awareness and management in culture, systems, procedures, protocols, reward and human resource systems and training. Embedding risk is similar to embedding quality, setting the tone at the top and using the cultural and systematic architecture to support it. The question was not about risk management nor did it require an explanation of what risk awareness was.

(c) should remind students that questions in Section B will often not be entirely located in a single area of the study guide. Most students could explain the benefits of PRP, but fewer were able to fulfil the second requirement, to comment on Mr Wang's reward package.

Marking scheme

					Marks
(a)	Risk strategies:				
	Half mark for identification of each strategy	max		2	
	1 mark for each strategy explained (From the five listed strategies needed to get maximum marks)	max		4	
	Risks in case: 2 marks for each risk identified from case with an appropriate strategy identified and explained. Strategies must be realistic for risks identified max			6	
					12
(b)	Marks given for each relevant point made on 'embedding' and for recognition of the importance of culture in embedding				
		max			5
(c)	1 mark for each relevant point made on benefits of PRP	max		5	
	1 mark for each relevant critical comment made on Choo's reward package	max		5	
		max			8
					25

(a) **Risk management**

Transfer

Risk transfer means limiting the impact of a risk by taking steps to ensure that others will bear the impact if it materialises. The best example of risk transfer is an insurance arrangement. The insurer will take on the risk in return for the business paying a **premium**, and possibly taking other steps to reduce the likelihood of the risk crystallising. Risk transfer thus generally has a cost, although this is regarded as necessary in order not to suffer the **severe consequences** of the risk crystallising; insurers will however only bear the risk if they believe that there is a **low likelihood** of the risk materialising.

Avoidance

Risk avoidance means taking steps to **avoid a risk** impacting on an organisation. It is an appropriate strategy for risks which will have **severe consequences** and are very likely to **crystallise if certain courses of action** are taken. Deciding not to undertake certain business activities, such as not operating in politically unstable countries, is an example of risk avoidance.

Reduction

Risk reduction means taking measures to **reduce the chances of a risk crystallising** or **reduce the consequences if it does materialise**. It is most appropriate for risks that are **likely to materialise** but the **consequences are not severe**. For example the chances of loss through theft of inventory can be reduced by searching staff and visitors as they leave the building.

Acceptance

Risk acceptance means taking a conscious decision to suffer the consequences of a risk should it materialise. It is appropriate when the consequences of the risk materialising are **not severe** and the **risk is unlikely to crystallise.** Businesses will also decide to accept risks when they consider the **costs of risk management** are **too high.** They may be unwilling to pay expensive insurance premiums, or may consider that an elaborate control system **undermines their flexibility.**

Risks

Burglary

The **consequences of a burglary** are unlikely to be **severe**, but the **likelihood** of a burglary happening is **high** if the factory is inadequately guarded. **Risk reduction** measures are therefore needed to prevent burglary, for example strong fencing. If strong fencing round the whole premises is impracticable, then **security guards** should be employed to patrol the premises when the factory is closed.

Supply of raw materials

If the material is strategically important for the business process and the board feels that the chances of running out of material are small, the risk may have to be **accepted.** If however shortages may lead to **frequent stockouts**, the board may take **risk reduction measures** such as **increasing the number of suppliers used or forward contracts**. If shortages may be **severe**, the long-term solution may be to **avoid the risk** by redesigning processes so that this material is not used.

Poisonous emissions

The **consequences of poisonous emissions** are likely to be **very severe**. The local environment will be affected, SCC may suffer **heavy legal penalties** and its **reputation** may suffer badly. Because of the severity of these consequences, if the board believes that it is at all likely that emissions will occur, it needs to take steps to **avoid these risks**. Not operating the factory at all would be too drastic an option. However certain activities may need to be **avoided**, and controls operated on other activities to **prevent emissions** such as filters or preventative technology.

(b) **Embedding risk**

Embedding risk awareness means ensuring that staff are thinking about **risk issues,** the **severity and frequency of risks,** as an **integral part of their work.** Staff should know that taking unnecessary risks will not only lead to disciplinary action, but be regarded as unacceptable by their fellow employees, who take risk awareness for granted. There are a number of ways in which risk awareness can be embedded.

Management example

Managers must set a good example and make it clear that they will not tolerate recklessness. Stephanie has identified the failure of the former manager as a key reason why **risk awareness is inadequate.**

Staff commitment

SCC needs to ensure that staff **acknowledge their commitment** to managing risks appropriately. **Signing a risk management code** would be a way of doing this.

Induction and training

It seems also that staff need better training to increase their **awareness of the major risk issues.** Risk awareness also needs to be built into the **induction process** so that staff are aware from when they start of the importance attached to risk management.

Assessment and remuneration

Staff assessment and the **remuneration packages** of staff need to be influenced by how staff handle risk management issues.

(c) **Benefits of performance-related pay**

Link with increased shareholder value

Performance related pay can be a means of resolving the **agency** problem, the idea that the director, the agent of the shareholders, may act in his own interests and not the shareholders. By linking directors' pay to improved profitability and hence **higher share and company value**, performance related pay ensures that **directors and shareholders' interests** are **aligned**.

Link with actual performance

Performance-related pay is also linked into the concept of responsibility accounting, the idea that managers should be **accountable** for what they can control. Performance related pay provides a means of **enforcing accountability.**

Motivation of directors

A generous profit-related package can **motivate directors** to achieve good results, and can also make **recruitment of good directors** easier, and **retention more likely.**

Risk management

PRP should mean that the risks of directors failing to perform adequately are being alleviated in a way that is **consistent with the strategic objectives of the company.**

Implications of Choo Wang's package

Links with performance

Choo is being rewarded only if the **acquisition is successful**, and this is better than rewarding him just for making the acquisition. He has clearly been motivated to make the acquisition successful.

Links with shareholder value

However the **link between shareholder value and Choo's bonus is not very clear.** Shareholder value depends firstly on whether the output from the factory links to enhanced business performance, and the nature of this link is uncertain.

Risk and return

Even if a link can be established, the increased **returns** may be at the expense of **unacceptable increases in shareholder risks** because of the possibility of environmental emissions. There is no scale of remuneration, just a single target, and this is not encouraging a **risk-averse approach.** The lack of an apparent link between risk and return may reflect a board failure to **define SCC's risk appetite adequately**.

Conflict of interest

Choo Wang appears to face a conflict of interest between his personal desire to maximise his remuneration, and his responsibilities as **chair of the risk committee**. As chair he is responsible for ensuring that risks are appropriately managed. Clearly there are serious risks connected with the factory; however Choo seems unconcerned that these risks may be unacceptably high, and have to be avoided rather than reduced or accepted.

28 Chen Products

Text references. Chapters 3,5 and 7.

Top tips. In (a) the marking guide differentiates clearly between a single line bullet point (which would be identifying each role) and a brief (2-3 sentences) description which would earn the full mark for each role described. Therefore a 6 line bullet point list would earn 3 marks at best.

In (b) it seems clear that the examiner favours the TARA framework. The problem you may have found with using this framework is that certain strategies seem clearly more appropriate than others. However the scenario highlights the disagreements among the risk committee, so it seems reasonable to suppose that the full range would be discussed.

As is actually quite common in exam questions, you are told some details about the products, but not actually told what they are, so don't let that put you off.

It's easy to spend too much time on (c) (i); note it is only worth 2 marks. The main issues in (ii) are weighing up the similarity of the roles of the audit and risk committee and the need for effective scrutiny by executives, against the clear problem of lack of industry knowledge on Chen's committee.

Easy marks. If you had revised risk management committees, the requirements in (a) are straightforward.

Examiner's comments. (a) asked candidates to describe the typical roles of a risk management committee. Some candidates failed to observe the verb ('describe') and produced a list (more like 'identify') thereby failing to achieve full marks. Others, perhaps misinterpreting the task, wrote about the purposes of risk management which is a slightly different thing. For five marks, the time budget of nine minutes should have been enough to write two or three sentences on each role by way of description. Again, I would remind candidates to obey the verb. If a question asks candidates to describe or explain, a bullet list of points is not an appropriate response.

(b) appeared to be straightforward but also required application to the case, and this was where some failed to gain marks.

(c)(ii) was not asking about the pros and cons of NEDs in general. Rather it was asking candidates to consider the pros and cons of the placement of NEDs on a particular committee (the risk management committee) and this raised slightly different issues than the general pros and cons. An approach taken by some candidates was to discuss the general advantages and disadvantages but to then fail to develop these into the more specific case of risk committees. Again, it is important to study what the question is really asking rather than assume that the sense of the task can be conveyed in a cursory glance at the key words in the question.

			Marks
(a)	0.5 marks for each role identified		
	0.5 marks for brief description of each role		6
(b)	0.5 marks for identification of each strategy		
	1 mark for definition of each strategy		
	1 mark for application of each strategy to Chen Products		10
(c)	(i) 2 marks for distinguishing between executive and non-executive directors		2
	(ii) 1 mark for each relevant advantage	max 4	
	1 mark for each relevant disadvantage	max $\underline{3}$	
			$\underline{7}$
			$\underline{\underline{25}}$

(a) **Approving the organisation's risk management strategies and policies**

The committee should ensure that risk management strategies and policies are **consistent with overall business strategies** determined by the full board. The committee should also obtain evidence that **risks and risk management strategies** have been **communicated** throughout the organisation, and that appropriate **staff training** has taken place.

Monitoring risk exposure

The committee should take a **portfolio view of risk** across the whole organisation, ensuring that **overall risk levels** do not exceed the levels deemed tolerable by the board, and that **opportunities to diversify and hedge risks** across the company are taken. The committee should also ensure that measures are taken to **limit the most significant risks or risks in particularly vulnerable areas**, for example placing trading limits on treasury function staff.

Reviewing reports on key risks

The committee should receive regular **reports from business operating units** and other key functions such as **information technology and treasury**. The committee should determine from these reports whether **appropriate actions** have been taken to **manage risks**, and the significance of risks crystallizing and control failures identified.

Assessing effectiveness of risk management systems

The committee needs to consider whether the **risk management systems** are fulfilling their **objectives**. Reports by internal and external auditors are an important source of evidence for this assessment .

Providing early warning on emerging risk issues

The committee should regularly review the wider business environment, including the activities of key competitors, legal, technological and economic issues. This review should aim to **highlight new risks or alterations in existing risks** that mean that risk management policies or systems need to change.

Reviewing external reports on internal control

The committee needs to satisfy itself that reports on internal control in the financial statements **fairly** reflect the systems in operation and include sufficient detail about **weaknesses in internal control.**

(b) **Transfer**

Transfer means taking action to ensure that **another party** bears some or all of the consequences of risks materialising, in return for that other party receiving some **benefit**.

Chen could **transfer liability for the costs of compensation to an insurance company**, on payment of a **premium** and subject to Chen accepting a **minimum liability**. However the insurance company may insist that Chen also takes action to **reduce risk,** as well as paying the insurance premium, before it accepts the insurance contract. Another method of transfer would be outsourcing manufacture of Product 2, with the outsourcing partner accepting liability for product problems.

Avoidance

Avoidance means **ceasing to undertake the activities** that could result in risks crystallizing and the company suffering losses.

Here avoidance of risk would mean ceasing to manufacture Product 2. The cessation could be **temporary**, lasting until the risk committee had obtained sufficient assurance that Product 2 would not fail. Alternatively the committee may consider that the **potential financial consequences** of compensation, plus the damage to Chen Products' **reputation** and **resulting falls in sales** of other products, are so great that Product 2 should be **permanently withdrawn**.

Reduction

Reduction means **reducing the chances of risks materialising,** by for example more stringent control measures or by becoming less dependent on the activity causing the risk.

If Chen was to reduce risks, it would continue to manufacture Product 2. However it would investigate why Product 2 had failed. The results of the investigation might mean that Chen introduced **stricter quality control procedures** or **checks by internal audit** that existing procedures were being applied correctly. Alternatively Chen could manufacture less of Product 2 and more of other products, although the directors would have to weigh up the **potential reduction in compensation claims** against the consequences of switching production to **possibly less profitable products**.

Acceptance

Acceptance means acknowledging that **some risks at a certain level** will be **inevitable** if Chen is to make profits and that the **costs of risk management outweigh the benefits** from reducing or eliminating the compensation claims.

If Chen's risk committee decided to accept risk here, the directors are likely to be acknowledging that some product failure is inevitable and the consequences are not sufficiently serious to warrant Chen taking further action to deal with the risks.

(c) (i) **Executive directors**

Executive directors are **employees** who are responsible for **managing the business** and **developing the company's strategy**, implementing the decisions of the board. Their value to the company lies in their **industry or role knowledge and experience.**

Non-executive directors (NEDs)

NEDs have **no managerial responsibilities** and their role is **part-time**. They are recruited from **wider, external backgrounds**. Their **independent scrutiny of the work of executive directors**, including their work on **board committees**, should provide reassurance to shareholders

(ii) **Advantages of NEDs**

Differing backgrounds and expertise

The variation in experience of NEDs will mean that they have seen **various risk management strategies** in action, and seen how the organisations they have worked for respond to various risks. These insights may be valuable given the changing risks Chen may face, and the need for its risk management to evolve.

Scrutiny of executive directors

A key role of the risk committee is to **scrutinise the operations of the risk management systems**, including the **performance of the executives** responsible for implementing the systems. If NEDs staff the committee, then the scrutiny should be **independent** and form an important part of NEDs' overall responsibilities to scrutinise performance.

Interaction with audit committees

Under governance codes, audit committee members must be NEDs. If the **audit and risk committees** have some common members, this should help ensure both committees take a **consistent approach to risk management issues**.

Discussion of sensitive issues

Having the committee solely staffed by NEDs means that they can discuss sensitive issues **without executives being present**, something identified in governance reports as being important for the audit committee as well.

Disadvantages of NEDs

Lack of experience of Chen's industry

The lack of industry knowledge appears to be the most serious weakness of the committee. As a result the committee's **decision-making** seems **deadlocked**, with no way of determining which of the strategies proposed is most appropriate.

Lack of time

Because of other commitments, NEDs **may not be able to spend enough time considering risk issues**, remembering that they may also have to staff the audit and nomination committees as well as attending full board meetings. Risk committee meetings may not be held frequently enough, and action to counter significant risks may thus be taken too slowly.

Improving risk awareness

Including executive directors on the committee should **improve the understanding of the executives** of the key risk issues that the committee is discussing. It should also provide the NEDs with key information relating to products and systems that helps them **understand the issues** involved in implementing their recommendations in this industry.

29 H and Z

Text references. Chapters 5 and 7.

Top tips. (a) (i) is basic book knowledge, but note the examiner required a description of the roles, which meant more than a single line bullet point list. On this occasion most students provided sufficient detail.

Some of the points in (ii) may appear slightly odd, but they do indicate that the risk manager's role goes beyond assessment of risks and simple recommendations. It does though bring into question H and Z's recruitment policies, recruiting someone to an important role whose understanding was so fundamentally flawed. Note also that a key theme of the June 2009 exam in which this question appeared was the shortcomings of important individuals, here the risk manager and in other questions the chairman and chief executive. Future exams may focus on the weaknesses of individuals holding other key roles.

In (b) the very strong hint in the question is for you to explain the likelihood-consequences matrix (the risk management framework) and then apply it. Risk appetite is an important issue to mention.

In (c) the requirement to evaluate requires (almost) the same number of points for and against. The answer includes the concept of STOP errors, a topic highlighted by the examiner as very important.

Easy marks. The role of the risk manager in (a) (i) and the likelihood-consequences matrix are what the examiner would describe as 'bookwork'.

Marking scheme

				Marks
(a)	(i)	1 mark for evidence of understanding in each type of role (0.5 marks for identification and 0.5 for description) max		4
	(ii)	1 mark for each relevant assessment comment on John's understanding of the role		4
(b)		Evidence of understanding of risk assessment (impact/hazard and probability)	2	
		Recognition of uncertainties over impact and probability information and description	2	
		Importance of return and recognition of lack of return/benefit information and description	2	
				6
(c)	(i)	Definition	2	
		Explanation of its importance	2	
				4
	(ii)	1 mark for each relevant point made in the case for Jane Xylene's view max	4	
		1 mark for each relevant point made in the case against Jane Xylene's view max	4	
		max		7
				25

(a)　(i)　**Establishing a RM framework**

The framework should **cover all aspects of risk** across the organisation, integrating enterprise risk management with other business planning and management activities and framing authority and accountability for enterprise risk management in business units. Development of policies includes the **quantification of management's risk appetite through specific risk limits**, **defining roles and responsibilities** and **participating in setting goals for implementation**

Promoting enterprise risk management competence

This includes **training managers and staff** to help them develop risk management expertise and, **helping managers align risk responses with the entity's risk tolerances.**

Dealing with insurance companies

The risk manager needs to deal carefully with insurers because of **increased premium costs, restrictions in the cover available** (will the risks be excluded from cover) and the **need for negotiations** if claims arise. If insurers require it, the risk manager needs to demonstrate that the organisation is actively taking steps to manage its risks.

Risk reporting

The risk manager is responsible for **implementing risk indicators and reports,** including losses and incidents, key risk exposures, and early warning indicators. He should **facilitate reporting by operational managers**, including **quantitative and qualitative thresholds**, and **monitor** this reporting process.

(ii)   **Flaws in risk assessment**

It is understandable that John wanted to carry one of the most important tasks quickly. However by doing it as soon as he started at H and Z, it seems he didn't give himself sufficient time to understand the company's **background and strategic aims**. The fact also that he had not had time to establish a risk management framework will have meant that his assessment of risk is based on inadequate information.

Form of advice

John's advice to the board is expressed too strongly. The board has responsibility for **taking key strategic decisions** and John is exceeding his remit by telling them so bluntly to stop the activity associated with Risk 3.

Support for advice

John's advice does not appear to be **backed by the supporting information** necessary for the board to take an informed decision on the risk.

Risk management

John is not responsible for **eliminating or minimising all the highest risks** facing the company. Some risks, for example the risks of operations being disrupted by natural disasters are risks John cannot influence much, if at all. John will also need to consider whether some high impact risks **cannot be effectively lessened**, but could be **transferred**, for example to **H and Z's insurers.**

(b)   **Probability-impact/Likelihood-consequences matrix**

This matrix is used to group risks and assess their relative importance. As such, it is a useful tool when you are considering, as John is, the **impact of major risks.**

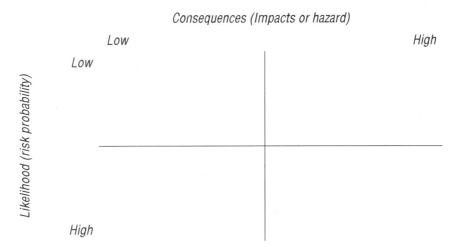

This diagram maps two continuums on which risks are plotted. The **nearer the risk is** towards the **bottom right-hand corner** (the high-high corner), the **more important** the risk will be. This profile can then be used to set priorities for risk mitigation.

Failure to consider probability

The most significant failure in John's approach to assessing risk is his failure to consider the **likelihood** that the risk will materialise. As Jane points out, in order for H and Z to continue in business, it will have to bear some **significant entrepreneurial risks.** However the investments can be justified if the risks are **low.**

Risk and return

John has also failed to take into account what the directors have established as the company's **risk appetite**. The directors may believe that taking significant risks is justified by the possibility of achieving **high returns** from the associated activities. Risk elimination or minimisation may not always achieve high returns. Instead better returns may be achieved by **risk reduction or transfer.**

Uncertainties of assessment

John has also not taken into account inevitable **uncertainties in the data used** to make the likelihood-consequences assessment. His strongly-expressed view fails to take into account the importance of the assumptions made, the likelihood of different scenarios and other issues surrounding the assessment.

(c)   (i)   **Entrepreneurial risks**

Entrepreneurial risks are the risks that arise from **carrying out business activities,** for example the risks of a major investment failing to deliver required returns or profits being lessened by competitor's activities.

Acceptance of entrepreneurial risks

Few if, any, business activities are risk free. For example in all business situations other than a monopoly, the business will face **risks arising from competition.** Also **shareholders** will have invested in a business on the grounds that they wish to **achieve higher returns** than those offered by risk-free investments. A business can only earn these returns if it takes risks.

(ii)   **Benefits vs costs**

Jane correctly identifies the needs to balance the benefits of risk management against costs. **Expenditure on over-elaborate risk management systems** may not be warranted by the **losses they prevent** or the **disruption to operating activities** that they cause.

Opportunity costs

Jane also correctly identifies the problems with taking a completely pessimistic view of risk, treating all risks as pure risks with only negative consequences. **Speculative risks**, the risks relating to doing business are risks from which **good or harm** may result. The upside of these risks needs to be taken into account when managers decide how to deal with them.

STOP errors

Jane's views also reflect the existence of **STOP errors**, of the adverse consequences of failing to take an opportunity that should have been pursued.

Lack of understanding

However Jane does not appear to understand the benefits of risk management and why corporate governance guidance insists that listed companies have appropriate risk management structures in place. Directors need to gain assurance that the decisions they take about **what risks** should be **borne** and how the **risks borne** should be **managed** are enforced. The risk management function helps to **give them this assurance.** The risk management function also **provides information** to the board to help decide on the risk implications of strategy, and also to operational managers so that they can recognise and deal with risks when they arise.

Risk-return relationship

Jane seems to be operating at the other extreme to John, and as such has an equally flawed view of the risk-return relationship. **Shareholder**s may require risks to be taken so that they can achieve an adequate return, but they will also judge some risks to be too high for the **potential returns from taking them**. Jane does not appear to recognise any limits to **H and Z's risk appetite.** John is right in saying that there are some risks that are too great for the company to bear, that will threaten its existence, and cannot be justified whatever the return.

Risk management strategies

Jane incorrectly views risk avoidance and the forbidding of activities as the only strategies recommended by risk managers. Risk managers can **recommend risk reduction strategies** that will increase the chances of commercial success, for example piloting a new product to a small audience before it is launched.

30 UU

Text references. Chapters 5, 6 and 11.

Top tips. There is some flexibility in this question about where material can be located in the answer. You could for example have expanded the discussion on industry issues in (a) and then said more in (c) about the pressures of keeping customers happy. Planning is certainly important here to ensure that you don't repeat yourself.

Our answer to (a) reflects the problems that many companies have during a recession, with the need to maintain liquidity conflicting with other priorities. Using knowledge from Paper F9 is helpful here. Given that the syllabus revision affecting exams from June 2011 places greater emphasis on financial risk management, knowledge brought forward from F9 is likely to be important in future questions as well.

In (b) and (c) the strength of the internal environment and information systems will determine how successfully risk can be embedded. In particular in (c) the lax attitude of senior management towards liquidity risk, which the scenario makes very clear, is a very significant factor.

Easy marks. You should have scored heavily on (b), as it is an important part of risk management, and questions like (b) have come up before.

Examiner's comments. Most candidates were able to define liquidity risk in (a) but fewer were able to explain its particular significance to UU, the fact that it was manufacturer with inventory levels not present in service industry companies.

(b) was done quite well by many candidates whereas (c) was less well done. (c) involved a careful analysis of the case to bring out the various factors that would make it difficult to embed liquidity risk management at UU. It was specifically about liquidity risk management and not risk management in general. The obstacles were relatively straightforward to find in the case and the highest marks were gained by those most able to show how the different attitudes of the company's managers put pressure on the different aspects of the company's working capital.

In (d) candidates had to point out why the policy wasn't a very good means of demonstrating CSR. The case contained a number of issues associated with the policy which the better-prepared candidates picked up on. Poor answers receiving few or no marks were those that simply defined CSR or used a textbook framework (such as Carrol's framework) in an attempt to answer the question.

Marks

(a) Definition of liquidity risk   2
    1 mark for each explanation of manufacturing vulnerability to liquidity
    risk max   3
                                                                                            5

(b) 2 marks for definition of risk embeddedness   2
    1 mark for each method of risk embeddedness max   5
                                                                                            7

(c) 2 marks for each obstacle identified and examined. 1 mark for
    identification only max   8

(d) 2 marks for each criticism made max   5
                                                                                            25

(a) **Liquidity risk**

Liquidity risk is the risk that an organisation is **unable to meet its day-to-day cash flow needs** and is **unable to settle or renew its short-term liabilities.** It is related to its **working capital**. Therefore significant influences over liquidity risk are the levels of inventory, receivables, cash and payables and how these are managed.

UU's position

UU has significant liquidity risk, because of its lengthy **cash operating cycle** – the period from ordering goods from suppliers to receiving monies from customers. As a manufacturing company, it has more significant working capital (particularly more inventory) than the service businesses that Bob Ndumo directs. There are problems in each area of working capital.

Suppliers

UU appears to have some leeway to **lengthen its payment period to suppliers** whilst still remaining within its credit limits. However any lengthening may give suppliers the impression that UU is in financial trouble, particularly as it has publicised its previous policy prominently. Suppliers may impose shorter credit periods than UU has had before, because UU is perceived to be of higher risk. Also if UU's inventory holding policies are to improve by, for example, the introduction of just-in-time ordering, then this will require the co-operation of suppliers.

Customers

The failure to enforce the debtor payment clearly has a significant impact upon UU's liquidity. 50 days would be regarded as an **excessively generous period** by many companies. The problem UU may face is that attempts to enforce a tighter policy may result in a **loss of customer goodwill**. It could also **threaten the liquidity of customers**. As short-term finance is difficult to obtain from lenders, some customers may be using the **lengthening credit period from UU** as an informal source of short-term finance. Loss of customers will result in falling revenues.

Inventory

UU is a manufacturer and hence inventory pressure will always be an issue. Here excessive inventory is another reason for the lengthy cash cycle, with amounts held **appearing to be too high.** Again however customer pressures appear to explain the high levels. Finished goods levels are high so that products are available for **customers to buy on demand**, reducing the risk of customers purchasing from competitors if UU does not have products available. The raw material levels are being kept high to minimise production time and **hence also minimise the time between customer order and receipt of goods.**

(b)   **Embedding risk**

Embedding risk means ensuring that risk **awareness and management** are innate elements of the **systems and culture** of an organisation. It means that **systems** should be **designed and operated** according to the **risk management objectives** of the organisation. It means ensuring that staff are thinking about **risk issues,** the **severity and frequency of risks,** as an **integral part of their work.** Staff should know that taking unnecessary risks will not only lead to disciplinary action, but be regarded as unacceptable by their fellow employees.

Methods of embedding risk

Management example and communication

Managers must set a good example and show that they will not tolerate recklessness. They should **discuss risk and associated risk responses** in regular communication with employees. **Risk management policies, standards and procedures** should be made **readily available to employees.**

Staff commitment

Staff should **acknowledge their commitment** to managing risks appropriately. **Signing a risk management code** would be a way of doing this. Risk management should be a part of everybody's **job description,** to ensure that staff's responsibilities are clearly defined.

Induction and training

Staff need regular **training** to increase their **awareness of major risk issues.** Risk awareness also needs to be built into the **induction process** so that staff are aware from when they start of the importance attached to risk management.

Information systems

Information systems need to make available **data about risks** and **performance indicators** that demonstrate to directors and managers how well risks are being managed. **Exception reporting** is an important element. This means the **immediate reporting** of certain risks if they rise above a certain level, and also having **channels available for staff to report poor risk management** directly to the board.

Assessment and remuneration

Staff assessment and the **remuneration packages** of staff need to be influenced by how staff handle risk management issues. In some instances staff will have to take risks as part of their jobs. The assessment procedures should consider whether they have handled risk appropriately – examining whether they have been too cautious as well as too aggressive.

(c)   **Attitudes of operational managers towards liquidity risk**

Operational managers appear to **underestimate or ignore the consequences of liquidity risk.** Both the manufacturing director and the sales manager appear to give sole priority to meeting customers' requirements at all costs. They ignore the need to take some action to **reduce liquidity risk** and balance this action against the need to keep customers happy. It would appear that liquidity risk management is not a major performance objective of senior operational managers.

Complex organisational structure

The way **responsibilities are allocated** may hinder a unified approach to liquidity management. Inevitably, given the complexity of UU's operations, different senior managers are responsible for control of different elements of working capital. However they all seem concerned with their own areas, and insufficiently focused on the wider corporate objective of maintaining liquidity.

Lax control environment

The **control environment over the sales department** appears to be **poor.** No reason has been advanced why credit periods are so lengthy. Whilst credit control staff may be taking account of the need to keep customers happy, the manufacturing director appears to imply that the long credit periods are due to laxness by credit control staff and poor enforcement of targets.

In addition the manufacturing director does not seem to have taken much action to limit the **decline in profit margins**, suggesting that targets and performance assessment of senior management may also be lax.

Attitude of Brian Mills

Brian Mills is **failing to give a lead in treating liquidity management** as important. He is prioritising the non-financial objective of demonstrating corporate social responsibility over the financial objective of proper management of working capital. Not only will this influence the attitudes of staff, but it may be difficult to change the policy as it is being promoted by the chief executive.

(d)   **Personal policy**

The policy has been **driven by Brian Mills** and does not enjoy the support of the other directors. The policy cannot be regarded as a long-term commitment and part of the company's **strategic positioning**, as it appears likely to change when there is a change of Chief Executive.

Costs and benefits of policy

The finance director has highlighted that the policy is **very costly** to UU. As far as the impact on the wider economy is concerned, it is debatable whether UU's policy is **making much difference**. Its suppliers will set credit periods for their own commercial reasons, and perhaps the main thing they require is the certainty that UU will pay within those periods rather than at some artificially early date.

Impact on reputation

How significant **damage to UU's reputation** would be if payment policy changed is **debatable.** As far as wide publicity is concerned, UU may be unlikely to suffer much damage if it merely reverts to paying within credit periods. The fact that one group of stakeholders (not perhaps the most vulnerable group) is being treated favourably may mean that UU does not gain much publicity benefit from its policy. Focusing social responsibility on different stakeholders or charitable causes, also examining more closely the environmental impact of its activities, may result in greater amounts of positive publicity and genuinely be more socially responsible.

31 YGT

Text references. Chapters 5-7.

Top tips. The examiner used the question to examine some of the new study guide content on risk, in particular the dynamic nature of risk and the idea of related risk.

(a) mentions dynamic risks, so you should be looking for signs in the scenario of risks that have changed recently. It is clearly stated that Risks C and D have been affected by recent events. As you're asked to criticise Raz's beliefs, you should also be looking for evidence that the risk assessment provided useful information, and the scenario again clearly emphasises that it did.

In (b) the descriptions of the risks are worded carefully to make clear where each fit on the impact/likelihood risk assessment map. None are marginal. Once the risks are correctly plotted on the map, the risk strategies should have been clear and the scenario again helps by indicating which activities are vital and which peripheral.

In (c) the point was that in some cases, increased environmental losses can result in deterioration of a company's reputation (i.e. a rise in reputation risk). Because both risks rise and fall together, they can be said to be positively correlated. However that does not mean their relationship is exact because of the different consequences that they have.

The key themes to bring out in (d) are that risk awareness is a way of thinking and that everyone in the organisation must have it. Being aware of risks that apply to day-to-day operations can be as important as awareness of strategic risks, and perhaps awareness of operational risks can easily be taken too much for granted.

Easy marks. The examiner highlighted coming up with criticisms in (a) and plotting the risks on the continuum in (b) as areas where easy marks should have been obtained.

Examiner's comments. (a) and (c) were done quite well on the whole and (b) and (d) were very variable.

For (a), many candidates were able to discuss the notion of risks arising as an organisation's environment changes but fewer were able to gain the 'criticise' marks.

ACCA examiner's answer. The ACCA examiner's answer to this question can be found at the back of this kit.

		Marks
(a)	2 marks for each evaluation point made max	4
	2 marks for each point identified and explained on dynamic max	4
		8
(b)	0.5 marks for correct strategy selection for each risk. 1 mark for each risk strategy correctly explained and justified method of risk embeddedness max	6
(c)	2 marks for explanation of related and correlated risks	2
	2 marks for each description of why correlated max	4
	max	5
(d)	1 mark for explanation	1
	2 marks for each relevant point for assessment max	6
	max	6
		25

(a) **Raz Dutta's beliefs**

Both Raz Dutta's assertions are incorrect.

Risks don't change much

It is untrue to say that the risks YGT faces do not change much. The new product, for example, has given rise to Risk C and the change in legislation has given rise to Risk D. Risk assessment is needed to translate these events in the environment into an analysis of the **consequences for YGT and the likelihood** that these consequences will occur.

Risks hardly ever materialise

The risk assessment that the consultants carried out revealed that this assertion is **incorrect,** which justified the assessment being made. Risk B is assessed as **highly likely to occur and with a high impact.** The risk assessment should **prompt action to be taken quickly**, perhaps abandoning the activity.

The assessment has also revealed that Risk C will have a high potential impact if it materialises. The risk assessment should therefore **prompt the board to weigh up this assessment** against **the low probability** of the risk materialising and see whether it is worth taking the alternative actions mentioned.

Why risk assessment is dynamic

Risk continuum

Most businesses **operate on a continuum** somewhere between highly static and highly dynamic. Few businesses operate very near the static end of the continuum, because of the **changing forces** in the outside world and the need for them to respond. These may include any or all of the PESTEL factors (political, economic, social, technological, environmental, legal). Risks may become more or less likely to materialise or have increased or decreased impact. Stricter legislation, for example, may increase the impact of the risk of non-compliance because it introduces tougher penalties for breaking the law.

Strategic decisions

The product launch, and the risks associated with that launch, will have arisen because YGT is seeking to gain a **competitive advantage.** Competitors are likely to take action in response to the product launch, resulting in further changes in risk levels.

Operational changes

The risks from the external environment will also prompt changes in the **organisation's activities and operations,** such as the introduction of procedures to comply with new legislation. Changes will carry their own risks, for example modifications in production processes when a new product is introduced may make machine breakdowns more likely.

(b) **Risk A**

Risk A should be **accepted.** Although the activity is marginal and could be abandoned, the **high returns** generated outweigh the low likelihood and impact and justify continuing with the activity.

Risk B

Risk B should **probably be avoided.** Although it generates high returns, it is not vital to YGT's continued existence. It is unlikely that the risk appetite determined by the directors should permit YGT to continue to be involved in an activity that is peripheral and which will probably generate large losses.

Risk C

Risk C should be **transferred.** Although it might have a high impact, it cannot be avoided. The scenario mentions alternative actions being taken. These could include insurance or outsourcing production, if the risk is associated with manufacture.

Risk D

Risk D should be **reduced.** Some action has to be taken to **avoid the business suffering frequent, small losses.** This action clearly cannot include transferring the risk. As the risk is associated with a change in legislation, the action could be whatever is necessary to comply with the new rules. The action could also include reducing the activity or carrying it out in a different way. The directors would need to weigh up the benefits of continuing to carry out the activity at the present level against the increased costs of doing so, and repeat this assessment at other levels or for other methods of performance.

(c) **Related risks**

A related risk is a risk that is **not independent of other risks.** Its level is linked to the level of the other risk, and its level will change as the level of the other risk changes. **Correlation** is an example of a relationship between risks.

Environmental risk links with reputation risk

Environmental risks are exposures to losses through the **impacts** the organisation makes on the environment or the **resources it consumes.** The organisation may suffer bad publicity, and hence a risk to its reputation, as a result of environmental risk arising. **Reputation risk** is thus likely to be **positively correlated** to environmental risk because they have a **common cause**, an impact or event that adversely affects the environment. Actions taken to reduce the likelihood of adverse environmental impacts or events occurring will also decrease the likelihood of reputation risk materialising.

Environmental risk distinction from reputation risk

The losses incurred from environmental risks materialising are separate from the losses resulting from damage to reputation. Environmental risk losses may include **clean-up costs or legal penalties,** reputation risk losses may include **lost sales** as customers boycott the business. The impact of reputation risk materialising is also not only dependent on the environmental impact or event that has occurred, but also how people have **reacted to it.** If there is no reaction, then reputation risk has not materialised.

(d) **Risk awareness explanation**

Risk awareness is the ability of an organisation and its personnel to recognise the risks facing the business. To be effective, there needs to be **risk awareness throughout the organisation.** Staff need to be thinking without prompting about the risks involved in what they are doing. Risk awareness needs to influence the ways they carry out their activities on a **day-to-day basis.**

Risk awareness assessment

Presence throughout the organisation

Risks are present in different ways within the organisation. They do not just arise from the strategic decisions directors make. There will be **risks present at every level of operations**. A culture of risk awareness will help employees understand the risks that affect them and identify these risks when they arise.

Dynamic risks

Directors and employees need to be aware that risks can change over time as a **result of changes in operations or changes in the business environment**. The most recent risk assessment may quickly become outdated. If employees have an awareness that risks can change, it will help them identify when risks have changed and this will aid risk assessment in the future.

Lack of board awareness

The fact that Raz Dutta feels that risk assessment is unnecessary indicates a **lack of awareness at board level** that will hinder the effective implementation of risk awareness lower down. This could mean that staff do not spot relevant risks and thus the company's exposure is higher than it should be. Alternatively they could wrongly assess risks and take unnecessarily costly actions to combat them.

32 Internal audit effectiveness

Text reference. Chapter 8.

Top tips. (a) brings in the issue of independence, which is likely to be a feature of most questions on internal audit, given the stress on independence in the syllabus. The question takes a different angle to the issue of who internal audit **reports to,** although the issue of internal audit-finance director relations is still very relevant.

(b) may appear to cover issues that you encountered in 2.6 or F8. However assessment of the effectiveness of internal control systems is an important requirement. You may well have to consider the role of internal audit when a question scenario presents you with internal control systems that you have to assess. We have grouped the objectives under the main headings given in Chapter 8 of the text, and also brought in material from the Turnbull report.

One problem is measuring internal audit's work in terms of it being a prevent control or detect control. Clearly internal audit is at least partly a deterrent, designed to prevent carelessness or fraud. But how much can the absence of fraud be used to judge internal audit (does the apparent absence of fraud mean that internal audit have failed to detect it?). Performance may be easier to measure in other areas, where internal audit recommendations can be assessed in terms of whether recommended improvements in value for money or behaviour have been implemented.

Be careful to pick up all that (b) is asking for, since the requirement is quite complicated. It's easy to forget to provide the example.

Easy marks. Based on your previous experience of auditing, you may have found the first section of (b), dealing with accounting controls, to be the easiest part. However note the majority of (b) deals with other areas of the control systems, and effective internal audit often needs to be an integral part of those systems.

(a)   **Who should carry out the assessment?**

Need for independence of reviewer

The IAD must **maintain its independence** from those parts of the organisation which it audits (ie most of the operations of the business). This independence must be maintained when the IAD is itself the subject of the audit for the sake of future IAD audits, and to obtain an objective result in this case. This criteria would exclude Meg as the Finance Director.

Use of audit committee

Other members of the board might be appropriate investigators, but the prime candidate would be a member of the **Audit Committee** (AC) as the IAD acts as almost an executive arm of the committee. A member of the AC with appropriate knowledge and experience would be required.

Another company's internal audit department

Alternatives to the AC that might be considered include the **IAD of another company**, which might be approached through contacts of Crucero's executive directors. **Confidentiality** might be an issue here. Crucero's board would need to make sure that the other company was not a competitor etc.

External auditors

Another option would be to use Crucero's own **external auditors**. If the auditors were happy with Crucero's IAD, then future co-operation between the two sets of auditors might produce a saving in the external audit fee. However, if they were unhappy with the work of Crucero's IAD, then the external auditors may decide that they need to perform extra audit work in future, and **fees might then rise**.

(b) **Objectives and performance measurement of internal audit**

Adequacy of internal control systems

Objectives

Internal audit will be concerned with the **design** of the systems, whether the systems are right in the first place, and monitoring the operation of systems by risk assessment and internal testing.

Performance measures

Internal audit will be judged by the **cost-effectiveness of the recommendations** it makes. One measure of this will be the **proportion of recommendations** that are **implemented**.

Adequacy of financial and operating information

Objectives

Internal audit's recommendations in this area relate very strongly to the general aims described above, of making sure that management are furnished with the **information necessary** to do their job **effectively. It also involves fulfilling external reporting and legal requirements that the business generates timely, relevant and reliable information.**

Performance measures

Important measures are **management reaction** to recommendations made and whether the improvements **change management behaviour** (for example management modifies plans because the information system identifies the probability of an overspend on budget). Recommendations for improvements in information systems should also lead to **improvements in the quality and timing of external reporting**, measured (hopefully) by external auditors giving the business an unqualified audit report, and raising few, if any, points in their letter to management

Economy, efficiency and effectiveness of operations

Objectives

A major part of internal audit's activities may well be a review of **value for money,** the economic, efficient and effective use of resources.

Performance measures

Performance measures should focus on **recommendations on each of the elements** of value for money, whether costs have been reduced, better use made of available resources and the desired results achieved. Excessive emphasis by internal audit on cost control, for example, may mean that costs fall, but sales fall as well because of reduced levels of customer service.

Compliance with laws and regulations

Objectives

The objectives here are similar to those for work on accounting controls, except that internal audit is seeking to **prevent non-compliance** with relevant laws and regulations. These laws and regulations may also demand that certain **specific controls** must be **operating effectively**, and so internal audit must check those controls are working.

Performance measures

The performance measures would be whether **breaches** that were not identified by internal audit have **occurred,** and the consequences of those breaches; payments of fines or penalties or time spent dealing with communications with regulatory authorities.

Safeguarding of assets

Objectives

Internal auditors will not only be concerned with security measures over physical assets and security systems; they will also be concerned with broader issues such as maintenance of customer base by responding to customer's changing requirements.

Performance measures

Specific performance measures would depend on the reports made by internal audit. Thus for example a satisfactory report on controls over the security of inventory could be measured against the level of **inventory loss**. Similarly reports on managing customer relationships could be assessed in the light of **losses of existing customers** and **acquiring new customers**.

Implementation of corporate objectives

Objectives

The areas of internal practices that internal audit may seek to consider include policies for **compliance with codes of best practice** such as the corporate governance reports. They also include **general business practices** such as planning, internal communication and staff problems.

Performance measures

Performance of internal audits will be judged by the activity being reviewed. Compliance with codes of best practice may be **reported on by external auditors or commented on by shareholders or the media,** and avoidance of adverse comments from these sources will be a measure of success. The results of review of staff policies can be measured by the rate of **staff turnover** or the number of staff grievances. Internal audit's comments on **planning** could be judged by the **quality of plans** produced, and **improvements in adherence** to those plans.

Risk identification and monitoring of risk management systems

Objectives

Internal audit review should provide evidence to support management review of internal control systems. Internal audit will be responsible for obtaining evidence that systems are in place to **recognise risks**, risk management systems appear adequate to manage these risks and whether actions are being taken to remedy weaknesses.

Performance measures

In some ways, this objective could be measured negatively; the absence of shocks, unexpected risks impacting significantly upon the business, for example the recommendations of internal audit acting to **prevent fraud**.

33 Audit committees

(a) **Limitations on the effectiveness of non-executive directors**

Qualities of non-executive directors

Having the same perspective as executive directors

The corporate governance reports stress the importance of non-executive directors possessing independent judgement and being appointed by a nomination committee. However the nomination committee may restrict its search to **directors** who will 'fit in' with the rest of the board, and may be **unwilling to recruit from a diversity of backgrounds,** for example stakeholders such as employees.

Support for chairman

Many non-executive directors will only agree to serve on the boards of companies if they admire the company's chairman or its way of operating.

Lack of independence

In many companies non-executive directors have been appointed through business or social contacts with directors. It may be difficult to find **non-executive directors** who **fulfil the independence requirements** of the corporate governance reports or freedom from any relationship that compromises independence.

Lack of business knowledge

This can be the other side to the problem of lack of independence. Potential non-executive directors who have **good knowledge of the business and industry** may have gained that knowledge through links with the company in the past.

Resource issues

Lack of director development

Non-executive directors may not have **proper induction** into the company, nor **proper updating and refreshment** of their skills and knowledge of the company. Their **performance may not be appraised** regularly; it should form part of an **annual appraisal** of the **board's activities**.

Limited time

The most knowledgeable and effective non-executive directors are likely to have other significant demands on their time. As directors they have to fulfil **certain legal requirements.** Apart from their contributions to the main board, they will also probably spend time at **meetings of board committees** such as the audit and remuneration committees. The limited involvement resulting from the lack of time may limit their ability to contribute to board meetings since they are **unable to obtain** a **broad enough picture** of what is happening throughout the organisation.

Information available

Non-executive directors' contribution will also depend on the information that is readily available to them as directors. This will be influenced by the **quality of the organisation's information systems**, and also the **willingness of executive directors** to supply information about their activities.

Functioning of board

Role of board

The corporate governance reports stress the importance of non-executive directors being involved in **strategic decisions.** If non-executive directors are involved in formulating strategy, they can fulfil what Sir John Harvey-Jones sees as their key role, of **warning of potential problems** and hence **preventing trouble**. However board meetings may focus almost entirely on **current operational matters and short-term operational results**.

Assessment of performance

In addition a focus at board meetings on short-term results may mean that non-executive directors **assess the performance** of the organisation using short-term indicators and its management, and do not focus on **longer-term issues** such as changes in product mix or re-engineering of the organisation's processes.

Inability to resist pressures

Non-executive directors have limited options when faced with a **united group of executive directors** who are determined to push through a policy with which the non-executive directors disagree. Their ultimate weapon is **resignation**, but if all or a number of non-executive directors resign, they may precipitate a **crisis of confidence** in the company. Alternatively they can **remain in office,** but then if serious problems arise, the executive directors may have to depart from the board, leaving the non-executive directors with the responsibility for **'picking up the pieces'**.

(b) **Improving the effectiveness of audit committees**

Appointment requirements

Appointments could be **recommended** by the **annual general meeting**. Alternatively certain stakeholders, for example employees could have the right to appoint a member. These measures might improve the independence of committee members. The **term of office** of committee members could also be **limited** to ensure the committee retained a fresh perspective.

Qualities of new directors

When nominating potential members, the selection process could be biased towards **recruiting members with financial accounting experience or experience of large control systems**. Members who have accountancy experience will be able to question the judgements management make when preparing accountancy information.

Expansion of responsibilities

There are various ways in which the committee's remit might be expanded. They could have responsibility for **reviewing compliance with laws and regulations** such as environmental legislation or ethical codes. Certain **transactions** could also be **referred automatically** to them for review.

Internal audit

As a major function of many audit committees is to oversee the role of internal audit, it follows that a **more effective internal audit function** will lead to more effective operation of the audit committee by improving the quality of information that the audit committee review.

Statutory backing

Audit committees may become more effective if their establishment by certain organisations is made **compulsory.** The recommendations of internal audit will also be **reinforced by stricter accounting and auditing standards.**

Improvement in operations

Changes that might improve the way audit committees operate include having **clear terms of reference** agreed by the board. The committee should establish an **annual plan** giving details of the areas on which it will focus. **Standards** should be established for the **frequency** and **form of reporting** to the main board. The board should carry out a regular **review** of the **effectiveness** of the audit committee including whether its recent work has been correctly focused.

(c) **Dealing with complaints**

One aspect of control systems improvement will be **dealing with complaints** from customers. However the control systems cannot just concentrate on dealing with complaints as even resolved complaints may lead to regulatory action, and poor experiences may influence the subsequent purchasing decisions of customers.

Customer feedback

Controls must also be implemented to obtain **customer feedback** on an ongoing basis. These may enable management to obtain a more representative view of customer reaction; those who complain may not be typical, and the regulatory body may take into account overall customer reaction. A variety of methods will be necessary as individual means may be unrepresentative (because for example only a small minority return customer service questionnaires).

Customer charter

The results of complaints and surveys must influence the controls that **prevent problems**. An enhanced regulatory regime means that this type of control is likely to be more important. A **customer charter** should be introduced. Other prevention controls may have to be better directed than they have previously; **training** may have to be focused more on staff in direct contact with the customer, and address specifically the issues that can cause problems with customers.

Change in audit committee role

Audit committees may have to spend more time on **reviewing compliance** with the **regulations** set down by the regulatory bodies, and also on compliance with the organisation's own customer charter. In their role as supervisors of internal audit, the committee should **check** that **internal audit adequately consider the procedures designed to prevent problems and to obtain evidence of customer views**.

Pro-active viewpoint of audit committee

Because audit committees are reviewing these matters, they may be able to **anticipate future developments** such as increased regulation or changes in customer demands. This intelligence will affect the discussions on strategy of the main board.

Membership of audit committees

If audit committees responsibilities are to increase in this way, there will be certain implications for the way they operate. Their **membership** is likely to be **expanded,** with the addition of members with the necessary knowledge of customer requirements and industry regulations. Audit committees may no longer be able to consider all matters as one body, and may split into **sub-committees** with one concentrating on financial controls and another on responses to industry pressure.

34 PNY

Text references. Chapters 5, 7 and 8.

Top tips. Previous knowledge from 2.6 or F8 may have helped you answer (a). Your answer needs to bring out the variety of features from an organisation's control environment, culture and information systems that will help prevent poor quality.

For (b) and (c) it is critical to review the information being provided in the scenario to identify risks in internal audit and the processes in the company. The scenario does provide plenty of clues (corporate governance shortcomings, independence of internal audit, problems with their work), so identify these.

To score well in (c), you should use the same headers as in (b) to link clearly each risk with recommendations for changes within the internal audit department.

Easy marks. The fraud discussion in (a) is fairly general, and the elements should hopefully be familiar.

(a) **Prevention of poor quality**

The fact that a risk management strategy for poor quality in place within an organisation may itself act as a **deterrent against poor quality**. Staff may be more careful if they know their errors are more likely to be identified.

Key methods of preventing poor quality

(i) **Organisational culture**

This means that all staff are encouraged to aim for the highest quality, ideally a **zero defects** policy. This aims should be **clearly communicated by management,** who should be seen to be supporting quality initiatives.

(ii) **Organisational structure and documentation**

The responsibilities of staff should be clearly defined. Staff should be made aware of what tasks they are **responsible for carrying out.** Quality processes (how staff carry out tasks) need to be defined in writing.

(iii) **Training**

Staff should be aware of the quality problems that can arise. They should receive appropriate induction when they join, which should be reinforced by **appropriate training programmes** within the entity. Training should ensure that staff are kept up-to-date so that technical errors do not occur and that courses highlight problems that have arisen and demonstrate how they can be prevented in future.

(iv) **Review systems**

All staff, but particularly **inexperienced staff,** should be subject to **peer or management quality review.** There should be also be quality checks or second opinions sought on specific issues, for example complex technical issues or areas of material where there have been significant recent developments.

(v)   **Human resources**

Feedback on quality should form part of the organisation's human resources procedures, being covered in appraisals and **influencing remuneration.**

Detecting poor quality

As noted above, good internal control systems will assist in preventing poor quality. However management cannot rely on operational procedures

(i)   **Reports to management**

Senior managers should receive **regular reports** on quality issues from operational managers.

(ii)   **Internal audit**

Internal audit work may be extended to cover issues of quality. This can involve checking to see that **operational quality procedures** (checklists, reviews) have been **carried out**, or it may extend to internal audit carrying out its **own quality checks** on books.

(iii)   **Customer feedback**

As well as responding to reports of errors, customer feedback should be proactively sought by **review forms** or **web forums.**

(b)   **Staffing of internal audit**

The internal audit department employs four staff. As noted in the scenario same staff have been working in the department for the last 10 years as they value the stability of the job and due to family and social commitments have no desire to move or seek promotion to move demanding roles. This implies two risks with the work of the internal audit department:

(i)   **Lack of continuing professional education**

Staff may **not have kept up-date** with the latest technology and therefore be unable to perform audits sufficiently well to test the newer systems in PNY. This comment is borne out by the lack of training within internal audit.

(ii)   **Lack of independence**

The internal audit staff may **no longer be sufficiently independent** of PNY or its staff to be able to produce a completely objective report. Internal audit may be too familiar with some systems to notice mistakes, and certainly too friendly with staff in PNY to want to criticise them too much in internal audit reports.

Role of internal audit

Auditing computer systems

The accounting systems in PNY have been **upgraded** in recent years, while internal audit staff have received only limited training. This indicates a risk that internal audit staff may **not have the skills or abilities to audit the new online systems in PNY**. The fact that audit trails are lost and may not be located again tends to confirm this view.

Physical inspection of assets

Even with a perpetual inventory system, audit testing of inventory appears to be **limited to the end of the year**. There is a risk that **inventory is misappropriated** during the year and this would not be identified until the year end.

Whistleblowing

The Head of Accounts sets the **risk management policy** in the company and also hears reports from potential whistle blowers. This in itself is not necessarily a risk within the systems of PNY as long as the Head of Accounts is seen to be **sufficiently independent** to be able to hear reports and take appropriate action. However, given that whistleblowing is not discussed with an audit committee, an independent body in a company, the Head of Accounts may appear to have a vested interest in **not taking action on reports**, especially if this adversely affects PNY.

Focus of testing

The **focus on substantive testing** by the internal audit department implies that there is **limited, or even no control testing being carried out**. This is a **weakness with audit testing** because the control systems within PNY, that are specifically designed to ensure that transactions are **appropriate, authorised and help prevent fraud**, are not being tested. Control weaknesses could be occurring without the internal auditors knowing about them.

Using substantive testing also implies that **audit testing** will be **time consuming** – it takes a lot longer to substantively test one invoice by tracing it back to source documentation, than it does to check that the appropriate signature has been placed on the document.

Reporting responsibilities of internal audit

PNY does not have an audit committee. Thus **internal audit reports are directed to the Finance Director**. This procedure raises **two specific risks** regarding the contents of internal audit reports:

(i)   **Finance Director's responsibility for internal audit**

Firstly, as the Finance Director is directly responsible for employing the internal auditors, the internal auditors may feel **uncomfortable about writing reports that are critical of the Finance Director**. There is the possibility, real or not, that an adverse report could adversely affect promotion or remuneration prospects of the internal auditors.

(ii)   **Lack of action**

Secondly, there is **no guarantee** that the Finance Director will **take action** on the reports. Again, the Finance Director may have a **vested interest in not making amendments to the control systems** and could block or amend any report prior to it being presented to the board.

(c)   **Ability and independence of staff in internal audit**

The problems could be avoided by **introducing new staff** into the internal audit department and possibly by providing internal audit staff with **secondments** into other areas of the company (eg the management accounting department) to ensure that they have an appropriate break from internal audit.

Auditing computer systems

Audit testing in the department needs to be upgraded to include **computer assisted audit techniques** to ensure that the new computer systems are audited appropriately. This may mean **employing new staff** in internal audit, **training existing staff** and certainly **purchasing new computers and audit software** to be able to carry out internal audits effectively.

Physical inspection of assets

The perpetual inventory system allows **physical inventory to be checked** to the book inventory on a regular basis throughout the year. Internal audit procedures should be amended to take account of this.

Whistleblowing

The **chief internal auditor**, being **independent of the executive board**, may be a more appropriate person to receive reports.

Focus of testing

To ensure that the **internal control systems in PNY** are working correctly, the internal auditors must **focus audit testing on control tests**. This will provide appropriate audit evidence that controls are working as well as being more time efficient.

Independence of audit reports

The problems could be avoided by **establishing an audit committee** or, if this is not feasible within PNY, **by sending internal audit reports to another board director**, possibly the Chief Executive Officer to maintain a division between the person employing internal auditors and the person reviewing their reports.

35 Franks & Fisher

Marking scheme

			Marks
(a)	1 mark for each factor identified and briefly discussed	7	
	1 mark for each factor applicable to Franks & Fisher	3	
			10
(b)	1 mark for each relevant point identified and briefly described		6
(c)	1 marks for each relevant point made		4
(d)	2 marks for definition of objectivity	2	
	1 mark per relevant characteristic identified and briefly described	3	
			5
			25

(a)   **Turnbull report**

The UK Turnbull report lists a number of considerations which will be taken into account when deciding whether to establish an internal audit department; most are relevant here.

Scale and complexity of operations

This has clearly increased recently with **rapid growth** meaning more products and activities being taken on, and possibly more that can go wrong. Internal audit review can act as a check on the decision-making processes, that all the **implications of the change in business** have been **fully considered**.

Number of employees

Increases in employee numbers are an indication of changes in size and the need for **development of human resource systems**, which internal audit would wish to evaluate.

Changes in organisational systems

Overall control systems will have to develop, and **internal audit** will be an important part of this change. Internal audit may be particularly needed as a check on the development of other parts of the system; with rapid growth, there is a danger that information systems for example may not develop in a way that is best for the company.

Changes in key risks

Changes in products and activities will bring changes in risks. There will be **risks associated with the production and sales of the new products**, such as production stoppages, health and safety considerations and distribution difficulties. There may also be **changes in the general risks** that Franks and Fisher faces, with possibly the **increased risk of inefficiencies and diseconomies of scale**. Internal audit can **review the adequacy** of the **overall risk management systems for** coping with these changes and carry out work on specific areas of high areas.

Problems with internal systems

The breakdown has highlighted possible problems with **quality standards**. The recent changes may mean that they would be **inadequate anyway even if rigorously enforced**. However they have not been employed conscientiously, and this calls into question whether other parts of the control systems are working as effectively as they should be. Internal audit should definitely investigate this.

Unacceptable events

Clearly the production breakdown was an unacceptable event because of its **consequences and its avoidibility**. Franks and Fisher is trying to establish itself in various product markets and therefore disruption in supply could have particularly serious consequences. If internal audit recommendations can reduce the chances of this happening in future, clearly this will be a major benefit.

Cost-benefit considerations

The fact that the board are talking about limiting internal audit's work may indicate that cost-benefit considerations are significant. Fears that internal audit will interfere with operational departments may well be exaggerated, and well-directed internal audit work should **bring benefits**. However if internal audit's work is going to be seriously limited, it may not be worthwhile employing an internal auditor.

(b) **Arguments in favour of external recruitment**

Other experience

An external recruit can bring **fresh perspectives** gained from working elsewhere. He can use his experience of other organisations' problems to **identify likely risk areas** and **recommend practical solutions** and **best practice from elsewhere**.

Independence of operational departments

An internal recruit is likely to have built up **relationships and loyalties** with people whom he has already worked, perhaps owing people favours. Equally he could have **grievances or have come into conflict with other staff**. These could compromise his independence when he comes to audit their departments.

Prejudices and biases

An internal recruit is likely to have **absorbed the perspectives and biases** of the organisation. He thus may be more inclined to treat certain individuals or departments strictly, whilst giving others the benefit of the doubt when maybe that is not warranted.

Auditing own work

Recruiting internally could mean that the internal auditor has to **audit the department** for which he worked, or **even his own work**. These would mean that he **lacked the detachment** necessary **to be objective**. This would not be a danger with an external recruit not previously involved with operations.

(c) **Inappropriateness of reporting to Mr Kumas**

There are a number of reasons why internal audit should not report to Mr Kumas.

Independence of internal audit

Internal audit's **independence** as a check on internal controls will be compromised by having to report to Mr Kumas, because he has **responsibility for operations** as an **executive director**. Instead internal audit should report to the chair of the audit committee, on the grounds he is, or should be, an **independent non-executive director** with no operational responsibilities. The corporate governance codes emphasise the importance of this.

Employment of internal audit

If internal auditors report to Mr Kumas, he will have **responsibility for establishing their pay and conditions**. Thus they will have a significant personal interest in not producing adverse findings and hence antagonising him.

Work of internal audit

Part of internal audit's work will be on the **finance function** for which Mr Kumas is responsible. If Mr Kumas is in charge of internal audit as well, he may be able to ensure that internal audit coverage of the finance function and his own work is **not as rigorous** as it should be, and may be able to **water down or suppress adverse audit findings.**

Using Mr Kumas' help

Even if internal audit did not report to Mr Kumas, he would **still have to supply them with the budgets and other control information** he has and generally provide assistance. However internal auditors should not rely on him for audit knowledge as they should themselves possess **sufficient knowledge and experience** to carry out their responsibilities effectively.

(d) **Definition of objectivity**

Objectivity means **not letting bias, conflict or undue influence of others** to override professional or business judgements. It implies detachment and not letting personal feelings intrude into professional judgements.

Demonstrating objectivity

Lack of favouritism

Internal auditors should **not accept gifts nor undue favours** from the departments that they are auditing.

Fairness

Internal auditors should avoid the perception that they are out to **'hit' certain individuals or departments**. They should **not take sides**, not being influenced by office politics in determining the work carried out and the reports given.

Not responding to intimidation

Internal auditors should choose which areas to audit based on their objectives and risk analysis, **and not be kept away** from certain areas by aggressive managers. Internal audit should also **cover the whole management process** and **not just audit the operational areas**.

Valid opinion

Internal auditors should aim to deliver a report that satisfies the needs of their principal (the audit committee).This means **producing a report based on all relevant factors** rather than one **designed to please operational departments**.

36 Gluck and Goodman

Text references. Chapters 4,7,8.

Top tips. (a) is very straightforward. You may have grouped the objectives of internal control under different headings, but your answer should have said much the same as ours. Other organisational factors relating to internal audit that the Turnbull report identifies include number of employees and problems with internal control systems.

In (b) the verb is criticise, a higher level verb, indicating you not only have to identify the problems but show why they are issues. Hence the mark scheme allocates 2 marks per point with the second mark being available for developing the point. In many scenarios, as here, the examiner drops some very clear hints about the problems; you need to highlight. They include blatant breaches of governance provisions (finance director chairing audit committee) failure to fulfil risk management responsibilities and also a lack of understanding of the importance of scrutiny by the internal audit function and audit committee.

The definition of market risk in (c) is taken from the BPP Study Text and is similar to the definition in IFRS 7, that market risk is the risk that the fair values or cash flows of a financial instrument will fluctuate due to changes in market prices. A wider definition of market risk would be risks from any of the markets in which the company operates, including resources, product and capital markets. Under this definition lack of an audit committee would have a strong impact upon the capital market risks affecting the company, since it would erode confidence that the company was a sound investment and hence affect its share price.

Easy marks. (a) is very much derived from the Turnbull report.

Examiner's comments. The first ten marks, (a) (i) and (a) (ii), were both level 2 verbs asking about what should have been core knowledge. I draw attention to the level of the verb because it was on misjudging this that some otherwise well-prepared candidates failed to gain marks. It was insufficient to merely identify the content requested in Q3 (a).

It was frustrating for markers, who always seek to award marks and give the benefit of the doubt where possible, to see an answer from a candidate clearly knew the answers to these parts but then failed to develop their answers according to the verb. Some candidates demonstrated their knowledge using a bullet list or a single paragraph for all five objectives.

(b) was the core of this question and employed the verb 'criticise'. In order to produce a criticism of something, the critic must know what good and bad practice is. Importantly, to criticise does not involve simply regurgitating the points in the case that were evidence of poor practice. That is only part of the answer. To produce a critique, candidates should discuss each point, perhaps in the context of other things (in the case of the exam scenario, regulations and code provisions) and why each point is important. One valid point of criticism in the case scenario, for example, was that the audit committee chairman considered only financial controls to be important. So the criticism begins with recognising that fact. In order to gain other marks, however, it is important to add why the criticism is valid. In this case, the audit committee chairman has failed to recognise the importance of other control mechanisms such as technical and operational controls.

In (c) I was surprised to see a lot of candidates unable to define market risk when it is clearly listed in the study guide as an examinable area. It was obviously difficult for candidates to explain its importance if they were unable to produce a correct definition. I would remind candidates and tutors that any part of the study guide may be examined and that all of it should be taught, learned and revised prior to the exam.

Marking scheme

					Marks
(a)	(i)	0.5 marks for the identification of each objective 0.5 marks for brief description (Maximum of 1 mark per objective)			5
	(ii)	0.5 marks for the identification of each factor 0.5 marks for brief description (Maximum of 1 mark per factor)			5
(b)		1 mark for identification of each criticism 1 mark for reason as to why identified behaviour is inappropriate (Maximum of 2 marks per criticism)			10
(c)		Definition of market risk – 1 mark for each relevant point made	max	2	
		No audit committee and risk – 1 mark for each relevant point made	max	3	
					5
					25

(a)   (i)   **Objectives of internal control**

Facilitate operations

Internal controls should ensure the organisation's operations are conducted **effectively and efficiently**. In particular they should enable the organisation to respond appropriately to **business, operational, financial, compliance** and other **risks** to achieving its objectives.

Safeguard assets

Controls should ensure that assets are optimally utilised and stop assets being **used inappropriately**. They should prevent the organisation **losing assets** through **theft or poor maintenance.**

Prevent and detect fraud

Controls should include measures designed to prevent fraud such as **segregation of duties** and **checking references** when staff are recruited. The information that systems provide should **highlight unusual transactions or trends** that may be signs of fraud.

Ensure quality of internal and external reporting

Controls should ensure that records and processes are kept that generate a **flow of timely, relevant and reliable information that aids management decision-making**. They should ensure that published accounts **give a true and fair view**, and other published information is **reliable** and **meets the requirements** of those stakeholders to whom it is addressed.

Ensure compliance

Controls should ensure that the organisation and its staff comply with **applicable laws and regulations**, and that staff **comply with internal policies** with respect to the conduct of the business.

(ii)   **Need for internal audit**

Scale, complexity and diversity of operations

Internal audit is more likely to be found in bigger, more diverse organisations, since the more complex the operations, the more that can go wrong. If operations are complicated, a key task of internal audit will be to assess the system as a whole to see if **risk management and internal controls** are **properly focused.**

Changes in key risks

If the business is developing in new areas, an internal audit assessment of how effectively it is **handling changes in risk** can be very valuable.

Increased number of unexplained or unacceptable events

Internal audit may have to investigate events that **cause problems with accounting records**, and problems that **delay production or result in inferior quality goods or services.**

Compliance with external requirements

An internal audit presence may be required to **comply with stock market or regulatory requirements.**

Cost-benefit considerations

The **costs** of employing internal auditors (salary, management time lost dealing with internal audit) should **not outweigh the benefits** internal audit work can bring.

(b) **Problems with internal control and audit arrangements**

Work of audit committee

The work of the internal audit committee is too heavily focused on financial controls. There appears to be **no review of other important aspects of the risk management systems,** such as the operational and quality controls in the production facility. The assumption that if the accounting systems are fully functional, then all other systems can be assumed to be working correctly, is extremely dubious.

Finance director chairing audit committee

The finance director should **not chair the audit committee.** One of the key aspects of the audit committee's work should be to review the financial statements and systems, for which the finance director is ultimately responsible. If the financial director chairs the audit committee, he is thus responsible for reviewing his own work, which means that the financial systems are not **independently scrutinised.**

Lack of information for audit committee

The audit committee appears not to be trying to obtain the information it needs to review internal systems effectively. In particular it trusts Mr Hardanger to **manage the production facility effectively**, rather than demanding the compliance information suggested by Susan Paullaos. As the production facility is a key element in the business, the committee **cannot rely on Mr Hardanger's reputation** as a good manager.

Lack of internal audit function

Gluck and Goodman's board has not given the question of whether to have an internal audit function the **serious consideration demanded by governance reports.** The board's belief that internal audit work duplicates the work of management accounting shows a flawed understanding of the different purposes of the two functions, in particular that internal audit should be **examining the quality of the management accounting function's work.**

Lack of support from chairman

The audit committee clearly does not have the support of Mr Allejandra. Ultimately the audit committee should report to him. As Mr Allejandra is a non-executive director, he should be aware of the need for non-executive directors generally, particularly board committee members, to **scrutinise** the performance of executive management.

(c) **Definition**

Market risk is the risk of loss due to an **adverse movement in the market value** of an asset – a stock, bond, loan, foreign exchange or commodity – or a derivative contract linked to that asset.
Audit committee and market risk

Review of risk

The audit committee is failing to review risks other than those connected with the accounting systems. If it fails to identify market risk that exists, it means that the risk exposure will **not be effectively managed.**

Lack of expertise

Even if the committee's remit is extended to review other risks, it still may not highlight market risk if its members **lack experience of the areas affected by the risk,** or if, as here, they do not even know what market risk is. One reason for having an increased presence of non-executive directors is that they bring wider experience of other business environments, including finance environments, which may help the audit committee conduct a more effective review of risk.

Inability to have recommendations implemented

Even if the audit committee correctly identifies risks and makes appropriate recommendations for dealing with them, it will be ineffective if it **cannot enforce the recommendations.** In this situation, Mr Allejandra's lack of support undermines the audit committee in the eyes of the rest of the board and company, and means that the audit committee may well find it difficult to ensure its recommendations are implemented by managers and staff such as Mr Hardanger.

37 Saltoc

Text references. Chapters 5 and 8.

Top tips. Although this question is primarily about risk awareness, management and audit, the scenario also illustrates the interactions between different elements of a company's systems that the examiner is keen to stress – here how board squabbling has undermined corporate governance and effective risk management.

In (a) the talk about embedding risk should have led you to discuss culture, and there are also obvious cultural problems as demonstrated by the loss of the computer data and the chief executive's attitude to risk management. The use of performance management as part of the control systems is not stressed particularly in the P1 syllabus, but is worth bearing in mind in promoting risk management, as the participation of all staff is required.

(b) explores the cultural factors that can undermine risk management, with most of the problems flowing from the lack of unity and the pressurising of board members.

In (c) as well as obtaining recommendations for better risk management, you also need to consider the need to reassure customers (who are mentioned in the scenario) and shareholders (who will naturally be concerned with their shares' value). Having an independent review is particularly important here as internal politics have compromised everyone working for the company.

Easy marks. The explanation of an external risk audit should have provided easy marks in (c), and you should go back over this area if you struggled.

Examiner's comments. (a) was not just asking for a description of embeddedness, but specifically mentioned 'with reference to Saltoc Company'. Many candidates failed to gain the application marks showing again the importance of carefully reading the question.

Time spent studying and scrutinising the case usually resulted in better answers to (b). It was not possible to gain a high mark without a careful study of the Saltoc culture based on the evidence of the case. Some candidates attempted a general discussion either about culture in general or about the importance of risk embeddedness but neither of these were well rewarded.

In (c) many candidates were able to get the 'contains' marks but then did less well on making the case for risk auditing at Saltoc. Given that the examiner had written an article on this, he was surprised and disappointed that some candidates were unable to recall the four stages in risk auditing. Candidates also had to study the case in order to place themselves in a position to make a convincing argument for external risk auditing. Again, a detailed analysis of the case was necessary to gain the highest marks.

Marking scheme

				Marks
(a)	1 mark for each relevant point describing embeddedness	max	3	
	1 mark for each relevant point of application	max	3	
				6
(b)	2 marks for each issue identified and discussed in context (1 mark for recognition only)	max		8
(c)	1 mark for each point of explanation of external risk auditing	max	3	
	2 marks for each relevant point in the construction of the argument (1 for recognition, 1 for development and application to the case)	max	8	
				11
				25

(a) **Interaction with control systems**

To have risk embedded in a system implies that appropriate steps need to be taken to assess and manage risks. This means that **risk management** should be seen as an **essential part** of an organisation's control systems. The operation of other control systems should reflect the requirement to manage risks effectively. With Saltoc the budgeting process needs to take account not only of the **costs of risk management** but of the **consequences of risks materialising** if management is inadequate.

Promoting risk culture

A further part of embedding risk culture is to make sure that all staff think about potential risks and consequences of risk materialising while they are carrying out their day-to-day work. The aim is that staff take **simple steps** that are not costly or bureaucratic, but can avoid serious risks materialising. The obvious example with Saltoc is **not leaving a computer containing sensitive data** in a **location** where it can **easily be stolen**. **Clear communication**, particularly a **clear risk policy**, and **targeted staff training** can all help promote awareness of risk.

Performance management

To reinforce managers and staff's awareness of risks, **metrics** should be built into the performance assessment system so that risk management is regarded as a normal part of employees' **job descriptions**. The **appraisal process** should include **accountability** for how risks have been managed, for example Laura being assessed on the effective operation of IT security arrangements.

(b) **Conflict between directors**

A significant barrier to effective implementation of risk management is the clear division in the board. For risk management to work a **coherent, unified approach** is required from the whole board. Here it seems Peter is most concerned with point-scoring over other directors. He also seems to be using his power over finances to reduce costs and make his own performance look good, while starving other directors of the **financial resources they need to manage risks effectively**.

Blame culture

There seems to be a widespread **blame culture** in place. When the disasters have occurred, the board has **not taken effective steps** to address the problems, but instead has concentrated on trying to blame each other.

CEO's view of risk management

Ken's view that risk management and control means **even more administration is misguided.** It explains why risk management has not been given a high enough priority, as other directors may well wish to comply with the chief executive's views, and it is difficult to see Ken leading attempts to embed more effective risk management. Ken seems to be unaware that effective risk management involves taking steps to manage **risks to company value**. The last few years may have been terrible for Saltoc, but the failure to manage these risks effectively could have even more devastating consequences.

Ability of managers to enforce risk management

If Peter is right, and Harry and Laura do not have the respect of their staff, then this will be a further barrier to **embedding risk systems.** A key aspect of Saltoc's control environment should be that the **tone** is set from the top, with management demonstrating through their words and actions **commitment to effective risk management**. However staff will only follow the example that managers should be setting if they respect them and that may not be the case here.

Staff problems

The frequent staff turnover will also not help the implementation of a risk culture. New staff will require **induction and training** and will also take time to gain the **necessary experience** to think about how to avoid effectively the risks that relate to their work.

(c)   **External risk auditing**

External audit

External audit means that the work will be carried out by **independent auditors** who are **not directors or employees** of Saltoc. The audit may be carried out by the firm that audits Saltoc's accounts, by another firm of accountants or by other risk specialists.

Identification and assessment of risks

Risk audit involves **identifying the main risks** affecting Saltoc. The risk audit should assess the **probability** of these **risks crystallizing** and their **likely impacts.**

Review of management and controls

The auditors will assess the operation and effectiveness of the risk management processes and the internal **controls** in operation to **limit risks.** A comprehensive risk audit will extend to the **risk management and control culture.**

The case for external risk auditing

Clear assessment of weaknesses

The recent problems have highlighted clear weaknesses in Saltoc's risk management systems such as **inadequate maintenance** and **deficiencies in the risk awareness** of staff with the result that Saltoc has been **exposed to the risks arising from the loss of data**. An external risk audit would assess the extent of the weaknesses. Internal personnel may have become **too familiar** with Saltoc's systems, and therefore be unable to see how they might change.

External expertise

External auditors would be able to bring **knowledge and experience** of other companies' methods of managing risks, something which internal auditors might well lack. External auditors would therefore be better able to **benchmark Saltoc's systems** against best practice elsewhere and base recommendations for improvements upon this.

Objectivity

External auditors would be able to take an **unbiased view** of Saltoc's problems. Their recommendations would not be affected by the **internal politics** at Saltoc, and they would not feel the need to protect their own positions and blame others for any problems.

Assurance to stakeholders

The **shareholders** of Saltoc are likely to be extremely worried by the threats to the value of the shares caused by the recent incidents. **Customers** are considering withdrawing their business from Saltoc. An investment by Saltoc in a risk audit should provide these stakeholders with the assurance that Saltoc will take **effective action** to remedy the risk management deficiencies, and may **reduce the damage** to Saltoc's **reputation**.

38 COSO

Text references. Chapters 2, 4, 7 and 8.

Top tips. Principles vs rules is often discussed in this exam in the context of corporate governance, but it shouldn't have been difficult to apply it to internal controls. Comply or explain is a key difference, as is the emphasis on applying objectives vs utilising specific controls. Key benefits to stress in the second part are flexibility and the cost-effectiveness of only having to operate necessary controls.

In (b) your answer needs to demonstrate why certain key features of operations apply whatever the industry. The second part brings out the importance of performance measurement of individuals in control systems.

Hopefully you should have remembered the first part of (c) from your F8 studies. The second part of (b) needs to bring out how internal audit testing contributes to an assessment of control systems design and operation generally, and also focuses on certain key features of systems, some of which you discussed in (b).

Easy marks. Hopefully the definitions of the principles and rules based approaches.

Examiner's comments. (a) was quite well answered overall although some became confused in their answers with rules and principles-based approaches to corporate governance in general. The second task was more challenging. This 'to an organisation' was important as it placed a particular perspective on where the benefits were obtained.

In (b) some less well-prepared candidates introduced a bullet list of 'purposes of internal control' from their study texts. This wasn't quite what the question was asking. In the context of the case, candidates were required to comment on the non-industry specific advantages. Most candidates who attempted the second part of (b) were able to provide something here but others seemed unprepared to explain a phrase that they had perhaps not encountered before, despite it being an important theme in internal control.

In (c) the COSO advice was simply used to introduce a notion that should have been familiar to a well-prepared P1 candidate. The first task on defining internal audit testing was done well by many candidates but the second task less so.

Marking scheme

				Marks
(a)	2 marks for distinguishing between rules and principles and 1 for application to the case		3	
	1 mark for each relevant advantage/benefit of principles-based	max	4	
				7
(b)	1 mark for recognition of each advantage and 1 for development of that point	max	8	
	2 marks per point for explanation of the statement	max	4	
				10
(c)	2 marks for definition of internal audit testing	max	2	
	2 marks for each internal role identified and explained	max	8	
		max		8
				25

(a)   **Rules-based approach**

A rules-based approach means what an organisation does is prescribed by legislation and compliance is **enforceable in law.** A rules-based approach will mean that organisations are **required to operate specific internal controls**, whatever their individual circumstances. It requires the **one size fits all approach.**

Principles-based approach

A principles-based approach is often based on stock market regulations, but non-compliance is allowed if it is fully disclosed. It means that the organisation's control systems should fulfil **general objectives.** To achieve these objectives however, organisations can adopt whatever controls are best and cost-effective for them.

Benefits of principles-based approach

Appropriate controls

The approach allows organisations to adopt the controls that are appropriate for them, based on their **size and risk profile.**

Avoidance of unnecessary controls

Organisations will **not have to spend money and time** complying with irrelevant legislation and operating controls that will not provide any benefits for them.

Development of principles

A principles-based approach allows **business sectors** to develop their own guidelines to meet the internal control challenges that are relevant to their sector.

Comply or explain

A principles-based approach allows companies some **flexibility and temporary periods of non-compliance** provided they disclose what they're doing. This puts the **emphasis on investors** making up their own minds about what businesses are doing.

(b) **Facilitate effective and efficient operations**

Whatever the business sector, well-designed internal controls should ensure that operations **run well.** They should do this by addressing the **risks to achieving objectives** that the organisation faces. These include waste and production of poor quality goods or services.

Ensure quality of internal and external reporting

Controls over accounting can help ensure the **correct and accurate processing of transactions** that is necessary to support reliable accounting records and ultimately true and fair reporting under local legislation. They should also help guarantee the quality of other external reports. They should also ensure that information is **captured and distributed in appropriate form and in good time.**

Ensure compliance with laws and regulations

All businesses have to comply with some laws and regulations. Internal controls should help them **address and demonstrate compliance.**

Aid shareholder confidence

Knowledge that internal controls are operating effectively should give investors and other stakeholders comfort that managers are **discharging their stewardship responsibilities effectively**. This should help reduce shareholder monitoring and agency costs. It should also provide comfort to other finance providers about the risk to their finance, resulting in a **lower business risk premium** and **lower cost of capital** as a result.

Deterioration of controls over time

Performance metrics

Continued operation of controls is most likely when they are monitored and the results used as part of the **performance measurement** of those who are supposed to be operating them. If they are not monitored, compliance becomes less likely over time as individuals' situation change.

Changing circumstances

Unmonitored controls will deteriorate, become less useful, over time, because **business circumstances change**. The controls in place will no longer be a **proactive** response to the problems the business faces. Even if they remain relevant, their **tolerance levels** may need to change.

(c) **Internal audit testing**

Internal audit testing means **obtaining evidence** about the operation of the accounting and internal control systems. It involves the use of audit techniques based on set measures and outcomes. It is part of the monitoring process over internal controls.

Roles of internal audit

Risk and control systems analysis

Internal audit work will involve **identification of significant business and financial risks.** It also includes **assessing the design of control systems** to ascertain whether they are appropriate for managing the risks faced and **testing internal control systems** to ensure that they are operating effectively.

Examination of financial and operating information

Internal auditors will test the **reliability and timeliness** of information. This includes review of the means used to identify, measure, classify and report information. It may also involve testing specific items (transactions and balances) for accuracy.

Review of compliance

Internal auditors will test **compliance with laws and regulations** and with internal policies and directives. Internal auditors may have to test the evidence provided of compliance to external regulators. It will also review compliance with specific internal requirements (authorisation levels), and measure actual performance against internal standards (safety measures or environmental issues).

Review of the implementation of corporate objectives

Internal auditors can analyse business planning, assess whether standards and objectives are relevant and review the implementation of corporate objectives. They can also **evaluate how well specific policies are operating,** such as communication of information

39 Crawley Gossop

Text references. Chapters 10 and 11.

Top tips. The main point to get across in (a) is that the rigour and independence of the EMAS standards should help satisfy critics. Remember that EMAS is based on verification and reporting of performance, though also covering corrective action by systems. (c) covers how the public interest should be defined, and who should define it, also the limitations of the auditors' role.

Easy marks. A number of the influences in (b) apply to any voluntary report.

(a) **Arguments in favour of EMAS**

Response to stakeholder concerns

Crawley Gossop appears to have suffered significant damage to its reputation, and adherence to EMAS should help to limit this damage. This is because EMAS represents an **independently established set of standards** that are widely acknowledged as rigorous. If Crawley Gossop establishes its own standards without reference to external guidance, it is likely to face criticism that its standards are not rigorous enough.

Continuous improvements

EMAS requires continuous improvements in environmental performance. Although having systems in place and compliance with legislation are important, they will not be **enough by themselves.** Environmental targets set will have to take account of impacts on the localities where Crawley Gossop operates and where it has **faced particular criticisms**.

Environmental policy statement

EMAS requires an **environmental policy statement** that should form the basis for action plans. Not only should the statement underpin systems, but it should help **embed environmental awareness in the company**. It should send a clear message to managers and staff that the board is committing to leading improvements in environmental performance. This commitment should help **convince external critics** that Crawley Gossop wishes to improve.

Review and audit

Under the EMAS regime, on-site environmental reviews have to be carried out regularly and full environmental audits need to be carried out every three years. The results of the audit will then form the basis of **future objectives and policy.** The link between the audit and **future targets** should demonstrate that objectives are not just being established in accordance with what is convenient for Crawley Gossop.

Reporting

Adherence to EMAS's reporting guidelines should help address the strong criticisms that **Crawley Gossop's disclosures are inadequate.** The EMAS requirements are wide-ranging, covering areas where Crawley Gossop's performance has been weak such as **pollution, waste and noise. External validation of the statement** will provide independent verification for critics that the disclosures are reliable.

(b) **Interests of users**

The board should take into account the differing requirements of the readers of the annual report. Shareholders will be interested in areas that will affect the value of their investment, for example areas where Crawley Gossop may **incur legal penalties**, or be forced to **bear cleanup costs**. Given the threat to Crawley Gossop's reputation and business from environmental groups, the board will also need to consider their wants.

Areas of change

Most users will be interested in areas where performance has changed significantly over the year, and the report should explain why changes have occurred. If the **changes in environmental performance** are adverse, the board should disclose what has been done to **address weaknesses** and how **systems are to be improved.**

Consistency with other information

As well as consistency with the financial data in the accounts, the report should **cross-refer to other areas**, such as the review of strategy in the business review, that have environmental impacts. Similarly the review of strategy should cross-refer to the environmental report. This will be particularly important for Crawley Gossop, since its strategy of rapid growth has had significant adverse environmental impacts, and taking strong action to curb these may have major impacts on future strategies.

Competition issues

What competitors are doing may have an impact on Crawley Gossop. Competitors' disclosures will provide a **benchmark** that the company can use to measure the adequacy of its own report. As part of its **competitive strategy**, Crawley Gossop may decide to disclose more than its competitors.

Wider community

The views of the external community, however expressed, will also have an influence. Crawley Gossop may arguably have a duty to (or feel it wise to) respond to public opinion.

(c) **Arguments in favour of viewpoint**

Firm's current moral position

Although it may not be explicitly stated in Broadfield Bewbush's current literature, it is likely that there are **some businesses that the firm would decline to take on as clients.** For example Broadfield Bewbush may not wish to be involved with any business that has links to the sex industry, as its partners may not want the firm to be criticised for connections with the exploitation of women. If this is the case, Broadfield Bewbush could be accused of picking and choosing what it regards as the public interest.

Transparency

A further criticism is that Broadfield Bewbush could be allowing its name to be associated with an annual report that lacks transparency, and does not provide the **information that stakeholders require**. This could be the case even if the accounts that Broadfield Bewbush reports on specifically show a true and fair view. Even if Broadfield Bewbush has limited responsibility to report on the rest of the annual report (just checking it for consistency with the accounts), arguably the firm should have no connection with an annual report that is judged as deficient. In addition professional bodies such as ACCA have been promoting sustainability reporting for some years, and partners who are members should arguably be seen to support their institute.

Arguments against viewpoint

Legal business

Although Crawley Gossop has suffered legal penalties, its basic business is undoubtedly **legal**. It is arguably the role of governments acting through legislation and regulation to make judgements about the desirability of activities, not auditors. It is not generally the intention of governments that businesses should be prevented from operating as limited companies because they cannot find an auditor.

Shareholders and investors

Auditors' main specific responsibility is to report to the investors on the **truth and fairness of the accounts**. In doing so they provide a function that is beneficial, by helping to ensure that directors are **accountable** to the shareholders who own the company's shares. This serves the purposes not just of the shareholders of that company, but also the wider public interest, since it promotes confidence in the capital market as a whole. Investors are more likely to purchase equities and hence provide funds to enable businesses to operate and invest if they believe directors' activities are monitored effectively.

Limitations of auditors' responsibilities

Auditors' legal responsibilities are to perform sufficient work to support their report on the **truth and fairness of the accounts.** They are not required to perform procedures testing other information in the annual report, and may not have the expertise to do so. In addition truth and fairness are clear concepts. Giving a reliable view on whether other information is sufficiently detailed can only be done against clearly laid down criteria, otherwise auditors will have to satisfy greatly varying stakeholder opinions.

Benefits of auditor involvement

Auditor involvement with a company like Crawley Gossop can help to **promote good practice**, since auditors can assist in advising on the development of **full cost accounting,** the **systems in place for reporting and disclosure** and the **work done by internal audit.**

40 Environmental and social issues

Text references. Chapters 1 and 11.

Top tips. Although it may seem difficult to find enough to say about this question, once you remember that environmental reporting impacts significantly upon reputation risk and think about the impact of stakeholder viewpoints, you can score well. In (a) one reason for disclosure is that the consequences may be worse if disclosure doesn't happen, as discussed at the start of the answer.

In (b) a good way of thinking through the environmental consequences is to go through the inputs, processes, outputs model and consider the likely environmental consequences at each stage. The social issues discussion is a good illustration of why background reading is useful; you can bring in topics that are currently areas of concern such as low-cost labour.

In (c) the range of business activity covered will depend on what is significant. The discussion about how the business can impact on its suppliers is an important acknowledgement that sometimes these issues cannot be tackled in isolation.

(d) draws a contrast between a compliance approach (hence data is needed to ascertain whether the business has complied) and a competitive approach (where the business is trying to improve and hence setting challenging targets, the board therefore requiring data about whether these targets have been met).

Easy marks. No particularly easy marks in this question.

(a)   **Reasons for the inclusion of environmental and social issues in the Annual Report**

Competitor disclosure

As the non-executive directors have observed, **many comparable companies** already **do include such issues** in their Annual Report and Z may attract adverse publicity if it does not follow this trend.

Attracting investments

There may be **positive benefits** to reporting such issues too. For example, an increasing amount of attention is being devoted to environmental and social issues. **'Green' and 'ethical' fund mangers** have increasing funds available for investment and Z may be able to demonstrate that it is suitable for such investment, thereby increasing its share price.

Strategic considerations

Moreover, the board should be constantly scanning the environment in which the organisation operates, including social and environmental areas, in order to assess the impact of any **changes on the future of the business.** Given that there is substantial interest amongst consumers and investment fund mangers in doing business with companies which are environmentally and socially responsible, the board may intend to report on environmental and social issues as part of its competitive strategy.

Government pressure

There have also been recent comments by a government minister that 'if all companies do not make progress', legislation on environmental and social issues will be introduced. If Z was to include such issues in its Annual Report it would **avoid being forced into providing damaging disclosures required by a more stringent regime.**

(b) **The range of environmental and social issues to cover**

Consumption of raw materials

The greatest focus from an environmental point of view is likely to be on **consumption of raw materials from tropical areas**. The directors may wish to consider the concept of **'sustainability'** – is Z replanting at a rate equal to or greater than that at which it is harvesting. If so, it is likely to be viewed favourably.

Costs of processing

The **costs of processing** should also be considered, in particular the percentage of **energy** coming from renewable and non-renewable sources and the steps taken to increase the efficiency with which Z uses energy.

Packaging

Packaging is of increasing concern to many consumers. The proportion of both Z's products and their packaging made from recycled material should be measured, as should the ease with which they can be **recycled after use**.

Social issues

Social issues to cover include minimum rates of pay, the minimum age of child labour, working conditions and living conditions, such as the availability of health care and education. The public's interest in consumer markets tends to focus on the **discrepancies between 'living standards' in their affluent market compared to those in less developed countries**. In setting standards the board needs to gather data about these issues in the source countries. Rates of pay expressed in relation to UK earnings may seem derisory but when expressed in relation to the local average they may seem much more acceptable. Using children aged just 14 as part of the labour force may seem less offensive if local schooling is provided up to the age of 12 and Z provides additional education as part of its benefits package.

Nature and extent of reporting

How well actual performance compares with what the board considers to be acceptable standards will determine the nature and extent of any reporting on these issues. If the board believes Z's performance is above average it may well make extensive disclosures in order to gain maximum benefit. The poorer the performance, the less it may choose to disclose. If there are any single issues that, were they disclosed would lead to adverse publicity, it may choose to make no disclosures until these issues are resolved to an acceptable level.

(c) **Business partners**

Z also needs to consider **whether to report on the activities of Z alone or on those of all of its business partners**, including those from whom Z sources its raw materials and the sub-contractors it employs during production. It could be argued that Z cannot control its sub-contractors, and therefore should not include their activities within its report. For example, it could be deemed unfair if Z was held responsible for contractors employing young children without the board's knowledge.

It is **unlikely that 'we didn't know' would be accepted as a defence were damaging information made public**, however. Once the range of performance benchmarks is established, Z should therefore provide it to all of its sub-contractors and advise them that they are expected to conform to such standards. These could be included as a requirement in the **supplier tendering process**.

Impact of other stakeholders

Problems are likely to centre on **identifying those issues that will be of concern in the future to stakeholders**. Z will also need to balance the demands of shareholders for maintaining a profitable activity with the concerns of pressure groups over the activity in question.

Changing viewpoints

The **popularity** or otherwise of environmental and social issues moves constantly with **changes in public opinion and government policy**. The board should endeavor to **anticipate the demands of its stakeholders**, however, rather than appear to be simply reacting to the current 'popular' issues.

(d) **Information requirements at board level**

Impact of attitude

The **additional information** to be supplied at board level will **depend on the board's ongoing attitude to environmental and social issues**.

Legal compliance

The board may take the view that Z should concentrate on **ensuring that current legal requirements are met and that the costs of adverse publicity are avoided**. If this is the case, an **individual should be responsible for monitoring social and environmental developments** and advising the board if or when the company is required to take additional steps. Disclosure would be kept to a minimum, and would concentrate on practices that are of benefit to the community at large, rather than those that may be of interest to competitors.

Competitive advantage

If the board intends to **report on environmental and social issues as part of its competitive strategy**, the information requirements at board level would then increase significantly. A **study** would need to be conducted into establishing what is considered to be **best practice**. This would **identify the investment requirements of the ethical investment funds** and the **current thinking on environmental and social issues by the various pressure groups**, such as Amnesty International and Greenpeace.

The value chain

The board needs to **identify the value chain** within Z, thereby allowing for all activities (from the sourcing of raw materials through to the selling activity) to be **assessed for their current and future impact on social and environmental issues**. High-risk areas are those that are likely to have a significant impact on profitability if appropriate contingency plans are not in place.

Impact on reporting

Z should then establish a **formal code of challenging targets** (such as 95% of packaging used should be made from recycled materials) to be achieved on these environmental and social issues and a **report on how these targets are being met should be included as part of the normal internal reporting package**.

41 Edted

(a)   **Corporate citizenship**

   Definition

   The concept of citizenship **shapes the values** that directors and employees are influenced by when participating in business and engaging with others outside the organisation. The concept of corporate citizenship recognises that there is a connection between the **everyday activities** of companies and the **wellbeing of society** as a whole, including minimising harm and maximising benefit.

   Issues affecting corporate citizenship

   Matten and al have suggested that there are two principal issues that determine organisational positioning on corporate citizenship.

   Whether citizenship is voluntary or imposed

   A limited view of citizenship would regard it as being **voluntary philanthropy**, likely to be undertaken at least partly in the organisation's self-interest. A more extended view would see it as **partly voluntary and partly imposed by society**. Society's views could be imposed by legal requirements or ethical codes, or more widely an organisation could respond to society's expectations on issues such as individual rights.

   In which areas and on whom citizenship impacts

   A limited view would see citizenship as meaning **undertaking limited focus projects**, addressed towards stakeholders particularly affected by the organisation's activities. What Matten defines as the **equivalent view** would see citizenship as broader corporate social responsibility with responsibility towards a broader range of stakeholders. The **extended view** would see corporations actively promoting social, civil and political rights, in some instances doing so in areas where governments have failed to provide safeguards.

(b)   **Significance of EMAS**

   Registration under EMAS demonstrates a **commitment to rigorous policies** for controlling the organisation's interaction with the environment. Companies that have adopted the EMAS scheme, particularly in countries where EMAS has not been widely used, are demonstrating the environmental aspects of corporate citizenship very seriously.

Internal procedures

Businesses should base what they do on an **environmental policy statement** that commits to **continuous environmental performance improvement** and goes beyond **compliance with legislation.** When EMAS is introduced, businesses should undertake an on-site environmental review. The management systems that businesses introduce have to be clearly linked to the policy statement and the review results; feedback must impact on policies.

Audit requirements

Feedback will not just come from internal review, but external environmental audits taking place every three years. **Rigorous external verification** is a principal reason why EMAS is regarded as a robust system. The audit does not just **test compliance,** but produces feedback that influences future objectives and targets. The environmental policy and management systems cannot therefore remain static, but must evolve in the light of the feedback from auditors.

Disclosure requirements

Disclosure requirements are the other key elements of EMAS, since the scheme is based on the idea of **rigorous public scrutiny.** Companies need to make detailed disclosure requirements about policy, management systems and performance in areas such as pollution, waste, raw material usage, energy, water and noise. Again external verification is required, **review of environmental statements** by **accredited environmental verifiers.** The disclosure requirements may (are perhaps designed to) make businesses confront tough choices. Will they seek to fulfil targets at the expense of profit maximisation, or will they risk falling short of their environmental targets if it means maintaining profit levels.

ISO 14000

The ISO 14000 group of standards encourages businesses to adopt many of the same elements as the EMAS standards, including an **environmental policy statement**, an **initial environmental review** and an **environmental management system**. However under these standards the system is policed by internal audit making reports to senior management. Disclosure requirements are less rigorous with the central requirement being a statement of compliance with ISO 14001. Critics have claimed that the ISO 14000 standards place excessive emphasis on systems, and do not emphasise sufficiently the need for **better performance.**

(c) **Basis for finance director's viewpoint**

The finance director's viewpoint is based on the idea that the ethical influences that individual employees have experienced over their lives are all-important, and that Edted cannot overcome these influences. The **level of personal integrity** staff have will have a significant impact, and there may be a number of influences on staff's ethical outlook. However Edted may be able to use some of these influences as a means of encouraging staff to act ethically.

National and cultural beliefs

Nations and cultures vary in the importance they give to different ethical issues, and it is likely that some of these variations will exercise a significant influence on individuals' attitudes. For example national society may place a lot of emphasis on **individual autonomy and fulfilment** rather than the individual striving towards group community goals. The extent to which **money and possessions** are valued in society as opposed to **people and relationships** will also be significant.

The directors may have difficulty overcoming deep-rooted cultural factors, but may be able to promote positive ethical culture by a mission statement, also **setting a good example**. Staff may be more likely to act ethically if their managers are driving good ethical behaviour.

Education

The individuals' education and the **degree to which citizenship** has been emphasised may also have a significant influence. However Edted can of course provide **ethical training** for individuals itself, and make ethical behaviour part of the **appraisal** system.

Cognitive moral development

Using the categories developed by **Kohlberg,** individuals with low moral development are unlikely to be influenced by concepts such as citizenship but by whether they will be **rewarded or punished** for particular actions. At a higher level, individuals' actions will be determined by what is **expected** of them by society so if concepts of citizenship are emphasised by society, individuals will try to be good citizens. At the highest levels, individuals will be making their **own decisions** about whether and how to act as good citizens.

However Edted's board can analyse the level of moral development that individuals have and tailor policies accordingly. **Disciplining staff** who act unethically should work well if staff are perceived to have low (pre-conventional) levels of moral reasoning. **Establishing the right culture,** communicating to staff that 'we don't do that sort of thing round here' should influence staff who see ethics as fitting in with whatever is accepted behaviour where they work. **Education and training** should be geared towards encouraging staff towards a higher level of moral development.

Locus of control

Individuals' **locus of control** may have a significant influence on how active their ethical position is. Individuals with a high internal locus believe that they can have a **significant influence over their own lives.** This could well mean that they are prepared to take more responsibility and hence are more likely to take an active ethical position (a high Kohlberg level) than those who believe that their lives are shaped by accident or circumstances that they can't control.

Edted's managers may have problems overcoming a very **deep rooted locus of control.** However the **overall management system** may have some influence. If the systems are very bureaucratic, then individual ethical beliefs will be of little consequence, overridden by rules and regulations. If however staff are allowed more autonomy, a system that promotes individual discretion and rewards ethical behaviour could persuade staff that their own actions could make a difference.

Moral imagination

Moral imagination is the **level of awareness** that individuals have about the moral consequences that could arise from their actions. **Education and previous experience** may have a significant influence on moral imagination. Moral imagination is likely to be a significant factor in ethical situations that are not clearcut, where for example individuals have to choose between options that all may have ethical problems.

Again **education and training**, also **ethical guidance and codes** that emphasise the need for individuals to consider difficult situations carefully may promote higher awareness.

42 Code of conduct

Text references. Chapters 8 and 10.

Top tips. The verb evaluate generally means that you should cover both sides of a case. Although the advantages of establishing an audit committee are numerous, there are one or two disadvantages of which you should be aware.

In (c) you need to consider what level of involvement internal audit ideally should have and what might be the problems limiting that involvement. The other steps are very important features of control systems. You will probably have to discuss them in any question scenario where directors are looking to improve the general control environment.

The recommendations in (d) covers an area of some interest to the examiner; how the ethical environment can be improved. This requires more than just tinkering with the code; the company also must consider communication and human resource issues.

Easy marks. Hopefully you should have been able to come up with plenty of advantages of establishing an audit committee.

(a) **Membership of audit committee**

An audit committee normally consists of the independent **non-executive directors** of the company, though there is no reason why other senior personnel should not attend on occasions.

The committee needs to consist of people who are senior enough to appreciate the delicacy of the position of defence companies in both security and political terms and therefore would have foreseen problems such as this.

Advantages of setting up an audit committee

Awareness of executive directors

The existence of an audit committee should make **executive directors** more **aware of their responsibilities**.

Contribution of outsiders

The audit committee should normally consist of **non-executive directors**, drawn from outside the company. They can apply their **experience** of other companies in recommending how problems such as failures of communication can be overcome.

Deterrent

The audit committee can act as a **deterrent** to the commission of **illegal acts by executive directors**, and may discourage directors from behaving in ways which could be **prejudicial to shareholders' interests**.

Liaison with auditors

The audit committee can act as a forum for **liaison with the external and internal auditors**. The auditors will have an opportunity to express any concerns or problems they might have, such as inability to obtain information or lack of confidence in executive management.

Review of financial information

The audit committee can **review financial documents** such as the year-end accounts or interim statements.

Review of systems

The audit committee can use their collective experience to **review objectively the operation of internal control and risk management systems** from a perspective outside any operating considerations.

Disadvantages of setting up an audit committee

Lack of transparency

Since the findings of audit committees are rarely made public, it is not always clear **what they do or how effective** they have been in doing it.

Brake on business

The audit committee's approach may prove somewhat **pedestrian**, resolving little of consequence but acting as a **drag** on the drive and entrepreneurial flair of the company's senior executives.

(b) **Audit committee assistance**

Prevention of problems

Prevention could have been achieved by a **review** of the company's operations, including sales reports and review of authorisation systems to ensure their adequacy.

Detection of problems

Detection could have been achieved by providing a **confidential listening post** for suppliers, customers and members of the public, but most particularly for employees. These roles would be carried out in tandem with the internal audit function.

Investigation of problems

After discovery of this kind of problem the committee has a role as **'independent' investigator**. The resources at the audit committee's disposal will be both internal and external audit. The investigation will try to discover **how such sales came to be made** on what was obviously a fairly regular basis, **who knew** about it and whether anyone on the board knew. The committee can also investigate **how the internal control and reporting function failed** to alert the board to the problem.

Management of outcome

The audit committee should also be in a position to help the company decide **what to do** about the situation. The sensitive nature of this area means that the company's public image may be badly affected and contracts, particularly with the government, may be threatened. In such a politically sensitive arena, the committee's **expertise** should be **invaluable**.

(c) **Involvement of internal audit**

Monitoring compliance

Whether the internal audit department is directly involved in ensuring compliance with the code depends to a great extent on the department's **terms of reference**. Normally, the central function of internal audit is to test the system of internal control. Ideally, the department should have been involved in **designing the code** and then **monitoring compliance with the code**. This seems unlikely to have happened here.

Reaction to breaches

It is more likely that internal audit will **react to reported breaches** of the code, or breaches uncovered by normal internal audit work on the control system. At worst, internal audit may have no reference to the code, although it is possible that the department is involved in occasional studies.

Problems with code

The ideal type of involvement of internal audit may be developed in future, but there are problems, particularly where the code is a very vague 'be good' document. **Internal audit** will need more **specific rules** in the code so that compliance can be judged more objectively.

Evidence seeking

Internal audit may also need to **abandon the usual standards of documentation** and **proof** as breaches of the code are unlikely to be very public or documented at all. The department is being asked to behave like a private detective, rather than an internal audit department.

(d) **Other steps**

Given the difficulty of implementing an ethical culture, a good code of conduct and of monitoring the situation, the following should be carried out.

Review and amend the existing code

The code should be amended as necessary to be as **specific and comprehensive** as possible.

Check that the code is disseminated

The code should be **distributed throughout the whole company**, from board level downwards. Board members and staff should acknowledge that they have **received a copy** and that they **agree to adhere to its principles.**

Whistleblowing

The company should **Implement a confidential reporting system for staff**, using the audit committee, internal audit department and possibly other more informal routes.

Internal processes

The board should **ensure staff are trained in ethical matters** and that ethics are included as a component in all managerial decision-making, including budgeting and reporting.

Rewards and deterrents

The board should **introduce** a **formal punishment and reward structure**. Staff should know that they will be punished for ethical breaches, but also that there is a positive reward for being ethical and reporting any breaches of the code.

Board support

The main board and the audit committee must clearly communicate to the rest of the company that the code has the **full authority** of the board and the committee behind it.

43 Drofdarb

Text references. Chapters 3, 8 and 10.

Top tips. (a) starts with a straightforward test of knowledge of the ethical principles; however the second half of (a) is more demanding and is a particular concern of the examiner, how an ethical culture is promoted. (b) requires focus on the role of the board in risk management, and an acknowledgement of the limitations of what the board can ensure.

Note in (c) that the independence issues are not clearcut and hence need some discussion if you are to score well. The grounds for making the recommendation are that there are too many potential threats to independence.

Easy marks. You need to learn the fundamental principles if you struggled with the first part of (a) as they really do represent core knowledge. Likewise the four main roles of the non-executive directors has been stressed by the examiner as important knowledge.

Marking scheme

			Marks
(a)	1 mark per principle up to a maximum of 6, plus up to 3 marks for recommendation of codes of conduct, and visibility		9
(b)	1 mark per point discussed up to a maximum of 4; up to 3 marks for reasons why risks may not be fully eliminated; 1 mark available if mention of links to best practice	max	6
(c)	1 mark per point discussed on role of NED up to a maximum of 4; up to 6 marks for discussions of suitability of NED candidate and conclusion		10
			25

(a)   **ACCA's ethical code**

ACCA's ethical code contains the following basic principles.

Integrity

A professional accountant should be **straightforward and honest in performing professional services.** A professional accountant should not be party to the falsification of any record, or knowingly or recklessly supply any information or make a statement that is misleading, false or deceptive in a material particular.

Objectivity

A professional accountant should be **fair** and should **not allow prejudice or bias** or the influence of others to override objectivity.

Professional competence and due care

In agreeing to provide professional services, a professional accountant implies that there is a level of competence necessary to perform those services and that his or her knowledge, skill and experience will be applied with **reasonable care and diligence**. A professional accountant is expected to **present information fully, honestly and professionally,** so that it will be **understood in its context**. She/he also **knows, understands and follows technical standards** and should ensure that all professional services are carried out in accordance with those standards.

Professional behaviour

A professional accountant should behave in a manner consistent with the good reputation of the institute. ACCA requires that its members **refrain from any conduct that might bring discredit** on the institute, especially with regard to their responsibilities towards employers, clients, third parties, other members of the accounting profession, employees and the general public.

Confidentiality

A professional accountant should **respect the confidentiality of information** acquired during the course of performing the professional services and should not use or disclose any such information without proper and specific authority, or unless there is a legal or professional right or duty to disclose.

Action by business

Commitment from business

The use of an ethical code for any business should tie in good behaviour by staff with the overall success of the company. In order for any ethical guide to be successful, **commitment** from senior finance managers is required, along with **visible evidence** that **those who follow the code prosper** while those that do not will be **disciplined.**

Need for ethical code

As well as organisational ethical guidance, there probably needs to be an ethical code specifically for the finance staff. Staff need to understand that there is a **clear rationale** for the code. The code should consist of a combination of **specific guidance** and **general expectations** on what constitutes acceptable and unacceptable behaviour. The code must be **freely available** to all staff.

Action by Mr McKenna

Mr McKenna needs to be asked what he has done to ensure this form of control is adopted and maintained within his department, and whether any departures from this code have either occurred or been missed in the last year. His assertions that there is no problem need to be based on more than just perception and supposition; **facts and evidence** need to be collected.

(b)   **Risk-based approach**

The UK's Turnbull Report is a good example of best practice. The Turnbull guidance follows a risk-based approach, highlighting the need for organisations to **identify and prioritise risks** and **deploy suitable controls**.

Board review

The Turnbull report suggests that boards should carry out regular and wider-ranging annual reviews of the effectiveness of **risk management and control systems.** The reviews should **cover all material controls** in respect of **financial, operational and compliance risks**. Boards should aim to ensure that **safeguards exist against loss of either assets or information** and that companies **comply with the relevant provisions** of the **UK Corporate Governance Code.**

Audit committee and audit

In addition to an annual review, the Turnbull guidance suggests that there should be an **audit committee** staffed by at least three NEDs with an **internal audit** function made up of employed staff. **Regular review of the systems of internal controls by internal audit** and **consultation with external audit** will help the organisation demonstrate that it is managing risks effectively.

Limitations of risk-based approach

The Turnbull guidance acknowledges the need to **manage risks by suitable internal controls.** However, it also acknowledges that there is **no perfect system** and that despite the best efforts of many key stakeholders, **risk** can only be **reduced**, not wholly eliminated. The reasons for this include **poor decisions** being made that result in losses. **Human error** can reduce the effectiveness of internal controls. There may be **deliberate circumvention of controls** by staff intent on fraud, malicious damage or **management override** for reasons of fraud or self – preservation. Controls may only be **geared to normal circumstances** and may **not be able to cope with unforeseeable circumstances.**

At best, a system of internal controls can **only give reasonable, not absolute, assurance** that systems are sufficient. It is up to the Drofdarb board to assess regularly the **uncertainties surrounding their business** to see how likely it is that systems will no longer be sufficient.

(c) (i) **Roles of NEDs**

The Higgs report identifies four roles of NEDs.

(1) They should **aim to participate in setting the strategy** of a company, in particular challenging the proposals of executive directors.

(2) They should **scrutinise the performance of executive management** in meeting goals and objectives, and monitor the reporting of performance.

(3) They are responsible for seeing that **risk issues are addressed** within the company, in particular that **financial information is accurate and financial management and systems of control are robust.**

(4) They should be **involved in the people side** of running the company, including their roles on the remuneration and nomination committees.

(ii) **Independence criteria**

Cross-directorship

Before Mr McDermott can be considered for the vacant post of NED at Drofdarb, his **independence** needs to be considered. His position as executive director of Sdeel plc calls into question whether he can keep information obtained in the course of his business at both Drofdarb and Sdeel separate and not suffer a **conflict of interest** This is known as **cross directorship**.

Audit partner

His previous position as **audit partner** for Drofdarb shows him to have had a **material business interest** in Drofdarb, although he would not necessarily have had the company's interests in mind, rather those of the shareholders instead. This is less easy to query independence over than cross directorships. The length of time since he has been an audit partner (two years) also means that this is less of an issue.

Family connections

Given that Mr McDermott has **family connections** with the Sdeel and Drofdarb founders, more would need to be known about these connections before his independence could be assessed.

Shareholding

A shareholding in the company is not normally a threat to a non-executive director's independence, as one of his roles is to **represent the interests of other shareholders**. However a very material shareholding might influence him significantly, particularly if he wants to dispose of it in the near future.

Conclusion

Because of the **threats to independence**, it is unlikely that Mr McDermott can be entirely independent and as such his appointment as NED is not recommended.

44 David Hunter

(a)   **What are the facts of the case?**

The facts are that the civil servants have made what is an apparently legitimate request for information. However the circumstances suggest that if the board supplies this information, it may be used by the governing party to **support its bid for re-election**.

What are the ethical issues in the case?

Independence. The main ethical issue is **independence**. The corporation exists to serve the **interests of the country as a whole** and should not be seen to be supporting one political party, even if the board believes that party's policies are best for EPC. The fact that the request has come via the civil servants will not be a defence, since the civil servants also have a (possibly stronger) duty of independence.

Obedience. The board also however owes a duty of **obedience** to the Ministry of Energy, which is its employer, and has a right to make legitimate business requests. **Confidentiality** may also be an issue, that the board may be instructed to treat the request and its response as confidential.

What are the norms, principles and values related to the case?

Objectives. The board must act in accordance with the **corporation's objectives**, which will be to **supply electricity** as **economically and efficiently as possible**. The board is entitled to consider whether major cost-cutting may increase the risk of the electricity supply failing.

Governance. As EPC is a nationalised entity, the directors are expected to **act in accordance with the wishes of the properly elected government**, since the democratic process confers legitimacy upon the government's wishes. This means **accepting major changes such as privatisation** if they wish to remain on the board, also accepting other obligations such as keeping certain information confidential if necessary.

Independence. The duty of **independence** means that the board **cannot actively intervene in the political process**, an issue of most relevance during a general election campaign.

Transparency. Ultimately also the board owes a duty of **transparency** about its policies to the public and consumers, as they are **primary stakeholders**. However the duty of transparency is not normally regarded as absolute; strategic business discussions may legitimately be kept confidential in the short-term for various reasons.

What are the alternative courses of actions for the board?

Supply the information on the grounds that the board is **not empowered to refuse a legitimate request** from the Department of Energy.

Supply the information provided that the board receives **prior assurance**, certainly from the civil servants and preferably from the Minister of Energy, that the information will not be used for political purposes during the election campaign.

Refuse to supply the information on the grounds that the board must be seen to be **neutral** when its future is a significant issue in the election campaign.

Refuse to supply the information on the grounds that it **cannot be expected to make a major commitment to cost reduction instantly**; review and discussion of possible options will be required and this will take time.

What is the best course of action that is consistent with the norms, principles and values?

The board seems to have **legitimate business reasons for asking for more time** to **consider cost reductions**. It is also entitled to be sensitive to independence issues and **seek assurances** before it supplies any information that could help the governing party.

What are the consequences of each course of action?

If the **information is supplied and then kept confidential**, the board's **independence** is **unlikely to be questioned**, although a hastily drawn up plan may later be **criticised for business reasons**. If detailed information is not supplied until the board has had the chance to consider its plans carefully, the decisions are more likely to be **in accordance with the corporation's objectives**.

If the **board supplies the information and it is used for political purposes**, then the board's **independence** will be **questioned**. If the opposition party then wins the election, some or all of the board may well be replaced and EPC may suffer **disruption to board decision-making and monitoring**. Similarly if the board **refuses**, the current government takes offence and wins the election, the **board** may also be **replaced**.

What is the decision?

The board may feel able to **supply some indications of how it might cut costs**. It should **refuse to supply detailed information** until it has had time to consider future planning carefully, even if this means the information is not available until after polling day. Before it supplies any information it should **seek guarantees** from the governing party that it will not use the information to forward its political platform. It should not reveal the request has been made unless the information is used for political purposes and the board therefore needs to demonstrate that it has acted independently.

(b)   The stages of Tucker's five question model are in the decision:

Profitable

Although the nationalised corporation will be a non-profit making body, it has the duty to control its costs. The costs of combating the protestors will include:

- The **costs of security**
- The **costs of taking action** to counter the bad publicity that may be a consequence of the treatment of the protestors
- The **costs of legal action** brought by the protestors as a result of the actions of the security guards

The other issue however is whether there is any alternative to **incurring these costs**. If the protestors are determined to protest, the alternative may be disruption to the country's power supply, which is likely to be regarded as being much more important.

Legal

The legality of the security guards' action depends upon local legislation, in particular the **rights to protest, to protect property and use reasonable force**. There is also the issue of how far EPC will be held responsible for the actions of **its agent**, the security firm. Because of the issues of poor publicity and also the costs described above, EPC's board should be wary if it appears that excessive force may be being used, since this is likely to be a legally grey area.

Fair

The pressure groups may claim that they have a **legitimate right to protest**. Their case may be weakened by the fact that they can currently take **political action in the general election campaign**, although perhaps they might argue that none of the major parties fairly represents their views. However even if the board was to accept that the pressure groups are **legitimate stakeholders**, it also has a duty to consumers, who are undoubtedly also legitimate stakeholders, to **preserve the continuity of electricity supplies**. These include consumers whose livelihoods and indeed lives may be threatened by power cuts (hospital patients for example).

Right

The main ethical issues are whether it is right for the pressure group to take potentially **life-threatening action** in order to advance a cause that has fundamental long-term consequences (action against global warming). From EPC's point of view the ethical issue is whether **force** should be used against the pressure group if its actions are life-threatening; if it can be, **how much force** would be right; ultimately would it be legitimate to take action that might jeopardise the lives of the protestors.

Sustainable

Because of the general election campaign and a possible change of government, the board cannot be expected at present to make long-term decisions about switching to a **more environmentally friendly method of electricity generation**. However if the managing director's attitude is typical of the board, then the viewpoint is **not sustainable**; continued use of coal will mean supplies are eventually exhausted and there is strong scientific evidence that the emissions are having **adverse climatic effects**. Many countries are investigating alternative sources of power. Whatever the result of the general election, EPC's board has a duty to ask the new government to review energy policies.

45 Penrice

Text references. Chapter 1 on transaction cost theory, Chapter 11 on environmental accounting and auditing.

Top tips. It's important to limit the number of points to the marks available, though it is not always easy to tell how many marks are given for each point. Generally, the examiner would give 2-3 marks for the opening explanation in (a). In evaluation questions such as (a), one mark per point for and against is likely be given, but in (b) and (c) it is more likely that 2 marks per point could be awarded if the points are developed and applied.

In (a) you need to bring out the different layers of full cost accounting. Remember that the information can be useful for internal purposes as well as satisfying the increasing demands of external users (although of course they may not like what they read).

In (b) an environmental audit can mean various things, and we have summarised features of many audits. As with other types of external audit, the value of an environmental audit lies in the independent and expert view which can provide assurance to important stakeholders such as the government.

(c) emphasises the implication of transaction cost theory, that an organisation's desire for control can lead to it being too cautious and failing to satisfy shareholder expectations. It links in with risk appetite and excessive avoidance of risks. The strategic implications mean that effective action is required by the board.

Easy marks. The content of a full cost accounting report and the main features of an environmental audit should be fairly easy book knowledge.

(a)   **Full cost accounting**

Full cost accounting is a system that allows accounts to incorporate all **potential and actual costs and benefits**, including environmental and social externalities, in order to arrive at cost figures that are fair and that can be used as a basis for realistic accounting.

The costs incorporated can include **usual costs,** that is basic capital and revenue costs. The next stage is identifying **hidden costs,** costs usually included as overheads such as costs of management systems and safety. There may be **contingent liabilities,** for example fines. The accounts may also bring in **less tangible costs,** other costs of poor environmental management, loss of goodwill by partners and suppliers. Lastly there are **costs of prevention**, costs that ensure activities have no environmental effect.

Arguments in favour of full cost accounting

Reduction of environmental footprint

Making data available about the **extent of the environmental footprint** provides an incentive to reduce the footprint in future years.

Knowledge of environmental footprint

Knowledge of the full extent of Penrice's environmental footprint should help **better decision-making** by the directors of, and investors in, Penrice. Investors will have more information about the risks involved in the company's activities, whilst full cost accounting will help the board make comparisons between the **externalities** of different investment options.

Favourable publicity

Producing full cost accounting information for external users will bring Penrice some welcome publicity for **demonstrating greater transparency** and hopefully demonstrate that the company's **products and processes do not have significant environmental impacts.**

Arguments against full cost accounting

Data required

Penrice will need to gather an increased amount of data, and **information-gathering costs may increase.**

Assumptions and parameters

It may be difficult to decide **which cost figures to use**, whether for example to include **costs of correction or costs of prevention.** Including **social externalities** would lead to further problems of **definition and measurement.** It also may not be easy to translate all of Penrice's activities into financial impacts.

Impression given

There is the risk that full cost accounting figures may give a poor impression of Penrice. This may **damage Penrice's reputation** and decrease the willingness of customers to buy from Penrice. It may also be used by the government as evidence of the need to take stronger measures against Penrice and other companies.

(b) **Nature of environmental audit**

Environmental audit can mean the audit of the truth and fairness of an environmental report. It can also be a general evaluation of how well control systems are safeguarding the environment, and whether the business is meeting targets and complying with internal policies and external regulations. It can include an environmental impact assessment of major projects as well as environmental surveys of the business as a whole.

Reasons for having an environmental audit

External expertise

External auditors would be able to bring **knowledge and experience** of other companies' methods of managing environmental impacts. External auditors would therefore be better able to **benchmark Penrice's systems** against best practice elsewhere and base recommendations for improvements upon this.

Gaining external recognition

If Penrice wishes to obtain **environmental accreditation** such as the EU's EMAS scheme it will need to have a periodic independent environmental audit. Gaining EMAS recognition would demonstrate Penrice's willingness for its activities to be submitted to **external scrutiny.**

Greater confidence to stakeholders

Independent verification of Penrice's activities should provide reassurance to interested parties such as the government that the information Penrice provides has been **independently verified,** and that Penrice is **committed to audited improvements** in its performance. This may be particularly important if full cost accounting has revealed Penrice's environmental footprint to be very significant.

(c) **Transaction cost theory**

Transaction cost theory indicates that the way an organisation is governed determines its control over transactions. Dealing with external parties will involve costs of finding new business partners, dealing with them and monitoring them. Companies may wish to avoid these costs by **pursuing vertical integration**, as has happened in Penrice. Under transaction cost theory managers will **organise their transactions to pursue their own interests**. Particularly in a vertically integrated company, they may have limited ideas of alternative strategies and may see their own interests as playing safe. This can result in their making 'Go' errors – failing to pursue profitable opportunities because of over-estimation of their risks.

Recommendations for improvements

Risk appetite

Strong leadership from the board appears to be required to change management attitudes here and as Pravina is the newly installed chief executive, she should be in a position to provide it. Firstly the board needs to **redefine Penrice's risk appetite,** which appears to be too cautious for its shareholders. This is likely to result perhaps in changes in strategy, with possibly **greater diversification of activities** and strengthening of links with external parties, possibly **outsourcing** of more activities.

Systems

Control systems may need to be changed to encourage managers out of their comfort zone. The **transfer pricing** system within Penrice may need to be reviewed as it may provide too great an incentive to use internal resources. Using market pricing may encourage use of **lower cost alternatives** elsewhere. **Tendering rules** may be introduced for specific contracts or activities, forcing managers to consider **supply by external parties** and justify decisions to use internal parties.

Performance appraisal

Targets set for management may need to become more challenging to encourage management to consider more **profitable or cost-effective alternatives.** Possibly there needs to be greater emphasis on managers demonstrating that they have sensibly **reduced risks**, rather than abandoning activities or not undertaking them.

46 JH Graphics

Text references. Chapters 1 and 9.

Top tips. (a) is a good example of how ethical theories may be applied to a situation. The difference between being ethical because one should be (normative view) and being ethical because it achieves a financial/strategic end (instrumental view) is very important in this exam. Without knowing this distinction you would score very poorly on this part (it's not worth guessing!).

(b) is also a good example of how ethical theory is applied in practice. The key distinction here is between being ethical because of benefit/harm considerations (pre conventional) and being ethical because one should conform with norms (conventional).

Ethical factors are of significance in (c), but you also need to think about strategic issues and reputation risk – very significant in a situation like this. Remember we stressed in the front pages that a key skill in this exam is identifying the most important features of the organisation and its environment; doing so here will mean your discussion of strategy and reputation risk is well focused. Assess in this context means saying something about the significance of these factors.

(d) does not require you to offer your own personal opinions; instead you need to say why the religious group may or may not have a claim on how widely accountability to stakeholders is defined.

Easy marks. (c) may have been the easiest part of this question as you could generate some ideas from your general business awareness rather than having to concentrate strictly on ethics.

		Marks
(a)	1 point for each relevant point made on normative	4
	1 point for each relevant point made on instrumental	4
		8
(b)	1 mark for evidence of understanding the terms	2
	1 mark for application for each to case	2
		4
(c)	2 marks for each relevant point made	10
(d)	1 mark for each relevant point made	3
		25

(a) **Jenny's view**

Jenny's view is based on a **normative view of ethics**, that the company should behave in an **ethical way as an end in itself**, and not a means to another end. Hence JH Graphics should not hesitate to adopt the code because it signifies that ethical behaviour is at the core of what it does. Her motivation is **altruistic** rather than **business strategic**.

The moral framework that supports this view is derived from **Kant's** notion of civic duties. Kant argued that these duties are required in maintaining good in society. Amongst these duties is the **moral duty to take account of others' concerns** and opinions; not to do so will result in a failure of social cohesion and everyone being worse off.

Extending the normative view to stakeholder theory, Jenny's view is that JH Graphics should accommodate stakeholder views because of its **moral duties** to its stakeholders, not because accommodating stakeholder concerns will help it achieve its own economic or other concerns.

Alan's view

Alan's view is based on an **instrumental view of ethics**. This sees the company taking ethical positions into account only when they are consistent with the overriding economic objective of **maximising shareholder value**. Hence Alan is concerned with the **strategic implications** of the code (will not adopting it place JH Graphics at a competitive disadvantage) and the **costs of drawing it up and implementing it**.

The instrumental view in relation to stakeholders suggests that shareholder concerns should be accommodated if not doing so threatens its ability to maximise shareholder value. Thus taking account of shareholder opinions is a **means to the end of maximising economic value**, not an end. Thus stakeholders are judged not in terms of whether it is ethically right to respond to their concerns, but how powerful they are in terms of how much influence they can have on JH Graphics achieving its economic objectives.

(b) **Conventional viewpoint**

Kohlberg identified the conventional viewpoint as one of the levels of moral reasoning. Using this perspective, individuals judge ethical decisions in terms of what is **expected of them** in terms of the norms of society or organisation. In this example Jenny would take into account what would be considered **good practice** in the industry; would other companies use similar images even if they did cause offence. She would also consider society's viewpoint as expressed in the law; would the images possibly break laws relating to good taste. Another viewpoint would be whether **members of society other than those belonging to the religious group** would find the image offensive.

Pre-conventional viewpoint

The pre-conventional reasoning viewpoint sees reasoning in terms of the **rewards or punishments** that will result from a particular act. The factors influencing the decision would be whether JH Graphics would suffer a **legal penalty** through its association with the advert, whether it would **lose business** because of the offence taken by potential client or whether (as Alan argues) it would **gain business** through the **free advertising**.

(c)   **Variety of factors**

The board will take into account a number of different considerations, some of which are not easily comparable. However one means of aiding the decision would be to consider the various stakeholders affected, and to analyse their viewpoints in terms of **Mendelow's stakeholder influence**, considering their **relative degree of power and influence**.

Relationship with customer

One obvious stakeholder with a strong economic relationship to JH Graphics is the **customer**. The board would need to consider whether business with the customer would be **threatened** if the advertisement was withdrawn and what the consequences would be in terms of **lost sales**. Another viewpoint would be that the customer's interests, that have been secured by paying the advertisement, should take precedence over the religious group's interest, as the religious group has **no economic relationship**. Of course the customer might prefer the advertisement to be withdrawn because it was damaging its interests. JH Graphics would presumably have to comply with the request, although then the issue would be whether there should be an apology.

Negative reputation consequences

The offence caused by the advertisement is an example of a reputation risk materialising, and the board therefore has to assess the consequences in terms of what stakeholders will do. Firstly would a **boycott by members of the religious group be significant**. More widely would actions taken by the **religious group and adverse press coverage** generated lead to other organisations **being unwilling to use JH Graphics** with further lost sales. The board will need to judge the **balance and strength of the coverage**.

Positive reputation consequences

However there may be an **upside to the reputation risk**. JH Graphics may **gain business** as a result of the advertisement with more clients being willing to use the company because it is seen as **forward-looking and daring**. Alan Leroy believes that the advertisement will be good for business. This may be jeopardised if the advert is withdrawn and an apology issued.

Organisational field

The board's decision may be affected by the organisational field of the advertising industry, the common **business environment**, **norms** and **values** within the industry. These appear to work in different directions however in this situation. On the one hand a lot of large companies are emphasising their **ethical commitment**; however there may be pressures within the industry to be **challenging and innovative**.

National culture

The board may also consider the **place of religion in the national culture**, how strongly religious ideas affect people's beliefs and actions.

Strategic considerations

Important strategic considerations include JH Graphics' positioning relative to its competitors. Does it wish to gain a **competitive advantage** through being seen as more ethical, or through being seen as more innovative or perhaps more subversive.

Company objectives

One particularly significant aspect of strategy is whether the objective of **profit maximisation** should be given precedence over everything else or whether JH Graphics exists to fulfil other significant considerations. This could be a very important decision for JH Graphics as there is evidently a dispute between the **purely capitalist, revenue-driven view** of Alan Leroy and the view of Jenny Harris that JH Graphics should express **ethical values through what it does**. The decision may end up having a significant influence on the company's future direction.

(d)   **Narrow stakeholders**

The religious group's viewpoint would be that they are **narrow stakeholders**, meaning that JH Graphics' activities seriously affected their own interests. They argue that the content and design undermines their system of beliefs and threatens the promotion of their faith.

Accountability to shareholders

How legitimate this claim is viewed as being depends on **how widely corporate accountability is defined**. **Society's views** will be a significant factor. The legitimacy of the claim would differ greatly in a **theocracy** compared with a society where the religious group represents a **minority view** and is seeking to impose its views outside the law or outside social norms. There is also the issue of whether the religious group needs to have a direct **economic claim** on JH Graphics, or whether the company is seen as having a **social contract** with society that implies a need for sensitivity on religious issues that groups in society believe to be important.

47 Professor Cheung's views

Text references. Chapters 9 and 10.

Top tips. (a) is a good example of how the examiner may use the requirement to evaluate. Remember the definition in the front pages of evaluation meaning to determine the value of in the light of the arguments for and against. The word 'critically' reinforces the need to look at the pros and cons.

In (a) you should get a certain amount of mileage from using Professor Cheung's arguments in the question. Partly the disadvantages of codes is that accountants pay too much attention to the examples and not enough to understanding the basic principles (this point is also picked up in the answer to Question 4 (c)). The impact of regional differences is interesting; you will remember that they impact upon individuals' ethical outlook, so how can codes respond. The arguments against the opinion bring out what codes can achieve, particularly minimum standards of behaviour.

(b) emphasises the key concept of integrity. The definition and the importance of integrity represent knowledge you must have; the examiner has laid a lot of stress on it.

(c) just asks for a definition of these two viewpoints. You may be asked in other questions to apply them to a situation where a deontological (absolute) perspective suggests one course of action, a consequentialist (teleological) perspective another.

Easy marks. (b) is the type of question that should represent easy marks; you need to be able to define key concepts and briefly explain their significance.

Marking scheme

			Marks
(a)	Award 1 mark for each valid point made supporting codes of professional ethics	6	
	Award 1 mark for each valid point made on limitations of codes of professional ethics	6	
	Up to 2 marks for using an actual code of ethics by way of example	2	
	max		12
(b)	Definition of integrity – 1 mark for each relevant point	4	
	Importance of integrity – 1 mark for each relevant point	4	
	max		7
(c)	Explanation of deontology – 1 mark for each valid point	4	
	Explanation of consequentialism – 1 mark for each valid point	4	
	max		6
			25

(a)   **In favour of Professor Cheung's views**

Stress on probity and integrity

Professor Cheung emphasises the **key principles** that should be at the heart of accountants' ethical thinking; arguably professional codes, with their **identification of many different situations** lack this focus.

Treatment as rules

Even if ethical codes stress that they are based on principles, evidence suggests that some treat them as a set of rules to be **complied with and 'box-ticked'**. In particular the examples codes give can be treated as actions to be taken in situations with different sets of circumstances where they may not be appropriate.

Situations outside the codes

Giving a lot of specific examples in codes may give the impression that ethical considerations are **primarily important** only when accountants are facing decisions illustrated in the codes. They may **downplay the importance of acting ethically** when facing decisions that are not clearly covered in the codes.

Limited values of codes

International codes, such as IFAC or ACCA, can **never fully encompass regional differences and variations** and thus are maybe of limited value. Focusing on the key principles of integrity and probity, which in all jurisdictions it is agreed accountants should possess, is a simple solution.

In addition the value of international codes may be limited by their not being legally enforceable around the world (although ACCA can **enforce sanctions** against members for serious breaches).

Against Professor Cheung's views

Building confidence in professions

Codes represent a clear statement that **professionals** are expected to act in the public interest, and act as a **benchmark** against which behaviour can be judged. They thus should enhance public confidence in the professions.

Fundamental principles

Both ACCA and IFAC's codes clearly state that they are based on **fundamental principles**, not a rulebook. These fundamental principles include integrity, also objectivity, professional competence, confidentiality and professional behaviour. Guidance is then in terms of **threats to adherence with these fundamental principles.** They emphasise the importance of professionals considering ethical issues actively and seeking to comply, rather than only being concerned with avoiding what is forbidden.

Minimum standards

The codes state that the ethical principles are **minimum standards** that can be **applied internationally**; local differences are not significant.

Need for application

Although clearly accountants should be following principles of probity and integrity, accountants facing ethical decisions may have **difficulty applying these concepts.** More detailed guidance, based on fundamental principles and with examples, should **assist ethical decision-making.**

Examples

Codes stress that the examples given are **not universal guides for action.** Although accountants may appear to be in very similar situations to those described in the examples, they should exercise their own ethical judgement actively rather than simply following the examples.

Prohibitions

Although a code may be based on principles, it can include explicit prohibitions if principles are not felt to be adequate.

(b) **Definition of integrity**

Integrity is a **strong attachment to morality**. It implies **sticking to principles** no matter what the pressures are to deviate from them. For accountants it implies **probity, professionalism and straightforward dealings in relationships** with all the different people in business life. Trust is vital in relationships and **belief in the integrity of others** is the basis of trust. It also implies qualities beyond a mechanical adherence to accounting standard and law; the post-conventional, highest level of Kohlberg's morality.

Integrity in corporate governance

As corporate governance codes cannot cover every situation, **maintenance of good corporate governance** will sometimes depend on judgements not backed by codes; in these instances integrity is particularly important.

As integrity is partly about proper dealing in relationships, it also underpins the principles of **fair and equitable dealings with shareholders** in corporate governance, particularly in relation to directors exercising an **agency relationship** in respect of shareholders. Good corporate governance is also about **maintaining market confidence** that the company is being run honestly; firm belief that directors have integrity will promote confidence in the company.

(c) **Deontological**

Deontology is concerned with the **application of universal ethical principles** in order to arrive at rules of conduct. It lays down in advance conditions by which actions may be judged. The criteria for judgement are separate from the facts of the situation, and are determined on the basis of **consistency**, **universal application** and **human dignity**.

Consequentalist

The consequentalist approach to ethics is to make moral judgements about ethical decisions on the **basis of their outcomes.** Right or wrong then becomes a question of **benefit or harm**. One example of a consequentalist approach is **utilitarianism** – the principle that the chosen course of action is likely to result in the greatest good.

Contrast between deontological and consequentalist approaches

The main contrast between the two approaches is that the deontological approach takes **no account of consequences**; the same ethical decision will be made in all situations no matter what the differing outcomes of the decision might be in each situation. Consequentalist ethics by contrast **depend on the consequences.**

48 Football club

Text references. Chapters 1 and 11.

Top tips. (a) brings in both viewpoints that are discussed in (b). It's necessary to carry out stakeholder analysis as part of risk and strategy, but there are also corporate social responsibility grounds for doing so – keeping stakeholders happy is seen as an end in itself.

The examiner highlighted a number of ways in which students misinterpreted the requirement to explain the importance of identifying stakeholders:

- Listing stakeholders
- Describing each stakeholder's position on the Mendelow matrix
- Explaining each stakeholder's claim on the stadium project

(b) is basically a discussion between the capitalist viewpoint which examines the (economic) power of shareholders over the business, and the social contract viewpoint which examines the impact of the business on the stakeholders and hence stakeholders' interests in the business. It sees a deal being done between the organisation and society: the organisation acts in tune with the norms of society in exchange for society allowing it to survive and prosper. A point the question is trying to make is that assessing the decision in terms of the impact made by the club means that the interests of community and (possibly) the fans should take precedence over those of the investors.

(c) covers an issue highlighted as a key issue, the limits of business accountability in the context of social responsibility. It requires you to construct a case ie argue in favour of the proposition of extending fiduciary responsibility. The examiner is keen on testing this skill and though you may not agree with extending fiduciary responsibility you have to support the view the question requirements specify. The arguments we've used can be related to some of the Gray, Owen, Adams viewpoints:

- Reputation corresponds to the expedient viewpoint, that a business's economic interests may benefit through acknowledging some social responsibility.
- Community footprint is based on the social contract position, the idea that the club exists only as a result of the will of those affected by its activities.
- The view that the club should not disrupt the local wildlife is based on the social/deep ecologist viewpoints.

An alternative approach might be to use Kohlberg's stances as a framework.

- A fiduciary responsibility to shareholders reflects a pre-conventional viewpoint, since they provide the finance that enables the club to operate.
- A conventional viewpoint would argue in favour in reflecting the opinions of those connected with the club (the fans) and having to take account of laws (local planning regulations).
- Taking account of the interests of the local community and the wildlife can be justified from, a post-conventional viewpoint, that it's the right thing to do.

Easy marks. There are quite a few marks for definitions in this question.

Examiner's comments. Students generally underperformed in this question because they failed to answer the question set. This was especially the case in the second part of (a), which asked students to place themselves in the position of the board considering all the benefits of knowing who the stakeholders were and what their different claims were. Students would have gained some credit for saying that the board would benefit from knowing the relative power and influence of stakeholders, in connection with progressing the stadium, but the question did **not** require a detailed analysis using the Mendelow framework.

(b) required students to apply two of Gray, Owen and Adams' positions, **not to** list the seven positions nor to explain any of the other five. Many students correctly described the two ethical positions, but failed to apply them to the football club's situation, which was essential for achieving high marks.

(c) was generally done poorly. Time pressure appeared to compromise the quality of many answers (the question was Question 4 on the paper and therefore done last), but students also struggled to construct an argument.

Marking scheme

				Marks
(a)	1 marks for each relevant point made on definition of 'stakeholder'	max	2	
	Up to 2 marks for each relevant point on the importance of Stakeholder identification	max	8	
				10
(b)	2 marks for description of pristine capitalist position		2	
	2 marks for description of social contractarian position		2	
	1 mark for each relevant point made applying the theories to the case	max	4	
				8
(c)	1 mark for each relevant point made defining 'fiduciary responsibility'	max	3	
	1 mark for each relevant point made in favour of extending fiduciary responsibility	max	4	
				7
				25

(a) **Stakeholders**

Stakeholders are any entity (person, group or possibly non-human entity) that can **affect** and/or be **affected** by the actions or policies of an organisation. The effect the stakeholder has on the organisation or vice versa may be **voluntary or involuntary**.

Importance of identifying stakeholders

Impact analysis

As the actions of stakeholders can affect an organisation, an organisation has to assess the **impact** of their possible actions as part of its **strategic analysis.** This includes the **risks** the stakeholders' activities may pose. For example with the stadium project there are the **legal risks** that the football club may have to defend an action brought by local residents. There is also the **risk to the club's reputation** resulting from the adverse publicity caused by the protests of the school and others.

Corporate social responsibility

There is also the argument that the football club needs to consider all those whom its impact might **affect**, as its activities may damage their rights or position. The **normative view** of stakeholders is that accommodating stakeholder concerns should be an end in itself.

Conflicts between stakeholder positions

Often stakeholder groups will have **competing interests**. In this scenario the economic interests of investors would appear to conflict with those of local residents and wildlife. The club needs to understand the nature of these conflicts to decide what further action to take.

Reconciling stakeholder positions

Only by identifying all stakeholders and attempting to **assess the levels of interest and power** each have will the club be able to make a fair decision about how to reconcile different interests.

(b) **Pristine capitalist position**

The pristine capitalist position is based on defence of the private property system, with the idea that companies should be able unhindered to **make profits** and **seek economic efficiency.** Companies are **responsible** to those who provide finance for its activities (its shareholders and creditors) and others who have **economic power** over it, and to no-one else.

Social contractarian position

The social contractarian position is that companies have a wider responsibility, to fulfil society's norms and beliefs. Companies can only operate with the consent of those from whom they derive their ability to make profits and **whom are affected by the companies' activities.** Companies should therefore act as if a contract exists between them and those who are affected by their activities, even if this reduces profits. Decisions such as the stadium project depend on the ability to address the concerns of those most affected, whose **level of interest** is therefore highest.

Football club position

Pristine capitalists

(i) **Investors**

Pristine capitalists would take the view that the company should proceed with building the new stadium if it **maximises economic value** for the most **important stakeholders**, the stock market **investors** who have bought the company's shares.

The importance of the views of other stakeholders would depend on how much **impact** they had upon **economic value.**

(ii) **Economic impact of other stakeholders**

Fans would **clearly be viewed** as **important stakeholders** because a boycott by fans leading to lower attendances would obviously **reduce revenues.** The local government would also be viewed as a significant stakeholder, given it has the power to grant the football club the **economic opportunity** to go ahead with the stadium. The club's view of local residents would depend how likely it was to incur **significant costs** as a result of the residents taking legal action. Other stakeholders would not be viewed as important unless they **influenced significantly** the views of stakeholders who could affect economic value.

Social contractarians

(i) **Local stakeholders**

The views of local government would be seen as particularly significant since local government has a democratic mandate to **represent the local community** as a whole. The views of local residents would also be very important on the grounds that the club's activities would definitely cause their **enjoyment of their properties** to be diminished. The importance of the wildlife centre would be assessed in terms of the **likelihood and scale of the impact of the stadium**, and the club's ability to reduce the impact of the construction process. The school's importance would depend on the disruption to their enjoyment of the wildlife centre.

(ii) **Fans**

The views of fans might not be seen as so significant since the main benefit they derive from the club is the **ability to watch football played there**, and this would apply whether the club moved to a new stadium or **stayed put.**

(iii) **Investors**

Social contractarians might also question how important investors were, since they would still be able to obtain returns if the **club remained where it was**, and the chance of making significantly increased returns from the move is by no means certain.

(c) **Fiduciary responsibility**

Fiduciary responsibility is the responsibility imposed on persons or organisations because of the **position of trust** they hold in relation to others. It refers to the **accountability** they have to others. The responsibility includes **full disclosure of information** and the **avoidance of conflicts of interest.**

Football club board

The football club's board clearly holds a fiduciary relationship to the shareholders to act in the best interests of the company. However there are a number of arguments in favour of the club acknowledging a **fiduciary responsibility to other stakeholders.**

Reputation

If the club is seen as acknowledging a responsibility to different stakeholders, it should **enhance its reputation** and make it more likely that stakeholders will **acquiesce in the development**.

Community footprint

As acknowledged by the chairman, the club participates in the local community and **derives benefits** from the local environment, for example the local infrastructure **facilitating access** to the ground. It therefore should have a duty to minimise the adverse activities of its affairs on the local community.

Environmental footprint

The club's activities may impose detrimental effects on the environment such as upsetting the wildlife's habitat. Since the club, like the wildlife, inhabits the environment, it has a responsibility to it to **minimise its environmental footprint**, the **impact** of its activities upon the environment.

49 Anne Hayes

Marking scheme

				Marks
(a)	1 mark for each relevant point on importance of independence made and briefly described. Half mark for mention only max		3	
	1 mark for each threat to independence identified max		3	
	1 mark for each threat briefly described max		3	
				9
(b)	(i)	1 mark for each organisational duty identified and briefly described	3	
		1 mark for each professional duty identified and briefly described	3	
		1 mark for each contrast or comparison drawn up	2	
		max		6
	(ii)	1 mark for each point made on inclination towards role as employee max	2	
		1 mark for each point made on inclination towards professional duty max	2	
				4
(c)	4 marks for evidence of understanding the two positions (whether as a definition or in the other parts of the answer)		4	
	2 marks for explanation of how the positions affect outcome		2	
	Cross marks between these two to reflect adequacy of overall answer			
				6
				25

(a) **Reliability of financial information**

Corporate governance reports have highlighted **reliability of financial information** as a key aspect of corporate governance. Shareholders and other stakeholders need a trustworthy record of **directors' stewardship** to be able to take decisions about the company. Assurance provided by independent auditors is a key quality control on the reliability of information.

Credibility of financial information

An unqualified report by independent external auditors on the accounts should give them more **credibility**, enhancing the appeal of the company to investors. It should represent the views of independent experts, who are not motivated by personal interests to give a favourable opinion on the annual report.

Value for money of audit work

Audit fees should be set on the basis of charging for the work **necessary to gain sufficient audit assurance**. A lack of independence here seems to mean important audit work may not be done, and thus the shareholders are not receiving value for the audit fees.

Threats to professional standards

A lack of independence may lead to a failure to **fulfil professional requirements** to obtain enough evidence to form the basis of an audit opinion, here to obtain details of a questionable material item. Failure by auditors to do this **undermines the credibility of the accountancy profession** and the standards it enforces.

Threats to independence

Familiarity with client

Zachary Lincoln has been partner in charge of the audit for **longer than the period recommended by most governance reports** (between five and seven years). His familiarity appears to have influenced his judgement, leading him to make the dubious assumption that because there has been no problem on this audit in the past, there cannot be a problem now.

Personal friendship – self interest

Zachary Lincoln appears to be **allowing his personal friendship** with Frank Monroe to **bias his judgement** on whether to investigate the questionable payment. There is a **self interest threat** involved in Zachary Taylor's wish to maintain the friendship, and also a **lack of objectivity**.

Non-audit services – self interest

Governance codes identify **provision of non-audit services** as a potentially significant threat to auditor independence. This scenario illustrates why; a **qualified opinion** on Van Buren's accounts may mean that the company stops using Fillmore Pierce to provide consultancy services. Thus it is clearly in Fillmore Pierce's **self interest to give an unqualified audit report**, and therefore it seems doubtful that the firm is truly independent.

(b)   (i)   **Obedience**

As an employee Anne owes the duty of **obedience** to her **managers**, and should comply with reasonable orders provided they do not breach her professional duties.

As a professional accountant Anne should comply with the **technical and ethical standards established by her professional body**, even if these conflict with what she is being required to do in the workplace.

Interests of employer and profession

As an employee, Anne has a responsibility to **promote the interests of her employer**. These include the **commercial, fee-earning, interests**, making efforts to obtain new work and keep existing clients happy.

As a professional accountant, Anne has a responsibility to maintain the good name of her accountancy body. This includes acting **honestly and objectively**, and not allowing herself to be associated with misleading information or a misleading report.

Obligations of employment and membership

As an employee, Anne owes a general duty to 'fit in', be part of a team and behave in ways that are in accordance with the **organisational culture** of her employer.

As a member of a professional accounting body, Anne owes the duty to act in accordance with the **norms** of that body, including its stress on **professional behaviour**.

(ii) **Acting non-commercially**

The main tension between the roles that Anne is experiencing is that if she acts in accordance with professional standards, and pursues a full explanation for the payment, she will not be acting in her employer's **commercial interests**. The audit will go on longer than budgeted, meaning that the assignment is **less profitable**. She also risks upsetting the client and **putting future income at risk**.

Anne's own interests

There is also the issue of whether Anne should take into account her own interests and if so how she should do this. She may feel that in order to make her life **easier as an employee** of Fillmore Pierce, she should allow the report to be signed. Against this is the **possibility of suffering disciplinary action** by her professional body if she allows the audit report to be signed, and it later turns out to be misleading.

(c) **Absolutist assumptions**

Definition

Absolutist dogmatic assumptions are based on the idea that there are **rules** which should be followed in all circumstances, **whatever the consequences**. This means that if an individual is facing an ethical dilemma, there should be a **'right' solution** to that dilemma.

Van Buren situation

Absolutist assumptions would indicate that an audit provides **independent assurance** on a business. Because of this, all material audit queries need to be resolved if an **unqualified audit report** is to be given.

Conclusion using absolutist assumptions

Resolving the query is the right course of action to take and thus should be pursued, even if it means a longer audit and problems with the client.

Relativist assumptions

Definition

A relativist position would be that there are a variety of ethical beliefs and practices, and that the ethics that are most appropriate in a given situation will depend on the conditions at that time. A **pragmatic consequentialist** position would consider the **consequences** of the various options available, and choose the option that on balance **produced the greatest benefits** or the **least degree of harm**. This may be benefits or lack of harm in general, or it may be defined more narrowly to mean benefits or lack of harm to Fillmore Pierce or even just to Anne herself (which would be egoism).

Van Buren situation

Using relativist assumptions would mean that Anne needs to assess the **consequences** of pursuing this point. The relativist viewpoint would take into account the argument that **not all audit trails** can **end neatly**. It would also consider the **other circumstances** surrounding the audit, including **previous experience of the client** and **personal knowledge of Frank Monroe**. That said, the relativist view would also consider the possible **adverse consequences to the reputation of Anne Hayes and Fillmore Pierce** if the firm gives an unqualified report when it later turns out it should not have done.

Conclusion using relativist assumptions

The decision using relativist assumptions therefore requires the weighing up of **different possible consequences**. Because of this, the outcome of the decision cannot be predicted easily.

50 Hogg Products

Text references. Chapters 9 and 10.

Top tips. Note in (a) that the purposes of the code of ethics are underlying themes across the whole of this exam. You could also have mentioned communication and other relevant purposes. Your discussion on contents could have included discussion of other key stakeholders such as suppliers of finance, other aspects of relations with the stakeholders identified in our answer (only buying from suppliers who provide quality guarantees or who meet ethical standards).

In (b) the examiner helpfully defines strategic positioning, although it is not so easy to see how many points you are required to make (five at maximum to generate seven marks). Our answer contains a combination of general points (a strong code of ethics means customers can have confidence in HPC's fairness) and specific issues linked to some of the content discussed in (a).

In (c) don't worry if you don't have all the points we identified; (c) will have been marked quite generously. The way to approach both viewpoints is to give a general description and then bring in the material from the scenario. The requirement to use the broad teleological viewpoint means that you can generate marks by looking at variations of the consequentalist viewpoint.

Easy marks. Using the contents of the example code of conduct in Chapter 10 of the Study Text would have generated most of the marks you needed in (a).

Examiner's comments. This question was the least attempted question on the paper and also the poorest done in terms of marks. The poor quality of many answers to this question suggests that candidates may have some difficulty with this section of the syllabus and this should be a challenge for future candidates and their tutors.

The content for (a) is clearly covered in published material so I was surprised that candidates overall did poorly on it. Some candidates confused corporate with professional ethics and introduced the elements of professional ethical behaviour (integrity, etc.) in place of the contents of corporate codes of ethics (policies towards suppliers, customers, etc.).

Many candidates who attempted (b) showed some misunderstanding of the term in question ('strategic positioning') despite it being briefly explained in the question itself. The question was referring to the ways in which some organisations use ethical behaviour and ethical reputation as a key part of the way they are perceived by their stakeholders.

In (c) the requirement was to 'assess' a particular belief (that employing child labour is 'always wrong') from deontological and teleological (consequentialist) ethical perspectives. It was therefore necessary to know what the two ethical perspectives were and also to be able to apply them. Where candidates did attempt this question, many answers consisted of a page or so of notes containing semi-remembered definitions of the two terms. The fact that some candidates entered into definitions of consequentialism by detailing 'egoism' and 'utilitarianism' demonstrated that the question was either misunderstood or that those candidates were unprepared for this question. Well-prepared candidates should not only be aware of the ethical theories but also to use them and apply them.

Marking scheme

			Marks
(a)	For purposes of corporate codes of ethics – 1 mark for each relevant point made	max 3	
	For contents – 1 mark for application of each to case	max 6	
			9
(b)	1.5 marks for relevant point made and explained	max	7
(c)	For deontological assessment, 1 mark for each relevant point made	max 5	
	For teleological assessment, 1 mark for each relevant point made	max 5	
		max	9
			25

(a) **Purposes of code of ethics**

Establishment of organisation's values

Ethical codes form part of the organisation's underlying environment. They develop and promote values that are linked to the organisation's mission statement.

Promotion of stakeholder responsibilities

Codes also demonstrate whom the organisation regards as **important stakeholders**. They show what action should be taken to maintain good **stakeholder relationships** (such as keeping them fully informed).

Control of individuals' behaviour

By **promoting or prohibiting certain actions**, ethical codes form part of the human resources mechanisms by which employee behaviour is controlled. Ethical codes can be referred to when employee actions are questioned.

Contents of ethical codes

Broad principles

Codes generally open with a wide statement stressing that it is company policy to conduct all of its business on ethical principles and it expects its employees to do likewise.

Role of employees

Codes normally stress the **core role of employees** in the organisation, often stating that they are the organisation's most important component. Because of this, the **duties of employees** to **follow the organisation's ethical ideals** are stressed in codes. Codes will also set out the concepts such as trust, respect, honesty and equality to which employees are expected to commit.

Relations with other stakeholders

Relations with customers and suppliers are often highlighted, since they are primary stakeholders with whom many employees deal. Codes stress the need for dealing with **customers courteously and politely** and **responding promptly** to their **needs**. They define relations with suppliers as being based on **mutual respect and truthfulness**, and stress various aspects of fair dealing including paying suppliers on time and in accordance with agreed terms of trade.

Legal and regulatory standards

Codes normally stress that it is company policy to **comply with industry legal and regulatory standards** and that employees are expected to do so. This emphasises that compliance should be regarded as **conventional behaviour.**

Fair business practices

Codes often develop wider ethical standards by stressing that the company aims to act as a good **corporate citizen in the markets** in which it operates. This is often defined as meaning being committed to open markets, promoting responsible competitive behaviour and prohibiting actions that undermine fair markets such as seeking or participating in questionable payments or favours.

Corporate social responsibility

Ethical codes often include statements that **define the basis** of the **organisation's corporate social responsibility commitment.** This may include commitments to **promoting sustainable development** and **preventing waste of natural resources.**

(b) **Ethical company**

Having a strong code of ethics, communicated throughout the business, to which employees are expected to adhere means that external stakeholders should be sure that they are dealing with people who **do business fairly**. Part of HPC's appeal to European customers seems to be that its strong code means that it has an outstanding ethical reputation and that it is a trustworthy business partner.

Social responsibility

Taking a **strong stance on responsibility and ethics** can enhance appeal to consumers in the same way as producing the right products of good quality can. Here HPC's chief executive believes that HPC has gained orders from European customers because it does not use child labour, orders which its local competitors cannot obtain as they do employ children.

Response to customers

As codes of ethics emphasise the importance of responding to customer requirements, drafting parts of the code to comply with customer wishes demonstrates that businesses are **responsive to customers.** Again HPC is obtaining orders from European customers on the basis of being able to give them guarantees that HPC is complying with their wishes

Avoidance of sweatshop labour

Central to many codes is the guarantee that labour will be treated fairly, and prohibiting sweatshop conditions shows that labour is valued. HPC can link this with its positioning on **product quality**, emphasising that employees are treated well and as a result produce high quality products.

Position of market leadership

As well as making specific commitments in its code, the strength of a code of ethics may be determined by where the business **wishes to position itself** overall in its market. Here HPC seems to wish to be the **market leader** locally, and as such has a stronger code of ethics than any of its competitors.

(c)   **Deontological viewpoint**

The deontological (Kant) viewpoint would stress that a decision such as whether to employ child labour was **absolutely right or absolutely wrong**, depending upon the ethical principle(s) that was relevant. This would mean that if it is **wrong in some circumstances**, then it is **always wrong**, even if in some situations there may be some arguably favourable consequences.

Child labour

Mr Hogg's viewpoint is that employment of child labour is ethically wrong by itself. This is partly based on the grounds that it exploits children as they **lack the ability to give informed consent to the terms** under which they are employed. They also do not have the physical and mental resources to cope with employment, and are traditionally paid much less than adult workers doing the same jobs.

Interruption of education

Mr Hogg has identified a further ethical principle, that a child's best hope in life is to receive a **proper education.** Child labour employment is therefore wrong since it denies children the chance to receive that education.

Contrary to code of ethics

In addition HPC has been able to **establish trading relations with European customers** on the basis of an ethical code prohibiting child labour. Deciding subsequently to use child labour could be seen as wrong, since HPC would not be honouring a commitment that underpins the trading relationship.

Capitalist viewpoint

However if the pure capitalist view is taken as to what is absolutely right, then HPC has a duty to its shareholders to **maximise profits**. Taking actions for reasons other than profit maximisation is morally wrong. Here as employment of child labour is legal, then if it ensures profits are maximised by minimising labour costs, then it is the right decision to take.

Teleological viewpoint

The teleological viewpoints stresses that the **consequences** of actions should be considered when an ethical decision is made. The correct ethical decision may vary according to the **situation.**   The complication is to decide which consequences are most important, and the significance of the various parties affected by the ethical decision.

Capitalist viewpoint

A consequentalist version of the capitalist viewpoint would be that pursuit of profit maximisation by all companies **generates the maximum amount of economic wealth**. The economic wealth can be distributed so that everyone benefits.

Wages

Mr Tanner raised the issue of HPC providing opportunities for children to **earn income** to support their families. The important consequences are thus that HPC is providing the opportunity for families to **increase their standard of living.**

Better working conditions

Mr Tanner also has highlighted the issue that HPC provides **better working conditions** than any of its competitors. If therefore children will work for HPC's competitors if HPC will not employ them, then the argument is that it is better for HPC to employ them as they will be treated better there than anywhere else.

Interference with education

Use of the teleological view may mean acknowledging that employment of child labour could have adverse consequences for the children's education. However it could be argued that these are **outweighed by the economic benefits** to children and their families, or that HPC can take steps to ensure **damage to education is minimised** by providing teaching and training itself.

51 Policy speech

Text references. Chapters 10 and 11.

Top tips. The definition in (a) is adapted from the IFAC definition.

(b) (i) is mostly a test of knowledge. However the question does invite you to use material from the scenario and it's best to avoid here making any reference to Mr Mordue's speech, since you'll be covering that part of the scenario in (ii). In (ii) we have also based our answer round the structure of the five threats. However the examiner's comments confirm that it would have been equally acceptable to structure your answer round the content of Mr Mordue's speech and then bring into your discussion the threats.

You may have found the requirement in (c) difficult to understand. What the examiner seems to want is an assessment of the remarks from the perspective of a deep ecologist.

Easy marks. You should have scored 5 out of 5 for the straightforward descriptions required in (b) (i).

Examiner's comments. The five general ethical threats asked for in (b) (i) were, where attempted, usually correct. Bullet lists of the threats were not well rewarded because they didn't respond to the verb 'describe'.

There was a wide range of responses to (b) (ii) in which candidates had to 'assess' the ethical threats implied by Mr Mordue's beliefs. Some candidates answered it by relisting the general threats and considering how Mr Mordue's beliefs might represent each threat. Others worked through Mr Mordue's beliefs and showed how each one was an ethical threat. Both approaches were rewarded by markers as long as they showed evidence of understanding of how some of Mr Mordue's beliefs were ethically wrong.

(c) on the deep green perspective was done poorly overall. Many candidates were able to say something about the deep green perspective but very few could show how Mr Nahum's remarks were deep green in nature. I would encourage candidates and their tutors to practice applying theories to cases as this tends to be how theory is tested.

				Marks
(a)		Definition/evidence of understanding of public interest	2	
		Explanation/application to accounting	3	
				5
(b)	(i)	1 mark for each type of ethical threat described (½ for identification only)	max	5
	(ii)	2 marks for assessment of each ethical threat in the case highlighted by Mr Mordue		8
(c)		Up to 2 marks for each area of agreement identified and assessed	max	7
				25

(a) **Definition**

The **public interest** is the **collective wellbeing** of the community of people and institutions that the professional accountant serves, including the business and financial community and others who rely on the work of professional accountants.

Trust

Trust is a key issue in terms of the public interest as it relates to accountants. The working of capital markets depends upon **reliable financial information,** as does business decision-making affecting jobs and supply. The public has to be able to believe that accountants' opinions are given on a basis of sufficient work and that they are **unaffected by external pressures**.

Audit and assurance

Mrs Ytrria is arguing that accountants who provide audit or assurance services must be able to demonstrate clearly their **detachment from the client**. They cannot do this if they are providing other services to the client.

(b) (i) **Self-interest**

Self-interest means the accountants' own interests being affected by the **success of the client,** or the **continuation of the accountant-client relationship.** An example would be a financial interest in a client.

Self-review

Self-review means the accountants auditing or reviewing work that they **themselves have prepared.** This could include auditing work that has been prepared as part of a non-audit service, something that prompts the suggestion that firms should not provide more than one service to a client.

Advocacy

Advocacy means **strongly promoting the interests of the accountants' clients** and undermining the accountants' objectivity. Accountants can be seen as acting in the client's, rather than the public, interest.

Familiarity

Familiarity means dealing with a client's affairs for a long time and developing a close relationship. This can lead to **reliance on previous knowledge** rather than a questioning approach to information supplied.

Intimidation

Intimidation means conduct of the assignment or conduct towards the client being **influenced by pressure exerted by the client.**

(ii)   **Self-interest**

Mr Mordue's comment about a firm providing multiple services highlights one threat to self-interest. If a firm providing audit and other services disagrees with the client over the accounts that it is auditing, it faces the risk of **not just losing the income from the audit**, but perhaps also the **much greater income from providing other services**. Mr Mordue's comments highlight how well financially firms can do out of providing multiple services.

Self-review

If the accountants provide other services that materially affect the content of the accounts, then they will have to **audit figures that they themselves have prepared**, for example valuations.

Advocacy

Mr Mordue mentioned providing **legal advice**. There are two problems. Firstly providing that advice could be seen as promoting the client's interests rather than the public interest. Secondly the accounts may need to contain **provision for, or disclosure about, legal actions.** This will depend on the likelihood of the success of legal action, which could in turn depend on the advice Mr Mordue had given. Therefore there is a clear possibility of the accountant not wishing to undermine the advice he has given by taking a prudent view of the issues' treatment in the accounts.

Familiarity

Mr Mordue **highlights his friendships** with his clients. Although he would claim that this made it more likely that clients would listen to his advice, critics could suggest the friendships meant that he placed **excessive trust** in what he was told, and would be **unwilling to raise awkward issues** that could jeopardise the friendships. The **provision of other services** may mean that accountants are less rigorous in auditing information with which their firm has been involved.

Intimidation

Mr Mordue comments that he got to know his clients very well and presumably they got to know him very well. This could mean that if they wished to **intimidate him** into giving advice that they wanted to hear, they would have a good idea of how to do so, by for example threatening to replace his firm as auditors.

(c)   **Economic priorities**

Mr Nahum is arguing that if accountants serve the **economic interests of clients**, then their priorities are fundamentally flawed. The deep ecologist perspective argues that giving the economic objectives of capitalists any priority over social and environmental degradation is immoral.

Environmental degradation

Mr Nahum's highlighting of environmental degradation links to the deep ecologist view that business must **not threaten the habitats of other species** or worsen the living conditions of humans affected by their activities.

Animal rights

The emphasis on the need for accountants to **address animal rights** is an important distinction between the deep ecologist and other positions, as it places animal rights on an equal plane with humans.

Poverty

The stress on making the relief of poverty and other social injustices a priority links in with the deep ecologist view that all humans, **living and yet-to-be-born,** are stakeholders in business. Businesses need to **recognise the needs of all stakeholders** rather than subjugating their requirements to the current economic interests of shareholders.

52 John Wang

Marking scheme

			Marks
(a)	Explanation and meaning	2	
	1 mark for each explanation of importance max	3	
			5
(b)	1 mar for each criticism identified in the context of the case. 1 mark for the development of the criticism with reference to practise or application		
	max		10
(c)	1 mark for recognition of each option max	2	
	2 marks for each relevant argument for or against either alternative		
	max	8	
			10
			25

(a) **Integrity**

The Cadbury report defines integrity as meaning **straightforward dealing** and **completeness**. IFAC's fundamental principles define integrity as being **straightforward and honest** in all business and professional relationships. Integrity means resisting any pressure to act unethically.

Importance in professional relationships

Reliability

Integrity should mean that colleagues should be able to **rely on a professional's word** and be sure that his **intentions are ethical.**

Promotion of control environment

As a partner, and hence being someone who is in charge of management, at Miller Dundas, Potto should be particularly concerned to promote integrity. Not only is his own integrity more important because of his position of power, but also he should set an example to other staff in order to **promote an ethical environment** at the firm on which clients and others can rely.

Efficiency and effectiveness

Integrity means that time does not have to spend checking the statements of a professional colleague against other evidence. Instead it should mean that other partners or staff who are unsure of an issue should feel they can obtain unbiased advice from Potto.

(b) **Agreeing to corruption**

It appears that Potto could be implicated in a **misappropriation of company funds** for Martin Mbabo's personal use. He has either agreed to this or accepted a weak explanation, raising issues about his **integrity or professional competence**.

Duty to shareholders

Potto seems to have allowed his relationship with Martin to override his duty to the rest of the shareholders. Potto is reporting to the shareholders to give them assurance of Martin's **stewardship** of the company and that he has acted reliably as their agent. He should therefore have taken an **objective** view of Martin's conduct and he has failed to do this.

Duty to tax authorities

As well as a duty to shareholders, Potto has a **duty to stakeholders** who have a legal or other right to rely on the reliability and completeness of information in the accounts. This particularly applies to the tax authorities in any regime, and in many regimes Potto could be charged with **colluding in tax evasion.**

Duty to professional colleagues

Potto has let down his partners and staff in a number of ways. Lisa's query was justified and Potto's initial response would have given the impression that he was **not taking the query seriously**. Potto then accepted what appeared to be an inadequate explanation, and **did not provide any reason** for his decision. Not only was this **poor conduct of professional relationships**, it was also a partner setting a **poor example** to a student.

Failure to fulfil accounting and auditing standards

Potto has breached auditing standards by allowing an **unqualified report** to be issued on accounts with a breach of accounting standards. IAS 24 requires all related party transactions to be disclosed regardless of value.

(c)   **The alternatives are:**

(i)   **Take no further action**

John could decide not to raise the issue with Potto. Possible arguments in favour of this are as follows:

Respect for Potto's judgement

Although Potto has failed to explain himself well, that may not mean that his decision was wrong. As a senior partner, Potto has **experience and knowledge of the client** that Lisa and John lack.

Destruction of working relationships

A confrontation with Potto without sufficient evidence is likely to destroy not only Potto and John's friendship, but also mean they **cannot work together in future**. It undermines the basis of trust that underpins the partnership in which they and others participate. Because of Potto's seniority, a dispute would also damage John's position in the firm. However if John allows these considerations to be the main influence in his decision, he clearly would appear to **lack objectivity** and have yielded to the threat of **intimidation**.

(ii)   **Confront Potto**

John's other alternative is to confront Potto and **demand an adequate explanation**. If Potto does not provide one, John would have to raise the matter with the other partners. Arguments in favour of this include:

Complicity in Potto's actions

The strength of the evidence suggests that at least John should seek an explanation from Potto, even if he accepts it in the end. At present it seems that if John takes no further action, then he, like Potto, is **complicit** in possible fraud, tax evasion and breaches of accounting, auditing and ethical standards.

Duty to other partners

If the transaction is found to be wrong, then sanctions may be taken not only against Martin and Mbabo Co, but also against Potto and Miller Dundas for failing to report the transaction and incorrectly giving a clean audit report. The firm may suffer **financial penalties** and a **loss of reputation** that would affect all partners. John therefore has a **duty to other partners** to deal with a potentially serious problem as soon as possible.

Duty to Lisa

As a training partner, John has a duty to Lisa to take her concerns seriously and make sure that they are **adequately addressed**. This is particularly important here as Potto has already set such a poor example. If John takes no action, Lisa may take the issue further herself, reporting her concerns to other partners or external authorities. John's position in the partnership and reputation may be damaged if he is found to have failed to investigate Lisa's concerns adequately.

Conclusion

John has a clear duty to seek an **adequate explanation** from Potto and take the matter further if Potto does not provide one.

53 Happy and healthy

Text references. Chapters 2 and 10.

Top tips. It's not easy to tell the split of marks between the two requirements in (a) (2:8) and you may well have spent too long differentiating a family business and public company. The points in the rest of (a) are fairly well sign-posted in the scenario (non profit maximisation, Ivan taking over, likely conflict).

In (b) 2 marks seems a miserly allocation for quite a challenging definition. Note the stress on what the accountant is expected to possess and the belief that the accountant will act in the public interest. A brief mention of relevant scenario detail will improve your answer to (b), though not all of the basic principles are relevant to the situation.

The recommendation in (c) confirms what Mr Shreeves appears to have already decided (he seems to know he has to recommend disclosures in the financial statements). This is perhaps the clearest issue you need to discuss. The other issues discussed are complications – split loyalties and an (arguably) ethical desire not to cause hurt. The discussion required in (b) should also have suggested that professionalism and the public interest needed to be brought into the discussion.

Note that speaking to Ivan before speaking to his parents could be construed as tipping off under money laundering legislation.

Easy marks. If you didn't know the fundamental principles of professionalism in (b) you need to learn them.

Examiner's comments. (a) was, in particular, about governance. It drew on content that should have been familiar to candidates that had carefully studied the study texts and many candidates were able to gain some marks for this distinction.

The first task in (b) was seemingly more challenging than the second. Most well-prepared candidates were able to do the second task. Fewer were able to explain the position of professionals in society and the importance of the public interest to a professional like Mr Shreeves.

(c) was done poorly overall. It required candidates to bring their ethical reasoning skills to bear on a problem. There were a number of professional and ethical issues that were relevant to the decision and it was a discussion of these that was required. More detailed preparation for ethical reasoning tasks would have benefited candidates and this should represent a challenge to tutors and future P1 candidates.

Marking scheme

			Marks
(a)	1 mark for each relevant point distinguishing between a family and listed business	max	2
	2 marks for each relevant point of explanation identified and discussed	max	8
			10
(b)	1 mark per relevant point explained on accountants as professionals	max	2
	1 mark for each relevant fundamental principle of Professionalism	max	5
			7
(c)	2 marks for each relevant issue identified and discussed	max	6
	1 mark for each relevant point made of the 'advise' point	max	2
			8
			25

(a) **Differences from public company**

Shareholder base

The majority of shares in a family company are held by a **small number of members of the family.** The shares in a public company are available to buy and sell on the stock market. As a result the shareholder base is likely to be much more widely dispersed, although in practice institutional shareholders could hold a significant proportion of shares.

Management

The family shareholders are likely to be **actively involved** in running the **company.** In a public listed company, there is a **split between management and ownership**. Most or all of the shares will be held by shareholders who take no part in the management of the company and instead they employ executive directors on service contracts to run the company on their behalf.

Governance issues

Agency

Because the shareholders are also managers, **agency costs** should be **reduced** as outsider shareholders do not need to check on managers whose interests may be different. However agency issues are not entirely absent if a manager-director operates **without adequate supervision** from the others, as here. The greater informality may allow a director to pursue his own interests without this being identified by the other directors, as has happened with Ivan.

Emphasis on financial performance

Manager/shareholders may be more flexible about when profits are earned. As with the Potters, they may seek to **satisfice** (ensure the company makes a certain level of profits) rather than **maximise profits**, which outsider shareholders would demand. Manager/shareholders may choose to **pursue other objectives instead.** Here the Potter family prefer to run the company to provide employment for themselves and a good service for their customers.

Succession planning

There are **unlikely to be formal mechanisms** for recruiting directors from outside to carry on the business. If the business is to continue, new family members have to take over from those who are retiring. This can **simplify long-term succession planning**, if new members are willing to assume responsibility. Ken and Steffi clearly hope that this is happening, with Ivan gradually being given greater responsibilities until he takes the business over. However Ivan appears to have other plans, throwing the company's future into doubt.

Mechanisms for resolving conflict

Family unity may be required for the company to continue to operate. There may be **no formal mechanisms for resolving conflicts** on the board. If the directors clash, the company may be deadlocked. Here it seems that a dispute over Ivan's conduct is probable, and it is difficult to see how a split with his parents would be resolved. Although his parents may be able to vote Ivan off the board as they hold a majority of shares, Ivan's holding of 40% is likely to give him a veto over several important issues affecting the company.

(b) **Why Mr Shreeves is regarded as a professional**

Mr Shreeves is regarded as a professional because he is making judgements, the value of which depends upon the **education, practical experience and professional and ethical qualities** that he holds himself out to have by virtue of calling himself an accountant and belonging to an accountancy institute. Society also expects these judgements to be exercised in the **public interest,** and the interests of his clients.

Professional competence and due care

Professionals have a duty to maintain **professional knowledge and skill** at a level required to ensure that they provide competent professional service **based on current developments in practice, legislation and techniques.** Professionals should **act diligently** and in **accordance with applicable technical and professional standards**, including **relevant ethical standards.**

Integrity

The public expects professionals to be **straightforward** and **honest** in all business and professional relationships. This means when they identify dishonest conduct such as Ivan's, they would not be expected to keep quiet and allow it to continue, but to deal with the problem.

Professional behaviour

Society expects professionals to **comply with relevant laws and regulations** and avoid any action that discredits their profession.

Confidentiality

Society expects professionals to **respect the confidentiality of information** acquired as a result of professional and business relationships and **not disclose any such information** to third parties without proper or specific authority or unless there is a **legal or professional right or duty to disclose**.

Objectivity

Professionals are expected not to allow **bias**, **conflicts of interest** or **undue influence** of others to override professional or business judgements. They are expected not to let **personal friendship** lead them away from the best course of action, which may be a problem with the Potter family.

(c) **Nature of problem**

Mr Shreeves appears to have **sufficient evidence** to establish that Ivan has been defrauding Happy and healthy. To seek explanations from Ivan may make Mr Shreeves liable under local money laundering regulations for **tipping off.** Mr Shreeves has therefore to decide whether to tell Ken and Steffi.

Public interest and interests of shareholders

One potential problem that can be identified is that Mr Shreeves **cannot act in the interests of the shareholders as a whole.** Ivan's interests clearly differ from his parents. Bringing the issue to light could also threaten the company's future. However considerations of **professionalism** and the **public interest** make Mr Shreeves' duty clearer. He is expected to act with **integrity,** and therefore act in accordance with the interests of the injured shareholders. Here the nature of the injury and conduct are clear. Ivan seems clearly to have committed a **fraud** and there is a clear **breach of trust** between him and his parents.

Professional competence

As well as being potentially fraudulent, the transactions with Barong are related party transactions which are **disclosable under accounting standards and possibly law.** Mr Shreeves does appear to understand that these rules mean he has to recommend disclosures.

Personal conflicts

The nature of Mr Shreeves' friendship complicates his decision. Even if Mr Shreeves wishes to do what is right professionally, he wants to **avoid causing hurt** to Ken and Steffi. They may decide not to pursue Ivan for the losses to Happy and healthy, but their relationship with their son may be destroyed.

Recommendation

Mr Shreeves must disclose what has happened to Ken and Steffi. He will be acting with **integrity** by disclosing the fraud. He will also demonstrate he is acting with **objectivity** by making the disclosure, since if the directors were not related and he was not a close friend, he would wish to disclose to the directors not involved in the fraud what had happened.

54 JGP

Marking scheme

			Marks
(a)	Explanation of sustainability	4	
	Criticism of the FD's understanding	2	
			6
(b)	3 marks for each of the 3 stages of the audit (1 mark for explanation of the stage, 2 marks for exploration)		9
(c)	Definition of environmental risk	2	
	Distinction between strategic and operational risks	4	
	2 marks for explanation of each reason why environmental risks are strategic at JGP — max	4	
			10
			25

(a)   **Sustainability**

Sustainability is ensuring that economic activities and development **meet the needs of the present without compromising the ability of future generations to meet their own needs**.

For businesses, sustainability means that the businesses' inputs and outputs should have **no irredeemable effects** on the environment. It involves developing strategies so that the organisation only uses resources (inputs) at a rate that allows them to be **replenished**, in order to ensure that they will continue to be available. Emissions of waste should be confined to **levels that do not exceed the capacity of the environment** to absorb them. It also involves recycling to **reduce the impact of product manufacturing** on natural resources. Sustainability can be assessed by measures such as triple bottom line reporting, **measuring financial, social and environmental performance**.

Finance Director's views

The Finance Director limits the definition of sustainability to **financial sustainability**, that based on past performance and current financial position, JGP should continue to go on making profits and operate as a going concern. The first problem with this view that it assumes that JGP will continue to be able to, or be allowed to, **pursue its strategies and operate in the way that it has done in the past.** Difficulties with resources (certain chemicals no longer being allowed or shortage of local labour) may mean that JGP has to make fundamental changes to its strategies or operations. In addition, in the context of environmental auditing, sustainability refers to whether JGP's environmental footprint is acceptable and sustainable, and that is the main issue here.

(b)   **Audit planning**

Audit planning involves deciding on the **areas (metrics) that the audit will cover and the measures that will be used**. The decision is more difficult because there are **no mandatory audit standards and no compulsory auditable activities** in an environmental audit. The scope of the audit will be influenced by the need to **produce sufficient evidence to satisfy key stakeholders**. This will determine the **targets** auditors consider when assessing performance and what and how much evidence is obtained, which in turn impacts upon the **length and cost of the audit**. A decision that has to be made at the planning stage is whether to extend the audit to **JGP's supply chain**. Not only will there be logistical audit issues in obtaining supplier co-operation and arranging the timetable with suppliers, the audit process may have serious impacts upon relations with suppliers that JGP's board may wish to consider.

Testing and measuring

The second stage of the audit is **measuring performance against the metrics established** at the planning stage of the audit. In order to increase the credibility of the audit, auditors are likely to focus on measuring **quantitatively** against targets where possible, for example in areas such as resource usage, waste disposal or emissions. However other areas of concern, for example how the business is perceived by key stakeholders, will **not be easy to measure quantitatively.**

Reporting

The last issue is deciding how the results of the audit should be reported. This means considering not only the **contents**, but also **to whom** the report should be circulated. Given the board wishes to make as much information as possible available to the public, it seems likely that the audit report will be included in the company's annual report, its primary document for communicating with stakeholders. The board will need to consider how the audit report will be included within the full environmental report that JGP makes. This report is likely to include a **high level of detail** to satisfy all significant stakeholders, but the board may need to take into account the **differences in information requirements of investors and other local community stakeholders**.

(c) **Environmental risk**

Environmental risk is the risk of loss to the business arising out of the **impacts of the natural environment upon it, or the impact of its operations upon the natural environment**. It includes the **effects of natural phenomena** such adverse weather or resource shortage. It also includes the risk of **fines** for polluting the environment, and also the risk of **incurring costs and using resources** to clean up the effects of operations or to dispose of waste. Environmental risk can also refer to the **consequences of bad publicity**, including loss of support from the community, boycotts of its products and employees leaving the company.

Strategic and operational risks

Strategic risks

Strategic risks derive from the **decisions the directors take** about the **organisation's objectives** and are the risks of **failing to achieve those objectives**. They link in with how the organisation is **positioned in relation to the sector in which it operates.** Many strategic risks are long-term and cannot be avoided if the business is to trade. They have **high hazards and high returns**.

Strategic risks include **longer-term risks** deriving from decisions the board takes about what **products or services** to supply, including the risks connected with developing and marketing those products. They also include risks connected with key sources of finance. **Reputation risk** can also be an important strategic risk, as here.

Operational risks

Operational risks are risks connected with the **internal resources, systems, processes and employees** of the organisation. They relate to the problems that can occur in the organisation's day-to-day business activities, such as human error or information technology failure.

Operational managers and employees will have responsibility for **managing operational risks**, whereas **management of strategic risks** will be the responsibility of the **board and senior management**, since they are taking the strategic decisions on which strategic risks depend.

Why environmental risks are strategic

Impact on primary stakeholders

Environmental risk is strategic because it affects the ways JGP is **viewed by its primary stakeholders**, those without whose support JGP will have difficulty continuing. These include here **the local community** because it supplies the key resource of labour. Withdrawal of community support could mean the loss of key staff and problems filling vacancies. The other significant primary stakeholders are **investors.** Loss of their support may result in them selling their shares and affecting JGP's market price. They may also seek to engineer changes in objectives by, if necessary, forcing changes in JGP's board.

Industry characteristics

Professor Appo's comments highlight environmental risks as structural risks that **underlie** the **entire chemical industry**. The methods of chemical processing used mean that the consequences of risks materialising are much higher than for other industries, leading in turn to **serious financial and reputational consequences.** Professor Appo emphasises also that JGP's and its suppliers' **usage of resources** may have serious environmental implications. JGP's strategies may be affected by the need to change the resources it uses, a shortage of resources or significantly greater resource costs.

55 Ann Koo

Marking scheme

				Marks
(a)	0.5 marks for identification, 1 mark for each threat identified and briefly described		5	
	2 marks for each relevant threat discussed	max	4	
				9
(b)	2 marks for each criticism identified and developed	max	8	
	2 marks for understanding of public interest		2	
				10
(c)	3 marks for evidence of understanding of insider dealing/trading		3	
	3 marks for explanation of why it is unethical		3	
				6
				25

(a) **Conflicts of interest**

Self interest

Self-interest occurs when accountants' decisions are **influenced by their own interests**, or those of close family members.

Self review

Self-review is when decisions and judgements are **reviewed by the same accountant** who made them or who prepared the data supporting them.

Advocacy

Advocacy is when accountants promotes a position or opinion **to so great an extent** that their **objectivity appears to be compromised.**

Familiarity

Familiarity is when a **close or long-standing friendship undermines the objectivity** of an accountant's judgements.

Intimidation

Intimidation is an accountant being **deterred from acting objectively** by actual or perceived threats.

Application to case

Self-interest

Ann has clearly acted in her own self-interest, by letting her decision to choose the supplier be **influenced by her family's financial needs.** It has meant that she has **failed to show objectivity** when taking the decision and not acted with **integrity.**

Advocacy

Ann's objectivity may also be impaired by **having to justify her decision** and defend the behaviour of the supplier if the supplier does not perform adequately. She may continue to defend the supplier's interests even though it is best for her company to take action against the supplier.

Intimidation

Ann may also face a threat of **intimidation**. The supplier, or someone else who gains knowledge of the bribe, may attempt to blackmail Ann by threatening to reveal that she took a bribe. This could mean that further decisions she makes are influenced by the threat of her conduct being revealed. She may be pressurised into awarding further contracts to the supplier, even though this is not in the best interests of her company.

(b) **Criticisms of Ann's beliefs and behaviour**

Illegality

The first criticism is that Ann has **deliberately acted illegally** in taking a bribe. Accountants have a duty to obey the law, even if it conflicts with their own interests. What makes Ann's behaviour more serious is that many governments have recently tried to promote the interests of society by strengthening anti-bribery laws, sending a clear signal that bribery should not be tolerated by society,

Fairness

Ann has not acted fairly in deciding between the competing contractors on the basis of her **personal interest** rather than the **objective criteria** of the value that they offer. Tucker's model, for example, highlights fairness as a key consideration when making an ethical decision.

Best interests of shareholders

Ann has not acted in the interests of her employers and the shareholders whose interests she is expected to promote. Their interests require that Ann should have ensured that all bidding suppliers had an **equal chance to win the contract.** Fair competition between suppliers would have offered Ann's employers the best chance of achieving value for money.

Low level of morality

By putting her desire to achieve a higher personal return first, Ann has acted on a **lower level of morality** than is expected by society. Kohlberg's framework puts making ethical decisions on the basis of personal benefit on a lower level than making them in accordance with the expectations of her professional peers (as expressed in her professional body's ethical code) or the expectations of society (as expressed in its laws). The rules laid down by government and professional bodies distinguish between legitimate pursuit of the career opportunities available and the earning of undeserved rewards through corrupt practice. The use made of the illicit rewards is not relevant.

Public interest

Ann has taken on **responsibilities as a company director and an accountant** which mean that others **rely** on the work that she does. In accepting these roles, Ann thus has a **duty to promote the common well-being, and not put her own interests first if they conflict with the interests of society**. This applies whatever the pressures are to pursue her personal interests.

(c) **Insider trading**

Insider dealing is **using inside information** as a basis for deciding to buy or sell shares in the stock market. Inside information is information that is specific and precise, has not yet been made public, and, if made public, is likely to have a significant effect on the share price. It is **price-sensitive information**. Directors will often know whether a company's current share price is over or under valued through knowing information that has not been released to investors. They will be guilty of insider trading if they deal in shares before they release the information publicly.

Why insider trading is unethical and illegal

Distortion of trading

Insider trading means that the market for trading shares may be seen as **unfair** and distorted in favour of those who have inside information. If investors are aware that insider dealing is happening, they may be less inclined to participate. Their lack of access to inside information means that the increased risks they face are not worth the returns they believe they can earn.

Agency

Insider dealing represents an **abuse of the directors' position as agents**. Directors are misusing knowledge, which they have gained as a result of accepting responsibilities as directors, to enrich themselves.

Conflict of interest

If directors believe that they can use information for their own benefit, this may mean that they make decisions in accordance with their own interests rather than the **interests of the shareholders which they should be promoting.** This may mean, for example, that they choose options that will guarantee them short-term gains rather than options that are likely to provide the best long-term value for shareholders. For example, directors may recommend that shareholders accept a takeover bid because they have previously bought shares in the company in the knowledge that the takeover bid would be made, and would make significant gains if the bid went ahead and the share price rose.

56 VCF

Text references. Chapters 1, 3, 4, 7 and 9.

Top tips. In (a) it is difficult to get away from the fact that the company is overwhelmingly dependent on Viktor but you have to try to make maximum use of the information in the scenario. The question is quite a test of your ability to assess a number of different types of control.

Your assessment has to be clearly grounded in the details in the scenario. So following the process of scenario analysis that we describe in the front pages is very important.

In (b) remember that this report is addressed to the board, in particular of course Viktor. Therefore to score well you need to explain your recommendations in terms that make it likely that the board will accept them. However the company is listed, and therefore needs to introduce more formal systems and not be so dominated by a single individual. There are some fairly obvious indications of poor corporate governance. The risk part can (as often) be tackled by following through the main aspects of the risk management cycle. The discussion on controls does link with (a) although there is not a one-to-one matching. This is because as well as suggesting improvements to existing controls, you also need to recommend new controls.

The professional marks would be available for putting your report in the right format and the persuasiveness of your answer; would Viktor act on it?

(a)   **Introduction**

The main features of the controls are much dependence on one person, and limitations in management accounting and human resource systems.

Dependence on Viktor

The main control and also the main weakness of the system is its **dependence** on **Viktor's knowledge and experience**. The biggest danger the company faces is that something happens to Viktor, perhaps as a result of the personal risks he takes, and the other directors and the company are left to cope without him.

Role of board

The board appears to play little if any role in **actively supervising** the company's activities. Viktor's reports appear to be unquestioned, and the rest of the board appears to have little involvement in decision-taking.

Sensitivity analysis

The **analysis undertaken** by Viktor to **manage cash flow** does **not appear to be linked** in with any **budget** and **management accounts** being produced. In addition VCF seems very dependent on this **analysis** being **reasonable**, particularly as costs are tight.

Pricing

The pricing system seems based on **customers' willingness to accept high prices**. If there is a risk of economic recession, customers may not be prepared to pay these prices and VCF will be forced to adopt **more sophisticated pricing methods**.

Balanced scorecard

Viktor is making some attempt to use a balanced scorecard to assess performance. A model scorecard focuses on four perspectives:

(i)   **Customer satisfaction** is being addressed, but it is difficult to see how it is being measured

(ii)   **Internal processes**; as suppliers are responsible for delivery of outsource service, VCF's processes are concerned with **how relations with suppliers are managed**. This issue does not appear to be considered very much, and may leave VCF vulnerable to problems with suppliers

(iii) **Innovation and learning**; VCF invests heavily in research and development but how the performance of research and development is assessed is unclear, apart from the vague measure of **maintaining technological leadership**

(iv)   **Financial**. Financial measures are a **major element in performance assessment**, but the weakness is that shareholders and the stock market may be more concerned with profit measures than Viktor is

Assessment of managers

Manager assessment appears to depend on Viktor's personal involvement; there seems to be no formal system of **appraising managers**. This is more of a problem as the achievement of **many of the responsibilities of management** cannot be measured in monetary terms; other than **Viktor's knowledge of competitors**, it is difficult to see how standards of **after-sales service** and **customer satisfaction** are being measured. In addition **cost control** does not appear to be a major element in the assessment of managers' performance.

Human resources

Identifying and dismissing staff who are 'not committed to the company's objectives' may be problematic unless carried out **formally**, and could result in **unfair dismissal claims** and **dissatisfaction** amongst staff who remain. VCF appears to rely on the assumption that staff will be happy as they are being paid well, which may not be correct.

Research and development controls

The fact that **research and development** is **not linked into any product** but is expensed suggests the link with specific product development lacks clarity and the benefits of R&D activity are uncertain. Some uncertainties are inevitable given the nature of the industry; however there seems to be risks that **activity is wasted** on projects that provide **no benefits**, that projects **fail to deliver the planned benefits and costs** are not adequately controlled.

Patent protection

The main control is the institution of legal proceedings but this may be a more effective control for limiting losses than **avoiding the risks of competitors** using VCF's technology in the first place. There do not appear to be any restrictions placed on **staff moving to competitors** and taking knowledge with them that competitors can use; the chances of this happening may be enhanced by Viktor's dismissal of unhappy staff.

(b) **Report**

To: Board, VCF
From: Consultant
Date: 1 August 20X5
Subject: Improvements in governance, risk management and internal controls

Introduction

This report offers recommendations for a number of ways in which systems can be improved, to enhance the efficiency of operations, manage risks more effectively and fulfil investor and stock market operations.

(i) **Corporate governance**

VCF fails to fulfil several aspects of **corporate governance best practice**. These should not just be seen as box-ticking requirements, but as contributing to the **well-running** of the company and its appeal to shareholders. The failure to follow requirements may mean that VCF is seen as riskier than it need be, and hence less appealing to investors, resulting in a lower share price.

Board

The board does not appear to be meeting often enough to be exercising effective supervision over the company. The governance reports recommend that in order to operate well, the board should **meet regularly (more than once a quarter)** and that the board's constitution should specify that certain major business decisions such as significant investments must be formally taken by the whole board.

Lack of division of responsibilities

Currently the board's operation is completely dependent on Viktor, and serious problems may occur if he is unable to **fulfil his responsibilities**. Viktor acting as **chairman and chief executive** does not fulfil the requirements that there is a clear division of responsibilities at the head of the company, with different directors acting as chairman and chief executive.

Non-executive directors

Although two out of four directors are non-executives, the connections both have with the company means that they cannot be classified as independent. Governance guidelines state that a majority of non-executive directors should be **independent**, and be able to contribute an **objective view** of the company.

In addition there is no indication that either of the non-executive directors has significant **financial expertise**; at least one non-executive director ought to have an accounting qualification to be able to analyse the accounting information with appropriate knowledge.

Committees

VCF does not operate the committee structure recommended by corporate governance guidance:

(1) A **nomination committee, made up of non-executive directors** whose role is to oversee the process for board appointments. The committee needs to consider carefully the best structure of the board including the balance between executives and non-executives, the range of skills possessed by the board, the need for continuity and the appropriate size of the board.

(2) An **audit committee made up of independent non-executive directors**. This committee would be responsible for certain control tasks including reviewing financial information and VCF's system of risk management, and liaising with, and reviewing, the work of external audit.

(3) A **remuneration committee, again consisting of independent non-executive directors**. Though salaries paid to directors could well be justified, the increased transparency that use of a remuneration committee can mean should deflect possible shareholder criticism of high salary levels.

Views of shareholders

There appear to be no mechanisms for **seeking the views of shareholders**, and damaging conflict may arise if shareholders are particularly concerned with short-term profitability.

(ii) **Risk management strategy**

Overall VCF does not appear to have a clear risk management framework. Identifying risks is one of the many responsibilities of Viktor, but risk identification and mitigation will be enhanced if VCF formalises its risk management procedures.

Risk appetite

It seems that the directors are prepared to tolerate a high level of risk being taken, but **do not appear to have a clear idea** of whether the **returns** the company is achieving justify the level of risks being taken. In addition the board does not appear to have considered whether the **benefits** of countering certain risks outweigh the costs – are the costs and resources required to pursue legal action for infringement of patents worth the benefits?

Risk identification

A key aspect of risk identification is **Viktor's analysis** of likely threats to cash flow. As this is so important, this analysis ought to be checked by someone else who reviews the figures, and considers the reasonableness of the assumptions made and whether there are any other possible scenarios that have not been analysed.

Risk acceptance

The **decisions** made on whether to accept exchange risk have been determined by historical balancing out of gains and losses, whereas VCF should also be considering the **likely future movements of exchange rates**.

Effectiveness of risk reduction methods

Outsourcing and personal contact may **not be very effective methods** for addressing some of the main risks the company faces. Even if Viktor has good contacts with customers and competitors, these will not do much to mitigate major economic risks. In addition competitors are themselves likely to have very stringent methods for **protecting their own technology** and it may be difficult for VCF to stay ahead if competitors develop market-winning technology.

Failure to reduce certain risks

In addition VCF does not appear to have mitigated the impact of certain risks. Although the company has tight cash flow quite often, there does not appear to be any identified source of **contingency funds**. There also appear to be **no contingency arrangements** if supplier problems arise.

(iii) **Internal controls**

Overall the control system needs to **depend less on Viktor's involvement** and have more formal procedures in place.

Role of board

Expanded board membership should enable the whole board to exercise more effective supervision over the company. This includes carrying out a formal process of **risk identification**, and **monitoring and considering the effectiveness of internal control**, including a formal annual review of internal control.

Internal audit

A small internal audit department could be established. Not only would it fulfil the requirements of corporate governance guidelines, but it could be used to review the **value for money** of a number of aspects of operations, including supplier procurement, marketing and research and development, thus potentially saving the business considerable costs.

Accounting system controls

Comparisons need to be made of actual costs with **budgeted costs** and **variances investigated.** A more formal **system of responsibility accounting** needs to be introduced with costs allocated to cost centres and ultimately to individuals for control purposes.

Scorecard

The system Viktor uses needs to be modified with more consideration being given to supplier performance and cost measures.

Area managers

The **responsibilities** of area managers need to be **clarified**; there appears to be confusion resulting in the managers being bypassed. The system for **appraising managers** needs to be formalised, and the scope of assessment widened, covering control over costs as well as the aspects currently appraised.

Staff controls

All staff ought also to be **formally appraised** and feedback obtained to ascertain whether staff are happy, since departure of dissatisfied staff to competitors may **jeopardise VCF's competitive position**. VCF should ensure that staff contracts are drafted as tightly as possible as regards use elsewhere of knowledge of VCF's operations, and **joining competitors**, although local employment law may limit how effective these restrictions can be.

Summary

Overall the company would benefit from **more formalised governance procedures, a wider base of directors** and developments in **accounting, human resources** and particularly **risk management systems**.

(c) (i) **Corporate governance ethical concepts**

Fairness

Fairness means taking into account the interests of all stakeholders that have a legitimate interest in VCF. The board certainly considers the interests of **shareholders** (the emphasis on cash flow) and **customers** (the emphasis on customer satisfaction). However whether all interests of employees are taken into account is less clear; Viktor appears to assume that all staff are interested in is high salaries, when they may also be interested in developing their own careers and contributing to decision-making in a way that is not allowed for by Viktor's personal rule. Perhaps staff potential exists that is not being fully realised.

Accountability

The board does not appear to recognise the significance of **accountability to shareholders,** nor that accountability extends beyond making high profits. Now that VCF is listed, and given that Viktor does not own a majority of shares, other significant shareholders who are discontented could combine and raise their concerns at general meetings or even seek changes on the board in attempt to limit Viktor's power. They might do so because they are **unhappy** about the **risk-return** relationship that is available from investing in VCF. Although sales may appear to be doing well, cash flows are tight, and the company's future success is dependent upon the outcome of uncertain research and development.

Transparency

Shareholders should be **reassured** if VCF fulfils another key concept, that of transparency. This not only means fulfilling all the requirements of law and accounting standards in relation to the content of annual accounts, but **maintaining a regular dialogue with shareholders and perhaps voluntarily reporting** on certain activities. Transparency may be limited to some degree by the need to maintain commercial confidentiality about research and development to keep the information from competitors. However the board may be able to give more details about their risk management processes and their long-term strategy; if shareholders are reassured that VCF has a **clear vision**, they may believe that the risks linked with strategy will be managed successfully.

Independence

The lack of independent non-executive directors means a lack of scrutiny not only of what the board is doing (which shareholders may be concerned about) but also the company's **risk and business analysis processes**. A non-executive director with experience of markets outside the Pacific home country may be able to contribute to suggesting improvements in the way VCF does business in those markets. An **IT specialist** may be able to monitor the activities of the research and development department in a way that current board members cannot because of their lack of expertise.

(ii) **Ethical viewpoint**

Instrumental viewpoint

The ethical viewpoint that regards good corporate governance as an mechanism for helping to ensure high profits is the **instrumental viewpoint.** This reflects the view that Viktor holds that organisations exist to fulfil **mainly economic responsibilities** towards shareholders plus the **legal responsibilities** that it needs to fulfil in order to continue trading. Thus the business does not have its own moral viewpoint; it adopts ethical attitudes towards corporate governance because not to do so would upset its stakeholders. Thus the instrumental viewpoint requires an assessment of the power and interest of stakeholders, and identification of the stakeholders that it cannot afford to provoke.

Normative viewpoint

The instrumental viewpoint can be contrasted with another key ethical viewpoint, the **normative viewpoint.** This sees ethical behaviour as reflected for example in good corporate governance as an end in itself and not the **means to the end** of making more money. Failing to take an ethical position leads ultimately to the breakdown of the cohesion that society requires to operate effectively.

57 Wilberforce Humphries

(a)   **Strategic risks**

Strategic risks are risks arising from the **failure to define a clear business strategy or the selection of an inappropriate business strategy**. Wilberforce Humphries faces the following risks in relation to its business as a whole or one or more segments.

Over-reliance on winning new contracts

This may be a big risk because of the **significant expansion** in the major projects sector. This division seems to be undertaking quite a lot of one-off building projects, which may well not lead to any repeat business.

Over-reliance in declining business sectors

It's also possible for Wilberforce Humphries to **rely too much on the office-building sector**, which appears to be in decline in its home country.

Over-reliance on risky markets

Again this may be a problem with **over-reliance on the major construction projects division**, where actual costs and profits may be the most uncertain.

Excessive investment in loss-leaders or in costly features

The board may feel that the major projects division in particular has to bid for projects offering limited returns, in order to **gain access to new markets** and to gain the opportunity of bidding for more profitable projects later on. Likewise the need for continual innovation may limit profits but may be **necessary to maintain competitive advantage**.

Operational risks

Operational risks are **risks of delays and disruptions to operations**.

Resource shortages

This could be a particular problem for the major construction projects division, which may be faced with **undertaking large projects at short notice**. The magnitude of the risks depends on the links with subcontractors and their ability to undertake work at short notice.

Loss of key managers, staff and contractors

This risk is clearly perceived to be a problem at **board level** judging by the enhanced terms given to some of the directors. Loss of key staff below board level may be a particular problem in the **design and development area**, since Wilberforce Humphries is looking to **gain competitive advantage** from the new features it introduces. Given that Wilberforce Humphries has been very reliant on **longstanding subcontractors**, problems with or loss of one or more of these may affect operations significantly.

Problems with subcontractors' work

Although Wilberforce Humphries has been dependent on its subcontractors, there is also a risk of delay caused by **slow working** by poorly-trained staff, or the need to spend extra time rectifying poor quality work once completed.

Freakish weather conditions

These could **delay building** and damage work that has already been completed. The magnitude of the risk will depend on the extent to which building has to take place in seasons of the year when **extreme weather** may occur or the ability to mitigate some of the disruption (for example backup power lines if power is disrupted).

Health and safety problems

As sadly shown by the recent fatalities, there is a risk of accidents in building work. As well as the **impact of accidents**, operations may also be slowed down by **stricter health and safety legislation or the demands of the health and safety inspectorate**.

Risk management framework

Establish risk appetite

The directors deciding on the company's risk appetite is vital for a proper **evaluation of the strategic risks** that it faces. The directors will be able to use this evaluation to decide whether opportunities carry too high a risk of loss, or whether the returns that are likely to be made justify the losses possible from the projects.

Assess risks

All divisions need to have a thorough process for assessing risks. This should include identifying the events that cause risks to materialise and **assessing the likelihood**, **severity and consequences** if they do. It is particularly important for there to be an effective **risk consolidation process** over the whole group in order to compare the **relative importance of the risks faced by the different divisions** and hence how to deal with them.

Develop and implement risk responses

Whilst different divisions will take their own decisions about dealing with certain risks, they must do so within a framework established by the board that reflects the risk appetite. The board is likely to take a **portfolio approach**, perhaps tolerating higher risks from certain projects if they are balanced by lower risks from other projects. The implementation process should clearly link the **risks assessed with the actions taken**; this should enable assessment of the effectiveness of systems and the costs and benefits of controls.

Monitor risks and controls

It is important to establish a **risk management committee**. Its functions should include reviewing reports on key risks, monitoring overall exposure to risks, assessing the effectiveness of risk management and warning on emerging risks. **Review of risks** also remains an important part of a **board's responsibilities**. Corporate governance best practice would be for Wilberforce Humphries' board to **review risk** as part of its **regular** agenda and conduct a **wider-ranging annual review** of how the group is tackling risk.

Obtain feedback and refine processes

The feedback obtained from monitoring process should be used to **enhance risk management processes**. For example feedback about the shortcomings of subcontractors may not just impact upon relations with those subcontractors; it may also be fed into the tendering process for **assessing and obtaining guarantees** from new subcontractors in the future.

(b) **Reasonableness of packages**

Corporate governance reports acknowledge the need for remuneration packages to be sufficient to attract, retain and motivate directors of sufficient quality. One aspect of this will be paying a **salary in line with market rates;** evidence that competitors are prepared to attract directors by paying more is an apparently obvious indication of what market rates are.

Balance of packages

One problem with the enhanced packages is that the elements that **do not depend upon company or individual performance**, basic salary and benefits, are a more important part of packages than they were. Whilst some increase in these may have been necessary, other elements that were dependent on performance such as bonuses on share options could also have been increased.

Service contracts

The length of service contract that has been granted presumably to tie the directors into the company is in excess of what is recommended by most corporate governance reports. **A maximum of twelve months is normally recommended**. If the directors subsequently underperform, then early termination could prove expensive.

Improvements in decision-making process

Remuneration committee

An important corporate governance recommendation is that a remuneration committee consisting of independent non-executive directors should be responsible for establishing the **overall framework of directors' remuneration** and **recommending the packages of executive directors.** Although the chief executive may make his views of the performance of individual directors known to the committee, he should not be responsible for deciding on their remuneration. The involvement of independent non-executives should ensure objectivity, and they can be held accountable at the annual general meeting.

Use of measures

Corporate governance best practice such as the UK regulations requires comparison of total shareholder return on the company's shares over a five year period with the total shareholder return on a holding of a portfolio of shares representing a named broad equity market index. Not only should this give shareholders comfort that **appropriate standards** are being used to determine remuneration, it also means that the remuneration committee is considering the wider environment. This should help the committee to determine the level of risks of directors being recruited by competitors. The remuneration committee may wish to employ **external remuneration consultants** to assist their decision-making.

(c)   **Use of external audit**

In some jurisdictions, such as America under the **Sarbanes-Oxley** legislation, companies are not allowed to use their external auditors for internal audit work. Even if it is permissible, Wilberforce Humphries' audit committee needs to consider carefully whether the external auditors' involvement, and the fees they earn, may **unacceptably jeopardise their independence**.

Work done

In a sense it does not matter whether an external auditor or an equally qualified internal auditor undertakes internal audit work as long as it is well-directed and concentrated on the areas that are **most significant to Wilberforce Humphries's business** and the **risks** it faces. The scenario seems to suggest that this is not happening, that the internal audit work is focusing on the financial risks associated with the accounting statements, rather than the more important risks relating to health and safety, building quality and development and innovation.

Qualifications

External auditors may however find it difficult to **staff internal audit work** that focuses on these risks. These are areas in which qualified accountants would not generally be expert. If an internal audit function was set up, Wilberforce Humphries could recruit staff for it who have industry knowledge of the building trade or specialist areas such as health and safety.

Knowledge of the company

Internal staff can gain **day-to-day knowledge of Wilberforce Humphries' operations and personnel** which external auditors visiting the company periodically will be unable to match. External audit staff may also be more likely to change from year-to-year.

Objectivity

A possible drawback of using internal staff is that they allow personal friendships or internal politics to **bias their findings**. External auditors may provide a **more objective view of operations and staff** that is therefore more valuable.

Conclusion

Given the nature of the main risks faced, Wilberforce Humphries's best policy may be to **establish an internal audit function**, and use its employees to check whether the company's risk management systems are operating as they should be. The company may however employ external experts, though not necessarily external auditors, to consider the adequacy of risk management systems in addressing the risks faced in high risk areas such as health and safety,

(d)   To: Board
      From: Accountant
      Date: 26 October 20X7
      Subject: Corporate responsibility framework

I shall cover our corporate responsibility framework using the headings in the latest report in the accounts.

Organisational framework

Having established the committee, any issues about its **terms of reference** need to be **resolved.** The committee needs to demonstrate that it has clarified Wilberforce Humphries' responsibilities to its shareholders, suppliers and customers.

Health and safety issues

Clearly the remaining subcontractors need to be trained, but the recent incidents mean that other measures will be required. The incidents may illustrate that **further training on specific areas** is needed; health and safety needs to be built into the **appraisal procedures** of staff and the **assessment of subcontractors.** **Enhanced procedures** may have to be introduced to combat the risks demonstrated by the accidents. As well as aiming to introduce better procedures, meaningful targets must be set to **reduce the number of accidents**, including of course a **nil target** for fatal accidents.

Environment

The training programme requires completion but also again the emphasis on training must feed through in the future into **improved performance targets** being set in specific areas. Examples may include recycling targets or increased use of technology to reduce energy waste during construction. Wilberforce Humphries should also **regularly review its own environmental policies** and **those of its subcontractors,** and consider environmental policies when deciding which subcontractors to use.

If external validation is required, the board should consider whether the company and its subcontractors should adhere to an environmental standard.

Employees

Having addressed the issues raised in the last employee survey, the next employee survey needs to be amended to provide **validation** for the measures taken by asking employees' opinions of how effective they've been. The increase in training also needs to be **validated by improved performance**, of which appraisals should provide evidence. The most significant measure of employee satisfaction may well be the number of employees leaving. **Reduction in departures** should be a target, particularly in areas where replacing employees will be most difficult.

(e) **Utilitarian perspective**

This means choosing the course of action that provides the greatest good for the greatest number of people.

Utilitarian justification

The government is arguing that a number of groups in society will directly benefit from this decision. These include people currently living in overcrowded cities who will enjoy **more space** if they move to the new settlement. Businesses who move will enjoy the benefits of **purpose-built office space** and a pool of employees from occupiers of the new houses. The economy as a whole could be said to benefit from the construction work given to Wilberforce Humphries and hence the increased employment, and also because it seems that using the land for business and residential purposes is a better use economically and environmentally than using it for tourism.

Criticisms of utilitarianism

Comparison of benefits and demerits

One criticism of utilitarianism is that it is **often not possible to compare like with like**. The existing inhabitants of the region will suffer disruption and the loss of their isolated environment; does this outweigh the benefits to the incoming inhabitants and businesses.

Effect on minorities

Even if a way could be found to **compare directly the effect on existing and incoming inhabitants**, and this method demonstrated that the development fulfilled utilitarian criteria, this decision would mean effectively that the impact on the minority (the existing inhabitants) did not matter. It could be argued that the harm visited on the minority would be ethically an unacceptable price for undertaking the development.

Absolute harm

A similar viewpoint would regard the development as unacceptable because of the adverse impact on the animals and plants. A deep ecologist view would be that man's economic requirements should not prevail over the life needs of other species. Such a view would be an absolute view, and this relates to another criticism of utilitarianism, that it does not allow for **absolute ethical rules**. What is defined as the greatest good can vary between time and place. Utilitarianism can therefore be criticised if it is felt that society's underlying values at the time are wrong, for example the promotion of material happiness above other considerations.

58 Partner

(a)   **Importance of stakeholder concerns**

Concerns of many stakeholders

Most stakeholders demand that companies' actions **match their rhetoric and aims**, that they engage actively in relations with stakeholders and fulfil internationally agreed values in core areas such as **labour conditions, human rights and environmental health**. Fulfilling these requirements is unlikely to involve companies in having to decide between the conflicting interests of different stakeholder groups.

Importance of different stakeholders

However business strategy will also be affected by the relative significance of different stakeholder groups, determining how much their concerns will impact upon strategy. Stuart Brand therefore needs to have in place a systematic method of stakeholder analysis. One such method is Mendelow's matrix where the axes are **power held** and **likelihood of showing an interest**. Stuart Brand's **business strategy** must be **acceptable** to **key players whose power and level of interest** is **high**. Stakeholders whose **level of interest is low** but whose **power is high** must be kept **satisfied**; stakeholders with **low power but high interest** must be kept **informed** since they may influence more powerful stakeholders, perhaps by lobbying.

Management of stakeholder relationships

As well as recognising stakeholder interest and power, Stuart Brand may wish to manage stakeholder relationships more actively, trying to **reposition certain stakeholders** and discouraging others from **repositioning themselves**. Environmental lobby groups for example may be placed in the low power, high interest segment; establishing better relationships with them may mean that they move to the low power, low interest segment.

Reporting of corporate social responsibility issues

(i)   **Transparency and accountability**

Better reporting can be justified on the grounds that stakeholders demand openness about companies' **economic, social and environmental performance.** It is an essential means of showing that Stuart Brand is responding to stakeholder concerns and keeping them informed.

(ii) **Response to standards**

The emergence of global principles and standards is a force **influencing stakeholder expectations** of companies. Guidelines such as the Global Reporting Initiative CERES principles or ISO 14000 on environmental issues have aimed to reduce confusion about what standards are appropriate to meet stakeholder demands and clarify what companies should be doing.

(iii) **Credibility**

As well as more detailed disclosures, the credibility of information is also enhanced by **external verification.** For example the EMAS environmental guidelines are seen as being particularly strong, since they require environmental audits with audit results forming the basis of setting revised environmental objectives, and a detailed environmental statement validated by accredited environmental verifiers.

(b) To: Pierre Renoir
From: Jaitinder Sharma
Date: 30 October 20X7
Subject: Assessment of control systems

Thank you for your query about control systems. Overall I would say that although the documentation will be helpful in making an assessment of how well run Loire Boucher is, you are likely to need further information to make a reliable assessment. The criteria you should use are summarised below.

Objectives

Firstly the controls in place need to help the company **fulfil key business objectives**, including **conducting its operations efficiently and effectively, safeguarding its assets** and **responding to the significant risks** its faces.

Links with risks

Links between controls and risks faced are particularly important. They imply that the company has to have a framework for dealing effectively with risks. Key elements are the board defining Loire Boucher's **risk appetite**, which will determine which risks are significant. There need to be reliable systems in place for **identifying and assessing the magnitude of risks.** The risks identified need to be clearly linked in with the controls. **Risk registers** can be used to list and prioritise the main risks, detail the action taken and show how risk levels have been reduced.

Control system compatibility

A detailed manual of control procedures is useful, but it could just sit on the shelf unused. It needs to be supported by other aspects of the control system, and the overall systems need to deliver a consistent message about the importance of controls. **Human resource policies and the company's performance reward systems** should provide incentives for good behaviour and deal with flagrant breaches.

Mix of controls

Detailed controls at the transaction level will not make all that much difference unless there are other controls further up the organisation. There should ideally be a **pyramid of controls** in place, ranging from **corporate controls** at the top of an organisation (for example ethical codes), **management controls** (budgets), **process controls** (authorisation limits) and **transaction controls** (completeness controls). Controls shouldn't just cover the financial accounting areas, but should include **non-financial controls** as well.

Human resource issues

How well control procedures operate will also be determined by the authority and abilities of the individuals who operate the controls. There need to be **clear job descriptions** that identify how much **authority and discretion** individuals have at different levels of the organisation. Controls can be also be undermined if the people who operate them make mistakes. Therefore managers and staff need to have the **requisite knowledge and skills** to be able to operate controls effectively; **documentation and training** will be required, and individuals' abilities assessed on a continuing basis as part of the **appraisal process.**

Control environment

The above issues all relate to the control environment, defined as the **overall actions and awareness** of directors and managers regarding the importance of internal controls. The control environment matters because the company's **culture** will determine how seriously control procedures are taken. Indeed certain aspects of culture may well undermine the control procedures in place. If there is evidence that directors are **overriding controls**, this will undermine them; if staff appear to resent controls, they may be tempted to collude to render controls ineffective.

Review of controls

Directors should demonstrate their **commitment to control by reviewing internal controls**. The UK Turnbull report suggests that this review should have two aspects. Review of internal controls should be a **regular** item on the board's agenda, focusing on the risks identified and how effectively controls are dealing with them. There should also be a wider-ranging **annual review** looking at changes in risk, the scope and quality of management review and possible impacts on the accounts. The financial statements should include details of the annual review and significant weaknesses identified.

Information sources

In order to carry out effective reviews of controls, the board needs to ensure it is receiving sufficient information. There should be a system in place of regular reporting by **subordinates and control functions, also reports on high-risk activities** such as systems developments. The board needs also to receive confirmation that weaknesses identified in previous reviews have been resolved. Finally there also needs to be clear systems of reporting problems to the board. These include **exception reporting** by managers, also **key stakeholders** (staff and customers) being able to raise concerns with the board.

Feedback and response

A basic principle of control system design is that the **feedback received** should be used as the basis for **taking action** to change the controls or modify the overall control systems. There are two aspects to this. Firstly there should be **rapid responses** if serious problems are picked up, for example involvement of senior management in reviewing possible fraud. Secondly management should as part of their annual review consider whether the **framework needs to be developed further**, for example by establishing an internal audit function.

Costs and benefits

Rational consideration of whether the costs of operating controls are worth the benefits of **preventing and detecting problems** should be an integral part of the board's review process. Directors may decide not to operate certain controls on the grounds that they are prepared to **accept the risks** of not doing so.

(c) **Strategic risks**

The main business risks that Garmeant 4 You faces can be grouped under the following headings:

Competitor risks

The ability of Chinese clothing manufacturers to produce goods of equivalent quality but at a significantly lower cost base means that they will compete with Garmeant 4 You on price. If Garmeant 4 You has to reduce its current pricing levels, it will either have to make a **significant reduction in its operating cost base** or face **increased financial problems.**

Customer risks

60% of all business activity is derived from only three major customers, with one of them stating their **possible intention to move their business.** The loss of one major customer would have a serious impact on the **scale of operations, revenues and cash flows**; it will also have an adverse impact on staffing, either by leading to **redundancies or by unsettling staff.**

Financial risks

Financial risk is the risk of running short of money. In the case of Garmeant 4 You the risks relate to falling operational margins, cash flow pressures and high levels of gearing. The cost of servicing the debt may place so much **pressure on cash flows** that the situation will not be sustainable in the long run; it will have to be remedied by improving the cash generation from operational activities (ie margins).

Human resource risks

The **skilful workforce** is critical to Garmeant 4 You's ongoing success. Therefore anything that unsettles them (eg job insecurity) may impact seriously on quality. In addition the impact on a business, that has relied so heavily on the diligence and skill of its workforce, being forced to shed staff through redundancy may be significant. **Recruiting new staff with the appropriate skills** may prove very difficult if business fortunes turn around and there becomes a need for higher staff levels again.

Operational risks

Changes to the supply chain management process at Garmeant 4 You will place **additional pressures** on staff and systems to deliver **high quality goods** in short lead times; there may in the end be a trade-off between speed and quality. The introduction of the computer-related design system also means that Garmeant 4 You is going to become more reliant on such systems (and the staff who operate them) to deliver the required level of performance. Garmeant 4 You is therefore not only vulnerable to the risk of the system breaking down; it also faces the risk of the system becoming **obsolete.** Garmeant 4 You will have to continue to **invest in, and upgrade, this system** to ensure it remains relevant.

Reputation risks

Any **failures relating to quality, supply,** etc could damage this business, which has built up a strong reputation and goodwill. Other customers may view for example a loss of the sales contract with the major customer as an indicator of declining fortunes in the firm and this could have further negative effects. Equally if quality reduces as a result of the loss of key staff then the **brand value** will suffer as a consequence.

(d) **Conflict of interest**

The discussions are not affected by a conflict of interest between Marie's concerns and the **chief executive's concerns**. Auditors have a duty to the shareholder body as a whole to take what action they see fit to protect their interests. In addition directors are entitled to **seek the professional advice** that they need to carry out their role effectively. Also the chair of the audit committee has the right to consult the auditors directly and to conduct discussions without the involvement of Quintus' executive management.

Features of Sarbanes-Oxley approach

The Sarbanes-Oxley Act is a rules-based approach where the key issue is whether or not there has been **compliance with the regulations**. Rules-based approaches provide clear guidance on certain situations; for example Sarbanes-Oxley clearly states which non-audit services cannot be supplied by auditors. They are less good at dealing with questionable situations that are not covered adequately in the rule book; Enron for instance was able to use some misleading accounting treatments because these were not contrary to the accounting rules then in place.

Features of European approach

The European **principles-based approach** places more emphasis on the **underlying objectives** of corporate governance; for example provisions would be drafted in terms of the need to treat minority shareholders fairly, rather than setting out a long list of actions to ensure this. A principles-based approach may **extend more widely** than a rules-based approach, since it can cover areas such as organisational culture that it is very difficult for a rules-based approach to cover effectively. Principles-based approaches also allow companies to **develop their own approach** that is relevant for their circumstances. Specific provisions in principles-based codes are generally established on a **comply or explain basis**; companies have to disclose fully if they have not complied and it is then up to investors to judge for themselves the significance of non-compliance.

Are the differences significant?

It has been argued that the differences between the two approaches are not really very great. Although codes based on principles may include statements that they are **not prescriptive**, stock exchanges have incorporated these codes within their regulations. Shareholders and stock markets may then be as intolerant of companies who fail to comply with principles as they are with companies that break rules.

Strictness of American and European approaches

There are a number of areas in which American legislation goes beyond European provisions.

(i) **Non-audit services**

As mentioned, Sarbanes-Oxley prohibits auditors from **providing a large number of non-audit services** to audit client listed companies including internal audit, human resources and legal services. Although there are limited provisions against providing certain non-audit services in guidance affecting European auditors, in the main it is left to the judgement of audit committees whether provision of certain services would unacceptably compromise auditor independence.

(ii) **Audit partner rotation**

The American legislation requires **rotation of the lead audit partner every five years**. European codes are not so strict, although auditors are subject to the requirements of their accounting bodies that are similar in fact to Sarbanes-Oxley. ACCA for example requires the engagement partner should be rotated after a pre-defined period, normally not more than five years,

(iii) **Internal control reporting**

Sarbanes-Oxley requires annual accounts to include an **audited assessment** of the effectiveness of the internal control structure and the procedures for financial reporting. European codes do not require opinion to be given publicly on control effectiveness.

(iv) **Certification of accounts**

Under Sarbanes-Oxley the **chief executive officer** and the **chief finance officer** are required to **certify the appropriateness of the financial statements** and that the financial statements fairly **present the operations and financial condition** of the company. If the accounts have to be restated, then both will forfeit their bonuses. European codes do not contain this provision.

Other issues

There are other issues that should be considered when deciding whether to transfer jurisdiction.

(i) **Costs**

The costs of delisting from the American stock market and relisting in Europe may be significant. Against this however may be the **lower ongoing costs of compliance** with a more flexible, and hence more appropriate, principles-based regime. Evidence suggests that lower cost has been the most significant influence on companies' decisions to change jurisdictions.

(ii) **Raising monies**

Quintus should not have difficulty raising the funds it needs in many instances from European stock markets, although it may have problems if it is **listed on a smaller stock exchange** and requires a massive capital injection.

(iii) **Investor reaction**

Provided investors feel that the European stock market is liquid, and that they will be able to dispose of their shares without any difficulty, they may not be too concerned about the **transfer of listing.** However some may be more concerned if they feel that the transfer is due to a lax attitude to corporate governance, so the public relations of the transfer may require careful management.

59 Integrated Broadcasting Organisation

(a)   **Strategic risks**

Strategic risk relates to the **potential volatility of profits** caused by the nature and types of the business operations. It therefore concerns the fundamental and key decisions that the board takes about the organisation.

Threats to income

Levy

IBO's income from the **levy on television and radio sales** may be **threatened** if the government decides that the levy is politically unpopular and **abolishes it** or **reduces it in real terms**. IBO also faces the threat from a decline in radio and television sales, as viewers and listeners use other technology to obtain IBO's programmes.

Sponsorship

Sponsors may **withdraw sponsorship** from programmes or IBO as a whole if they feel their investment appears tainted because of ethical problems surrounding IBO. In the UK for example, Carphone Warehouse ceased sponsoring the programme Big Brother after a scandal. Sponsorship income may also be at risk if competitor action results in **audiences for IBO's programmes falling**.

Donations

Donation income may be threatened if donors believe that IBO is **not giving sufficiently high priority** to the programmes they wish to see on air, for example broadcasting them at times when the audience will be low. Like sponsors, donors may also be put off by the recent scandals surrounding IBO.

Subscriptions

Subscription income will depend on IBO's ability to **supply programmes** that audiences wish to pay for directly. The income from sports channel subscriptions may be most vulnerable if competitors acquire the rights to major sports.

Increased expenditure

New technologies

Because of the threats to income, IBO may have no choice but to **develop its services and technologies**. The expenditure and benefits of these may be uncertain; the technology investments may prove to be greater than expected as technology develops quicker than expected. Expenditure on new channels to attract a fresh, for example younger, audience may not be justified by the income received if the channels do not prove popular.

Rights

IBO may face a bidding war with an uncertain cost outcome if it wishes to **retain the rights to major sports**.

Confusion of strategic decision-making

The strategic decision-making process may also be a factor increasing the level of strategic risk. Because IBO has a number of **different key stakeholders** who provide **financial support** for its programmes and who are represented on its management board, its strategy has to satisfy all of them. This may lead to sub-optimal decisions being taken.

Role of Management Board

Risk appetite definition

The acceptability of the risks involved must be integral to the board, in particular the **strategy committee's**, decision-making. The **pay-off between risk and return** must be considered carefully, particularly where the benefits may be rather **less tangible** than the costs.

Risk and control management systems and environment

The board is responsible for establishing **appropriate risk management systems** that combat the main risks IBO faces. It is also responsible for overseeing the **environment** within which risk management takes place; is the focus on **innovation** and making programmes that may not be popular or is the focus on **achieving large audiences**. This needs to be communicated clearly to staff through **training and publicity**. The board is also responsible for ensuring that the IBO's **core values** are clearly stressed to staff and that they demonstrate their own **adherence** to these values. Clearly the IBO does have a management hierarchy, but the board also needs to ensure that the accountabilities and authorities within the hierarchy are understood.

Risk review

Review of major risk issues should be a **regular part of the board's agenda**. The board should review the risks, the strategies for identifying the risks and the controls and the other actions being taken to **reduce risks**. The board should obtain information by regular reports on different areas by senior managers and reports on key risk areas, also from staff expressing concerns. A better system of information gathering might have lead to the current problems being identified earlier. The board should also conduct an annual review covering longer-term issues such as **changes in risk** and the **scope of management monitoring**.

(b) To: Ben Jackson
     From: Consultant
     Date: 26 November 20X7
     Subject: **Corporate governance arrangements**

Introduction

You asked me to advise on current governance arrangements and to recommend appropriate improvements.

Lack of independent non-executive directors

Half of the Management Board are trustees, equivalent to non-executive directors (NEDs) in companies. However governance reports specify that half of the board should be not just NEDs but independent NEDs. A number of the trustees cannot be classified as independent because of their connections with key stakeholders in the IBO. Peri Brown is connected as managing director of a company that **supplies programmes** to IBO. Harry Sullivan is a director of a **competitor** of IBO and will have duties towards the competitor. Jamie McCrimmon is a **representative of the governing party of Tara**, which makes decisions on how the IBO is meant to be financed. Victoria Waterfield is connected for similar reasons, as Director of one of IBO's **main sources of finance**

Further non-executive directors therefore need to be appointed to ensure that the IBO has **sufficient independent trustees.**

Conflicts of interest

The analysis about non-executive directors must be taken further and questions asked whether it is appropriate that certain non-executive directors are on the Board at all. Directors have a **fiduciary duty** to act in accordance with the best interests of the organisation for which they are directors. It would appear to be impossible for Harry Sullivan to serve effectively both the IBO and its rival the Network Group. Peri Brown has a duty as MD of the supplier which may conflict with the best interests of the IBO, if for example the supplier is tendering in competition with rivals. Since one of the three Is fundamental values of the IBO is **independence**, Jamie McCrimmon's position seems doubtful as it lays the IBO open to suspicions of party political influence, as there does not appear to be a representative from the opposition parties on the board.

It seems vital for the IBO to avoid accusations of political bias so Jamie McCrimmon should **resign from the board.** Harry Sullivan's conflict of interest is so fundamental that he too should **leave the board.** Peri Brown's conflict of interest is confined to the area of programmes that her production company makes. She can therefore remain on the board provided her position is **clearly disclosed** and she is **not involved in any decisions that affect her production company.**

Roles of non-executive directors

The major corporate governance reports believe that NEDs should be involved in discussions about **strategy**; as directors they are responsible for supervising the company and the experience they bring from other companies is helpful. However governance reports also stress the monitoring role of NEDs, implying that their main role is to scrutinise rigorously the proposals made by NEDs. The involvement of trustees in the strategy committee may be a weakness, since if trustees are actively involved in setting strategy, they will then find it difficult to **criticise their own decisions.**

A trustee presence on the strategy committee may be valuable, but there should also be a strong trustee presence on the main board that is not involved in the strategy committee, and can therefore **monitor its activities effectively.** Possibly also the specification of the duties of trustees requires amendment to clarify their role in determining strategy.

Board committees

Although the IBO has established the main board committees, the membership of the appointments and audit committees are not in accordance with governance best practice. Best practice recommends that a majority of the members of the appointments committee should be **independent NEDs,** and all the members of the audit committee should be **independent NEDs,** as these committees play a vital role in scrutinising management.

The membership of these committees should therefore be **changed** to be in accordance with **governance best practice.**

Risk committee

Although other board committees deal with aspects of risk, IBO lacks a **risk committee**. Having a committee of directors and trustees specifically responsible for overseeing the risk arrangement framework should mean risk management is supervised more effectively, and that problems like those that have happened recently are avoided.

A separate risk committee should be established, staffed mainly by the trustees. Its remit should include approving **risk management strategy and risk management policy, reviewing reports on key risks, monitoring overall exposure to risk** and **assessing the effectiveness of risk management systems.**

(c)   (i)   **Conventional perspective**

This means individuals living up to what is expected of them.

(1)   **Immediate circle**

It is not easy to define the immediate circle whose expectations IBO will try to meet. It could be IBO's **commercial rivals**; would they film in Landra? It could also mean IBO's **viewers** or **stakeholders who are involved in financing programmes**; would they be happy to be associated with a channel that films in Landra?

(2)   **Social and cultural accord**

This would mean acting in accordance with what the people of Tara wished. One aspect would be obeying any **legal restrictions or prohibitions** on doing business in the country. Alternatively it would mean acting in accordance with **public opinion,** expressed in support for a boycott or divestment of interests in Landra.

Post-conventional perspective

A post-conventional perspective means individuals **making their own decisions** in terms of what they believe to be right, rather than acquiescing in the views of society.

(1)   **Ethical values of society**

If IBO made the decisions using the ethical values of its society, it would be in terms of what was believed about doing business with unethical regimes, and what action should be taken against them.

(2)   **Wider ethical principles**

This means the board **deciding for itself** on what ethical principles the decision should be made. Board members may believe for example that it is wrong to do business with an oppressive regime.

(ii)   **Utilitarian perspective**

The utilitarian perspective can be summed up in the principle of the **greatest happiness of the greatest number**; the course of action chosen should result in the greatest good for the greatest number of people.

(1)   **Good enjoyed**

The utilitarian arguments would be based on **economic benefits for IBO** of making a popular show, and **economic benefits for the population of Landra** from the filming and resultant tourism. Utilitarians might also think in terms of the enjoyment derived by the viewing public from watching an authentic adaptation of the novel.

(2)   **Limited demerits**

The utilitarian approach might acknowledge the **risk to IBO's reputation** through its perceived association with the Landran government, but might see the economic impact of that as small compared with the benefits from making the production. Utilitarians might also accept that boycotting Landra may **worsen the country's economy** and **undermine the country's oppressive government**, but may argue that IBO acting by itself could have little impact on the government.

Deontological approach

The deontological approach is concerned with the **application of universal ethical principles** to arrive at rules of conduct. A critic taking this approach would question IBO on various grounds, linked with Kant's formulations.

(1) **Dealing with corrupt government**

Deontological critics would say that IBO should not have any dealings with a corrupt, oppressive government and should certainly not enter into any business arrangements that might **enhance the government's popularity**.

(2) **Using people as means to an end**

The deontological view would also criticise IBO for ultimately being concerned with the **profits on the production** rather than the impact on the people involved. Even though locals in Landra would benefit, supporters of this view would argue that the impact on locals, good or bad, was not a relevant factor in IBO's decision.

(3) **Setting an example**

The deontological view would be that IBO has to act as if what it does will make a difference and **establish rules of conduct** for others to follow; only by doing that will ethical principles be established.

(d) **Criticisms**

Vague terms

The problems faced by IBO appear to indicate that staff **lack understanding** of the basic concepts, suggesting that they have not been well-defined.

Contradictions with current situation

Arguably two of the three Is are controversial and IBO's current situation and policies may appear to contradict them. IBO's **independence** is questionable given the presence of a government-supporting politician and representatives of its finance providers on its governing board. Almost inevitably in today's climate, some of IBO's popular programming may well be accused of 'dumbing down, suggesting a questionable commitment to **intelligence**.

Lack of specific examples

Most corporate codes begin with very broad ethical principles, but these only represent a starting point on which more specific provisions are built. IBO appears to have relied too much on staff understanding and applying the broad principles, and has **failed to develop comprehensive supporting guidance** to deal with situations that may reasonably be expected to occur.

Improvements

Increased guidance

Clearly the specific provisions in the code need to be more comprehensive. This does not necessarily imply a change to a rules-based approach. Instead the IBO could adopt a similar approach to ACCA with the code including guidance on **minimum standards of behaviour** and **prohibitions** as necessary; the code can also include examples to show how the principles are applied, whilst stressing that different behaviour may be appropriate in other circumstances.

Support mechanisms

The messages in the code need to be reinforced by **training** and employees making a **formal commitment** to the code. They should be reinforced by **disciplinary mechanisms** to discourage bad behaviour.

Need for change

As new situations occur at IBO and elsewhere, the code may need to evolve in response. The **editorial standards committee** possibly should take on a **wider, more proactive role** in regularly reviewing the code and considering changes and events in the industry environment.

Management commitment

The board needs to **take the lead in promoting the code** and stressing to staff that unethical behaviour will not be tolerated.

60 ChemCo

Marking scheme

				Marks
(a)		Up to 2 marks per valid point made on the inadequacy of JPX's governance		10
(b)		1 mark for identifying and describing each risk to ChemCo in the JPX acquisition	6	
		Up to 1 mark per relevant point on assessing each risk and a further 1 mark for development of relevant points	10	
		max		15
(c)		Award 1 mark for each relevant point made		
	(i)	Up to 4 marks for an explanation of the advantages of a unitary boards	4	
	(ii)	Up to 5 marks for the case concerning the advantages of a unitary board at JPX	5	
	(iii)	Up to 2 professional marks for the clarity and persuasiveness of the argument for change in the JPX board	2	

			max	10
(d)	Award 1 mark for each explanation of the four roles of non-executive directors	4		
	Award 1 mark for each specific benefit of NEDs to JPX up to a maximum of four marks	4		
			max	7
(e)	Memo to Leena Sharif			
	Explaining environment footprint – 1 mark for each relevant point made	3		
	Explaining importance of environmental reporting – 1 mark for each relevant point made	5		
	Up to 2 professional marks for the form of the answer (memo in which content is laid out in an orderly and informative manner)	2		
			max	8
				50

(a) **Reasons for inadequacies**

The shortcomings in JPX's corporate governance arrangements can be seen as largely due to its **development from being a family-run company**. As JPX has increased in size, its corporate governance arrangements do not seem to have developed.

Non-executive directors

There are no non-executive directors on the boards of JPX. Corporate governance reports recommend that there should be a strong presence of non-executive directors on the board. The result of having no non-executive directors is that JPX's upper board is too **inward-looking** and may well **lack balance in terms of skills**. It is also very difficult to say that JPX's board is **objective**, and this undermines its role as a monitor of JPX's activities.

ChemCo is also likely to be concerned that there are **no non-executive directors** to **counter the influence of the dominant family clique.**

Board committees

The lack of board committees may indicate that JPX is **paying insufficient attention** to some aspects of corporate governance.

(i) **Audit committee**

The **lack of an audit committee** would be against the law in America, and may mean that **insufficient attention** is being paid to **reviewing financial statements, risk management and internal control**. It also means that internal and external audit are **unable to report to independent directors.**

(ii) **Nomination committee**

The **lack of a nomination committee** may be a factor in the lack of balance of the boards. A nomination committee should address issues such as **director recruitment** and an **enhanced role for department heads.**

(iii) **Remuneration committee**

The lack of a remuneration committee may mean that **inadequate scrutiny** has been made of **directors' remuneration**, and directors may be receiving remuneration packages that shareholders consider unwarranted.

Organisational structure and communication

Corporate governance is also about encouraging a proper control environment. This includes an **appropriate and effective organisational structure.** Although there is a structure in place, the **lack of involvement of department heads in strategic decision-making** indicates **shortcomings in communication** and organisational practice differing from organisational structure – as directors, department heads should be involved in decision-making.

Annual general meeting

Under corporate governance codes, the annual general meeting should be the principal forum for **communication** between the **board and shareholders.** However at JPX's annual general meeting discussion has been stifled.

As controlling shareholder, ChemCo would expect to communicate through other channels as well as the annual general meeting, but may be concerned with the AGM as a **means of communication** if other shareholders still hold shares after the takeover.

Reporting

The limited evidence available of JPX's accounts, the unclear comment about environmental impact, may indicate a **lack of transparency** and **insufficient disclosure** for the purposes of shareholder decision-making. Given that ChemCo is uncertain about the **risks inherent in the investment**, risk disclosures in JPX's accounts may also be inadequate.

(b) **Risks**

Market risks

Whenever ChemCo invests in JPX, there is a risk that it will be paying a **higher value** for JPX's shares than they are intrinsically worth. This risk could be quite high, because JPX has only recently been floated, and its shares may not **yet have found their equilibrium price;** also ChemCo's **lack of experience** in dealing with the region where JPX is located may mean that it is more likely to make a mistake in deciding an acceptable price to pay.

Exchange risks

As JPX is operating in a different part of the world to ChemCo, the value of ChemCo's investment in JPX may fall. The **present value of future cash flows** from the **investment in JPX** may be reduced by adverse exchange rate movements.

Integration risks

There appear to be a number of risks that may arise from **integrating JPX into the ChemCo group.** These include ChemCo **management time being taken up** dealing with resistance from JPX, that **diseconomies of scale arise** due to the larger group being less easy to control and that **JPX's culture** does not change in the ways that ChemCo's board desires. The results of these risks may result in the investment **yielding lower returns** than were expected when it was made.

Environmental risks

The comment about negative local environmental impact indicates the existence of environmental risk, the risk that the environment will suffer **adverse consequences** through JPX's activities and also that JPX will suffer adverse financial consequences. These may include **legal costs and fines, also clean-up costs.**

Reputation risks

The poor corporate governance arrangements and the potential threat to the environment may also mean that JPX acquires a **reputation** as a company to avoid. This could have various financial consequences. Shareholders, frustrated by the lack of communication, could sell their shares, **forcing the price of shares down. JPX** could be subject to a **consumer boycott** because of its adverse environmental impacts, leading to **falling revenues and profits.**

Risk assessment

There are various frameworks for assessing risks, but most follow similar stages with maybe slightly different terminology

Risk identification

Companies need an awareness of **familiar risks,** also to look out for unfamiliar risks. This implies knowledge of **what conditions** create risk and what **events** can impact upon **implementation of strategy** or **achievement of objectives.** Methods of doing this include inspections, enquiries, brainstorming, also monitoring conditions that could lead to events occurring and trends. With JPX, it is likely to mean consulting with directors, senior managers and other stakeholders.

Risk analysis

Risk analysis means determining what the **consequences and effects** will be of a risk materialising. This includes not just financial losses, but opportunity costs, loss of time.

Risk profiling

This involves making an assessment of the **likelihood** (low or high) of the risk materialising and the **consequences** (low or high) of the risk materialising. This will help the organisation to decide whether the risk is acceptable in accordance with its **appetite** for taking risks. If it isn't acceptable, profiling will help the organisation decide what it should do about the risk (take risk reduction measures, transfer the risk by means of insurance.) Again consultation with managers and stakeholders should help determine the best strategies.

Risk quantification

For more significant risks, this stage involves trying to calculate the **level of risks** and **consequences**. Organisations may wish to **quantify** the **expected results**, the **chances of losses** and the **largest expected losses.**

Risk consolidation

Risk consolidation means aggregating at the corporate level risks that have been **identified or quantified at the subsidiary or divisional level.** This stage may involve further analysis such as **sorting risk into categories.** The consolidation process will support board decisions on what constitute appropriate control systems to counter risks and **cost-benefit analysis of controls.**

(c)   **Advantages of a unitary board**

Equal responsibility

A unitary board structure implies that all directors having **equal legal responsibility** for **management and strategic performance**. All directors can be held **accountable** for board decisions. This avoids the potential problem of confusion over responsibilities if more than one board is responsible for performance.

Equal role in decision-making

If all directors attend the same meetings, it is less likely that some directors will be **excluded from making important decisions** and **given restricted access to information**. Boards that take all views into consideration and scrutinise proposals more thoroughly hopefully should end up making better decisions. It also **enhances the role of non-executive directors.**

Reduction of dominance

If all directors are of **equal status**, this **reduces the chances** of the board being **dominated by a single individual or a small group.** It fulfils the requirement of governance reports such as the UK Corporate Governance Code that there is a **balance of power and authority.**

Better relationships

The **relationships between different directors** may be better as a single board promotes easier co-operation.

Case for JPX adopting a unified board structure

Removal of family dominance

Combining JPX's boards should **dilute the influence of the controlling family** and enable other viewpoints to be heard. At present the family's domination of the upper board appears to be stifling debate.

Involvement of department heads

A unitary head with department heads will mean that their **views are heard when strategy** is devised, which should improve the quality of decision-making.

Consistency with ChemCo

Adopting a unified board structure would make JPX's board structure consistent with ChemCo's. This would help solve the problem of **integrating JPX** into ChemCo's culture and structure. It should also give ChemCo more confidence that JPX's governance is effective.

Signalling

A unitary board would signal to stakeholders such as JPX's managers and employees, also ChemCo's shareholders, that the acquisition would mean that ChemCo intended the **management culture at JPX to alter.**

(d) The UK's Higgs report summarises the role of non-executive directors under four headings.

Strategy

Non-executive directors should contribute to discussions about the strategic direction of their organisation, and be prepared to **challenge the viewpoints of executive directors.**

Scrutiny

Non-executive directors should **scrutinise the performance of executive management** in **meeting goals and objectives**, and **monitor the reporting of financial performance.** They should ensure that **shareholders' interests** are represented, and that managers are not taking advantage of the agency relationship to under-perform or to reward themselves excessively.

Risk

Non-executive directors have a general responsibility to satisfy themselves that **financial information is accurate and that financial controls and systems of risk management are robust.** They will have further, specific, responsibilities if they are members of the **audit or risk management committees**.

People

Non-executive directors are also responsible for **manning the nomination and remuneration committee**. As members of the nomination committee, they will be responsible for considering whether the board is well-balanced in terms of **skills, experience etc**. On the remuneration committee, they should consider overall policies, and the appropriate level of remuneration for each director.

Contribution to JPX

Better balanced board

Non-executive directors will **dilute the seemingly reactionary dominance of the family**. They also could **widen the perspectives of JPX's board**, which appear to be rather narrow at present, and bring new skills and experience. These extra contributions should **improve the quality of decision-making**. They should also address the point that important views are not being heard when strategy is discussed.

Representing shareholder interests

At present there is little opportunity for external shareholders to **express any concerns** about the direction JPX is taking. Non-executive directors can **put shareholders' viewpoints** in board discussions, and **act as a contact point** for shareholder representatives. This addresses the issue of board **accountability** raised by Leena Sharif.

Monitoring function

Non-executive directors can focus on ensuring the board **monitors risks, controls and operations effectively**, and also monitor the performance of executive directors.

To: Leena Sharif
From: Chief Accountant
Date: 12 March 20X7
Subject: Environmental footprint and environmental reporting

Introduction

The purpose of this memo is to explain the term environmental footprint and to discuss the importance of environmental reporting.

Environmental footprint

Environmental footprint can be defined as the evidence of the **impact a business's activities have upon the environment.** It can be seen in terms of a business's direct inputs and outputs, also its indirect effects. Input effects relate to the business' **resource usage**, for example water and land usage, and whether it **replenishes the environment** in any way. Output effects relate to matters such as **emissions causing pollution**, also the impact of **using and disposing of any packaging.** Indirect effects include effect on local transport systems of JPX's employees attempting to get to work.

Importance of environmental reporting

Good governance practice

Environmental reporting can be seen as fulfilling the key governance principle of transparency, and the requirement of various governance codes for the board to provide a **balanced and understandable assessment of the company's position**. This includes negative impacts such as environmental impacts.

Impact on operations

The need to **specify the impact on the environment** builds environmental reporting into internal control systems, and hence provides a spur, encouraging reductions in environmental impact.

Stakeholders

Investors and other stakeholders are becoming more interested in the level of environmental disclosure, seeing them as **disclosures** relating to **risk management and strategic decision-making.** This can lead to investors seeing companies as lower risk as more risks are known about and reported, and hence companies' cost of capital falling.

Reputation building

An increasing number of companies see voluntary environmental reporting as a means of demonstrating their commitment to good practice and hence **enhancing their reputation**, leading to **marketing opportunities** as green companies. Surveys such as Sustainability's Tomorrow Value surveys provide useful publicity for companies.

If you have any further questions, please do not hesitate to contact me.

61 Worldwide Minerals

Text references. Chapters 1, 3, 4 and 9.

Top tips. (a) is quite tough; 10 marks is a lot to award for a question on a single concept. The key point relating to corporate governance that the question requirement highlights is that transparency helps solve the agency problem. The advantages of transparency in relation to financial reporting should be easy to discuss. However the question requirement asks for an evaluation, which means examining in detail by argument, so you have to give consideration to the arguments against transparency as well as the (more obvious) points in favour. Note that the mark scheme gives as much credit for arguments **against** transparency as it does for arguments in its favour, which may seem slightly strange.

In (b) Kohlberg's pre-conventional stance implies letting ethical decisions be guided by the **consequences**; a conventional stance implies acting in accordance with **generally accepted behaviour in society**, in particular here **obeying regulations and codes**; a post-conventional stance using **ethical principles** as the basis for ethical decisions. The argument that Martin Chan puts forward is **not** self-interest; instead it is the golden rule ethical principle 'Do as you would be done by'.

The requirement to critically discuss in (c) means giving some indication of what's needed for each role to be effective, discussing certainly two elements of each role. The most significant tension is between pragmatic business interest and acting in good faith towards the shareholders, but there may also be a short-term, long-term objectives conflict if the problem cannot be permanently concealed. The UK Cadbury and Hampel reports also identified a tension between NEDs monitoring executive activity and contributing to the development of strategy. However the UK Higgs report thought in practice, NEDs contributed most effectively if they balanced the two roles. An over-emphasis on monitoring would lead to NEDs being seen as 'an alien policing influence' detached from the rest of the board; too much emphasis on strategy would lead to NEDs becoming too close to executive management and hence undermining shareholder confidence in their independence.

(d) requires some quite general points on the purposes of internal control (links with strategy and risk, information management, also the qualitative human resource controls). You could define the purposes in terms of Turnbull's guidance on internal control, and so include safeguarding assets, compliance with laws and regulations and operating efficiently and effectively as your main headers. The scenario gives only limited information about the failings, so only a couple of well-explained action points would be needed to score 4 out of 6 for part (ii). Note that the question sets out very clearly what you need to do to gain the professional marks, you would get 1 mark for the letter layout, 3 marks for the right structure, content, and style/tone. There's a reminder in the kit front pages of the key elements of letters and other forms of business communication.

Easy marks. The four roles of NEDs, taken from the Higgs report, also came up in the pilot paper so you should earn easy marks for describing these.

Examiner's comments. In (a) most students were able to define transparency and explain its relevance, but many did not fulfil the requirement to evaluate, to cover arguments for and against full reporting. A lot of answers failed to explain why disclosure is not appropriate at times.

In (b) students explained Kohlberg's three levels well, but some were less good at applying the three levels, failing to interpret the evidence in the case study correctly.

In (c) again students did not answer the more demanding second part of the question well, many answers containing descriptive content rather than serious efforts to consider the problems NEDs faced.

(d) demonstrated that professional presentation skills will be a part of future P1 exams. Future P1 papers will ask candidates to 'draft' or 'write' content in the form of various types of written communication.

'One professional mark was available for the basic form of a letter, meaning it was correctly headed, finished, addressed and physically laid out. The other three were awarded for the composition, flow and persuasiveness of the narrative itself. The letter was from a company chairman to the company's shareholders and those gaining all four professional marks were those that read most like a letter of its type would read in 'real life'. A good answer contained an explanatory introduction, a discussion in the form of narrative (rather than bullet points) of the content of parts (i) and (ii) of the question finished off with a brief paragraph drawing the threads together.'

Students failed to obtain the full quota of professional marks for various reasons:

- Their answers did not read like a letter (perhaps more like a memo)
- They were not in the form of a formal letter to shareholders which would typically have a beginning and an end with a logical flow of content in the 'middle'.
- They were addressed to the wrong audience ('Dear Mr Blake')
- They used bullet points and short, unconnected paragraphs with no sense of 'flow' between them.'

(d) (i) tended to be done less well than (d) (ii) with students discussing internal control components rather than discussing importance. A range of approaches was rewarded in (ii).

			Marks
(a)	Up to 2 marks for definition of transparency		2
	1 mark per relevant point on advantages of transparency	max	3
	1 mark per relevant point on reasons for confidentiality or concealment	max	3
	Up to 2 marks for relevance to the case		2
			10
(b)	Up to 2 marks for each Kohlberg level identified and described		6
	Up to 2 marks for each person's position identified with reasons/evidence from the case 0.5 marks for identification only		6
			12
(c)	2 marks for each NED role identified and briefly explained	max	8
	4 marks for discussion of tension in advising on reserve overestimate		4
			12
(d)	(i)	1 mark for each relevant point made on importance of control	max	6
	(ii)	Up to 2 marks for each relevant point identified and examined	max	6
	Up to 4 professional marks for structure, content, style and layout of letter		4
			16
			50

(a)   **Transparency**

Transparency means **open and clear disclosure** of relevant information to shareholders and other stakeholders, also not concealing information when it may affect decisions.

Advantages of transparency

Agency problem

In order to exercise effective control over those who **manage the company**, the owners-investors who are not involved in corporate governance need guarantees that they are receiving sufficient, accurate information. Without these guarantees, the position will be weighted towards managers who have the detailed knowledge from supervising the company's affairs that the investors lack. The importance of keeping investors informed appears to be acknowledged by WM publishing investor relations literature, and seemingly making efforts to produce accurate reports.

Stock market confidence

Linked with the agency issue, publication of relevant and reliable information **underpins stock market confidence** in how companies are being governed and thus **significantly influences market prices.** WM's literature talks about trust and reputation influencing the stock market.

Truth and fairness

International accounting standards and **stock market regulations** based on corporate governance codes require information published to be **true and fair.** The information can only fulfil this requirement if adequate disclosure is made of uncertainties and adverse events. Previous estimates, even those made in good faith, need to be corrected when more accurate information becomes available, as here.

Arguments for concealment

Commercial rivalry

Sometimes information has to be kept secret, because disclosure of board discussions would benefit commercial rivals. This is particularly true of discussions relating to **future competitive strategy**.

Resolving strategic problems

There is a significant strategy problem here, since if the problem is publicised and the market loses **confidence in the survey department**, WM will not be able to make changes by employing better qualified surveyors, as it already employs many of the best qualified surveyors. Possibly this may justify postponement of disclosure until the board has had a chance to resolve the problem.

Misinterpretation of information

One argument for concealment is that the market will **misinterpret bad news**, as seems to be possible here. It appears that the market may place too much emphasis on bad news affecting a single mine; a general loss of confidence in the geographical survey department appears unwarranted in the circumstances, and the market appears to be taking too little notice of otherwise good results. However taking a position of transparency does mean **trusting the market** to make the right decisions based on full disclosure.

(b) Kohlberg's moral development

Pre-conventional

Pre-conventional development means judging ethical problems in terms of the **drawbacks and benefits** that may affect the individual taking the decision. The individual sees the decision in terms of whether he or she will be **punished** for ethically wrong behaviour, or **rewarded** for behaving in an ethically acceptable way.

Conventional

Conventional development means taking ethical decisions on the basis of what is **accepted as ethical behaviour** by those who have a relationship with the person taking the decision. It means following the **ethical norms** in the **workplace or the local community**, or **obeying the laws of society** on the grounds that they **codify ethical behaviour** that the community accepts to be right.

Post-conventional

Post conventional development means taking autonomous **ethical decisions** in accordance with **relevant ethical principles.** These ethical principles may be **ethical principles that are applied in the individual's society**, or they may be **universal ethical principles.**

Gary Howells

Gary Howells demonstrates he is at a **pre-conventional level** by focusing not on ethical principles, but on the **consequences of the decision**. He is arguing that there will be **certain harm** from disclosure, but that **harm is unlikely to arise** from non-disclosure as investors will probably not find out.

Vanda Monroe

Vanda Monroe is taking a **conventional viewpoint**. She sees disclosure in terms of obeying the ethical norms that are **codified in codes of governance and stock market rules.** She sees the decision as wrong since it will mean breaching these rules.

Martin Chan

Martin Chan is taking a **post-conventional stance.** He is arguing that it is wrong to deceive investors because of the **ethical principle** that you should not treat others in a way that you would not like to be treated yourself. The consequences of the decision and whatever the codes say or don't say are not relevant to the decision.

(c) **Four roles of non-executive directors (NEDs)**

The UK Higgs report has summarised four roles of NEDs.

Strategy

As members of the full board, NEDs should contribute to discussions about **developing future strategy to maximise company value**. However NEDs should not automatically support executive directors; instead they should **evaluate**, and if necessary **challenge**, the proposals made by executive directors, using their own business experiences to reinforce their contribution.

Performance scrutiny

NEDs should **scrutinise executive directors' performance** in the light of the strategic objectives that have been established, and also **monitor how the company's performance is reported**. They should represent shareholder interests and seek to **ensure that agency problems do not arise between shareholders and executive directors.**

Risk

NEDs should satisfy themselves that **financial controls** and systems of **risk management** are **robust.** This includes satisfying themselves that systems can **produce accurate financial information,** linking in with the scrutiny role. Executive directors will have ultimate line management responsibility for the implementation of control systems; NEDs should carefully assess systems developments proposed by executives. They should enquire into and **monitor** the **operation of control and risk management systems**, using their own business experience to help them assess whether they remain adequate.

People

NEDs are responsible for **determining appropriate levels of remuneration for directors**, linking with their scrutiny of directors' performance. They will also make recommendations about the **appointment and removal of executive directors and senior managers**. In order to ensure that NEDs can review these issues effectively without being pressurised by executive directors, governance reports recommend that boards operate **nomination and remuneration committees**, consisting wholly or mainly of independent NEDs.

Potential tensions

Strategy and shareholder protection

Having participated in strategic decisions, NEDs have a duty to support the **strategy** the board has chosen on the basis of **collective responsibility**. Some directors may believe that disclosure will undermine the current business strategy; however, as part of their **performance scrutiny** role, the NEDs should be protecting investor interests by insisting on full disclosure.

Short-term risk management and long-term strategy

Arguably disclosure will **increase short-term risk** by **threatening WM's reputation** and **decrease short-term shareholder value**; maybe Gary Howells is correct in suggesting that concealment is the less risky option at present. However the longer-term strategy suggested of **hoping new reserves will be found may be optimistic.** If there continues to be a problem, the consequences of the problem eventually being exposed may be much more severe.

(d) WM Ltd
WM House
Anytown

9 January 20X8

Dear Investors

Consequences of Mallerite reserves problems

I would like to reiterate the board's earlier apology for the publication of inaccurate information about the Mallerite reserves. As a result of this, the board has undertaken a thorough review of internal control systems in order to prevent a similar problem recurring. The aim of this letter is to reassure you that the board regards robust controls systems as being very important, and to inform you of how we intend to improve internal control systems in the light of the overestimation of mallerite reserves.

(i) **Importance of internal controls**

Maintaining investor confidence

We acknowledge that your **confidence** in the company depends on your belief that the board is taking all reasonable steps to safeguard your investment and manage WM's resources effectively.

Implementing strategy

The controls in place should contribute to the company fulfilling its business objectives by **facilitating operations** and at the same time **preventing and detecting problems**.

Management of risks

We see **effective risk management systems** as an integral part of control systems, in particular systems that manage the risks associated with **safeguarding of WM's assets.**

Management of human resources

Staff are a **key asset** of the business. Controls are therefore designed to ensure employees know **what is expected of them** and **their freedom to act.** Controls should also ensure that staff have the **necessary knowledge, skills and tools** to do their jobs well.

Guaranteeing quality of internal information

In order to make the correct strategic decisions and to manage WM effectively, the board and senior management need to be able to **rely on the information** they receive. Ensuring the quality of management information is therefore an important aim of control systems. Part of this is encouraging a **culture of openness and transparency**, with staff and business partners reporting problems when they arise.

Guaranteeing quality of external reporting

A key aim of control systems is to ensure that the financial and non-financial information we report to you is **reliable and objective**, and that **full disclosure** is made of relevant information.

(ii) **Improvements in control systems**

Review of mallerite evidence

We shall insist, if at all possible, on our geological surveys department conducting **detailed audits of reports** rather than taking the word of others without further enquiry.

Review of purchase procedures

The problems over the mallerite mine have also emphasised the importance of thorough review of any purchase we are considering. We shall strengthen our **due diligence** procedures, carrying out **more robust work internally** and calling on **external help** if necessary. We shall consider making the terms of future purchases dependent on the accuracy of representations.

Reporting problems

We shall review our internal mechanisms to ensure that staff have **adequate opportunity** to report problems when they arise. We shall also stress to those with whom we do business WM's **commitment to a culture of transparency.** If we do not believe that our business partners will be open and honest, then we shall cease to do business with them.

I would like to thank you for your continued support of our company. I emphasise again that the board understands your concerns and will take the necessary steps to prevent the problem over the mallerite reserves recurring.

Yours faithfully

Tim Blake

Chairman

62 Rowlands and Medeleev

Text references. Chapters 1, 6 and 11

Top tips. Note that (a) required you to identify external stakeholders; employees are internal, not external, stakeholders, so you would not have gained marks for discussing them. However you would also have gained marks in (a) for discussing the claims of shareholders. Remember that there is a **two-way** relationship between the organisation and its stakeholders.

The examiner described (a) (ii) as more ambitious and the question does offer scope for misinterpretation. The term stakeholder claims means what the stakeholder wants R&M to do, not how much power the stakeholder has, for example First Nation not wanting the dam to go ahead.

In (b) the examiner has used the word assessment quite narrowly, to mean considering the likelihood and consequences of each risks (a stage described as risk profiling in the BPP Study Text). This use of assess is problematic, as in ChemCo in the pilot paper the examiner takes risk assessment to mean the whole process, from initial identification of risk through to risk consolidation. The clues in this question are that only 6 marks are available, which would not give you time to describe all stages adequately, and the mention of the diagram means that you should concentrate on the profiling stage.

The requirements in (c) clearly oblige you to make good use of the information in the case. Although clearly many risks affect R&M, you shouldn't have discussed them if they weren't mentioned in the scenario.

(d)'s requirement to prepare a statement to be read out at a general meeting will have surprised a lot of students, although the examiner has emphasised that students may be asked to prepare different types of business communication in the exam. The examiner explained what he wanted to see in this statement:

'It would begin with a formal introduction and provide an overview of what he was going to cover. As he spoke, the sections would be connected with narrative designed to make the speech sound convincing, logical and persuasive. It would obviously not contain bullet points (how would they be delivered in a speech).'

(d) (ii) in a sense is really the heart of the question; the examiner chose a big civil engineering project to test environmental implications, asking students to explore the pros and cons of the development. Make sure that you can define sustainability. Bear in mind that flooding habitats and farmland is an environmental impact, whereas forcing First Nation out of their homes is a social impact and therefore you would not have gained marks for discussing it.

The main point to bring out in (iii) is the conflict between the two important ethical principles. Confidentiality is needed for protecting commercial interests.

If you struggled with (e), think about the prevent-detect-correct categorisation of controls; that may help you generate ideas. In our answer culture is a prevent control, budget reports and quality inspections are detect controls and the discussion on dealing with problems is effectively saying that it will be difficult for R&M to remedy delays if they occur.

Easy marks. There are a few easy marks for definitions and descriptions of the risk analysis framework in (b), but overall the question is quite a rigorous test of your application skills.

Examiner's comments. Most candidates did well on (a), although some confused internal and external stakeholders. In (b) some students confused the likelihood-consequences matrix with Mendelow's mapping of stakeholders.

In (c) some students failed to address the specific risks described in the case; the scenario gave details of three risks with enough information to make an assessment, and those risks were what was rewarded: 'It was thus crucial to analyse the case. If a requirement asks candidates specifically to use information from the case as this one did, then they will not be awarded the best marks unless they do what the question requires.'

The professional marks in (d) could make the difference between passing and failing. Students should spend some of the time allocated to professional marks planning how they are going to fulfil the question requirements. Most students were able to define what sustainable development was, although a few thought sustainability referred to R&M being able to continue as a going concern. In (d) (ii) the requirement to discuss environmental and social sustainability implications meant that the question was not concerned with the fate of 'First Nation' nor the archaeological sites.

(e) was about how the lack of internal controls in subcontractors could delay the project's progress. Many students gained marks for discussing issues such as the subcontractors having different corporate cultures, structures and control regimes to R&M.

				Marks
(a)	(i)	1 mark for each relevant point made on definition of stakeholder max	2	
		1 mark for each relevant point made on definition of stakeholder claim max	2	
		0·5 marks for each stakeholder correctly identified max	2	
				6
	(ii)	1 mark for a brief description of each claim max		4
(b)		1 mark each for recognition of impact and probability as the two variables max	2	
		1 mark each for explanation of each variable in context	2	
		2 marks for a correct diagram (axis labelling may vary)	2	
				6
(c)		1 mark for identification of each risk max	3	
		2 marks for assessment of each risk (1 for impact, 1 for probability) max	6	
				9
(d)	(i)	1 mark for each relevant point made		3
	(ii)	1 mark for each environmental impact identified (2 positive, 2 negative factors)	4	
		1 mark for description of each up to a maximum of 4	4	
				8
	(iii)	1 mark for each relevant point on the 'normal duty of transparency'	3	
		1 mark for each relevant point on the importance of confidentiality in the case	4	
		max		6
		Professional marks for layout, logical flow and persuasiveness of the answer (ie the professionalism of the statement)		4
(e)		1 mark for each difficulty briefly identified and explained (half mark for mention only)		4
				50

(a) (i) **Stakeholder**

Stakeholders are any entity (person, group or possibly non-human entity) that can **affect or be affected by** the achievements of an organisation's objectives, here to build the dam. The relationship is thus **bi-directional**.

Stakeholder claim

Stakeholder claims mean the **demands** that stakeholder interests make upon organisations, based on the view that the impact of companies is so great that they have responsibilities to different sections of society, not just to shareholders. Management has to decide on the **legitimacy and relative strength** of different stakeholder claims.

Four stakeholders

Four stakeholders are:

- Government of the East Asian country
- Stop-the-dam
- First Nation people
- Banks

(ii)   **Stakeholder claims**

Government of the East Asian country

The government is the most important **primary stakeholder** in the development, since without its desire to invest in the dam, the project would not go ahead. The government wants the project completed on **time and to budget**. The government evidently believes that the project will service the greater good of the whole community and also the wider world, and this outweighs the detriment suffered by some other stakeholders.

Stop-the-dam

Members of the Stop-the-dam group are **active stakeholders**, seeking to prevent the dam being built on the grounds that its **negative environmental and social footprint** will be greater than the benefits derived from changing to hydroelectric power. The group would argue that its interest in environmental matters means it can make an **informed assessment** of the consequences of the project. The imperatives to protect the environment mean that it has the right to protest if the project is wrongly given the go-ahead.

First Nation people

The First Nation people are **narrow, involuntary stakeholders**. They too do not want the dam to proceed and wish their current lives to continue. They are protesting that they have had **no say in a decision** that has a fundamental impact on their lives.

Banks

Banks are also **primary stakeholders** since they will be providing the funding the R&M needs to invest in the dam. They wish to provide the funding at a level of **risk** to themselves that is **consistent with the return on lending**. It is clear here that banks are not only concerned about the risk of default; they are also worried about the **threats to their reputation**.

(b)   **Risk assessment**

Risk assessment involves considering how significant risks are. This means considering the **likelihood** of risks materialising and the **consequences** of risks materialising, the hazard involved.

The organisation has to **profile risks**, compare them on the basis of their likelihood and consequences. This should indicate to the business the action that should be taken to tackle risks and also **prioritisation** – which risks are the high likelihood, high consequences risks that must be tackled first.

Likelihood-consequences matrix *Consequences (hazard)*

Low   *High*

Low

Likelihood (risk probability)

High

(c)   **Disruption to the project**

The Stop-the-dam pressure group could take the action described of blocking access to the site, and hiding in tunnels and then having to be evicted before work could continue. This clearly represents a risk to the **progress of operations**, involving delays to the actual work, and staff having to spend time dealing with the protestors.

The **risks of disruption materialising** appear to be **high**, as the Stop-the-dam pressure group is being organised to disrupt the project. The **consequences** may be **low to medium**, depending on the tightness of timetables to complete the dam (is any allowance at all being made for delays from external sources). The consequences will also be influenced by the measures that the country's government is prepared to take to support R&M.

Treatment of First Nation people

The First Nation people are likely to try to undermine the project by highlighting the adverse impact on themselves and the environment that the dam will have. This poses a **reputation risk** to R&M. It may be more difficult for R&M to find business partners, since some may wish to demonstrate their commitment to corporate social responsibility by declining involvement in a questionable project.

The **likelihood** of this risk materialising seems high, as clearly the First Nation people have **strong reasons for protesting**. The **consequences** are **less likely to be high**, since sub-contractors, for example, would have strong business reasons for involvement in such a large project.

Financial risks

The financial risks that R&M faces are that the banks may be reluctant to lend sufficient money to invest in the project, not only because of fears about **bad publicity**, but also **concerns about the viability of the project**. This risk will be more significant if **additional finance** is required during the project or existing finance needs to be renewed; banks will have additional evidence to make their decision and as a result finance may not be available at that point.

The **likelihood** of these risks materialising can be assessed as **low to medium**. It may depend on the **risk attitudes of banks**, how easy it is to discover which banks are financing the project, and also whether the project keeps within budget limits. The **consequences** of finance not being available are **high**; the project will not be able to begin if no finance is available and R&M may expend substantial resources without full reward if funding is withdrawn midway through the project.

(d)   (i)   **Chairman's statement at the annual general meeting**

Good morning. Thank you for attending this Annual General Meeting

I am speaking to you today to explain our **potential involvement in the Giant Dam project**. I understand that as shareholders, many of you are naturally interested in our involvement; not only is this project one of the largest R&M has ever undertaken, but I know that many of you are concerned with the **impacts upon the environment** that this project will have. I therefore feel that I should demonstrate why this project reflects R&M's commitment to sustainable development.

Because of the **sensitivity of the project**, obtaining the finance necessary has not been straightforward. Therefore I shall also explain issues surrounding the project's funding and our relationship with lenders.

Sustainable development

I shall begin by clarifying what is meant by sustainable development. Sustainable development means investing in developments that will **safeguard the needs of those living in the future as well as those living in the present**. Society has to try to ensure that those living the future have the opportunity to experience the same quality of life as those in the present. Key issues in sustainable development are energy, usage of land and natural resources and waste emissions.

(ii) **Implications of the Giant Dam project**

Resource depletion

One of the most important benefits of the project is that it means that the country can **rely on hydroelectric power and not fossil fuels**. This has important sustainability implications. Future generations will have **equal opportunities** to our own to use hydroelectric power. On the other hand the supply of fossil fuels is **finite**; if we continue to use them, they will eventually be exhausted and hence unavailable to future generations to use to maintain their lifestyle.

Global warming

The burning of fossil fuels also has a significant impact upon the environment, **inevitably releasing greenhouse gases** and hence **contributing to global warming**. The government places a high priority on **meeting its obligations to reduce carbon emissions**. Effective worldwide action is needed if carbon emissions are to decrease. We believe governments will need to support major projects like the building of the dam to make a sufficient impact on the amount of carbon produced.

Impact on natural environment

At the same time your board is aware that the dam will **destroy several rare plant and animal habitats** and may therefore result in a **wider loss of balanced environmental conditions**. We do regret this. We are also sensitive to the view that building the dam maintains the economic sustainability of the human race by providing a supporting power source, but does so at the expense of the sustainability of other species. However we believe that this needs to be weighed against the **impact on the natural environment of global warming**, with threats to many plants and species being well-documented.

Loss of productive farmland

I also acknowledge that building the dam will **destroy farming land** that has been occupied by the First Nation people for hundreds of years. We acknowledge that the loss of productive farmland will impact upon the country's ability to sustain itself by producing its own food. Again however the long-term **consequences of global warming** could well be much more significant, resulting in the loss of a lot of productive land due to flooding or erosion.

Conclusion

As you can see there are arguments for and against development. Our client, the government, has weighed the arguments up and believes that the country's future prospects and also wider global interests are best served by going ahead with the dam. **Choosing to change the source of power**, the government believes, will make a greater **contribution to sustainability** than preserving the original environment at all costs, which is the belief of the Stop-the-dam pressure group. I emphasise that in accepting the contract, the board is happy that the decision has been made on the basis of full and fair consideration by the government.

(iii) **Confidentiality**

In order to undertake this significant project, we shall require **significant funding**. We shall have to incur early project costs before receiving our first payment from the government. We shall also from the start of the project need to pay our sub-contractors.

It seems likely that we shall only be able to obtain this funding if we keep the **identity of the finance supplier confidential**. Even if this condition is not built into the terms of lending, your board feels honour bound to comply with it. Without the guarantee of early funding we cannot begin this project.

Conflict with transparency

Your board is however aware that keeping the **identity of the finance supplier secret** conflicts with our normal duty of **transparency**. We are committed to disclosing all relevant information to you, not concealing any information that may affect your decision-making, in order to **retain your confidence**.

As suppliers of equity finance, we understand that you will wish to be aware of what the **other main sources of business finance** are and what conditions are placed on its availability; it impacts upon the **risk of your investment**. However although our accounts give details of the length and conditions attached to loan funding, they do not normally disclose the identity of individual lenders.

Resolution of conflict

We believe that obtaining funding from banks on conditions of confidentiality will **minimise the risk to the project** due to lack of continuing funding. Project failure would certainly have a major adverse impact on the **market value** of the company and the **value of your investment**. We shall be taking all the steps necessary to ensure that the Stop-the-dam pressure group does not obtain knowledge of our lender.

Conclusion

I hope I have addressed all the concerns that you have about the Giant Dam project. However I shall willingly answer any questions now or separately after the meeting. Thank you for your time today; are there any questions?

(e) **Culture**

The subcontractors may not have the same attitudes to risk and control as R&M. The control environment and culture may be **laxer**, with subcontractor staff being encouraged to finish jobs as quickly as possible and failure to operate controls being ignored.

Agency costs

In order to ensure that the subcontractors are working to an acceptable standard, R&M will have to review their work. Given the sensitivity of the project, it is unlikely that self-certification by the subcontractors will be strong enough evidence. R&M will therefore have to incur costs and use staff time sending staff out to check on the subcontractors' work.

Tracking progress

A number of different subcontractors may be used on the project. This will make it difficult to see if the project is within **time and budget limits**, even if the information supplied by subcontractors is reliable, and that cannot be assumed.

Dealing with problems

If problems do arise, for example time going over-budget, R&M may find it difficult to take action to remedy the situation. Subcontractor staff are not under R&M's direct control so it may not be easy to ensure that they **start working more efficiently**.

63 Swan Hill

Top tips. The mark guide in (a) indicates that it is possible to get 5 marks out of 10 for demonstrating understanding of Tucker's criteria. However the obvious way to demonstrate understanding is to apply the criteria to the scenario. Note that the discussion on fairness links in with the effect on stakeholders.

The key difference in (b) is between the risks that are affected by where the directors position SHC, and those that arise out of normal business activities.

In (c) we have tried to save time by using the same introduction to both sections. You would be rewarded for the introduction as part of the four professional marks. The main thing to emphasise in (i) is the responsibility to maximise profits, whilst in (ii) you need to consider who are legitimate stakeholders. Note the differing perspectives on the need for competition in the two parts.

You may have thought of various alternative disclosures in (d) (i), using your knowledge of financial accounts and corporate governance. The main advantage of voluntary disclosure is increased information provision, and it can also enhance participation by shareholders.

Easy marks. The definitions of strategic and operational risks, and the disclosures in (d), should offer good mark scoring opportunities.

Examiner's comments. (a) was the question that candidates did the best on with many achieving all ten marks. Some candidates failed to gain high marks because of a failure to relate the answer to the case or by misunderstanding one or more of the criteria. Some, for example, wrongly construed 'sustainable' as referring to the continuance of the SHC business rather than the environmental implications of the option.

In (b) there was a recent article in *student accountant* on strategic and operational risks by Nick Weller so it was good to see many candidates achieving good marks on the theory. It was disappointing to see that many candidates were less able to use their theoretical knowledge of strategic risk by relating it back to the case. In order to attract maximum marks, candidates had to show how the secrecy option would be a *strategic* risk and not just a general risk.

(c) was the most ambitious component of this question. Candidates therefore had to be aware of what each ethical perspective was 'about' and also to apply it to the case. This application of ethical theory to the case proved difficult for many candidates. A common approach was to attempt to make the business case for the two options and then to include a paragraph briefly providing the candidate's understanding of the two ethical stances but failing to develop those by referring to the case. Again, it is the application of ethical theories to the case that was the reason why many candidates did not perform well in (c). Candidates will usually be required to apply them in some way to get the majority of marks in P1 ethics questions.

(c) also contained 4 professional marks. Candidates should ensure they are familiar with formats. Here some candidates wrote a letter from chief executive Nelson Cobar while in other cases the answer was more like a memo. Neither of these incorrect approaches was rewarded with professional marks.

(d)(i) asked candidates to distinguish between mandatory and voluntary disclosures with examples and it wasn't surprising that most candidates were able to do that to some extent. In (d)(ii) many candidates were unsure as to the link between voluntary disclosure and accountability. Once an item is disclosed it means that stakeholders gain information on which to hold the business to account.

				Marks
(a)		1 mark for evidence of understanding of each of Tucker's criteria		5
		1 mark for application of each to case		5
				10
(b)		1 mark for each relevant point demonstrating understanding of operational risk	max	3
		1 mark for each relevant point demonstrating understanding of strategic risk	max	3
		1 mark for each reason explaining why the secrecy option is a strategic risk	max	4
				10
(c)	(i)	1 mark for each relevant point making the business case	max	4
		1 mark for each relevant point making the stockholder (shareholder) case	max	5
			max	8
	(ii)	1 mark for each relevant point making the business case	max	4
		1 mark for each relevant point making the stockholder (shareholder) case	max	5
			max	8
		Professional marks: up to 2 marks per part		4
(d)	(i)	1 mark for definition of each (mandatory and voluntary)		2
		0.5 marks for each example up to a max of 2 marks per category (allow latitude for jurisdictional differences)		4
				6
	(ii)	1 mark for each relevant point made and briefly explained (0.5 marks for mention only)	max	4
				50

(a) **Tucker's five criteria**

The stages of Tucker's five question model are is the decision:

Profitable

Edwin Kiama is arguing that the secrecy option is the option offering the chance of the highest profits and so should be pursued for that reason. However SHC's board also needs to take into account the relationship between **profits and risks**, and consider whether the option that offers highest possible profits also involves taking unacceptable risks. Sean Nyngan's viewpoint is that the licensing option is preferable, as it offers **acceptable profit levels** in return for **zero risks**.

Legal

Clearly developing new environmentally-friendly technology in secret is legal. Apart from the risks of not filing a patent, the other legal concern may be the consequences of SHC creating a **global monopoly**. Competition authorities may well be concerned, and may have the power to force SHC to share the technology.

Fair

SHC has valued its relationship with its stakeholders in the **workforce** and the **local community**. However the secrecy decision means that **some stakeholders are likely to benefit at the expense of others**. Certainly SHC's workforce may well benefit from higher profits through their remuneration packages. However the local community may, as an **involuntary stakeholder,** suffer various consequences of SHC's attaining a monopoly such as a significant increase in traffic congestion. There is also the issue of SHC's **position**

versus its competitors. Is it fair for SHC to keep all the rewards for its investment in research and development, or should competitors be given the chance to develop the sink method further and benefit their employees and shareholders.

Right

It seems very difficult to treat the secrecy decision as a morally absolute one without having regard for the **consequences**. The issue is whether the board should pursue the secrecy option if it believes certain consequences will result. Alison Manilla for example believes that SHC may not have the right to put its competitors out of business. On the other hand the **pristine capitalist** view would be that secrecy was the right option if it was the **profit-maximising option**.

Sustainable

One of the main justifications for developing the new process is that it will enable SHC to produce lower unit emissions, so in that respect the development is **environmentally sustainable**. However if the secrecy option is pursued and SHC does become the single global supplier, the **carbon footprint** from transporting the products round the world may be higher than if customers continued to be supplied by local manufacturers. SHC's decommissioning its old plant may also have adverse environmental impacts.

(b) **Strategic risks**

Strategic risks derive from the **decisions the directors take** about an **organisation's objectives** and are the risks of **failing to achieve those objectives**. They link in with how the organisation is **positioned in relation to its environment**. Many strategic risks are long-term and cannot be avoided if the company is to trade; they have **high hazards and high returns**.

Strategic risks include **longer-term risks** deriving from decisions the board takes about what **products or services** to supply, including the risks connected with developing and marketing those products. They also include risks connected with key sources of finance.

Operational risks

Operational risks are risks connected with the **internal resources, systems, processes and employees** of the organisation. They relate to the problems that can occur in the organisation's day-to-day business activities such as human error or information technology failure.

Operational managers and employees will have responsibility for **managing operational risks**, whereas **managing strategic risks** will be the responsibility of the **board and senior management**, since they are taking the strategic decisions on which strategic risks depend.

Why secrecy option is a strategic risk

Changes in processes

The secrecy option represents a **fundamental change in the method of operations**, leading to major alteration in SHC's **cost base**, the **technology** it uses and hence its **pricing policy.**

Changes in sales

The much higher volumes of production that the new process will enable may mean that SHC has to change its **distribution networks significantly.** SHC may have to move a much greater number of products to a significantly expanded number of outlets.

Place in market

The secrecy option will also **change the product market** in which SHC operates. SHC may move from being one of a **number of competitors** to a **monopoly supplier**, with a fundamental change in its **risk profile.** However its competitors could take **retaliatory action** with uncertain consequences.

Requirement for funds

The level of capital investment that the secrecy option needs means that SHC is likely to require a **major injection of long-term funds, probably debt.** This appears to mean a significant alteration in SHC's capital structure, with the company becoming more dependent on debt and possibly facing a **significant increase in its finance costs.**

(c)   (i)   **New production method**

Background

Our research and development function has recently made an important discovery connected with the manufacture of our most important product that will revolutionise production of the product. This discovery meant that your board had to take a decision that will have a fundamental impact on the future of the company:

(1)   To **develop the technology ourselves** and keep the technology secret from competitors
(2)   To **share the technology with competitors** under a licensing arrangement

Having given this decision very serious consideration, your board decided to develop the technology ourselves for the following reasons:

Business issues

Enhanced position in marketplace

We believe that implementing the new technology will lead to **significant falls in the company's cost base** and mean that SHC can **meet greatly expanded demand**. This means that SHC can move from being the market leader to taking a **dominant position** in the market, enabling us to gain **pricing power** and **guaranteeing large profit levels** for the foreseeable future. Your board believes that this is the logical outcome of acting competitively, and that our competitors would take the same decision were they to discover a revolutionary new method.

Higher customer satisfaction

We also believe that our customers will benefit through **lower prices and higher quality goods**. These higher levels of customer satisfaction should also generate **increased sales.**

Benefits to shareholders

This fundamental shift in SHC's position will, we believe, result in **significant increases in dividends** and also a major increase in SHC's market valuation and hence in the value of its shares.

Ethical issues

Responsibility to shareholders

Your board is committed to **pursuing shareholders' economic interests**, and hence seeking to maximise profits, since the shareholders are SHC's legal owners who have risked their own money by investing in the company.

Dilution of responsibility to shareholders

Your board also acknowledges its responsibility as **agents** of the company's shareholders. We believe that our loyalty is therefore to our shareholders. If we take into account responsibilities to other external stakeholders, and as a result take actions that result in lower than optimal profits, we should be **abusing our position as agents**.

Responsibility to employees

We also believe the development offers **major opportunities to our employees**. They can benefit materially and develop their skills. This in turn will aid recruitment in future years. This commitment to our employees will also benefit the locality in which we are situated.

Commitment to competition

Your board believes that society's interests are best served by the pursuit of **economic efficiency**. We believe that economic efficiency is most likely to be attained by companies making every effort to **maximise their own performance** by pursing maximum profits.

(ii) **New production method**

Our research and development function has recently made a most important discovery connected with the manufacture of our most important product that will revolutionise production of the product. This discovery meant that your board had to take a decision that will have a fundamental impact on the future of the company:

(1) To **develop the technology ourselves** and keep the technology secret from our competitors

(2) To **share the technology with competitors** under a licensing arrangement

Having given this decision very serious consideration, your board decided to share the technology with competitors for the following reasons:

Business issues

Legal protection

We believe that the option to develop the method ourselves would involve overall risk levels that would be greater than your board regards as acceptable. One risk would be being unable to protect the technology. The need to keep the development secret means that we would be unable to file a patent, and hence possibly **lack legal redress** against competitors who obtained and used the technology.

Financing the development

Developing the technology ourselves would also have required capital investment that would have been larger than anything SHC has previously undertaken. This investment would initially have required a **large injection of debt finance**, raising debt to levels greater than your board deems desirable. We believe that the need to pay interest to service this debt would impact upon the funds available for distribution as dividends.

Low risk of licensing option

By contrast we believe that the licensing option can generate very significant royalties in return for minimal risk. We believe that it can generate a **smoother flow of funds** in the medium to long-term; these funds can be invested in further research and development to enhance our position as market leader.

Consequences of improvement sharing

Finally we believe that enabling our competitors to share our technology means that the process can develop quicker, since several manufacturers will be implementing the processes and **pursuing improvements.**

Ethical issues

In addition we are conscious that there are significant ethical issues connected with the decision. Your board is sensitive to these and in particular to the need to consider the interests of stakeholders whom SHC's activities significantly affect.

Responsibility to local community

SHC has always been committed to working in partnership with the local community. We felt that this partnership might be broken if SHC developed the technology by itself. To do so could have put our competitors out of business, and we are sensitive to the **increased unemployment** that might result. In addition the huge increase in sales that we believe could result from developing the new technology would lead to greatly increased activity around SHC's premises, impacting adversely on the community by for example **causing increased traffic**.

Commitment to fair competition

Your board has always been committed to **fair competition** within the industry. We believe that high customer service levels and commitment to research and development are best stimulated by a number of competitors operating within the industry. We believe that if any company, ourselves or any competitor, held a monopoly, then this would inhibit developments in the industry that benefit customers and other stakeholders.

Wider social responsibility

In addition we believe that the technology could have a major impact on the **environmental footprint of production**, significantly reducing unit emissions. This is perhaps the most important consequence of developing the new method, and therefore your board needed to consider how best to develop the technology to enhance further the positive environmental impact. We have decided that allowing competitors to share our technology is the best way to benefit society, since it will give competitors the opportunity to make further improvements, which could then be shared.

(d) (i) **Mandatory disclosures**

Mandatory disclosures are disclosures that listed companies are required to make by legislation, regulation, accounting standards or stock market requirements. In most jurisdictions the annual report should include the identity of directors and information about the directors including interests in shares. The directors should make a statement of whether the company has **complied with the corporate governance requirements** that apply to it, together with details of, and justification for, any examples of non-compliance. The report should also include **accounting information**, such as a statement of comprehensive income and a statement of financial position, and the audit report on the accounts.

Voluntary disclosures

Voluntary disclosures are disclosures that are not required by regulation but are made to **enhance the usefulness of the accounts** and **provide information of interest to key stakeholders**. Examples include:

- A **chief executive's report** providing a commentary on what has happened and the company's future strategy that is wider and more detailed than required by law or regulation

- A **social and environmental report**, setting out the company's social responsibility objectives and the progress made in fulfilling the targets it has established for itself

- Information about the policies adopted towards the company's employees including **anti-discrimination policies** and ways in which employees are **involved in decision-making**

- Details of the company's **code of business ethics**, and how it affects relations with key stakeholders such as customers and suppliers

(ii) **Wider information provision**

Disclosures covering wider areas than those required by law or regulations should give stakeholders a **better idea of the environment** within which the company is operating and how it is responding to that environment. This should enable investors to carry out a more informed analysis of the company's **strategies**, **reducing information asymmetry** between directors and shareholders.

Different focus of information

Voluntary information can be focused on **future strategies and objectives**, giving readers a **different perspective to compulsory information** that tends to be **focused on historical accounting data.**

Assurance about management

Voluntary information provides investors with further yardsticks to **judge the performance of management**, and its disclosure demonstrates to shareholders that managers are **actively concerned with all aspects of the company's performance.**

Consultation with equity investors

The voluntary disclosures a company makes can be determined by consultations with major investors such as **institutional shareholders** about what disclosures they should like in the accounts.

64 Global-bank

				Marks
(a)	(i)	2 marks for each Kohlberg level identified and explained. ½ mark for identification only max		6
	(ii)	0.5 marks for correct identification of Mineta's level. 1 mark for each relevant justifying point max		4
	(iii)	Correct identification of stage 4 in conventional level with brief explanation. 0.5 marks for identification of conventional only	1	
		Explanation of why it is most appropriate level	1	
				2
(b)		1 mark for each cause of failure identified and briefly explained (0.5 marks for identification only) max	5	
		1 mark for each internal control failure at Global bank identified and briefly explained (0.5 marks for identification only) max	5	
				10
(c)		Evidence of understanding the principal-agency relationship	1	
		Explanation of principal side max	2	
		Explanation of agency side max	2	
		max		4
(d)		Distinguishing between narrow and wide stakeholders	3	
		0.5 marks for each narrow stakeholder identified max	1.5	
		2 marks for assessment of the loss and refinancing on each identified narrow stakeholder	6	
		max		10
(e)		1 mark for each CEO role identified and briefly explained max	4	
		1 mark for each relevant criticism of Mrs Keeler's performance linked to case max	6	
				10
Professional marks				
Physical layout of the letter, address and signoff			1	
Flow, persuasiveness and tone			3	
				4
				50

(a)   (i)   **Pre-conventional**

The decisions individuals make on ethical matters will have nothing to do with the ethical issues involved, but will instead depend on the **personal advantage or disadvantage to the individual**, including rewards, punishments and deals.

Conventional

When taking ethical decisions individuals live up to what they think is **expected of them,** by their **immediate circle,** or by society as expressed in **laws or social customs.**

Post-conventional

Individuals make ethical decisions in terms of what they **believe to be right in line with higher or absolute ethical principles**, not just acquiescing in what others believe to be right.

(ii)   **Pre-conventional**

Mr Mineta appears to have operated at Kohlberg's pre-conventional level for the following reasons.

Lack of ethics

Miss Hubu's evidence that Mr Mineta **didn't believe in right and wrong** indicates that his decision-making was not influenced by whether a course of action was ethical.

Reward

Miss Hubu's evidence indicates instead that the decisions made were determined by how much **personal reward** they would bring him.

No pressures to act at conventional level

Mr Mineta **ignored internal control systems** and did not face any pressures to act at a **conventional level,** as trading rules were not enforced in his office. Instead he was encouraged to take risks in return for a trade-off of high rewards.

(iii) **Desired level**

Mr Mineta should have operated at the **Conventional level Stage 4** making decisions in accordance with the ethical norms expressed in **trading rules and internal guidance.** Stage 3 here would not be sufficient due to the possibility of office pressures to ignore the rulebook.

(b) **Poor judgement in decision-making**

Poor control decisions can sometimes be made because the **information** supporting those decisions has been inadequate.

Human error or fraud

Adequate controls may be in place, but staff may **not operate them properly** either through **making mistakes** or in **order to commit a fraud**.

Collusion between employees

A system that depends on one employee checking or monitoring another's work will be ineffective if the employees **connive together** so that the checks are not carried out.

Management over-ride

Managers may **ignore the controls in place** and instruct the staff working for them **not to operate the controls.**

Routine transactions

Control systems may be **designed to deal with routine transactions.** They may **not recognise or highlight problems with non-routine transactions or unforeseeable circumstances.**

Performance of Global-bank

Judgement

Mr Mineta demonstrated **poor judgement** by breaching trading rules.

Failure to apply controls

The controls that should have applied to all traders, **trading limits and authorised products,** were **not applied to Mr Mineta** because his trading made such large profits.

Culture

The culture in the Philos office promoted by the manager, Mr Evora, focused on **maximising profits** at all costs, even if it meant controls were **not enforced or bypassed**.

Information provision

The Philos office did not provide the information to head office that head office needed to **monitor its activities effectively.** Head office did not insist that this information be provided.

Role of head office

Head office **accepted without question the high level of profits** made in Philos, and did not investigate warning signs of potential problems, such as the persistent failure to provide information. It seems also that there were **no whistleblowing channels** that worried employees in the Philos office could use to voice their concerns.

(c)   **Agency relationship**

The two parties in the agency relationship are the **agent** and the **principal,** with the agent being **accountable** to the principal.

Principals

In this situation the trustees are the human representatives of the principal, the Shalala pension fund. Their aim is to **maximise the value of the fund,** so that its members' fund values are also maximised. This means maximising the value of Shalala's investments, including its investment in Global-bank. However the trustees cannot do this by managing Global-bank itself. Instead Shalala's agents, Global-bank's directors, run the bank on its behalf and are **accountable to the pension fund.**

Agents

As agents, the directors of Global-bank are responsible for running the bank with the aim of achieving the objectives of their principals, the Shalala pension fund and other shareholders, the **maximisation of long-term value**. The directors have a **fiduciary duty** to act solely in their principals' interests and are accountable to the principals for failure to achieve objectives. Here the bank has failed to achieve the objectives of maximum capital growth because of the failure of internal controls.

(d)   **Distinction between narrow and wide stakeholders**

Narrow stakeholders are the stakeholders who are **most affected** by the organisation's strategy and policies, including shareholders, managers, suppliers and important customers. **Wide stakeholders** are those who are **less affected** by the organisation's strategy, including government and the wider community.

Investors

The impact on investors' interests is that the **market price of their shares has presumably already fallen.** They now face a choice between paying out for additional shares to fund the losses made by Mr Mineta, or refusing to support the rights issue and increasing the risk that the company will become insolvent and wipe out their existing investment. They will presumably wish to gain more assurance before subscribing to the rights issue. The rights issue itself does not guarantee Global-bank's continued existence. If Shalala or other investors refused to subscribe to an issue that goes ahead, then their holding will be **diluted**, reducing their influence over the bank.

Employees

If Global-bank is in financial trouble, many of its employees could **lose their jobs.** Those that remain could find themselves operating under **more restrictive controls**, with **more stringent limits** being placed on their **performance-related bonuses.** Employees based in the Philos office who are found to have known what was going on could **lose their licence to trade.**

Directors

Directors who are up for re-election at the next annual general meeting may find themselves being **voted out of office**. The whole board may face a **vote of no confidence** at a **general meeting.** Even if they avoid this, they may experience **increased scrutiny and intervention by investors.** This may adversely affect their **remuneration or bonuses**. Some or all of the directors may face **local legal sanctions for** making an inaccurate statement about internal control effectiveness.

(e)

Shalala Pension Fund
1 Any Street
Alltown
12 October 20X8

Global-bank
1 Every Road
Capital city

Dear Mrs Keeler

Internal controls at Global-bank

I am writing to express the concerns of the trustees of the Shalala Pension Fund over the losses made in the Philos office and the fall in the value of the shares held by the fund that resulted from this. We do not accept your argument that what happened was a genuinely unforeseeable situation. We are sorry to say that we hold the board responsible for the shortcomings in control, and feel that prime responsibility for these failings must rest with yourself as chief executive.

We would like to define the roles and responsibilities that you should assume in relation to internal control and set out our assessment of how you have discharged those responsibilities.

Risk assessment

As chief executive you should have ensured that the board **assessed and monitored areas of greatest risk** to the company as part of its review of the company's activities. We are sorry to see that the board appeared to have **no idea of the risks** that were being borne in the Philos office, particularly since the area of derivatives trading would normally be an **area of high risk** that the board should monitor.

Risk appetite

The chief executive is **responsible for ensuring** that the activities of the company **reflect the risk appetite** that the board has established. However the situation in Philos appears to illustrate that the board's wishes were **not communicated effectively.** Mr Mineta's activities were not **regarded as those of a rogue trader in Philos,** but as being in accordance with an ethos of taking undesirably high risks to achieve large profits.

Lack of enforcement

The board does not appear to have enforced the control systems that were in place **effectively**. Mr Mineta felt that he could break trading rules unpunished and in addition Mr Evora appears to have totally **ignored normal trading rules** instead of enforcing them.

Monitoring of internal controls

As chief executive you need to ensure that you receive **sufficient information** to be able to **monitor the bank's controls** effectively and **report on its controls fairly in its accounts.** We are very disappointed that you have **failed to obtain the assurance** that controls were operating properly in Philos because of the office's failure to submit the information it should have sent to head office. We are particularly disturbed that this has resulted in an **inaccurate report** on the strength of internal controls.

Audit committee

In addition there are flaws in the bank's corporate governance arrangements that have helped prevent effective scrutiny of the activities of the Philos office. We are disturbed that **no attempt has been made to replace the two directors** who have left the audit committee, especially because this has resulted in criticisms of the effectiveness of the audit committee by the external auditors. We would emphasise. that we regard the **proper functioning of the audit committee** as a key control.

Internal audit

We also are disappointed that the **internal audit function** at Global-bank has been ineffective. We regard internal audit as a particularly important part of corporate governance.

I would stress again that we are deeply concerned with the apparent failures of control that the events in Philos have illustrated. We look forward to receiving your response to the comments we have made.

Yours sincerely

Millau Haber
Chairman of the Shalala trustees

65 Mary Jane

Text references. Chapter 9 on the AAA model, Chapters 4 and 5 on internal control issues and Chapter 8 on information.

Top tips. The mark schemes for this exam are worth studying in detail. In most question parts, the examiner draws a clear distinction between demonstrating knowledge and understanding (worth perhaps up to 50%), and demonstrating the higher level skills of analysis and application.

If you couldn't remember the AAA model in (a), be warned that it was examined in the compulsory section of the paper. (Note also that the other decision-making model highlighted in the syllabus, Tucker's five questions, has also been examined in the compulsory section). In the exam, if your mind does go blank, the best method is to analyse the problem logically and hope you will gain some marks for application. If you did remember all the questions, you needed to give at least a comment to demonstrate your understanding. The norms, principles and values in Question 3 relate to care to customers, compliance with law, good governance and acting in accordance with the values the company proclaims it has.

The examiner expected you to consider the case for non-disclosure and so your answer should have considered the threat to shareholders and the company. However a note from the examiner indicated that although some credit would have been given for coherently arguing in favour of non-disclosure as the final decision, you would not have got full marks as 'alignment with the stated values of the company' required disclosure.

(b) requires you to make good use of the 15 minutes reading time, as you will undoubtedly require it here to sort out all the detail in the scenario. It certainly will have helped to have read through the requirements before reading the scenario in detail, as the requirements would have told you that you need to look out for internal control failures, and that is important here as the failures you need to discuss are scattered throughout the scenario. If you did go through the process and identify the weaknesses, you would have scored well. However knowledge dumping the content of the Turnbull report would not have scored marks, as all the points you discussed needed to be derived from the scenario.

In (c) your answer needs to discuss what NEDs bring to Sea Ships and what they can do. Here technical expertise and the lack of independent scrutiny are highlighted in the scenario to help you. As with (b), just dumping your knowledge of the relevant governance report, in this case the Higgs report, and making bland general statements would not have scored marks as the justification needed to be related to the scenario.

In (d) the format of the memo should not have caused you any problems. The introduction should emphasise the regret felt at the tragedy. (i) relates to the strategy and objective setting, and monitoring roles of the board, as well as the need for external reporting to be supported by reliable information flows. There are various ways to describe the qualities of good information in (ii) and the examiner allowed leeway for different descriptions. The mnemonic ACCURATE is one checklist you can use. However (d) was not about implementing risk management and better controls, however desirable that is. If you discussed issues that were not related to information provision, you would not have scored any marks for them.

Easy marks. Hopefully your knowledge of what non-executive directors can provide and do will have helped you in (c). If you struggled to think of points, you must revise this important area.

Examiner's comments. In (a) all of the information needed to conduct the analysis was in the case scenario. Candidates that could only recall some of the 7 steps did receive some recognition but it was disappointing to see some candidates reproduce the seven steps but then either ignore or misinterpret the ethical dilemma. A careful reading of the question should have indicated exactly what the requirement was to consider 'whether or not to disclose this information [about the independent consultant's report on structural changes] publicly' but some failed to recognise that this was the dilemma to be considered and thereby did not achieve high marks for this part.

(b) required a careful reading of the case but the internal control failures were relatively clear to many candidates. Some candidates missed out on some of the internal control failures at the Sea Ships Company itself (such as the failure to ensure adequate insurance cover).

In (c) candidates that based their answers on the unique governance situation at Sea Ships were rewarded whilst those that reproduced an auto-response ('strategy, scrutiny, risk and people') tended to achieve few or no marks on this question. Again, it was important to analyse the case and read the question carefully. The question was not asking about the roles of NEDs but rather the contribution they (rather than executive directors) could make given the governance failures at Sea Ships Company.

In (d) the two requirements were poorly done overall with some candidates refusing to attempt them at all. Both areas asked about were well covered in the study texts so I was surprised and disappointed that some candidates did so poorly. The range of answers on (d) (i) suggested that some candidates misinterpreted its meaning. The key words in the question were 'importance of information'. d)(ii) was also done poorly overall but was relatively straightforward in what it was asking. However many candidates failed to see what the question was asking them to write about. Again a careful reading of each question is crucial.

One of the most disappointing things to report was the poor attempts to gain the professional marks.. The question required the answers to be in the form of a memo. The various forms of narrative communication should be taught to, and learned by, P1 candidates, It was evident that many candidates were unsure of how to frame and draft a memo to management and this was reflected in the professional marks awarded. A common error was to write the answer in the form of a letter

Marking scheme

			Marks
(a)	1 mark for recognition and evidence of understanding of each question.		
	1 mark for correct application to case	max	14
(b)	mark for identification of each control failing.		
	1 mark for analysis of each failing	max	12
(c)	1 mark for recognition of each area where NEDs could improve matters.		
	1 mark per area for application to case	max	8
(d) (i)	1 mark for each point on importance.		
	1 mark for application of each point to case	max	6
(ii)	For each quality of information, ½ marks for recognition, 1 mark for development of quality based on content of case, 1½ marks per quality recognised and developed	max	6
			12
Additional professional marks for the layout, logical flow, persuasiveness and tone of the memo			4
			50

(a)   **Step 1 What are the facts of the case?**

The Mary Jane ship has sunk with much loss of life. This disaster could have been **prevented** if **structural changes** had been made to the ship to make it safer for the ship to operate in the rough seas of the Northport route.

Step 2 What are the ethical issues in the case ?

The main ethical issue is a conflict in responsibilities to stakeholders. Particularly as Sea Ships has stressed its ethical credentials, there is a **duty to the passengers who survived and the relatives of the victims** to make full disclosure of the circumstances to allow them to arrive at a better understanding of what has happened. On the other hand this exposes the company to a greater risk of huge damages, which will **destroy the value of shareholders' investment.**

Step 3 What are the norms, principles and values related to the case?

The norms are that the directors have a **duty of care to passengers**, and if that duty has been breached, then passengers and their relatives have a right to know the full circumstances. Sea Ships also should have ensured **compliance with safety legislation** because of the potential risk to life of breaches. It would also be **socially responsible** for Sea Ships to disclose the circumstances so that other shipping lines could take steps to prevent a similar disaster happening with another boat. Sea Ships has claimed to be maintaining the highest standards of corporate ethics, including **integrity and honesty.**

However the directors' primary duty is to **protect shareholder value**, and **keeping the report confidential** may mean that there is less chance of a successful action for negligence and the company's future being threatened by huge fines or damages.

Step 4 What are the alternative courses of action?

The first alternative is to **publish the consultant's report**.

The second alternative is to **keep the report confidential** and hope that there will be no leak.

Step 5 What is the best course of action consistent with the norms, principles and values?

If the directors place any value in Sea Ships' **commitment to social responsibility**, then they should **publish the report,** whatever the consequences to Sea Ships and its directors may be. It will be consistent with the **duty of care** to customers, and it will provide other external stakeholders (other shipping lines, insurance companies, regulators) with important information that may help to prevent a similar disaster in future.

Step 6 What are the consequences of each possible course of action?

If the report is disclosed, the consequences for Sea Ships and its directors will probably be severe. The **fines and damages** may be higher because the report provides additional evidence of **negligence**. These financial penalties may well force the company out of business and at minimum there will a severe loss of shareholder value. The **loss of reputation** may threaten Sea Ships' ability to operate the route in future and threaten the jobs of Sea Ships' workforce. The directors may be liable to prosecution on the grounds of **negligence.**

Non-disclosure may give the company a better chance of continuing, although if the **evidence of other control failures** is made public, the company and directors may be **liable anyway**. Non-disclosure by the board also carries the risk that **someone else**, possibly the consultant who wrote it, will **disclose the report.** This may result in the company and directors incurring **further liability** for non-disclosure of material evidence.

Step 7 What is the decision?

The board should disclose the report and the circumstances surrounding their failure to act on it. This will act to **protect passengers** who travel on Sea Ships or other lines in the future, and be consistent with the company's ethical values.

The alternative of non-disclosure is very **risky**, as it is likely that the report will be leaked by someone acting according to their conscience or with a grudge against the company. Non-disclosure would also be **against proclaimed ethical and governance values** and will not protect long-term shareholder value.

(b) **Design fault**

The first control failing was that the **design fault** was **highlighted** in the consultant's report, but the **consultant's report** was **not acted upon** because it was 'lost' in the company. This suggests a **serious failure in information provision** within the company.

Problems with loading

Control systems prior to departure also were inadequate as they allowed vehicles to be **loaded wrongly** onto ships. Well-trained staff or physical controls such as better signing would have prevented this happening. These problems contributed to the time pressure that led to the disaster.

Failure to secure doors

The accident was caused by the failure to secure the doors, and the **checks** over door **security** were inadequate. A design flaw meant that no review could take place from the deck of the ship. There was no formal requirement for acknowledgement that the **doors** had been **checked**, instead reliance was placed on someone else carrying out the **check** and the **confusion over responsibilities** meant the control was not carried out.

Reporting system

The ship's reporting system relied on **reporting by exception** – assuming all was well to sail unless the bridge heard otherwise. However if communications were faulty, problems may not have been reported to the bridge. The **previous system of positive reporting** by each department head being required should **not have been abandoned** just because it was **inconvenient to operate.**

Emphasis on speed

The systems were ineffective in allowing captains to give speed of departure and sailing priority over compliance with the law. There were **no control systems** on board to prevent the ships **breaking local speed limits.**

Failure to insure

Controls also failed to operate over Sea Ships' legal department with the result that the liability was not properly insured. The legal department should have **annually reviewed the insurance arrangements** to check that they covered all liabilities and recommended **major changes in cover or terms.**

(c) **Technical expertise**

Caroline Chan's comments highlight one failing of the board, the **lack of technical expertise.** Having a technically qualified nautical officer as a non-executive director would mean that the board was better able to assess the **technical and operating implications** of **major strategic decisions** such as **operating on different routes.**

Independent input

It appears that the current board were very complacent and placed unwarranted trust in the company's control systems. A non-executive director, recruited from outside, would have the **objectivity and independence** required to **challenge the board's strategy and question the company's approach to risk management.**

Improvement in control systems

It is debatable whether the current board could be relied on to review current systems to see how they could be improved, and as Caroline Chan implies, it is poor practice to rely totally on executive directors. Strong non-executive directors can work on board committees (audit and risk) to **monitor exposure to risk** and **review regularly overall control systems**, assessing whether they were as good as the executive directors thought they were. Their outside experience could enable them to **benchmark Sea Ships systems** against better practice elsewhere and therefore recommend improvements. It would also help Sea Ships comply with **local governance requirements** for listed companies.

Legal compliance

Because of the importance of compliance with health and safety legislation, non-executive directors should focus on the company's procedures for complying with **key legislation affecting operations.** They should also review the accounts to check not only compliance with accounting rules, but also that the **narrative in the accounts** gives a **fair picture,** in particular here whether statements about corporate responsibility are warranted by actual performance.

(d) **Memo**

From: Wim Bock, CEO
To: All Sea Ships senior officers
Date: 22 December 20X9
Subject: Information on internal control and risks

Colleagues

I know we are all grieving at the sinking of Mary Jane and of the terrible loss of life. I realise that we all would want to send our sympathies to the families and friends of those involved.

As a result of the tragic events the board has reviewed the internal control systems. One result is that I am writing to you now to remind you of the importance of proper **information provision.**

Board requirements

The board of Sea Ships requires information of good quality in order to be able to discharge its duties effectively. The directors need to place particular reliance on information provision to support the following areas.

Strategy setting

In order to establish **effective strategies**, the directors require **reliable information** about the business environment in which Sea Ships operates. This includes information about the major issues affecting the operation of ships. This allows the board to establish **what changes in working practices or design of the ships** will be necessary if the company is to operate new routes, and to **weigh the costs of these changes against the revenues** that new business may bring.

Monitoring of activities

Governance best practice requires the directors to regularly monitor the company's **activities and performance**, the **risks** it faces and how **efficiently and effectively** the control systems respond to risk. We therefore need information on a regular basis on how control systems are operating, and whether there are any problems or inefficiencies with systems on board ships or elsewhere. If the directors are made aware of issues, then we can take action to address them with your assistance.

Reporting on risks, internal controls and corporate responsibility

The board remains committed to fulfilling the highest standards of corporate governance and ethics. One important aspect of this is transparency, including full reporting of relevant information in the company's annual report. This incorporates a **full report on risks and controls**, including information about weaknesses in control and improvements that are being made. Users of the accounts must be able to place reliance on this report if the company is to repair its reputation. They can only do this if we can provide assurance that report is based on information with a number of qualities, which I shall now go on to discuss.

Qualitative characteristics of information

In order for the board to be able to make best use of the information you provide, that information must possess a number of features. The content of the information should be **clear** to the board, and the board should quickly be able to establish its **significance**. In particular the information you supply should have the following qualities.

Accuracy and reliability

Firstly to be reliable information must be **correct factually**. It must be **unbiased,** meaning that you should not try to play down news of weaknesses or problems with controls.

Timely

Information should be available when it is needed. This means **submitting routine reports on control and safety on time**. Completion of these reports should not be regarded as a bureaucratic chore but as an essential duty. Also if there are problems of which the directors should be aware, you should **report them immediately** while the directors can take action, for example problems over loading arrangements at ports.

User-directed

Information should be **clearly presented** and not **excessively long.** It should also contain **sufficient explanation of necessary technical and nautical detail** to enable board members without operating experience on ferries to be able to understand it. As already indicated, information needs to be **relevant** for board decision-making.

Complete

You must supply on a **timely basis all the information** you think the board needs to know. I would ask you to supply all necessary details of **risks, systems weaknesses and accidents**, even if you believe that you may cause difficulties for other personnel. It is essential that you do not suppress important information, however bad the news it appears to convey.

The future

The tragic loss of the Mary Jane has emphasised the importance of full provision of information on controls and risks in ensuring the safety of our ships and the commercial future of this company. I know I can rely on your full co-operation in supplying information when required and responding to information when it is provided. If any of you have any questions, please do not hesitate to contact me.

Wim Bock

66 Hesket Nuclear

Text references. Chapters 1, 7 and 11.

Top tips. A general definition of stakeholders would not have been awarded any marks in (a). The scenario makes clear in (a) who are the involuntary stakeholders. The key determinants of strength of claim are proven impact and ability to avoid that impact.

In (b) note that the requirement specified employee representatives/trade union's role in corporate governance so each point you made needed to be relevant to governance. As the answer demonstrates governance includes control systems and representatives can act within these in various ways, highlighting bad board behaviour and helping to manage human resources. The scenario makes it clear that FT's support has greatly benefited HN, but that in exchange perhaps it has used its position to force up wages and cause HPC's board to consider alternative solutions.

Your answer to (c) needs to bring out the competing objectives HN faces. Since the government is the only shareholder, these reflect the government's problems, particularly unemployment reduction versus expenditure (subsidy) reduction.

In (d) both parts of your answer needed to clearly counter NNN's arguments. There is plenty of information in the first couple of paragraphs of the scenario to support arguments by HP. (d) (i) shows how risk management builds on accurate risk assessment, (ii) corrects the impression that NNN's statements give that the footprint is wholly negative. It's difficult to do given limited time but you need to be careful that you don't give NNN opportunity to hit back – any statement about accepting risks could be twisted.

Easy marks. Any definitions in this paper, such as voluntary and involuntary stakeholders and agency should generate 2 or 3 straightforward marks.

Examiner's comments. The issues raised in the case were similar to those present in many such situations in a number of European countries and elsewhere where nuclear facilities are present. As in previous diets, the 50 mark question covered a number of sections of the P1 study guide.

In (a) the first task (distinguish) was done quite well in the majority of cases but after that, candidates often became confused over which stakeholders were in which 'camp'. A common mistake was to nominate the anti-nuclear group NNN as an involuntary stakeholder when it is obviously voluntary: it chose to engage with HN of its own free will.

(b) was one of the better questions in terms of candidate answers but the highest marks went to those able to show how FT had helped and challenged HPC using the evidence from the case. It was important to recognise that the union had been helpful to HPC in some respects but unhelpful in others.

In (c) most successful candidates achieved a pass mark on this part although others failed to see the difference between a government being the principal rather than shareholders.

Common errors in (d)(i) were to explain what risk assessment is rather than its importance or to fail to link the answer strongly enough with the case. Those achieving the highest marks were able to show the links with the NNN assessment and the effects that this flawed assessment might have.

For (d)(ii) many candidates were able to explain 'social and environmental footprint' but fewer were able to do well on the second task which was a level 3 intellectual outcome: to construct a case.

Despite my highlighting a poor 'professional marks' performance in previous examiner's reports, many candidates failed to approach the answer as required in order to gain all of these marks. In this case, the required format for the answer was a response statement for a website. This means it was NOT a letter or a report.

Marking scheme

			Marks
(a)	2 marks for distinguishing between the two types of stakeholder	2	
	½ mark for each voluntary stakeholder identified	max	2	
	½ mark for each involuntary stakeholder identified	max	2	
	2 marks for each assessment of the three involuntary stakeholders (1 mark for explanation of why it is involuntary and 1 mark for assessment of claim)	6	
			12
(b)	2 marks for each relevant role identified and explained	max	6	
	Critical evaluation		
	2 marks for each helpful/positive role identified and discussed	max	2	
	2 marks for each unhelpful/negative role identified and discussed	max	2	
	2 marks for conclusion/summary	max	2	
		max	10
(c)	1 mark for each relevant point on explaining agency relationship	max	2	
	1 mark for each relevant point in the exploration of HPC's agency with the government of Ayland	max	6	
	1 mark for each relevant point on HPC as a conventional company max	2	
			10
(d)	(i) 1 mark for each relevant point identified and 1 mark for explanation in the context of the case	max		8
	(ii) 2 marks for evidence of understanding of footprint in context	max	2	
	1 mark for each relevant positive social and environmental impact convincingly argued for	max	4	
			6
	Professional marks		4
			50

(a) **Voluntary stakeholders**

Voluntary stakeholders are those who **engage with the organisation of their own free will and choice,** and who can detach themselves from the relationship.

Voluntary stakeholders in HN

They are Forward Together, HN employees, Ayland government, local authorities, HPC board and No Nuclear Now.

Involuntary stakeholders

Involuntary stakeholders are those **whose involvement with the organisation is imposed** and who cannot themselves choose to withdraw from the relationship.

Involuntary stakeholders in HN

They are the Beeland and Ceeland governments, the seal colony and the local community.

Assessment of claims

Beeland's government

Beeland's government is representing its people, and it cannot move all of them and its capital city far away from the plant. The short distance 70 km suggests that it is very possible that **low level emissions** could affect Beeland. Scientific opinion suggests that a major incident could have **serious consequences for Beeland**. The government's claim that it can be affected by the plant is therefore **strong**.

Ceeland's government

Ceeland's government also have to represent its people and some of them would be worried about the plant and their inability to move from where they are. However Ceeland's government's claim is clearly **much weaker than Beeland's**, Ceeland is **much further way from the plant** (500 km) and reliable scientific evidence suggests that even a major incident will not impact significantly upon Ceeland.

Seal colony

Any emissions from the plant could affect the seal colony and more significant incidents may destroy it. Their **dependence on the local ecosystem** means that the seals cannot move away. These factors influence the strength of the claim of the colony. However the most important determinant of the strength of the claim is how much human interests should take priority over non-human interests, which is a matter of individual opinion.

Local community

Some local citizens will have had to put up with the plant being developed nearby, but others will have moved there since and **can move away again.** The plant also provides the local community with **jobs.** The most important factor strengthening the local community's claim is that it will be the most affected by a major incident.

(b) **Role of employee representatives in corporate governance**

Support for management

When board and employee representatives interests are **aligned**, the trade unions' support for the board can **strengthen the business's case against external threats.** For example a board's case against a hostile takeover can be strengthened by trade union opposition to the potential owners.

Critic of poor governance

Employee representatives are part of the safeguards for shareholders or owners over governance, since they are in a **strong position to protest** about aspects of poor governance. For example they will be concerned about a **lax control and risk environment**, which may jeopardise health and safety. They can raise the issues of **poor communication** by directors or **failure to protect whistleblowers who report wrongdoing.**

Control over human resources

Employee representatives can be part of the control systems over the key resource of staff. Most importantly they can advocate staff's interests, and seek to ensure staff are **content and therefore productive**. They can also be involved in **communication of information to staff**, and can be used by the board to ascertain the **views of workers**

Evaluation of Forward Together's (FT) role

Positive contribution

FT has **consistently supported HPC's board over time** on safety issues. FT has **stressed its members' role in ensuring compliance** and has supported the views put forward that Ceeland's fears are **unfounded.** This may help reassure Ceeland's government, as FT would clearly be concerned if the **risks were substantial**, since its members would be first affected by an incident.

Negative contribution

FT's attitude towards staffing issues has been **inflexible.** FT's demands have **driven wages up**, but FT has been **unconcerned with the impact on costs** and the need to stay within its subsidy. The views that foreign workers are not as reliable appear to **lack foundation** and are not based on a valid legal argument.

Conclusion

FT's support for the way HN is operated has strengthened the board's position over time. However FT appears to have **taken advantage of this** by driving up pay so much that the board has been forced to **recruit from overseas.** Whether overseas employees are as experienced as workers from Ayland is questionable.

(c) **Definition of agency relationship**

Agency is a relationship under which a principal engages another person (the agent) to **fulfil the principal's objectives,** and which involves **delegating decision-making authority** to the agent. The agent has a **fiduciary relationship** to its principal.

Board's agency relationship

Agent and principal

HPC's board are acting as the **agents** of its principal, the government of Ayland, the sole owner of HPC.

Accountability to electorate

In turn Ayland's government, and therefore its board, are **accountable to the electorate in Ayland.** Their principal concerns will be the taxes paid to **subsidise HN and their energy supply.**

Objectives

Determined by government

As Ayland's government solely owns HPC, it has the **right to determine its objectives**. These need not be, and are not, solely commercial.

Operational objectives

The most important objective that HPC's board has is that HN needs to be **kept operational** as it is a **key part of Ayland's energy strategy**. This increases the pressure on the board to ensure HN **operates safely.**

Political and environmental objectives

The board is working within the **objectives or constraints determined** by the government. These may change as the government approaches an election and probably will change if there is a change of government.

Social and economic objectives

One reason why HN has stayed open appears to have been that it **provides a great deal of local employment and boosts the local economy**. Ayland's government would have to provide unemployment benefits to many workers if it shut and also cope with other impacts on the area's economy. However the board also faces the economic objective of trying to find ways of **minimising the subsidy** it receives. This has meant that it has had to seek the lower cost solution of using foreign workers, reducing local employment opportunities.

Difference if private shareholders

If HN was owned by private shareholders, it would be assumed that its prime objective was to **maximise profits.** The board would therefore be concerned with **ensuring HP was profitable.** Since HP is currently loss-making, it would mean that the business would need to undergo **substantial restructuring** if it were ever privatised.

(d) **Statement**

HPC's response to NNN's report

We are aware that concerns have recently been raised about the operations of the HN power station following the recent report by NNN. We appreciate the reasons for those concerns. However we believe that NNN's risk assessment was inaccurate and we also strongly disagree with the conclusions of the report, that HN has a wholly negative impact and should be shut down.

Importance of accurate risk assessment.

Our own risk assessments do not support the figures published by NNN. We feel that we need to emphasise to **stakeholders** the importance we place on accurate risk assessment at HP and therefore our belief that our assessments are trustworthy.

Impact of problems

The most important reason why we seek to assess risks accurately is because we are aware of the **impacts** HP's activities could have. We appreciate that a major incident could have a devastating effect on the areas affected. We are also concerned about the impact of low-level emissions, since we understand the impact these can have on communities near the power station and on local eco-systems.

Use of money and resources

We are also aware that HP **receives a large subsidy and employs significant resources** in its operations. It is vital therefore that we demonstrate that we are carrying out our activities efficiently and economically as well as effectively. Accurate risk assessment helps us do this by forming the **basis for resource allocation**. Accurate assessment ensures that most resources are allocated to managing effectively the areas of highest risk.

Methods of managing

We also need to carry out accurate risk assessments in order to determine **the best ways to manage risks**. It helps us decide which risks should be avoided (because their potential impact is large) and which risks should be reduced by appropriate controls (because the risk is smaller).

Avoiding over-reaction

Lastly our risk assessments need to be accurate because we **do not wish to cause concern** by substantially over-rating risks. We believe that the assessment carried out by NNN greatly exaggerates the risks HP faces and has resulted in unnecessary alarm.

Social and environmental footprint

Our social and environmental footprint relates to the **net impact** we have on local communities and the wider natural environment in which we operate. The net impact is made up of a number of positive and negative interactions. Although NNN has sought to portray our footprint as wholly negative, we believe that we have several positive impacts externally that have to be considered when assessing our net footprint.

Employment providers

We remain a **very large employer** in an area where employment opportunities are relatively few. Our contribution to the regional economy is thus very important, and this is recognised by many regional and national stakeholders.

Clean energy strategy

Nuclear energy is a **renewable source of energy** and generates a **negligible amount of greenhouse gases**. It is an essential part of the government of Ayland's **clean energy strategy**. We have to fulfil stringent legal regulations that require us to ensure that emissions from HN do not harm the local environment. The alternative to provision of nuclear energy would be the burning of fossil fuels which would generate more pollution and would eventually be exhausted.

Reprocessing fuel

We provide reprocessing facilities for nuclear fuel that enable us to provide developing countries with a much **cheaper source of fuel.** By making it available, we are therefore **promoting economic development** in these countries.

Our safety record

We would remind our stakeholders that we have **fulfilled the high safety standards** to which we are subject. The FT trade union has recently highlighted our clear safety record since the 1970s. We intend to continue to live up to these high standards.

67 ZPT

Text references. Chapters 1-3, 8-9.

Top tips. The question is based on actual details from corporate governance scandals in America about ten years ago, that led to the development of the Sarbanes-Oxley legislation, including the requirement to report on internal controls over financial reporting.

In (a) a threat to the value of shareholdings is the main reason for intervention, with most of the other reasons ultimately resulting in a loss of value. Note also the thread about institutional shareholders having the opportunity (and maybe the responsibility) to enforce their views.

(b) required you to bring out the differences between absolution and relativism clearly. In (b) an important point with the relativist viewpoint is that although Shazia weighed up her options from an ethical perspective, you should disagree with her decision. Although she was facing conflicting ethical pressures, accountants should never take bribes.

(c)(i) did **not** require a list of the corporate governance failures in ZPT. A key word in the requirement is **by**. It meant that the way you had to make your case was to give examples of the consequences of ZPT going out of business due to its governance failures. The main theme behind (c) (i), which the scenario emphasises, is the loss to innocent internal and connected stakeholders. The other theme reflects what happened in America, the potential disruption to the whole economy of a large company's bankruptcy. This links to market confidence, a key theme in (ii) along with greater accountability and mandatory reporting making it more difficult to tolerate control failures. Our answer to (iii) is mainly based on the Turnbull report. If you used a different framework, it was important nevertheless to stress the responsibility of directors, the processes of internal control and the explanation of weaknesses.

The speech needs to read like a speech, so professional marks will be awarded for tone, flow and persuasiveness. Note the weaknesses highlighted by the examiner.

Easy marks. The examiner has published a question like (a) (i) before. Definitions, such as the different approaches to ethics, should always provide easy marks in this exam.

Examiner's comments. A similar situation happened in 'real life' some years ago and so some candidates may have been familiar with some of the issues already. This does show the value of studying current cases from the business news in preparing for P1 exams as 'real life' themes are sometimes borrowed in framing exam case studies.

(a) (i) was not a requirement to define 'institutional shareholders' as some candidates did (scoring nothing for their efforts in doing so). The content should have been well-known to any well-prepared candidate. For (a)(ii), candidates had to study the case to see which factors applied to ZPT and use these to 'construct the case', which means to produce arguments in favour of investor intervention because of the identified weaknesses.

In (b) from an absolutist perspective, it is obvious that no accountant should ever be complicit in bribery, fraud or mis-statement. From a relativist perspective and this is where the case raises an interesting ethical conundrum, it maybe right in some circumstances to show compassion and to carefully consider the consequences of actions, not merely their legality. Shazia used the money not to enrich herself but to pay for medical treatment for her mother. This in no way excuses her actions but it does raise the issue of trading one ethical good (upholding her professional and legal duties) against another (assisting in the medical care of her mother).

All parts of (c) were done poorly overall. What surprised me about this is that all parts are clearly 'core' areas in the P1 study guide and whilst some candidates addressed the questions correctly and scored highly, many did not.

In (c)(i), it seems that many candidates saw the first part of the requirement but ignored the second part. So they described the nature of 'sound corporate governance' whilst neglecting the second part which was to do this 'by assessing the consequences of the corporate governance failures ay ZPT'. This question is essentially probing the main purpose of corporate governance: without sound corporate governance, companies go bust, employees lose their jobs, investors lose their investments and can be financially ruined, and a number of other terrible outcomes. So the 'consequences of CG failure' was often overlooked by candidates, which meant that they failed to gain those marks.

(c)(ii) highlighted that poor internal controls were in part responsible for the situation at ZPT and that mandatory reporting to an agreed reporting framework would have made it much more difficult for the IC failures to have occurred. The accountability created by having to report on internal controls could have made it much more difficult for the ZPT management to have got away with the bad practice that they did.

In (c)(iii) the essential components should have included, in all cases, an acknowledgement statement (whose job is it?), a description of the processes (how is IC done?), it should be accurate and reliable, and, specifically, it should explain any particular IC weaknesses.

The professional marks were awarded for framing the answer to (c) in the form of a speech by a legislator. There was some evidence of improvement in candidates taking this seriously and setting out their answer accordingly, but others made errors like setting it out as a memo or letter, or else by using bullet points (in a speech?) or unlinked statements.

Marking scheme

				Marks
(a)	(i)	1 mark for each reason identified and explained (½ mark for identification only)	max	6
	(ii)	2 marks for each point identified and argued in context (½ mark for identification only)	max	6
				12
(b)		Distinguishing between absolutism and relativism (2 marks for each)		4
		Evaluation of Shazia Lo's behaviour from an absolutist perspective		3
		Evaluation of Shazia Lo's behaviour from a relativist perspective		3
				10
(c)	(i)	2 marks for assessment of each consequence of ZPT's governance failures (1 mark for brief explanation only)	max	10
	(ii)	2 marks for each argument identified and made	max	8
	(iii)	2 marks for each broad theme identified and explained	max	6
				24
		Additional professional marks for the structure, flow, persuasiveness and tone of the answer to (c)		4
				50

(a) (i) **Active intervention**

Active intervention by an institutional shareholder by making an attempt, for example, to change the board is regarded as a serious step, and may result in a **significant increase in agency costs**. However there are a number of reasons why it might happen.

Concerns about strategy

Institutional shareholders may intervene if they perceive that management's policies could lead to a fall in the long-term value of the company and hence the **value of their shares**. There could be concerns over **strategic decisions** over products, markets or investments or over **operational performance**. They could be concerned that management was taking **excessive risks** or was **unduly risk-averse**. Although institutional shareholders can sell their shares if they are unhappy, in practice it may be difficult to offload a significant shareholding without its value falling.

Poor ethical performance

Institutional investors may intervene because they feel the board cannot be trusted. At worst they may fear **management fraud.** They may also be concerned about the company showing **poor corporate social responsibility**. This may make it vulnerable to social and environmental risks and **harm its reputation** in the long-term.

Poor non-executive performance

Institutional investors may take steps if they feel that non-executive directors are exercising **insufficient influence** over executive management. This is particularly significant when there are concerns over the executive directors, for example a very strong chief executive.

Remuneration concerns

Another sign of limited non-executive influence may be **excessive executive pay**, with non-executive directors on the remuneration committee failing to enforce limits. Shareholders will also be concerned about executive greed and **failure to align remuneration with shareholder interests**.

Internal control failures

Intervention would be justified if institutional investors had **serious concerns about control systems**. They may be worried that control systems do not appear to have changed as the circumstances of the company have changed. They may also be worried about obvious failures, for example high-level fraud or failure to control expenditure on, and development of, major investments.

Compliance failures

The institutional investors may be concerned that they will **suffer criticism** if they are perceived as conniving in breaches of stock market requirements or governance codes because they have not taken action.

(ii) **Threat to share price and investment value**

The downgrading of the results represents a **clear threat to share price** and to the **value of the investment of institutional shareholders** and indeed all other investors. Not only were the results poorer than first announced, they also were below market expectations rather than above. A restatement of this magnitude was not guaranteed to have just a short-term effect on share price, whatever Clive Xu's views. Institutional investors should have intervened to find out why the restatement had happened.

Flaws in accounting and control systems

The restatement calls into question the **accuracy of the accounting and financial control systems.** Institutional investors should have intervened to find out why the systems supported figures used in the initial announcement that were clearly inaccurate. Institutional investors should also have aimed to find out why the auditors failed to identify the misstatement, as it appears that the **audit report may be worthless** and the accounts not therefore verified by an effective independent firm.

Senior management concerns

Again the restatement is of such a magnitude that it calls into very serious question the **competence and integrity of management**. The fact that the authorities were known to be investigating ZPT for **fraud** could have warranted intervention by itself. Even if there was no investigation underway, a misstatement of such seriousness would appear to require the **connivance of at least some of the executive directors.** Some directors, particularly non-executive directors, may have no knowledge of any fraud, but failed to identify problems and intervene. The investors should have been most concerned with the role of Clive Xu, on the grounds that his bonus was based on **artificially inflated figures,** and his failure to repay it raises doubts over his integrity.

(b)   **Absolutism**

Absolutism is the view that there is an **unchanging set of ethical principles** that will apply in all situations, at all times and in all societies. The principles should be applied whatever the pressures on the decision-maker.

Relativism

Relativism is the view that a **wide variety of acceptable ethical practices** exist. The ethics that are most appropriate in a given situation will depend on the **conditions** at the time.

Absolutist evaluation of Shazia Lo

Shazia Lo's conduct was ethically correct from an absolutist viewpoint in these ways.

Concern about over-valuation of contracts

She was right to ask herself whether the valuation of contracts was warranted. As a qualified accountant, she is subject to **high ethical and technical standards**, and also **public expectations** that she will act professionally and not be associated with misleading information. Questioning figures that she thought might be wrong fulfils these responsibilities.

Reporting to the finance director

Having become concerned about the problems, Shazia was right to raise the issue with the finance director. She was acting correctly from an absolutist viewpoint in **not being influenced by the impact on her position at ZPT** if her actions were unpopular with management.

Disclosure to press

Threatening to disclose the information outside the company was also correct from an absolutist viewpoint. Again professional ethical guidance makes clear the circumstances in which the **duty to disclose takes precedence over a duty of confidentiality**. These include **false accounting,** since remaining silent would mean that the owners of the company, the shareholders, are being **defrauded.**

Relativist evaluation of Shazia's actions

Shazia's eventual action can be seen from a relativist viewpoint as follows.

Weighing up conflicting ethical outcomes

Relativist viewpoints acknowledge that because a wide variety of ethical practices exist, it is possible that the decision-maker may find that there is a **conflict between two different ethical outcomes**. Here Shazia had to **weigh up** the conflict between the requirement to disclose the fraud, and the morally good ways in which the bonus could be used.

Taking an ethical decision

Shazia's conduct appears to indicate that, having weighed up the two outcomes, she took what appeared to her to be the **best ethical outcome.** She did not keep any of the bonus for herself, but used the money to alleviate her mother's suffering. She gave precedence to reducing her mother's pain over the professional considerations she faced.

Taking the right ethical decision

However it is also possible to question from a relativist viewpoint whether Shazia **weighed up the outcomes correctly.** Her eventual decision meant that she not only **failed to fulfil her professional responsibilities,** she also **accepted a bribe.** The view here is that Shazia should not have had the opportunity to help her mother, since the money she needed to do so was obtained **illegitimately,** through **dishonesty,** and this over-rides the ethically good use of the money.

(c)   **Speech on consequences of poor corporate governance**

Introduction

Honourable members, the case I am making today for enhanced corporate governance is a response to the major problems in our country's business environment. These have resulted from the collapse of one or our largest companies, ZPT, and one of our major audit firms, JJC. Apart from the significant impact on all those involved with ZPT or JJC, we should not underestimate the **general impact on business confidence** in this country.

(i)   **Consequences of corporate governance failure in ZPT**

I believe that what happened in ZPT demonstrates the **importance of better corporate governance to prevent the damage caused by management recklessness and incompetence,** The case for stricter regulation can be made by examining in detail the consequences of governance failure at ZPT.

Shareholders

Firstly, ZPT demonstrates that a lack of control over arrogant and negligent directors results in a **loss of shareholder investment**. The shareholders in ZPT received no payments when the company was liquidated. I would remind you that many who lost out were not rich people and big corporations. Instead they were small investors who placed their money in good faith with pension funds and insurance companies, institutional investors, who invested significantly in ZPT. These small investors have seen their potential future income significantly reduced as a result of the collapse. Better governance legislation is needed to protect them.

Employees

Secondly, it will be obvious how much ZPT's and also JJC's employees have lost as a result of the company's collapse. Not only have they lost their jobs without termination payments. ZPT's employees have also **seen the value of their income in old age depleted** because they invested in a pension fund that has proved to be vulnerable to the directors' poor decision-making. We will need to consider stronger protection for employees' pension funds. However for now not only are many of these employees suffering the problems of unemployment, the **burden on our taxpayers is higher,** in terms of unemployment benefit and perhaps future old age support.

Suppliers and customers

Thirdly, those have done business with ZPT have also suffered significant losses. **Suppliers** who provided goods and services have gone unpaid. In the current economic climate this may have threatened their future existence. The lack of money left to repay legitimate business debts indicates that **excessive risks** were taken, and that stricter governance requirements are necessary to force directors to focus on effective risk management. Customers too are **no longer receiving the services and support** for which they have paid, causing personal inconvenience and difficulties to businesses. Again, it is unacceptable that excessive risk-taking has meant that customers have **not received value** in return for their payment.

Impact on wider economy

I would also like to remind you of several broader impacts on our economy. **Confidence in other telecommunications providers as sound investments** has been **damaged**. JJC's failure to report the problems with ZPT may also have caused a **loss of confidence in the audit profession**. This undermines one of the supports to investors being able to deal in shares confidently. Investors need to be sure that the **financial information** they are using as a basis for their decisions is **reliable**. A

key source of reassurance is that the information has been effectively and independently verified by strong audit firms. Is an audit firm that also provides lucrative consulting services to its client truly independent? The collapse of JJC has also caused **short to medium-term disruption in the audit profession.** JJC's former clients have needed to find other accountants, and other major firms have struggled to cope. With one fewer major firm, the audit industry has also become less competitive.

Dishonest culture

Supporting better corporate governance will also send out a message that we support a **business culture based on honesty and trust.** The lax governance arrangements in ZPT placed employees in impossible positions. Although we may deplore Ms Lo's conduct in accepting a bribe, we should condemn all the more a system where it was considered best for directors to offer her an inducement. We should also ask ourselves why there were **no internal mechanisms** for Ms Lo to report concerns with impunity, rather than being forced to talk to the media to express her worries. Better corporate mechanisms, such an audit committee, will ensure channels exist for honest employees to report their concerns in the knowledge that they will receive a fair hearing and not be victimised.

(ii)   **Case for mandatory control reporting**

I shall now concentrate on the need for compulsory reporting on internal controls and risks. ZPT's problems arose not only from accounts that gave **inaccurate data**, but accounts that **did not provide sufficient information** about the risks it faced and how these risks were being controlled. There are a number of reasons for requiring major companies to report on risks and controls.

Enhanced confidence

The first reason should be obvious from my previous remarks, that **better reporting improves the confidence of investors.** Investors need to know that boards are **managing risks responsibly**, and that the **information companies provide is reliable.** ZPT's bankruptcy illustrates how rapidly things can go wrong if confidence in directors and controls collapses.

Good practice

Secondly if companies have to report on controls, they know that many investors will scrutinise the report carefully and pursue any weaknesses or problems that the report appears to indicate. This will act as a clear incentive for companies to **eliminate problems by developing effective control systems** and therefore keeping investors happy. The requirement to report annually will mean that review of internal controls has to be a permanent element of companies' systems.

Holding directors to account

Linked in with this, a compulsory report provides ammunition to those that have most power to hold **directors accountable.** These include **stock market regulators**, who can investigate poor practice. They also include **institutional investors** such as pension funds, whose role in ZPT has been criticised significantly. Better reporting would assist greater shareholder activism by institutional investors. It would enable earlier intervention than was possible with ZPT, where the complexities of the group structure and the lack of requirement to report on controls, may have made it difficult for investors to find reasons to intervene.

Need for legislation

Some members might argue that if best practice was publicised rather than enforced by law, that investors would note which companies gave most information and invest in those companies. Companies that were less transparent would see their share prices fall. However there would still be the risk of a similar situation to ZPT developing again. In time there may be another company whose apparently excellent results drive up its share price, with insufficient attention being paid to **possible control weaknesses and lack of transparency** that enable directors to **publish inflated figures.**

(iii)   **Content of report on controls**

I do not have time during this speech to do more than outline the broad areas that I believe that a report on internal control should contain. Further details will be included in the bill that I intend to introduce. The areas I recommend have also featured in other guidance on governance around the world, and have resulted in improved reporting in many countries.

Statement by directors

Firstly the report should include an **acknowledgement by the directors** that they are responsible for the company's system of internal control and reviewing its effectiveness. If ZPT's directors had been obliged to make this statement, it would have emphasised to them their **responsibility** for making sure that the systems were working well. Directors making this statement would not easily be able to play down a major restatement of the financial accounts as due to' regrettable accounting errors.' The statement also emphasises that the board supports the development of effective control systems, and board support is a very important impetus towards developing effective systems.

Process for managing risk

Secondly the statement needs to confirm that there have been **processes in place for managing risks** and highlight and explain any unusual features. Mr Xu alleged some time after ZPT went bankrupt that its complex group structure was a method of managing exchange rate risks. Had ZPT been required to explain this in full, stakeholders would have had a better understanding of how the company was being run, and been able to form their own judgements on whether the structures used were appropriate.

Monitoring by directors

In order to make sure that risk and control systems have been continuing to operate effectively over time, directors **need to review how they have worked.** A major problem identified at ZPT was a **lack of effective oversight** of the controls over the external reporting process. To provide users of accounts with confidence that monitoring has happened therefore, the report on controls needs to include a **summary of the process** that the directors have used to review the effectiveness of control systems. This may include use of a board committee, often the **audit committee,** and also drawing on the work of **internal audit** to support the review.

Problems and weaknesses

If the board review has identified **significant weaknesses in internal control,** then the report needs to give details of these. Significant weaknesses include problems that have resulted in major losses or uncertainties that are, or should be, disclosed in the accounts. One of the major reasons for ZPT's misleading accounts was a failure to follow accounting standards. A board review should have highlighted problems with compliance and explained the implications if these problems had previously affected the accounts.

Conclusion

I would like to thank all of you for your time today. I hope the case I have put for enhanced corporate governance legislation has persuaded you of its necessity. Our economy cannot afford the damage that results from further big corporate scandals. I believe therefore that we have a urgent duty to take steps that will help to prevent another ZPT.

68 Bobo

Text references. Chapters 3, 6, 7, 9 and 11.

Top tips. (a) illustrates the value of systematically reading the scenario as the risks are clearly flagged and some strong hints given about the controls. Any reference in this type of question to cost cutting or rushing work should ring alarm bells and you need to keep an eye out for the consequences of these. Be alert also for signs of intimidation as this illustrates a poor culture and often results in serious consequences. The examiner uses the verb explore to give you some flexibility in how you discuss the issues.

In (b) many students clearly thought that there had to be one person at each Kohlberg level, but this wasn't the case. Vernon's positioning is very clear given his overriding concerns with personal rewards. The key determinant of James's position is that 'he is complying with the expectations of shareholders ie stakeholders close to the company. Although Kathy's stance appears more ethical than James, she is arguing her position on the basis of the expectations of customers, which places her in the conventional category as well.

In (c) the term extraordinary general meeting is not used in all jurisdictions, but it is clear from the context what is happening. The key justification is that the issues discussed at the EGM must be discussed now and not some months later at the AGM. These will generally be matters that pose a serious immediate risk to shareholder value, such as very poor management decision-making.

With (d) (i) it is important to understand the limitations placed by the question requirements on discussing the chief executive roles. Although the answer covers many of the general roles, it is important to link each of them to James's involvement in the Bobo Foo development. (ii) is an excellent example of the examiner asking students to argue from a viewpoint with which many will have disagreed. With both parts, it is important to try to make as strong a case as possible, emphasising the interests of shareholders and the commercial success of the new car, even though you can see some obvious flaws. Our answer does not mention the failure to act on the test result, which is probably the weakest part of the company's position.

Easy marks. The requirement to explain the different levels of Kohlberg has been examined in a number of questions, and you must revise this area if you struggled with it.

Examiner's comments. As usual, I used the scenario to examine a number of outcomes which not only sampled the study guide and also required candidates to answer at more than one level intellectual level. Also as previously, the requirements were based heavily upon the case, meaning that candidates had to study the case in some detail to gain marks.

In (a) the verb 'explore' was used here to enable candidates to have latitude in responding to this task. Many candidates were able to correctly pick out and explore the causes of the problem. The second task in (a) was less well done than the first task. A careful consideration of the specific problems at Bobo was the secret to gaining marks. Candidates that attempted to answer this using a memorised list of points from a study text or other notes were less well rewarded.

ACCA examiner's answer. The ACCA examiner's answer to this question can be found at the back of this kit.

Marks

(a) 2 marks for each cause identified and described max   8
     2 marks for each internal control measure identified and described   max

                                                                                                 6
                                                                                         max
                                                                                                         12
(b) 2 marks for each Kohlberg level identified and described   6
     2 marks for each level correctly assigned to a person with evidence, 1
     mark for correct recognition only max   6
                                                                                                         12
(c) 2 marks for distinction between AGMs and EGMs   2
     1 mark for purpose of AGMs   1
     1 mark for purpose of EGMs   1
     1 mark for each advantage max   4
                                                                                                         8
(d) (i)   1 mark for each role identified and 1 for placing in context or 1
     mark for each role identified and briefly explained max   8
     (ii)   2 marks for each point of defence identified and developed max   6

     Up to 4 professional marks for clarity, logical flow, persuasiveness and
     appropriate structure   4
                                                                                                         18
                                                                                                         50

(a) **Cost reduction**

James **emphasised that cost reduction** not safety, was the top priority. This was done to be able to market the car as cheap to buy. James sought to **embed cost savings** as the most important consideration in the thinking of the production team by his poster campaign. **Key decisions** were **determined** by the need to limit costs, particularly the reduction of the testing period, the positioning of the fuel tank and the decision to proceed after the test results.

Reduction in development time

The **significant reduction in the development period** from 43 to 25 months resulted in not enough time being provided to test all the design features satisfactorily. The lack of a sufficient testing period was more significant in relation to the positioning of the fuel tank, since it was proposed in order to save costs and not because it was safe.

Crash test results

The crash tests provided clear evidence that the **positioning of the fuel tank** was **unsafe.** If Bobo had acted in accordance with what the tests indicated, production would have been delayed. However the board decided that **the cost involved in retooling the production line** was the most important consideration in determining whether production went ahead, on the grounds that the directors wished to make a return on the investment as soon as possible

Intimidation

Kathy's actions were determined by the pressures placed on her by James's poster campaign. She was **intimidated** into going ahead with the testing process despite having inadequate time and not protesting about, and making public, the results of the fire safety test. Other directors also failed to raise concerns about the impact of the reduced testing period and the results of the fire safety test. If the board had included strong-minded, independent non-executive directors, they would have felt able to challenge James's decisions.

Internal control measures

Embedding safety

The board needs to ensure product safety is **embedded in the thinking of all staff.** Public statements, such as adverts, should highlight product safety as a key feature of all Bobo's cars. The board should emphasise to staff the need to ensure that products are safe, so that it influences all actions taken by staff. All designs for new cars must include an appropriate safety metric.

Development time

Adequate time needs to be budgeted for testing of vehicles. The minimum period to market should be determined by the time **required to complete thoroughly** all safety tests. The designers should be encouraged to protest if they feel that the testing period allocated is too short.

Testing sign-off

Safety testing, such as the crash test, should be built into the development process at various key stages. As part of the sign-off process before production is allowed to go ahead, management should **obtain evidence that all necessary tests** have been **completed** and **review the results for any problems.** Management must not allow production to go ahead if weaknesses identified by the safety testing have not been rectified.

(b) **Kohlberg's moral development**

Kohlberg provides a framework for classifying responses to ethical issues, based on the moral development of the individual. Kohlberg argued that there are three levels.

Pre-conventional

Pre-conventional development means judging ethical problems in terms of the **drawbacks and benefits** that may affect the individual taking the decision. The individual sees the decision in self-serving terms of whether he or she will be **punished** for ethically wrong behaviour, or **rewarded** for behaving in an ethically acceptable way.

Conventional

Conventional development means taking ethical decisions on the basis of what is **accepted as ethical behaviour** by those who have a relationship with the person taking the decision. It means following the **ethical norms** in the **workplace or the local community**, or **obeying the laws of society** on the grounds that they **codify ethical behaviour** that the community accepts to be right.

Post-conventional

Post conventional development means taking autonomous **ethical decisions** in accordance with **relevant ethical principles.** These ethical principles may be **ethical principles that are applied in the individual's society**, or they may be **universal ethical principles.**

Levels of Bobo management

James

James is exhibiting a **conventional level** of moral development. He believes that the decision should comply with the expectations of those with whom the board has a close business relationship, that is the **shareholders as key stakeholders.** He has argued against the recall option because investors and stock markets would form an adverse view of Bobo as a result.

Kathy

Kathy is exhibiting a **conventional level** of moral development. Her decision again depends on the views of **key stakeholders**. However she is most concerned about **customers**, not shareholders. Her argument is not based on compliance with society's ethical principles as an end in itself. Instead she takes the **pragmatic** line that the decision should be determined by the need to **convince customers** that the cars are safe, and also society that Bobo is acting in line with **society's expectations** about its corporate social responsibility.

Vernon

Vernon is exhibiting a **pre-conventional level** of moral development. He believes that the decision should be determined by the impact on the rewards, the bonuses, that he and the other board members receive. Ethical principles or the expectations of shareholders appear to play no part in his thinking.

(c) **AGM and EGM**

The annual general meeting (AGM) is a **statutorily guaranteed** opportunity for the shareholders of a company to be informed of its affairs and hold its management **accountable.** It is part of the financial calendar of a company.

Extraordinary general meetings (EGM) are one-off meetings, held if there is a **matter of great significance or grave concern affecting the company's present position or its future.** In most jurisdictions, directors can summon an EGM. However if members wish to compel the directors to hold an EGM, they need to hold a certain percentage of share capital holding voting rights.

Purpose of AGM

The AGM is the **most important formal means of communication** with shareholders. AGMs give directors the opportunity to discuss with members the results of the company, present its audited accounts and explain its future outlook. Shareholders vote in proportion to their holdings on the appointment and remuneration of directors, the appointment of auditors and the level of dividends.

Purpose of EGM

EGM are often convened to **discuss issues that cannot wait until the next annual general meeting**. They may be called to allow the shareholders to vote on whether the company should pursue a major business opportunity, such as an acquisition. They may also be called if the company is facing significant risks to its future or the shareholders have major concerns about the decisions directors have taken, to inform shareholders of what is happening and hopefully reassure them.

Advantages of holding EGM

Matters of concern to shareholders

The EGM gives shareholders the chance to be informed about, and discuss, the **safety problems.** The negative publicity surrounding these problems may seriously affect the **value of the shareholders' investment**. Shareholders may also have serious ethical concerns about what has happened.

Accountability

The EGM offers shareholders an opportunity to **hold James to immediate account** for **serious errors of judgement**. These include the decision to proceed with the production of the Bobo Foo despite the safety concerns and the decision not to discuss the choice of the compensation option in public.

Publicity

Although the board tried to keep the decision to pursue the compensation option secret, this has proved counter-productive and has led to much bad publicity. The EGM offers the chief executive and the board a **public opportunity to respond to the bad publicity.** It also offers the board the chance to speak directly to shareholders and answer their questions. It therefore may be a better way to reassure shareholders than written communication.

Resolving the position

The EGM gives shareholders the chance to pass a **vote of no confidence.** If shareholders are not satisfied with the explanations given by James, they can vote him and also other directors out of office. This will quickly **resolve the issues of shareholder dissatisfaction with the board and allow Bobo to move forward,** rather than have uncertainty over the company and board's situation drag on until the next AGM.

(d) (i) **Statement at EGM of chief executive's roles**

Thank you for taking the time to come to this extraordinary general meeting. I appreciate that you have a number of serious concerns arising from the recent media coverage about the Bobo Foo. I intend to address these concerns in my statement today.

The first area I shall cover is my own role as chief executive leading the company over the recent period. One of my most important responsibilities is to lead the **development of the company's business objectives and strategy.** I was recruited on the basis that I would oversee Bobo's entry into the economy car market. It was believed that developing a new model for this sector would enhance Bobo's profitability and brand, as a supplier providing cars in all the main market segments.

The second aspect of my role is to **lead the management team** who, amongst other tasks, are responsible for developing new models. Although I was closely involved in the development of the Bobo Foo, the model could not have been developed successfully without the expertise of those involved with all aspects of the project. I believe in particular that Bobo is lucky to have Kathy Yao on the board and in charge of an excellent team of car designers.

As chief executive I am also responsible for overseeing the operational performance of Bobo. This includes **effective management of the company's financial and human resources** and ensuring that appropriate risk management and control systems are in place, weighing the benefits of control systems against their costs. I therefore took a close interest in the development of the Bobo Foo. I emphasised to the management team the factors that were necessary to achieve good performance in the economy car market. The sale of half a million units a year in a very competitive market represents a strong commercial performance.

The last aspect of the role that I want to discuss is my responsibility for dealing with a **range of stakeholders.** This of course very importantly includes addresses the concerns of you, our shareholders. It also means dealing with legal authorities, suppliers and of course customers. It was therefore my responsibility to deal with the legal issues and compensation claims that have been made against Bobo as a result of issues with the Foo's design.

(ii) **Justification of decision**

I shall now therefore explain the reasons behind our decision not to issue a universal recall of the Foo but to continue dealing with compensation claims.

Firstly, as I have indicated, I have a number of accountabilities to different stakeholders, but my **primary accountability** is to you, our shareholders, as owners of this company. When I am faced with a **range of conflicting views** from different stakeholders, I must remember that my most important responsibility is to **protect shareholder value**. The decisions I take must be taken with this duty always in mind.

The decision not to recall the Foo was therefore taken on the basis of fulfilling my responsibility to take the course of action that would provide the **best value for shareholders.** The detailed calculations that our Finance Director, Vernon Vim, has produced, showed that the expected value of the costs of a universal recall would be approximately $750 million over 10 years. This would represent a very significant loss of shareholder value. The costs of continuing to deal with compensation claims are less certain. However on the basis of the incidents with the Foo so far, it is most likely that the costs of the compensation claims would be around $200 million, over half a billion dollars less than the recall option.

I therefore would justify the decision to continue to deal with compensation claims on the basis of the **huge difference between the costs of the two options.** As a result of my fiduciary duty to preserve shareholder value, I had to choose the option that is virtually certain to result in a much smaller loss of shareholder value. I appreciate some of you may have wanted us to take the decision on other criteria. However I hope you will understand that I took a very difficult decision in good faith, on the basis of my responsibilities as chief executive to opt for the most commercially and financially realistic decision.

If any of you have any questions you would like me to answer, I will now gladly do so.

Mock exams

ACCA Professional Level

Paper P1

Professional Accountant

Mock Examination 1

Question Paper	
Time allowed	
Reading and Planning Writing	**15 minutes** **3 hours**
This paper is divided into two sections Section A This ONE question is compulsory and must be attempted Section B TWO questions only to be attempted	
During reading and planning time only the question paper may be annotated	

**DO NOT OPEN THIS PAPER UNTIL YOU ARE READY TO START UNDER
EXAMINATION CONDITIONS**

Section A – This question is compulsory and must be attempted

Question 1

SeaShells is a small company operating from an island near continental Europe. SeaShells is a private company with 25 shareholders; its shares are not traded on any stock exchange. The main shareholders of SeaShells include relatives of the company's first CEO, and also private investors from whom the first CEO sought finance and who have since retained their shares. 25% of the share capital is held by members of the current board.

Although SeaShells is a private company, its board is constituted in accordance with good corporate governance practice. Half of the directors are executive directors and half of the directors are non-executive directors who are independent in accordance with the guidance in the UK Corporate Governance Code. The board also operates nomination, remuneration and audit committees. The members of all these committees are all non-executive directors.

The main business of SeaShells is packaging of fresh seafood (fish, oysters, crab etc.) and selling these to supermarkets and other retailers. The company employs 750 people, mainly in the packing departments. Packing is labour intensive due to the need to clear and prepare fish etc. by hand prior to packing. Supplies of seafood are obtained from the island's fishing fleet. Previously the fleet supplied a number of companies on the island. However recently a couple of the fleet's other major customers have closed down, and the result is that SeaShells is now the only significant customer of the fleet. SeaShells is also one of the island's major employers. There is some concern that SeaShells' increased demand for seafood is causing over-exploitation of some fish species, and that the population of these fish may "crash" or decrease dramatically in the near future.

In the last few weeks, the directors of SeaShells have decided to transfer almost all of the packaging of seafood to another country. The seafood will be moved by refrigerated ships to this other country, packaged by workers there and then moved back by ship to SeaShells for resale as before. The rationale behind this move is that labour costs are only $1/10^{th}$ of the costs on the island. Even taking into account transportation costs, this move will halve the packaging costs of SeaShells. As a result of the move, the workforce will decrease to 200 people. The decision has resulted in significant adverse publicity for SeaShells on the island. The trade union representing the employees has threatened strike action, saying that this is a typical example of exploitative employment practices. However the reaction from customers has been positive as the company can offer reduced prices on many products. A government minister on the island on which Sea Shells is based has recently welcomed developments that limit the price of food to consumers. However the government has recently come under attack from the opposition for allowing jobs to be exported from the island. Both these issues are expected to be campaign issues when an election is held on the island next year.

The directors of SeaShells believe that the decision to transfer the packaging of seafood is correct because, as the CEO explained, the decision is "best for the company, best for the shareholders and best for the directors". The CEO has dismissed the objections to the transfer of employment as' predictable whinging and politician grandstanding.' He has noted that the move has been very popular in the country to which employment will be transferred.

However a couple of the non-executive directors have raised doubts about the move. One has raised the objection that SeaShells depends on sales on its island. However it is removing purchasing power from the island by transferring employment overseas. The other non-executive director has wondered about the impact of moving the packaging operations on SeaShells' environmental footprint and whether it can be regarded as sustainable. He has also wondered about the impact of the move on SeaShells' financial accounts. If the impact on the figures in the accounts is limited, he has raised the issue whether, on grounds of corporate social responsibility, the accounts should include more information about the impact on the environment, or whether this information should be included in a separate report.

The CEO's comment concerning directors is certainly true in terms of directors' remuneration. 75% of the total remuneration package of the directors is based on performance related pay, the main element of this being the net profit of SeaShells. The chairman of the remuneration committee believes that it is important that directors' bonuses can clearly be related to tangible measures. 'Our shareholders want profit, so if the company makes profits, it's only fair that the directors should benefit.' The remaining 25% of remuneration relates to salary and is based on a 3 year contract with SeaShells. Other (non-salary) remuneration includes company contributions to a pension scheme and a share option scheme, with options being exercisable in 5 years based on the share price 1 year ago.

The CEO believes that it is important that the board of SeaShells continues to be staffed by high-calibre executive directors. He believes that the package offered to executive directors must be more than competitive, since SeaShells is a private company. He feels that there is a risk that directors who are seeking to develop their careers may seek to do so in companies listed on an international stock exchange, because of a perception that the opportunities, and therefore the rewards, at these companies are greater. The CEO's arguments have persuaded the remuneration committee and a number of features of directors' remuneration packages are designed to bind them to SeaShells in the longer term.

There have recently been two changes to the board of SeaShells. The Finance Director has retired, and has been replaced by his deputy, who was previously Financial Controller. SeaShells has also recruited a new Marketing Director. The director was previously a senior employee at a large marketing consultancy on the European mainland.

Required

(a)   Explain Mendelow's theory of stakeholder power. Identify the stakeholders involved in the decision to transfer packaging of seafood to another country, and assess the response of each group to this decision.

(14 marks)

(b)   Using Gray, Owens and Adams' viewpoints on social responsibility as a framework for your answer, evaluate the decision to transfer packaging seafood to another country. **(14 marks)**

(c)   Prepare a memo for the board that:

(i)   Defines the concept of ''sustainability'' and assesses the extent to which SeaShells' activities can be considered sustainable **(7 marks)**

(ii)   Evaluates methods of reporting that can be used by SeaShells to explain the environmental impact of its activities. **(7 marks)**

(part (c) also includes 4 professional marks)

(d)   Explain corporate governance best practice in terms of directors' remuneration and assess the extent to which remuneration in SeaShells meets these requirements, making any recommendations you consider appropriate. **(4 marks)**

(Total = 50 marks)

Section B – TWO questions ONLY to be attempted

Question 2

HiT is an information technology company set up in the Dotcom boom in the late 1990s. Unlike many other companies, it did not expand too quickly at first as the proprietors were cautious and hence did not seek external funding other than venture capital. As a result the company has been well-placed to pick up business that has become available in the IT sector and has done well since the millennium.

The directors have now decided on a policy of expansion both internally and by acquisition. They appreciate that they will need more external funding, and believe the company will soon be in a healthy enough position for them to seek a stock market listing.

The chairman understands that a listing will mean that the company's corporate governance structures need to become more formal. Previously the board has just consisted of the original shareholders plus a representative from the venture capitalists. The chairman appreciates that if HiT is listed, the company will need to recruit some non-executive directors to the board, but are unclear about their role and why most of them need to be independent.

In addition the chairman has doubts about a number of comments that were made at a recent board meeting by executive directors.

'In order to maintain board unity, the whole board should set directors' remuneration. Any other arrangement would be divisive.'

'As we're paying the finance director a large sum of money, we should be able to rely on him to get the figures right. The external auditors will pick up any errors.'

' Any new directors we recruit have to fit in, otherwise we'll destroy board unity. The board as a whole needs to decide on and interview possible candidates.'

The chairman has also recently spoken informally to someone who may be interested in becoming a non-executive director. This person has expressed interest, but has stated that he wants part of his remuneration to be in the form of shares or share options.

Required

(a)   Explain the board position and desirable attributes of non-executive directors and their role in the corporate governance of a listed company.   **(7 marks)**

(b)   Explain the distinction between independent and non-independent non-executive directors.   **(3 marks)**

(c)   Assess the corporate governance issues that are linked to the comments made at the recent board meeting, and advise the chairman on how non-executive directors can help resolve any problems.   **(11 marks)**

(d)   Discuss the objections to paying non-executive directors in shares or share options.   **(4 marks)**

(Total = 25 marks)

Question 3

HOOD sells a wide range of coats, anoraks, waterproof trousers and similar outdoor clothing from its 56 stores located in one country. The company is profitable, although the gross profit in some stores has declined recently for no apparent reason.

Each store uses EPOS to maintain control of inventory and provides the facility to use EFTPOS for payments. However, about 55% of all transactions are still made by cash. Details of sales made and inventory below re-order levels are transferred to head office on a daily basis where management reports are also prepared.

Inventory is ordered centrally from Head Office, details of requirements being obtained from the daily management information provided by each store. Orders are sent to suppliers in the post, inventory arriving at each store approximately 10 days after the re-order level is reached.

Recent newspaper reports indicate one of the chemicals used to waterproof garments releases toxic fumes after prolonged exposure to sunlight. The board of HOOD are investigating the claim, but are currently treating it with some degree of scepticism. The product range has generally sold well, although there has been little innovation in terms of garment design in the last 4 years.

Required

(a)   Explain the different risks facing HOOD and identify which risks are strategic risks and which risks are operational risks.   **(10 marks)**

(b)   Assess the potential effect of each risk on the company and recommend how the impact of that risk can be minimised.   **(15 marks)**

(Total = 25 marks)

Question 4

LMN is a charity that provides low-cost housing for people on low incomes. The government has privatised much of the home building, maintenance and management in this sector. The sector is heavily regulated and receives some government money but there are significant funds borrowed from banks to invest in new housing developments, on the security of future rent receipts. Government agencies subsidise much of the rental cost for low-income residents.

The board and senior management have identified the major risks to LMN as: having insufficient housing stock of a suitable type to meet the needs of local people on low incomes; making poor property investment decisions; having dissatisfied tenants due to inadequate property maintenance; failing to comply with the requirements of the regulator; having a poor credit rating with lenders; poor cost control; incurring bad debts for rental; and having vacant properties that are not earning income. LMN has produced a risk register as part of its risk management process. For each of more than 200 individual risks, the risk register identifies a description of the risk and the (high, medium or low) likelihood of the risk eventuating and the (high, medium or low) consequences for the organisation if the risk does eventuate.

The management of LMN is carried out by professionally qualified housing executives with wide experience in property development, housing management and maintenance, and financial management. The board of LMN is composed of volunteers with wide experience and an interest in social welfare. The board is representative of the community, tenants and the local authority, any of whom may be shareholders (shareholdings are nominal and the company pays no dividends). The local authority has overall responsibility for housing and social welfare in the area. The audit committee of the board of LMN, which has responsibility for risk management as well as internal control, wants to move towards a system of internal controls that are more closely related to risks identified in the risk register.

Required

For an organisation like LMN:

(a)   Analyse the purposes and justify the importance of risk management and explain its relationship with the internal control system.   **(9 marks)**

(b)   Discuss the importance of a management review of controls for the audit committee.   **(5 marks)**

(c)   Explain the principles of good corporate governance as they apply to the board's role:

   (i)   in conducting a review of internal controls; and
   (ii)   reporting on compliance.   **(11 marks)**

Illustrate your answer with examples from the scenario.

(Total = 25 marks)

Answers

DO NOT TURN THIS PAGE UNTIL YOU HAVE
COMPLETED THE MOCK EXAM

A plan of attack

We know you've been told to do it at least 100 times and we know if we asked you you'd know that you should do it. So why don't you do it in an exam? 'Do what in an exam?' you're probably thinking. Well, let's tell you for the 101st time. **Take a good look through the paper before diving in to answer questions.**

First things first

What you must do in the first five minutes of reading time in your exam is **look through the paper** in detail, working out **which questions to do** and the **order** in which to attempt them. So turn back to the paper and let's sort out a plan of attack.

We then recommend you spend the remaining time analysing the requirements of **Question 1** and highlighting the key issues in the question. The extra time spent on **Question 1** will be helpful, whenever you intend to do the question, If you decide to do it first, you will be well into the question when the writing time starts. If you intend to do it second or third, probably because you find it daunting, the question will look easier when you come back to it, because your initial analysis should generate further points whilst you're tackling the other questions.

The next step

You're probably either thinking that you don't know where to begin or that you could have a very decent go at all the questions.

Option 1 (if you don't know where to begin)

If you are a bit **worried** about the paper, remember you'll need to do the compulsory question anyway so it's best to get it over and done with.

- You can score well on part (a) of **Question 1** if you use the information in the scenario – there is plenty of information about the stakeholders. There's also enough detail about remuneration to jog your memory in part (d) about corporate governance remuneration requirements.

- If you have think you have some knowledge of non-executive directors, **Question 2** could be a good choice. However a couple of the parts bring in wider practical and ethical issues so it's not just a straightforward test of knowledge.

- Although the scenario in **Question 3** may appear quite short, there is in fact lots of information about potential risks. If you think widely and make realistic suggestions in (b) that clearly link into your answer in (a), you can score well on this question.

- There's a number of fairly basic points you make in part (a) of **Question 4,** and you can get significant credit in (c) for setting out your knowledge of the corporate governance guidelines. Think when you're planning how you can bring the scenario information in.

What you mustn't forget is that you have to answer **Question 1** and then two questions from Section B.

Option 2 (if you're thinking 'I can do all of these')

It never pays to be over confident but if you're not quaking in your shoes about the exam then **turn straight to the compulsory question** in Section A. You've got to do it so you might as well get it over and done with.

- Make sure you make the most of the information you're supplied with in parts (a) and (d) of **Question 1**; a general answer won't score well. You may well have very good knowledge of the issues covered in parts (b) and (c) but allocate your time carefully; it's important not only to avoid running over time for each question part, but also to ensure you cover a sufficient breadth of points within the time allowed.

Once you've done the compulsory questions choose two of the questions in Section B.

- Although **Question 2** may look straightforward, parts (c) and (d) require a bit more thought about wider governance issues, so be careful if you choose this question.

- Careful reading of the question and planning is the key to success in **Question 3**. Make sure you identify all the risks hinted at for part (a) and provide realistic suggestions for managing those specific risks in part (b).

- If you've got good knowledge of the corporate governance requirements relating to control reviews, you can score well in **Question 4**. Part (a) is about the fundamentals of risk management, so knowledge of these basics will help you as well. However make sure that you include references to relevant scenario information.

No matter how many times we remind you...

Always, always **allocate your time** according to the marks for the question in total and for the parts of the questions. And always, always **follow the requirements exactly** and indicate which questions you're answering **clearly**.

You've got free time at the end of the exam.....?

If you have allocated your time properly then you **shouldn't have time on your hands** at the end of the exam. If you find yourself with five or ten minutes spare, however, go back to **any parts of questions that you didn't finish** because you ran out of time.

Forget about it!

And don't worry if you found the paper difficult. More than likely other students would too. If this was the real thing you would need to forget the exam the minute you leave the exam hall and **think about the next one**. Or, if it's the last one, **celebrate**!

Question 1

Marking scheme

			Marks
(a)	Up to 3 marks for explanation of Mendelow's matrix	3	
	Up to 2 marks for each stakeholder identified and analysed	<u>12</u>	
	max		14
(b)	Up to 2 marks for each Gray, Owen and Adams position discussed		14
(c)	Up to 2 marks for definition of sustainability	2	
	Up to 5 marks for assessment of whether company's position is sustainable	5	
	Up to 7 marks for evaluation of methods of reporting – to achieve high marks detail must be given of a number of different methods	7	
	Up to 4 professional marks for the form of the answer (memo in which content is laid out in an orderly and informative manner)	<u>4</u>	
	max		18
(d)	Up to 2 marks for each relevant point. To achieve 2 marks points must include application to company and recommendations	max	<u>4</u>
			<u><u>50</u></u>

(a) **Mendelow's matrix**

Mendelow classifies stakeholders on a matrix (shown below). The matrix is used to identify the type of relationship the organisation should seek with its stakeholders, and how it should view their concerns. The two axis show the **level of interest** the stakeholder has in the company and the **amount of power** that stakeholder has to influence the decisions of the company

Using these two axes, stakeholders can be divided into four groups as follows:

Level of interest

	Low	High
Low	A	B
High	C	D

Power

Section A

Stakeholders in this section have a **low level of interest** in the company and have **minimal power** to influence the decisions of the company.

Government

For SeaShells, Section A stakeholders may include the **government** of the island. As long as SeaShells pays the correct amount of taxes, the government may not be able to interfere with the company.

Section B

Stakeholders in this section have a **high level of interest** in the company, but have **minimal power** to actually influence its activities. This group will normally attempt to influence the company by lobbying groups that have high levels of power.

For SeaShells, stakeholders in this category include the following.

The local community

SeaShells is a major employer on the island. This means the community has an interest in the company **maintaining that level of employment**. It is unlikely therefore that the community will agree with the decision to decrease the number of jobs at SeaShells. However, apart from applying pressure in terms of adverse publicity, the community cannot actually stop SeaShells taking this action.

Suppliers

SeaShells purchases from the fishing fleet on the island. As SeaShells is the **only major customer** of the fleet, then the fleet has little power to affect SeaShells. While in theory the fleet could refuse to sell to SeaShells, the lack of an alternative buyer decreases the effectiveness of this option.

Employees

This group is obviously **interested in the success of the company** as they receive a salary from SeaShells. However, the only method of influencing SeaShells is by **withdrawal of labour**; this is ineffective given that transferring the packing to a different country has this effect anyway for Seashells. The only other option for influencing the company appears to be generating bad publicity, as for the local community above.

Section C

Stakeholders in this section have a **low level of interest** in the company, although they have the **ability to exercise power** over the company if they choose to do so. The group will have to be kept satisfied to ensure that their power is not used.

Shareholders

In SeaShells, this group is likely to include the shareholders. As long as the **return on investment** from SeaShells is **acceptable**, and the directors are running the company effectively, then the shareholders will be happy. Certainly the decision to decrease input costs will be acceptable if this also means increased profits and dividends. Given that knowledge of cost savings is now available, it can be argued that the directors must take this option, or else the shareholders may become dissatisfied and attempt to remove the directors.

Section D

Stakeholders in this section have a **high level of interest in the company** and also a **high level of power**. These stakeholders are therefore able to influence the company. For SeaShells, this group will include customers and directors.

Customers

Customers have high power because they can presumably **obtain supplies of seafood from other companies**. SeaShells must therefore keep this group satisfied or lose important sources of income. The decision to decrease packaging costs will be supported by customers as SeaShells' prices will also fall.

Directors

Directors can influence SeaShells because they **make decisions regarding the running of the company**. In this sense, moving packaging to a different country is in the interests of Seashells, as it provides the company with additional competitive advantage in terms of price and therefore helps ensure its survival.

(b) **Viewpoints of social responsibility**

Gray, Owen and Adams in their book *Accounting and accountability* identify seven viewpoints of social responsibility. These viewpoints can be applied to many situations, including the actions of companies, as explained below.

Pristine capitalists

Pristine capitalists support the idea that in a liberal economic democracy, the **private property system** is the best system. This means that companies **exist to make profits and seek economic efficiency**. Businesses therefore have **no moral responsibilities** beyond their obligations to shareholders and creditors.

In terms of moving packaging to another country simply on the basis of cost, then SeaShells has acted in terms of this belief; the obligation to maximise shareholder profit has been met and the social issues of making people redundant and the adverse effect on the island community are irrelevant.

Expedients

Expedients believe in a modified liberal economic democracy, noting that economic systems do generate some excesses. This means that businesses have to **accept some, albeit limited, social legislation** and moral requirements, particularly if this is in the businesses' best interests.

Seashells is potentially caught between two countries here. On the one hand in its home country Seashells does not appear to be acting morally because the loss of jobs will adversely affect employment and the island's overall economy. However, in the country to which the packaging is being moved, more jobs will be created, potentially in areas of lower employment. In these terms Seashells is acting morally.

Proponents of the social contract

Proponents of the social contract believe in a **contract between society and organisations**. Both parties must therefore **interact to their joint benefit**.

Seashells is continuing to provide employment in terms of purchasing fish etc from the fishing fleet – and the island is providing support services to Seashells (some employment, land etc.). Seashells has possibly breached the contract by removing some employment from the island; some adverse impact in terms of bad publicity is therefore expected.

Social ecologists note that **economic processes** that **result in resource exhaustion, waste and pollution must be modified**. In other words, the transfer of seafood to another country for packaging only to be returned to SeaShells for distribution is not environmentally friendly. To be responsible in this area Seashells should continue to package the seafood at its current location.

Socialists

Socialists see two classes in society – **capitalists owning businesses exploiting workers**. Within this framework, equality is difficult to achieve. In Seashells, shareholders and directors appear to be capitalists because they stand to "win" from the packaging decision. However, the workers on the island stand to "lose" in that their employment is terminated (although other workers will gain in the overseas country).

Radical feminists

Radical feminists see a trade off between **masculine qualities such as aggression and conflict** and **feminine values of cooperation and reflection**. Moving the packaging work to another country does appear to create conflict. However, whether the feminine view of cooperation is better is unclear – even if say only half the packaging function was moved, there would still be conflict on the island. Similarly, not moving the packaging function could create resentment in the other country as Seashells is not taking advantage of their cost advantage in terms of labour wages.

Deep ecologists

Deep ecologists believe that human beings have **no greater rights to resources or life than other species**. At the extreme therefore the entire business of SeaShells cannot be justified, especially where fish populations are threatened. Similarly, the economic decision to move packaging cannot be justified in environmental terms. The viewpoint that businesses cannot be trusted to maintain something as important as the environment is therefore correct.

(c) To: Board
     From: Accountant
     Date: 23 May 20X7
     Subject: Sustainability and environmental reporting

Definition of sustainability

Sustainability involves developing strategies so that the company only **uses resources at a rate** that **allows them to be replenished**. This means that those resources will continue to be available into the foreseeable future. Similarly, emissions of waste are confined to levels that do not exceed the capacity of the environment to absorb them.

In other words, sustainability has been defined as ensuring that development meets the needs of the present without compromising the ability of the future to meet its own needs. **Sustainable development is development that meets the needs of the present without compromising the ability of future generations to meet their own needs.**

In terms of the activities of SeaShells, they could be termed to be not sustainable on two counts.

Demand on fish stocks

In terms of capitalism, the fishing fleet will continue to try to meet this demand and SeaShells will continue to sell seafood as both parties are making a profit from these activities. However, the warning that some **fish stocks may crash** indicates that fishing and the economic activity of SeaShells as a company are not sustainable. How activities can be amended to be sustainable is unclear, unless there is some way to limit demand for fish or limit the amount of fish actually used by SeaShells.

The transport of seafoods for packaging in another country

The use of fuel simply to take seafood to a different location and back again to be packaged does **not appear to be justifiable economically**, and is not sustainable given that oil is a limited resource.

Disclosures

The extent to which SeaShells may actually want to disclose the environmental impact of its activities is unclear; in other words **entirely voluntary disclosure is unlikely**, particularly in view of the lack of sustainability referred to above. Methods of reporting the environmental impact of SeaShell's activities include the following.

Financial accounts

The basic financial accounts of SeaShells will disclose **the financial impact of its activities**, although these will only show the direct costs in terms of fuel used to transport fish for packaging etc. As many environmental costs are intangible e.g. pollution or potential over-fishing, these will not be included in the financial accounts, making this method of reporting incomplete.

Full cost accounting

This is a system that allows current accounting to include all **potential/actual costs and benefits** including environmental and possibly social externalities. The aim is to arrive at a 'full cost' of the activities of an organisation.

While the idea is good, it is not necessarily clear what the 'full cost' of an organisation's activities are. Full cost accounting suggests various 'tiers' of costs from the tangible through to the intangible. Using this system SeaShells would disclose not only **actual costs** incurred (transport, wages etc.), but also **hidden costs** of maintaining environmental monitoring systems. The accounts would also disclose contingent **liability costs**, such as fines for any environmental damage.

More widely the accounts would show **intangible costs**, including loss of customer goodwill (possible given the packaging policy) and reputation risk (again this risk will be there with the packaging policy). However, it is unclear how these costs will be 'measured'. Lastly the accounts would show **environmentally focused costs** – prevention costs, the costs of ensuring the company's activities have a zero environmental impact. The transport of seafood for packaging is likely to be environmentally negative; there is then the query of how these costs are 'offset' – should SeaShells plant trees to offset CO_2 emissions?

The emphasis on costs and the difficulty of estimating some of those costs again implies that this method of disclosure may not be effective.

CSR / GRI

An alternative to financial reporting is to provide information in a separate, predominantly narrative, report. The Corporate and Social Responsibility (CSR) report in the UK or the recommendations of the Global Reporting Initiative (GRI) are examples of this type of report. The GRI has a vision that reporting on economic, environmental and social importance should become as routine and comparable as financial reporting. The emphasis is therefore on **voluntary disclosure**, but based **on some ethical standards**. The additional information may be expected by society, and therefore perhaps companies should provide it.

SeaShells appears to be under some pressure at present, although this is more in terms of economic pressure on jobs than on environmental reporting. Either additional legislation or social pressure appears to be required to ensure that additional environmental reporting is provided.

(d) **Remuneration**

The overriding requirement is that **adequate remuneration** has to be paid to directors in order to attract individuals of sufficient calibre. Remuneration packages should be structured to ensure that individuals are **motivated to achieve performance levels that are in the company and shareholders' best interests** as well as their own personal interests.

Within SeaShells it is difficult to determine whether total **remuneration is sufficient** to meet this objective. However, the fact that there does not appear to be any problems recruiting directors indicates that remuneration is sufficient, or may even be excessive.

Setting remuneration

Directors' remuneration should be set by a **remuneration committee**, which SeaShells has. The reason for this is to ensure that there is **no bias in setting remuneration levels**.

Performance related remuneration

Corporate governance guidelines indicate that a **significant proportion of the rewards** should be focused on **measurable performance**, which SeaShells does. What is meant by a significant amount is not always stated but 50% is a reasonable figure. A 75% amount may again be considered as excessive.

The other element of guidance regarding the performance element of remuneration is that this should be **balanced and not relate to the short term only**, as short term performance can be manipulated. The current focus simply on net profit is therefore inappropriate.

Share options

Share options give directors the right to **purchase shares at a specified exercise price over a specified time period in the future**. If the price of the shares rises so that it exceeds the exercise price by the time the options can be exercised, the directors will be able to purchase shares at lower than their market value. This provides a good incentive to the directors to increase share prices.

However, corporate governance regulations normally suggest a **three year maximum term** for share options. The five year term in SeaShells may be unrealistic as the **term is too far in the future** to motivate the directors now. Decreasing the term for future option grants should be considered.

Service contract

Length of service contracts can be a particular problem. If service contracts are too long, and then have to be terminated prematurely, directors may receive **excessive payments for breach of contract**. Most corporate governance guidance therefore suggests a 12 month term.

The **current length of service contracts** in SeaShells of three years therefore appears to be **excessive**. Although there is no indication that directors are looking for compensation for loss of office, decreasing the term to one year would be advisable.

Question 2

Text references. Chapter 3.

Top tips. Whilst ACCA has stated that it's most important that you're aware of the general principles of corporate governance without getting too involved in the details of individual reports, it is fine to quote **selectively** from them as we have done. The length of each part of your answer should roughly reflect the marks available.

Note how the system of committee (audit, remuneration, nomination) is designed to counter key threats to independence. The most basic control though is recruiting sufficient independent non-executive directors, so look out for threats to non-executive independence if you are given scenarios about the corporate governance situation in a particular organisation.

Easy marks. All parts require some thought: even in (a) you could obtain a few marks through quoting the corporate governance reports, but would need to go beyond these for higher marks.

			Marks
(a)	Position of NEDs	3	
	Attributes of NEDs	3	
	Role of NEDs	3	
	max		7
(b)	Up to 3 marks for relevant explanation, answer should stress lack of connection		3
(c)	Up to 2 marks for each relevant point. To obtain high marks answer must contain assessment of issues and solutions that alleviate problems identified max		11
(d)	Problems with shares	2	
	Problems with share options	2	
			4
			25

(a)   **Position of NEDs**

The board of directors of a listed company has the purpose of leading and controlling the company. The board will normally be made up of **executive directors** who work full time for the company and have specific roles, such as finance director or sales director. The board should also consist of **some NEDs** who will be part-time and have no specific operational role in the company.

The board should include a **balance of executive and NEDs** (and in particular independent NEDs) such that no individual or small group of individuals can dominate the board's decision taking. Some corporate governance guidelines suggest that at least half the board should be NEDs.

Attributes of NEDs

NEDs should be **independent in judgement** (even if they are not independent according to governance guidance) and have **enquiring minds**. They need to be **well-informed** about the **company and the external environment** in which it operates, with a strong command of issues relevant to the business.

Role of NEDs

The main roles of NEDs are **to develop strategy** and **monitor performance**.

(i)   **Development of strategy**

In terms of their strategic role they are working with the executive directors in order to **determine the future** of the company.

(ii)   **Monitoring**

The monitoring role of NEDs takes on many forms. In general terms they are there to **challenge the decisions** of executive directors where they do not agree and to highlight any bad practice or poor performance.

NEDs should also **satisfy themselves** on the **integrity of financial information** and that **financial controls and systems of risk management** are robust and defensible. They therefore need to ensure that **sufficient, accurate, clear and timely information is provided in advance of meetings** to enable thorough consideration of the issues facing the board.

(b)   **Non-independent NEDs**

A NED is not independent if he or she is on the board **representing the interests of a major shareholder**, because the views given by the director will be made in the interests of that shareholder. Similarly, it is debatable whether a director is independent when he or she has a **close relationship** with the company or any other executive director. For example, a former chief executive of a company might be given a non-executive role after retirement. He would not be independent.

Independent NEDs

In contrast, an independent NED is a person who has no connection with the company other than as a non-executive director, and who should be able to give an **independent opinion** on the affairs of the company, without influence from any other director or any shareholder.

(c)   (i)   **Remuneration**

If executive directors are allowed to decide their own remuneration, they could be inclined to pay themselves as much as possible, without having to hold themselves to account or to justify their high pay. Where incentive schemes are in place, there is a risk that incentive schemes devised by the executive directors for themselves will be linked to **achieving performance targets** that are not necessarily in the shareholders' interests. For example, rewarding directors with a bonus for achieving profit growth is of no value to shareholders if the result is **higher business risk** and a **lower share price**.

Remuneration committee

Corporate governance in many countries, such as the UK Corporate Governance Code, calls for a remuneration committee of the board to be established to decide on **directors' pay**, including **incentive schemes**, and for this committee to comprise at least three, or in the case of smaller companies two, members, who should all be **independent non-executive directors**.

The remuneration committee should have **delegated responsibility** for **setting remuneration** for all **executive directors** and the chairman, including pension rights and any compensation payments. The committee should also recommend and monitor the **level and structure of remuneration** for **senior management**. The NEDs should, in principle, be able to devise fair remuneration packages that include an incentive element, in which the performance targets bring the objectives of the executive directors more into line with those of the shareholders.

(ii)   **Financial reporting**

The finance director and other executive directors might be tempted to **'window dress'** the results of the company, in order to **present the financial results** in a way that reflects better on themselves and their achievements.

Audit committee

There should be an **audit committee** of the board, consisting of non-executive directors, whose task should be to consider issues relating to financial reporting and financial control systems. This committee **should be responsible for maintaining regular liaison** with the external auditors. The UK Corporate Governance Code says that the audit committee should **comprise at least three**, or in the case of smaller companies two, members, who should all be **independent NEDs**. The board should satisfy itself that at least one member of the audit committee has recent and relevant financial experience.

(iii)   **Nominations to board**

A powerful chairman or chief executive could be tempted to appoint their supporters or 'yes men' to the board, and so strengthen their position on the board.

Nomination committee

The UK Corporate Governance Code recommends that there should be a nomination committee of the board, manned by NEDs. The nomination committee should consider objectively the **balance** between executives and independent non-executives, the **skills**, **knowledge** and **experience** possessed by the current board, the **need for continuity** and succession planning, the desirable **size** of the board and the need to attract board members from a **diversity** of backgrounds.

(d) **Share payments**

In many companies, NEDs receive a fixed cash payment for their services, without any incentives. However, some companies pay their NEDs in shares.

They would argue that the more equity the NEDs hold, the more likely they will be to look at issues from the point of view of the shareholders. There is a risk that a NED holding shares could become more concerned with **short-term movements** in the share price and the opportunity of making a **short-term profit from selling their shares**. However, a suitable precaution against this could be to obtain the agreement of a NED **not to sell his or her shares** until after leaving the board.

Share options

The argument that NEDs should be rewarded with share options is more contentious, but it has been widely practised in the UK and is even more common in the US. The argument against rewarding NEDs with share options is that this form of remuneration **could align the interests of the NEDs more closely with the executive directors**, who also hold share options. NEDs should give independent advice, and it can be argued that it is therefore not appropriate to incentivise them in the same way as the executives.

The UK Corporate Governance Code points out that holding of share options could be relevant to the determination of a non-executive director's independence. It states that remuneration for non-executive directors **should not include share options**. If, exceptionally, options are granted, **shareholder approval** should be **sought in advance** and any shares acquired by exercise of the options should be held until at least one year after the non-executive director leaves the board.

Question 3

Text references. Chapters 6 and 7.

Top tips. The framework used in (a) is a good way of identifying the most important risks. Other frameworks may be used, although it will be important to ensure that the risks identified are clearly related to the situation outlined in the scenario.

For (b) if you are faced with a question of the format:

Part (a) Identify risks

Part (b) Assess effects of identified risks and what the organisation can do to mitigate them, ensure your answer plan shows consistency in format. Your answer to (b) needs to be a mirror image of your answer to (a).

Don't worry also if you haven't thought of, or had time to discuss, all the possible risks we have. Remember a score of 15 out of 25 is a comfortable pass. It's safer from the viewpoint of passing to cover each risk in reasonable depth, making reference to the scenario rather than just briefly listing all possible risks. A long list of risks without any explanation carries the possibility of obtaining no marks as you haven't shown why what you said is relevant.

Easy marks. Evidence suggests most students find it easier to identify risks than to come up with ways of reducing and controlling them. However to improve your chances of passing, you must be able to come up with realistic ways of tackling risks at some stage in your answer.

			Marks
(a)	Up to 2 marks for each distinct risk identified.		
	Max 2 marks for well-organised categorisation of risks	max	10
(b)	Up to 3 marks for discussion of effect and reduction of each risk		
	identified. To gain 3 marks, both effect and reduction should be		
	discussed. Risks discussed should be those described in (a).		$\frac{15}{25}$

Risk can defined as the possibility that events or results will turn out differently from is expected.

(a)   The risks facing the HOOD Company are outlined below.

Operational risks

These are risks relating to the business's day-to-day operations.

(i)   **Accounting irregularities**

The unexplained fall in gross profit in some stores may be indicative of **fraud** or **other accounting irregularities**. Low gross profit in itself may be caused by **incorrect inventory values** or **loss of sale income**. Incorrect inventory levels in turn can be caused by **incorrect inventory counting** or **actual stealing of inventory** by employees. Similarly, **loss of sales income** could result from **accounting errors** or employees **fraudulently removing cash** from the business rather than recording it as a sale.

(ii)   **Systems**

Technical risks relate to the **technology** being **used by the company** to run its business.

(1)   **Backup**

Transferring data to head office at the end of each day will be **inadequate for backup purposes**. Failure of computer systems during the day will still result in loss of that day's **transaction data**.

(2)   **Delays in ordering**

Although inventory information is collected using the EPOS system, **re-ordering of inventory takes** a **significant amount of time**. Transferring data to head office for central purchasing may result in some discounts on purchase. However, the average 10 days before inventory is received at the store could result in **the company running out of inventory**.

Non-business strategic risks

These are risks that arise for reasons beyond the normal operations of the company or the business environment within which it operates.

(i)   **Production**

The possibility of sunlight making some of HOOD Company's products potentially dangerous may give rise to **loss of sales** also inventory recall.

(ii)   **Event**

HOOD may be vulnerable to losses in a warehouse fire.

Business strategic risks

External risks relate to the **business**; they are essentially **uncontrollable** by the company.

(i)   **Macro-economic risk**

The company is **dependent on one market sector** and **vulnerable to competition** in that sector.

(ii) **Product demand**

The most important social change is probably a **change in fashion**. HOOD has not changed its product designs for 4 years indicating some lack of investment in this area. Given that fashions tend to change more frequently than every four years, HOOD may experience falling sales as customers seek new designs for their outdoor clothing. HOOD may also be vulnerable to **seasonal** variations in demand.

(iii) **Corporate reputation**

Risks in this category relate to the overall **perception of HOOD in the marketplace** as a supplier of (hopefully) good quality clothing. However, this reputation could be damaged by **problems with the manufacturing process** and a consequent high level of returns.

(b)   **Profiling**

By identifying and profiling the effects of the risks, HOOD can assess what the consequences might be, and hence what steps (if any) are desirable to mitigate or avoid the consequences.

The potential effects of the risks on HOOD and methods of overcoming those risks are explained below.

Operational risks

(i)   **Accounting irregularities**

The potential effect on HOOD is **loss of income** either from inventory not being available for sale or cash not being recorded. The overall amount is unlikely to be significant as employees would be concerned about being caught stealing.

The risk can be minimised by introducing additional controls including the necessity of producing a **receipt for each sale** and the **agreement of cash received** to the **till roll** by the shop manager. Loss of inventory may be identified by more frequent checks in the stores or closed-circuit television.

(ii) **Systems**

(1)   **Backup**

The potential effect on HOOD is relatively minor; **details of one shop's sales** could be lost for part of one day. However, the cash from sales would still be available, limiting the actual loss.

Additional procedures could be implemented to **back up transactions** as **they occur**, using online links to head office. The **relative cost of providing these links** compared to the likelihood of error occurring will help HOOD decide whether to implement this solution.

(2)   **Delays in inventory ordering**

The potential effect on HOOD is **immediate loss of sales** as customers cannot purchase the garments that they require. In the longer term, if running out of inventory becomes more frequent, **customers may not visit** the store because they believe inventory will not be available.

The risk can be minimised by letting the stores **order goods directly** from the manufacturing, using an extension of the EPOS system. Costs incurred relate to the provision of Internet access for the shops and possible increase in cost of goods supplied. However, this may be acceptable compared to overall loss of reputation.

Non-business strategic risks

(i) **Production**

The effect on HOOD is the possibility of having to **reimburse customers** and the loss of income from the product until the problems are resolved.

The risk can be minimised by HOOD taking the claim seriously and **investigating its validity**, rather than ignoring it. For the future, **guarantees** should be obtained from suppliers to confirm that products are safe and **insurance** taken out against possible claims from customers for damage or distress.

(ii) **Event**

The main effects of a warehouse fire will be a **loss of inventory** and the incurring of costs to replace it. There will also be a **loss of sales** as the inventory is not there to fulfil customer demand, and perhaps also a loss of subsequent sales as customers continue to shop elsewhere.

Potential losses of sales could be avoided by **holding contingency inventory** elsewhere, and losses from the fire could be reduced by **insurance.**

Business strategic risks

(i) **Macro-economic risk**

The potential effect on HOOD largely depends on HOOD's **ability to provide an appropriate selection of clothes**. It is unlikely that demand for coats etc. will fall to zero, so some sales will be expected. However, an increase in competition may result in **falling sales,** and without some diversification, this will automatically affect the overall sales of HOOD.

HOOD can minimise the risk in two ways: by **diversifying into other areas**. Given that the company sells outdoor clothes, then commencing sales of other outdoor goods such as camping equipment may be one way of diversifying risk. It can also look to resume **operational gearing**, fixed cost as a proportion of turnover.

(ii) **Product demand**

Again the **risk of loss of demand and business to competitors** may undermine HOOD's ability to continue in business.

This risk can be minimised by having a **broad strategy to maintain and develop the brand of HOOD**. Not updating the product range would appear to be a mistake in this context as the brand may be devalued as products may not meet changing tastes of customers. The board must therefore allocate appropriate investment funds to updating the products and **introduce new products** to maintain the company's image.

(iii) **Corporate reputation**

As well as **immediate losses of contribution from products** that have been returned, HOOD faces the consequence of loss of future sales from customers who believe their products no longer offer quality. Other clothing retailers have found this to be very serious; a **reputation for quality**, once lost, undoubtedly **cannot easily be regained**. The potential effect of a drop in overall corporate reputation will be falling sales for HOOD, resulting eventually in a **going concern problem**.

HOOD can guard against this loss of reputation by **enhanced quality control procedures**, and introducing processes such as **total quality management**.

Question 4

Marking scheme

		Marks	
(a)	Up to 3 marks for analysis of purposes of risk management	3	
	Up to 3 marks for justification of importance of risk management	3	
	Up to 3 marks for explanation of interaction of risk management and internal control system.	3	
			9
(b)	Up to 3 marks for need for, and significance of, management review	3	
	Up to 2 marks for other sources of assurance	2	
			5
(c)	Up to 8 marks for explanation of different elements of review. To obtain high marks, answer must include details of regular and annual review and relate to information in the scenario	8	
	Up to 4 marks for explanation of different disclosures. To obtain high marks, answer must include statement of board's responsibilities, what has been done to manage risk and that board has reviewed risk management	4	
	max		11
			25

(a) **Purposes of risk management**

Alignment of risk appetite and strategy

LMN's board should consider what risks it is prepared to **tolerate** in the light of the organisation's strategy. Risk management comprises the systems and processes for dealing with the risks that the board is prepared to tolerate in order for LMN to fulfil its **strategic objectives**.

Develop a consistent framework for dealing with risk

A coherent risk management framework can help LMN compare risks with **obvious financial consequences** (poor cost control, loss of income due to bad debts) with risks whose financial consequences are less obvious (dissatisfied tenants). It also should provide guidelines that can be applied by staff operating across all areas of LMN's activities.

Develop risk response strategies

The risk management process should **identify and evaluate risks** (for example by the high-medium-low method described) and therefore provide the information necessary for management to decide what the best **response to risk** should be – bearing, reduction, elimination or transfer.

Importance of risk management

Improve financial position

The risk management framework can provide a means of judging the costs of **treating the risks** measured against the **benefits**. It can also help LMN's directors judge whether to take advantage of opportunities, for example property investment.

Minimise surprises and losses

By identifying risks in the **risk register**, the risk management process should reduce the occurrence of unexpected shocks. For example identifying property maintenance as a risk issue should encourage a programme of regular maintenance designed to deal with the risks associated with the types and ages of property.

Maintain reputation

As LMN is a charity, its reputation as a good corporate citizen is very important. Risk management should help it avoid risks to its reputation such as **poor treatment of tenants** or failing to comply with **regulatory requirements**.

Risk management and the internal control system

Internal control is action taken by management to achieve organisational objectives and goals. Internal control thus is bound up with the organisation's strategies, and is therefore also bound up with risk management that is dependent upon the organisation's strategies. Internal control is made up of two elements:

(i) The **control environment**, the framework within which controls operate and within which attitudes towards risk are an important elements. **Communication** between directors and employees is a key element of the control environment.

(ii) **Internal controls**, which should be operated when their **benefits outweigh costs**; controls focused on dealing with the most significant risks will have obvious benefits. Because risks as here affect different areas of activity, controls of different types will be required; financial controls, although significant, will not be enough.

Given the risks LMN faces, key controls will include **debtor management, maintenance inspections and logs, financial appraisal of new investments** and **tenant satisfaction questionnaires**, as well as **accounting, compliance** and **cost limitation** controls.

(b) **Audit committee's role in internal control**

Under corporate governance guidelines audit committees are responsible for creating a **climate of discipline and control.** To do this, they have to obtain assurance that internal control is working **effectively** and providing an **adequate response** to the **risks** faced.

Importance of management review

The management review provides the audit committee with evidence of whether the **control systems** appear to be effectively managing the most significant risks. It also gives the audit committee an indication of the **scope and quality** of management's monitoring of risk and internal control; does the report appear to be an **adequate review** given the risks faced. The review should provide **feedback** that the audit committee should confirm has led to improvements in the control systems.

Other sources of evidence

However management's review of internal control is only one source of evidence that the audit committee should use to gain assurance. The committee should also receive reports from **staff** undertaking important and high-risk activities such as property investment. They should also receive reports from **control functions** such as human resources or internal audit (if any). Feedback from external sources such as **external audit** or **regulatory visits** will also provide information.

(c)   (i)   **Review of internal controls**

The UK's Turnbull committee emphasises the importance of a regular review and an annual review of internal control as part of an organisation's strategy for **minimising risk, ensuring adherence to strategic objectives, fulfilling responsibilities to stakeholders** and **establishing accountability at its senior levels.**

Regular review

Regular review is an essential part of the strategy for minimizing risks. The audit committee is likely to have responsibility for this review, and as best practice recommends at least **three audit committee meetings a year**; this is thus how often the review should take place. Its findings should be communicated to the board.

The review should cover the following areas:

(1)   **Risk evaluation**

Whether LMN is **identifying** and **evaluating** all key risks, financial and non-financial. This is a very significant task given the variety of risks faced, and also the need to devote limited resources to the most important risks.

(2)   **Management response**

Whether **responses and management** of risks are **appropriate**; for example what level of risks should LMN bear without taking any steps (just low likelihood, small consequences risks or any others).

(3)   **Control effectiveness**

The **effectiveness of internal controls** in countering the risks. The board should consider how much controls could be expected to **reduce the incidence** of risks, any evidence that controls have **not been operating effectively** and how **weaknesses are being resolved**. The board would consider evidence such as incidence of bad debts, records of property occupation and complaints from tenants.

Annual review

The annual review of internal control should be more wide-ranging than the regular review, taking into account the **strategic objectives of the charity** and undertaken by the **whole board** rather than just the audit committee. It should examine controls and risk management systems in all major areas, covering in particular:

(1)   **Changes in risks**

The **changes** since the last assessment **in risks faced**, and the charity's ability to **respond to changes in its environment**. For example the board would consider any changes in the charity's credit ratings, also longer-term trends such as changes in the incidence of low income earners.

(2) **Monitoring**

The **scope and quality of management's monitoring of risk and control**, also whether internal audit is required. In particular the review should consider whether the **scope and frequency of the regular review** should be increased.

(3) **Reports to board**

The **extent and frequency of reports** to the board; should reports on high incidence, high likelihood risks be made more regularly.

(4) **Significant aspects**

Significant controls, failings and weaknesses that may materially impact on the financial statements, for example problems over its property portfolio management.

(5) **Communication to shareholders**

Communication to stakeholders of **risk objectives, targets** and **measures** taken to counter risks.

(ii) **Disclosures in the annual report**

The report on compliance is a key part of the annual report by which LMN demonstrates its **compliance with regulations** and how it has **fulfilled the differing requirements of its stakeholders**.

Responsibility

The board should also **acknowledge its accountability** for LMN's system of control and **reviewing its effectiveness**.

Risk management

The Turnbull report recommends that as a minimum the board should disclose what has been done to **manage risk** and how the board has **reviewed the effectiveness of the risk management process**. The board should explain the limits of the process (it aims at risk management rather than risk elimination) and disclose any **material problems or weaknesses** that have been found.

ACCA Professional Level

Paper P1

Professional Accountant

Mock Examination 2

Question Paper	
Time allowed	
Reading and Planning Writing	**15 minutes** **3 hours**
This paper is divided into two sections	
Section 1 This ONE question is compulsory and must be attempted	
Section 2 TWO questions only to be attempted	
During reading and planning time only the question paper may be annotated	

DO NOT OPEN THIS PAPER UNTIL YOU ARE READY TO START UNDER EXAMINATION CONDITIONS

Section A – This question is compulsory and must be attempted

Question 1

Pacific Goods is a large retail company, selling a wide range of goods from small household items such as cleaning materials to garden tools and a limited range of gifts and chocolates. The company was founded in the 1800's and now trades in 23 countries with more than 250 stores. The company's image has in the past been one of being 'cheap and cheerful' – that is staff have been seen historically as always happy to assist customers, although the goods themselves are moderately priced.

Although the company is not a listed company, it has a number of shareholders with significant holdings who are not actively involved in running the business. Most of the shareholders are descendants of the original founders of the company.

In terms of corporate governance, Pacific Goods also maintains an appointment committee and an audit committee. Each committee comprises two executive directors and one non-executive director. Mr Beckett, the Chairman of Pacific Goods and a major shareholder, has always maintained that it is important to follow the principles of corporate governance rather than follow rigorous regulations. The fact that Pacific Goods is not a quoted company confirms his belief that it is the 'spirit' of corporate governance only that needs to be followed. He has argued that it is to Pacific Goods' credit that it seeks to apply the spirit of governance guidance. However as much governance guidance is specifically targeted at listed companies and designed to satisfy the major institutional shareholders who have invested in those companies, it is not really relevant to Pacific Goods' ways of doing business.

The country in which Pacific Goods' Head Office is based follows a principles-based approach to corporate governance, with most of the guidelines being based on the OECD principles of corporate governance. Other local companies, with trading interests in America, have however chosen to adhere to the Sarbanes-Oxley legislation, and this is regarded as acceptable by the company's local stock exchange.

Over the past three years, Mr Carson (the CEO) has attempted to take Pacific Goods more 'up-market'. Ranges of cheap goods were discontinued and more expensive items placed on sale. A new company logo and corporate slogan were implemented in an attempt to re-brand the company. The board of Pacific Goods provided Mr Carson with unanimous support. The directors believed that Pacific Goods would be able to benefit from being able to open stores in upmarket shopping developments. One director commented; 'We should move away from the local malls and into the exclusive ends of large retail developments.' The directors however ignored warnings from some store managers concerning the demographic profile of their customers and how the move would adversely affect that profile.

The risk committee was also concerned that this strategy was not fully evaluated and raised the issue of whether the company was too committed to a speculative course of action and whether the changes to what had previously been successful policies were justified. However, the committee was not provided with the time or information to make an effective evaluation of most of the decisions associated with the strategy. Generally the committee only saw the papers the board saw and discussed the decisions once the board had already made them. The committee comprises one non-executive director and three store managers.

To complement the new image, Mr Carson required store managers to provide detailed monthly reports on achievement of profit and budget variances and insisted on downsizing the number of shop staff to achieve an enhanced level of profit. Remaining staff were also required to work longer hours with only minimal pay increases on an annual basis. Store managers were also to refer a range of decisions (although the exact list was never published) to the newly appointed human resources director, the son of Mr Carson. Mr Carson jnr was 24 years old when appointed and had just graduated from business school. Mr Carson jnr had not previously been in paid employment, apart from working in Pacific Goods' head office in a couple of summer vacations from business school. The appointment of Mr Carson jnr was made without the involvement of the appointments committee. Mr Carson snr justified his son's appointment , stating that he had all the necessary skills to assist store managers in their difficult task of managing budgets and people. Mr Carson snr commented that his son had all the qualities needed to 'shake things up at the stores.' Some of the other directors had their doubts about the appointment, but kept quiet as they knew Mr Carson snr rated his son's abilities highly and they did not wish to upset Mr Carson snr.

Unfortunately, the store managers (rather than the board's optimism) were proved correct and the move upmarket was disastrous. Sales at Pacific Goods have fallen by around 25% in the last two years. 40 stores have closed, including upmarket stores that had been opened in large retail developments. One of the reasons for the failure of the upmarket stores according to the trade press has been customer perception of a poor level of service, As a result of these problems, Mr Carson (snr and jnr) resigned their positions. The remaining board members are attempting to 'rescue' the company. Mr Beckett collapsed from a heart attack at about the same time and is now convalescing; he does not expect to work for at least six months.

In response to the problems facing the company, the appointment committee has taken the unusual step of appointing Mr Staite to be the company's chairman and CEO. Mr Staite has had significant previous experience in re-focusing corporate strategy; it is the appointment committee's belief that this is the most effective way of ensuring Pacific Goods survives as a going concern over the next few years.

At a recent shareholder meeting, a number of the external shareholders expressed concern about the corporate governance arrangements that the company had been operating, saying that the basis of corporate governance appeared to be very vague and that they needed to enforce some definite rules on the directors. One of the non-executive directors on the board has also indicated that he will not seek re-election next year. He has accused the rest of the board of 'paying lip service to corporate governance best practice, in order to make Pacific Goods appear to be a good corporate citizen.'

Required

(a)   Prepare a memorandum for the board explaining what is meant by the term 'control environment' and criticising the control environment within Pacific Goods.   **(17 marks)**

(including 4 professional marks)

(b)   Explain to the external shareholders the principles-based approach to corporate governance, and construct a case for using this approach. Advise the external shareholders on whether a principles-based approach is appropriate for Pacific Goods.   **(13 marks)**

(c)   Define strategic and operational risk. Identify and describe the strategic and operational risks facing Pacific Goods.   **(13 marks)**

(d)   Identify the ethical and corporate governance issues resulting from Mr. Staite's position on the board of Pacific Goods and recommend how the issues can be resolved.   **(7 marks)**

(Total = 50 marks)

Section B – TWO questions ONLY to be attempted

Question 2

Hammond Transport, a road haulage company, is likely to be seeking a stock exchange listing in a few years' time. In preparation for this, the directors are seeking to understand certain key recommendations of the international corporate governance codes, since they realise that they will have to strengthen their corporate governance arrangements. In particular the directors require information about what the governance reports have achieved in:

(i)   Defining the role of non-executive directors
(ii)   Improving disclosure in financial accounts
(iii)   Strengthening the role of the auditor
(iv)   Protecting shareholder interests

and the factors that have limited the ability of governance reports to achieve these objectives.

Previously also the directors have received the majority of their income from the company in the form of salary and have decided salary levels amongst themselves. They realise that they will have to establish a remuneration committee but are unsure of its role and what it will need to function effectively.

The directors are also considering whether it will be worthwhile to employ a consultant to advise on how the company should be controlled, focusing on the controls with which the board will be most involved.

Required

(a)   Discuss whether the main corporate governance reports have achieved the objectives (i) – (iv) listed above.
(9 marks)

(b)   Explain the purpose and role of the remuneration committee, and analyse the information requirements the committee will have in order to be able to function effectively.
(9 marks)

(c)   Explain what are meant by organisation and management controls and recommend the main organisation and management controls that the company should operate.
(7 marks)

(Total = 25 marks)

Question 3

Tim Teddie is a course leader on a professional development course on corporate governance and ethics, aimed at directors and staff who are working for companies that have recently been listed, or are about to be listed. Tim has circulated attendees in advance to ask what topics they would like covered. The most popular suggestion has been for Tim to cover the role of the audit committee.

One of the attendees has brought to Tim's attention a comment she had read in a newspaper article:

'In many companies with poor corporate governance, there is insufficient reporting of exceptions and problems'

She suggested that Tim could cover exception reporting as part of his review of corporate governance.

Another attendee has contacted Tim with details of a problem that a 'close friend' of his is currently facing. He wonders if it can be used as a case example on Tim's course. The 'friend' is an employee in the internal audit department of a recently-listed company. During the course of the audit of the computer-based financial control systems, he discovered that €1.1 billion of revenue expenditure has been treated as capital spending. He reported this finding to the head of internal audit and then to the chief accountant, but as far as he is aware, no action has been taken by the company. The external audit is due to commence in the next few weeks, and he has been instructed by the head of internal audit not to disclose this information to the external auditors.

Required

(a)   Describe the membership and explain the role of the audit committee in a listed company.   **(8 marks)**

(b)   Discuss the importance of exception reporting as part of an organisation's information systems.   **(6 marks)**

(c)   Assess the alternative actions available to the attendee's 'friend', and how these may conflict with ACCA ethical guidance.
(11 marks)

(Total = 25 marks)

Question 4

LP manufactures and supplies a wide range of different clothing to retail customers from 150 stores located in three different countries. The company has made a small net profit for the last three years. Clothes are made in three different countries, one in Europe, one in South America and the last in the Far East. Sales are made via cash, major credit cards and increasingly through the company's own credit card. Additional capital expenditure is planned in the next financial year to update some old production machinery.

In order to increase sales, a new Internet site is being developed which will sell LP's entire range of clothes using 3D revolving dummies to display the clothes on screen. The site will use some new compression software to download the large media files to purchasers' PCs so that the clothes can be viewed. This move is partly in response to environmental scanning which indicated a new competitor, PVO, will be opening an unknown number of stores in the next six months.

As a cost cutting move, the directors are considering delaying LP's new range of clothes by one year. Sales are currently in excess of expectations and the directors are unwilling to move away from potentially profitable lines.

Required

(a)   Describe a process for managing risk that could apply to any company of a similar size to LP.   **(10 marks)**
(b)   Assess the business risks affecting LP and recommend how these risks can be managed.   **(15 marks)**

(Total = 25 marks)

Answers

DO NOT TURN THIS PAGE UNTIL YOU HAVE COMPLETED THE MOCK EXAM

A plan of attack

We've already established that you've been told to do it 101 times, so it is of course superfluous to tell you for the 102nd time to **Take a good look at the paper before diving in to answer questions.**

First things first

Remember that the best way to use the 15 minutes reading time in your exam is firstly to **look through the paper** in detail, working out **which questions to do** and the **order** in which to attempt them. Then spend the remaining time analysing the requirements of **Question 1** and highlighting the key issues in the question.

The next step

You may be thinking that this paper is a lot more straightforward than the first mock exam; however, having sailed through the first mock, you may think this paper is actually rather difficult.

Option 1 (Don't like this paper)

If you are challenged by this paper, it is still best to **do the compulsory question first.** You will feel better once you've got it out the way. Honest.

- There are a lot of application marks in **Question 1**. Having read the requirements carefully, mark against each paragraph the part of the question to which it relates. Use this as the basis of your plan as hopefully the material in the scenario will jog your memory about the corporate governance theory that you need to discuss.

- The scenario in **Question 2** gives you the framework you need for your answer to part (a); you just need to flesh it out with some ideas. In (b) there's quite a lot you could say about the role of the remuneration committee. Whether you choose this question may depend on whether you think you can attempt part (c); if you are struggling to define these controls or think of relevant examples, you may choose to avoid this question.

- Part (a) of **Question 3** may appear to be one of the easiest sections of the paper. However you will also need to think about wider information systems issues in (b) when discussing exception reporting and make practical recommendations in (c). Remember in (c) that you have to discuss a number of possible solutions and will get two to three marks for each.

- Part (a) of **Question 4** is fairly general, but you do have to bear the company's details in mind. Although the scenario is quite short, there are lots of ideas in it that you can use to generate points for (b).

Option 2 (This paper's alright)

Are you **sure** it is? If you are then that's encouraging. You'll feel even happier when you've got the compulsory question out the way, so why not **do Question 1 first**.

- Although **Question 1** appears to require some fairly basic knowledge, you won't get all that many marks for it. Make sure therefore by marking the question that you identify the relevant issues in the scenario for each part of the question and that you maximise your score by including them within your answer.

- Yes, there is potentially lots to write for **Question 2.** However read the question and scenario carefully to make sure that you realise all the elements that your answer has to contain. Check when you've completed your plan that your answer is complete. Also make sure when answering part (c) that the examples of controls that you suggest are relevant.

- You may think you know enough about audit committees to tackle a 25 mark question on the subject. However part (a) of **Question 3** is only worth 8 marks so take care! You have to discuss wider issues in (b) when considering exception reporting, and discuss a number of alternatives in (c), coming up with some practical arguments.

- Remember to bear in mind the circumstances of the company when answering part (a) of **Question 4**, although your answer can be fairly general. Analyse the scenario carefully in part (b) to ensure you've identified all relevant risks.

Once more

You must must must **allocate your time** according to the marks for the question in total, and for the parts of the questions. And you must must must also **follow the requirements exactly** and indicate which questions you're answering **clearly**.

Finished with fifteen minutes to spare?

Looks like you slipped up on the time allocation. However if you have, make sure you don't waste the last few minutes; go back to **any parts of questions that you didn't finish** because you ran out of time.

Forget about it!

Forget about what? Excellent, you already have.

Question 1

Marking scheme

			Marks
(a)	Up to 3 marks for definition of control environment	3	
	Up to 2 marks for each issue covered in company's control environment	12	
	Up to 4 professional marks for the form of the answer (memo in which Content is laid out in an orderly and informative manner)	4	
	max		17
(b)	Up to 3 marks for explanation of principles-based approach	3	
	Up to 2 marks for each advantage identified	8	
	Up to 2 marks for each point about application of approach to company	4	
	max		13
(c)	Up to 3 marks for definitions of strategic and operational risk	3	
	Up to 2 marks for each risk described	12	
	max		13
(d)	Up to 3 marks for identification of issues	3	
	Up to 4 marks for alternative solutions suggested	4	
	max		7
			50

(a)   **Memo**

To: Board
From: Consultant
Date: 5 May 20X8
Subject: Control environment in Pacific Goods

You have asked me to give my views on whether there are underlying causes that help or hinder the operation of controls at Pacific Goods. I therefore will explain the significance of the control environment, and comment on the control environment at the company.

Control environment

The **control environment** is the **overall attitude**, **awareness and actions** of directors and management regarding internal controls and their importance in the entity. The control environment encompasses the **management style**, **corporate culture and values** shared by all employees. It provides the **background** against which the various other controls are operated.

Control environment Pacific Goods - overview

While there appear to be the **correct structures** in place to **identify and implement control systems,** such as the risk committee, the structures do not appear to be effective. Specific matters that need to be addressed are noted below.

Risk identification

The risk committee appears to be ineffective because it **lacks clear strategies** for either identifying or dealing with those risks that have been identified. For example, the strategy of attempting to move Pacific Goods 'upmarket' was not fully considered, and the **possibility of failure** was **not considered** by the board.

Company culture

Pacific Goods' standard of customer service has been good. The fact that staff were prepared to assist customers provided a **good company reputation** and **repeat business**. However, the new emphasis on **profitability and cutting of expenses** (including the number of staff in each store) will have **adversely affected the company's image** and **contributed to falling sales**. Similarly, basing store manager performance entirely on **profit** rather than a range of indicators has meant a cultural emphasis on profit, again decreasing the good customer service ethic.

Reporting requirements

The **requirement to send monthly reports on profitability** with detailed comments on variances further implies a change in the company's culture. The detailed review implies a **lack of trust in the store managers**, which will also **decrease the motivation** of those managers. Staff **motivation will also have fallen** as they see an **increased focus on selling** rather than customer service, to say nothing of **redundancies** further decreasing motivation.

Consequences of poor appointment

The appointment of Mr Carson jnr may have been premature. While business school will provide some skills, the director **lacked the real world experience and therefore credibility** within the role. It was unlikely that store managers would trust Mr Carson jnr with the effect that they may not have deferred decisions to him and neglected to implement his advice.

Authority levels

The **lack of clear explanation of what decisions** would be made by Mr Carson jnr was also not helpful. Store managers would have been in the situation of being **accountable for their budgets**, but **not having the authority** to make the decisions they need to manage those budgets effectively. Not only will this have further decreased their motivation, but also it will have **decreased the store manager's credibility** with shop staff as the managers would have been seen to lack the authority to run the store.

Appointment committee

There are two specific weaknesses within the control environment at Pacific Goods in relation to corporate governance. Firstly, the appointment committee can be **over-ridden by the board of directors**. The appointment of Mr Carson jnr clearly shows this. There is the risk that inappropriate staff/directors will be appointed into the company, increasing the risk that their duties will not be carried out appropriately.

Risk committee

Secondly, the **risk committee appears to be ineffective** regarding the identification or evaluation of risks. This is due partly to lack of information provision, but also to lack of sufficient senior staff on the committee. Even if a full evaluation of the change in company image had taken place, it is unlikely that one non-executive director could sufficiently influence the rest of the board.

Conclusion

As a matter of urgency, the board needs to address a number of issues to improve the control environment in Pacific Goods. These include taking steps to ehnance the profile and the terms of reference of key board committees. At an operational level, store managers' authority needs to be clarified and customer service levels assessed as well as cost control.

(b) **Principles-based approach to corporate governance**

The principles based approach focuses on **objectives of corporate governance** rather than **enforcing the mechanisms** by which those objectives should be achieved. The idea is that principles are easier to integrate into strategic planning systems than detailed rules and regulations.

Advantages of principles-based approach

Difficulty of applying rules

The principles-based approach is particularly useful where **rules cannot easily be applied**. For example, it is relatively straightforward to define rules for internal control systems, but not for areas such as organisational culture or maintaining relationships with stakeholders. Similarly, principles can be **applied across different legal jurisdictions** rather than being based on the legal regulations of one country.

Comply or explain basis

Principles-based approaches are also normally in force in corporate governance terms **on a comply or explain basis**. The extent to which a principle has or has not been applied can therefore be clearly explained, rather than simply stating that a rule has not been followed.

Ease of implementation

The approach is also **easier and cheaper to implement**. Being able to state principles removes the need for detailed or complicated legislation to attempt to cover every possible eventuality and is therefore cheaper from the legislative point-of-view. The law making body of each jurisdiction does not have to spend large amounts of time (and money) producing detailed legislation. From the point of view of companies, the benefit is less 'red-tape' or form filling.

Flexibility for companies

Using principles allows **each entity to decide how to implement those principles**, without having to follow detailed rules or guidelines that may simply not be applicable to that entity.

Investors' decision-making

The principles-based approach means that **emphasis is placed on investors** to decide what a company is doing, rather than the company providing lots of data about rules being followed, but no overall impression of the success or otherwise of the company.

Appropriateness for Pacific Goods

It is unclear whether the principles-based approach is applicable for Pacific Goods. Clearly, the benefits of the approach should apply to the company in terms of being able to **implement procedures appropriate** for the company, particularly in softer areas such as stakeholder communication and employee management.

Lack of commitment

However, the risk of this approach, as identified in Pacific Goods, is that the company may either choose **which principles to apply** from the longer list, or apply those principles in de-minimis form rather than being serious about corporate governance. For example, Pacific Goods does have an appointment committee and risk committee, but the members of those committees **do not have sufficient power to carry out their duties** correctly. Having only one non-executive director on each committee for example means a 'uphill' battle in persuading the board into a course of action and leaves the executives with the easy option of vetoing any suggestions.

Use of rules-based approach

Taking the alternative, a rules-based approach may be more appropriate for Pacific Goods as **compliance** with a set of rules would have to be stated. In other words, the extent of compliance would not be left up to the company; the **extent would be inherent within the rules or regulations**. Taking this approach would mean, for example, that the appointment committee had the 'correct' numbers of non-executive directors. Obviously areas such as internal controls would still be difficult but at least 'lip-service' could not be paid.

Advice

Overall, a principles-based approach would be appropriate if the directors **actually were happy to follow the appropriate corporate governance guidelines**. Without that compliance, a rules based approach may be preferred, at least in the short term.

(c)   ### Strategic risks

Strategic risks are risks that relate to the **fundamental and key decisions** that the directors take about the future of the organisation.

Company strategy

The main strategic risk relates to the **change in company strategy** at Pacific Goods. The directors have in effect risked the entire business in the attempt to move the company 'upmarket'. A strategy change in this way is notoriously difficult (for example even after the attempt to move 'upmarket' Skoda cars are still considered cheap and unreliable even though the company has won reliability awards). As the scenario appears to indicate, it has not worked.

Company culture

There has also been a significant change in company culture. There have been two key changes in this area; firstly the additional requirements placed on store managers and secondly the overall philosophy of customer service being reversed. The new emphasis on profit may succeed although there has been **considerable damage to morale** with respect to redundancies and treatment of store managers.

Liquidity risk

There is some liquidity risk relating to the falling sales, although **no financial information** is **available** to identify any effect on cash flow. However, a fall in volume may indicate that overheads **take a higher proportion of expenses**. In the longer term, Pacific Goods may have **cash flow problems** as falling inflows are insufficient to pay for fixed cash outflows.

Legal risk

There is the possibly of **legal risk** in relation to pay and working hours of staff. Most jurisdictions have **legislation on minimum wage and maximum working hours** and Pacific Goods may be in breach of these. There is specific concern regarding extension of working hours with minimal pay increase as the hourly rate payable is likely to fall, and this fall could be below the minimum wage. Breach of legislation would result in adverse publicity for Pacific Goods.

Operational risks

Operational risks relate to matters that can go wrong on a **day-to-day basis** while the organisation is carrying out its business.

For Pacific Goods, operational risks focus mainly on the business of ensuring that the correct goods are available for sale in its shops at the correct time. Given the focus on profit and downsizing, specific risks in the supply chain include late or **inappropriate orders to re-stock products** (mistakes made in reading inventory levels). In addition **inappropriate orders could be placed** (store managers not being aware of the product ranges that could appeal to slightly more upmarket customers). **Products could also not be placed** on shelves quickly enough (insufficient staff for restocking)

In other words, overworked staff may cause an increased number of manual errors.

(d) **Issues arising**

Mr Staite is currently the **chairman and CEO of Pacific Goods plc**. Codes of corporate governance indicate that the roles of chairman and CEO should be taken by different people to avoid excessive power being vested in one individual.

In Pacific Goods plc, there is a risk that Mr Staite could **abuse his power** on the board, either to further his own interests in Pacific Goods, or to adversely affect the strategy of Pacific Goods without proper discussion at board level. Mr Staite will effectively dominate the board meeting.

Alternative options

There are two options available to Mr Staite.

Firstly, he can **resign from being either the chairman or the CEO** as soon as the appointment committee can identify and appoint a suitable replacement.

Secondly, he can **continue to be chairman and CEO to see out the crisis** at Pacific Goods. This course of action is allowed by codes of corporate governance in the short term only and has been used occasionally. For example, in the early 2000's, Marks & Spencer appointed a chairman/CEO in an attempt to revive the company.

Recommendations

Given Pacific Goods' current problems and Mr Staite's experience in alleviating similar problems in other companies, then it appears reasonable that he can **continue as chairman / CEO at least in the short term**. However, the appointment committee should be seeking suitable candidates to be CEO within a timescale of say 18 months from now.

This action allows Mr Staite to **attempt to see Pacific Goods through the current crisis**, while at the same time identifying the corporate governance requirement of keeping the roles separate wherever possible.

Question 2

Text references. Chapters 1,3 and 4.

Top tips. As well as illustrating the key features of governance codes, (a) illustrates some of their limitations, the lack of detailed practical guidance and the realities of board power.

(b) is a good summary of the guidance on remuneration committees. The requirement relating to information is effectively asking what the remuneration committee should consider when setting levels of remuneration.

(c) deals with the SPAMSOAP controls that are of most relevance for this paper, the organisation and management controls.

Easy marks. The role of the remuneration committee should have provided easy marks in (b) even if the information requirements proved more difficult, so make sure you revise this area if you struggled.

			Marks
(a)	Up to 3 marks for each issue discussed. 3 marks only awarded if limitations of each measure analysed		9
(b)	Up to 2 marks for each relevant point made about role and functioning of remuneration committee	7	
	Up to 4 marks for information requirements	4	
	max		9
(c)	1 mark for definition of organisation controls, 1 mark for definition of management controls		
	1 mark for each reasonable example given of an organisation or management control		7
			25

(a) **Main concerns**

Most of the corporate governance reports have addressed concerns about the system of **financial reporting** and the **safeguards** provided by **auditors**. Other concerns that governance guidance has addressed have included **unexpected failures of major companies** and **lack of accountability of directors** towards shareholders and other stakeholders.

Features of governance reports

(i) **Role of non-executive directors**

Governance reports have stressed the **role of independent non-executive directors**. Independent non-executive directors should constitute **a strong presence on a board** (a third or more in numbers, depending on the governance regimes). They should be prepared to challenge the views of executive directors, and also **staff the key board committees** that monitor executive directors (the audit, remuneration, nomination and risk management committees).

However there are a number of examples of companies failing with a **significant non-executive presence** on board. The impact of the governance codes may thus be limited, for the following principal reasons.

Limited nature of role

The role of non-executive directors is essentially a **part-time**, **limited** involvement.

Position on board

Whilst the report recommends that certain tasks should fall specifically within the remit of non-executive directors (membership of the audit and remuneration committees) their impact on the main board depends on the **constitution** of the board and the **division of power** amongst executive directors

(ii) **Improvement of disclosure in financial accounts**

Certain recommendations in the area of financial reporting have been further developed. Listed companies in some regimes are required to produce an **operating and financial review**; most regimes require the board to comment on the **operation of internal controls** and the entity's future as a **going concern**. There should be **improved disclosure of directors' remuneration**.

Undoubtedly there is more information but its added value remains uncertain. In particular some of the guidance on internal controls does not lay down the form of report, and does **not require** directors to make any statement on **effectiveness**. In addition there is **little guidance on design and implementation** of controls; industry-specific guidance may be helpful in this area.

(iii)   **Strengthening the role of the auditor**

Undoubtedly the codes have demonstrated how **auditor concerns can be raised** with **independent directors**, and have demonstrated the importance of links between the external and internal auditors and the **audit committee**.

However whether the reforms have increased the value of audits to shareholders is doubtful for the following reasons.

Strength of board position

The audit committee's ability to express concerns will depend on its **members' position and influence on the main board**.

Increase in scope of audit

It is doubtful whether in most instances changing the auditor will mean the scope of the audit will increase significantly. 'Big Four' spokesmen have indicated that their fears about increased exposure to liability meaning that they are unwilling to take on extra reporting responsibilities.

(iv)   **Protection of shareholders**

The codes have stressed that **shareholders** can take advantage of their rights to **speak** at Annual General Meetings. They have also acknowledged the influence of **institutional shareholders**, stressing how institutional shareholders could be a force for good within companies.

However many codes have **not addressed** the question of whether the **interests** of different types of shareholders, would **differ**, and, if so, how each type could be protected.

(b)   **Purpose and role of remuneration committee**

The purpose of the remuneration committee is to provide a **mechanism for determining the remuneration packages** of executive directors. The scope of the review should include not only salaries and bonuses, but also share options, pension rights and compensation for loss of office.

The committee's remit may also include issues such as **director appointments** and succession planning, as these are connected with remuneration levels.

Constitution of remuneration committee

Most codes recommend that the remuneration committee should consist entirely of **non-executive directors** with no personal financial interest other than as shareholders in the matters to be decided. In addition there should be **no conflict of interests** arising from remuneration committee members and executive directors holding directorships in common in other companies.

Functioning of remuneration committee

Corporate governance such as the UK Corporate Governance Code states that remuneration should be set having regard to market forces, and the packages required to **'attract, motivate and retain' the desired calibre of director**. The committee should pay particular attention to the setting of performance-related elements of remuneration.

Reporting of remuneration committee

In addition a **report** from the committee should form part of the annual accounts. The report should set out **company policy** on remuneration and give details of the **packages for individual directors**. The **chairman** of the committee should be **available to answer questions** at the annual general meeting, and the committee should consider whether **shareholder approval** is required of the company's remuneration policy.

Information requirements

In order to assess executive directors' pay on a reasonable basis, the following information will be required.

(i)   **Remuneration packages given by similar organisations**

The problem with using this data is that it may **lead to upward pressure on remuneration**, as the remuneration committee may feel forced to pay what is paid elsewhere to avoid losing directors to competitors.

(ii) **Market levels of remuneration**

This will particularly apply for **certain industries**, and **certain knowledge and skills**. More generally the committee will need an awareness of what is considered a minimum competitive salary.

(iii) **Individual performance**

The committee's **knowledge and experience of the company**, will be useful here.

(iv) **Organisation performance**

This may include **information about the performance of the operations** which the director controls, or more **general company performance information** such as earnings per share or share price.

(c) **Main concerns of board**

The board's principal concern is with controls that can be classified as organisation or management.
Organisation controls

Organisation controls are designed to ensure **everyone is aware of their responsibilities**, and **provide a framework** within which lower level controls can operate. Key organisation controls include the following.

(i) **Structure**

The board should establish an **appropriate structure** for the organisation and **delegate** appropriate levels of authority to different grades.

(ii) **Internal accounting system**

The board should ensure that the system is providing **accurate and relevant information** on a regular basis. Good quality information will enable the board to assess whether targets are being met or losses are possible.

(iii) **Communication**

Communication of organisation **policies** and values through manuals and other guidance to staff is essential.

Management controls

Management controls are designed to **ensure** that the **business** can be **effectively monitored**. Key management controls include the following.

(i) **Monitoring of business risks on a regular basis**

This should include **assessment of the potential financial impact** of contingencies.

(ii) **Monitoring of financial information**

Management should also be alert for **significant variations in results** between branches or divisions or significant changes in results.

(iii) **Use of audit committee**

The committee should actively **liase** with the external and internal auditors, and **report on any weaknesses** discovered. The committee should also regularly **review the overall structure** of internal control, and investigate any serious weaknesses found.

(iv) **Use of internal audit**

Internal audit should be used as an independent check on the **operation of detailed controls** in the operating departments. Internal audit's work can be biased as appropriate towards areas of the business where there is a risk of significant loss should controls fail.

Question 3

Marking scheme

			Marks
(a)	Up to 3 marks for membership of audit committee, focusing on independence and financial knowledge	3	
	1 mark for each of the major tasks carried out by the audit committee	5	
			8
(b)	Up to 2 marks per point discussed		6
(c)	Up to 3 marks for identification of problem	3	
	Up to 6 marks for discussion of possible solutions	6	
	Up to 2 marks for recommendation which should be relevant and related to previous discussion	2	
			11
			25

(a)   **Membership of audit committee**

According to the UK Corporate Governance Code, the **audit committee should have at least three members**, all Non Executive Directors. At least one member should have **relevant financial knowledge**; generally this would mean holding an accountancy or similar qualification. A majority of the membership should be **independent NEDs**. The head of the internal audit department and the external auditor may also form part of the committee, especially where internal and external audit reports are being discussed.

Role of audit committee

Review of financial statements and systems

The committee should review both the **quarterly/interim** (if published) and **annual accounts**. This should involve assessment of the judgements made about the overall **appearance and presentation of the accounts**, **key accounting policies** and **major areas of judgement**. The committee should also review the financial reporting and budgetary systems.

Liaison with external auditors

The audit committee's tasks here will include being responsible for the **appointment or removal of the external auditors** as well as fixing their remuneration. The committee should consider whether there are **any threats to external auditor independence,** particularly **non-audit services.** The committee should **discuss the scope of the external audit** prior to the start of the audit and act as a **forum for liaison** between the external auditors, the internal auditors and the finance director.

Review of internal audit

The review should cover **standards** including objectivity, technical knowledge and professional standards, the **work plan** and **scope**. The review should also cover adequacy of **resources, reporting and results** and **liaison** with external auditors. The head of internal audit should have **direct access** to the audit committee.

Review of internal control

Committee members can use their own experience to **monitor the adequacy of internal control systems,** focusing particularly on the control environment, management's attitude towards controls and overall management controls. The committee should also **consider the recommendations of the auditors** in the management letter and executive management's response.

Review of risk management

The audit committee should check whether there is a **formal policy in place for risk management** and that the policy is **backed and regularly monitored** by the board. The committee should also review the arrangements, including training, for ensuring that **managers and staff** are **aware of their responsibilities**. Committee members should use their own knowledge of the business to confirm that risk management is updated to reflect the current business environment and strategy.

(b) **Risk management**

Exception reporting means highlighting variances from standards of performance that have been established or events or conditions that have been forecast. By highlighting variances, exception reporting allows for **action to be taken** to correct the situation and get conditions and performance back towards what was predicted or standards. Exception reporting should aim to avoid important information that requires action being buried within routine information. Exception reporting is therefore most important where the consequences of a risk materialising are **very severe** and action needs to be taken to prevent the risk materialising if it appears that the risk is likely to materialise.

Monitoring

A sound system of exception reporting aids management by indicating the areas upon which **management monitoring and internal audit** work needs to focus. It shows the areas where **separate evaluation** of control systems and performance may be required, in addition to routine monitoring. **Whistleblowing** directly to the board may be an important form of exception reporting where systems have failed to indicate problems.

Performance evaluation

Exception reporting will be part of the performance evaluation of management and staff, highlighting areas where performance has been better or worse than expected. The data however needs to be used with care, with assessments being made about the **controllability** of variances found and the **interrelationships** between different information that is reported.

Cost-benefits

As with other elements in control systems, the **costs** of operating the system and of investigating exceptions need to be **weighed against the benefits.** The exceptions highlighted may relate to risks that do not have severe consequences, and thus are not very relevant to senior managers.

Routine reporting

Exception reporting should be seen as being only part of information systems. The board and senior managers need to **receive routine reports from operational managers and staff** in order to obtain assurance that there are no exceptions and that the organisation is functioning as expected in situations that have been correctly predicted. Gaining this positive assurance is particularly important in areas of high risks, for example the development of major investments.

(c)   **Importance of ethical code**

Actions that the employee can take must be **weighed against the ACCA ethical code**. While disclosing information about financial irregularities to a third party may appear to be attractive, the employee must bear in mind the overall ethical principles of integrity and confidentiality.

(i)   **Integrity**

The principle of **integrity** implies that the employee will act honestly and that any action can be trusted. Any disclosure must therefore be made in good faith and not for financial gain and without malicious intent.

(ii)   **Confidentiality**

The concept of **confidentiality** implies that information obtained during the course of employment in a company will be kept confidential, unless there is an appropriate reason to disclose this information. 'Normal reasons' will include client authorisation, breach of specific laws such as money laundering, and due process of law in a court.

The employee must therefore consider whether any disclosure will be believed. It appears in any case that the duty of confidentiality has already been breached, albeit the disclosure has been to a single person who has apparently been instructed to keep the company details private. The employee must consider if a further breach of the duty of confidentiality is appropriate.

Possible actions

Assuming that disclosure is thought appropriate, then the employee can consider the following reporting options:

(i)   **Board of directors or the chairman**

However, these people may be **swayed by the opinion of the chief accountant** and may not wish disclosure due to the adverse impact on the company.

(ii)   **External auditors**

Disclosure to a third party would appear to **go against the explicit instructions** of the head of internal audit. There is also no guarantee that the external auditors will be able to obtain appropriate audit evidence due to limited audit procedures or alteration of evidence prior to their visit.

(iii)   **Audit committee**

Given that the company is a listed company, then the principles of good corporate governance should be followed. Specifically, there should be procedures within the company to **allow employees with genuine concerns** about the operations of the company to make a confidential approach to the audit committee. As the committee is comprised of non-executive directors, then they should be able to take appropriate investigative action without conflict of interest regarding their stewardship of the running of the company.

Recommendation

It is **therefore recommended** that the **employee makes disclosure** to the **audit committee**. This action will **not breach confidentiality** against the company as **external disclosure** is not being made, and given that disclosure is made in good faith, then it will also **maintain the employee's integrity**.

Question 4

Marking scheme

		Marks	
(a)	Up to 4 marks for description of risk identification procedures	4	
	Up to 4 marks for description of risk evaluation procedures	4	
	Up to 5 marks for description of risk management procedures	5	
	Up to 3 marks for description of risk control and review procedures	3	
	Give credit in all stages for relevant procedures		
	max		10
(b)	Up to 3 marks for each risk. Only award 3 marks if assessment of risk's significance has been made and means of managing the risk have been identified		15
			25

(a) There are four main principles for effective risk management in a business context.

Risk identification

Any organisation needs a procedure for **reviewing** the **risks** it faces and **to identify what those specific risks are**. The board of the company also needs to be aware that those risks will change over time, so it must be on the lookout for new risks. This is particularly true with more widespread terrorist activities (eg the 11th September attacks in the USA) and changes in the nature of global competition (eg outsourcing of call centres from Europe to the Middle and Far East).

Risks may also **vary depending on the country** in which the company operates. For example it may be difficult to establish a new brand in a new country, or there may be different employment, environmental or other legislation that must be followed.

The use of **internal audit** and **environmental audit programmes** will help to **identify different risks** enabling the company to keep up-to-date on the different risks facing it.

Risk evaluation

Risk evaluation involves the **use of various procedures to try and identify the size of the risk**. For a downside risk, the extent of any loss depends on:

(i)   The **probability of the outcome of the loss making event**, and
(ii) The **size of the loss in the event that the risk crystallises** – that is occurs

Where the probability of the outcome is remote and the actual loss small, then no action may be taken regarding that risk. However, a high probability of the event and potentially large losses will mean that some risk management measures are required.

Risk management measures

Risk management measures are the **responsibility of managers and the board in an organisation**. The actual measure taken vary depending on the risk:

(i) **Transfer of risk** by **Insurance** may be available so that a third party pays should the event occur, eg loss of company assets.

(ii) **Avoidance** by removing that risk from the company. For example, a company may avoid the possibility of losses in a subsidiary by selling that subsidiary.

(iii) **Reduction** of the risk. Many financial risks can be minimised, by hedging or use of forward contracts. Other risks such as over-reliance on a single product may be minimised by expanding the product range or purchasing competitors to diversify.

(iv) **Acceptance** of the risk as a feature of business. Some risks such as acts of terrorism may not even be insurable.

Risk control and review

Control systems should be established to monitor risks and to identify situations where actions are required to minimise new risks or existing risks that are becoming more significant. The Turnbull report indicates that a good system of internal control should be established to monitor risks, but that risk reviews should also be carried out on a regular basis to ensure that the control system is operating correctly.

(b) **Business risks**

These are risks that a **company's performance could be better or worse than expected**.

(i) **The new business venture to sell clothes on the Internet using 3D models to display the clothes**

There is the risk that demand will be far short of that anticipated or that costs of developing the Internet site will significantly exceed budget. Previous experience in this area is not positive, with the dot.com company Boo.com collapsing after only a few weeks trading due to lack of ability of servers to cope with demand.

LP should have assessed the 3D project for feasibility. Budgets should have been established and **actual expenditure regularly compared with budgets**. If actual expenditure is unavoidably significantly in excess of budget, the board should consider whether the **project should continue**. Thorough **testing procedures** should have been built into the plan, and these should ensure that the site is capable of coping with anticipated demand. Once the site is operational, LP should monitor the level of sales generated by obtaining customer feedback through the site, and comparing sales generated with the costs of keeping the site updated.

(ii) **Product obsolescence**

The decision to lengthen the time of sale for each product may appear to decrease development costs. However, the board of LP must also take into account **demand** for the goods. The fashion industry tends to issue new clothes and designs every few months, and certainly in temperate climates, fashions will change according to the season. There is a risk that not amending the style of products sold will **reduce sales far in excess of the reduction in expenditure**. The overall going concern of the company may also be adversely affected if customers perceive the clothes to be 'out of date' and change to other suppliers.

LP should **monitor the performance of products** in detail, and look for evidence of falling sales and other evidence that its products are viewed as old-fashioned, for example adverse customer or press comment. The board should also consider whether work on developing new products should continue to some extent, so that new lines can be launched quickly if demand falls.

(iii)   **New competition**

The new company PVO appears to be aggressively attacking LP's market place. While the overall effect of the new competitor is difficult to determine, having a new range of clothes available is likely to attract customers with little if any brand loyalty to LP.

LP should make sure that **competitor activity** is **carefully monitored** and responses are made to known or predicted competitor activity, for an example an advertising campaign to counter new products being launched by the competitor. LP's board should also **review very regularly the performance of products** which are most vulnerable to competitor activity and decide whether to invest more in these or concentrate on other less vulnerable products.

The overall going concern of the company may again be affected.

Financial risks

Financial risks arise from the **possibility that the financial situation of the company will be different from what was expected**. Financial risks will include:

(i)   **Credit risks**

These arise from the use of the **company's store card**. If there is an economic depression then there may be an increased risk of card holders defaulting on their payments.

LP should carry out **credit checks** before consumers are allowed a credit card. The **initial credit limits** should be **set low**, and increased over time if the customer's level of business and repayment record warrant it. The company's systems should **reject payments** that take customers in excess of their credit limits. LP should insist on a **minimum amount** being repayable on the card each month. There should be **specified procedures** for pursuing overdue debts.

(ii)   **Foreign exchange risks**

These occur because LP purchases raw materials and some finished products from **overseas**. Depending on how these purchases are financed, there will be a risk of **exchange rate losses** if the main currency LP uses moves adversely compared to the supplying country's currency.

LP's board should consider changing purchasing arrangements, so that more purchases are made in countries where LP has significant sales, thus reducing exchange risks by **matching**. However this should be weighed against the possibility that purchase prices may increase from using different sources. Payments on large purchases not made immediately could be covered by **forward contracts**.

(iii)   **Interest rate risks**

This results from an **increase in bank base rates**. An increase in rates may affect LP adversely, especially where there are significant **loans or overdrafts** where the interest rate follows the base rate.

LP's board should review the company's pattern of lending. Ideally if interest rates are expected to rise, it should look to replace **overdraft and floating rate finance** with **fixed rate loans**. LP may also hedge borrowing that will be required in some months' time by means of **interest rate futures and options**.

ACCA Professional Level

Paper P1

Professional Accountant

Mock Examination 3

December 2011

Question Paper	
Time allowed	
Reading and Planning Writing	**15 minutes** **3 hours**
This paper is divided into two sections Section A This ONE question is compulsory and must be attempted Section B TWO questions only to be attempted	
During reading and planning time only the question paper may be annotated	

DO NOT OPEN THIS PAPER UNTIL YOU ARE READY TO START UNDER EXAMINATION CONDITIONS

Section A – This question is compulsory and must be attempted

Question 1

Coastal Oil is one of the world's largest petrochemical companies. It is based in Deeland and is responsible alone for 10% of Deeland's total stock market value. It employs 120,000 people in many countries and has an especially strong presence in Effland because of Effland's very large consumption of oil and gas products and its large oil reserves. Coastal Oil is organised, like most petrochemical companies, into three vertically integrated business units: the exploration and extraction division; the processing and refining division; and the distribution and retailing division.

Because of the risks and the capital investment demands, Coastal Oil has joint venture (JV) agreements in place for many of its extraction operations (i.e. its oil and gas rigs), especially those in the deep-water seas. A joint venture is a shared equity arrangement for a particular project where control is shared between the JV partners. In each of its JVs, Coastal Oil is the largest partner, although operations on each rig are divided between the JV member companies and the benefits are distributed according to the share of the JV.

As a highly visible company, Coastal Oil has long prided itself on its safety record and its ethical reputation. It believes both to be essential in supporting shareholder value. Its corporate code of ethics, published some years ago, pledges its commitment to the 'highest standards' of ethical performance in the following areas: full compliance with regulation in all jurisdictions; safety and care of employees; transparency and communication with stakeholders; social contribution; and environmental responsibility. In addition, Coastal Oil has usually provided a lot of voluntary disclosure in its annual report and on its website. It says that it has a wide range of stakeholders and so needs to provide a great deal of information.

One of the consequences of dividing up the different responsibilities and operations on an oil or gas rig is that Coastal Oil does not have direct influence over some important operational controls. The contractual arrangements on any given oil rig can be very complex and there have often been disagreements between JV partners on some individual legal agreements and responsibilities for health and safety controls. Given that Coastal Oil has JV interests in hundreds of deep-water oil and gas rigs all over the world, some observers have said that this could be a problem should an accident ever occur.

This issue was tragically highlighted when one of its deep-water rigs, the Effland Coastal Deep Rig, had an explosion earlier this year. It was caused by the failure of a valve at the 'well-head' on the sea floor. The valve was the responsibility of Well Services, a minor partner in the JV. Eight workers were killed on the rig from the high pressure released after the valve failure, and oil gushed into the sea from the well-head, a situation that should have been prevented had the valve been fully operational. It was soon established that Well Services' staff failed to inspect the valve before placing it at the well-head at the time of installation, as was required by the company's normal control systems. In addition, the valve was attached to a connecting part that did not meet the required technical specification for the water depth at which it was operating. The sea bed was 1,000 metres deep and the connecting part was intended for use to a depth of up to 300 metres. There was a suggestion that the need to keep costs down was a key reason for the use of the connecting part with the inferior specification.

Reports in the media on the following day said that the accident had happened on a rig 'belonging to Coastal Oil' when in fact, Coastal Oil was technically only a major partner in the joint venture. Furthermore, there was no mention that the accident had been caused by a part belonging to Well Services. A journalist did discover, however, that both companies had operated a more lax safety culture on the deep-water rigs than was the case at facilities on land (the 'land-side'). He said there was a culture of 'out of sight, out of mind' on some offshore facilities and that this meant that several other controls were inoperative in addition to the ones that led to the accident. Information systems reporting back to the 'land-side' were in place but it was the responsibility of management on each individual rig to enforce all internal controls and the 'land-side' would only be informed of a problem if it was judged to be 'an exceptional risk' by the rig's manager.

The accident triggered a large internal argument between Coastal Oil and Well Services about liability and this meant that there was no public statement from Coastal Oil for seven days while the arguments continued. Lawyers on both sides pointed out that liability was contractually ambiguous because the documentation on responsibilities was far too complex and unclear. And in any case, nobody expected anything to go wrong. In the absence of any official statement from Coastal Oil for those seven days, the media had no doubts who was to blame: Coastal Oil was strongly criticised in Effland with the criticism growing stronger as oil from the ruptured valve was shown spilling directly into the seaoff the Effland coast. With no contingency plan for a deep-water well-head rupture in place, the ruptured valve took several months to repair, meaning that many thousands of tonnes of crude oil polluted the sea off Effland. Images of seabirds covered in crude oil were frequently broadcast on television and thousands of businesses on the coast reported that the polluted water would disrupt their business over the vital tourist season. Public statements from Coastal Oil that it was not responsible for the ruptured valve were seemingly not believed by the Effland public. Senior legislators in Effland said that the accident happened on 'a rig belonging to Coastal Oil' so it must be Coastal Oil's fault.

A review by the Coastal Oil board highlighted several areas where risk management systems might be tightened to reduce the possibility of a similar accident happening again. Finance director, Tanya Tun, suggested that the company should disclose this new information to shareholders as it would be value-relevant to them. In particular, she said that a far more detailed voluntary statement on environmental risk would be material to the shareholders. The annual report would, she believed, be a suitable vehicle for this disclosure.

Because of the high media profile of the event, politicians from Effland involved themselves in the situation. Senator Jones's constituency on the coast nearest the rig was badly affected by the oil spill and many of his constituents suffered economic loss as a result. He angrily retorted in a newspaper interview that Coastal Oil's CEO, Susan Ahmed, 'should have known this was going to happen', such was the poor state of some of the internal controls on the Effland Coastal Deep Rig.

As the oil spill continued and the media interest in the events intensified, CEO Mrs Ahmed was summoned to appear before a special committee of the Effland national legislature 'to explain herself to the citizens of Effland'. The Coastal Oil board agreed that this would be a good opportunity for Mrs Ahmed to address a number of issues in detail and attempt to repair some of the company's damaged reputation. The board agreed that Mrs Ahmed should provide as full a statement as possible on the internal control failures to the special committee.

Required

(a)   Describe the general purposes of a corporate code of ethics and evaluate Coastal Oil's performance against its own stated ethical aims as set out in its code of ethics.   **(10 marks)**

(b)   Explain, using examples, the difference between voluntary and mandatory disclosure, and assess Tanya Tun's proposition that additional voluntary disclosure on environmental risk management would be material to the shareholders.   **(10 marks)**

(c)   In preparing to appear before the special committee of the Effland national legislature, CEO Mrs Ahmed has been informed that she will be asked to explain the causes of the accident and to establish whether she can give assurances that an accident of this type will not re-occur.

Required

Prepare a statement for Mrs Ahmed to present before the committee that explains the following:

(i)   The internal control failures that gave rise to the accident;   **(10 marks)**

(ii)   The difference between subjective and objective risk assessment (using examples). Argue against Senator Jones's view that Mrs Ahmed 'should have known this was going to happen';   **(8 marks)**

(iii)   'Health and safety' risk and the factors that can increase this risk in an organisation;   **(4 marks)**

(iv)   Why Coastal Oil cannot guarantee the prevention of further health and safety failures, using the ALARP (as low as reasonably practicable) principle;   **(4 marks)**

Professional marks will be awarded in part (c) for logical flow, persuasiveness, format and tone of the answers.   **(4 marks)**

(Total = 50 marks)

Section B – TWO questions ONLY to be attempted

Question 2

There has been a debate in the country of Geeland for some years about the most appropriate way to regulate corporate governance. Several years ago, there were a number of major corporate failures and 'scandals' caused in part by a number of single powerful individuals dominating their boards. Business leaders and policy-makers were sceptical about a rules-based approach, and this led the Geeland stock exchange to issue guidance in the 'Geeland Code' as follows:

'Good corporate governance is not just a matter of prescribing particular corporate structures and complying with a number of rules. There is a need for broad principles. All stakeholders should then apply these flexibly to the varying circumstances of individual companies.'

Given the causes of the Geeland corporate governance failures, there was a debate about whether the separation of the roles of chairman and chief executive should be made a legal requirement. This resulted in the stock exchange issuing guidance that whilst a rules-based or 'box ticking' approach would specify that 'the roles of chairman and chief executive officer should never be combined… We do not think that there are universally valid answers on such points.'

One company to take advantage of the flexibility in Geeland's principles-based approach was Anson Company. In July 2010, Anson Company announced that it had combined its roles of chairman and chief executive in a single role carried out by one individual. In accordance with the Geeland listing rules, it made the following 'comply or explain' statement in its 2011 annual report:

'Throughout the year the company complied with all Geeland Code provisions with the exception that from 1 July 2010 the roles of chairman and chief executive have been exercised by the same individual, William Klunker. We recognise that this has been out of line with best practice. We understand the concerns of shareholders but believe that we have maintained robust governance while at the same time benefiting from having Mr Klunker in control. On 31 July 2012 Mr Klunker will step down as executive chairman, remaining as chairman until we conclude our search for a non-executive chairman to succeed him, no later than March 2013.'

Required

(a) Briefly distinguish between rules and principles-based approaches to corporate governance. Critically evaluate the Geeland stock exchange's guidance that 'all stakeholders should then apply these flexibly to the varying circumstances of individual companies.' **(12 marks)**

(b) Explain why a separation of the roles of chairman and chief executive is considered best practice in most jurisdictions. **(8 marks)**

(c) Assess the 'comply or explain' statement made by Anson Company in its 2011 annual report. **(5 marks)**

(Total = 25 marks)

Question 3

After the government of Haitchland decided to privatise its monopoly gas supplier (transferring it from government control to private ownership by issuing and selling shares), there was a period of transition as the new board took shape. A great deal of internal reorganisation and culture change was deemed necessary as the company moved to the private sector. The new company, called Dale Gas, set up a committee structure in readiness to comply with stock exchange listing rules. During this transitional period, some directors left and new ones, more familiar with operating in listed companies but unfamiliar with the gas industry, joined the board.

It was unanimously agreed by the new board that the previous chief executive, Helen Evans, should continue in her role after the privatisation. Tom Nwede, a fund manager at XY Investments, one of the company's major new institutional shareholders, said that the company would be exposed to higher market risk if she were to leave the company, so it was very important that she stayed on. She was seen as a highly competent CEO with excellent strategic and communication skills. She commanded the confidence and trust of the employees and also the new institutional investors.

One of the first actions of the new remuneration committee was to propose a doubling of Mrs Evans's salary. The committee said that she had been underpaid when the company was state-controlled because of government constraints on the salaries of public servants. The committee said that she now needed to receive a salary commensurate with the importance of the job and in line with other public listed companies of similar size. This proposal was widely publicised. Some criticised it on the basis that if her previous salary was considered sufficient then, why was it now felt necessary to double her rewards after privatisation?

Her new salary was put to the vote at the company's first annual general meeting after privatisation. Although many small shareholders (some protesting at the AGM itself) voted against her salary increase, it was easily passed by the proxy votes of the large institutional shareholders who did not attend the meeting in person. Tom Nwede, the XY Investments fund manager, said that the votes of the institutional shareholders were crucial in ensuring that Mrs Evans was retained, thereby mitigating market risk.

Required

(a) Explain the purposes of a chief executive's reward package and review the factors that might influence the level of reward for Mrs Evans after the privatisation. **(10 marks)**

(b) Define 'market risk' and justify, giving reasons, Tom Nwede's belief that retaining Mrs Evans was crucial in mitigating market risk. **(10 marks)**

(c) Define, and explain the advantages of, 'proxy voting' in the context of the case. **(5 marks)**

(Total = 25 marks)

Question 4

When Biggo Manufacturing (a public listed company) needed to build an extension to its factory, it obtained planning permission to build it on an adjacent field. The local government authority was keen to attract the new jobs that would go with the expansion and so granted the permission despite the objections of a number of residents, who were concerned that the new factory extension would mean the loss of a children's play area.

When the board of Biggo met after the building approval had been given, the chief executive read out a letter from Albert Doo, leader of the local government authority, saying that although permission to build had been given, the company should consider making a sizeable contribution towards creating a new children's play area in a nearby location. Mr Doo said that Biggo 'should recognise its social responsibility'. He said that the company should consider itself a citizen of society and should, accordingly, 'recognise its responsibilities as well as its legal rights'.

One of Biggo's directors, Robert Tens, said he thought the request was entirely reasonable given the displacement of the play area. He also said that they could use the donation strategically to help cultivate the company's reputation locally to help in future recruitment. It might also, he said, help to reduce resistance to any future expansion the company might need to make.

Margaret Heggs, in contrast, argued that the company should not make the donation as it was likely that company profits would be low in the current year. She said that the acquisition of the land and the gaining of planning permission were done through the normal legal channels and so the company had no further contractual or ethical duties to the local government, nor to the local community. She said that Biggo provided local employment and produced excellent products and so it was unreasonable for the request for a donation to have been made. 'This board is accountable to the shareholders of Biggo and not to the local community or the local government authority', she said.

Required

(a) Explain the meaning of 'rights' and 'responsibilities' in the context of Biggo and describe how these terms are interpreted at the two ends of the Gray, Owen & Adams 'continuum'.   **(10 marks)**

(b) Justify, using evidence from the case, which of Gray, Owen & Adams's positions are best described by the comments made by Robert Tens and also Margaret Heggs.   **(6 marks)**

(c) Define 'social responsibility' as used by Albert Doo. Contrast how short and long-term shareholder interest perspectives may affect Biggo's attitude to the requested contribution for the children's play area. **(9 marks)**

(Total = 25 marks)

Answers

DO NOT TURN THIS PAGE UNTIL YOU HAVE
COMPLETED THE MOCK EXAM

A plan of attack

Yes we know you've heard it 102 times but, just in case for the 103rd time: **Take a good look at the paper before diving in to answer questions**.

First things first

Again remember that the best way to use the 15 minutes reading time in your exam is firstly to **choose which questions to do** and decide the **order** in which to attempt them. Then get stuck into analysing the requirements of **Question 1** and identifying the key issues in the scenario.

The next step

You may be thinking that this paper is OK compared with the previous two mocks. Alternatively you may like this paper a lot less than the other two.

Option 1 (Don't like it)

If you are challenged by this paper, it is still best to **do the compulsory question first.** You will feel better once you've got it out of the way. Honest.

- You should allow yourself a full 15 minutes' reading time in answering **Question 1** in addition to the 90 minutes, as it would have been available in the exam. You would have needed to use it because of the amount of the information in the question. If you are struggling for ideas, try to make the most of the material in the scenario, because there are lots of hints in it. If you can remember what you read about BP and the Gulf of Mexico spill in the text, it will help as this scenario covers similar circumstances.

- Most of **Question 2** can be answered from knowledge without a need for much application to the scenario. There are enough pointers in the statement to give you a couple of ideas for part (c), and that's all you need as it's only worth 5 marks.

- There are also a number of hints in the scenario that can generate ideas for **Question 3**, particularly for part (b). If you're not sure on proxy voting, don't worry too much about part (c) as it's only worth 5 marks.

- If you have some knowledge of Gray, Owen and Adams, that will certainly help in **Question 4**. Part (c) tests knowledge of the Johnson and Scholes classification. If you can't remember this, it's probably worth avoiding this question. What not to do is to attempt this question and waffle generally about social responsibility, as that approach won't get you many marks.

Option 2 (It's a pleasant surprise)

Are you **sure** it is? If you are then that's encouraging. You'll feel even happier when you've got the compulsory question out the way, so why not **do Question 1 first**.

- Allow yourself the full 15 minutes' reading time for **Question 1**, as there is quite a lot of detail in the scenario that you need to absorb and that will inform your answer. If you can remember what you read in the text about BP and the Gulf of Mexico oil spill, that will help as well.

- If you are comfortable with the subjects tested in **Question 2**, you could well choose this question as it's possible to score heavily. Make sure you leave yourself enough time to gain the marks for part (c), as the question provides some clear pointers that you can slot into your answer.

- One trap with **Question 3** is to look at part (a) and think the question is mainly about directors' remuneration. The principal topic of the question is the contribution that a chief executive can make and how shareholders respond to her.

- If you are comfortable with Gray, Owen and Adams, you may choose **Question 4** although the question is different in form from the other questions that you've practised in this kit. Note however that you also need to be comfortable with Johnson and Scholes's stances, as part (c), which tests them, is worth a significant 9 marks.

Once, once more

You must allocate your time according to the marks for the question in total, and for the parts of the questions. And you must also **follow the requirements exactly**. It's easy to waffle on this exam if you don't follow the requirements strictly. If your answer contains irrelevant material, you will not be scoring marks efficiently and you will put yourself under **time pressure**. Also make sure you show **clearly** which question you're answering.

All finished and quarter of an hour to go?

Your time allocation must have been faulty. However make the most of the 15 minutes; go back to **any parts of questions that you didn't finish** because you ran out of time. Always write something rather than nothing if you possibly can and try not to leave questions unanswered.

Forget about it!

Just wipe it from your mind.

Question 1

Marking scheme

				Marks
(a)	1 mark for each purpose of code of ethics max		5	
	1 mark for evaluation of each point max		5	
		max		10
(b)	Distinguishing between voluntary and mandatory disclosure		2	
	½ mark for each example of mandatory disclosure max		2	
	½ mark for each example of voluntary disclosure max		2	
	2 marks for each benefit to shareholders identified and assessed (½ mark for identification only) max		8	
	max			10
(c)	(i)	2 marks for each internal control failure identified and explained (½ mark for identification only)	10	
	(ii)	Distinguishing between objective and subjective risk	2	
		1 mark for explanation of each and/or evidence of understanding max	2	
		2 marks for each argument developed against the senator's statement	4	

	(iii)	Explanation of health and safety risk	1
		1 mark for explanation of each factor (½ mark for identification only) max	3
	(iv)	Evidence of understanding of ALARP	2
		Explanation of why health and safety risks cannot be completely eliminated under ALARP	
			2
			26

Professional marks for logical flow, persuasiveness, format and tone of answer

4

50

(a) Purposes of corporate code of ethics

Establishment of organisation's values

Ethical codes are part of an organisation's **internal environment**. They should be in a form that makes their content easy to remember. They promote **values** that link to the organisation's mission statement and strategic purposes.

Promotion of stakeholder responsibilities

Codes explain who are regarded as legitimate stakeholders and define stakeholder rights and responsibilities. They emphasise the importance of maintaining good relations with stakeholders.

Conveying values to stakeholders

Codes can act as communication devices, increasing the **transparency** of an organisation's dealings with its stakeholders. They help stakeholders understand how the company will react in particular situations.

Control of individuals' behaviour

Codes can promote or prohibit certain actions and therefore help to **control management and employee behaviour.** They are meant to guide internal stakeholders towards acting ethically on a day-to-day basis and achieving ethical outcomes if problems arise.

Promotion of business objectives

Codes can be part of **strategic positioning.** Taking a strong stance on responsibility and ethics and earning a good reputation can enhance appeal to consumers.

Coastal Oil's performance

Compliance with regulations

Coastal Oil aimed to achieve full compliance with regulations in all jurisdictions. The complexity of the arrangements with Well Oil meant that **health and safety and environmental regulations** may have been **breached** even though the company was not criminally negligent.

Safety and care of employees

The **lax safety culture and the health and safety failures** on the rigs contributed to the eight deaths and the bereavements for the employees' families. Controls were not operated properly. Coastal Oil's management appears to have been unaware of what was happening on the rigs and did not enforce standards of care on its partner and its managers and employees.

Transparency and communication with stakeholders

Coastal Oil **failed to communicate well** in the days after the explosion. Its priority appears to have been trying to avoid liability rather than providing full information to stakeholders. Many stakeholders would have been anxious to see a statement, including the families of those killed and injured and those living in the surrounding area.

Social contribution and environmental responsibility

Coastal Oil **failed to demonstrate environmental responsibility.** It showed **insufficient commitment to enforcing internal controls** that could have prevented the breach from happening. It had no contingency plan in place for dealing with the effects of a deep-water rupture. The problem took a long time to repair. It caused severe environmental damage, and also had adverse social impacts on the local area's community and economy. Businesses were damaged during the tourist season and the local community therefore had less income to support it.

(b) **Mandatory disclosures**

Company annual reports contain a mixture of mandatory and voluntary disclosures. Mandatory disclosures are those required by legislation, listing rules or accounting standards. They include:

- **Financial statements**

- **Directors' and auditors' reports**

- **Policies** that the company has adopted in particular areas, including the policies it has adopted when preparing its accounts

- **Significant transactions or situations in the context of the accounts,** for example material transactions with related parties or events occurring after the date of the accounts

Voluntary disclosures

Voluntary disclosure can be defined as any disclosure above the **minimum required by legislation and standards**. It can mean giving more information than is required by regulations on particular areas or making disclosures that are not required by regulations. Voluntary disclosures are often narrative in form rather than numerical, as some information that is material to stakeholders cannot be adequately summarised numerically. Examples include:

- **Chairman's statement**

- **Chief Executive's report** going into detail about important aspects of performance

- **Risk reporting** – highlighting the main risks that the company faces

- **Social and environmental reporting** – where guidance is not compulsory but companies may be reporting in line with established good practice

Reasons for voluntary disclosure

Material risks

Even if there had no explosion, shareholders will still welcome detailed disclosure about environmental risk. Interaction with the environment is **inherent** to operating in the oil industry. As sadly demonstrated by the accident, the consequences of risks materialising can be severe and the impact on shareholder value very large. Shareholders therefore require information on the risks that affect Coastal Oil. A detailed statement can also reassure shareholders that Coastal Oil's **risk assessment** policies are effective.

Risk appetite of shareholders

A more detailed environmental report can give shareholders a better idea of the **likelihood and consequences of the risks** the company faces. They can therefore make more informed judgements about whether the overall risk profile of Coastal Oil matches their own appetite for risks, and whether the returns from Coastal Oil are sufficient for the risks of investing in it.

Costs of better systems

Shareholders will wish to see more information about the measures that Coastal Oil will be taking to improve the systems after the disaster, in order to be able to judge what their **costs** will be. Increased costs may have a very material impact on profits, dividends and the value of shareholder investment. Better systems will include better external reporting and this may have a **cost or benefit** too. Greater knowledge about Coastal Oil's activities may have a material impact on market opinion and hence share price.

(c) **Statement to special committee**

Introduction

I would like to start by expressing the deep regret of the board of Coastal Oil for the accident at the Effland Coastal Deep Rig, and the associated loss of life, injuries and environmental damage.

The board accepts the need for **full disclosure** about the circumstances surrounding the accident, in accordance with Coastal Oil's commitment to transparency in its ethical code.

First I want to discuss issues with the internal controls that were operating on the rig.

(i) **Complexity of control arrangements**

Although Coastal Oil accepts its share of responsibility for problems with controls, I would highlight to the committee that we were acting as a **major partner in a joint venture** and did not have complete control over what happened on the rig. Other partners had responsibilities for maintaining controls over operations and safety. However discussions after the accident have highlighted a **lack of clarity in the responsibilities** of ourselves and our joint venture partner. Because we must place some reliance on the controls maintained by our partner, we acknowledge the need for clearer agreements in future.

Inspection of valve

The second failure of control was a **failure to inspect the valve** that failed before it was installed. The inspection was part of the control systems that our partner, Well Services, operated, but we understand that staff failed to carry out this inspection.

Wrong connecting part

A further issue was the use of a connecting part for the valve that was **not suitable for the depth at which it was operating**. It appears also that the connecting part was not chosen by accident, but was selected on grounds of **cost** despite not having the right specification for that depth.

Information systems

Fourthly, Coastal Oil has had a reporting system in place for rig managers to report problem to management on land (that is land-side management). However rig managers have been allowed to **use their discretion** in reporting problems. It seems that some rig managers have only reported problems to land-side management in exceptional circumstances. Regrettably this can also be seen as part of a picture where rig managers failed to enforce certain necessary controls. The board is considering changing the reporting system and requiring regular reports from rig management, with issues that need to be reported clearly specified. We are also examining how we can obtain greater assurance that the **controls in place are being operated properly.**

Contingency plan

Lastly we acknowledge that there was **no contingency plan** in place to deal with the effects of the explosion and above all to prevent the oil spillage that resulted from the rupture. We failed to take urgent steps to seal the well-head or stop the flow of oil and we very much regret the environmental damage that resulted. Although we believe that the control improvements that we are making will reduce the risks of an accident occurring, we also acknowledge that we need a plan for taking immediate action if the worst occurs.

(ii) **Distinction between subjective and objective risk assessment**

The next area I would like to cover is how we assess risks and respond to Senator Jones's comment that we must have known that an accident would happen. Risk assessment is a complex process, involving the assessment of both the **likelihood** of a risk materialising and the **impact** if it does materialise.

One important distinction in risk assessment is between **objective and subjective risk assessment.** **Objective risk assessment** involves measuring the **likelihood and impact** of risks precisely or at least to a high degree of accuracy. Subjective risk assessment means using judgement to assess risk levels that cannot be determined using objective criteria.

Objective risk assessment

To expand on this definition, objective risk assessment may involve mutually exclusive outcomes, where the probability of each outcome can be assessed with certainty. To take a very simple example, tossing a coin has two outcomes with a 50% chance that each will occur. Impacts of risk occurring can also be measured objectively, for example if a company was to go into liquidation, each shareholder could lose at maximum the amount he paid for his shares.

Subjective risk assessment

By contrast subjective risk assessment involves assessing risks that **cannot be measured with quantitative precision**. The accuracy of the judgement will depend on the **knowledge and skills of the risk assessor**, also the **information available** and the **factors influencing the risk levels**. An example of a subjective likelihood assessment is the risk of a train being late on a particular day. An example of a subjective impact assessment would be how much the stock market might fall during the next month.

Argument against Senator Jones's view

I must respond to Senator Jones's comment that I, as the company's chief executive, 'should have known that the accident was going to happen.' I accept that the Senator is very angry because of the impact of the disaster upon the area he represents. However I must disagree with his comment because it fails to take into account the complexities of risk management.

Subjective assessment of accident

The probability of a workplace accident occurring is not something that can be assessed with precision. It has to be assessed subjectively and I could therefore never therefore be certain that an accident would happen. **Subjective assessment** of the probability and impact of a risk occurring is also very difficult. Coastal Oil operates hundreds of rigs worldwide and does so in conjunction with a number of joint venture partners. The nature of the processes are such that it is very difficult to predict the probability that an accident will happen on any rig, and even more so that an accident will occur on a specific rig such as the Effland Coastal Deep Rig. Similarly it is virtually impossible to predict the scale of the impact if an accident occurs.

Lack of information

Assessment of the risk of accidents was also made more difficult by the information systems we have had in place. As I have already explained, the rig's management informed us of problems **by exception.** They failed to report internal control failures on their rigs to land-side management and hence the board was unaware of these failings. In future we intend that the information that the board receive from the rigs will be enhanced. They will include reports by management on the operation of controls, even if there have been no incidents caused by lapses in control.

(iii) **Health and safety risk**

As a responsible company, we are particularly concerned about the health and safety risks that are connected with our operations. Health and safety risks are the threats of injury or death to employees or others that could arise from our operations.

- Factors increasing health and safety risk
- Health and safety risks can be increased by a number of factors.

Lack of health and safety policy

The lack of a policy for dealing with health and safety risks is one factor. However **legislation** in most countries requires companies participating in the oil industry to have effective health and safety policies in place. In addition it is in companies' best interests to enforce policies, because of the loss of working time caused by injuries to employees or the possibility of legal action. We believe that there were robust policies on the rigs.

Unexpected situation

The second factor is the failure of policies to deal with an **emergency or unexpected situation.** This can come about, for example, through a lack of emergency procedures or failures of the procedures in place to deal with new threats or impacts that arise because of **changes in technology.**

Lack of health and safety culture

The third factor relates to the fact that even if policies and control procedures are appropriate for the demands placed on them, their effective implementation also depends on the **knowledge and the care of the individuals** involved in operations. A lax culture can lead to a lack of care and a failure to

operate controls properly. As a board we take very seriously the press reports of a poor health and safety culture on the rigs. We shall be assessing the steps that need to be taken in conjunction with our joint venture partners to improve culture, for example by an enhanced training programme and disciplinary measures.

(iv) **Impossibility of eliminating risk**

I share the committee's desire for an accident like this not to happen again. However I cannot guarantee that the risk can be reduced to zero. It is impossible for us to avoid undertaking hazardous activities. The controls that we have in place cannot eliminate the risks associated with these activities, since for example the company may face extreme circumstances or errors may be made by staff operating controls. Governance best practice acknowledges that sound control systems can reduce, but not eliminate, risks and that the **costs of operating elaborate controls may outweigh their benefits.**

ALARP

Our risk management procedures are instead based on the **ALARP** (the as low as reasonably practicable principle). This is based on the idea that the **higher the level of the risk**, the **less acceptable** it is. If risks are judged as high, then **effective control measures** are required to reduce their likelihood and impact. We can for example reduce the likelihood of a risk to health and safety materialising by training staff so that they are aware of threats and less likely to make mistakes that will jeopardise safety. We can reduce the impact of a health and safety risk materialising by taking measures to protect staff, for example by insisting that they wear safety clothing.

Judgement

However, as I have already explained, the assessment of the risks that we face is a subjective process. It therefore follows that judgements about the controls necessary to reduce risks are also a matter of **judgement.** This means that I cannot guarantee that the probability of health and safety risks materialising is zero, but it would emphasise that we intend to maintain vigilance in order to keep risk levels low.

Conclusion

Thank you for listening to me today. I will now take any questions.

Question 2

Text references. Chapters 2 and 3.

Top tips. In (a) the Geeland guidance appears to be very much like the Hampel report in the UK and the answer reflects the debate on that report. As usual, critically evaluate means give points for and against. Here the arguments and marks are weighted more evenly than in other 'critically evaluate' questions. Cost vs consistency and lack of clarity are issues that have to be weighed up. Note also flexibility can be seen as a point for **and** against a principles-based approach.

(b) and (c) cover a favourite corporate governance topic, which sometimes features in the news. Hopefully you are familiar with the practical and ethical arguments in (b), but note also the point about compliance with governance guidelines. Comply or explain is only satisfactory if the shareholders accept the explanations. They are less likely to do so if companies do not explain why non-compliance has occurred (a significant issue in (c)). In some cases though the best way to keep shareholders happy is to assure them that non-compliance is temporary, as has happened here.

Easy marks. (b) is textbook knowledge and you should have scored well on this part.

		Marks
(a)	Distinguishing between rules and principles-based approaches	4
	2 marks for each argument in favour of or against remark max	10
	max	12
(b)	2 marks for point of explanation (½ mark for identification only) max	
		8
(c)	1.5 marks for each relevant point of assessment (½ mark for identification only)	5
		25

(a) **Rules-based approach**

A rules-based approach, known as **box-ticking,** requires companies to comply with regulations. There are **no exceptions** apart from those allowed for in the regulations. A rules-based approach is generally underpinned by law. Companies which do not comply will face **legal sanctions.**

Principles-based approach

A principles-based approach is likely to be underpinned by some company law, but the principles will also cover areas not included in legislation. Principles-based approaches emphasise the **objectives of governance**, rather than good governance being achieved by taking a number of prescribed actions. Companies operating under a principles-based code cannot however just ignore it. The code will often be incorporated into listing rules. They have to state that they have complied in their accounts or identify and explain the areas where they have not complied. Investors will then decide whether they accept the company's justification for non-compliance and may take action that impacts upon share price.

Geeland's approach

The guidance in the Geeland code clearly identifies that the code is **principles-based,** as it states that there is more to governance than complying with rules. Good governance requires broad principles which should be applied flexibly to individual companies.

Arguments in favour

Areas of application

A principles-based approach can **extend more widely** than a rules-based approach and can focus on areas where it would be unrealistic to apply rules. For example a principles-based approach can require directors to undertake professional development to extend their knowledge and skills without laying down how many courses they should go on each year. A principles-based approach can require boards to maintain good relations with major (institutional) shareholders without laying down how much contact there should be each year.

Cost to companies

A principles-based approach is also less costly in terms of time and expenditure. Companies in a rules-based jurisdiction may have to invest considerable time and monies in developing information and reporting systems that evidence compliance. There is evidence that companies have turned away from US stock markets, where they would be under the rules-based, Sarbanes-Oxley, regime on the grounds of cost of compliance. To be effective also, a rules-based regime has to have bodies to **monitor and enforce compliance.** The costs of maintaining these bodies are often passed on to companies in the form of listing costs.

Flexibility of approach

A principles-based approach can require companies to maintain adequate structures, for example effective risk management systems, but allow what is adequate to vary by company or industry. For example in some industries companies will avoid hazardous activities and will not therefore require **elaborate health and safety control systems**. Other industries, for example extractive industries, inevitably involve hazardous activities and so require complex risk management systems, to ensure that risks are reduced to levels that are as low as reasonably practicable.

Flexibility in application

Principles-based codes can allow for flexibility in application of provisions in circumstances where non-compliance can be justified. Companies may have to deal with a period of transition, for example where a Chairman leaves the board suddenly and it takes time to recruit a permanent successor. In these circumstances having the same person act as Chairman and Chief Executive on a temporary basis may be felt to be the most **practical solution.** Provided the non-compliance is explained clearly, investors may accept the justification.

Arguments against

Consistency of approach

A rules-based approach means all companies are **complying with the same standards.** It should be easy for investors to see that **compliance** has been **achieved.** Comparison between companies should be **straightforward.** Some investors may have **more confidence in a rules-based approach** as a result. It is also therefore easier to enforce a rules-based approach on companies.

Broad principles

The principles in a principles-based code may be so broad as to mean that companies have excessive leeway in following the code. Some companies may therefore try to do as little as possible to comply with the code, and therefore gain **cost and competitive advantage** over other companies that have been more conscientious.

Compulsory requirements

Where principles-based codes include specific recommendations, for example that the role of **chairman and chief executive be split**, there may be confusion over whether these recommendations are compulsory or not. Recommendations that are underpinned by company law requirements will be compulsory, but the status of recommendations that are not underpinned may be unclear. In some countries, the adoption of governance codes by stock exchanges means that specific recommendations in codes have been seen as **listing rules requiring compliance**. Companies that lack compliance expertise may find it difficult to judge whether and how they should comply.

Explanations

Explanations for non-compliance may not be adequate for shareholders. Shareholders **may not understand** the **reasons for, and consequences of, non-compliance.** Accounts may provide unclear explanations, with directors knowing that, even if some shareholders are unhappy, their positions are guaranteed by having the support of sufficient large shareholders.

(b) **Power**

Having the same person in both roles means that **power** is **concentrated** in one person. A common feature of governance scandals that have prompted the development of guidance has been an individual exercising excessive power The board may be **ineffective in controlling the chief executive** if it is led by the chief executive. For example the chairman is responsible for providing information that the other directors require to manage the company. If the chairman is also chief executive, the directors cannot be sure that the information they are getting is **sufficient and accurate.** Separation of the role also means that the board can **express its concerns more effectively** by providing a point of reporting for the non-executive directors.

Accountability

The board cannot make the chief executive **truly accountable** for management if it is chaired and led by the chief executive. The chairman carries the **authority of the board** and the chief executive carries **authority delegated by the board.** Separating the roles emphasises the chief executive's accountability to the board's leader, the Chairman, and also the shareholders whose interests the Chairman represents. Separation should **reduce the risk of conflicts of interest** where the Chairman/Chief Executive focuses on his own self-interest.

Demands of roles

Splitting the posts between different people reflects the reality that both jobs are **demanding roles** and no-one person will have the **skills and the time** to do both jobs well. The chief executive can concentrate on running the company's operations, developing business and risk management strategy, reviewing investment policy and managing the executive team. The chairman can concentrate on running the board effectively and ensuring that directors develop an understanding of the views of major investors.

Under governance best practice, the chairman should be an independent non-executive director, and hence well-placed to adopt a **supervisory and monitoring role.**

Governance requirements

Splitting the roles **ensures compliance with governance requirements and reassures shareholders.** Investor confidence is important in maintaining company value and sometimes compliance with governance best practice is needed to maintain confidence. Although Marks and Spencer in the UK sought to justify Sir Stuart Rose acting as Chairman and Chief Executive for a few years, a number of institutional investors objected to this arrangement, saying that such a leading UK company should set an example by complying with this important governance requirement, rather than explaining why it had not complied.

(c) **Comply or explain**

Compliance with governance requirements

Anson has fulfilled the requirements of the listing rules to identify areas of non-compliance. The statement **clearly highlights the issue** where Anson has not complied. It unambiguously states that it is not in accordance with governance best practice. It specifies as well that Mr Klunker is the individual concerned. This may be significant for shareholders who may be less concerned about the breach because they have confidence in Mr Klunker.

Why it has happened

However the statement does not state clearly **why** Anson has not complied. It does not explain the reasons for the company benefiting from having Mr Klunker in control. The statement that the company has maintained robust corporate governance is also vague. Stating the company understands the concerns of shareholders is not the same as saying that the company has responded to them.

Time limit to non-compliance

However shareholders will be reassured by the fact that Anson is planning to **comply with governance requirements in future.** Anson has made a clear commitment to separate the roles and has set a time limit on this.

Question 3

Marking scheme

			Marks
(a)	1 mark for each purpose max	3	
	2 marks for each influencing factor reviewed in context (½ mark for identification only) max	8	
	max		10
(b)	Definition of market risk	2	
	2 marks for each relevant point of justification max	8	
			10
(c)	Definition	2	
	1 mark for each advantage max	3	
			5
			25

(a) **Purposes**

Attract

Remuneration packages are designed to persuade an individual with **appropriate skills, knowledge and experience** to join the company. If the package is too low, the company will not be able to recruit a chief executive with the qualities it desires. If it is pitched too high, it may attract applicants who lack the required qualities.

Retain

Packages are designed to **retain the chief executive's services** and to avoid the **discontinuity** arising from a chief executive leaving unexpectedly to take a role with another company that offers more generous remuneration.

Motivate

Reward packages should motivate chief executives to remain loyal and to lead the company to achieve objectives that are **consistent with shareholders' interests.** This may be done by **linking part of remuneration to achievements,** for example bonus to profit levels.

Influences on Mrs Evans' remuneration

Previous performance

Past performance in the role will influence the salary levels of a chief executive. Here Mrs Evans is felt to have **performed very well.** This has influenced the value that the remuneration committee has placed on her services. In particular she has demonstrated strategic and communication skills and gained the trust of employees and investors, which will all be very important in the new circumstances of Dale Gas.

The market rate

Remuneration will be influenced by the remuneration paid to chief executives in comparable positions, in other words what Mrs Evans would be paid if she moved to an **equivalent position in another company.** The remuneration committee believes that doubling Mrs Evans's salary would bring her package into line with what other public companies of similar size are paying.

Government constraints

The scenario highlights that **government constraints** were an influence on the chief executive's salary when the company was a nationalised monopoly. These constraints may be imposed by **legislation,** or governments may **impose a pay policy** on salaries to limit expenditure levels or avoid political unpopularity from having a government servant paid what is viewed as an excessive amount.

Stakeholder views

Some organisations may take into account the **views of stakeholders such as the small shareholders** in this case. This is most likely in a case of a public interest organisation, such as a charity, where the use of funds raised for non-charitable purposes is very sensitive. However it may be an issue here if a large salary increase occurs at the same time as significant price increases to consumers and the new company is vulnerable to the charge of continuing to exploit a monopoly position.

(b) **Market risk**

Market risk is the risk of loss on capital markets due to an adverse movement in the market value of an asset, here the shares in Dale Gas. Market value will be sensitive to a number of factors, including views on the leadership of the company. If Mrs Evans were to be replaced, the share price and return on investment could fall.

Advantages of retaining Mrs Evans

Tom Nwede's belief

Tom believes that it is important for the future of Dale Gas and the market value of its shares that Mrs Evans be retained and motivated by an appropriately increased salary.

Knowledge of sector

Investors need assurance that the company is being directed and its strategies being developed by a board that includes directors with expertise in the gas industry, particularly during a time of change. Retaining Mrs Evans would mean that the leading executive director in Dale had the **necessary expertise** in the sector.

Knowledge of company

Mrs Evans also provides **continuity in the leadership of the company** because of her previous experience of the nationalised supplier. She can **guide the new directors** who are unfamiliar with the company. Mrs Evans is also well-known to the company's key internal and external stakeholders.

Strategy

The board's role of developing strategy would be especially important as Dale enters the private sector and seeks to **reposition itself strategically**. Mrs Evans clearly has the **strategic skills** necessary to lead this development and the **communication skills** to keep institutional investors informed of what is being planned.

Internal communication

Mrs Evans' skills will also be important in **maintaining internal morale.** The uncertainty and culture changes resulting from privatisation are likely to unsettle staff. Key individuals may leave. Staff who are left behind may become demotivated and resist change. Mrs Evans' communication skills, and the trust staff have in her, appear to mean that she is the most likely person to **persuade staff to adapt to the new circumstances.** The belief that Mrs Evans is able to implement a necessary change in attitudes is likely to enhance the confidence of investors.

(c)   **Proxy voting**

A **proxy** is a person appointed by a shareholder, who is **unable or unwilling to attend company general meetings**, to exercise the votes of that shareholder at the meetings. The shareholder completes a proxy form that transfers the right to vote to a board member or another person. The proxy may or may not have **specific instructions** on how to vote on each motion.

Advantages

Attendance

Institutional shareholders often hold shares in hundreds of companies. It is impractical to expect their representatives to attend every annual general meeting. Even if they could, the **associated agency costs** would be considerable and the usefulness of being present would be limited if all the votes were routine. Using a proxy means that **their votes can be exercised**, in accordance with best practice.

Representative of shareholders' views

If only those who attend the annual general meeting are allowed to vote and only a small number of shareholders attend, the votes taken may **not be representative** of the views of the shareholder body as a whole. Proxies mean that the views of those not attending the annual general meeting are reflected in the general meeting votes and the votes should thus be more representative of shareholder opinion.

Question 4

Text references. Chapters 2 and 11.

Top tips. (a) is a reminder about rights as well as responsibilities. An important point here is how far the business is entitled to the support of society and what it needs to do to earn that support. The Gray, Owen and Adams discussion is very much in terms of rights and responsibilities, ranging from absolute economic rights to perhaps no meaningful economic rights at all. You needed to discuss the issue of the play area in the context of the extreme positions to gain high marks.

It is quite easy for your answer to (b) and (c) to cover much the same ground, given the similarities between the pristine capitalist and the short-term shareholder interest, and the expedient and the long-term shareholder interest perspectives.

Hopefully in (b) you did recognise and discuss the clear indications of the position of each director. The emphasis on responsibilities to shareholders and no other responsibilities apart from meeting legal requirements is a clear sign of the pristine capitalist viewpoint. The argument that showing social responsibility can be justified as being for the company's strategic benefit is characteristic of the expedient position. Note that both positions do not see social responsibility as inherently justified, but the expedient position acknowledges that in the real world, stakeholders other than shareholders may have considerable power over the company.

In (c) the short-term position does not really look beyond the next profit statement. Note that the examiner included detail in the scenario that reinforced this position. Biggo was facing low profitability and therefore could not afford the expenditure. It was listed and its market price might be vulnerable. The longer-term perspective can be justified as being in the best interests of shareholders by maximising longer-term value. Here strategic considerations, principally here good stakeholder relations, come into play and the plan for future expansion means that these are particularly important.

Marking scheme

		Marks	
(a)	1 mark each for an explanation of rights and responsibilities and up to 3 marks each for explaining these in the context of Biggo max	6	
	½ mark each for identification of the two ends of the continuum	1	
	½ mark each for explanation of terms (pristine capitalist and deep green)	1	
	2 marks each for descriptions of the pristine capitalist and deep green ends of the continuum max	4	
	max		10
(b)	1 mark for correct identification of position of each person max	2	
	2 marks for justification for selecting position of each person from the case information max	4	
			6
(c)	1 mark per relevant point on social responsibility max	3	
	Recognition of short and long-term perspectives max	2	
	Discussion of short-term effects	2	
	Discussion of long-term effects	2	
			9
			25

(a)   **Citizenship**

Albert Doo's concept of citizenship is that it extends to companies as well as to individuals.

Rights

The rights that a corporate citizen has include **being able to take actions that are lawful and to enjoy the protection of the law**. As a company, Biggo's rights include the right to exist as a separate legal entity and carry on a lawful business. Society will grant it protection under the law and will also permit it to develop and expand.

Responsibilities

Responsibilities are the **duties owed to society** by the citizen as a consequence of the citizen belonging to the society and enjoying rights within it. In order to enjoy the protection, Biggo has to **comply with the laws** that affect it. It also has to recognise that it is **developing its business within society** and must therefore act in accordance with society's norms.

Gray, Owen and Adams's viewpoints

Gray, Owen and Adams identified seven viewpoints on social responsibility and relationships with stakeholders, the viewpoints differing on who were regarded as **important stakeholders** and a business's **rights and responsibilities.** There is greater emphasis on rights at the pristine capitalist end of the continuum and on responsibilities at the deep ecologist end.

Pristine capitalist position

This position emphasises the business's rights to pursue economic ends with the support of society and the law. It **limits business's responsibilities** to achieving maximum value for shareholders by producing goods and services profitably. It does not acknowledge wider responsibilities to society beyond compliance with its laws. It would see a business incurring costs to pursue social responsibility ends, as conflicting with its responsibilities to its shareholders.

Deep ecologist position

By contrast the deep ecologist position is that a business has no **greater rights to existence or consumption of resources** than the rest of humanity and other species. It does not have the right to exploit social and environmental systems for the ends of wealth creation. It has a fundamental responsibility to act in accordance with the **interests of human and non-human stakeholders** and cannot pursue economic objectives that threaten the interests other stakeholders. It would therefore be morally wrong for Biggo to build on the play area, as it would be exploiting the resource of land in conflict with the rest of the community's right to enjoy the use of that land.

(b) **Robert Tens**

Robert Tens is arguing from an **expedient viewpoint.** This position is that the **business's strategic and economic interests are of prime importance** and the business does not have an implicit duty to be socially responsible. However the business has to recognise that its activities have some **adverse consequences,** for example displacement of the play area. These may be unpopular with the stakeholders with whom the business deals. The expedient position is that it may therefore be necessary to show a limited degree of social responsibility, for example to make the donation, **in order to maintain or enhance the business's wider strategic interests,** for example here to reduce the risk of future local opposition.

Margaret Heggs

Margaret Heggs is arguing from a **pristine capitalist position**. This viewpoint only recognises **accountability to shareholders** and does not recognise accountability to the local community (the social ecologist position) or the local authority (the social contract position). The focus is on **maximising profits for shareholders** and, as a by-product, providing other economic benefits such as employment and products. Provided the business operates correctly through legal channels, it does not have wider responsibilities and should not get involved in costly social responsibility activities, such as the donation for the play area.

(c) **Social responsibility**

This phrase means that companies should act in the **general public interest** as well as the specific interests of shareholders. Social responsibility can be interpreted narrowly (as by Margaret Heggs) or widely (as by Albert Doo). It can refer to how the company is **governed** or the impact the company has on the **natural environment** through consumption of resources or through its externalities. In this instance the focus is on Biggo's **social footprint**, the impact it is making on the local community.

Johnson and Scholes

Johnson and Scholes drew distinctions between different social responsibility stances based on whether they acknowledged responsibility to shareholders or other stakeholders, and whether they were exercised over the short or the long-term.

Short-term shareholder interest

A short-term shareholder perspective would see the company's principal concerns as being profits or dividends in the near future, perhaps up until the **end of the next financial year**. Its actions would be judged on the basis of the impact they had on **profitability.** Hence the requested donation would not be viewed favourably as it would reduce profits without having any obvious financial benefits. Biggo is currently facing a period of low profits and probably low dividends as well. It has to keep costs under control and **cannot afford to make unnecessary expenditure,** such as the donation. As a public listed company, it has to be especially sensitive to the impact on share price of low profits and dividends.

Long-term shareholder interest

A longer-term perspective would emphasise the importance of pursuing strategies that maximise shareholder value over a number of years. It would not see socially responsible actions such as the donation as **inherently beneficial**, but accept that they could be justified on the grounds of the **strategic opportunities** they provided, particularly here the opportunities arising from good relationships with key stakeholders such as the council and local community. These might include:

- **Benefits from a good public image,** persuading consumers to look favourably on the company and attracting high-quality new employees. The donation might therefore be seen as promotional expenditure

- **Reducing the possibility of future opposition** to Biggo's activities from the local community or local government. It appears that Biggo may need planning permission for future expansion, which it cannot take for granted that it will receive, and in any case it has to co-exist with the local community.

ACCA examiner's answers:
June and December 2011 papers

Note: The ACCA examiner's answers are correct at the time of going to press but may be subject to some amendments before the final versions are published.

Question 1

(a) **Internal controls**

Circumstances leading to the problem

The case describes four clear causes of the fuel tank problems with the Bobo Foo.

The first one was the brief given by the board in which cost reduction was emphasised above all other considerations. This was underpinned in the design team by a 'tone from the top' conveyed on posters that said 'keep it cheap'. The key concepts for the car also conveyed the message of cost and Mr Tsakos's seniority in the company had the effect of cementing the cost message into the design team including Kathy Yao.

This was exacerbated by the second cause which was a radical reduction in the normal development time. Whereas the design team were used to working with timetables of 43 months, Mr Tsakos imposed a 25-month time limit on the project. This in itself conveys a powerful message that the board wants the project completed as quickly and cheaply as possible.

Third, the board ignored the crash test result for reasons of cost. In order to hasten the product launch, presumably to make a return on investment as early as possible, the company tooled up the factory as early as possible. This meant that it was too late to make changes to the fuel tank positioning without incurring excessive cost.

Fourth, Kathy did not speak out when pressured by Mr Tsakos to reduce the development time. She, and other directors involved in the project, should have stood up to Mr Tsakos, but they failed to do so. She was also complicit in ignoring the crash test and allowing the Bobo Foo to go into production before all the tests were completed. Had she felt able to challenge Mr Tsakos, the problems with the car could have been avoided. An effective non-executive presence on the board would also have been a way of countering Mr Tsakos's persistence in 'forcing' the development time for the car.

Internal control measures

Establishing a standard development time sufficient to meet a range of agreed metrics on all new car models. Kathy Yao's private comments to colleagues about her fears for the safety of the car given such a short development time are relevant. If the company places a minimum time to market for a new model (say 40 months or thereabouts), it would ensure that there was sufficient time or all proposed features of any product feature could be fully safety tested. Being so rushed was presumably a factor in the incorrect and unsafe positioning of the fuel tank.

Embed safety metrics into all design briefs in future. None of the key concepts underpinning the Bobo Foo were concerned with safety and none of the messages conveyed in the key design concepts ('cheap to buy, economical to run', etc) included a reference to product safety. Risk mitigation is most effective when it is placed as a normal part of any role. For a car design team such as that led by Kathy Yao, the introduction of a safety metric into the brief could have prevented such an unsafe feature as the badly positioned fuel tank being allowed to happen.

Procedures to sign off each stage of the development process based on safety criteria. Without an effective 'sign off' for each identified stage, the next stage cannot continue. This would involve establishing an agreed set of stages in a development process at which safety criteria should be applied. The crash test would be an obvious such stage. Once the crash test had taken place, it should be made a mandatory procedure that any failings in the vehicle should be addressed before it can be 'signed off' to go into production (unlike at Bobo where the factory was tooled up regardless of the crash test failure).

Tutorial note: allow latitude in candidate's answers. Reward points that address the causes of the risks.

(b)   **Kohlberg**

Explain Kohlberg's levels

Kohlberg's theory of moral development is a framework for classifying a range of responses to ethical situations. Kohlberg argued that these were indicative of the moral development of the individual. Kohlberg identified three levels that people can operate at.

At the preconventional level of moral reasoning, morality is conceived of in terms of rewards, punishments and instrumental motivations. Those demonstrating intolerance of norms and regulations in preference for self-serving motives are typically preconventional.

At the conventional level, morality is understood in terms of compliance with either or both of peer pressure/social expectations or regulations, laws and guidelines. A high degree of compliance is assumed to be a highly moral position.

At the postconventional level, morality is understood in terms of conformance with perceived 'higher' or 'universal' ethical principles. Postconventional assumptions often challenge existing regulatory regimes and social norms and so postconventional behaviour can often be costly in personal terms.

Levels of people in the question

James Tsakos is exhibiting a conventional level of moral development. His main concern is with compliance with the expectations of shareholders. The 'good boy-nice girl' orientation component of the conventional level is that which is concerned with how society sees the company and with shareholders being a prominent stakeholder, Mr Tsakos's expressed concerns are about placating and managing their concerns. He is against the universal recall option because of the signal it would send to markets.

Kathy Yao is also exhibiting a conventional level of moral development. Although her concern was driven by a personal concern arising from her part in the design of the Bobo Foo's fuel tank, her motivations were concerned with compliance and strategic interests. Whereas Mr Tsakos was more concerned with the expectations of shareholders, Kathy Yao was more concerned with the expectation of customers. Her concern was rooted in what customers thought of the company. She framed her concerns in terms of product safety whilst also pointing to the importance of a reputation for social responsibility and compliance with the interests of society.

Vernon Vim is exhibiting a preconventional level of moral development. He pointed to his personal loss of bonus if the recall option was taken and quantified the choice in purely financial terms. It was 'because the board's bonuses were partly based on the company's annual profits' that he opposed the recall option. He was unconcerned with any compliance or higher ethical purpose.

Tutorial note: allow James Tsakos to be described as preconventional if his motivations are seen as self-serving with the loss of shareholder value.

(c)   **AGMs and EGMs**

Distinguish between

Annual general meetings (AGMs) are a part of the normal financial calendar for all limited companies and take place on the occasion of the year-end results presentation and the publication of the annual report. Extraordinary general meetings are called to discuss strategic and other issues with shareholders outside the normal financial calendar.

Purposes of each

Both types of meetings are formal meetings between company directors and the shareholders of the company. They typically involve presentations by the board (typically the chairman and/or CEO) and a chance for shareholders to question the board.

AGMs

The AGM is a formal part of a company financial year. Its purpose is to allow the board to present the year's results, discuss the outlook for the coming year, present the formal, audited accounts and to have the final dividend and directors' emoluments approved by shareholders. Shareholder approval is signalled by the passing of resolutions in which shareholders vote in proportion to their holdings. It is usual for the board to

make a recommendation and then seek approval of that recommendation by shareholders. The dividend per share, for example, is recommended by the board but only paid after approval by the shareholders at the AGM. Institutional shareholders may employ proxy voting if they are unable to attend in person.

EGMs

Extraordinary meetings are called when issues need to be discussed and approved that cannot wait until the next AGM. A full year can be a very long time. In some business environments when events necessitate substantial change or a major threat, an EGM is sometimes called. Management may want a shareholder mandate for a particular strategic move, such as for a merger or acquisition. Other major issues that might threaten shareholder value may also lead to an EGM such as a 'whistleblower' disclosing information that might undermine shareholders' confidence in the board of directors. In this case, given the nature of the disclosure, there is a case for James Tsakos to answer in terms of shareholders continuing to have confidence in him as CEO.

Advantages

In the case of Bobo, the shareholders will be able to gain reassurance that the public disclosure of important safety concerns being ignored will not threaten shareholder value because of lost sales or damaged reputation. There is a clear risk to the reputation of the company as a whole if it is associated in the public mind with unsafe product designs.

The shareholders can hold James Tsakos accountable for his actions and demand explanations. There is a prima facie case to answer that he presided over the development of a car with a safety risk to its occupants and then opted to resist suggestions to recall the vehicles to have the safety problems addressed.

Mr Tsakos, in return, will be able to speak directly to shareholders rather than through written communication and this may be a more convincing way of explaining his position. Given that the shareholders 'wanted to hold James Tsakos accountable for the decision' and wanted to hear from him directly, the EGM will enable him to address these demands.

Resolutions of confidence or no confidence can be passed if proposed and this would 'clear the air' one way or the other to enable the company to resolve its issues quickly. Shareholders have the right to remove Mr Tsakos if they are not satisfied with his explanations and this could be resolved quickly at an EGM rather than having it drift on to the next AGM, which could be many months away.

(d) (i) **Role of CEO**

Thank you for attending this EGM. I know that you will have questions in the light of recent media reports about our economy car model, the Bobo Foo, and I hope to address some of these questions in my remarks.

As your chief executive, you will understand that it is my job to lead the company and to protect shareholder interests above all others. These are responsibilities I take very seriously.

In particular, and in explaining how your board arrived at the decision it did, I would like to briefly outline my roles. It is my role to develop and implement policies and strategies capable of delivering superior shareholder value and to assume full responsibility for all aspects of the company's operations. It was I who commissioned the Foo in the first place in pursuit of the strategy that Bobo should be represented in all of the main car segments. The correctness of that decision is shown by the outstanding sales of the model at half a million units a year in what is a very competitive part of the market.

I must also manage the financial and physical resources of the company, monitor results, and ensure that effective operational and risk controls are in place. Bobo is a profitable company and in designing and developing the Foo, I personally took a direct interest in maintaining its low cost ethos. I assigned our expert design team to create the product and we then submitted it to the crash test to gain information on its safety vulnerabilities.

My role also involves overseeing the management team, co-ordinating the interface between the board and the other employees in the company, and assisting in the appointment of directors to the board. In a large company such as Bobo, it is obviously vital that we have the best people at all levels and I am pleased to be able to have Kathy Yao on the board. She leads our talented team of car designers and the excellent design of the Foo is testimony to their talents.

Finally, it is my role to relate to a range of external parties including the company's shareholders, suppliers, customers and state authorities. The legal issues that have confronted us with regard to compensation claims against the Foo's design are mainly my responsibility and it is to these matters that I now turn.

Tutorial note: these paragraphs contain two roles in each. Allow for different ways of expressing the roles.

(ii) **Defence of company decision**

I am very aware of the reason we meet today in this EGM and I want to explain to you why the board took the decision it did, resisting the idea to issue a universal recall of the Foo.

As your chief executive, it is my responsibility to take a wide range of opinions and viewpoints into account, some of which are conflicting. The protection and maximisation of shareholder value is, however, my highest and most important duty in all contestable cases. I have many potential accountabilities, but my primary accountability is to you, the shareholders.

Accordingly, the decision I took was that which I thought would provide the best value to shareholders. This was only my view of course and others will disagree, but given the calculations made available to me, the choice was clear. It would have been an abdication of my fiduciary duty to allow an option to be adopted that reduced shareholder value as significantly as the recall option would have. In making this judgement I took into account the very small number of incidents that have occurred with this product as a proportion of all the Bobo Foo cars sold to date.

The margin between the two options was not close with the choice of resisting the recall outweighing the other option by a factor of three in terms of costs to the company. If it were a more finely balanced financial calculation, I may have opted for the recall option but given the projected difference of half a billion dollars over 10 years, I really had no choice because I had no right to erode shareholder value to that extent. I do not necessarily expect you all to agree with me, especially those who may have alternative ethical perspectives on these issues, but I do hope you can accept that the decision was taken in good faith as the most financially prudent and commercially responsible of the two stark options available to us.

Tutorial note: allow different ways of expressing these thoughts within the pristine capitalist perspective.

Question 2

(a) **Criticise and explanation of dynamic**

Criticise Raz Dutta's beliefs

Raz Dutta is wrong in both of her assertions. The belief that risks do not change very much is only true in static environments. In reality, the changeability of risks depends upon the organisation's place on a continuum between highly dynamic and completely static. The case mentions changes in some of YGT's risks and this suggests that there is some dynamism in its environment. Clearly then, her belief is very difficult to defend.

Her belief that risks 'hardly ever' materialise may be historically true (but this is also unlikely) but the risk assessment highlighted at least two 'likely' risks which could well materialise. Risk D was assessed as 'highly likely' and Risk B was also likely with a high potential impact. Neither of these variables would be known were it not for intelligence gained as part of the risk assessment. Importantly, Risk B was a 'high/high' risk meaning that it is a likely risk with a high impact once it materialised. Being unaware of this could have caused great damage to the organisation.

Why risk assessment is dynamic

Risk assessment is a dynamic management activity because of changes in the organisational environment and because of changes in the activities and operations of the organisation which interact with that environment. At YGT, the case describes Risk C as arising from a change in the activity of the company: a new product launch. The new product has obviously introduced a new risk that was not present prior to the new product. It may be a potential liability from the use of the product or a potential loss from the materials used in its production, for example.

Changes in the environment might include changes in any of the PEST (political, economic, social, technological) or any industry level change such as a change in the competitive behaviour of suppliers, buyers or competitors. In either case, new risks can be introduced, existing ones can become more likely or have a higher impact, or the opposite (they may disappear or become less important). The case describes Risk D as arising from a change in legislation which is a change in the external environment.

(b) **TARA**

The strategies for each risk assessment are as follows:

Risk A is accept. This means that the likelihood is low and the impact is low such that even if the risk materialised, it would not have a high severity. The case says that the activity giving rise to Risk A is capable of making good returns so given that both likelihood and severity are low, there is no obvious reason to pursue any of the other strategies with regard to this risk.

Risk B is avoid. When the likelihood and impact are high, it would be irrational to accept the risk and so the risk should be avoided. This may involve changing behaviour or discontinuing a certain activity. The case says that the activity giving rise to Risk B is capable of making good returns, but importantly, it is not strategically vital. Given this, and because the case information does not mention the possibility of viably transferring the risk, there is no reason to bear the risk unless the potential return is very large and the company has a high risk appetite.

Risk C is transfer. YGT says that the activity giving rise to the risk must not be discontinued (so avoidance is not an option) and specifies that it can be transferred ('alternative arrangements for bearing the risks are possible'). To transfer risk is to share it with another party. The most common way to do this is to insure against losses or to outsource or licence the activity to a third party thereby transferring that risk to that third party.

Risk D is reduce. The case emphasises that the risk cannot be transferred (by insurance or outsourcing) but that the activity that gives rise to the risk can be reduced. Reduction involves reducing the risk exposure by carrying out the activity in a different way, doing less of the activity that gives rise to the risk or adopting behaviour that, whilst still exposing the company to the risk, results in a lower impact if the risk is realised.

(c) **Related and correlated**

Related risks are risks that vary because of the presence of another risk. This means they do not exist independently and they are likely to rise and fall in importance along with the related one. Risk correlation is a particular example of related risk.

Risks are positively correlated if the two risks are positively related in that one will fall with the reduction of the other and increase with the rise of the other. They would be negatively correlated if one rose as the other fell. In the case of environmental risks and reputation risk, they may be positively correlated for the following reasons.

Environmental risks involve exposure to losses arising from an organisation's consumption of resources or impacts through its emissions. Where an environmental risk affects a sensitive situation, (be it human, flora, fauna or other), this can cause negative publicity which can result in reputation damage. These two risks can have a shared cause, i.e. they can arise together and fall together because they depend upon the same activity. They are considered separate risks because losses can be incurred by either of both of the impacts (environmental or reputational).

Activities designed to reduce environmental risk, such as acquiring resources from less environmentally-sensitive sources or through the fitting of emission controls, will reduce the likelihood of the environmental risk being realised. This, in turn, will reduce the likelihood of the reputation risk being incurred. The opposite will also hold true: a reduction of attention to environmental risk will increase the likelihood of reputation loss.

(d)   **Risk awareness**

Explanation

Risk awareness is a capability of an organisation to be able to recognise risks when they arise, from whatever source they may come. A culture of risk awareness suggests that this capability (or competence) is present throughout the organisation and is woven into the normal routines, rituals, ways of thinking and is taken-for-granted in all parts of the company and in all employees.

Assessment

Risks can arise in any part of the organisation and at any level. Not all risks are at the strategic level and can be captured by a risk assessment. A culture of risk awareness will help ensure that all employees are capable of identifying risks as and when they arise.

Risks are dynamic and rise and fall with changes in the business environment and with changes in the company's activities. With changes to the company's risk profile occurring all the time, it cannot be assumed that the risks present at the most recent risk assessment will remain the same. Being prepared to adapt to changes is a key advantage of a culture of risk awareness.

A lack of risk awareness is often evidence of a lack of risk management strategy in the organisation. This, in turn, can be dangerous as the company could be more exposed to risk than it need be because of the lack of attentiveness by staff. A lack of effectiveness of risk management strategy leaves the company vulnerable to unrecognised or wrongly assessed risks.

Question 3

(a) **Charities and public listed companies**

Differences

Firstly, the two types of organisation are different in terms of regulation. Listed companies are subject to all the provisions of company law plus any listing rules that apply. Listing rules, such as the need to adopt the UK Corporate Governance Code in the UK, impose a number of obligations upon listed companies such as non-executive directors, committee structures, a range of reporting requirements, etc. Charities, in contrast, must receive recognition by a country's charity authority to operate and they then receive the concessions that charitable status confers. This often involves favourable tax treatment and different reporting requirements. Because charities are not public companies they are not subject to listing rules although, depending upon the country's rules, they may be subject to audit and have some reporting requirements.

The second difference is in the strategic purpose of the organisation. Listed companies exist primarily to make a financial return for their investors (shareholders). This means that they employ and incentivise people, including directors, to maximise long-term cash flows. Value is added by the creation of shareholder wealth and this is measured in terms of profits, cash flows, share price movements and price/earnings. For a charity, the strategic purpose is to support the charitable cause for which the organisation was set up. It is likely to be a social or benevolent cause and funds are donated specifically to support that cause and this expectation places a different emphasis on the purpose of governance.

Thirdly, the two are different in terms of stakeholders and societal expectations. Society typically expects a business to be efficient in order to be profitable so that, in turn, it can create jobs, wealth and value for shareholders. Society expresses its support for a business by participating in its resource or product markets, i.e. by supplying its inputs (including working for it) or buying its products. A charity's social legitimacy is tied up with the charity's achievement of benevolent aims.

Stakeholders in a business often have an economic incentive to engage with the organisation whereas most stakeholders in a charity have claims more concerned with its benevolent aims.

Governance arrangements

There can be a number of substantive differences between the governance structures of public companies and charities. In a public company, a board consisting of executive and non-executive directors is accountable to the shareholders of the company. The principals are able to hold the board accountable through AGMs (annual general meetings) and EGMs (extraordinary general meetings) at which they can vote on resolutions and other issues to convey their collective will to the board. In a charity, the operating board is usually accountable to a board of trustees. It is the trustees who act as the interpreters and guarantors of the fiduciary duty of the charity (because the beneficiaries of the charity may be unable to speak for themselves). The trustees ensure that the board is acting according to the charity's stated purposes and that all management policy, including salaries and benefits, are consistent with those purposes.

Tutorial note: allow latitude and 'cross marking' between these points

(b) **Transparency**

Define transparency

Transparency is usually defined in terms of openness and adopting a default position of information provision rather than concealment. This means that unless there is an overwhelming reason not to disclose information of any kind (perhaps for reasons of commercial sensitivity) then information should be disclosed or made available upon request to any interested stakeholder.

The case for greater transparency at HHO

Transparency is an important principle in corporate governance, including at HHO, for a number of reasons.

In general, transparency has the effect of reassuring investors that their funds are being responsibly stewarded and used for worthwhile investments. In the case of a charity, such as HHO, without shareholders in the conventional sense, donors give money to support the charity's stated aims and purposes. With the relief of suffering to animals being a prominent reason any donors give to HHO, the amount of money diverted for other purposes, such as salaries, would be information of considerable interest.

Transparency would inform and placate HHO's critics, including the journalists who are investigating it. Public commentators like journalists are capable of causing damage to HHO's reputation and this in turn can affect donations and support for the organisation.

There are a number of potentially damaging allegations made against Mr Hoi including the likelihood of large payments to himself and some profligacy in the purchase of the private jet. These allegations could be rebutted if the organisation were to make the accounts public and explain the case for the purchase of the jet. For a charity receiving money from 'well-meaning individuals that care greatly about animal suffering', the allegations have the potential to do much reputational damage to the charity.

The publication of the financial data is an inadequate expression of transparency and appears to be a poor attempt to give the appearance of providing information whilst providing no useful detail at all. This would not meet any stakeholder's information needs and fails to address any of the concerns raised about HHO. It does not give any absolute financial figures, for example, in terms of income and costs. Such a truncated summary actually gives the impression, to any informed observer, of an attempt at concealment and this provides a strong reason to provide a full financial statement.

(c) **Audit committee and internal controls**

There are a number of apparent internal control deficiencies, although the case does not permit definite and specific allegations of IC deficiencies to be made or to conclude that a complete lack of governance structure exists at HHO. However, any such organisation would benefit from having an audit committee with wide-ranging powers and responsibilities when reviewing internal controls. With regard to the situation at HHO, the most important areas for audit committee attention are monitoring the adequacy of internal controls, checks for compliance with relevant regulation and codes, checking for fraud and reviewing existing IC statements for accuracy.

Monitoring the adequacy of internal controls involves analysing the controls already in place to establish whether they are capable of mitigating risks. In the case of HHO, there are internal risks that the controls need to be capable of controlling. The risk of fraud and the risk of compliance failure are relevant internal risks.

To check for compliance with relevant regulation and codes refers to HHO's compliance with its legal and other regulatory constraints. It is likely that HHO has a number of regulatory constraints as a result of its charitable status. It may also have voluntary codes it seeks to abide by, perhaps made public through its marketing or reporting literature, and the audit committee could also test for compliance with these.

Checking for fraud is also within the remit of an audit committee and this would, at first glance, be a priority at HHO. There are grounds for believing that inadequate remuneration policies exist at HHO and grounds for suspecting some financial dishonesty. There also seems to be a lack of accountability for the behaviour and actions of Horace Hoi, especially if the claims about his lavish lifestyle are accurate. The misuse of donations for personal enrichment would be outside of what is allowed under his charitable status and this could be reviewed by the audit committee.

Finally, an audit committee could play a more supervisory role if necessary, for example reviewing major expenses and transactions for reasonableness. This might include measuring transactions against its regulatory regime and the reasonable expectations of its trustees and donors.

Question 4

(a) **Ethical threats**

The five generally accepted types of ethical threat under the IFAC and ACCA codes of ethics and conduct are:

(a) Self-interest threats, which may occur as a result of the financial or other interests of a professional accountant or of an immediate family member;

(b) Self-review threats, which may occur when a previous judgement needs to be re-evaluated by the professional accountant responsible for that judgement;

(c) Advocacy threats, which may occur when a professional accountant promotes a position or opinion to the point that subsequent objectivity may be compromised;

(d) Familiarity threats, which may occur when, because of a close relationship, a professional accountant becomes too sympathetic to the interests of others; and

(e) Intimidation threats, which may occur when a professional accountant may be deterred from acting objectively by threats, actual or perceived.

The IFAC code highlights self-interest threats and intimidation threats as relevant in accepting gifts or hospitality.

260.1. 'Self-interest threats to objectivity may be created if a gift from a client is accepted; intimidation threats to objectivity may result from the possibility of such offers being made public.'

A self-interest threat is one in which a person's interests in him or herself obscures objectivity and the need to act with integrity. Clearly the promise of personal gain can be a threat to ethical behaviour, especially if, as in the case of Ann, it can be a large amount of money.

An intimidation threat can arise when the party who has given the inducement seeks to exercise power over the recipient in the belief that further advantage can be taken. In the case of a bribe, the recipient can be induced to take further unethical actions with the threat that their first bribe will be exposed if they do not comply. Ann may be induced to award other contracts to the contractor, for example, and this could act against the interests of the company, its shareholders and other contract providers.

There may also be an advocacy threat in addition to the self-interest and intimidation threats. An advocacy threat occurs when objectivity is impaired because of a person's advocacy for a certain interest (e.g. client, bidder, person, etc). In this case, the fact that Ann awarded the contract seemingly on the basis of a bribe, means she will have to defend (act as an advocate for) the successful bidder against her own management if the contract does not go well. In so doing, she may well be acting against the interests of her employer and the company's shareholders.

(b) **Criticise Ann Koo**

First, she did not allow the contract to be bid for by all competing parties equally. This is a failure of her duty to the public interest, to her employers and, as an accountant, to her professional body. Her employers and other stakeholders expect to gain the best value for money and this requires a fair tendering process giving all potential contractors an equal chance of winning the contract.

Second, she accepted a bribe to award the contract. This undermines the contract bidding system and offers poor value to the organisation's principals, which in the case of a public company are the shareholders.

Third, she exposed herself to ethical threats that may result in more unethical behaviour in the future. Safeguards are put in place to ensure that ethical threats are not incurred. Her family's personal financial misfortunes are of no direct concern to her employers and should have had no bearing on her management of the contract process.

Fourth, her belief that she deserves a 'higher personal return' suggests she is seeking more than just the career opportunities that come with being a qualified accountant. This belief or expectation may apply to most qualified professionals but acceptance of additional rewards in the manner that this case describes is totally unacceptable and is not a generalisable ethic in terms of Kant's deontological understanding of ethics.

What if everybody sought to make a 'higher personal return' on their training through abusing their responsible position in this way?

Public interest

Ann Koo owes a duty to the public interest both as an accountant and as a company director. This means that it is her duty to behave in such a way as to maximise the public good and not act in terms of pursuing personal interests only. Accounting and other professionals are bound to recognise this duty and to comply with it regardless of the temptation or inducement to act otherwise.

(c) **Insider trading**

Insider dealing/trading

Insider dealing (also called insider trading) is the buying or selling of company shares based on knowledge not publicly available. Directors are often in possession of market-sensitive information ahead of its publication and they would therefore know if the current share price is under or over-valued given what they know about forthcoming events. If, for example, they are made aware of a higher than expected performance, it would be classed as insider dealing to buy company shares before that information was published. Similarly, selling shares in advance of results publication indicating previous over-valuation, would also be considered as insider dealing.

Why is insider trading unethical and often illegal?

By accepting a directorship, each director agrees to act primarily in the interests of shareholders. This means that decisions taken must always be for the best long-term value for shareholders. If insider dealing is allowed, then it is likely that some decisions would have a short-term effect which would not be of the best long-term value for shareholders. For example, businesses which are about to be taken-over often see a significant rise in their share price. In this situation directors might purchase shares in their own companies, seek potential buyers for the company and recommend the sale to shareholders, in order to make a profit on their own share investments. For this reason, a blanket ban on insider dealing ensures that such short-term measures are not taken.

There is also the potential damage that insider trading does to the reputation and integrity of the capital markets in general which could put off investors who would have no such access to privileged information and who would perceive that such market distortions might increase the risk and variability of returns beyond what they should be.

Question 1

(a) **Corporate code of ethics.**

Purposes

A corporate code of ethics (sometimes contrasted with a professional code) has five general purposes.

The first is communicating the organisation's values into a succinct and sometimes memorable form. This might involve defining the strategic purposes of the organisation and how this might affect ethical attitudes and policies.

Second, the code serves to identify the key stakeholders and the promotion of stakeholder rights and responsibilities. This may involve deciding on the legitimacy of the claims of certain stakeholders and how the company will behave towards them.

Third, a code of ethics is a means of conveying these values to stakeholders. It is important for internal and external stakeholders to understand the ethical positions of a company so they know what to expect in a given situation and to know how the company will behave. This is especially important with powerful stakeholders, perhaps including customers, suppliers and employees.

Fourth, a code of ethics serves to influence and control individuals' behaviour, especially internal stakeholders such as management and employees. The values conveyed by the code are intended to provide for an agreed outcome whenever a given situation arises and to underpin a way of conducting organisational life in accordance with those values.

Fifth, a code of ethics can be an important part of an organisation's strategic positioning. In the same way that an organisation's reputation as an employer, supplier, etc. can be a part of strategic positioning, so can its ethical reputation in society. Its code of ethics is a prominent way of articulating and underpinning that.

Evaluate Coastal Oil's performance

In the case of Coastal Oil, the company appears to have failed its own code of ethics in terms of its pledge on safety and care of employees, transparency and communication with stakeholders, and being environmentally responsible.

The deaths of eight employees on the Effland Coastal Oil Rig resulted from health and safety failures because of a number of internal control failures. If Coastal Oil saw the protection of employees as an ethical issue, it might have adopted, or ensured that its JV partners adopted, the 'highest standards' of performance in ensuring their safety.

Because of the internal arguments between Coastal Oil and Well Services, it took seven days to make a public statement about the event. Clearly, there would be many stakeholders eager to hear Coastal Oil's view on what had happened, including the families of those killed and injured, and the delay caused by the internal arguments was a breach of its own code of ethics on this issue.

The valve failure caused an oil leak on the sea floor which took several months to stop. This is an environmental failure and, given that Coastal Oil stated that environmental responsibility was a key heading in its code of ethics, stakeholders will be reasonably entitled to conclude that it has failed against its own ethical standards. Given that the company operates in such an environmentally sensitive industry, it would clearly require a high level of commitment to internal controls to maintain this, whether directly by Coastal Oil employees or through the partners in the JV such as Well Services.

(b)   **Voluntary disclosure and environmental risk**

Difference between

Company reporting, usually in annual reports, interim reports or on websites, contains both mandatory and voluntary disclosures. Mandatory disclosures are those statements that are compulsory under relevant company laws or stock market listing rules. In most jurisdictions, mandatory items are the main financial statements such as income statement, statement of financial position and statement of cash flows. Listing rules in many jurisdictions, such as in the UK, also mandate some corporate governance disclosures such as directors' shareholdings and emoluments, and details of directors' contracts.

Voluntary disclosures are not required by any mandate but are provided, usually in narrative rather than quantitative form. There is a belief that some information of interest or relevance to shareholders or other stakeholders cannot be conveyed numerically and so additional information is needed. The chairman's statement, chief executive's review, social and environmental disclosure, intellectual capital reporting and risk reporting are all examples of voluntary disclosure in most jurisdictions.

Tutorial note: mandatory and voluntary disclosures vary slightly between jurisdictions.

Material to shareholders

Voluntary disclosure is of interest to shareholders because it provides information that cannot be easily conveyed in statutory statements or in numerical form. In the case of environmental risk reporting at Coastal Oil, it is likely that shareholders will welcome the environmental risk measures put in place after the accident as reported in the annual report.

First, in the case of Coastal Oil, the fact that there has been a recent and expensive environmental accident means that environmental risk is clearly material to shareholder value and is likely to remain so while the company continues to extract and process oil. This is a 'structural' risk resulting from the company's core activity. This makes environmental disclosure potentially highly material and capable of affecting the value of the company. The extent of potential exposure (total impacts), and hence the potential losses, would be a key piece of information needed, and also the previous environmental accident statistics.

Second, it will allow the shareholders to understand the extent and nature of the risk which clearly wasn't fully known before the accident. By knowing this, shareholders can assess whether the risk profile of the business matches their own attitudes to or appetite for risk. In a portfolio of shares, some investors will want to blend certain risks and returns, and knowing about a company's risks is important in making these judgements.

Third, the additional environmental risk information will allow the shareholders to judge how the risk might affect company value and hence the potential volatility and attractiveness of the share. The case says that the disclosure would contain 'value relevant' information meaning that the risks described will be capable of affecting returns, costs or both. The materiality of environmental risk reporting is potentially quite high: shareholders were unaware of the poor internal controls on the Effland Coastal Oil Rig and, had they been more aware, may have discounted the share price accordingly.

Fourth, risk reporting can explain the new risk controls put in place. After a confidence-threatening event such as the valve rupture and oil spill on the Effland Coastal Oil Rig, the explanation of these measures could be vital in restoring investor confidence. In particular, they should reassure shareholders that the accident should not re-occur, or that if it were to re-occur, further controls would be in place to offset the worst of the damage. It is likely that more detailed and granulated environmental reporting would be valued by shareholders, especially those specialist institutional shareholders made cautious by the Effland accident.

(c)   (i)   **Internal control failures**

In keeping with Coastal Oil's stated commitment in its code of ethics to transparency, I have been authorised by my board to provide a full and frank statement on the internal control failures that led to the accident on the Effland Coastal Oil Rig. I will be happy to explain any particular point in more detail if required, but if you will allow me I will outline where I believe our internal controls were below standard.

I should inform the committee that the ownership and management of the oil rig was complicated by the fact that Coastal Oil was part of a joint venture in which, despite being the major partner, we did not have complete control. This means that other partners had responsibilities, including control of some operations crucial to the safety of staff and the oil supply.

The complexities of ownership may have led to the first of the failures which was a lack of clarity on individual and collective legal responsibilities. Accordingly, liability for the valve failure was ambiguous even though it was another company, Well Services, who directly caused the problem. We work very closely with joint venture partners on projects such as the Effland Coastal Oil Rig and rely on each other's controls. In this case, the situation was made worse for Coastal Oil by a lack of clarity on these agreements and this is salutary for future projects.

It is my understanding that the engineers belonging to Well Services failed in regard to two operational controls. The valve that was the site of the pipeline's rupture was not tested in accordance with their normal procedures. Also, a connecting part was deployed at a depth beyond that at which it was designed to operate (i.e. beyond its safety tolerance). I was troubled by the suggestion that cost may have been a partial explanation for this. In both of these cases, a failure of operational controls contributed to the failure of the valve.

I sadly have no reason to doubt reports suggesting that the culture on the rig was less rigorous than it should have been. It is important that stringent controls are operated throughout Coastal Oil and it is especially important at the sites of operation where hazardous work takes place. There are issues with the reporting of exceptions to the land-side and hence the management style of a rig's individual manager becomes the defining issue on whether a certain internal control problem is reported to us. On reflection, this could have been more robust and it relied more on objective measures and less on human judgement.

Finally, we had no effective contingency plan in place for sealing the well-head or stopping the flow of oil from the well after the valve ruptured. This was the cause of the leakage of oil into the sea over several months. Contingency plans or system backups may have helped in this regard but we were unable to respond with the speed necessary and this resulted in such environmental and economic damage.

(ii) **Subjective and objective risk assessment**

I would like to respond directly to Senator Jones's remark in the media that I as the company's CEO 'should have known this was going to happen'. Whilst I understand the senator's anger at the events that have so badly affected his constituency, I owe it to Coastal Oil's shareholders to respond to him for the purposes of clarity.

Risk assessment is an important but complicated process and involves establishing both the probability of a particular risk event happening and also the impact or hazard that would arise if it was realised. A key point is that some of these calculations can be made with some degree of objectivity whilst others rely more on subjective assessment. There is an important distinction, then, between objective and subjective assessments. A risk can be objectively assessed if we can 'scientifically' measure the probability of a given outcome or predict, with some certainty, the impact. I can predict with some confidence, for example, based on past data, the number of working days likely to be lost in a given year through absenteeism of employees. I can predict with much less certainty, the probability that the stockmarket will rise or fall on a given day. In such a situation, I must use more subjective judgement.

Similarly with regard to impact, I might be able to assess the impact of my loss should my car get stolen but I could much less accurately predict the number of people hurt or injured in an accident. Again, I would use a more subjective figure for assessing that risk. The probability of having my car stolen would increase if I were to leave it unlocked and this underlines the importance of controls to help reduce the probabilities of adverse events happening.

Argue against Senator Jones

This brings me to Senator Jones's remark that I 'should have known' the accident was going to occur. I'm afraid that his remark does not recognise the complexities of risk management and risk assessment. I have outlined the reasons for uncertainty in both assessing the probabilities and impacts of risk events.

Accidents do occur in many industries including in the petrochemicals industry. Given that Coastal Oil operates hundreds of similar deep sea rigs in waters all over the world, I could not, with any degree of certainty, predict the probability of a fatal accident on a given oil rig and much less could I have known about the probability of an accident on the Effland Coastal Oil Rig. Similarly, there is no information that I could have received that could have predicted the scale of death or injury in the event of a given incident.

I concede that there were a number of internal control failures on the rig in question, but would point out to the senator that I was unaware of those failures because of the nature of the information systems linking rigs to our land-side operations. It is the responsibility of each rig's management to enforce safety controls on that rig and no such information would have reached me except by exception. He may be justified in criticising these, and I have explained already that I view these information failures as an internal control issue that we must resolve.

(iii) **Health and safety risk**

The board of Coastal Oil was deeply saddened to hear of the loss of life on the Effland Coastal Oil Rig. As a petrochemical company involved in each stage of the extraction, processing and distribution of oil products, we are naturally very aware of the health and safety risks that we face. These are risks to individuals, employees or others, arising from any failure in our operations giving rise to compromised human welfare.

Health and safety risk, and particularly the probability of a given health and safety risk materialising, is generally increased by a number of factors. The first is a lack of a health and safety policy. In some industries, including petrochemicals, large parts of this policy are underpinned by legislation, depending on jurisdiction, but it is also in the interests of a business to ensure that robust policies are in place covering all aspects of health and safety and indeed this was the case on the oil platform in question. The second is a lack of emergency procedures or a failure to deal with hazards that arise. Once identified, a new hazard or impact must be addressed with a policy or a way of dealing with it. Ineffective operational controls, such as was the case on the Effland Coastal Oil Deep Rig, contribute to this failure.

Third, a poor health and safety culture can undermine an otherwise good policy if management and staff are lax towards health and safety, or believe it to be unimportant. There is some evidence that this was sadly the case on the rig.

(iv) **ALARP**

I understand and share the committee's desire to ensure that an accident of this type does not happen again. However, risk management is partly a trade-off between the cost of control and level of perceived risk. We operate to a principle known as ALARP or that risks should be 'as low as reasonably practicable'. There is an inverse relationship between a risk and the acceptability of that risk or, in other words, a risk is more acceptable when it is low and less acceptable when it is high. Accordingly, risks assessed as 'high' in terms of probability and/or impact, must have credible and affordable strategies put in place for their management. The extent and cost of that risk strategy is a matter of judgement and you will appreciate that as the chief executive of Coastal Oil, I owe it to our shareholders and customers to control costs. This means that risks cannot be completely eliminated, much as I might wish that they could.

Accordingly, then, each risk is managed so as to be as low as is reasonably practicable because we can never say that a risk has a zero value. It would be financially and operationally impracticable to completely eliminate health and safety risks, and so we must live with the ever-present possibility that they can happen. This does not mean we would ever become complacent, of course, but merely that I should be honest in saying that the probability of occurrence cannot be zero. Because of this, we maintain a number of controls that should reduce the probability of the risks materialising, such as by having a policy in place and enforcing it. We also have protections in place, such as the compulsory wearing of safety equipment, to reduce the impact of an event should it occur.

Thank you for listening to this statement. I am now happy to take questions.

Question 2

(a) **Rules and principles**

Distinguish between

There are two broad approaches to the regulation of corporate governance provisions: rules-based and principles-based. In a rules-based country (jurisdiction), all provisions are legal rules, underpinned by law, transgression against which is punishable in law. Often characterised as a 'box ticking' approach, full compliance is required by all companies at all times (excepting where dispensations are granted, again, under the provisions of the law).

In a principles-based jurisdiction, legal force applies to the provisions of company laws but additional listing rules are enforced on a 'comply or explain' basis. It is important to note that compliance is not voluntary in that the provisions can be ignored, but that provisions may not be complied with in full, usually for a limited period if the full reason for non-compliance is explained to the shareholders. This allows for the market to judge the seriousness of the non-compliance and to potentially re-appraise or revalue the company as a result.

Critical evaluation of remark

The remark in the Geeland Code strongly argues in favour of a principles-based approach to corporate governance. In particular, it is critical of rules-based codes that would, for example, place a blanket ban on combining the roles of chairman and chief executive. In order to allow for differences between circumstances, it is arguing for flexibility and 'common sense'.

The arguments in favour of the remark.

In most cases, compliance with general principles is cheaper than compliance with a detailed 'box ticking' regime. A common criticism of rules-based approaches is the expense of compliance including the establishment of information systems to meet reporting requirements (for example on internal controls), consultancy costs, increased management costs and reporting costs. Where some flexibility is possible, the principles-based approach allows some 'common sense' to be employed in the extent of detailed compliance.

A principles-based approach is flexible and allows companies to develop their own approach, perhaps with regard to the demands of their own industry or shareholder preferences. This places the emphasis on investor needs rather than legal demands. There may be no reason, for example, why companies in lower risk industries should be constrained by the same internal control reporting requirements as companies in higher risk industries. As long as shareholders recognise and are satisfied with this, the cost advantages can be enjoyed.

An example of the flexibility afforded by a principles-based approach is that it allows for transitional arrangements and unusual circumstances. Details such as the contract terms of directors may need to be varied to meet individual needs or the notice periods might similarly be varied. In the event of a sudden, unexpected change such as a death in service, a company can enter a phase of technical non-compliance but, with suitable explanation of the reason for non-compliance, most shareholders will nevertheless be satisfied.

It avoids the need for expensive and inconvenient monitoring and support structures, the costs of which are ultimately borne by the companies themselves (through stock market or regulatory bodies) or by the taxpayer. The costs and inconvenience of policing compliance with rules has been shown to be material in some situations, especially in smaller companies. Similarly, the costs of a large national 'watchdog' to monitor and enforce detailed compliance is considerable.

Arguments against

There may be confusion over what is compulsory under law and what is principles-driven under listing rules. A lack of clarity might be present, especially where compliance expertise is not available to management (such as in some smaller companies) between legally-required compliance and listing rules which are subject to comply or explain. This may confuse some management teams and cause non-compliance borne of lack of advice and information.

A principles-based approach assumes that markets are capable of understanding the seriousness of any temporary or more lengthy periods of non-compliance and of revaluing the shares as a result. Non-specialist shareholders may not understand why a given provision is not complied with nor appreciate the potential consequences of the non-compliance. Cleverly-worded comply or explain statements might mislead shareholders.

A 'box ticking' approach offers the advantage of gaining full compliance at all times (i.e. all boxes are actually ticked) whereas a principles-based approach allows some bad practice to continue. A full compliance regime is likely to provide a greater overall confidence in regulation and this, in turn, will further support long-term shareholder value.

A rules-based approach provides standardisation and prevents any individual companies gaining competitive or cost advantages with lower levels of compliance. This creates a 'level playing field' in which all competitors in an industry understand what is required.

Tutorial note: allow individual arguments to be used for or against as appropriate

(b)   **Separation of roles**

The strongest and most common reason for the separation of these roles is to avoid the dangers of unfettered power that may arise when power is concentrated in a single, powerful individual. The original proposition for the separation of roles was in the UK's Cadbury Report in 1992 which was itself a response to a number of corporate 'scandals', similar to those in Geeland, involving unfettered power and the abuse of shareholder wealth as a result.

Accountability is better served by the separation of roles because the chief executive has a named person, in addition to the non-executive directors, to whom he or she must account for the company's performance and his or her own behaviour. This serves to protect against conflicts of interest where chief executives may be tempted to act in their own self-interest rather than to serve the best interests of the shareholders.

Third, both roles are complex and demanding. In large companies, it is likely that the two roles cannot be carried out effectively by one person. By gaining the advantages of a separation of duties (and hence a division of labour), the performance of the company's management in total will be enhanced. The two roles are materially different in terms of their skills, and it enhances organisational effectiveness for one to chair the board (chairman) and another, with different skills, to manage the strategy of the company. It is usual for the chairman role to be undertaken by a non-executive director, whilst the chief executive is an executive director. Having this distinction at the top of the company allows the chief executive to be hands on and directly involved in the management of the company, whilst the chairman can adopt a more supervisory position.

Finally, it is considered best practice because it provides a reassurance to investors and ensures compliance with relevant codes. Investor confidence in company management is very important and this is enhanced by having a transparent and clear

separation of roles. Where codes specify separation and this can be demonstrated, unlike at Anson Company, unqualified comply or explain statements can be issued thereby promoting investor confidence.

(c)   **Comply or explain**

The statement clearly identifies the one area of non-compliance and represents a full discharge of the company's reporting obligation to comply or explain. In a principles-based jurisdiction, this statement is required under listing rules and involves informing shareholders of the level of compliance and also specifying any areas of non-compliance, which the company has done in this case.

It is clear and free of ambiguity in what it says. Clearly though, one area of non-compliance is explained. The area of non-compliance is identified and the individual is named. The naming of William Klunker may be material because if he is known and trusted by shareholders, the breach may be less important than if he were less known and less trusted.

It does not provide a good reason for the non-compliance other than saying that it was 'benefiting from having Mr Klunker in control' which might be seen as weak by some investors. The reasons for combining the roles in July 2009 are not given and so it could probably be argued that this is not a full explanation.

It does, however, provide a date for returning to full compliance against which management can be held accountable for failure. This will reassure investors that its period of non-compliance is temporary and the default position of the company is to remain in full compliance with the relevant code.

Question 3

(a) **CEO's reward package**

Purposes

Reward packages are generally considered to have three purposes: to attract, retain and motivate. To attract means that they must be set at a level adequate to ensure that people with suitable skills will find the post attractive. If the salary is too high, a number of people with the wrong skill levels will be attracted and if it is too low, too few suitable applicants will be attracted.

Retention means ensuring that the level is adequate to prevent a good chief executive from seeking employment elsewhere in order to find a level of reward more suited to his or her skills and experience. Finally, rewards serve to motivate. This means that there must be enough reward to provide loyalty and a desire to achieve in the role. This is often done by providing a part of the reward in the form of a variable payment linked to corporate performance.

Influencing factors

The market rate is the first factor that influences the reward level. This is what the case meant when it said 'commensurate with the importance of the job and in line with other public companies of similar size'. The market rate is the transfer value of Mrs Evans if she were to move to a comparable position in another company. In the case, it is evident that the remuneration committee believes this to be double the previous salary she was paid when the gas supplier was owned by the state.

Legal, fiscal or regulatory constraints are relevant in many situations. Public servants, including those employed by state monopolies, are sometimes constrained in their earnings by legislation or maximum differentials (i.e. a compulsory multiple between the highest and lowest paid in an organisation). Mrs Evans's salary had previously been limited because of 'government constraints on the salaries of public servants', but the privatisation meant she was now free of this limitation.

The third influencing factors are previous performance in the job (if relevant) and the outcomes of performance reviews. The recommendation of the remuneration committee has clearly based its value of Mrs Evans on her past performance. Based on this, it has not only decided to recommend her retention in post but also the substantial pay increase. The knowledge of her strategic and communications skills is based upon observing her in post when she worked for the nationalised company and, based on these, there is a belief she will perform well in future.

Fourth, stakeholder opinion and ethical considerations are also relevant factors in some situations. Where a CEO is highly visible or in charge of a politically-sensitive organisation, the opinions of stakeholders is sometimes a constraint on what can be paid. This might apply to charities, for example, non-governmental organisations (NGOs) and similar organisations. In the case, Dale Gas appears to be seeking to pay Mrs Evans the increased salary despite the concerns of some in society.

(b) **Market risk and retaining Mrs Evans**

Market risk

Market risk concerns potential losses on capital markets from changes in the value or volatility of a share price or other security. A number of factors give rise to market risk, sometimes referred to as 'market or price sensitive' factors including a range of external opportunities and threats. In the case of Dale Gas, an internal factor, the potential loss of a trusted CEO, is thought, by Tom Nwede, to be a source of market risk because her loss would cause a devaluation of Dale Gas shares.

Tutorial note: Market risk is usually defined as risk connected with the share market, but in some circumstances could be defined as risk associated with the market for products and with the competitive environment. Where candidates have taken the latter approach appropriate credit will be given.

Justify the remark

In the context of the case, Mr Nwede was referring to the increased market risk and loss of shareholder value that may arise were the experienced Mrs Evans to be replaced because of the public concern. Increased volatility or a reduction in share price could result in a lower company value and a lower return on investment for the clients of XY Investments and other shareholders in Dale Gas.

Mr Nwede is clearly of the view that Mrs Evans is important for the stability of Dale Gas after its privatisation and for the mitigation of market risk. He is saying that it was important that the protestors and opposing small shareholders did not win in opposing the salary increase as that increase was, he felt, important in retaining and motivating Mrs Evans in the important period ahead.

Shareholders greatly value competent leadership in the companies they invest in, and Mrs Evans was clearly held in high regard by XY Investments and other institutional shareholders. The case highlights her excellent strategic and communication skills, both of which are valued by shareholders. The company will be strategically repositioned because of the privatisation and her communication skills will be necessary in managing the business and in conveying information to shareholders and others.

There were several board changes resulting from the privatisation. This would have meant that some new members were unfamiliar with the gas industry and would need to learn their new roles at a strategically important time for the company. Market uncertainty and hence market risk will be reduced by the continuing presence of an experienced and trustworthy CEO. This would, accordingly, be valued by shareholders in that she would be a source of valuable experience, continuity and stability.

She was respected by, and had the trust of, employees meaning that necessary internal changes could be made. These would be more difficult were a new and less trusted CEO to be brought in (although in other cases, a new CEO can have a positive effect). These changes are deemed necessary and so future shareholder value is likely to depend upon them being competently and fully implemented.

(c) **Proxy voting**

Proxy voting

A proxy is a substitute or 'other person' that can be nominated to attend a company meeting to exercise the votes of shareholders unable or unwilling to attend in person. The proxy can be the company chairman (where the shareholder agrees with the directors' recommendation on a particular vote) or another person so nominated. It requires the completion of a 'proxy form' transferring the shareholder's voting right to the proxy person. A proxy other than the chairman will almost always have highly specific instructions of how to vote on each motion in the meeting. The validity and the number of votes for each proxy is essential in calculating the outcome of each vote.

Advantages

The advantages of the appointment of a proxy include a lower agency cost if fund managers do not need to attend each AGM in person. This becomes more important as the number of individual stocks in a fund increases. Where votes are routine and uncontested, there is no need for fund managers to attend in person and proxy voting (where the proxy is a company officer, e.g. chairman) facilitates this absence. In addition, the use of proxies in the case means that fund managers would not need to face the added pressure of being confronted by the smaller shareholders' protest. These are likely to be seen as an irritation by Mr Nwede with no possibility of them changing his voting were he to attend in person.

Question 4

(a) **Rights and responsibilities**

Rights and responsibilities

The comment by Albert Doo identifies rights and responsibilities as being two essential characteristics of citizenship, be it human or organisational in nature.

A right is an expectation of the benefits the citizen can receive, by virtue of citizenship, from society. In most civil societies, rights include the freedom to conduct business by engaging in resource and product markets, to enjoy the protection of the law and the goodwill of other members of society in supporting the right of the organisation to exist, to innovate and grow.

A responsibility is a duty owed, by the citizen, back to society as a quid pro quo for the extension of rights. These are owed by virtue of the citizen's membership of society. In most societies, responsibilities extend to compliance with all relevant laws and regulations, including the payment of taxes, and compliance with the behavioural norms of that society.

Gray, Owen & Adams's perspectives

Gray, Owen & Adams described seven possible positions that can be adopted on a company's relations with its stakeholders. These concern the ethical assumptions of the roles of a business in society and are as follows: the pristine capitalist, the expedient, the social contractarian, the socialist, the social ecologist, the radical feminist and the deep green. The range of views along this continuum are primarily characterised by the ways in which they interpret the rights and responsibilities of business.

Broadly speaking, the nearer to the pristine capitalist end of the continuum, the greater the rights of shareholders and the fewer their responsibilities to a wider constituency. Conversely, the nearer the 'deep green' end of the continuum, the fewer the perceived rights and the greater the responsibilities of the company and its agents to a more widely defined group of stakeholders.

At the 'pristine capitalist' end of the continuum, rights and responsibilities are understood principally in terms of economic measures. The company has the right to pursue its legal business activity and to develop that business with the support of society and the governing authorities. In return, its responsibilities are limited to the profitable production of goods and services and, accordingly, the generation of profits that are entirely attributable to shareholders. It is not the responsibility of businesses to pursue any other social, environmental or benevolent end. In this context, it is clearly not the company's responsibility to use shareholders' money to contribute to the new children's play area.

At the socialist-to-green end of the continuum, it is argued that businesses like Biggo have fewer (and contestable) rights and much greater responsibilities. According to positions at the deep green end, Biggo, does not, for example, have the right to consume non-sustainable resources 'simply' for the purposes of wealth creation. They may not have the moral right, even if they have a legal right, to build on the community's play area. At the same time, Biggo has a wide responsibility to society and to the environment that might seriously constrain their behaviour and activities.

(b) **The two comments**

Robert Tens is closest to the expedient position. The expedient position is one in which social responsibility is seen in terms of what return can be gained from social responsibility policies and actions. In other words, it may be expedient to adopt social responsibility actions but only if by doing so, it furthers its strategic interests. The expedient position does not recognise any implicit social responsibility as such and social policies are therefore only pursued if a clear strategic rationale can be identified for them.

His comment considers the actions towards the community in terms of cultivating current and future employees: it is an exercise of specific stakeholder management with the key stakeholder being the local community. By engaging in activities that give the appearance of being socially responsible, i.e. making the requested donation, other economically advantageous ends can be achieved. He highlighted three strategic benefits that might arise: it might 'cultivate the company's reputation' specifically in order 'help in future recruitment'. Third, it might 'help to reduce resistance to any future expansion the company might need to make.' He clearly sees the donation in instrumental terms.

Margaret Heggs's comment is closest to the pristine capitalist position. Her comment suggests that she believes that the social responsibilities of Biggo do not extend beyond the social benefits it already provides through employment and the provision of 'excellent products'. The purpose of Biggo is not to engage in costly social responsibility measures such as community donations, even if they can be shown to have a positive strategic benefit. That is not the purpose of a business. In accepting that the company had 'no further contractual or ethical duties to the local government nor to the local community', she was demonstrating a pristine capitalist perspective.

(c) **SR and short/long term**

Social responsibility

This phrase refers to the belief that companies such as Biggo must act in the general public interest as well as in the specific interest of their shareholders. This can apply to the company's strategy and the way in which the company is governed, but Mr Doo is referring to the specific social footprint that the company has locally. It can also apply to the environmental footprint that a company has, i.e. the effect of company activities on resource consumption or the effect that emissions from operations have. It is possible to interpret this phrase narrowly, as Margaret Heggs has done, or more widely, as Albert Doo has.

Short and long-term perspectives

This question recognises that the attitude that a company may take towards a particular stakeholder claim can vary when a time perspective is introduced.

A short-term perspective is likely to consider a time period of days, months or perhaps up to a given financial year in terms of an action affecting short-term performance. A longer-term perspective, typically looking to years rather than months ahead, is likely to consider the legitimacy of a claim in terms of its effect on long-term shareholder value.

In the short term, Biggo may see the claim from Mr Doo, on behalf of the community, as a cost because a 'sizeable' contribution would have an effect on the profit for the year and hence the return to the shareholders. The case mentions that profits are likely to be low in the current year and so all costs should be carefully scrutinized for value for money and reduced or eliminated if possible. As Biggo is a public listed company, a short-term reduced profit can erode shareholder value because of reduced dividends and a potential reduction in share price.

In the longer term, Biggo can be seen to be cultivating two potentially key stakeholders (Mr Doo and the local community) and hence may create longer term value in terms of the advantages identified by Robert Tens (such as local employees and lower resistance to future factory enlargements). The case mentions the resistance from the local community and, given that the company will have to 'live with' the community for many years to come, it may be in Biggo's long-term strategic interest to do what it reasonably can to reduce any friction with this key stakeholder. There may, therefore, be a strategic case for making the contribution as requested.

Review Form – Paper P1 Governance, Risk and Ethics (01/12)

Name: _____ Address: _____

_____

_____

How have you used this Kit?
(Tick one box only)

☐ Home study (book only)

☐ On a course: college _____

☐ With 'correspondence' package

☐ Other _____

Why did you decide to purchase this Kit?
(Tick one box only)

☐ Have used the complementary Study text

☐ Have used other BPP products in the past

☐ Recommendation by friend/colleague

☐ Recommendation by a lecturer at college

☐ Saw advertising

☐ Other _____

During the past six months do you recall seeing/receiving any of the following?
(Tick as many boxes as are relevant)

☐ Our advertisement in *Student Accountant*

☐ Our advertisement in *Pass*

☐ Our advertisement in *PQ*

☐ Our brochure with a letter through the post

☐ Our website www.bpp.com

Which (if any) aspects of our advertising do you find useful?
(Tick as many boxes as are relevant)

☐ Prices and publication dates of new editions

☐ Information on product content

☐ Facility to order books off-the-page

☐ None of the above

Which BPP products have you used?

Text	☐	*Success CD*	☐	*Learn Online*	☐
Kit	☑	*i-Learn*	☐	*Home Study Package*	☐
Passcard	☐	*i-Pass*	☐	*Home Study PLUS*	☐

Your ratings, comments and suggestions would be appreciated on the following areas.

	Very useful	Useful	Not useful
Passing P1			
Planning your question practice			
Questions			
Top Tips etc in answers			
Content and structure of answers			
Mock exam answers			

Overall opinion of this Kit	*Excellent* ☐	*Good* ☐	*Adequate* ☐	*Poor* ☐

Do you intend to continue using BPP products?   *Yes* ☐   *No* ☐

The BPP author of this edition can be e-mailed at: nickweller@bpp.com

Please return this form to: Nick Weller, ACCA Publishing Manager (Professional papers), BPP Learning Media Ltd, FREEPOST, London, W12 8BR

Review Form (continued)

TELL US WHAT YOU THINK

Please note any further comments and suggestions/errors below.